THE *CTR* ANTH

Fifteen Plays from *Canadian Theatre Review*

THE *CTR* ANTHOLOGY

Fifteen Plays from
Canadian Theatre Review

Edited by
Alan Filewod

University of Toronto Press

Toronto, Buffalo, London

Printed on acid-free paper

Canadian Cataloguing in Publication Data

Main entry under title:

The CTR anthology : fifteen plays from Canadian
theatre review

ISBN 0-8020-6812-X

1. Canadian drama (English) – 20th century.*
2. Canadian drama (French) – 20th century –
Translations into English.* I. Filewod, Alan
D. (Alan Douglas), 1952–

PS8307.C88 1993   C812'.5408   C92-095004-3
PR9196.3.C88 1993

This book has been published with the help of a grant
from the Woodlawn Arts Foundation.

This volume is dedicated to

FLOYD S. CHALMERS

Journalist, publisher, and indefatigable supporter of the arts, his patronage has recognized and benefited a great many artists, and his generosity and enthusiasm have left an indelible mark on all the arts in Canada. His many honours, including Companion of the Order of Canada, the Order of Ontario, and various honorary degrees, are tributes to the wide range of his philanthropy. This volume attests to his love for Canadian theatre.

Contents

Acknowledgments ix

Introduction xi

Michael Cook: **The Head, Guts and Sound Bone Dance** 3

John Palmer: **Henrik Ibsen on the Necessity of Producing Norwegian Drama** 35

Hrant Alianak: **Passion and Sin** 47

George F. Walker: **Rumours of Our Death** 107

Jack Winter and Cedric Smith: **Ten Lost Years** 133

Betty Lambert: **Jennie's Story** 191

The Anna Project: **This is for You, Anna** 249

Paul Ledoux and David Young: **Love is Strange** 283

Cindy Cowan: **A Woman from the Sea** 339

René-Daniel Dubois (translated by Linda Gaboriau): **Being at Home with Claude** 389

Arthur Milner: **Zero Hour** 435

Baŋuta Rubess: **Boom, Baby, Boom!** 479

Sky Gilbert: **Lola Starr Builds Her Dream Home** 531

Richard Rose and D.D. Kugler: **Newhouse** 573

Marie Brassard and Robert Lepage (translated by Gyllian Raby): **Polygraph** 647

Acknowledgments

The Head, Guts and Sound Bone Dance © 1974 Michael Cook. Originally published in *CTR* 1

Henrik Ibsen on the Necessity of Producing Norwegian Drama © 1976 John Palmer. (Author's agent: Rhonda Cooper, The Characters Talent Agency, 150 Carlton St, Toronto, Ont., M5A 2K1.) Originally published in *CTR* 14

Passion and Sin © 1976 Hrant Alianak. Originally published in *CTR* 19

Rumours of Our Death © 1979 George F. Walker. Originally published in *CTR* 25

Ten Lost Years © 1974 Jack Winter and Cedric Smith. Originally published in *CTR* 38

Jennie's Story © 1981 the estate of Betty Lambert. Rights are retained by The New Play Centre, P.O. Box 34091, Station D, Vancouver, BC, V6J 4M1. Originally published in *CTR* 40

This is for You, Anna © 1985 The Anna Project (c/o Baṇuta Rubess). Originally published in *CTR* 43

Love is Strange © 1984 Paul Ledoux and David Young. Originally published in *CTR* 44

A Woman from the Sea © 1986 Cindy Cowan. Originally published in *CTR* 48

Being at Home with Claude English-language version © 1987 René-Daniel Dubois and Linda Gaboriau. (Authors' agents: L'Agence John C. Goodwin et

Associés, 839, Sherbrooke est, suite 2, Montréal, Que., H2L 1K6.) Originally published in *CTR* 50

Zero Hour © 1986 Arthur Milner. Originally published in *CTR* 53

Boom, Baby, Boom! © 1988 Baņuta Rubess. Originally published in *CTR* 58

Lola Starr Builds Her Dream Home © 1989 Sky Gilbert. Originally published in *CTR* 59

Newhouse © 1989 Richard Rose and D.D. Kugler. Originally published in *CTR* 61

Polygraph English-language version © 1990 Robert Lepage, Marie Brassard, and Gyllian Raby. Originally published in *CTR* 64

Introduction

Alan Filewod

Of the fifteen plays in this anthology, most have been out of print since they originally appeared in the pages of *Canadian Theatre Review*. A few have been republished elsewhere but are no longer available; a smaller number are currently available in book form or in other anthologies. This volume therefore serves two purposes: to recover a number of significant plays that have gone out of print, and to offer a representative overview of the development of Canadian drama and theatrical practice as recorded by the several editors of *CTR* since 1974.

These fifteen plays, which comprise approximately twenty per cent of the journal's canon to date, represent the tastes, prejudices, and analyses of three different editorial regimes at *CTR*. Four of them (*The Head, Guts and Sound Bone Dance, Henrik Ibsen on the Necessity of Producing Norwegian Drama, Passion and Sin,* and *Rumours of Our Death*) were published while *CTR*'s founder, Don Rubin, served as editor (with occasional associates, most notably Alan Richardson) from 1974 to 1982. Six (*Ten Lost Years, Jennie's Story, This is for You, Anna, Love is Strange, A Woman from the Sea,* and *Being at Home with Claude*) were originally published under the direction of Robert Wallace, editor from 1982 to 1987. The remaining plays (*Zero Hour, Boom, Baby, Boom!, Lola Starr Builds Her Dream Home, Newhouse,* and *Polygraph*) have appeared since 1987, when Wallace was succeeded by an editorial collective consisting of Alan Filewod as editor, and Natalie Rewa, Wallace (until 1988), and Ann Wilson (until 1992) as associate editors. Although the selection of the plays for this volume was made by one person, in a very real sense it is a collective effort that reproduces the work of all of the editors who have been involved in the journal since its inception.

Each year *CTR* has normally published four plays – with occasional fluctuations – and the choice of plays has always been subjective. They were published because the editors involved considered them significant, either because of their textual and thematic values, or because they documented important developments in theatrical production.[1] Each editor's choice is justified by a personal analysis of Canadian drama and theatre. In that sense, *CTR*'s mission has consistently been one of advocacy: to publish deserving plays that demonstrate what we as editors have seen as important in Canadian theatre, and to record how Canadian theatre changes.

At the same time, the selection of plays to be reissued raises the question of canonization, a topic that has provoked considerable debate in recent years. The process of canonization is necessarily exclusive, for certain texts are made available at the expense of others, and during the existence of *CTR* the field of new Canadian plays to choose from has expanded rapidly. The canon of Canadian drama – the body of available texts that together define the conceptual borders of the discipline – is in a constant state of change, somewhat stabilized by the lists of the playtext publishers and the few anthologies available for use in university and college courses.

All canons enshrine identifiable values and in this *CTR* is no exception. At the same time every addition to or rehabilitation of the canon both expands and subverts notions of Canadian theatre. The *CTR* canon represented here offers several narratives of Canadian theatre. In particular, these plays can be read in terms of the evolution of *CTR*'s discourse of nationalism and regionalism as the defining conditions of modern Canadian drama, and as an expression of the changing nature of theatrical practice in Canada. In both cases, these plays document a growing pluralism that corresponds to the phenomenal growth in Canadian theatre since the early 1970s, a period which has seen Canadian playwrights move from a marginalized minority to become the dominant presence on Canadian stages. That growth has produced a diversity of styles, thematic concerns, and theatrical approaches that has radically transformed the conceptual notions that informed *CTR* at its founding.

In its first years, under Don Rubin, *CTR* advocated a notion of Canadian theatre in terms of the arrival of a professional institution committed to producing Canadian drama. In Rubin's analysis the idea of a canon was crucial; although the "alternate" theatre movement of the 1970s produced hundreds of new plays, few of them were seen on the boards of the larger institutionalized theatres that accounted for the lion's share of theatrical funding. In his editorial in *CTR* 2, Rubin addressed this issue directly, using the horticultural vocabulary of cultural maturity common to post-colonial societies:

> We're speaking here about developing a culture and the fact is that until we have a strong culture of our own to share with the world, we must be extraordinarily careful not to let its potential disappear through colonial thinking or misguided liberalism. The Massey Commission was well aware of this danger nearly a quarter century ago and it aided immeasurably in planting the seeds for a truly Canadian culture. But we can have no real culture until these seeds reach some kind of maturity. And theatrical maturity means the creation of a drama (playwrights) as well as the continued growth of a theatre (actors, designers, directors). Canada does have a Canadian theatre right now, and the possibility of creating a Canadian drama to go with it is closer now than ever before.[2]

Rubin's choice of plays articulated a cultural nationalism that accorded with the prevailing theory that Canadian culture was best comprehended in terms of aggregate regional cultures. The orthodoxy of regionalism that *CTR* (which by 1976 was calling itself "Canada's National Theatre Journal") helped define in the 1970s implied an ideological centrality, its emblem, the undefinable phrase "national unity"; the decentralizing impulse of regionalism was stabilized by the proposal of a national community that finds its unity in nationalism, multiculturalism, and bilingualism. In effect, this was the ideology of the Trudeau Liberal governments that subsidized the formative years of the contemporary Canadian theatre.

Rubin departed from the Trudeau vision in one important regard. In his selection of plays, Rubin made it clear that while *CTR*'s mandate was to cover the whole of Canada, it could not pretend to speak for Quebec, where the *jeune théâtre* movement offered incontrovertible proof that, in the theatre at least, Quebec had already achieved cultural autonomy. *CTR*'s subsequent editors continued this recognition of Quebec as a distinct culture, to be addressed on its own terms. Robert Wallace and Natalie Rewa in particular brought a close familiarity with Québécois theatre to *CTR*, but a journal that defined Canadian theatre in terms of colonialism was from its beginnings sensitive to Québécois cultural autonomy. When *CTR* published Quebec plays, they were plays that had enjoyed success in translation in English Canada, and therefore could be counted in the anglophone repertoire. Such was the case with René-Daniel Dubois' *Being at Home with Claude* and Marie Brassard and Robert Lepage's *Polygraph*, both of which are included in this volume.

Canadian federal governments, both Liberal and Progressive Conservative, have adhered religiously to the idea that Canada cannot exist without Quebec, neither materially nor ideologically; in accepting the existence of two separate cultures, *CTR* proposed an idea of an essential anglo-Canadian cultural identity. The journal has continually been engaged in a project of defining, interrogating, and documenting that culture, which now appears much more complex and pluralistic than it did in the mid-1970s.

The complexity of that pluralism can be seen in *CTR*'s evolving understanding of the significance of regionalism. As Trudeau's policies were inscribed into legislation and critical orthodoxies, the contradiction between regionalism (seen at its most extreme in Quebec, where regional difference could be seen as the expression of a separate nation) and the need for a unifying national sentiment was apparently resolved in the cliché, "unity in diversity." For *CTR*, regional difference was the defining condition that proved the existence of a Canadian culture. Only by legitimizing a national mythos could the hegemony of the colonizing "other" be resisted. *CTR* defined that "other" in the same way it was defined by the new theatre movements: the "other" was superficially British but substantially American. The earliest issues of the journal were preoccupied with the question of nationalism and colonialism; in fact the first issue coincided with the hiring of Robin Phillips at Stratford, a move seen at the time as one more example of what Tyrone Guthrie had called "the send-for-the-governor syndrome" afflicting Canadian middle-class theatres. Rubin perceived the Phillips hiring as the colonial antithesis proving the legitimacy of an imperilled indigenous theatre. (One marker of the ideological distance we have since travelled is the changing meaning of "indigenous," which then meant "Canadian" and now pertains almost exclusively to the aboriginal First Nations.)

On the face of it, Canadian theatre in the 1970s was subject to British colonialism: the artistic directors of the larger theatres were British, the repertoires were largely derived from British experience, and as *CTR* never failed to point out, the largest theatres in the country were dedicated to the work of dead British playwrights. But this colonialism was in a sense self-imposed; it had nothing to do with Britain per se, and everything to do with the obsessive post-colonial construction of a "mother" culture. Nowhere was this attitude more clearly, nor more cleverly, expressed than in John Palmer's one-act dramatic lecture, *Henrik Ibsen on the Necessity of Producing Norwegian Drama*, in which Ibsen methodically demolishes the cultural arguments that kept Canadian playwrights marginalized and argues that a dramatic canon is the proof of nationhood.

The colonialism that afflicted theatre often spoke with a British accent, but as critics had observed from the beginning of the century, the real hegemony to be resisted was that of American commercial culture. More than anything else, it was the threat of absorption into American popular culture that gave the nationalism of the 1970s its sense of urgency. This in turn led to an essentialist notion of Canadian culture that defined itself in terms of historical experience and localism. It is in this context that *CTR*'s emphasis on regionalism can be understood: regionalism sought to prove the existence of specific cultures that combine to form a coherent cultural narrative with, at its core, a repudiation of the narrative of American culture. Significantly, the first play published in *CTR* (and the play that begins this volume) was written by a British immigrant to Newfoundland, which had joined Canada only twenty-five years earlier. Michael Cook's *The Head, Guts and Sound Bone Dance* seemed to define a new genre of regionalist drama in its use of dialect, its minimalist plot, and its localist specificity, all expressing a deeply romantic cultural myth of survival and (as Cook wrote in his original preface) a "satanic struggle to impose order upon experience rendered frequently chaotic by a blind or savage nature."[3]

Rubin's choice of plays in those first issues continued to express the notion of a national community making itself known through the process of canonization. Gradually, however, *CTR* began to interrogate the premises of its nationalism. Rubin's analysis began to examine the class distinctions within Canadian theatre, between the heavily subsidized "regional" theatres and the small new theatres that produced the bulk of Canadian plays; in his last issues, when the issues of nationalism seemd less urgent, he broadened his scope to embrace international topics.

When Robert Wallace assumed the role of editor in 1982, the process of interrogation accelerated. Canadian theatre had evolved to the point where a quarterly journal could not pretend to cover it comprehensively. Wallace therefore began focusing on a particular theme in each issue, and often sought plays that illuminated that theme. For example, *Ten Lost Years* was selected to complement an issue on Toronto theatre; Cindy Cowan's *A Woman from the Sea* was chosen by guest editor Richard Paul Knowles to illustrate the work of the Mulgrave Road Co-op in an issue on "Atlantic Alternatives"; and *This is for You, Anna* was the centrepiece of an issue on feminist theatre. This policy of thematically related playtexts, which continues to this day, has not always been applied rigidly but in each issue editors have generally tried to establish a relationship between the play and the cover topic.

This principle had the effect of further questioning the premises upon which *CTR* had been founded, because the theme issues attempted to dig beneath the surface and offer several different perspectives on their respective topics. Critical notions that in 1974 seemed straightforward could be seen in retrospect as ideologically situated; the 1970s idea of nationalism, for example, had in the 1990s fragmented into several interconnected discourses. In *CTR* 62, on the subject of "Nation and Theatre," Ann Wilson argued that the idea of nationalism, which not too many years before had seemed self-evident, was in fact a cipher for "that which reinforces and perpetuates the power of those whose status within the society is predicated on a particular sense of the political entity called the nation."[4] If in the 1970s *CTR* was radical because it called for cultural nationalism, in the 1990s it was radical in its questioning of "whose nation(s)?" In this regard, the editorial team that succeeded Wallace has continued his practice of interrogating the vocabularies and conceptual frameworks in which Canadian theatre operates.

Reconsideration of the meaning of nationalism may be seen to indicate that the battles that had launched *CTR* had been won: by the 1980s the primacy of the Canadian playwright was an established fact, and critical attention could turn to the task of defining the trends and developments that were constantly changing the theatre. The earlier idea of regionalism was supplanted by a new understanding that accepted the principle of regional difference but freed it of geographic determinism. The first indication of this in the *CTR* canon came early with the recognition of women playwrights as a struggling minority within the theatre who express their own "region" of experience. Although *CTR* has always sought and published women playwrights, they comprised a minority in the journal's evolving canon, as they did on the stages of Canadian theatres. Happily that trend has been reversed, or at least substantially modified, in recent years, but the disproportionate ratio of male to female playwrights in this volume reflects the overall ratio throughout *CTR*'s history.

The plays by women in this volume show clearly that the region of experience shared by women is itself pluralistic and must be considered in terms of cultural difference. *Jennie's Story*, *This is for You, Anna*, *A Woman from the Sea*, and *Boom, Baby, Boom!* can all be analysed as feminist plays but their notions of women's experience and the construction of gender in them are very different. Both *Jennie's Story* and *This is for You, Anna*, for example, deal with abuse and violence against women but in two very different contexts.

In *Jennie's Story*, by the late Betty Lambert, notions of region, in this case of gender and geography, intersect and draw strength from the localist specificity of the script's dialogue and characterizations. Its realist form and use of dialect expand the parameters of conventional dramaturgy by resituating the marginalized (the victims of sexual and institutional abuse) into the centre. Like many realist plays written by women, it reclaims a dramatic form that has long been dominated by male concerns. The same holds true of Cindy Cowan's *A Woman from the Sea*, which modifies realism with poetic sparseness to imbue traditional dramaturgy with mythic resonances that the play defines as essentially feminine. *Anna*, in contrast, is a collective creation that repudiates realist dramaturgy as the aesthetic technology of patriarchy and therefore incapable of expressing women's experience. Its imagistic, non-linear structure is both an expression of subjectivity and a process of discovering a feminist performance vocabulary.

The concern for cultural difference and the redefinition of the conceptual boundaries of Canadian drama have led the editors of *CTR* to examine other regions of experience, many of which can no longer be analysed in terms of an essentialist national culture. *Zero Hour* is included here as an example of the topical political drama typical of the popular theatre movement that emerged in force during the 1980s; *Lola Starr Builds Her Dream Home* is an example of the distinct genre of gay parody encouraged by Buddies in Bad Times Theatre in Toronto. In both cases, as with many feminist plays, the "regional" concerns of the play are trans-national; *Zero Hour* examines American intervention in Central America, and *Lola Starr* expresses a gay cultural experience that must be understood in a broader North American context. This is also true of many of the Native plays that have been written in recent years (several of which have been published in *CTR* in the course of the past two years, too recently to be included in this anthology). Although they do not explicitly address questions of Canadian culture and regionalism, they call into question the critical premises that have evolved to explain the development of Canadian drama. There is, for example, a growing body of plays that reflect the experiences of immigrants and cultural minorities, and while these can be analysed in terms of changing perspectives on Canadian identity, they might be more usefully read along with similar Australian, Caribbean and British plays in terms of global post-colonialism.

Taken together, the plays in this anthology can be read as a narrative of the development of the idea of Canadian nationalism, which progresses from the essentialist notion of a national identity arising out of regional difference, to a pluralistic intersection (and often conflict) of community interests. As such, this volume both constructs an idea of Canadian culture and deconstructs it as a contradictory notion that may in the end elude any attempt at definition (or in narrative terms, at closure). No longer can an editor of *CTR* write confidently, as could Rubin in 1974, of "our culture," because "our" today implies a monolithic and hegemonic analysis that many of these plays resist.

This same principle can be read into the narrative of theatrical practice the plays offer. The rapid expansion of Canadian theatres over the past several years can be traced in the *Canada On Stage* series initially published by *CTR* and more recently by the Professional Association of Canadian Theatres. In its first volume covering the 1974 season, *Canada On Stage* recorded the seasons of fewer than 100 theatres; in its latest (covering the seasons of 1986–8) it documents close to 350. This in part reflects improved documentation, but it also demonstrates that the breadth of theatrical production has so expanded that no one person can assume to comprehend the totality. This blossoming (to return to horticultural imagery) has brought with it an unprecedented diversity in theatrical and dramaturgical styles which undermine any generalizations about Canada playwriting.

The earliest plays in this volume are typical of the dominant approaches to playwriting in the early 1970s, although *CTR* was quick to publish alternative textualities. *The Head, Guts and Sound Bone Dance* may be considered representative of the traditional displacement of the playwright from the theatre that *CTR* sought to rectify in its early years. When Cook wrote his play, Newfoundland had no professional theatre (other than the collective Mummers Troupe) that might have worked with him to explore other modes of writing, nor did he miss it. (In his preface to the play, he wrote, "I don't, mind you, give a damn if someone decides to alter this or switch that in production. The Director has carte blanche. I just want to be left out of it, that's all.")[5]

But as theatrical practice evolved, mainly in small companies committed to new drama, the traditional understanding of literary textuality was enriched by a growing awareness of the textuality of performance. *CTR* saw this happening as early as the second issue, which published James Reaney's *Sticks and Stones*, still a model of theatricalist collaboration between a writer and a collective. *Ten Lost Years*, originally produced in the same year that *CTR* was founded (but not published until a decade later) similarly owed much to collaborative creation; the textuality that delighted audiences across the country was as much a product of George Luscombe's unique staging techniques as it was of Barry Broadfoot's oral histories, Jack Winter's narrative adaptations, and Cedric Smith's songs. (In this case, the complexities of the collaboration resulted in a long and bitter dispute over the ownership of the play, between the accredited authors of the written text, which *CTR* published, and the author of the *mise-en-scène*, which is essentially unpublishable.) Hrant Alianak's *Passion and Sin* can be read as a clever inversion of the traditional approach to textuality: the playwright has specified the physical actions and subtexts of his characters in minute detail, with occasional lines of dialogue included in the manner of stage directions. This playing with dramatic conventions is representative of the adventurous spirit that governed the early years of Toronto Free Theatre, a company founded by playwrights to create opportunities to work closely with actors and directors. Similarly, George F. Walker's ironic fable of colonialism, *Rumours of Our Death*, characterizes the break-the-rules attitude of Factory Theatre (before it dropped the "Lab" from its name). Walker has always written his plays with a close relationship to an ensemble of actors and directors, but *Rumours* is without question the least conventional, the least "textual" of his plays – so much so that the published text can only provide a glimpse of the play as seen on stage, for it omits the songs that gave the performance its distinct theatrical style. The text itself is nevertheless of interest for its witty examination of colonialism and for its place in Walker's development as one of Canada's foremost play-wrights.

The centrality of music, which defies reproduction on paper, is also a factor in *Love is Strange* and *Boom, Baby, Boom! Love is Strange* is a rare published example of the new approach to musical theatre, in which music is contextualized in the realist confines of the play but defines the style of the production. *Love is Strange* (which was in its first version called *I Love You, Ann Murray* until legalities forced a major revision) uses popular songs to interrogate mass culture, as did the authors' subsequent hit musical *Fire. Boom, Baby, Boom!* is a post-modern reflection on multiculturalism in the 1950s, which uses a jazz band to establish performance ambience. As in *Love is Strange*, music is used in this play as an integral element of both the narrative and the performance. In this case, music had an even more intangible result: Baṇuta Rubess, who directed as well as wrote the play, imposed on the production a stylized movement pattern to the rhythms of the band which expressed meaning that can only be suggested in the published text.

Music may be the most elusive textual element to be considered in the publication of a play, but it is not the only one. Robert Wallace originally published *Being at Home with Claude* in an issue that focused on what he called "image theatre," an approach which locates textual meaning in the visual and aural images of the performance. *Being at Home with Claude* may seem at first glance to be a naturalistic two-hander, but René-Daniel Dubois' extremely precise stage directions reveal the play to be a dense choreography of visual imagery; without careful attention to these imagistic structures, the play might well collapse under its own weight in performance. This same principle of imagistic performance is taken even further in Marie Brassard and Robert Lepage's *Polygraph*, which uses filmic techniques (including montage, shifting angles, and changing speeds) to challenge the structures of perception we bring to performance, and to the unravelling of its narrative mystery.

The final example of non-literary textuality in this volume is *Newhouse*, in which two canonized texts, *Oedipus* and de Molina's *Don Juan*, are plundered to construct a political fable of a near-future Canada in the grip of political crisis caused by an AIDS-like sexual plague. *Newhouse* can be read in strictly literary terms; in fact, its use of the source texts invites such a reading. In performance, however, the "literary" quality of the text was subverted by the environmental staging (in which actors processed their way to various platforms, around which the audience wandered at will) and by the integration of live-feed video.

For a number of the plays in this volume, then, the published text derives from the conditions of the performance itself, and is presented in a tentative form offering tantalizing clues to the variables of performance. In some cases, the written text changed considerably over the course of performances. In particular, the versions of *Ten Lost Years*, *This is for You, Anna*, and *Polygraph* published here are best read as documentations of performances at one point of development.

In a sense, this is true of all published playtexts. Because the development of modern Canadian playwriting was made possible by the expansion of theatres committed to producing their work, even the most traditional dramatic forms are created with a strong awareness of the textuality of performance. It has always been an editorial principle of *CTR* that plays are normally selected because of significant productions, and very often playwrights have been approached after an editor has seen the play performed. It sometimes happens that the qualities that attract notice in the first place are the very ones that cannot be captured on the page. What published text can suggest the theatrical intensity and centrality of Sky Gilbert's drag performance in *Lola Starr*, the jazz band in *Boom, Baby, Boom!*, the actor-created sound effects of *Ten Lost Years*, or the chilling presence of the television monitors of *Newhouse*? In such cases the texts are offered as a glimpse of what struck us as important theatrical events. It is hoped that they will be read in that light. And it is hoped that all of the plays in this volume will be read not only for their historical and critical values, but also for the considerable pleasure they can offer the reader.

This volume would not have been possible without the active collaboration of a number of valued colleagues, beginning, of course, with the playwrights themselves, and their agents. In the process of editing the anthology, I have been keenly aware of the debt owed to the editors to *CTR* who over the years have worked passionately to document the theatre they love: to Don Rubin, Robert Wallace, Natalie Rewa, and Ann Wilson I offer my deepest respect and admiration. I could not hope for finer colleagues, and I have learned much from all of them.

This book was made possible by University of Toronto Press, who as publishers of *Canadian Theatre Review* encouraged its compilation. Two colleagues from the Press have been invaluable; Olive Koyama's painstaking copy-editing and Beth Earl Rose's visual design are as important to this book as they have been to *CTR* over the years.

Finally I would like to thank Floyd S. Chalmers, who provided the subvention that made this project feasible, and to whom it is dedicated.

NOTES

1 A more complete analysis of the process and implications of canonization as it pertains to *CTR* can be found in my article "Undermining the

Centre: The Canon According to *Canadian Theatre Review*" in *Theatre History in Canada* 11, 2 (1990): 178–85

2 Don Rubin, "Creating the Impossible," *CTR* 2 (Spring 1974): 6
3 Michael Cook, preface to *The Head, Guts and Sound Bone Dance*, *CTR* 1 (Winter 1974): 74
4 Ann Wilson, "Notions of Nationalism," *CTR* 62 (Spring 1990): 3
5 Cook: 75

THE *CTR* ANTHOLOGY

The Head, Guts and Sound Bone Dance

Michael Cook

Anglo-Irish in Valentine's Day in Reichstag fire, educated at various schools before he ish army in 1949. In service in Korea, origin, and born on the year of the Michael Cook was Catholic/Jesuit enlisted in the British army twelve years he saw Japan, Malaya, and Europe. Upon his release he studied Drama at Nottingham University. Emigrating to Canada in 1966, he worked as Drama Specialist for Memorial University of Newfoundland's Extension Service, before transferring to the Department of English Language and Literature, where he remains as an Associate Professor. He is the author of a dozen stage plays and over a hundred radio and television plays and adaptations. His plays have been performed across North America (including Mexico), and in Poland, Sweden, Germany, Hungary, the United Kingdom, and Ireland. In 1977 he was awarded the Queen's Medal for Service to the Arts; he is also the

PHOTO CREDIT: RICHARD STOKER

recipient of the Government of Newfoundland and Labrador Achievement Award 1985, the National Radio Award for best original play 1990, and the Labatt's Award for best original play, which he has won three times. In 1989 he was Playwright in Residence at the Stratford Shakespearean Festival.

The Head, Guts and Sound Bone Dance was first performed at the Arts and Culture Centre, St John's, Newfoundland, 4 March 1973.

PRODUCTION
Director / **Tony Chadwick**
Set Design / **John Roddis**
Lighting / **Tony Duarte**
Sound / **Sharon Buehler**

CAST
Clyde Rose / Skipper Pete
Pat Byrne / Uncle John
Flo Edwards / Rachel
Dick Buehler / Absalom
Kelly Buehler, Paul Kelly, Perry Fowler / Children
Geoff Seymour / Lew
Leslie Mulholland / Aiden

CHARACTERS
Skipper Pete, 80
Uncle John, 60
Absalom, 60
Aiden, Lew, men of the village
Child
Wife to Uncle John

ACT ONE

The curtain rises on a typical splitting room on a fishing stage. The room rises from the landward side and runs generally to one third of the way out on the stage. At high tide, water runs beneath its whole length. At low tide, the sea-ward end (rear) still is far enough over the water for guts to be emptied, buckets hauled to wash down. They're low, noisome, dank. The external timbers are skeleton grey. Inside a luminous green dampness masks the same grey. The largest entrance is at backstage centre. When the door opens the platform can be seen – widely spaced pine logs dropping smartly into the sea after a few yards. Inside, stage right is a jumble of gear of all kinds, rope, barrels, heaps of netting, buoys. Downstage right is the second entrance, effected by climbing (or jumping) a few feet from the outside up onto the main platform level. At centre right is an ancient pot-bellied stove. Backstage left is the splitting table. Down from that, a couple of salt barrels. The left wall has a ragged window, once a church window, saved from an abandoned church somewhere and put to use by a crude insertion into the room. Low beams spread the rear towards the auditorium. From them too hang a variety of implements, pots, grapples, gaffs. Downstage left is a frame from which hangs a net in the process of completion. At left centre a small trap, opened, reveals a drop to the sea. The whole effect must be one of apparent mess and confusion, an immense variety of gear representing man, and fish, and the sea in a tottering, near-derelict place, and yet also reveal, as we become accustomed to it, an almost fanatical sense of order.

Morning light. A faint sound of sea. Skipper Pete *enters downstage right (does not yet open the door). He stands listening. An explosive screech of gulls. It dies away. He tramps on upstage and disappears. Another explosive screeching of gulls. He opens the door at rear, takes one pace into the room. The door swings back on him. He swears.*

Skipper Pete: God damn door!

(He disappears back through the door. Seizes it from behind, and fastens it – out of sight from the audience. Re-appears in the door frame. Takes one pace inside then turns his back. Looks seawards. Gives a deep grunt – perhaps of satisfaction. Turns – moves a few paces downstage. Pauses. Scratches himself in the crotch. Shakes his head. Unzippers his fly. Turns. Moves back to the doorway. Urinates over the water. Turns. Does up his fly. Gives another grunt of satisfaction. Moves towards the stove. He lifts the stove lid. Puts it to one side. Moves into the jumbled stage right straight to a barrel containing splits. Takes a yaffle. Moves back to stove. Puts the wood in the stove. Moves back up stage right, straight to bottle containing stove oil. Moves back to stove. Pours the oil liberally but carefully onto the wood. Takes back the bottle. Returns to the stove. Extracts a match and throws it in. Stays a moment, waiting to make sure the oil has caught. Grunts again. Replaces the lid. Moves across to net and frame. Picks it up exactly where he left off and begins to knit the net.

He stands facing off stage left through the cracked frame of the church window. The light, growing stronger, betrays the presence of sun. He begins to sing, fragments of an old ballad ... Looking out as his fingers move amongst the netting ...)

Skipper Pete: At the tender age of sixteen years,
                         I had to sail away,
                 All on a banking schooner – *(Hums)*

(He frowns – as if recollecting the words. Smiles. Hums the tune again loudly. Pauses to cough. Then spit. The hands all the time working.)

All on a banking schooner,
In the morning light of day,
All on a banking schooner *(Hums to himself)*
I stowed my gear away –

Funny – can't remember it now.

(Begins to hum the tune again with concentration ... half-way through he's interrupted ... Uncle John appears downstage right. Looks up at the sky. Nods at the smoke. Enters the room downstage right. He carries a can slung over his shoulder by a rope. He shuts the door behind him. Pete, still humming, has continued to look out of the window. Uncle John nods in his direction.)

Uncle John: 'Ow do, Skipper.

(Skipper Pete nods back without turning his head.)

Skipper Pete: 'Ow do.

(John moves up to the splitting table, swings the can from his shoulder. Puts it squarely in the middle. He comes and stands by the stove, rubbing his hands. A moment's silence.)

Uncle John: Fine morning.

Skipper Pete: Seen worse.

Uncle John: Better than yistiday.

Skipper Pete: Not so good as Wednesday afore last.

(A pause. John ponders this.)

Uncle John: No. I grant you that. Not as good as Wednesday afore last.

(A pause.)

Uncle John: Last Saturday weren't too bad neither. Got a gallon of berries.

(Skipper Pete pauses in his work. Turns and looks at John. Spits thoughtfully.)

Skipper Pete: Partridge?

Uncle John: Marsh.

Skipper Pete: I allow. Last Satiday weren't too bad.

Uncle John: Sunday were half decent. Act of God I s'pose. For the Bishop.

(Skipper Pete *begins at the net again. Spits.*)

Uncle John: I saw the Bishop.

(*Without waiting for any kind of reply he goes into the gloom stage right and emerges with an armful of birch chunks. He puts two on the stove. Places the remainder carefully at its feet.*)

Uncle John: Did you see the Bishop?

Skipper Pete: I didn't bother. No arches.

Uncle John: No. It's not the same.

Skipper Pete: I mind when we used to make 'em all along the path 'e'd come. T'ree, four arches ... bigger'n old church door they was. And all the maids wid flowers.

(*Uncle John goes to door stage right. He throws it open. Looks for a moment. Then from the side of the door where it has been leaning takes a gaff, and props the door open, in such a way that it makes two triangles of the entrance. Stands framed in the door.*)

Uncle John: He'd come by boat.

(*No response. A pause. He raises his voice.* Skipper Pete *is slightly deaf.*)

Not the same by road.

Skipper Pete: No. The road's not the same.

Uncle John: Might a meant something then.

Skipper Pete: It did. We made the arches for'n to go under. All the way up the road. Past the houses. It meant something.

Uncle John: I remember the Bishop standing up in the boat in his robes. The cross in front of him. The whole place turned out in their best. The harses and sheep driven to top pasture. (*Chuckles*) The hooman sheep to the wharf. (*Chuckles*) Even the pigs clean. Old dogs on chains. (*A pause. Scornfully*) This one now. Didn't matter how much shit was on the road. Came by car. (*Indignant. Strides across to* Skipper Pete.) A Bishop. Can you imagine that now. Confirmation by car. Where's the God in that I'd like to know.

Skipper Pete: No arches. That's what it was. (*He suddenly drops the net. A pause.*) Time for a mug?

Uncle John: Aye ... (*Half absently*) Aye.

(*Unhooks a kettle – ancient black kettle from the beam. Goes back stage right. Dips kettle into barrel of water. Brings it still dripping back to stove. Takes off lid of stove. Places lid to one side. Puts kettle on hole thus exposed. Turns upstage to his can on the splitting table. Extracts the makings for tea. Brings them back to stove. Moves downstage right of door. Hanging on two hooks are four mugs. He brings back two mugs to stove. Stands thinking. Goes back. Gets the other two mugs.* Skipper Pete *moves left. Selects a barrel. Rolls it towards stove, between the net and the stove. Sits, taking his cap off. Watches* John *preparing tea. Suddenly sees the other two mugs.*)

Skipper Pete: Where's Absalom?

(*A pause.* John *is uncomfortable.*)

Skipper Pete: Should be here.

(John *busies himself with tea.*)

Skipper Pete: (*Getting angry. He begins to twitch.*) He's never late. Ye are. Often. That woman of yours I s'pose. Useless as the day ever was. God damnedest child I ever did raise. Glad to be rid of 'er. But Absalom.

Uncle John: (*Sharply*) He's gone.

Skipper Pete: Gone?

Uncle John: Fishing.

Skipper Pete: Fishing? (*Half rises, turns to window. A pause.*)

Uncle John: Lard Jesus Christ, where else 'as the poor bastard got to go?

Skipper Pete: But dey's no fish.

Uncle John: You knows it, I knows it. And he knows it.

Skipper Pete: But what's he coddin about at ... (*Sits slowly. Puzzled. Pained.*)

Uncle John: (*Bitter*) He 'as dreams. Didn't you know? Dreams of all the fish once. Of the mackerel thicker'n on the water than moonlight, whispering together. Then 'e 'as to go. Here's your tea.

(*Hands* Skipper Pete *his tea. Goes back to stove. Takes kettle off. Puts in two birch chunks. Replaces stove lid. Puts kettle on floor. Takes up his own mug. Walks across* Skipper Pete *to the net. Looks at it thoughtfully. Turns.*)

Uncle John: You've nearly finished.

Skipper Pete: Should've finished yesterday.

Uncle John: Wednesday.

Skipper Pete: I allow as how Thursday's all right.

Uncle John: It's a civil enough day.

Skipper Pete: How's the killick?

Uncle John: Binding to do. That's all.

Skipper Pete: Should finish together then.

Uncle John: Celebrate then eh? Bit o' shine. Just like the old days.

Skipper Pete: Aye. We'll have a time!

Uncle John: If Absalom's back.

Skipper Pete: Can't understand it. We agreed. Next year. New nits. Gear. Four'n us. We'd manage. We'd show the youngsters.

Uncle John: (*Walks back to stove. Sinks on his haunches.*) Aye. They're useless. Bloody great boats they can't handle. Can't hold their liquor. Feared of animals. Like the fella said, wed to music and misery.

Skipper Pete: My Absalom. Fishing! Without me! Jesus. The lad'll ... (*Pause*)

Uncle John: What will he do?

Skipper Pete: Nivir did grow up, see. Had to lead'n all the way. That time he fell off the harse on the way out of the woods ...

Uncle John: (*not without sardonic mirth*) And ye sent him back in, didn't ye. " 'Ow many sticks boy" ye said. "Ninety-five" he said, and it fifteen below and blowing and coming on dark. I remember it now. "Holy Christ" ye roared ... I was just coming from the stage hid then and I heard ye. "Holy Christ. Get back on that damn harse and git another five or by God I'll leather you." And him already taller than you.

Skipper Pete: All right for ye to talk now John. But ye knows ye had to bring 'em up 'ard else they wouldn't survive. Look at 'em now – they's nothing to survive against. I had to do it, John.

Uncle John: I remember the harse coming back on his own. And it blowing a blizzard then. And us saying we'd better go in and look for'n. And ye saying: "Let the young bugger get here by hisself." (*Chuckles*) I remember it well. "Let the young bugger get here by hisself."

Skipper Pete: (*Gets to his feet and glares at* John *malevolently*) My Jesus John. Ye watch. I'm not past giving ye a punch in the mout'.

Uncle John: Don't be so Jesus foolish. Ye'd die of a heart attack.

(Pete *sits again, breathing heavily. Ancient leader of a savage pack with the instincts still there but the ability in pitiful disrepair.*)

Uncle John: And what'd be the pint. I got nar tooth left anyhow ... (*He laughs*) Eh boy? (*Goes across to* Skipper Pete *and punches him in the shoulder.* Skipper Pete *begins to laugh. They laugh together. Cough. Fall out of breath. Breathe heavily. Suddenly outside – a sudden explosion of gulls.*)

Skipper Pete: Blast them gulls. Seems as if they do be mocking a man. All the time. Time was ... (*Memory fades – comes back*) Time was ... Got me own back on a few of 'n though.

Uncle John: Aah! Bit of bait on a bobber ...

Skipper Pete: Down they'd go. Greediest buggers in the sea ...

Uncle John: (*Screeches like a gull – raises his arm*) There they'd be. The hook in their t'roat. (*A pause. They both remember meals of seagull.*)

Skipper Pete: They never seemed to mind it once the wings was broke ... Tame as chickens some of 'n, and the bread they'd eat ... Get fat as a goose.

Uncle John: Aye. Seems the law's agin anything a man might do to help hisself to a good meal. (*Gulls screech*) Listen to'n. Got worse since they was protected. (*Gulls screech*) Dam' sight worse.

Skipper Pete: Not so bad as the Funks – even now!

Uncle John: No, not so bad as the Funks.

Skipper Pete: I stayed there once all night. For a bet.

Uncle John: I 'lows I heard that.

Skipper Pete: Screeching. All night screeching. Up to me arms in shit.

Uncle John: (*Laughs*). I'd like to have seen that. (Pete *glares.* John's *laugh dies slowly in his throat.* Uncle John *moves back toward rear door.*)

Uncle John: S'pose I'll go get the killick then. (*No reply from* Pete.)

Uncle John: Will I git the killick? (*No reply.*)

Uncle John: Finished wit yer tay? (*No reply.*)

Uncle John: Is ye finished wit yer tay er what?

Skipper Pete: Eh?

Uncle John: Is ye finished wit yer tay? (*No answer.*)

(John *crosses. Takes* Pete's *mug. Goes back and picks up his own. Places both mugs on the hatch. Goes back. Comes back with bucket on the end of a rope. Moves mugs. Lifts hatch. Lowers bucket. Draws up water. Closes hatch.*

*Washes mugs in bucket. Lifts hatch. Pours water away. Is about to close it.
Pauses. Decides he wants to urinate. Raises it. Turns back to* Pete, *facing
right. Lowers zip carefully. Is about to commence ...)*

Skipper Pete: (*Savagely*) Can't you go outside.

Uncle John: (*Startled*) Eh?

Skipper Pete: Can't you go outside. Always was a dirty bugger. Tanned
your arse once on the Labrador for pissin' into the wind. Sprayed all on
us. Dirty little bugger ye was.

Uncle John: (*Defensive – a child as then*) I were only fourteen then.

Skipper Pete: Aye. And you've got the same habits now. There's things
better done in private. That's why they're called privates.

Uncle John: I never called 'em privates. They's in the army.

Skipper Pete: What do you know about that, eh? Never was in the army.
I was there. Beaumont Hamel. The Somme. You'd never have survived
there. Unless I was wid yer. Ye might have stood a chanst then. Privates.
What do you know about privates?

Uncle John: If ye're talking about the same thing I'm talking about I
knows as much about 'em as any man. An 'right now I want to know what
business it is of yours where I pisses, when I pisses and how I pisses.

Skipper Pete: I told yer. There's a lot of things done better in private, an'
pissin's one of 'em. Dey's places in the world you'd get arrested for doing
that. I know. I was there.

Uncle John: Same sea in't? Sea's a big place.

Skipper Pete: Not the pint. I 'low the sea's a big place. Now a man's a
small place. You've got to have order. Decency. There 'as to be a way of
doing things. A man's way. That's why we're here isn't it? They's only we
left.

(Uncle John *grumbles and fumbles with his fly. His sense of order has received a setback. He begins to move backstage.*)

Skipper Pete: Hatch.

Uncle John: (*Turning*) Eh?

Skipper Pete: The hatch then. You've left the hatch open.

Uncle John: Jesus Christ!

Skipper Pete: S'pose a sea hove in. What then?

Uncle John: (*Turning back disgusted*) Sea. It's like a bloody pond. (*He
slams the hatch down.*)

Skipper Pete: Ye never know. I mind the time – thirty-two was it, or three? Me'n your father was bringing the schooners back from St John's. Ye was on my boat. Not yet twenty-one ye were. Ye were safer with me. 'Twas as well I took ye. Yer father an they was so god-damned drunk after selling the catch they nearly hit the Battery on the way out through the Narrows.

(John *moves as if to protest but* Pete *waves him away.* John *moves stage right and urinates out over the diagonal across door stage right and stays there, a sullen shadow.*)

Skipper Pete: Your father, mind, was a Godless man.

Uncle John: (*Interrupting*) Ye old hypocrite.

Skipper Pete: (*Unmoved*) A man without a decent sense of order. I mind he had a couple o'pigs aboard. And for sport they run 'em up the mainmast in a barrel and let'n go. Down come the pigs – I saw it, ye didn't. Ye was down below cooking. The worst cook I remember, as was ever sent aboard a boat. Smash! All over the boat. Barrel. Pigs and all. An' they laughing, drunken fools, the guts flying. I tried to hail 'em. "Look out to your trim John b'y. They's weather coming." None of 'em took no heed. Shouted back over the water, "Don't ye mind us Uncle. We's all right. Just knock some fear and God into that boy of mine and leave us be." (Pete *gets up. Goes forestage ... staring out ... reliving the event ...*) "Damn fools," I shouted, "Damn fools. Go to Hell then." (*He's almost dancing with self-satisfaction.*) "Devil's bait," I shouted. "That's what ye'll be afore marnin'." Then the first gust came an' she with all canvas flying ... ripped her mains'l off and she keeled over. An they still laughing and staggering. I'd a prayed then and there, but I reckoned it would 'ave done no good. Aye. (*He stomps slowly back to his seat.*) Saw no more of'n after dark. Wind came on Nor E. Driving snow an' a sea raging like a barren woman. She got fed that night ... (*Grim satisfaction*) Not a body ever found. Not a spar.

Uncle John: (*Turning in from door*) Not even a piece of pig eh? But Skipper Pete, the Iron Man, come through. Never lost a ship; lost one man in fifty years. Ice and fire, storm and flood – Skipper Pete come through. The legend of the coast! Trips to St John's. Signed pictures of Joey Smallwood – God knows why, he couldn't stand drinking water! CBC cameras and wet-eared pups praising ye on yer birthday. And what for, eh? What for? (*In a sudden movement almost throws himself face to face with* Pete) It was for ye, wasn't it. Not the ships. Not the men. Ye didn't give a damn for none of it, but for yer own pride.

Skipper Pete: I saved you, boy. Don't ye forget that. More than once. And many another walking the world because o' me.

Uncle John: (*Anguished*) I would to Christ Jesus ye'd let some of the poor

bastards drown. Like me father and they. Drown free. But ye broke 'em
ye did. Like bits of driftwood. Ye saved 'em all right. But not to stand up.
Not to walk the world. Crawl! Ye made 'em crawl. Ye made me crawl.
(*Turns back upstage. Turns back. He is crying.*) We should have hung you.
But no. I remember me father saying – saying ... We escaped the rule of
others. And exchanged it for the rule of our own kind. No escape, boy, he
said. No escape. Except to kill 'n or run away agin. And they's nowhere to
run. Merciful God!

Skipper Pete: (*Roaring*) God is not merciful. (*He gets up trailing the net
after him. Goes to* John) Don't ye ever forget that. "The Lord is a strong-
hold to him whose way is upright, but destruction to evildoers." Isn't that
what I've just told ye? "He who spares the rod hates his son." Can ye say
I didn't love ye?

Uncle John: I'll give ye back your Proverbs. "A man's pride will bring
him low, but he who is lowly will gain honour."

(*A pause.* Pete *turns back, slowly pulling the net together.*)

Skipper Pete: Ye can't say I didn't teach ye neither.

Uncle John: (*Coming after him*) But what does it mean? What does it
mean? (*Grips him by the shoulders and turns him. They face each other. Still
in command,* Pete *throws* John's *hands off. They stand facing each other.*)

Skipper Pete: It doesn't matter what it means. It's enough that it's there.

Uncle John: It's not enough. Ye use it when it's convenient. Like people.
But I knows ye well enough. When ye wants to cuss ye cusses. And when
ye wanted a woman ye took'n. And when ye wanted a drink ye got drunk
like the rest of us.

Skipper Pete: No. Ye damn fool. I did those things when I had to ...

Uncle John: When ye had to! Why – you're making an excuse! An excuse!

Skipper Pete: No. It was to show ye it was possible for a man to fall *and
rise.* (*Suddenly chuckles*) An' it kept ye all guessing. (*Goes back to his seat.*)

Uncle John: (*A light dawning*) So that's it. When ye'd druv us to the point
o' mutiny ye'd always do something – human. You bastard.

Skipper Pete: It has to be done! Ye just agreed yourself. To survive. I did
what was best. An they was order to it. Like ye said. About the Bishop.
And the youngsters. They's got no arches now ye see. Just space. And
they flop about like broken birds hither and yon, lost. I made an arch for
ye. Aye – an' I wasn't the only one either. They was others.

Uncle John: Arch! 'Twas a bloody prison. (*Confused*) Dey's something there though. (*Walks forward right.*) Something. Can't quite put me finger to it. Is it because I'm what I am that they is what they is. Because o' ye and them.

Skipper Pete: It's all of it. It's ye and the Govermint wid its eddication and its handouts and the women snivelling after hot air stoves and 'lectric ovens and motor cars and Bishops goin' from altar to altar and seein' nothing between ...

Uncle John: (*Unhearing*) They was either hypocritical God-driven old tyrants like ye or wild men like me fader who cursed God and man and the sea until one o' the three took'n.

(*A pause*)

Skipper Pete: (*Sighs*) We'se old men now, me son. No pint in us fretting now. Just do what we have to do. That's all they is. Relive the good times. (*A pause*) They was good times. (John *does not answer.*) They was good times. (John *is staring painfully out.*) Canvas − salt-stiff cracking in the wind. Fish in their t'ousands. The voyage home wid a fair wind and the holds full. Walking thru' the skinny clerks o' St John's, they feared to look at'n. Aye they was good times.

Uncle John: Were they? (*A pace towards* Pete) I need to know, Pete. God help me, I don't know myself. Was they good times?

(Pete *looks at him. Then down at the net in his hands.*)

Skipper Pete: I'll finish me net now, son. It's time. (*This is said with an air of finality.* John *pauses a moment, indecisive. Then moves backstage area. Exits onto stage head.*)

Skipper Pete: (*Singing-humming*)

Eternal father strong to save
Whose arm does bind the restless wave ...

(*Pauses − puzzled. To himself*)

That's no good fer today. Today's fer celebratin'. The end of the voyage. The journey. (*Hums again.*)
At the tender age of sixteen years,
I had to sail away,
All on a banking schooner,
In the morning light of day,

(*A woman's voice outside.*)

Woman: John. John.

Skipper Pete: (*Looks up sharply. Cocks his head, spits with disgust.*) Get in anywhere they will.

(John *staggers back through rear door carrying a huge killick. Places it right centre.*)

Woman: (*Off*) John. Are ye there?

Skipper Pete: Don't let that in 'ere.

Uncle John: 'Tis yer own daugher. (*Bitter*) Remember?

Skipper Pete: Kin be the Divil's for all I know. Jest don't let it in here.

(*The woman appears in D/S right doorway.*)

Woman: There you are.

Skipper Pete: (*Laughing without mirth*) Go to her, boy. Go to her. (*Mimics*) John. John.

Uncle John: (*Angry*) Ye mind, Skipper. Ye mind. She wouldn't 'a come unless it was important.

(Pete *spits emphatically once more.* John *crosses to his wife. She's still standing outside the door.*)

Wife: I jist wanted to know, John, if ye was coming to Aunt Alice's funeral. It's at three o'clock.

Uncle John: (*Uncertain*) Oh aye. I'd forgotten. We was finishing up ye see. I s'spose we'd better go then. (*Turns to* Pete) Will we be done by three, Skipper? (Pete *doesn't bother to answer.* John *takes a pace towards him.*) Aunt Alice is to be buried at three.

Skipper Pete: When did she die?

(*Wife climbs across entrance, and goes right of John.*)

Wife: Last night, poor soul. And her as frail as a bird. "Put another quilt on me for the Lard Jesus Sake" she said, not meaning it blasphemous, mind, "For I'm so thin I'm sure I'll fly to Heaven afore me time's up." And she laughed then ye know – just like a poor sick chicken the sound was, a little whispering in the throat, and then she closed her ...

Skipper Pete: (*Abruptly*) Which cemetery?

Uncle John: (*Anxious to prevent his wife getting into full flow again*) That'd be the Pentecostal wouldn't it, maid? Alice and they was all Pentecostal.

Skipper Pete: (*As if unhearing*) What cemetery did ye say?

Uncle John: (*Shouting*) Pentecostal. She's to be put down in the Pentecostal.

Skipper Pete: I'll not be going. Never been to a Pentecostal service in me life an I'm too old to start that foolishness now.

Wife: She was kin, father. Ye should be ashamed of yerself. And she did many a good turn for our poor mother, God rest her soul.

Skipper Pete: (*Suddenly raging*) Ah, to the Divil with the lot o' ye. What she did fer yer mother on this earth might help her in the next and I wish her good luck wc' her good deeds. But she did nothing for me, and she's a Pentecost. And I'll not be going to any arm-raising mumbo jumbo like that. (*As an afterthought*) Not while I'm alive anyways.

Wife: Ye haven't changed. (*She pushes past John and crosses to Pete.*) Not one bit, father. Only one breath away from God or the Devil hisself and still as spiny as a whore's egg.

Skipper Pete: Mind yer place, girl. Ye're in my house and don't forget it.

Wife: (*Hurling across stage right*) House is it? (*Laughs*) A house. Oh sure, 'tis where ye spend time making fools of yourselves, the two of ye. Coiling and uncoiling the same rope day after day. Knitting nets you'll never use. Making killicks. And they's only fit now to make ornaments in the homes of the stuck-up in St John's and upalong. Talking about things that once were and will never be again, Thank God. (*She is flushed and angry. Storms over to the killick and with one heave pushes it over.*)

Uncle John: That's enough, maid. Ye've no right to be saying those things.

Wife: Enough! Oh, 'tis enough all right. I saw ye with the can on yistiday. Time for another celebration is it? A drunk at the end of the voyage and ye nivir moving from the stage hid from one day – no, year, to the next. An' poor simple Absalom the only one can stand upright in a boat. What'll the catch be today, boys? Three, four fish!

Uncle John: That's enough, woman. 'Tis no business of yours. We don't harm no one.

Wife: Just ye, John. (*Softening, putting her hand on his arm*) Can't ye see? That's the way he holds onto ye now. Just like it used to be. Smash yer face in if he caught ye with a drink on the voyage, and then encourage you to riot yer last cent away at the end of it, so ye had to go back. He's still doin' it, John. And ye should be at home now, on the daybed, or out on the bridge. With a nice cup of tea and a few squares I'd make ye. Living comfortable. Talking to yer neighbours. Waiting to see yer grandchildren.

(Pete *gets up. The conversation has taken a dangerous turn. He points his stick at her.*)

Skipper Pete: I niver wanted ye in my house. When ye were born. And I still don't want ye. Get out. (*He moves as if to strike her with his stick but she is unflinching, unafraid. Scornful.*)

Uncle John: Come on, maid. Come on out now. I'll think about the funeral ... (*He takes her by the arm as if to propel her to the door.*)

Wife: Get your foolish hands off me. I'll find me own way to the door. Aye, and home. And to me Maker when the time comes. (*She moves to the door. Turns back.*) Don't forgit yer supper will be waiting. *And* the television ye're ashamed to tell him ye watch. And the electric blanket the doctor told ye to get to keep your arthritic bones from paining at nights. (*Makes one last desperate effort.*) For the love of God, John. Leave off this foolishness and come home.

(John *pauses, uncertain.*)

Skipper Pete: Go home, John, for the Lard Jesus sake. Go home. I'll celebrate the end of the voyage by meself.

Uncle John: I'll be along by and by now, maid.

Wife: An' I knows when that'll be. (*Almost in tears*) Theys times, so they is, when I wishes you'd fall into the water to be bait fer the connors and the tansies. If theys anything more foolish than a drunken young man 'tis a drunken old one. An if theys anything more foolish than a fine young man thinking he can make a living from the sea, 'tis an old man who can't stop lying to himself about the living he used to make. (*She turns, exits, pausing on the other side of the barrier to say*) I'll say a prayer at the graveside for ye, father. But I doubt it'll do any good.

(*We hear her as she walks back along the rim of the stage and down the steps.*)

(*A pause.*)

Skipper Pete: (*Savage*) I told ye not to let her in.

Uncle John: (*Defensive*) She's your daughter.

Skipper Pete: Useless bitch. Always was. Can't understand why ye married her.

Uncle John: (*Angrily raising the killick and dragging it towards his seat*) Ye was happy enough fer it to happen at the time.

Skipper Pete: (*Laughs*) Thought I'd get rid of both of ye at once. Killing two birds with one slingshot.

Uncle John: No. No. That's not it. (*He stumps up stage right. Finds some heavy twine. Comes back and begins to fasten the four ends together*) Ye thought ... (*viciously tightening the tope and punctuating his words with the actions*) Ye thought that ... with two of your responsibilities under one roof ... that it'd be easier to bend'n.

Skipper Pete: (*Is enjoying himself. Is enjoying John's anger*) John! John!

When your father was drownded, I took ye fer me own. Treated ye just like me own sons ...

Uncle John: (*Bitter*) Aye. That's true enough.

Skipper Pete: Now they's you and Absalom. And me. That's all they is left of all of us. And I thought, if ye married me daughter, ye might be able to shut her blather long enough to give me a grandson, even two maybe ...

Uncle John: (*Stung*) There you goes again. Give you a grandson. Not me. Not for her and me. No. D'ye know what ye did? Ye came between us even there that's what ye did. It was like (*he struggles for words – feelings. Desperation*) I'd be lying atop her and I'd hear your voice. Roaring. Give it to her son. Give it to her. Don't stop now. Don't give up. And she felt the same ... We had to stop ...

Skipper Pete: (*Still goading*) Two daughters. And ye had to stop! What a man!

Uncle John: There was no love in it. Ye killed it. In her. In me ...

Skipper Pete: (*Mock rage*) What's love got to do with having sons. They's necessary. To make things continue as they were. To ...

Uncle John: Then why in Jesus name didn't ye knock her up yerself?

(*A shocked pause.* John *is shocked at himself.* Pete, *however, is not.*)

Skipper Pete: That's blasphemy, son. The real kind. Not a man's kind.

Uncle John: (*Tormented*) God damn it. I didn't mean it. Not that way. (*Desperate*) Ye knows I never meant it that way.

Skipper Pete: What way did ye mean it ...

Uncle John: (*Raging around like a tormented animal, touching something here, throwing rope down there, spinning a barrel across the floor*)

This is it isn't it? This is us. God damn it, this is the answer to the sum the teacher could never knock into me stupid skull. And I hates it. I hates it. (*Throws more gear about.*) But I don't understand anything else. It's too late.

(*A pause. He goes and slumps by the killick, his head in his hands.*)

Skipper Pete: (*Rises. Crosses to him. Puts a hand on his shoulder. Goes backstage, speaks out of the gloom*) Ye do understand son. We understand. The old way. The only way. The proper way to do things. Greet the day at cockcrow. The sea, no matter the weather. Stack the gear. Mend the nets. Make the killick. Keep the store in order. They's nothing without it. (*A moment of insight*) The new ways is for new people, that's all. We don't want their sympathy. And I don't give a damn if anyone understands it or not. It's just the way things always was. (*Softly*) When fish was t'ousands, that was the time. Sea and wind howling like the Devil after a man's soul but the traps was out and the fish waiting ... (Pete *comes down and takes* John *by the arm and raises him up*). Look boy. Look. (*He turns him round and they stand facing out through the church window over the sea.*) The sun's on the water. Just like it always was. Days like this when we've given her every stitch of canvas and foamed down the sound – the water alive with boats about us all rushing to git to the grounds first. Good men, John b'y. Good men. But they's gone. And their boats gone wid'n. And the land gone wid'n too. The fences broken. The trees marching back over the hayfields.

(*There is a noise outside. A shouting. A child's voice.*)

Child: Somebody, quick. Jimmy Fogarty's fallen off the wharf.

Skipper Pete: (*Unhearing*) People kin laugh at us, John b'y. But we knows what we is.

Child: (*Offstage*) Help! Quick somebody. (*Appears in doorway stage right. Rushes in*) Uncle John. Uncle Pete. Jimmy Fogarty's fallen off the wharf fishin' for connors and he can't swim. He's drowning.

Skipper Pete: (*He and* John *still facing out,* Pete *with his arm gripped tightly on* John*'s. They don't turn around. The child is behind them.*)

Skipper Pete: I mind when young Amos fell overboard from his father's schooner on the Labrador. Remember that, John? Wind a bit fresh. They wasn't watching the sail. Jibed a bit sudden and took him straight over the side into a school of dogfish.

Uncle John: Aye. I remember that all right.

Child: (*Tugging at them from behind*) Uncle John. Uncle Pete. Please come quick. Jimmy's drowning.

Uncle John: Stripped clean in ten minutes. Took three of us to hold his father down from going in after him.

Skipper Pete: Aye. No pint in two of 'em feeding the devils.

Child: (*As any child ignored by adults persistently ... less forcefully*) Jimmy Fogarty's in the water ... (*They ignore him. The child rushes off ... his cries for help fading in the distance.*)

Skipper Pete: Every time they'd haul a dogfish in the nit after that he'd hack it to pieces ...

Uncle John: Aye. Like a wild man. Or he'd cut his belly open just enough for the blood to show then fling it back overboard and watch his brothers eat'n alive.

(*A pause. There's a commotion outside which continues as* Pete *comes down slowly to his net,* John *to his killick. They begin to finish their work.*)

Skipper Pete: We shouldn't be too long at it now.

Uncle John: Not long. (*He wrestles with the twine.*)

Skipper Pete: Absalom's not so foolish he'd stay out all day.

Uncle John: I 'lows he'll come in directly now, when he's caught something.

Skipper Pete: Then we'll have our own Thanksgiving.

Uncle John: (*Laughs, without mirth*) Well. We'm alive. We can give thanks for that.

(*The noise outside is punctuated by a long high-pitched woman's howl ... An outburst of voices which dies away.* Pete *gets up and looks out of the window. Turns.*)

Skipper Pete: I 'low that the day is as civil as Wednesday afore last.

Uncle John: I allow that it is. (*Nods. Smiles*) I 'low 'tis.

(*He works on in silence as ...*)

Blackout

ACT TWO

The finished net is looped and draped from the beams stage left. The killick, finished, is now downstage left. Pete and John are sitting on two barrels on either side of the stove. In front of them another, smaller barrel on which rests three glasses and the jug of shine. As the curtain opens they are sitting, staring ahead, saying nothing. In the distance a bell begins to toll. John, after a moment listening, gets up slowly, goes to window left and stands looking out.

Uncle John: That's the bell for Aunt Alice. (*No response*) Quite a crowd too. They's Faheys. They's Catholic. Culls. They's Anglican. An' all the Pentecosts o' course. Looks like it's goin' to be one of they mixed services everyone keeps on about. (*A snort from* Pete.)

Skipper Pete: That's easy for funerals.

(John *turns from the window, surprised.*)

Uncle John: Eh?

Skipper Pete: Mixed funerals. They's easy. Don't mean nothing when the party's dead.
Christenings now – that's different.

Uncle John: How is it different?

Skipper Pete: You never heard tell of the Pope attending a mixed christening now, have you.

Uncle John: (*Puzzled*) No – I can't say that I have.

Skipper Pete: Well. Until he do I'll stick to what I know. I thought I'd taught you that.

(*The bell is still tolling.* John *turns his head back and looks out. He says, with a trace of irony.*)

Uncle John: Ye taught me so much, Skipper. I 'lows it's difficult to remember all of it.

Skipper Pete: (*Unaware*) Never change a habit or an opinion until someone proves there's a better one.

Uncle John: You and the Pope 'as got something in common after all then, Skipper ...

(Pete, *surprised, is about to query this when there is the unmistakable sound of a four horsepower Acadia.*)

Skipper Pete: Listen, John. Listen.

(*Still it can be heard – amongst the bells.*)

Skipper Pete: Damn those bells. Enough to jangle the wits from the living.

(*The bells suddenly stop. The Acadia has the world of sound to itself.*)

Skipper Pete: It's Absalom. Absalom, I'll be bound.

(John *too is excited. He rushes backstage to the stage head door. Shouts back.*)

Uncle John: It's him. It is Absalom.

Skipper Pete: Any fish?

Uncle John: What?

Skipper Pete: Any fish?

Uncle John: Can't tell from here.

Skipper Pete: Then ask him, ye fool.

(John *cups his hands.*)

Uncle John: Absalom. Hey, Absalom. Any fish?

(*The sound of the engine is quite close now.*)

Uncle John: Fish, boy. Any fish? (*A pause*) Skipper. He's holden'n up. He's got – one, two – my God he's got six. And they's big'uns.

Skipper Pete: That's my Absalom. Six, eh? A harvest. John, me son. The pan ...

(John *scuttles to the table. Gets the pan. Brings it reverently down to the stove. Puts it on. Goes down right. Fetches bucket. Lifts hatch. Lowers bucket. Fetches up water. Puts bucket down. Lowers hatch. Pours some water from the bucket into the pan ... Pauses ...*)

Uncle John: Skipper. The table.

Skipper Pete: (*Lost in reverie*) 1931 now, that was the year. 900 quintals, boat loaded until she was awash. Weather perfect. The sea like glass. The icebergs rearing up and folding in the sun. Lost a man that trip – that's all. Tommy Burns from Greenspond. Fell overboard. Drunk. A single man, though, not as if he'd a family to keep. We divided his share among the rest of us.

Uncle John: Skipper. The table!

Skipper Pete: Eh? Oh, aye. The table.

(*He gets up slowly and goes back to* John. *With difficulty they raise the table and bring it down right centre. The gear is left on it.* John *unhooks oilskins from right wall, hands them to Pete, who begins to draw them on.* John *sets three plates, knife and fork and places them up stage left. Busies himself sharpening the splitting knife. Just as he's done this the sound of the motor stops. For a minute only the sound of the sea, and the occasional gull cry.* Pete *turns on his barrel and stares at the doorway.* John – *standing – does the same thing.* Absalom *stands framed in the stage head door, six fish hanging from a hook in his huge hand. He is gaunt and bent. Despite the age of* Pete *and* John, *we've been expecting, because of the conversation, someone much younger. But he is, of course, sixty, or near to it. He has still, however, the face of a child – a characteristic of some aspects of retardation. He speaks slowly, with difficulty, and has trouble looking his father in the face.*)

Absalom: I got some fish, father.

Skipper Pete: Good boy. That's a good boy. Bring them here, Absalom. Bring them here me son.

Absalom: I forgot to tell you I was going fishing, father.

Skipper Pete: That don't matter now boy. Bring them here.

(*Absalom advances cautiously into the room towards the table. Places the fish upon it.*)

Absalom: You see, father, the sun was shining.

Skipper Pete: (*His eyes gloating over the fish*) That's all right boy. All right.

Absalom: And I had a dream of fishes, father. Just like you talk about and

I can never remember. The sea was all fish, father. There was no water hardly.

Skipper Pete: (*Impatient*) It doesn't matter, son. Dreams don't matter. Fish – that's all that matters.

Absalom: (*Persistent, like a child*) But you were in the dream, father.

(Pete *takes a splitting knife from his trousers and a small sharpening stone. He begins to sharpen it with slow, deliberate actions, ignoring Absalom.*)

Absalom: I told ye. The sea wasn't the sea. It was fish. And ye were there, picking them up in your hands. Your hands, I couldn't tell what was fish and what was your hands (*Agitated*) I had to go, ye see, father. On account of yer hands.

Uncle John: I told him Absalom. And it was the right day to go. A good day to go. The one day ... (*He eyes* Pete *furtively, slides round table to barrel with mugs and shine on it.* Pete, *humming now, still sharpening knife.* John *pours. He whispers.*)

Uncle John: Drink, Absalom?

(Absalom *reaches for the mug eagerly, both lift mugs to their lips when ...*)

Skipper Pete: Nobody drinks. Not yet.

(*Like guilty school boys, both pause.*)

Skipper Pete: The fish, first.

(*The two hold a tableau, mugs to mouth almost. Put mugs down. Move to table.* Pete *splits, guts and removes the sound bones of the fish.* Absalom, *at a word from* John, *draws water. With a swish of his hand he sweeps the offal to the floor.* John *guts remainder of fish, passes to* Pete *who splits them.* John *takes the fish to the bucket still containing salt water and rinses them.*)

Skipper Pete: Water ready?

Uncle John: She's bilin'.

Skipper Pete: Put this one in the pot. Keep the rest for another day.

(John *puts the fish into the pan on the stove. He takes the remaining three backstage to a salt barrel, lifts the lid, drops the fish in. Replaces the lid.* Absalom *clears off the knives.* Pete *removes oilskins.* John *comes down, rinses his hands in the bloody water in the bucket, then joins* Pete *and* Absalom *who have moved right to drinks. The two look at him expectantly.* Pete *pours himself a mug of shine, raises his glass to his lips. The other two, with audible sighs of relief, do the same, when ...*)

Skipper Pete: No.

(*In pained disbelief they watch* Pete *lower his mug.*)

Skipper Pete: The table first. John. Absalom.

(*With reluctance they lower their mugs.* John *opens the trap. Throws down the bloody water. Lowers the bucket. Raises it. Swills down the table, wiping the remnants away with his hand.* Absalom *fetches a mop. Sweeps water and offal towards the trap.* John *raises bucket again, washing down floor. The operation complete, the trap is lowered.* John *and* Absalom *return to the drinking barrel. They pause — ancient fishing soldiers awaiting orders ...*)

Skipper Pete: Well, b'ys.

Uncle John: Well.

Absalom: (*After a pause*) Well.

Skipper Pete: The end of the voyage.

Uncle John: The end of a voyage.

Skipper Pete: A drink.

(John *once again pours three mugs of shine. Once again the three mugs are tipped slowly, deliberately, and drained. Moment of silence and intense inner satisfaction.*)

Skipper Pete: Well, b'ys, what's the news?

(*A pause.*)

Absalom: Father. I heard Aunt Alice died.

Skipper Pete: That's not news. That's history.

(*A pause.*)

Uncle John: They's catching plenty of herring in Placentia Bay.

Skipper Pete: They are?

Uncle John: I heard it on the news. The big boats. They's all there, catching herring.

Skipper Pete: Why ain't there none here then?

Uncle John: I don't know. (*The drink has made him more belligerent.*) How the hell do I know. You always ask foolish questions. All I know is they's herring in Placentia Bay.

Skipper Pete: That'll be the last place.

Uncle John: I 'low it will.

Skipper Pete: None after that. They stripped her clean, boys.

Absalom: Can we take the boat, father? Can we catch herring in Placentia Bay?

Skipper Pete: (*Roaring*) It's four hundred miles away, boy. (*Laughs*) And if they heard ye was coming they'd all swim away. Absalom, the fisherman.

Uncle John: He got today's fish. And they isn't any fish. Give the boy credit.

Skipper Pete: I'll give him credit. I taught him all he knew. If there was just one fish left in the ocean he should be able to find it. That's what I taught ye. And them damn politicans, and their stupid industries; and that damned Ottawa letting every bloody foreigner in the world drag the beds clean – they don't know nothing.

Uncle John: Ye should have taught them too. To spill their guts out into the ocean.

Skipper Pete: (*Unmoved*) Relief. (*Spits*) Welfare. Education. What was wrong with these, eh? (*Holds up hands*) What was wrong with these?

Uncle John: But ye knows, Skipper – they's no fish now. We're playing a game, that's all. A death game. The woman's right.

Skipper Pete: (*Suddenly strikes* John, *who stumbles and falls*) It's not a game. Ye cursed blind fool. We gits ready fer the fish year after year, that's all. And we waits. And out there, they knows we're waiting. And one day, they'll come back, in their t'ousands, when all the boats has gone away, and nobody thinks they's anymore. They's waiting for the old days like we is. When the trap and the handline and the jigger was something they understood and we understood. We took what we could get. They knew us, and we knew they, and they bred faster than we could take them. They bred enemies too, theirs and ours. (John *rises slowly, holding his head.*) We understood each other – the sea, and the cod, and the dog fish, and the sculpin, and the shark, and the whale. They knew us and we knew they. And if we keep ready, and we keep waiting, they'll come again. We can't give up on 'em. We can't give up on ourselves. I nivir give up on ye.

(Pete *is nearly in tears. He stumbles and puts an arm round each shoulder –* John's *and* Absalom's.)

Uncle John: Christ. Ye're mad, Skipper. Mad. I knew it all along. But God help me, I prayed ye might be right. (*He too in tears*) I still prays. I looks out over the sea, and it looks the same, but it isn't. It's dead. The hulks rotting on the shore. Maybe, maybe we should give it all up, eh? Should turn our backs on this and lock the door and nivir come back no more. Die decent. We got our memories, Skipper. No one can take they ...

Skipper Pete: Memories ain't no good unless you can see someone else working out the same ones.

Absalom: Father, Father ... when we going into St John's?

(*A pause.*)

Uncle John: Ye see. Six fish. When we going into St John's? Jesus Christ – it's funny. If it wasn't Absalom, it'd be funny.

Skipper Pete: They's nothing funny about it. The boy just remembers, that's all.

Uncle John: Oh yis. We'll take the schooner now. We'll go down through the sound out into the bay and sail right round to St John's and there we'll sell our season's catch. Six fish. It's all right to get drunk here because this is us. And I don't mind. But I'm dying, Skipper. And so is ye. And the trouble is the god damn place has died afore us. We can't git that out of our guts, can we?

(*A pause.*)

Skipper Pete: Drink. (*He pours three more mugs. Once again they drain the cups. All are tangibly drunk.*)

Skipper Pete: (*As if talking to a child*) Ye remembers sometimes ye'd plant potatoes in a dry year. No rain. And the tops burnt before they had a chance to flower?

Uncle John: Aye, I can remember that.

Skipper Pete: Did that stop ye planting next year?

Uncle John: 'Course not. Every year's different.

Skipper Pete: (*Triumphant*) There ye are. And suppose we didn't mend nets, and make the killicks, and then come a year when even we could take to the boat and haul fish out like in the good old days. Suppose we wasn't ready then. And they's no young men to go out and get their hands dirty. What then?

Uncle John: Skipper. Ye haven't been in the boat for two year now. They's only Absalom got the strength in his arm to heave the engine over. Every year the same, roll her down, tie her to the collar, and then pukin' 'cos you can't crawl aboard'n. Why you was blarin' at him 'cos he went out on his own ...

Skipper Pete: I don't care. We've got to be ready. I got one more trip to make. I don't know when. But I got one more trip to make.

(*He slumps into the chair. For a moment he looks tired and defeated.* John *makes a move towards him – half puts out a hand. Draws it back. Turns.*

Pours out three more mugs of shine. Looks at Absalom. *Looks at* Pete. *Conspicuously puts both the other mugs together but makes no move to offer them to anyone. Picks up his own glass with great care. Walks down front right. Raises glass to his lips, lowers it. Belches with satisfaction. Looks round slyly towards* Pete. *Looks front. Raises mug and drains it. Walks back, a little unsteadily towards the table. Thumps the mug down hard!* Absalom *jumps like a rabbit. No response from* Pete. *Slowly and deliberately goes right. Unzips his fly, and stands as if about to urinate ...)*

Skipper Pete: (*Without raising his head*) I told ye ... I told ye before. Dirty bugger.

(John *sighs with relief. Doesn't turn yet.*)

Skipper Pete: (*Raising his head and glowering malevolently*) Never learn, will ye? Only yistiday I told ye.

Uncle John: Today. (*With satisfaction*) It was today.

Skipper Pete: (*Roaring*) Today. Yistiday. What's the difference?

(Absalom *picks up his father's mug and proffers it gingerly. After a moment,* Pete *grabs it and drinks.*)

Skipper Pete: (*To Absalom*) And I told ye. No more fishin' on yer own. Ye wait fer me.

(John *lets out a sharp burst of laughter.* Absalom *nods in agreement. Picks up mug. Drinks. There is a general silence. All three are waiting.*)

Skipper Pete: Well. (*No response*) (*To* John) Are ye going to stand there with yer cock out all day?

Uncle John: It's not out. (*A pause*) I nivir got'n out. (*A pause*) I couldn't fin'n. (*Begins to laugh.* Pete *digests this but if the information means anything, doesn't show it.* John *moves unsteadily across left and looks out of the window.*)

Uncle John: They's lots of fun out there. Big crowd. Half the place on the wharf. (*A pause*) Looks as if they's fishing for something. That's odd now.

(*He turns, and there's a moment of uncertainty as if trying to recollect something. He shakes the thought away. Staggers back down to the table. Discovers that his fly is unzipped. Zips it up, catching his finger in the process. Curses ...*)

Uncle John: (*To* Pete) I bet you can't find it neither. I bet it's all covered with kelp and barnacles. (*Laughs. Pours another drink.*)

(Absalom, *after having been perfectly still throughout this interchange, suddenly falls against the table. Straightens himself in slow motion.*)

Absalom: Father. (*He speaks with some difficulty.*) Father. Aren't ye going to sing, father.

Uncle John: Oh Absalom, my son. Absalom. Absalom. (*Going to him and putting his arm round his neck*) What did he sing to ye, boy. When ye was in the cradle. Rocking ye to and fro in his clammy hands ... (*He sings in a mutilated voice*)

I sailed out to the Labrador
When I was but thirteen (*Pauses*)

I never could sing. And now I can't find it neither. (*A pause*) Yer father now. Like a goddam foghorn. Could hear him right across the Bay. (*Sings again*)

I sailed out to the Labrador
When I was but thirteen ...
Me mother wept ...
Me mother wept ...

Aw to hell we' it.

(*Lets go of* Absalom *and collapses heavily on to the bench. Suddenly* Pete *begins to sing ...*)

Skipper Pete: I went out to the Labrador
When I was but thirteen. (*He stops*)

Absalom: (*Claps his hands together*) That's it, father. That's it.

Skipper Pete: No, son. No. I've forgot the words.

Uncle John: Forgot the ... ye nivir forgot a word ye spoke or sang in yer whole life. Sing, ye old walrus ... Sing. (*He bangs his mug on the table.*)

(Pete *rises slowly. Takes a few paces. Starts to sing the first two lines again. Stops.* Absalom, *slowly and unsteadily, goes around the table and down to him. He holds his arm, and the pair slowly start to shuffle their feet.* Pete *starts the song again, growing in power and intensity.* Absalom *joins in softly on the end of words.* John *stops banging his mug and becomes absorbed, murmurs encouragement at intervals.*)

I sailed out to the Labrador
When I was but thirteen,
Me mother began to keen
I raised you at my tender breast
I loved you deep and strong
And now I fear my own true dear
The sea will drag you down.
Oh the sea will drag you down my son
Like your father long ago

And I'll be left on the wild shore
To wander to and fro.

(*As* Pete *begins the second verse he holds out his hand to* John. John *slowly moves forward, and the three now form a kind of misshapen circle swaying, stamping their feet, shaking each other's hands and arms up and down. All three raise their voices in triumph for the chorus at the end of the second verse. For a moment they are all one. All free.*)

(*Second verse of song*)

I didn't go home that year boys
But stayed out on the sea
And was down in the West Indies
When a message came to me
"Your mother she was drowneded
While looking out for ye"
A wild wave is all her grave
But still I hear her plea ...

Oh the sea will drag you down me son
Like your father long ago
And I'll be left on the wild shore
To wander to and fro.

(*At the end, all three break into chin music, and step dance appropriately. At the end of the dance they stand as in a trance. The woman enters silently right. They don't notice her, holding their trance a moment longer.*)

Woman: (*Very quietly*) Young Jimmy Fogarty's lost. (*No response*) He fell off the wharf. (*And again there is no response.*)

(*The woman moves down a little, speaks with a growing intensity.*)

Woman: John! Ye were here. They're saying ye could have saved him.

(*With a violent movement* Skipper Pete *explodes out of the group and swings on her.* John *staggers and falls on all fours.* Absalom *sways but stays upright.* Pete *raises his arm as if to strike her. She doesn't flinch or move.*)

Skipper Pete: They! Who's they?

Woman: Aiden. Lew. Old Mr Fogarty himself. They say ...

Skipper Pete: And ye just couldn't wait to bring the news, could ye. (*He turns and stomps to the table.*) Absalom, the fish should be ready. (*He sits. He spits.*) Daughter. Hop the Lard Jesus out of here.

(Absalom *shakes his head and moves to the stove, lifts the lid, inspects the fish. Starts to serve the fish.*)

Skipper Pete: John! Come and have a bite to eat. Get on yer feet, man.

(*The* woman *goes towards* Pete *a pace or two.* John *gets to a sitting position.*)

Woman: But ye could have got there. Just a few yards. And ye were told. But you didn't even try.

Skipper Pete: (*Roaring*) Mind yer own business d'you hear. Blood of mine. Jesus, I'll carry the shame o' ye to the grave. Go tell the others what ye want, but I'll tell ye .. (*He lowers his voice, passionately believing what he wants to believe*) The sea wanted him. Old Molly. She took him in her good time. She marked him down. Today, tomorrow, next year ... it doesn't matter. She touched him the day he was borned.

(*The woman stares at him as if for the first time seeing the soul of him. And she is both frightened and horrified. He raises his head and locks eyes with hers. Challenging he suddenly roars:*)

Skipper Pete: John! Ye drunken fool. Yer meal's spoiling.

(*For a few seconds he holds her with his gaze. She struggles to break the hold, summoning up the one emotion she has inherited from him but rarely used – hate. It flares up and breaks the spell, rushing her to action. She almost runs to* John, *still sitting dazedly on the floor, only dimly aware of what has been said, of what's going on.*)

Woman: Ye heard that, did ye? (*She shakes* John, *bends over him, pouring the words into his ear as if they are hot oil to be used for melting the wax that has deafened him for years.*) So. It's God's will, is it, to leave a poor mite like that struggling in the water while two grown men – if I durst call you that – let him drown. All it needed was a walk and a rope. Look at ye. (*She stands up – raging*) He curses the day I was born. But I curse the day I took ye for a man in my bed. Thank God I dropped me son before me time. Did ye ever tell him that. Did ye? Stupid, selfish, drunken ...

(John *has struggled to his feet. One phrase scratches through the fog of his brain ...*)

Uncle John: Drown? Let him drown? We never let nobody drown – dog-fish got'n. Skipper ... (*He looks uncertainly round for* Pete. *Confused. Looks back at his wife.*) I never let nobody ... Let who drown?

Woman: (*Fiercely*) Jimmy Fogarty, that's who. (*Lets it sink in*) Little Jimmy with the freckles and the foxy hair and the big smile with no front teeth. Well – the waters filled that gap now and the connors'll be mouth-ing at his eyes. And the pair of ye ...

Skipper Pete: (*Very sharply*) Absalom!

(*Throughout this interchange* Absalom *has been sitting at the table, knife and fork raised, ready to eat the fish but he won't eat until his father does. Slowly he puts the knife and fork down.*)

Absalom: Yes, father?

Skipper Pete: Go bail the punt, my son.

Absalom: (*Surprised*) But the fish, father.

Skipper Pete: (*Surprisingly gentle*) We'll have it when ye get back. Put it in the pot now, back on the stove.

Absalom: (*Puzzled, but obedient. Almost to himself*) This morning all shining. When I had that dream of fishes. (*He just pours the fish back and replaces the pot on stove. Turns to* Skipper Pete) Father. It's all broken ... the fish ... And this morning it was whole.

Skipper Pete: (*Impatient*) It'll keep. Fer Chrissake it's kept for a year. We'll have it when ye get back. All of us. We'll have it together. When she's gone.

(Absalom *turns and goes out up stage centre. The* woman *crosses up to* Pete *and confronts him across the table.*)

Woman: Ye knew, didn't ye? All the time. The little feller was in beggin' and pleadin' wit' yer. But ye'd filled that fool of mine with your dirty ravings of a dead past. Dead ... dead ... that past. And now ye've added another little body to yer tally. If we ever find him, we should hang him round your neck, so we should, until he's rotted away like an ould fish.

(John *crosses up to* Skipper Pete, *still a bit dazed.*)

Uncle John: What are ye saying, woman?

(*He is confused now. And a little afraid. That recollection which nearly emerged as he looked out at the crowd at the wharf is stirring.*)

Uncle John: Say it's not true, Skipper. (*He pauses, struggling*) Tell her. (*He puts an arm round him, as if trying to recapture the truth of the dance.*) Tell her! Nobody came. We didn't see nobody.

(Pete *stands up suddenly shaking himself free and goes upstage left, turning his back, looking out of the window.*)

Woman: (*Softly*) He can't tell you. He only lies in the head. But never out loud. Never. (*Shouts*) Go on! Tell him! Tell him that nobody came! That Jimmy Fogarty didn't drown! That ye didn't know!

(Skipper Pete *does not move.*)

Uncle John: (*An agonized shout*) Skipper!

(*A silence. In the silence the fog drifts away and* John *confronts the truth he always knew ...*)

Uncle John: My God. (*A pause*) He did come. (*A pause*) The little feller.

(*A pause*) Pulling at me leg. (*A pause*) Shouting, he was. (*Horrified at himself*) Why didn't I go. Why didn't we ... (*He crosses up behind* Skipper Pete.) Skipper. Why didn't we – hear him? Why?

(*No response from* Skipper Pete. *Suddenly, like a man demented,* John *spins him round.*)

Ye've got to say, Skipper. This is real. We owe it to him. Young Fogarty. We owe it to us. You owe me!

(Pete *stares at* John, *crosses down below him to the table. Pours himself a drink.*)

Skipper Pete: I don't owe ye a thing. (*Spins on him*) Don't ye ever forget it. I don't owe a living soul a thing.

Woman: No. They're all dead, that's why. Your bad debts are people, and they're all dead.

(Absalom *enters from the rear. In his arms he carries* Jimmy Fogarty. *He is quite happy and excited.*)

Absalom: Look, father. Look what I caught by the side of the boat.

Woman: Oh Lord bless us.

Absalom: I nivir caught a boy before. (*He advances down stage towards his father.*) What shall I do wid him, Father.

(*For a moment all are paralysed, a terrible tableau. Then the woman rushes out calling ...*)

Woman: (*Off*) Aiden ... Aiden ... Lew ... They've found him. Absalom's found him ... they've found him ...

(Absalom *is facing* Skipper Pete, *the dead boy in his arms. The grandson he might have had!* Skipper Pete *puts out his hand slowly, traces the blind, wet face with his horny hands. Then he turns, the hand that touched the dead child's face to his throat, as if it is a weight that will choke him. He crosses* John *and goes back up to the window, facing out. Two men,* Aiden *and* Lew, *come in right. They are both wearing waders which are wet. They pause a moment.*)

Aiden: (*Advancing slightly*) Here, Absalom. Here, boy ... (*A silence.* Absalom *looks uncertainly between the men and the turned back of his father.*)

Aiden: Bring him to me, Absalom.

(*There is an element of urgent anger in his voice. Outside, the murmur of a crowd, men and women.* John *crosses quickly, and restrains* Aiden *who is about to move to* Absalom *to take the boy from him.*)

Absalom: What shall I do, father?

(*A silence.*)

Lew: (*In a whisper – as if anything louder would snap a thread that seems to have tied them all and provoke violent reaction.*) Fer Chrissake, John. We've got to do something.

Absalom: He is mine, isn't he father. I caught him. I nivir caught a boy before. Can I have him?

(*A silence. Is there a quiver from* Pete? John *crosses slowly to* Absalom.)

Uncle John: Go wid them Absalom. Ye can take him. Ye caught him. Go on now. (*Gently he turns him in the direction of the door.*)

Absalom: Father ...

Uncle John: Don't matter what he says. Not any more. Anyways, he don't know nothing about boys. Only fish. Go on now ... (*Slowly he propels* Absalom *towards the door. He crosses the two men and goes on out. Lew follows him.* Aiden *turns to go, then turns back.*)

Aiden: We wants to talk to ye, John. And Skipper there.

Uncle John: Aye. I know.

(Aiden *goes out.* John *turns.*)

Uncle John: Skipper, are ye coming? (*No answer*) Skipper? No – they's nothing out there b'y. (*No answer*) I 'low it wasn't too bad a day after all, Skipper. One hell of a catch. But I don't think I'll be shareman wid ye any longer. (*He is nearly crying.*) I'm going home, ye see. Home ...

(*He pauses one last time waiting for a response, or any indication from* Pete *that they have ever known each other at all. But there is nothing.* John *crosses to the killick. Picks it up. Goes to the door right. And then, a flash of the old sardonic mirth returns ...*)

Uncle John: I'm taking the killick. I'm going to tie it to me goddamn leg, that's what. In Memoriam, dat's what they say ...

(*He goes out. The murmur of the crowd dies away. After a pause* Pete *turns. Slowly goes across right and shuts the door. He pauses. Comes across to stove, checks it for flame. Checks the fish. Goes back up stage and disappears partially from view as he undoes and fastens the upstage door. There's just a shaft of light left now coming in through the church window. He goes right and finds an oil lamp, lights it and puts it on the table. He begins to sing ... two or three lines of the opening song. Stops. Takes the fish off the stove, fills his plate and begins to eat ...*)

THE END

Henrik Ibsen on the Necessity of Producing Norwegian Drama

John Palmer

As a director and playwright, John Palmer was a major force in the formation of the alternative theatre movement in Toronto during the late 1960s and early 1970s. With Martin Kinch he co-founded the brief lived Canadian Place Theatre in Stratford, where his play *Memories for My Brother, Part 1* premièred in 1969. In 1971 he was one of the co-founders of Toronto Free Theatre (TFT) (along with Kinch and Tom Hendry). His plays at TFT include *The End* in 1972 and the collective *The Pits*, which he directed. John Palmer was also closely involved with the other experimental theatres in Toronto, including Factory Theatre Lab, which premièred his *A Touch of God in the Golden Age* in 1971 and *Henrik Ibsen* in 1976, and Theatre Passe Muraille, where he directed a celebrated production of Fabian Jenning's *Charles Manson a.k.a. Jesus Christ* in 1972. His most recent play is *A Day at the Beach*, produced in 1987.

Henrik Ibsen on the Necessity of Producing Norwegian Drama was first produced on 10 October 1976 at Factory Theatre Lab. The play was originally conceived as a curtain-raiser for George F. Walker's *Bagdad Saloon*.

PRODUCTION
Director / **Martin Kinch**
Designer / **Miro Kinch**

CAST
Chapelle Jaffe / Henrik Ibsen

CHARACTERS
Ibsen
A woman
A man

A plain wooden podium. On the front of it, facing the audience, is a simple sign attached to the podium. The sign reads: "The Society For The Encouragement Of The Norwegian Theatre." On the top of the podium, to the right, is a small Norwegian flag inserted in a little stand. Under the top of the podium and not visible to the audience is a Union Jack the same size as the Norwegian flag. Beside the podium is a plain glass jug of water and a perfectly plain shapeless glass on a small pewter tray. Beside this is a small wooden gavel.

Ibsen should be introduced by a Woman in modern dress, i.e. a costume similar to whatever the audience is wearing. She is a very timid woman, obviously out of place before others. She carries a little white card on which her "introduction" is written. She stands beside the podium, not at it. She tries to smile at all times. She gets the audience's attention by waiting silently for it. When everyone is quiet she bangs the gavel once.

Woman: I have the privilege this evening of introducing to you ... (*She checks her card*) ... one of our Norwegian playwrights and lecturers ... (*She checks her card*) ... Mr Henrik Ibsen who will speak to us on the subject of ... (*She checks her card*) ... the necessity of producing Norwegian drama. Mr Ibsen has written a number of plays and has travelled extensively in Italy. I know you will appreciate what he has to say. (*She checks her card.*) Thank you. (*She steps away, applauding silently.*)

Henrik Ibsen *takes the podium. He is a short giant of about seventy, a vile, crotchety, condescending, glowering, impatient, and explosive man. He is the very cliché of aged genius. He is dressed in his own period, very conservatively (c. 1900). If he ever smiles, it is the malicious glint of one who knows that his audience will have difficulty following him. And yet he loves what he is doing, what he is talking about. He looks quickly about and starts talking. During the course of his speech he will work up to fever pitches, loosen his tie and collar, take off his coat, and have to take frequent drinks to calm himself down.*

Ibsen: I should like to thank Miss —— for her magnificently accurate introduction. The question that has disturbed my waking hours for the last two weeks is both tangential and relevant: shall I prefix this address with "Ladies and Gentlemen"?

The reality in the prefix "Ladies and Gentlemen" is a complex system of repression and psychological absurdity; a clever subterfuge by which the speaker and the audience are placed under the illusion that the speaker is in fact addressing, in the same way, both ladies and gentlemen; but as any serious discussion is not considered fit for female ears and as no real power has been delegated to women and since men do not listen to these other folk in the same way as to the images of god himself, the exercise of addressing women on any other subject than strudel seems pointless.

The problem is not solved by shortening the prefix to "gentlemen" which I consider an ironic term for success in business or luck in ancestry or both. It also excludes the ladies in a profoundly puerile sense. But perhaps the main excuse for dispensing with the prefix altogether is that except for the 25 Kronen I need and am being paid as a token of your appreciation which I neither expect nor require, I consider none of you gentlemen and I am aware that I am wasting my time.

I therefore find myself in the untenable position of trying to address something vital to a gathering of no one, for no equitable reward, to no apparent purpose. However, since my subject is the necessity of producing Norwegian drama, all is in its place.

It is not necessary to produce Norwegian drama: it is hardly necessary to produce anything. A bushel of potatoes, the odd musk-ox, and a cave ensure a kind of survival. What civilization has presumed to be about is an improvement in the quality of survival, or existence as we call it, having replaced caves with houses. This social order has now developed into what we call nations.

It seems to me that we in Norway are having difficulty with the definition of a nation. This is not surprising as we have been a part of first Denmark and then Sweden up until the present year. We have not, in fact, been a nation since the middle ages, long enough to have forgotten the sensation.

What is a nation? Sardines? Reindeer? Is it the quality of sunsets or the funny head-dresses of peasants? But I speak to an educated audience who cannot possibly confuse these banal sentimentalities with the harsh necessities of nationhood, an audience who no doubt demands a sterner definition of that sacred state of independence in which they claim to abide. A nation is numbers of people either of diverse backgrounds or sharing a common history, language, and aspirations etc., living in a territory defined by specific boundaries. The soul of humanity is in its diversity and each nation's uniqueness is an added happy factor to the sum total of the human genius. It should therefore cause little mental effort to see that while art in general is an international commodity, it is produced by an artist of a particular culture and there is, in fact, no such thing as an international work of art. (*He takes a drink of water.*)

I proceed.

It is presumably in the interest of most nations to concern themselves with their own self-preservation. I am stating the obvious because it seems to me that most Norwegians are labouring under the illusion that a nation is a very peculiar sort of tree needing only boundaries and no water to sustain it. Self-preservation is manifested by nations in three basic areas: the political which is a concern for boundaries, the economic which is a concern for material prosperity and may involve boundaries, and the cultural which is a concern for being ourselves as opposed to others and which keeps us from reverting entirely to the first two concerns, that is from becoming

ordinary animals such as sheep. Thus it is no accident that the great nations of the world have taken the greatest care in the protection of all
three areas. While there is no proof positive that indigenous drama is a
necessity to a great and civilized state, there is conclusive evidence to
show that historically a nation has not achieved recognition in the world
solely on the basis of its armed might or successful economy. Thermopylae
and Marathon have become mere thorns for schoolboys; Epidaurus will
live forever. Louis XIV flattened Europe and bankrupted France but made
her diadem of the world by establishing for all time a significant body of
dramatic literature for the stage – oh yes, and funding a little painting and
sculpture as well. We have yet to hear anything of import from those
United States of the New World except to remark that, being but a century old, they have exhibited neither unity, nor any inclination to exert an
influence on the rest of mankind, nor the least spark of indigenous drama,
all of which, when considered in the same breath, must lead one to specu-
late on what must go hand in hand with what in the development of new
societies, if they are not to be mere appendages of the old.

Self preservation in all its aspects is the cornerstone of any national policy.
(*He takes a drink of water.*) It is, in fact, the only logical approach to social
existence. Now that we in Norway have finally decided on independence
in the recent plebiscite, it is crucial to see that more is involved than
boundaries and a flag, indeed, that these are only trappings: the true test of
our existence is in the art of self-preservation: it is nothing more nor less
than nationalism itself. Do not be fooled by the sanctimonious and hysterical cries of those Norwegians who seek to brand nationalism as evidence
of the devil. Look closely and see if their interests are not with Denmark
or Sweden or Germany or even England; powerful interests, my friends,
in search of more civilized colonies than Africa or Asia. What they are
doing is a malicious attempt to confuse a just and natural set of aspirations
felt by every people on the fact of the earth and I mean nationalism, with
a scurrilous monster called patriotism, which is indeed the last refuge of
the scoundrels who seek to allow our integration with those nations such
as England and Germany who in the name of this same patriotism of
which they accuse us, are gobbling up the globe whether it will or no. The
attempt to subvert and pervert nationalism in Norway is nothing less than
a call to national suicide. It is nonsense. It is greed. In any sane society it
is perfect treason. (*He dabs his handkerchief in the water and touches his forehead with it.*) A nation that does not covet and cherish its own culture
does not deserve to be a nation, nor will it so exist for long. A nation that
emulates all but itself is the true homeland of decadence and dictatorship.
(*He fills his glass which should now be empty, full. He does not drink.*)

I am almost ready to discuss Norwegian drama, which, if you remember
was purportedly my subject for this evening. First, however, I must reassure you that I am not a socialist and secondly I wish to perform a modest

little act involving our flag, which, if you remember, is Norwegian. I would like to show you first the flag of another nation, oh any other one will do, it doesn't matter which – a random flag. (*He takes out a small Union Jack from behind the podium.*) I have obtained this flag at my own expense to make a point although I must in all honesty tell you that it was more easily obtained than our own which you have provided. This is a Union Jack. It is the flag of Great Britain although you may see it waving over approximately 27 other territories round the globe whose inhabitants are presumably too stupid to have invented their own. This ... (*He points carefully to the little Norwegian flag on the podium*) ... is our flag, the flag of Norway. Please note that while the resemblance between these two flags is so uncannily exact as to make a perusal of it esoteric there are a few small differences such as colour, intensity, and design. It is important to remember these inconsequential variants when one sees a flag in public, if only to ease anxiety as to one's location. Now this random flag ... (*He holds up the Union Jack*) ... is reasonably attractive if a little cluttered and may understandably hold more fascination than our own. (*He points to the Norwegian flag.*) How pitiful it must be to wander about under the constant blandness of this flag ... (*He points to the Norwegian flag*) ... when what truly waves in your heart is the dashing familiarity of this one. (*He points to the Union Jack.*) I would suggest that a movement be initiated to convince the Norwegian parliament to adopt the flag of your choice. After all, a flag ought not to be merely a scrap of quilting to be waved about for parades, but a true indication of the aspirations and determination of a people to exist. A second solution is more radical: that is to give up the luxury of Norway and go where the flag of your choice legitimately flies. Norway must cease its terrible coercion of would-be emigrants. I hope not to cause undue alarm as I put away this flag ... (*He replaces the Union Jack where he got it. Out of sight.*) ... so I will remind you that it can easily be recalled should it be needed and that I am not a socialist. Now as you will note, I shall take in my hand our own flag, that of Norway. (*He picks up the Norwegian flag.*) You will find absolutely no need for smelling salts. I am aware there are ladies present and I have no wish to be called out by any of the gentlemen – I warn you that I am about to wave this Norwegian flag. I warn you so that any who wish to do so may leave the room. I assume you are prepared. I shall count from five. Five, four, three, two, one ... (*He gives the Norwegian flag a small quick wave and replaces it on its stand on the podium.*) There now, that wasn't so bad, was it? (*He slowly drinks the whole glass of water.*)

I move rapidly to the necessity of producing Norwegian drama. Since this vital question seems to demand a proof for the necessity of any drama at all and since there is no proof but what I have already offered in the name of civilization, I should like to pose a few pertinent questions on the subject after first defining the term "Norwegian drama."

There seems little doubt as to what is French drama or German drama or English drama; it is often what we see on the stage in France, Germany and England. (*He fills the glass again.*) And though it seems odd to me to raise the question as to what is Norwegian drama, it is not I who have raised it, but, even more oddly, those who claim it does not exist, thereby placing themselves in the rather untenable position of demanding a definition of nothing. Since I know that it does exist I shall not insult anyone's intelligence by trying to define a self-evident term such as "Norwegian drama" except to observe that it may or may not portray sardines or fjords, may or may not transpire in Norway itself, even may or may not portray Norwegians; it is the sensibility that is Norwegian, not the cut of the maid's apron.

Other hysterics have prophesied that the production of new Norwegian drama will mean the demise of the classics and the best of contemporary foreign drama. Do they infer that once our new drama is widely produced, nothing can compete with it? Whatever their idiotic fear may be, it has been trumped up by those who know they are incompetent in dealing with new work. There is no precedent for these prophesies in 2,000 years of history. (*During the following paragraph he dabs himself with his handkerchief.*)

Why has the lie been propagated that there are no Norwegian playwrights who are any good? I think for the same reason that there are supposedly no women playwrights of merit. Well, there are very few Jews in the Vatican; if you want more you have only to advertise stipulating the salary.

The Norwegian theatre is paid for by the Norwegian people in taxes yet it is largely run by Germans and Englishmen who are bent on giving the Norwegian people German and English versions (I refer here to an all-important sensibility) of German and English plays. I suppose we must be thankful they have sometimes bothered to have them translated into Norwegian.

I must here timidly inquire as to the purpose served by performing Norwegian in an English accent. Am I supposed to be impressed by that air of rigid respectability? I find it odd to live a Norwegian life the way I do and enter a Norwegian theatre to find not a jot that is Norwegian. Why do we not simply tour entire productions from England and Germany 52 weeks a year? Better the real thing than a copy of it? Why is our largest theatre controlled by a foreigner? Why are many regional theatres, all subsidized as well by Norwegian taxpayers, similarly manacled? Why is this not tolerated in any other nation on earth? Why do these aliens overwhelmingly produce drama originating in any other nation than Norway? Why is their much touted genius not automatically used in the development of Norway? We, after all, are employing them at the disastrous expense of ignoring those who have consistently pledged themselves to precisely that indigenous labour which these carpetbaggers disdain. (*He crumples the handker-chief violently in his fist.*) Who is using whom? Why is government condoning this state of affairs with subsidy and indifference? Why not subsidize Drury Lane directly? Why is this intolerable in any other nation on earth? What is suicide? (*He picks up the glass and puts it down again.*)

If the government were to heavily subsidize the importation of sardines and allow our own fishing industry to fend for itself as best it could, the nation's economy would collapse. Do not think that art has no relation to politics. It is the barometer of the times. In a healthy society, art is a min-ister created by the people, answerable only to the nation and before whom kings and presidents tremble alike. Why is the barometer in Nor-way being ignored? The main reason, as I have stated, is that Norwegians are not able to see it since our stage is at present cluttered with the lords and ladies of other lands, whose glitter, ambience, and humour are irrele-vant to Norway.

Another reason is that the state of criticism here is even more unhealthy than that of the theatre to which it owes its keep. It is a sad fact that Nor-wegian criticism is irrelevant to Norwegian theatre because the critics themselves are yearning after something they will inevitably not see on the Norwegian stage since it is not the English stage or the German stage. Why this tautology should cause them so much anguish and confusion is beyond my modest powers of comprehension. I cannot pierce the darkness but a little stumbling about may be helpful. First of all, the criteria these critics use in diagnosing our indigenous drama are from other times and other places. You cannot find a liver ailment if you are looking for a bro-ken heart. (*During the next two sentences he takes out a number of old, tiny newspaper clippings and holds them up to the audience.*) Again and again the critics rail against the fact that they can find no sentiment in my work, no honouring of mothers, no tender lament over lost daughters or aging loyal hounds. The answer is very simple. There is none in it and that is why they do not find it. (*He puts the clippings away.*) Similarly they ruffle up considerable feathers when our modern playwrights, not only Norwegians, choose to deal with violent or sexual matters. Mr Strindberg has been con-stantly abused because his portraits of life are too violent, passionate, and despairing. Too passionate for whom? Too passionate for England, cer-tainly, and hence for acceptable taste everywhere. Yet England, the most hypocritical society ever to deface the globe, is precisely where Mr Strind-berg is needed most. Anton Chekhov is sending us a beautiful new drama of stasis and character exposition as has never been seen before in the world in such exquisite detail. But our critics are buried in mud at the bot-tom of the sea under 700 steam engines. They complain that there is no plot! No story. No sudden thrilling revelations at the end of the second act. Perhaps they have mistaken the titles. It is not the three bears but the three sisters, not the dance of the *Sugar Plum Fairy* but *The Dance of*

Death. He is not Shakespeare, he is Chekhov, and Strindberg is Strindberg and I am Ibsen and that lady to my right is not the gentleman to my left nor the headwaiter at the Metropole. If the critics would rather be presented with Valhalla than Norway they should not address themselves to the public but to God.

But the most important reason for the production of our own drama and at the same time for the lack of such, lies deeply within ourselves. You cannot invite locusts to dinner and expect them to eat like birds. Are we governing ourselves or are we not? You are either for independence when it is threatened or against it: there is no such animal as a "little freedom" for modern man. A nation must say who it is in a loud clear tone or it will be readily swallowed up by the milieu of those who are not doubtful of their existence. The much touted "identity crisis" which we in Norway are said to suffer is a foul and inane lie propagated by those who stand to profit by it. It does not exist. I certainly know who I am. If you do not know who you are then, according to the laws of psychiatry and the state, you are insane and have no rights in the affairs of Norway.

Norwegian art is abundant and at this very moment is clearly defining Norwegian existence for those who choose to see: to remain deaf to it is the prerogative of any citizen: to claim its non-existence is either to be blind or wicked, but to oppose its legitimate growth and establishment is a criminal act against the people of Norway. (*He removes his tie and stuffs it in his pocket.*) Yet this is precisely the program of these powerful émigrés running our cultural institutions, who, curiously enough, have arrived here with a regularity that suggests they are somehow unacceptable in their own countries and while it is the perverse norm to deport one's undesirables to one's colonies, I should expect any Norwegian (no matter to what degree a toady he may be) to object to the establishment on his territory of an international garbage dump. (*He unbuttons his collar.*) These people are not content to populate the Norwegian stage with trivial manuscripts from bygone seasons in foreign capitals nor even with scoring a puny success by costuming Plantagenets in waistcoats or getting up Italianate Elizabethans as American Indians. They have been lauded by critics from afar who see not Norway's show but their own. They have fooled our own critics by reproducing third-rate ideas long since worn out in the countries from which these little foreign fish come looking for a little pond presumably because they can no longer swim in their own oceans. (*He picks up the glass and holds it, continuing.*) But our imported beribboned masters are not even content with this. They bring in their friends and acquaintances to play with yet another theatre, another gallery; any toy will do it seems in this eternal soirée given by an obsequious Norwegian government and boards of governors as culturally lobotomized as they are impressed and grovelling in awe of foreign titles. A veritable fiesta for everyone save Norwegians. (*He puts the glass down.*)

No one is suggesting that some influence on the theatre from abroad is not necessary or beneficial; we do not wish to live in a vacuum. But we must control our own theatre for ourselves and give the main thrust of it to indigenous work.

There is an easier solution. Why are we bothering with borders at all? Or for that matter with the tiresome pretence of self-government? Why do we not obtain in one bold stroke the most powerful army in the world, the most successful economy, and the proudest cultural heritage by voting ourselves out of existence as a nation altogether and seeking incorporation by either Germany or England? This would instantly solve all the problems to which we are heir. We must make up our minds. We cannot have it both ways. (*He takes off his collar and stuffs it in another pocket.*) We either are or we are not. (*He drinks the glass of water.*)

I realize that in speaking here tonight I am to some extent preaching to the converted. Your invaluable organization, the Society for the Encouragement of a Norwegian Theatre is to be much admired for what it has accomplished so far. I think the time has come to review exactly what has been accomplished in the interest of what has yet to be done. I should respectfully like to point out that what you have established to this date is a small number of small institutions producing Norwegian drama on a tiny island in Norway. It will not do. It is not enough. If you think that this great enterprise has been solidly secured you are under an illusion and you had better think again. If you believe that you may work quietly in your little huts without being affected by those in the palaces across this nation then you are naïve. Is anyone that naïve? If you cannot see that what you have established in five or ten years can be as easily swept away in less than half that time, then look out your windows: while you have been snuggling comfortably, the laurels of your past have withered and throughout the land retrenchment is the order of the day. You are marching backwards into a bog because you are too self-satisfied to move forward and therefore cannot see that by staying where you are it is only a matter of time before you will be nowhere. (*He dips the handkerchief right into the jug and dabs himself erratically.*) And what do we see, as a lackadaisical farewell is bid to the eleventh hour? Bickering among you as to who is big and who is small: that is nonsense: you are all small. Who is best? Who is cleverest? You are all fools abdicating your potential. Who will grab the most scraps left by those who control the real resources in this country? It is lugubrious to consider a hierarchy among slaves. (*He fills the glass of water full.*) And yet none of you have surfaced without sacrifice, without fight. What on earth could lead you to believe you can get any further in any other way? Little schemes for self-aggrandizement will avail you nothing but soulless fat. Some of you have told me that you simply wish to work and be left alone, that you are artists and not politicians. Your sentiments are as irrelevant to the real situation as those of the critics are to your work.

Do you think they will hand you a national theatre because that is your right? (*He picks up the glass.*)

It is necessary to give it another push. It is necessary to look united to the problems of establishing on a national scale a system of theatres devoted to the creation of a significant body of dramatic literature with all that that entails: administrators, technicians, designers, directors, actors, and playwrights. This is necessary. You must take what you have started to every handful of this Norwegian earth, to newspapers and periodicals, to schooltexts, to publishing houses, to painting, to dance, to music, and to whatever forms of human expression are yet to come, to those who administrate and control cultural subsidy, to their lieutenants, and to their secretaries' children, to the grocers, the doctors, and the boardrooms of the nation, to the judges, to the ministers, to the very government and the people itself. (*He pours the glass of water back into the jug and throws the handkerchief in after it.*)

I have dreamed of going to any Norwegian theatre across this land and seeing a plenitude of Norwegian drama from all regions, from all walks of life, in a multitude of styles, moods, and attitudes. I have dreamed of my grandchildren attending a theatre in which there is another kind of conflict, in which young playwrights will say of us – enough – the Norwegian theatre is sinking in the mire of its own aging – enough of Ibsen and all the old fogies – produce one a year if you like, but let us have a new Norwegian drama better than the old – yes, we can do better.

We have embarked on nothing less than a fight for our own culture. I can think of nothing sadder than inaction now. We must be able to make our own mistakes. We will produce well and badly but we must produce. And in the same breath we must fight or become feathers in the wind.

Voltaire has said that God is on the side of the strongest legions. In true Norwegian fashion let us take no chances: let us pray to God and gather our legions. Thank you.

(*He glares around for a long moment as if lost in thought, as if there was something crucial left out. He decides it would be pointless to add anything in any case and so he leaves. A very well dressed Man of 37 with slight greying at the temples comes to the podium smiling broadly. He speaks smoothly with a slight British accent, very polite, always smiling, dressed modern.*)

Man: I would like to thank Mr Ibsen for his most interesting and provocative opinions. I am sure his speech has given us much food for thought not only in the realm of philosophy but in his valuable hints for practical suggestion. I would like to welcome him to return again to speak to us whenever he wishes. I know that we are always ready to listen. Thank you. (*He steps down, sharing a joke with a man at one of the tables nearby.*)

THE END

Passion and Sin

Hrant Alianak

Born in the Sudan in 1950, Hrant Alianak moved to Canada in 1967, and studied at McGill and York universities. He has worked widely as an actor, writer and director in theatre, television, film, and opera. His plays, all produced under his own direction, include *Lucky Strike, Night, The Blues, Passion and Sin, Christmas, Mathematics,* and *Tantrums.* He has directed for Theatre Passe Muraille, Factory Theatre Lab, Buddies in Bad Times, and NDWT Theatre. As an actor he has appeared in numerous television dramas and films, and his performance in Atom Egoyan's *Family Viewing* won him a Genie nomination.

Passion and Sin was first produced at the Toronto Free Theatre on 4 March 1976.

PRODUCTION
Director / **Hrant Alianak**
Designer / **Ralph McDermid**
Lighting / **Sholem Dolgoy**

CAST
Diane Dewey / The Mother
Miles Potter / The Military Man
Booth Savage / The Son
Allan Aarons / The Man on the Run
Diane Lawrence / The Monkey
Ann Lantuch / The Other Woman

CHARACTERS
The Mother, beautiful, listless, angry
The Military Man, suspicious, brutal, slow
The Son, spoiled, scared, restless
The Man on the Run (The Man), violent, famous, betrayed
The Monkey, innocent, fascinating, animal
The Other Woman, hostile, suicidal, craving

COSTUMES
All clothes worn by all have been permanently marked with the dried stains of salt-soaked sweat.

SET
The Shack: Once a place to live in, ripped in two by a tornado, put together again with anything. Renovations consist of creating the fourth wall and ceiling out of corrugated metal sheets, cardboard and the odd piece of wood hammered on. The walls that have remained standing after the tornado are broken down: plaster, woodwork, paint fallen off in many places.

Heavily barricaded with planks hammered on windows and doorways, from within, against the outside.
A small totally barricaded window on centrestage right.
A large window dead centre on upstage wall, with heavy wooden shutters and nothing else.

A place of shelter and refuge, difficult to enter, even more so to exit.

Boxes, crates all around particularly downstage area, boxes downstage right forming an exit partially, and more boxes upstage right. Crates unopened mostly, some opened full of unseen possessions. Bundles of five-year-old yellowing copies of "The Havana Times" around the crates. The odd plank of wood.

Four exits, upstage right, upstage left, downstage right, downstage left.
Upstage right to front door, only a hallway.
Upstage left to bedroom, a solid door.
Downstage left to bathroom, curtained.
Downstage right, the back exit, an exit hidden by crates, no door.

A couch, two armchairs.
Crates underneath window, alongside walls, to sit on.

Faded linoleum on floor.
All colours brownish, pinkish, yellowish.

Outside the central window another shack. The balcony to it. The railing
of the balcony. Also deserted, broken-down.

Beyond, the beach, the sea.

LIGHTS
Lots of sneaky rays hitting the room from outside through the many
cracks in the walls.

SOUNDS
The sound of the waves outside, constantly present, capricious, at times
turbulent, at times passionate, at times gentle and soothing. The occasional
screech of a sea gull.

WEATHER
Brooding heat. Oppressive. Night after night. Day after day. Relentless.
Unalterable. Affecting. Hovering afternoons and evenings of sweaty listless
thoughts of sex, religion, philosophy, frustration, fury, and malaria.

SCENE ONE: GUILT

1957. *Havana. A hot summer. On the Beach, in a broken-down deserted condemned shack ...*
Black ... Silence ... Pause ...
*Suddenly, out jumps the angry drama of the giant humourless notes of repen-
tant violins and punishing drums.*

Music: *Past, Present and Future* Loud.

The silent rage of shadowy ominous red lights follow. Dim. Fuming.

*The figure of a woman is revealed in faded pink night robe, thigh and cleavage
visible. Still for a second, then tottering forward dazedly. Blind and unsteady,
pleading for the support of a chair that remains hostile and distant. Stumbling
in anguish to the grubby hot wall that feels her sweat-drenched breasts sticking
to its rotting plaster in relief.*

*Right hand weakly clawing the wall above her, she hugs the wall in despair,
feeling guilty and soiled. Wanting to undo what has just happened, knowing
she'll have to live with it for the rest of her life.*

*Eyes closed, rubbing her cheek along the cheerless wall, the friendless woman
turns around slowly to reveal a small, wooden crucifix hanging around her
neck by a string and resting against her moist chest.*

*The woman opens her eyes, feeling an internal revulsion ripping her soul to
shreds, as she now leans back against the wall, revealing to all her identity –
The Mother.*

*The Mother listlessly dries the uncomfortable sweat on her neck and chest
when for a moment she can feel the crucifix under her palm.*

*The guilt of mortal sin pierces her heart as she lets her hand fall to her side
very slowly because she now wonders whether she truly feels penitent, and
knows she doesn't fully.*

*Hugging the walls with her arms, she can feel her back sliding down the wall
and her knees giving in as she slowly lets her body ease down along the wall.*

*Her mouth twists with anger as she once again recollects her folly in the other
room, and her whole face projects the disgust that every woman must have felt
once for all the men that walked the face of the earth.*

*The twisting chords agonize shrilly as the shadow of a man steps in front
downstage right. The shadow moves forward but stops and backs out again as
the naked figure of a man slowly moves into the room – downstage left.*

*Big, muscular and angry, he stands rooted firmly to the floor in his black
socks, and gazes at the Mother with wide flaming accusatory eyes.*

He stands with his back to the audience, his face not to be seen for now. His hands tightly clenched into fiery red knobs that are in truth the fists of a man in fury. Fury that is controlled, suppressed, abnormally suppressed, raging to fly out of control, ready to wreak the venom that every man must have felt once for all the women that walked the face of the earth.

The chords, the strings vanish as the furious drums pound, pound, pound.

The Man slowly looks over to his left to a bundle of clothes lying on a chair, then back at the Mother who keeps looking at him, her disgust being slowly shrouded by her deep unhappiness.

The Man slowly, tensely walks over to the chair and clutches it tightly with his left hand. For a moment he leans forward as he feels the unbearable cloak of vertigo draping him.

He angrily, tightly clutches the unlucky chair and combats his vertigo – successfully.

He looks up tensely, then at the clothes on the chair – his clothes.

With intent, searing eyes he commands his left hand to clutch a pair of brown shorts.

Tensely clenched in his fist, he looks at them, then at her, when he feels this unbearable impulse to get dressed and get out as fast as he can.

He angrily, quickly puts them on.

He then tensely clasps his brown t-shirt and raises that up, his raging fury interfering with his burning desire for speed, and causing his fast moves to appear almost jerky and crisp, very crisp.

He puts his t-shirt on as fast as he can, with clean, sure, definite sweeps. However, his fury demands a tense pause of controlled rage after the completion of each and every move.

He grabs his pants and swings them open in front of him. A tense pause. And zoom, swish they're on. Tense pause. Snap. Zip. Tight.

He grabs a boot. Puts boot on. Crisp, fast, angry but sure tight doing up of laces, tucking pants in boot.

Other boot grabbed. Put on. Other foot tense crash land on floor with boot on. Stamp. Stomp.

Both feet rooted, planted firmly on ground. The rest of his dressing continues independent of his feet which do not budge an inch.

Angry chords join the drums and cymbals as he slowly, tensely grabs a coat and looks at it and slowly, tensely, now sudden, fast puts it on to reveal the nature of the coat – brown army, and to reveal his identity – The Military Man.

The red fury of the lights now slowly change colour as they give in to the tougher white rays of rage.

The Military Man crisply does up the buttons to his huge, bulky canvas coat, then briskly produces an angry green belt and buckles it over his coat.

Crisply then grabs knapsack, crisply puts it on.

Tense pause.

Slow seething tension, the speed of his reach abruptly arrested as he slowly reaches and produces his helmet, with angry netting and jetting twigs ominously displayed, and with one continuous flowing move slowly places it on head, pauses tensely for a moment then angrily secures it.

Now slowly moves hand to his right and from behind a crate produces his menacing machine-gun.

Brings it front of him.

Cocks it.

Holds it out, facing it to his left.

Long, tense pause.

And he moves. Alert. Ready. In a fighting mood. Aware of his hostile surroundings.

Slowly tensely moves for a few steps facing the Mother.

Stops.

A lengthy exchange of looks. Looks of mutual disgust.

He slowly slides to his left still looking at her. Then turns to disappear upstage right, having successfully managed not to reveal his face, when the shadow creeps out again, slightly from downstage right.

Military Man tenses and stops. The shadow quickly disappears. Suspicious Military Man decides to pursue enemy as he runs out upstage right. The Mother looks on with anticipation at the danger that still lurks around her.

The lights fade as the Mother backs a step ... The music fades in ...
Black.

SCENE TWO: TRAPPED

The previous music crossfades into new.

Music: *Family Man.*
A hot, unpleasant sticky morning.

The Mother, leaning against the shutters in the throes of despair, feeling trapped, feeling the smallness of the room.

She slowly walks forward, listless, robe parted provocatively, yet not enough. The aftermath of an evening of unimaginable events.

The music wails along, equally jaded, yet quivering for more.

The Son.
Slowly enters from the shadowy upstage right, in white shirt, sleeves rolled up, light brown pants and white sneakers.
The Mother is unaware of him.
The Son looks on longingly, gloomily, suppressing desires, breathing heavily.

The Mother hears him breathe and tiredly turns to look at him.
The Son shudders as he catches a glimpse of the Mother's left nipple. He guiltily looks down, only to linger most obviously at one of her brazen pubes that had escaped concealment.

The Mother bravely tugs her robe shut, disgustedly looks away, and dejectedly stumbles towards the bedroom.

The Son feels unbearably guilty, unable to conceal his blush.

Son: Ma ... I'm sorry ...

The Mother looks at him for an instant, sees his blush, softens a little, but feels more than ever the urgency to be alone, as she reaches for the door knob to her bedroom.

Son: Ma, please ...

A moment of hesitation, but then she welcomes the dark recesses of her private bedchamber as she enters and closes the door after her.

Son: *Weakly.* Ma ... I'm sorry.

The music ends equally weakly, and the sound of the waves is heard.

The Son feels aimless for a moment, when a light flicks on and off very quickly, three times, from outside the downstage centre shutters.

The Son is shocked at this strange phenomenon as he anxiously rushes against a wall, away from the shutters.

He waits — anxious, tense, scared. Nothing happens. He slowly approaches the window, and worriedly wonders if he should call Ma, but decides to peer out through the cracks of the closed shutters of the window.

His anxious peeks don't disclose much of the outside. He shows his frustration as he agonizes over a decision, now hurling a cautious, guilty glance towards the bedroom door, knowing he doesn't really want to call Ma. Coast clear.

He turns back to the shutters and cautiously, slowly opens them partially, making certain he's not visible from the outside as he leans back against the wall and cranes his neck to see outside, the thrill of fear piercing through his bones.

He parts the shutters some more to reveal the balcony of a deserted shack immediately across and the beach beyond. He looks at the shack opposite cautiously but with great interest, trying to see inside.

When, unknown to him, the shadow of a man slowly moves forward (downstage right) and a man dressed in a dark brown suit enters sideways, back to audience, stops and looks on at the Son. The Man seems to be very tense, yet very quiet and still.

The Son, about to wipe the accumulated sweat of heat and anxiety off his chest, tenses as he suddenly becomes aware of a presence and turns with a start to see the Man.

The Son is about to speak, when the Man's voice pierces the silence with the constrained tension of urgency and the hushed immediacy of desperation.

Man: Close the window!

The Son is about to speak again, very indignant now.

Man: Close the window! Close the window, close that goddamn window (*produces gun*) before I blast your goddamn head off!

The Son immediately closes the window. The Man no longer restrains his violence as he hurriedly moves around checking the place, now rushing to the window anxiously listening for approaching sounds. Underneath his violence, panic and fear lurk, plainly evident. His tie poorly done over his white shirt, a two-day growth of beard, eyes betraying three sleepless nights. He is The Man on the Run.

Son: Who ...

Man: Shut up!

Son: Hey, I've seen you before.

Man: Shut up!

Son: *Eyes brighten in recognition.* Hey, you're that ... *Man clicks gun, pointing it right in his face. The Son shuts up. A tense pause.*

Man: (*Referring to shack opposite*) Who lives in there?

Son: No one. (*An obvious lie.*)

The Man notices the obvious lie and is about to be even more menacing.

Son: No one, no one, I swear.

The Man sizes him up. Not much, he thinks.

Man: Where's the dame?

Son: (*Points to bedroom, reluctant*) In there.

Man moves to check.

Son: She's asleep.

Man opens door and peers in anyway. Closes door, and walks over to Son, beginning to feel more and more at home now.

Man: She any good?

Son: (*Angry blush*) She's my stepmother.

Man: You live here all year?

Son: She does.

Man: All alone?

Son: Ye ...

Man: (*Yanks him forward by shirt.*) She get other visitors besides you?

Son: I ... don't know.

Man: You don't know.

Son: I don't think so.

Man: You don't think so.

Son: No one ever comes here.

Man: The milkman.

Son: There's no milkman.

Man: The mailman.

Son: There's no mail.

Man: No mail. Goddamn right there's no mail, and you know why there's no mail, cause this goddamn joint's condemned, has been for years. No one's supposed to be living here any more. (*Getting progressively more violent as he almost screams.*) So what the hell are you two doing in here? Huh? What the hell are you doing here? (*He beats up the struggling Son.*)

Son: Please.

Man: How long have you been here?

The Mother enters from the bedroom, rushing in in panic. White slip, bra, panties underneath gown.

Mother: No!

Man immediately hurls Son aside and brutally grabs Mother by gown, ripping it in the struggle.

Man: What are you doing here? What? What are you two here for?

Son makes a move forward in her aid.

Son: Leave her alone.

In a split second the Man hurls the Mother down to her knees and has his gun pointing right in the Son's face. The Man's hand is shaking with pent-up fury and the gun threatens to go off any minute, despite the enormous self-control that the Man is trying to exercise.

Man: Get out! Get out!

Son: No I ... I can't.

Man: Get the hell out and don't come back, don't ever come back. Move. (*He points to downstage right exit.*)

The Son reluctantly starts to move towards requested direction.

Man: And hey, don't try anything. Go on, out.

The Son is extremely reluctant to go, but has no choice and leaves, afraid and concerned for his mother, hating himself for his impotence.

A lengthy pause as the Man's tension slowly seeps away leaving him naked in his trapped despair as he looks up and around the room, almost scared.

The sound of the waves crossfade with the foreboding notes of menace.

Music: *Do A Thing* (*excerpt*)

The Man slowly replaces gun in belt and wearily removes coat.

He sees the Mother, still on her knees, looking at him through anxious eyes. Eyes that don't seem to hold fear, only an anticipation and a readiness to cope.

The look at each other for a long time. Very hostile.

The Man slowly walks to her, slightly unnerved by her show of guts.

He stands over her and slowly, menacingly caresses her hair.

She slowly gets up moving her hair sideways as she drops her hands defiantly, letting her white bra be seen under her ripped gown.

The Man sees this defiance and decides to find out just how tough she can be as he brutally grabs her by the hair and yanks her towards the bedroom.

Lights fade very fast.
Music continues through opening of next scene in
Black.

SCENE THREE: SECRETS

Same music continues.
Lights fade up slowly on the empty room.
Late afternoon.
Pause.

The Son slowly creeps in from upstage right, sliding against the wall cautiously.
He silently walks to the bedroom door and pauses against it, trying to listen in.
He decides to take a gamble and slowly, cautiously turns the door knob, and very gently opens the door, slightly and as silently as possible.
He peers in. Too dark. Can't see.
Parts door open some more.
Stunned shock! For a moment his emotions are unclear, a mixture of pain, revulsion, and anger, as he stands there immobile just staring in.

Music stops.

Man: (*From inside bedroom.*) What the hell!

The dismayed Son seems to be suddenly jolted back out of his immobility, as he moves back apologetically, placatingly.

Son: (*Mumbling.*) I ... I'm sorry, I'm sorry.

He dazedly walks to a chair and weakly leans on it, when the Man hurriedly steps out of bedroom, buttoning up his shirt.

Man: What the hell!

He zooms over to the Son and brutally punches him in the guts.

Son: No, I'm sorry, I'm sorry.

The Man is about to punch him a second time, when he suddenly decides to hurl him aside.

The Man anxiously walks to the window and tries to peer out through the cracks of the shutters.

Man: You fool! (*Pause.*) Anyone see you?

The Son shakes head listlessly.
The Man looks at him, then out the window once more, then slowly moves in, more relaxed.

The Son sadly lifts himself up on a chair.

The Man stares at him as he produces a cigarette from his pocket.

Son tries not to stare back, but finally musters up the gumption to return the stare.

The Man blankly wipes some sweat off his neck and continues staring back.

The sound of the waves can be heard once more in the distance.

The stares are interrupted when the Mother slowly walks in from bedroom, her faded pink night robe on.

The Son sees her. She sees him. The Son dares not accuse her in the presence of the Man but his thoughts are plainly accusatory. His eyes angry at her treachery.

The Mother guiltily looks the other way as she reaches the window. But she knows she must face him sooner or later and bravely turns to look at him once more and sees underneath his moist angry tears, his deep sorrow.

He no longer accuses but asks "why?" and even "what did he make you do?" as he dazedly approaches her.

The Man tenses and steps forward menacingly. The Son stops and backs impotently.

The Mother melts and decides to go over by her Son's side, the side where she really belongs, but the Man grabs her left arm and brutally yanks her over next to him, and feeling extra big, gives the Son a look of utter contempt.

Man: I don't want you here. C'mon, c'mon scram.

Son: Why don't you just shoot me, buster?

The Man continues to stare at him for a while. He then stubs out his cigarette and gets up, about to go into bedroom, when he stops dead in his tracks.

A slight shuffling noise, from around the crates (downstage left), from in particular a large crate which is draped and covered completely.

More shuffling noises.

Crossfade sound of waves out and into the jingly shuffling percussion sounds of menace.

Music: *Suite Revenge; Part D: "Last Stop"* (excerpt)

All tense up in fear.

The Mother, the Son slowly back off slightly.
The Man slowly walks forward to crate.

The shrill music punctuates the ominous mystery as the Man, with one fell swoop, removes the drape and hurls it aside to reveal a metal cage, and within, on all fours – a woman – circling around in the narrow cage, now startled. In long dark purple lacy skirt and turn of century long sleeved, three sizes too large, blouse. Somehow it looks incredibly erotic. The woman, early twenties, but still a baby in many ways, her speech for one, all words being variations of sounds like vij, sheesh, cheej, ffy, byy, etc. – is The Monkey.

Brown lights envelop the cage, shrouding the rest of the room in deep gloom.

The Monkey is happy at the sight of company as she meekly emits some friendly sounds at the Man.

The Man, puzzled but more so shocked, looks at the Mother and Son for an explanation.
They guiltily offer none.

The Man cautiously approaches the cage for a closer look at her.
She seems to be quite harmless and very friendly, exuding an innocent incomprehension as she crawls in her cage to him, placing face against bars.

The Man crouches in front of her and looks at her.
Friendly Monkey tentatively reaches out her arm from behind the bars, causing the Man to tense for a moment, and innocently, playfully holds his nose, making friendly, childish noises.

The Man gently sways his face aside as she playfully persists to grab his nose.

The Man thinks for a minute, then cautiously decides to open the door to the cage.

The Mother and Son are horrified. The Son tries not to reveal it. The Mother can't hide it.

Son and **Mother:** Don't!

This sharp word causes the Man to stare at them and reconsider his decision as he sees their deep concern, but he feels the Monkey has been unjustly caged and continues unbolting door. He opens door wide and moves aside, beginning to feel scared himself.

The Monkey sees the open door but is a little hesitant, scared. She backs away from the door slightly, but then, smiling meekly, she slowly, tentatively approaches the door. Stops. Looks at the Man. Continues crawling out into freedom.

Outside the cage now she slowly turns around on all fours inspecting her new perspectives.

She sees the cage. She sees the Man. She tentatively moves to him, smiling gently.

She stops as she sees the Mother. She makes a slight move.

The Mother tenses incredibly wanting to back off, too scared to do it.

But Monkey stops again and changes direction as she sees the Son. With an extra happy smile she starts to crawl over to him.

He parts window ever so slightly.

The Son has not experienced any greater horror than this as he weakly, incredibly scared, terrified, face turned pale white, backs off.
But
She approaches – hand outstretched to him.
He backs, backs, backs.
She comes closer, closer, closer.

The menace of the music peaks as the lights slowly fade to
Black.

The music continues as it slowly dissipates the menace in
Black.

SCENE FOUR: WATCHERS

The previous music tapers off in slight tinkly sounds, as lights fade up on Son lying on couch, face out, eyes wide open, unable to sleep.

Night.

The door to the empty cage is open.

The Son is somewhat in control of his fear. Nonetheless he is extremely tense and uneasy and wishes he weren't alone (although he won't admit it).

He suddenly sits upright on couch.
Long silence, as he stares out in worried thought. Suddenly glances to the right, in direction of arm chair.

Music: *The Lost Man* (main title) *Very faint.*

Bolts up, springs to chair, lifts cushion and produces a chocolate bar which he quickly unwraps and frenziedly takes a much needed bite.

Still tense, when he abruptly stops mid-bite and stares intently at the cage.
A mischievous smile, and he's down on his knees at once, placing chunks of his chocolate bar on the floor in a sneaky trail that leads straight to the cage.
Rapidly smearing the entrance of the cage with the bar, he then tosses rest of chocolate in cage and steps aside to inspect his trap.

He looks warily at the cage. He looks at crates downstage right, and the exit.

He paces along upstage wall, back and forth, restless, worried, tired. He sees the closed bedroom door. He becomes enraged once more. Stops by it, listens in. Volume of music slowly increases. Ominous creepy undertones becoming more and more pronounced.
Peaking.

Suddenly lights bang on outside the window from the deserted shack opposite.

The music peaks again.

The lights in the room markedly decrease, equally suddenly.

The Son is still unaware as he continues pacing, when it hits him. He stops dead still. His widening eyes wanting to pop right out of his head, his whole body quivering, shaking.

He suddenly turns, sees light as suspected, crashes his body away from front of window to side of it with a horrified jolt, sweat pouring out of his body.

He wants to scream, still trying to reject the obvious fact of the light across.
He looks to bedroom door, wincing for aid.
He turns back to window.
He tries to peer through cracks. Impossible.
His shaky hand slowly, reluctantly grabs the latch.
Should he, shouldn't he. O cruel dilemma.
He slowly undoes latch.
Tries to peer through.
Parts window slightly some more.
Peers. Can't see.
Backs. Decision. Decision. Arms slowly move, hold shutters.
Tension.
Music shatters into another peak.
Son crashes shutters wide open very fast.
The sight outside bolts his stunned body a mile back with the impact of sheer terror.

The Son cries in fear, helpless horrified fear.

A woman, the Other Woman — naked, dead, her left side, her guts bloodied, tied up by her arms to a rope suspended from above, head lolled to side, immobile.

The Son's wailing cry is ripped out of his guts into a prolonged terrified soul-splitting scream as he jumps forward, slams shutters shut, stays there a moment and crashes to his knees, intensifying his crazy scream.

The bedroom door is flung open as the Man and the Mother rush out. The Man with gun in hand.

Both horrified and electrified for a moment at the shock of seeing the light.

The Man then suddenly rushes to the Son and hurls him away from in front of the window, crashing his own body against the wall to the side of the window. He takes a cautious peek and looks at the Mother seeking refuge on opposite side of window. The Man tentatively reaches out his hand to open the window, impulsive decision, zooms to it and flings shutters open, as he bolts backwards.

Both the Mother and the Man see the Other Woman tied up, dead.

Shock.

The Man just stands there dumb-founded.

The Mother dazedly unknowingly stumbles towards the window, strangely drawn forward by the sight, drawn by a dangerous magnet.

The Man immediately grabs her and tosses her back on the couch.

The music peaks again.

The Other Woman suddenly lifts her head up in one smooth rise and stares at them with a strange sensuous smile, her eyes wide open. Eyes that are black with yellow pupils shining, blazing widely inside.

The two turn to be stunned with this new sight.

The Mother screams hysterically.

The Man rushes to window and slams shutters shut, body shivering all over.

For a moment, he's very confused, not knowing what to do, a quick look at the Mother, still screaming, a quick look at the shutters closed and window light off, a quick look at the gun in his hand, a quick decision and he zooms out the upstage right door.

The lights fade very fast.
The music fades in
Black.

SCENE FIVE: CLAUSTROPHOBIA

The lonely sound of the waves.
The same night.

The Mother and the Son – in exactly the same positions. The Son splayed on the floor – his sobs now subsided. The Mother by the window clutching her night robe, looking very strange, feeling very strange.

Her head shaking nervously, her insides burning deep holes in her, a despairing haunting look in her eyes, a need to scream – oppressed by claustrophobia.

She walks slowly, sombrely, steadily forward. She sits on the couch. She looks all around her suddenly, swayingly, she looks above her, the ceiling, the walls, her cell, she clutches the couch firmly, battling her malaise, wanting to scream, managing once a wince, shaking her head, slowly, slowly, endlessly.

The Son sees her from his dusty misery on the floor. He watches her attentively then clambers up to his knees, a quick look at the open bedroom door, and he crawls over to her, ending up on his knees in front of her. He peers at her face studiously, misery written in his eyes, the searching, yearning derelict eyes of the orphan he is.

He holds her hair trying to keep her face still, but she keeps shaking her head.

Son: Ma ...

She keeps shaking. He holds her face with both hands and keeps her squirming head as steady as he can.

Son: Ma ... I'm gonna get the police.

She keeps shaking her head, looking at him blankly, listlessly, not acknowledging him. He holds her by the shoulders, caressing her arms gently.

Son: Ma, please, listen to me. I'm gonna get the police.

She keeps shaking her head, listlessly, sadly. He becomes very sad as he holds her and lifts her almost closer to him, his hands firmly under her arms, slowly caressing the side of her body, with a burning urgency.

Son: Please, let's end it all. Let's go somewhere else.

She slowly stops moving and stares deep in his eyes, her face an inch away from his. The Son holding her firmly, holding her body, close to him, but not touching him, holding her, quelling a feverish desire with great difficulty. He looks at her, like the unwanted, desperately needing to be wanted. He parts his lips slightly, his moist tongue visible to her.

She slowly looks up behind him at the Man standing at the doorway to the bedroom, shoulder holster on with gun, hands in pockets, staring at the two of them intently, sombrely.

Son spins around guiltily and jolts up and backs against the wall. The Man looks at him stonily. He heard. There's a trace of violence in his stare.

The Son is feeling equally violent.
He wants to ...
He wants to ...

The son bolts out the upstage right door angrily and disappears, seething with frustration.

The Man was almost going to follow him. He knows he should, but he doesn't.

Half-sad, half-thoughtful, he wonders what the Mother is thinking about as he slowly walks over to her.

The Mother is confused, wanting to rush out, at the same time compelled to stay.

A moment of apprehension as the Man stops next to her, his eyes making clear that without her it would be a different decision.

They keep staring at each other, the Mother becoming increasingly saddened by her fate, feeling all hope gone.
The Man feeling guilty at having to hold her captive, yet more firm than ever, he also becomes sad, wishing there were other alternatives.

The Mother looks away and down.
The Man looks at her and away, very tired.
The Mother feels her eyes get moist, her head quiver slightly.
The Mother sees his hand close to her face.
The Mother making a point of looking the other way slowly, timidly raises her own hand and tentatively holds his.
A pause.
She slowly, almost guiltily, with suppressed yearning places her cheek against his hand and slowly caresses her cheek against it.

The Man simply looks down at her, gentle yet emotionless. She looks out ahead of her, vulnerable.

The sound of the waves fade as the lights fade to
Black.

SCENE SIX: SIN

Dim lights jump out of the black to reveal the loneliest latest hour of that same night. The angry drums of combat jump out loudly with the lights.

Music: Battle Scene

To reveal the Military Man — seated on some crates upstage right, leaning against the wall, head drooping in sleep — in full combat outfit, machine-gun in hand on knees.

The moment the light hits him, his head slowly moves up to reveal the black charcoal marks on his stony face of suspicion.

He has a chocolate bar in his mouth. A Mars Bar. He had just finished taking a bite of the bar and his right hand is now in the process of lowering the bar.

He munches on it. Each chewing motion of the jowls tinged with the anxiety of his hostile enemy territory. Fear kept at bay only by the explosive potential violence kept boiling in him. Lid down but ready to overflow any minute without warning.

The Military Man is ready for battle, as his eyes remain fixed on the bedroom door.
He checks his watch.
One more bite of Mars.
Checks watch once more.
Time.
Mars 'tween teeth, he bolts up, cocks gun and begins to move.

He slowly, silently moves forward, eyes fixed intently at bedroom. He reaches the bedroom door and pauses. Tense.

Nothing. No sound.

He cautiously leans against wall by door and slowly reaches door knob, ready to twist it open.
Hand on knob, about to open, when he turns around, gun pointed at down-stage right door.
He heard a sound. He's sure of it.
He slowly, crouchingly moves to door.
Has idea.
Kneels behind armchair, gun pointed at door ready to blast a round and waits. Tense beads of perspiration forming on his forehead.

Tense angry chords accompany the drums now. The volume of the music increases.

All the lights turn red!

Upstage right, from behind the shadows of the moody, unfriendly doorway out lurks a figure — Monkey.

She pops her head out quizzically, holding on to the wall and unsteadily moves out of hiding. She has a limp in her left leg and has to hold on to objects occasionally.

Military Man, tense, is unaware of her presence, and sits tight as Monkey slowly, tentatively moves closer to him.

Monkey's nostrils flare suddenly and her eyes pop out.
She smells chocolate.
A quick look around and the trail on the floor is detected.
She blissfully retrieves each chunk on the floor, following the trail, not to the bar in the cage, but the bar in Military Man's mouth.
Monkey is perilously close to Military Man as she mumbles sweetly to him, like the irresistible beggar she is.

Military Man's eyes flare for an instant as he senses her, before he suddenly turns around pointing rifle at her, his pent-up violence ready to be released through his trigger finger.

Monkey backs frightened and almost stumbles down as she tries to allay his fears now by a shy smile, mustered up with great difficulty.

Tense Military Man just stands there pointing rifle at her, defensive fear roaring through his eyes.

Monkey is no longer startled, as she now mumbles gently, trying to make friends with him as she hesitantly, shyly points to the chocolate bar twist his teeth, and meekly inquires with her gentle continuous "pshpshpsh" mumbling noises whether she could have a bite.

Tense, cautious, suspicious Military Man looks down at the bar 'tween his teeth, slowly removes it and cautiously, after much deliberation, extends it to her.

She hesitantly comes forward and with shy gratitude slowly takes it. A friendly giggle escapes her as she takes a tiny bite.

Slightly relieved Military Man, still staring at her with disbelief, slowly takes seat on couch and reaching for knapsack produces second Mars Bar for himself.

Military Man seems to have relaxed a little. Monkey senses this as she hesitantly ventures nearer, hobbling and limping closer to him, more curiosity having gripped her inquiring head, as she tentatively touches his helmet, fascinated by the complex netting and twigs. She makes herself comfortable as she sits on his knee, munching her chocolate with one hand and playfully trying to remove the helmet with the other.

Military Man moves his head back slightly, signifying that's a no-no. Monkey tries to cover up her guilt by giving it a last playful tug.

The giggly kid is now fascinated by the charcoal lines on his face and starts to follow the lines with her finger mumbling her curious questions to him.

He remains stonily impassive, as he places rifle beside him.

Time for another bite thinks Monkey as she now begins to mumble the story of her life to him. However, she's not looking at him because at this point she's busying herself with the complexities of lowering the wrapper round the bar. All her attention is focused there now.

An appropriate moment thinks Military Man. For he has for the past few seconds been himself fascinated with the sight of her bare left breast, which her blouse had unconsciously uncovered.

Putting his Mars Bar in coat pocket, he sneakily makes a very subtle move, under the guise of helping her remove the wrapper from her Mars Bar.

His left arm fumbling with wrapper from behind her back, his right in front of her. Mars wrapper ripped, his right arm ends resting on her knee, his left hand on her left breast.
He stonily notes she is unaware of the move.
He decides to make his move more obvious as he stonily squeezes her breast, a trace of guilt passing through his eyes.
He notes once more a lack of suspicion from the opposite camp and is about to grin.

Just then, Monkey's attention is caught as she notices him playing with her breast. He stops. She giggles however and gives him a tiny wet kiss on the cheek and continues with the business of removing the wrapper altogether, mumbling about the difficulties chocolate bars sometimes pose. Her irritation shows as she moves up and down on his knee. Military Man decides to placate her as he starts to rock his knee, his eyes now definitely inflamed with lust.

He decides to gamble and make a strategic move as he slowly fumbles with the buttons on her blouse.

The friendly Monkey's attention is once more diverted as she sees Military Man's hand slip underneath her blouse and rest on her breast once more.

Monkey inquires as to his intentions.

Military Man's eyes only brim with grim uncommunicative determination. Monkey decides to stop asking questions and see what he's up to, as she watches on clueless but, with an unmistakable feeling that a surprise is due as his caresses move downwards along the side of her body. The air is full of excitement and anticipation.

His hand slowly moves along her thigh. His face darkens. He feels the thigh once more, very firmly. His heart seems to stop beating for an instant, his eyes seem to be gripped with a strange look of anxiety, he can feel the hair on the back of his neck standing upright. He now does not move his open palm but keeps holding on to her thigh firmly, trying to confirm his suspicions.

They are confirmed. Something is unmistakably very strange. His head quivers tensely. His neck muscles strain to break. His teeth grind and bite his lips. His eyes bulge. He shivers, trembles all over as he stares at his hand on her thigh, in terror.

He moves his hand down to the hem of her skirt, grips a handful tightly and without warning pulls up the skirt with a quick move to her waist, and reveals the horror underneath.

Monkey's left leg is not made of skin but of fur! Black fur! Like a furry black cat's fur! Not hair but fur!

Military Man screams like a maniac as he hurls her off his knee to the ground and bolts a mile back, himself seeking refuge against the distant wall.

The dropped girl cries in fright. Startled, clueless, frightened, she sobs, afraid of him, as she backs off on the floor slightly.

The Military Man has stopped screaming, but is looking on at her furry leg in open-mouthed terror.

He slowly looks up at her and sees the bawling kid even more scared than him. He sees her try to wipe a tear as she looks on sad and trembling.

Military Man keeps looking at her leg for a while longer, then slowly, slowly, very, very cautiously dares to move forward towards her.

This scares the sniffling Monkey as she starts to move back. Military Man stops. She stops. He moves a little slower now. His slow move reassures her slightly that he means no harm. Still, she's very cautious.

Military Man reaches her and crouches, and then kneels slowly in front of her thigh staring at it intently. Monkey stares at her leg too now, wondering curiously at the reason for all this undue attention to her leg.

Their eyes meet for a moment. They stare at each other.
Military Man slowly tentatively reaches out his hand over her thigh and with great deliberation forces himself to hold it.
Monkey attentively watches on, now beginning to wonder if something might be wrong with her leg.
Military Man caresses the furry thigh slightly. He hates to admit it, but it feels good. He suddenly clambers down to her foot and removes her shoe.
A paw!
He's going to get scared again.
She smiles naïvely.
He removes the other shoe.
A normal foot.

He quickly, frenziedly lifts up her skirt to have a good look at her naked body. He's slightly relieved at the lack of any more surprises.
But that leg.
Pink at the hip, slowing getting covered up with smooth black fur, but light at the thigh and blossoming into a full-fledged regular cat's leg and paw.
A second glance at the paw and now he thinks it's cute. But the perversity of the whole thing confuses him tremendously.
Still he's fascinated by it as he holds her paw and caresses her leg and thigh.
Monkey is reassured of his friendly intentions and giggles playfully, seeming to say, "That's me, whadya think?"

Military Man's caresses slowly, imperceptibly become firmer and more passionate. His eyes recapture their former gaze of lust. Desire slowly seems to conquer perversity. Although he can never quite shake off that voice in him that keeps saying, screaming in fact, no, that's wrong, No.
He's almost delirious now as he holds her tightly by the waist and brings her closer to him, his hand once more roving furiously alongside the length of her body, his rein over his passions now surely going beyond control, a beastly, animal frenzy overtaking him in its tight grip.

Without warning he kisses her on the mouth with violent almost brutal passion as his hand fondles the opiate fur of her thigh.
The smiling friendly Monkey now becomes very confused, welcoming his friendliness on the one hand, but pleading in her mumbles for less force.
His brutal fury scares her and pains her.
She's almost sobbing now as things begin to go out of control and she becomes very frightened of him.

His hand violently grips her hip, then he turns her to her back and mounts her, as he brutally claws the thigh all over.

Monkey's mumbling, gentle pleas are now lost in her frightened sobs and now tortured by the pain, trying to push him away almost wanting to scream, to run away.

A brutal shove pins her to the ground and there is no escape.

Music ends.
Black.

SCENE SEVEN: HATE

Late afternoon. The following day. Very hot.
Silence.
The Son, the Mother, the Man.

The Son standing by the shuttered window centrestage right, back to audience, brooding. Angry at himself, angry for having come back, feeling out of place, feeling like a fool.

The Mother is seated on the couch, feeling extremely uneasy.

The Man is peering out through the shutters of the central window. He turns in, looks at Mother, at Son.

They're all staring at each other, leaving countless things that must be said, unsaid.

The Son is slowly seething inside.
The Mother now tries only to look at neutral things. The Man's stare is defiant, but recklessly defiant, the kind of self-assured stare that would want to make anyone in his right mind squash that fact to bits. Only he's wearing a gun.

The Man can't understand the Son's persistent masochism, which is beginning to get on his nerves.

Man: Why did you come back?

Son: Yeah, well, home is where the heart is.

The Man doesn't like his joke as he stares at him with steely eyes. He then glances over at the Mother and slowly goes and sits next to her, very close, arm around her. He continues to size up the Son and his short supply of guts. The seething Son tries to be calm.

The Man slowly turns to the Mother, turns her face to him and kisses her — slowly.

The Mother's open eyes guiltily see the Son see this and she tries to squirm out of it.

The Man holds her face more firmly and kisses her twice as passionately and twice as slowly, making a point of tonguing her as wetly as he can.

His hand now wanders down and he starts to caress her breast over her robe. The Mother decides best to go along with his whims as her resisting hand no longer tries to pry his grip loose, but slowly weakly drops.

The Son looks on seething with rage, hate, disgust. Boiling. Boiling.

The Man's hand wanders inside her robe.

The Son can't take it any more as he starts to mutter under his breath.

Son: (*Slow mutters – deliberate.*) Fucking cunt ... fucking ... fuck ... cunt ... cunt. (*The Man stops kissing and all stare. To Mother.*) Fucking cunt. You cunt. *No longer mutters.* You fucking cunt. You fucking cunt. Fuck. Fuck. Fuck, get fucked. Go on, get fucked you fucking cunt. You fucking pig, you slut. You fucking slut. You pig. You fucking pig. You filthy, slimy, fucking cunt. (*The Son moves around very rapidly; bolts, jumps, starts, very unpredictably all round the room. He periodically rushes out and continues shouting offstage then runs back in throwing crates around, being dangerously maniacal.*) Cunt. Fuck. Fuck, go on fuck. Suck cock. Go on, you pig, suck cock, suck his cock, you fucking pig, you fucking cocksucking pig. You bitch. Suck cock, suck cock all the way to fucking hell, you motherfucking cunt. You fuck. You cunt. You shithole garbage slut. You fucking pig cunt. (*Slowly having built his vituperation to a shouting spit-spouting frenzy, jumps up suddenly as the angry Man produces gun. The Son backs up in rage, hurling a crate down and keeping his furious distance. Then to Man.*) You fucking asshole, you make one more fucking move I'm gonna rip your fucking balls off, you fucking cunt sucking pig, you fucking shit. Asshole. You motherfucking asshole. You motherfucking cocksucker, fuck off, you fucking shitface, fuckface pigass cocksucking cock eating pile of shit. You motherfucking cocksucking asshole. Fuck off. Fuck off. (*Man cocks gun, Son enraged comes and shouts in his ear.*) You fucker. You want me to drag you outa here, you fucking bastard, you fucking shit. You fuck. You motherfucking, cunt lapping asshole licking piece of shit. Hey, fuckface you deaf or what. You asshole, I'm gonna kick you outa here so hard you're gonna fucking slide in your piss, you fucking flatfoot cocksucker. (*Son makes a move forward. Man makes a move with gun. Son bolts back to behind a chair, even angrier.*) You motherfucking shit. You cunt sucking motherfucking cocksucking fucking asshole shit. You garbage fuck. You shit reaming pigfucking dogfucking cocksucking motherfucking asshole cunt. Motherfucking fuck. Fucking cocksucking cocksucker. (*Son is getting very tired now, but keeps it up.*) Cunthole fuck. Fucking, fuck fucking, fuck fucker, fuck. Fuck. (*Winded, out of breath, almost crying. The mother and Man now just sit and look away. The Man patiently waits for him to finish as he inspects the ceiling. A slow comeback from Son. To Mother.*) Filthy slut. You cunt. Cunt. Get fucked, you cunt, you slut, you pig. Come on, spread your fucking legs and let him suck you off, you cunt. Let him suck your fucking cunt, your snatch. Fuck your snatch slit twat quim pussy cunt. Fuck your cunt, you fucking pig. (*To Man.*) Fuck her cunt, asshole. (*Weary now.*) C'mon asshole grab your motherfucking prick and shove it in her motherfucking cunt and fuck the shit outa that motherfucking bitch.

You motherfucking, cocksucking cunt. Fuck. Cunt. (*Pause.*) Cunt. (*Pause.*) Fuck. Fuck. (*Long pause.*) Fuck cunt. Cunt. Cunt. (*Pause, all mutters now, as he sinks down on his knees behind the armchair, all worn out, and very sad.*) Fucking Cunt. (*Pause.*) Cunt. Cunt. Fuck. (*Pause.*) Fuck. (*Pause.*) Fuck. (*Pause.*) Fuck. (*Pause.*) Fuck. (*Lengthy, lengthy pause.*) Get out. (*Pause.*)

The sound of the waves is heard in the distance.

Pause.
All remain quiet.
The exhausted Son is crying silently.
The Man awkwardly sits.
The Mother impassive; no longer offended; deeply hurt and sad.

When some shuffling noises are heard and Monkey crawls in, on all fours, from entrance (upstage right).
Monkey is very subdued and far from her usual cheerful self.
She pauses as she sees the three and senses the gloom in the heavy air.
She quizzically looks from one to another, almost asking for an explanation. None is offered.
She now stares at the Son who remains immobile, but tenses a little.
She smiles weakly as she tentatively crawls over to him, feeling her usual particular extra special friendliness towards him.
He starts a little and tenses a lot, causing her to stop.
Mumbling softly she extends her hand and shyly touches his knee.
She starts to caress his thigh, when the Son can no longer control his horrified disgust and screaming loudly kicks her brutally away.
Crying Monkey backs fearfully as the Son jumps up and away still screaming.

Son: Leave me alone, leave me alone.

He sees a broom, rushes, grabs it and brutally prods her towards the cage.

Son: Get in there, come on, get in there.

Monkey whimpers, scared and in pain, when the Man interjects, violently grabs the broom away from him, pushing him back.

Man: Leave her alone. I said leave her alone.

Son backs to the wall in impotent unsatisfied rage. He angrily looks at him for a second.

Son: Go to hell!

And gets out downstage right very fast, very angry, slamming door behind him.

The Man looks after him for a while then turns to the Mother to see her very tense standing way upstage left as the sniffling Monkey sadly approaches her.

The Man watches intently.
Monkey is sad and craving for the Mother's compassion.
The Mother tenses up, full of revulsion.
Monkey tentatively touches her thigh.
With a groan of disgust, the Mother pushes Monkey down and is about to move away when she notices the Man staring at her with disbelief.
She realizes the severity of her attitude and takes a seat on an armchair instead, trying not to make the situation any worse.

Music: ***The Lost Man***

The music of the window gently creeps in as Monkey once more attempts a plea for sympathy and creeps close to Mother and gently, timidly caresses her hand.

Mother remains immobile, trying to fight the repulsion. Helpless, not wanting to, but not being able to help it. Horror, disgust mounting up in her unbearably. Yet trying to suppress it, not moving on purpose.

Monkey's eyes plead, a few silent mumbles escaping her, but in vain, for there is nothing coming from the Mother. Sad and rejected, she persists as she attempts one last move, getting up on her knees, wanting to kiss her cheek.

The Man sees the Mother quiver with unbearable, painful revulsion.

The Mother can't stand it any longer as she violently tosses Monkey away and backs up against the wall, on the brink of hysteria.

The rejected Monkey rocks herself a little, not knowing what to do.

The Man slowly walks over to Monkey, who backs a little, scared, but the Man's reassuring pat allays her fears. He gently caresses her hair for a while, then pats her off.

Man: Go on, go on.

Monkey is cheerful now as she slowly wanders upstage, curiously inspecting the room, on all fours, touching, mumbling, sniffing, content with the search and the discoveries the room offers.

The Mother moves off downstage right quickly, in disgust, in tearful suppressed anger at Monkey, at herself, at her lack of love for her.

The Man looks at her, puzzled, uncomprehending, feeling disdain, contempt for her attitude.

The Mother sees his accusatory look and hugging her shoulders tries to hide her tears, her whole body trembling.
Something tense on the brink of explosion can be felt when Monkey affectionately decides to rub her body against the Man's legs and receives another absent-minded pat.

At the same instant the volume of the music increases.

The creepy menace slides out, the ominous cue occurs.

*The light from the shack across the window goes on, the lights in the room dim.
And only Monkey notices the light.*

*For at that precise moment, the Man decides to have a confrontation with the
Mother and angrily walks over to her.*

*Monkey mumbles at the Man in warning, but he doesn't hear her.
Monkey feels something very wrong in the air, feels scared, instinctively knows
the light to be an omen of some sort.
Monkey anxiously calls out after the Man some more, but he can't hear her,
for he is now immersed in an angry, loud, violent argument with the Mother.*

*Although the ongoing argument between the Man and the Mother is literally
screamed, it is nevertheless barely audible under the crushing impact of the
music's violently loud volume.*

Man: What's going on here? Huh? What the hell is going on here? Hey,
I'm talking to you. (*Grabs her and turns her around to face him.*) Answer
me when I talk to you.

Mother: Please don't ask me anything, I can't explain.

Man: You can't explain! Whadya mean you can't explain?

Mother: (*Mumbling, turns face away.*) I can't, I just can't.

Man: Look at me, now you look at me ...

*Meanwhile the lights have crossfaded so that the Man and the Mother are in
relative darkness, whilst Monkey's urgent appeals are highlighted.
But to no avail.
Monkey now has to go check herself as she scurries to the window and tries to
peer out through the obstinate shutters.
No luck. Nothing can be seen. A decision must be made and soon thinks Monkey as she makes a half-hearted attempt to reach for the window latch.
But no. The fear. Too much.
One more plea at Man. No use.
When she notices her favourite rubber duck lodged beneath the couch. She retrieves it and absent-mindedly fondles it, but thoughts of the window are becoming more and more persistent, and she finds she is mentally beginning to
gradually overpower her initial fears. A mischievous glint can now be detected
in her eye as she gives the couple downstage right a furtive glance.*

Man: ... When I first got here, I see you and your stupid kid shacked up
here. Here in this shack. Out of nowhere I find you two cooped up in
here. Why, why, huh? What the hell are you two doing here? Huh, what?

Mother: I can't explain. I can't tell you. Can't you understand, I just can't.

Man: Whadya mean, what are you talking about, you gone nuts or what? What's all this mystery? What? What? (*Shakes her some more and tosses her down on chair.*) Then there's this other kid of yours. Jesus Christ, what the, what's the matter with you, you're treating the poor kid like she was some animal. I mean, Christ, just 'cause she's a cripple, you put her in a cage. (*Walks over to cage.*) A cage. A goddamn cage, for Christ's sake. I oughta put you in a cage. (*Angrily walks back to her.*)

An opportune moment, thinks the mischievous Monkey, her mind now definitely made up to open the window. On the sly. Before anybody realizes it or changes their mind. The incredible necessity to see what's on the other side of the window only bringing new unexperienced thrills now, fear thrown at bay altogether.

With a naughty smile, she slowly, slowly crawls over to the window, climbs up a crate lying underneath, and barely able to suppress her guilty giggles begins to fiddle with the latch, her adventures totally unnoticed by the two.

Man: What kinda crazy setup is this? What kinda lousy way is this to treat a poor kid? Nobody treats their kid like that. Nobody.

Mother: That's not my kid. It's not mine.

Man: Whadya mean, not yours?

Mother: Please stop asking me all these questions. I told you you wouldn't understand.

Man: Don't give me that crap again. Start talking right now. You got no feelings, you got no feelings at all.

Mother: How would you know? How dare you talk about feelings. I hate her, don't you understand. I hate her. I can't stand her. I can't stand to have her near me. I can't bear to have her touch me. She disgusts me. I wish she were dead.

Man: (*About to slap her.*) You bitch!

Utter contempt for her, he doesn't even slap her but disgustedly goes to sit in an armchair, confusion gnawing at his guts.

That abrupt cross to the chair was a close call for Monkey as she guiltily lost her balance and almost fell, noisily.
But she managed to regain her balance in the nick of time, still unnoticed by the two.

And so, amidst more guilty giggles, she cheerfully fiddles some more with that obstinate latch, trying to pry the difficult thing open.

The music approaching its climax. Nearing, nearing, ever closer.

The latch is open.

Monkey parts the shutters lightly. Tries to. They seem to be stuck. She uses all her strength to pull them open.

The music peaks.

The Mother turns to offer yet another explanation to the Man about why she can't explain, when she notices the window being opened and screams at the top of her lungs.
The Man bolts out of his chair.
Too late, for Monkey just met with success.

The shutters fly open all the way to reveal ...

The Other Woman, no longer bloodied and very much alive, still tied, but in the throes of blind ecstasy.

And the Son, naked from the waist up, behind her, passionately caressing her body, her breasts, her belly, her thighs and kissing her neck.

The Son immediately lifts his head the moment he notices the window opened and looks in at the three with blind hate, staring right at them through black-yellow eyes.

Jolted to motion once more, both the Man and the Mother zoom to the window in utter panic.
The Man hurls Monkey away, hurls interfering Mother away and slams shutters closed.

Face white with fear, feels his brain swimming, grabs gun and unthinkingly rushes out (upstage right).

Monkey is too stunned to complain and just stares at his exit and at Mother, very scared.

The Mother, weakly holding on to the wall, breathing with difficulty, dazedly looking at window, suddenly turns to look the other way.

A strange, strange claustrophobic, hysteric look.
A look of a person about to burst.

The music fades as the lights fade to
Black.

SCENE EIGHT: BURST

Music: *Fill Your Hand* *Top, furious volume.*

The manic rage of a pianist crashes the bass notes in the **Black**.

Lights fade up to reveal Mother, Man, Monkey.
A deep angry orange glow.

The Man seated upper right on a crate, by the door, feeling very spent.
Monkey on the floor centre, facing them upstage.
The Mother against, in front of the window.
The Mother.
The Mother is pent-up with rage and fury. The fury of the countless years.
But no longer. Dangerously on the brink of letting go. Dangerously meaning
business. Dangerously about to explode and detonate all in sight in the process.

She slowly, slowly raises her painful tense quivering head, murder, death, viol-
ence shining in her eyes.

A second frenzied crash of piano notes.

The Mother slowly, slowly walks ahead of her, staring ahead of her, her mind
is made up, only a matter of time. The screws have spun loose and spiralled
into nowhere. It will happen. Definite.

A third jolt from the chords.

She tensely clutches the back of a chair, looking down ahead of her, determined
eyes calculating all. Still keeping it in, all in, readying herself for that gigantic
eruption. Now boiling. Boiling.

A fourth frenzied quiver of chords.

She tensely angrily murderously looks up and focuses all her attention on
Monkey.

Monkey, scared out of her wits, whimperingly scurries out on all fours to bath-
room (downstage left), and safety, she hopes.

A fifth jolt from the chords.

The Mother slowly, slowly turns her head and focuses on the Man, who very
tense also, knows what is about to happen. Aware, afraid, stubborn.

The Mother's eyes go to the door upstage right. Breathing heavy.
The Man's too.
Both look at each other.
Mother makes a start.
Man does just as quick.
Both stop.

A silence in music. The silence before.

Both know.
Both wait.
Both tense.
Both determined.

The music suddenly explodes in crazy manic hysteria, no more stops, just one
long extended string of shrieking frenzy.

Mother screams like a maniac as she lunges at the door. All reason gone now forever. Just one clawing burning pressing urgent need to get out of that door, no matter what. Just getting out.

Screaming, yelling, "Lemme go," "Lemme out," constant screaming panic, hysteria, she lunges.

But the Man is equally determined and just as stubborn, also having lost all reason, his one aim in life, to stop her from getting out, stop her at all costs.

The Man grabs the Mother by the waist, her body in constant non-stop motion, frenzied hands, legs, all over, must escape out of clutches. Out of door. Hands clawing his face, feet kicking his shins. The Man oblivious to pain, all strength, takes all punches and persists in holding her motionless.
He drags her all the way to upstage left. A very, very long way. As she strains at the chains of captivity, manages to turn entire body around, so Man holding her by waist from behind, having more difficulty.
The force of her straining makes him turn around so that she is once more facing the door. A violent clawing of his eyes and she's out of his grasp as she zooms to door.

Man lunges after her, loses grip on slippery robe, grabs her once more and drags her back again as far away as possible from door.
Mother kicks, punches, going bananas, fury, pounce out of his clutches once more, bringing him to floor.

But not long, for Man grabs her by the leg and causes her to stumble on couch between her and door.
Mother holds to couch trying to jump over it.
Man on floor in frenzy grabbing her leg for very life pulling back, back.
Mother getting pulled back, only able to hold leg of couch. Almost tentative. A sudden summoning up of energy and pulls herself forward, now dragging him along forward.
Violent kicks of fury.
One on face and released from grasp.

Mother lunges once more over couch, climbing over and down.
Man leaps up suddenly and tackles her legs. He falls back on couch, causing her to fall back on couch as well, over him.
Mother still trying to get loose, breaks forth from over him.
Grabs back of couch, lifts herself, knocking him down.
Free once more.

Man holds her by left arm dragging her back, he stumbling, now fallen on seat on floor.

Agony, frustration of Mother.
Fear. Fear. Fear.
Suddenly sees plank lying by crates.
Still being held by arm, lunges, grabs wooden plank with right arm, squirming out of his grasp frenziedly.
Man loses grip, unprepared.
She holds plank with both hands "pow" breaks it, landing it on his head.
Man unconscious, very hurt.

Mother free at last. No more restraint. Free to run to door. To run out.
She lunges to door running.
She suddenly stumbles and falls.

Frenzied clamber up and lunge to go.
Legs unsteady, wobbles, falls flat down on face.

Frenzy, hysteric. Frantic.
Why legs unsteady?
Trying to get up. Clamber. Up.
Like in puddle of oil.
Legs slippery. Fall off.
Up again. Fall, slippery.
Scream agony, frustration.
Must get up. Fall, slippery.
Hands on floor, frenziedly steadying herself up, up on feet, about to go, slips, falls.
Cry in frustration.
Up. Fall.
Up. Fall.
Up. Fall.
Frenzy of holding to couch for support to get up.
All force on couch. Lifts herself up. Fall.
Hold on to couch once more. Hysterical. Help support couch. Props herself up.
Lets go of couch. Falls again.

Lets go of couch. Just try to get up on own again.
Up. Fall.

Frenzy of clambering up, legs slipping underneath, falling. Hands, knees, prop up to feet.
Can't move now.
Feet stuck to ground.

Electrocuted in the puddle almost.
Electric shocks running up her legs, up her body, through her extended, shaking waving now stiff arms, hands, fingers.
A gigantic shiver running through to guts, doubling up, falling down.

Frenzy once more, clamber up.

Again lengthy, immediate electrocution.
Sparks, electric shocks. Stiffening her body, extended arms causing her to lose balance, trying to rise out of puddle on tips of toes.
Tremble back, fall.

Man coming to.
Man seeing her.
Man getting up to come to stop. To hold her back.
Panic.
Nightmare. The Blob. Coming. Coming. Nearer.
Frenzy. Fear, as Mother hurling frightened looks at him, holding on to couch, clambers up, tries to run, falls.
Crying terror, Man nearer nearer nearer, clambers up couch, to legs, fall.
Up, run, fall.

Man reaches her, holds her by the arms, lifts her up, holding her tight, firm grip unescapable. Mother hysterical as Man holds her by waist, tight against him.

Mother move, move, gyrate, squirm, pound fists on chest, legs move, slip, trying to get away, away, away.
Cry despair, desperate, tired, slowing holding on snivelling almost, must get out of clutches.
Move, move, move, now faster, faster again, faster.
Cry. Scream. Frenzy.

Suddenly raging rips his shirt open. Violently rips down his back. Violently trying to remove, press down.

Frantic sudden stick glue press angry violent desperate press her body tight tight against him.
Frenzy. Need. Desperate. Must have. Furious frenzy of sticking, pressing tight, herself on him, sap him, drain him, get him, get his energy, stick, must.

Frenzy of motion, move, tight press now electric shock-like. Her whole body electrified, energized, stick tighter, drain tighter, drain out of his body, drain out his pain.

Rip body, claw chest, furious, frenzy claw rip skin off. Jump on him, legs around, tighter, in him, into him.

But exhausted. Spent. Slipping. Slowly reluctantly slipping. Sliding down him. Down his chest. Down his thigh. Down his leg. Down to the floor. Still holding to his leg. Angry tired frustration.

The Man breathes heavily in relief. Slowly moves back, unable to shake her loose.
Kicks her away tiredly. Falls on couch. Dead-beat. Breathing heavily.

Mother stubbornly, weakly crawls along the floor to him, weakly grabs his leg once more, weakly climbs up his leg, up on couch beside him, about to climb up to his mouth, falls, flops on his lap. Beat.

The Man tiredly flops a protective arm over her.

Slow slow fade to **Black**.

The music rages, rips, roars in black for 30 seconds, slowly evaporates, trembles rage off, exhausted.
Fades in
Black.

SCENE NINE: PASSION

The sound of the waves.
A hot evening.
The room is empty.

Slowly Monkey appears out of the bathroom, hesitantly limping in.

She is quiet, quizzical and very cautious after that scare she got from Mother.
She listens around. Nothing.
She's about to doublecheck that "nothing" as she slowly starts to limp towards the bedroom (upstage left), holding on to crates and wall for support.

Noises of movement are heard and without warning the Son enters from upstage right, dragging in the semi-conscious Other Woman. He's holding her under her arms and constantly trying to make her stand. She refuses. All she can do is shiver.

The Other Woman is totally drenched, head to toe.
She's wearing a white slip, white bra, white panties, and one white shoe.
She's prone to using mascara by the bushel and the price is now paid as heavy dabs trickle wetly down her cheeks.

The Son, busy dragging the Other Woman starts slightly as he sees Monkey.
A tense, unfriendly look backs the frightened Monkey against the cage.

Son is tense as he takes Other Woman and seats her on couch.
He stands and stares at Monkey who stares back.
Finally convinced that danger is at bay for the present, gives his attention to the Other Woman.

Son: C'mon, take your clothes off. Hey! C'mon, you're gonna catch cold.

She's not that conscious and just sits, all glassy-eyed, dopey-like, in another world, shivering constantly, helplessly.

Son has to do it all himself. He's a little annoyed as he decides to go to the bathroom to fetch something.

Wiping sweat off his brow, he unthinkingly moves to find himself perilously close to forgotten Monkey.
He tenses. He stomps his foot threateningly, causing scared Monkey to lose balance and topple on all fours.
Son is equally scared, however, as he backs away almost as quickly.
Using the longest, furthest way possible he exits to bathroom and re-enters with towel in hand, and again using furthest route from Monkey goes over to Other Woman.

A moment of indecision and finally he stands Other Woman up, who, shivering and tottering, needs to be almost constantly held up by Son. He mumbles pleasantries to her constantly, trying to soothe her as he raises her wet skirt above her head and removes it, bending her slightly to get it off from around her arms.

Son: Gotta undress you, don't mind me. Off it goes. Soon get you all dried up.

Son is no longer aware of Monkey, who watches every little detail most attentively.

Son throws slip on floor. Steadies her straight. Shivering, Other Woman manages to keep standing. Son goes behind her, undoes bra, lowers it very slowly, removes, squeezes water out of it, throws down with slip. Gets down on knees next, about to remove panties, sees shoe, decides to remove that instead, lifts her foot up, off with the shoe.

A silent moment, then he lowers her panties very quickly, raises her right foot, removes panties, lifts up left leg, removes panties completely, throws over with other clothes.

Other Woman shivers a lot now as she makes feeble attempts to hug her shoulders.

Son takes towel and starts to dry her, thoroughly.

First her hair and face and ears.

Son: Dry your ears. (*Then neck.*) And now your neck. There we go. (*Then right arm.*) Skinny arms. Should eat some more. (*Then left arm. Then chest and belly.*) Belly button all dried up. (*Then sides of body. Then back. All very thoroughly. Then he seats her back on couch.*) Sit you down now. (*Dries her thighs, down leg and foot.*) Do up your toes. (*To other foot and thigh. A silent reverent moment. A small dab between the thighs. Hair once more. Wonders if he missed anything. Bends her forward. Goes over back again. Lifts her up. Dries bum.*) The bum. (*All dry now.*) There we go. (*Throws towel down.*) Oh, get you a blanket now.

Gets blanket from beside a crate, drapes it over her, and sits her on the couch once more, and cuddles next to her, warming her up, rubbing her lovingly over blanket.

She's regained some consciousness now and looks like she's in a very unsociable mood.

Son sits on couch beside her, looking at her quietly. Now strangely subdued and sad.

He holds her cheeks gently and gently caresses her hair, murmuring. She looks away dazed, unfriendly.

Son: You O.K. now? All warm! Ah baby! Why did you wanna kill yourself, huh? Why baby? I told you not to do anything silly like that didn't I?

She wishes he'd let go of her cheeks.
Son is feeling very hurt as he stares deeper and deeper into her eyes.

Son: I told you not to kill yourself. Didn't I? I told you not to kill yourself. (*Angrily grabs her by the shoulders and brutally shakes her around.*) Why did you wanna kill yourself? (*He stops shaking as she winces in pain. Son cuddling up again.*) I'm sorry baby, I'm sorry. Sorry baby, sorry. (*Tenderly places her head against his chest, arms holding her head close to him, protectively, tightly kisses her hair and starts to rock her gently.*)

But she won't have any of it as she angrily tries to get out of his clutches, whimpering and wincing her impatient annoyance.
He persists in his tender sentimental caresses.

Son: C'mon baby, I'm sorry.

Other Woman is suffocating as she winces loudly and manages to muster up enough strength to bite his arm and shove him away in disgust. "Leave me alone, don't touch me," scream her eyes.

Son is very hurt as he slowly digests her reaction. He sadly, slowly moves off and away from her. He feels embarrassed and just moves around aimlessly for a while, too late to retract his sentiments now, he moves upstage right and flops on a crate by the window, threatening to cry any minute as he gives her a coupla pouting sidelong glances.

Other Woman isn't even aware of his existence at this moment.

Monkey is, however.
She has watched the turn of events, and of course having that soft spot for the Son decides he's in the right and feels very sympathetic towards him. She does exercise caution though as she crawls over to him now, very timidly, inching her way slowly.

The Son tenses as he sees her approach.
She stops. They look.

He murmurs, mutters weakly "Go away, leave me alone, get away."
Even though her tender sympathetic look softens him slightly.
She cautiously inches for some more. He persists muttering "No, no."
Son is tense, but decides not to pursue a hostile course this time around, as he sits back, spent in his misery.
She inches forward some more.
Perilously within touching distance.
Both get a little tense.

Son: No, please, don't. Please.

She becomes shy as she timidly ventures to touch his knee.

Son: Argh. No. Please.

The contact rips like a sharp needle through him, but he grits his teeth, determined to be brave, determined not to be sick.

Monkey is murmuring softly now as she smiles at the encouragement and hesitantly, like the unwanted child helplessly in need of affection, slowly climbs on his lap.

Son backs off as far as the chair will allow, back straight as a rod, spine ready to snap, extremely tense, scared, breathing heavy, wanting help, looking weakly at Other Woman for aid who's too immersed in her solitary moodiness to notice, now turns to look at Monkey, face quivering slightly, afraid to guess what she'll do next, wanting her off, yet impelled, obliged somehow to try and fight his hatred and disgust for her.

She gently touches his cheek.
He moves away tense, weakly crying "leave me alone, please."
Monkey is hesitant, smiles, mumbles gently, sweetly, touches cheek again, very soft.
Tenderly caresses his face.
Her eyes well with tears as she slowly caresses his hair, murmuring, smiling, almost pleading with him to be friends.
Monkey kisses him on the cheek.
Son is still very tense but moved by her sweetness and truly guilty by his attitude, helpless, wanting to change, finding it impossible to, wanting, ordering himself to try.
He stops his mutterings now.

Deadly silent except for the sound of the gentle waves hitting the shore.

With great effort he decides to touch her.
He slowly moves his hand to her shoulder, within touching distance, but he doesn't, he just holds his hand there, next to her shoulder.
He slowly, slowly moves his tense hand closer, closer, closer, touching her now, touching her arm, pressing his hand against her.

He almost sighs with relief as he masters his fear.
It's OK, he seems to say to himself. OK.
He starts to caress her shoulder slowly, her neck, her cheek, telling himself each step of the way, it's OK, reassuring himself, urging himself on.
Almost happy and proud that he's slowly able to master his fear.
He urges himself onwards, he knows he must go much, much further to be able to really master it.
He slowly caresses her breast, along the side of her body, down her waist, down, he feels the tension mount, his hand can't go down any more, refuses to.
He looks up at her who looks back innocently, friendly, unaware.
He looks down at the leg.
Very tense again.
Holds the leg.
Feels it.
Feels a revulsion.

Fights it, makes himself feel the leg.
Makes himself slowly raise the skirt.
Eyes filling with tears of fear.
The leg, the fur, the black fur, bare, visible.
The revulsion, can't, can't, don't want to.
Must, makes, forces himself slowly.
Touch the fur.
Brow perspiring.
Head, face, body quivering with pent-up held-in held-back revulsion.
Too much.
Can't.
Shaking all over.
But must.
As he forces himself to hold on to the fur
The palm of his hand pressed tight against the fur
Rubbing on that fur.
The fur.
Fur.
Blind with tears.
Wanting to be sick.
Disgust.
Puke.
Touching the fur.
Caressing hand tight against the fur.
Can't.
Forcing himself.
Can't.
Can't.
The disgust — too much — disgust.

He screams violently with all his might, screams like a lunatic, screams as he brutally pushes her, throws her off his lap, screams, screams as he pounces back up far away against the wall his whole body quivering with disgust, screams, screams.

Lunges forward like fury, lunges at her, grabs her by the neck, grabs her from behind as she tries to escape, wrings it, wrings it, wrings it furiously wrings it, wrings her neck, wrings it, tears it off her body.

She screams in agony, panic, unaware panic, pounced on her, her whole body moving side to side to side like straw, her head, her arms, her body, flying around out of control.

He knocks her forward against the back of the couch.
His grip fails.
A moment.
She lunges up forward on couch grasping for escape for life.
He lunges over her again from behind her wringing her neck, strangling strangling furiously.
Her body fluttering about helplessly, choking.
Over the Other Woman, who screaming tries to scramble away in panic, falling on the ground, crawling away.
The bedroom door flying open.

The Man, the Mother rushing in.
The Mother petrified.
The Man trying to grab Son.
Son furiously thrashing him, knock him off.
Screaming back to strangle Monkey.
Monkey choking breath, face terribly contorted, eyes bulge, squash noises, escape, frenzied trying.

Monkey falls limp in his hands – Motionless.
Son still wrings her neck and screams like a maniac.
He suddenly realizes she's dead as he stops dead for a second.
With a huge scream of disgust, violently hurls her up and against the wall, tossing her by the neck.
She flies up in the air and lands, crashes, flops down on the floor like a rag doll.
Dead.
A one second pause.

Music: *Paint Her Mouth* *Very loud.*

Three violent screaming crashes of strings and chords.

Son lunges downstage to the couch, crying in huge gushes, crying, sobbing off his disgust, wiping the contact of the fur off his palms onto the couch, wiping the touch of her, the disgust still fresh on his hands off off off.

A long extended rise rise on the strings unbroken slowly slowly leading up.

The Son, whole body shaking with horror looks at the Mother, who looks away in shock at the limp body of Monkey.

Sharing his disgust of her, yet shocked at what he's just done.

The Son turns away in guilt.
She was harmless, why did he, why, why couldn't he help it, why did he have to, but the disgust, unbearable.

The Man slowly walks over to Monkey, crouches by her and feels her pulse —
dead. He holds her in his arms and tenderly lifts her up as he stands, her lifeless body splayed in his hold.

He slowly walks towards downstage right door.

As he passes Mother, Mother backs, not wanting to be touched by Monkey.

Man looks at her strangely, contemptuously.
He stops and stares down at the Son on his knees.
He looks up at him, crying in gasps, gushing huge chunks of air.
Man just looks at the Son.

The Son bites his own hand as he growls trying to keep his emotions hidden, feeling naked, bared, guilty, apologetic, and yet not because he couldn't have helped it, turmoil, internal turmoil, private now being paraded.

The Son stares back at the Man and angrily rises and backs slowly, but with a dangerous look in his eyes.

Music climaxes.
Angry chords clash.
Black.

A last angry chord
and music dissipates in
Black.

SCENE TEN: VULNERABLE

Very late at night.
Very hot.
Very windy outside.

The sound of waves raging outside.
Inside — a deathly silence.

The Other Woman seated on couch, scared and cold, shivering uncontrollably.

The Man, standing by the cage, holding the bars, looking grim, feeling hot and sweaty, not wanting to speak, tired, sad.

Thirty seconds.

Wind rages outside, shutters move.

The Other Woman, feeling alone under her blanket, whimpers a little.

The Man turns to look at her and is almost surprised at seeing her there.

He slowly walks over to her, giving an unconscious glance at the window, trying to connect her, place her from somewhere.

The Other Woman looks at him intently through big wide innocent eyes.

The Man is scared.

The Other Woman pulls blanket tighter around her shivering helplessly, as she continues to look at him, through her hypnotic waif-like eyes.

The Man can't resist her eyes.
He shakes himself out of his reverie, however, as he realizes she is indeed shivering a lot and hesitantly walks over to her behind the couch and tentatively touches her shoulder.

The unresisting Other Woman looks deep deep in his eyes.

He slowly starts to rub her shoulders.
A little faster.
Slowly takes a seat beside her and rubs her arms and back, feeling her body very close to his, smelling the salty sea in her hair, staring back at her wide-eyed attentiveness, noticing her stop shivering as violently as before, touching the soft flesh of her arm.

He slowly stops rubbing and just looks at her, seated close to her, entranced by her gaze.

He doesn't realize the gentle move forward that he's unconsciously making. Almost imperceptibly his face moving closer to her slightly parted moist lips.

He's hardly aware of the Mother who has silently crept out of the bedroom and is silently taking it all in.

Neither he nor the Other Woman notice her as she silently walks to the window and leans there looking at them, not accusingly but almost guiltily, feeling sad and very out of place; feeling like the intruder she is, wishing she hadn't stepped out in the first place.

The Mother tries to look away, when the Other Woman notices her and now stares at her.

The Man senses a presence and turns to see the Mother as well.
He doesn't know why he feels so guilty as he uncomfortably sits back away from the Other Woman and tries to be unobtrusive.

The two women stare at each other for a while, silently.

The Other Woman tiredly clutches her blanket, weakly gets up and dazedly walks off into the bathroom (downstage left), above all not wanting to complicate things or get involved. She doesn't even look at the Man on her way out.

She just goes.

The Man is beginning to get angry as he looks accusingly at the Mother, who returns the accusation with a look of contempt and mistrust and betrayal.

The Man, boiling, seething inside, feeling suddenly shackled quickly gets up, gives her another look, a look that dares her to say anything and spitefully starts out to the bathroom himself.

Grim, confused, outraged – he exits.

The Mother looks down at the floor and doesn't follow his exit. Not angry, hiding that under her uncaring show of pride.
She slowly turns around to face the window and listlessly peers out through the shutters, trying hard not to cry.

Music: *Fujiyama* *Very, very soft.*

The music fades in from the distance, the lonely wail of a sax, later accompanied by a subdued piano.

The Mother slowly turns around, back against window and stares blankly ahead of her.
Thinking, feeling bitter, sad, alone.
A helpless smile fading into a silent cry as a tear flows down her cheek.

Thirty seconds.

The Man slowly comes out of the bathroom, stands there and sadly looks at her.

She glares at him accusingly, angrily, in pain, in love.

He looks down, he's very sad, sad that he hurt her. He slowly walks over to her, but still can't look at her. He stands there beside her trying to muster up some face, wanting to be vulnerable with her, wanting to explain, trying to explain why he needed to hurt her, angry, lonely. He, standing facing window. She, standing, leaning against window facing room. Both silent. Both immobile. Both wanting, needing so much to love each other, to be loved. Both already very much in love. Both needing to say it. The Man slowly turns and leans against the window beside her.

(The following dialogue is only barely audible and most of the time not audible at all. It's all whispered sounding like soft murmurings. Very private, said very slow, laboured. At times passionately fast, but more often said with difficulty and weakness and helplessly saddened by what is said)

Man: I'm sorry. *(Pause. No answer.)* Hey c'mon ... I'm sorry. *(Slightly touches her arm.)*

Mother: (*Shrugs him off.*) Leave me alone. (*Pause.*)

Man: (*Touching her again.*) C'mon ...

Mother: (*Shrugging him off, moving a step away.*) I said leave me alone. (*Long pause.*)

Man stays by the window, sadly looking at her.
She tries to avoid looking at him.
Man slowly walks over beside her, hands in pockets, stands there awkwardly next to her.
Looks at her, but she won't meet his gaze.
Gently touches her shoulder. She's about to be capricious again as she prepares to resist, but he won't allow it this time as he holds her by both arms and turns her to face him.
She tries to get out of his grasp, as she winces.

Man: Hey.

She stops and looks at him angrily.
He looks at her with sad sincere loving eyes. Eyes that repeat "I'm sorry."
But she refuses to believe him as she looks away once more.
He holds her cheek and turns her face to him once more, softening as he looks deep in her eyes, and softening her too.
She looks at him poutingly, her sad eyes still persisting in saying "You're lying." Still refusing to believe.

Man: (*Tenderly caressing her cheek.*) Baby.

Her moist eyes can no longer resist. The need in her heart overpowering all, not caring any more for the truth, as he draws her close to him, and they kiss passionately, hungrily, desperately.

She draws him close to her, holding him tight, as she now hugs him fervently, crying and needing him close, very close.

She kisses his cheek, small furious kisses, cheek, neck, mouth, holding his cheeks in her palms now, tightly holding his face close as she looks at him, needing him so desperately, and trying to get one more reassurance.

Mother: Oh baby ... baby ... don't leave me.

Man: I won't.

She gently caresses his face and buries her head against his chest, letting him hold her close to him, wanting him never to let go.

Slow blackout.
Music fades in
Black.

SCENE ELEVEN: TIME

Early morning.

Dim rays of sunshine coming into the room through the many cracks in the walls.

The distant sound of waves.

The Man, seated on the couch, arms around the Mother, curled up against him, half-asleep.

The Man is awake as he tenderly caresses her hair.

In the distance, very faint, the sound of a siren wailing persistently.

The Man tenses as he gradually becomes aware of the siren.

The Mother wakes up as the sound of the siren once again fades away in the distance.

They look at each other, both a little scared. He gently pushes her aside, gets up and tries to peer through the shutters.

He looks grim as he decides to go into the bedroom for his gun.

Music: *The Lost Man*

The creepy window music gently wafts in once more as the Mother sits tensely at the edge of the couch, terribly frightened and lost.

The Man re-enters the room checking his gun and leans against the wall by the window, once again trying to detect some movements outside.

The Mother gets up, about to look as well, when the Man motions her tensely to get away from in front of the window.

She quickly does as she leans against the wall on the opposite side.

Both look out anxiously as the Man very carefully undoes the latch and very, very slowly begins to part the shutters, very slightly.

The first music cue happens and the light bangs on from the shack opposite the window.

The Man immediately closes shutters again and backs against the wall.

Neither is aware that at the same moment the Son has silently entered the room through the downstage right entrance, and hands in pockets is silently standing there looking at the two.

The Man slowly begins to approach the window once more when he suddenly becomes aware of a presence and turns with a start, gun pointed at the Son.

The Man looks at the Son who looks back grimly.

For a moment the Man is at a loss as he realizes the Son's betrayal.

Looking out the window an instant, then back at him, his face full of despair and grief now, a realization of the end.

He wants to squeeze the trigger, he wants to pull it very badly as he keeps pointing the gun at the Son who remains totally motionless and looks back at him, with the look of a damned man.

The Man feels his arm drop to his side as he leans against the wall wearily with a sigh, smiling bitterly.

The Mother has a sense of loss as she looks at the now guilty Son. Too sad to be angry.

Mother: Why?

The Son is beginning to regret his action bitterly. She walks over to the Son, tears in her eyes and looks at him. Standing lost, close to him, eyes pleading.

Mother: Why?

The Son looks back with equally pleading eyes, trying to make her understand as he gently tries to draw her near, tenderly reaching her waist.

The Mother abruptly gives him a stinging slap across the face.

The Son is stunned as he holds his cheek in disbelief.
The Mother glares at him angrily as she stumbles back a few steps aimlessly.

Stops. Far from the Son. She sadly walks back upstage right looking at the Man. Yet far from the Man.

The volume of the music is very loud now.

No one moves.

The Man looks at the Mother.
She looks at him.
Both needing that last moment together, close to each other. Instead they just remain still and look at each other, both trying not to be emotional.

Slowly the Man raises his gun hand, rechecks if it's loaded and slowly rises and positions himself against the side of the window.

The Man grimly focuses all his attention at the shutters as he slowly, cautiously gets ready to open them once more.

The Son is now looking on with great anxiety. Tense, almost about to stop him.

The Man slowly parts the shutters very slightly.

The music is approaching its final peak.

The Man readies himself next to the window, readies himself to fling the shutters open.

The Son getting tense, scared, aimlessly wanting to undo things.

The Man suddenly flings the shutters open and has gun ready to shoot out the window as the music climaxes, when the Son impulsively runs up to hurl him away from the window, screaming.

Son: No, don't.

Man: Get away.

The Man determinedly hurls him aside and is about to shoot out the window, a split-second too late.

The flame of a gun is seen from outside the window as a shot is fired at him.

The Man's gun goes off at the direction of the flame at the same instant and almost immediately the Man finds himself reeling back in pain, shot in the guts, as the Mother screams in horror.

The Man staggers and steadies himself, doubling forward slightly as the music passes the climactic moment and is slowly becoming more subdued.

The Man slowly straightens himself.
He slowly walks forward a few steps, holding his guts.
He slowly, slowly sinks to his knees.
Slowly lets go of his gun.
Slowly doubles forward and rolls to left side and tries to stretch and slowly rolls to his back.
Dead.

The Son stands by the upstage wall looking on.
The Mother slowly walks to him and kneels beside him, crying silently as she tries to hold his cheek but keeps her hand just barely away from him, not touching him, sighing in unbearable pain.

Mother: Oh ... Oh ...

She slowly touches his cheek and caresses his face tenderly as she looks on helplessly.

Pause.

The Military Man is seen outside the window, coming out of the shack to the balcony.

He does not carry his knapsack or helmet and his coat is unbuttoned to reveal a gun wound over his bloodied t-shirt.

Machine-gun in hand he dazedly stops as he thuds against the wall. His shaky hand slowly raises his machine-gun pointing it ahead, straight at the Mother.

The Son sees him first as he backs with a frightened sigh.

The Mother is suddenly aware as she turns and sees the gun pointed at her. She is too stunned to move as she just stares at him waiting, when the gun falls off his hand and the Military Man sinks to his knees, falling limp – dead.

The fading music is slowly crossfaded into another piece.

Music: *Vio*

The music is slowly, slowly increasing in volume.

The lights slowly, slowly brighten as the Son cautiously approaches the window, looks at the dead Military Man and closes the shutters.

He stands there looking at the Mother wanting to make up to her somehow.

Mother gives him an "I hate you" look, turns back to the Man, closes his open dead eyes and sadly goes to flop on the couch.
The Son tentatively approaches her, trying to offer sympathy but the Mother won't have any of it.
The Son is angry, full of hate, as he now stares at the Man's corpse, slowly walks over to him, sees his gun, picks it up, feels renewed strength, energy, angrily places gun in belt, angrily grabs Man's legs and angrily, quickly drags his corpse off and exits (upstage right).

The lights keep brightening steadily. The music, angry, cantankerous, cacophonous, shrill, noisy, irritating, berserk, speeding, reeling, going bananas, spinning everyone in sight out of balance, zooming steadily ahead, crashing, bursting frenziedly, exploding, never letting up, volume increasing steadily steadily peaking to angry ear-splitting violent high peaks.

All the action slowly becomes faster and faster and faster till everyone is crazily zooming through the paces like frenzied speeded up violent maniacs.

Ma.
Ma slowly precipitates all.
Slowly starts the wheels spinning.
Spinning out of control.
Ma.

Ma about to cry.
Despair, loneliness, emptiness.
Uneven breathing.
Slow get up, back to audience, stand in middle of room, feels claustrophobia, reels around, gasping heavily, 'bout to sob, scream or do something unpredictable.

Ma hold it in, hold it in, let go, stumble, stumble faster and faster, sc, scr, scream, disappear into bathroom (downstage left).

Lights bang up full glaring level.

Zoom in Other Woman from downstage left, in dried slip, panties and bra.
Stumble forward dazedly to exit (upstage right).
Stop, about to faint.
Not allowing herself to, quickly looks at bottle of aspirins in hand, rips lid off,
empties forty pills in palm and throws all in mouth.
Son re-enters from upstage right, sees this and becomes angry.
Guilty Other Woman removes forty pills from mouth, replaces them in bottle,
closes lid and defeatedly throws bottle away.

Glaring Son reprimands her folly as he comes to her, slaps her, shakes her
around.

Wincing, Other Woman resents her lack of freedom and hits back, pounding
away at him and escaping his grip.

Music screaming now.

Other Woman screaming as one thought only remains – get out the door (up-
stage right).

Lunge for it, Son hold her by waist, drag downstage left.
Other Woman turns round in grip, claws Son's eyes, causing both to fall.

Other Woman rips eyes out, out of his grasp, runs over couch.
Son drag her back by leg.
Other Woman grab couch, drag Son forward, kick knee, jump up couch.
Son jump up, pin her down.
Other Woman kicks him in guts, sends him reeling back, lunges off couch, Son
holds her arm, girl drags him forward, grabs plank, crashes it over head, knocks
him unconscious.

Lunge to go out. Stumble, fall.
Get up.
Hold on to couch, up and away and out (upstage right).

Revived Son sees no Other Woman and goes to run off (upstage right).
Window light bangs on.
Petrified Son in the throes of dilemma, to go after Other Woman or to peek
out window.

The thrilling gasp of rashness urges him to wrong decision as he rips window
open impatiently.

Electrified by shock, plasters back to wall next to window.

Outside – Monkey, naked, tied up, yellow eyes and fangs with an evil growl,
trying to lunge for him.

Son bangs window shut.

Knees give in — vertigo.

Decision. Runs downstage right, grabs planks, hammer, nails, runs to window and starts to nail plank over shutters.

Immersed in frenzy does not notice anything.
Not even Ma.
Who dazedly stumbles out of downstage left in slip, panties, bra and rushes upstage right, aspirin bottle in hand, about to open it.
Son sees Ma. Son is confused.
Ma sees Son, throws bottle away, zooms off upstage right.
Son throws plank down and zooms off after her.

Empty room.
Window shutters being furiously rattled from outside, someone wants to get in.
Rattling stops.
Enter Son dragging in dazed Other Woman, takes her, places her on couch, tries to revive her.
Rattling again.
Son petrified.
Son quickly goes to peek out of shutters, now in throes of terror.
Decision, hurls shutters open.
Moment of immobility.
Swings around, arm still out and crashes flat against wall, eyes of horror, splitting in half.

To reveal, in identical position, eyes of horror, arms open, Military Man in exact same outfit as Son, looking like twin brother.

Son spins back again, arms still open and seeming flat, to face Military Man-Son and immediately shuts window.

Turns face out, vertigo, knees give in.

Rattling outside, furious.

Son frenzied, grabs planks, hammers over shutters. Rattling stops.

Son intent on job.

Sudden glance upstage right and planks drop off his hands as he backs, knees giving in.

Military Man-Son enters dragging in dazed Mother.
Military Man-Son throws some four-letter words of frustration at Son, admonishing him for making life difficult.

Son can only look on open-mouthed.

Military Man-Son takes Mother to couch and plunks her down next to Other Woman, trying to revive her.

Military Man-Son sees Son still at wall and impatiently calls him over:
"Don't just stand there, dum-dum, come and gimme a hand" *as Military Man-Son desperately slaps Mother's cheeks.*

Son awkwardly comes forward and doesn't know what to do, starts slapping Mother too.

Impatient Military Man-Son is amazed at Son's stupidity as he shouts, "Not her, that one."

Son goes and does some slapping at Other Woman.

The two Sons look at each other as they absent-mindedly slap the dames.

When window light bangs on.
The two petrified Sons look at window, look at each other and both cautiously run to window, with backs at opposite sides of window.

A quick exchange of looks.
Both grab a shutter each and hurl window open.

The Man, both hands on gun, trying to keep gun in control, but gun controlling him, making him point it from one Son to the other and back and forth frenziedly, threatening to shoot a load any minute.

The two Sons rush out of petrification and slam shutters shut and bang backs against wall staring out with open eyes of terror.

Panic.
Son urges planking the shutters.
Smarter and more aggressive Military Man-Son knows his priorities, however, as he urges idiot Son to help him barricade the entrances. Son agrees readily as both lunge at the crates and frenziedly begin to pile 'em up in front of doors, Son at downstage right, Military Man-Son at upstage right. Scaredycat Son, being scareder, piling up faster than Military Man-Son.

Unnoticed to both, the two women have now revived themselves and find the two Sons' turned backs an opportune moment to get out.

Both lunge out towards entrance (upstage right).
Unlucky Ma gets caught in alert Military Man-Son's clutches and his kicks send frenzied Other Woman for another alternative as she lunges to window.

Military Man-Son screams at Son to nab the kid at the window. Son lunges at Other Woman and grabs her, but too late, for Other Woman had thrown shutters wide open.

And fully-clothed, very violent, yellow-eyed, fanged Monkey has now dived in the window, with death scream and is now over terrified pinned on ground Son, intent on biting him to bits.

Panicky Other Woman zooms to safety of bedroom.

Unlucky Son screaming at Military Man-Son for aid.

Military Man-Son has principles and pushes Mother on couch, then reluctantly goes to drag ferocious Monkey off Son by leg, knowing full well Ma will rush off upstage right, which she does.

Military Man-Son rips the evil Monkey off Son, grabs her by the arms, urges now freed, but reluctant Son to help him.

Son joins in, now him holding her by arms from behind her, as unwieldy Monkey almost gets out of Military Man-Son's grip.

Military Man-Son now manages to hold her down by legs, both Sons in total agreement to toss her back out window.
However, Military Man-Son enraged by her defiance, becomes violent and rips top part of dress open and instantly decides a gang-bang in order before the tossing out.

Military Man-Son urges Son to hold her as still as possible while he takes a first go.

Enraged Son screams that the time and place are totally wrong for his inclinations.

Military Man-Son does not listen, however, as he buries head in her, already commencing to unzip fly.

Son now knows Military Man-Son is bananas as he angrily hurls him away and tosses Monkey out of window on his own, amazed at his sudden show of strength.

Furious Military Man-Son lunges forward to Son but too late, plus Son kicks Military Man-Son in nuts, buys extra time to close shutters, and turns to face Military Man-Son and give him a piece of his mind.

Military Man-Son is in a murderous mood.
Both Sons convinced of the total insanity of the other and now full of hate for each other.

The two Sons can't stand each other any more and the inevitable happens.

A fight.

Punches, ripping of hair, nose, ears, biting, clawing eyes, both end up rolling on ground, furiously beating each other up, totally immersed in their biting growling fury.

Neither notices Monkey's re-entrance downstage right, crawling on all fours, minus fangs and eyes and usual friendly self again.

Monkey creeps in and watches with extreme curiosity as the two continue to fight.

When suddenly both Sons tense and are aware of Monkey's return.

Both rush to feet, in terrified panic as friendly, mumbling Monkey, creeps forward to them.

In identical moves the two Sons, close to each other, backs to window, frenziedly dig in pockets, produce their guns and point at Monkey.

Stupid Monkey thinks they're toys and comes even closer.
Two Sons back, back, point, point, gun, gun, left, left, right, right, left, left, at her, at her.

The wall won't budge, however, and the two scared Sons are petrified and can't pull the trigger, trigger.

Vertigo for both as Monkey caresses their legs, holds their hands, waists.

Unbearable disgust.

The two Sons unanimously kick her away, fight with their trigger fingers and win the battle, when two shots ring out, simultaneously, one from each gun and Monkey shot in guts, reels back dead.

The two Sons immobile for a moment, then both rush to couch and rub Monkey off touched parts of their bodies on couch.

Both pant heavily.

The two Sons look at each other and decide they gotta do what they gotta do and go over to Monkey to remove her outa room.

Pocketing guns, they bend to pick her up, moment of reluctance, gotta touch her again, oh let's get it over with and both summon up an extra portion of guts, grab her and rush out upstage right.

Empty room.
A hand with gun punches the wall (downstage right) to pieces and bursts in. The hand and the gun are thrashing about but the rest of the man can't get in, efforts to burst in thwarted.

Plaster falls from walls and ceiling.
The whole house shakes.

Angry frustrated growls are heard.
But to no avail.
The furious gun and hand disappear.

The two Sons, faces showing they've been through a lot, slide in from upstage right and seek relief against the wall.

Both pant awhile.

Military Man-Son, a responsible guy, tells Son, their troubles ain't over, and says to get to work planking shutters.

Son agrees as Military Man-Son holds plank while Son gets hammer but can't find nails.

Son runs to crates (downstage right) to dig for some nails when two hands zoom out of the hole in the wall and grab Son's throat and immediately commence to throttle screaming Son.

Military Man-Son immediately throws planks down and zooms to aid, managing to get hands off neck, both Sons now holding and wringing an arm each.

When Other Woman decides now is opportune moment to rush out of bedroom and zooms out (upstage right).

Military Man-Son sees this and unthinkingly zooms out after her, leaving the cursing Son on his own once more.

Son no match as hands grab Son's throat once more toss him forward on floor, disappear, door (downstage right) slams open and the man behind the hands enters the Man, punching away freely, hurling Son to window area, producing gun, menacing away like crazy, zooming from one entrance to other, check, check, checking all the rooms, zooming back to Son, lifting him up by shirt, interrogating him violently, Son crying and denying all.

When Military Man-Son re-enters dragging dazed Mother, contentedly remarking that he nabbed one of them anyway.

When he sees the Son's dilemma, and his smile fades, an oh-oh escaping him as he decides to get out again.

But the Man's gun say not so fast, bud.

The Man violently yanks the Mother off his clutches and claims her for his own.

The Mother gets revived rather quickly this time as she finds herself thrown on her knees (downstage left).

The Man menaces the two Sons some more, both backed against window, identical moves.

Man asks questions, two scaredycats deny knowledge. Man angrily slaps both, one slap that flows from cheek to cheek and asks them to leave.

The two Sons panic, very reluctant to go.

The Man gets ready to shoot.

The two Sons, identical moves, quickly walk to door (downstage right), give Ma one last look and exit.

Man, very impatient grabs Mother by hair and throws her in bedroom, entering in after her.

Empty room – one second.

The two Sons creep in, identical moves from upstage right, sliding against the wall, looking around, quick, quick glances, not relating to each other at all, but mirroring each other's moves, both very close to each other, almost one person.

The two Sons approach the bedroom door, listen cautiously, slowly open door, get shocked, mutter apologies and back.

The Man angrily enters buttoning up shirt and violently punches two Sons down to ground.

Zooms to window to check for signs of danger – none.

Advances to two Sons, wondering what to do, when enter Mother from bedroom with robe, and guiltily looks at the Sons and away.
The two Sons bawl "Maaa."
Son backs off on floor, on verge of tears.
At same moment Military Man-Son cranes forward, on verge of rage and screaming zooms at Man.

Man kicks Military Man-Son in nuts, easily subduing him.
Son feels sympathy pains as he drops in armchair holding own nuts.
Military Man-Son in tearful rage, gets up, curses Mother and Man and rushes out (downstage right).

The Man advances on Son and screams.

Man: Why did you come back?

Son screaming back at top of his lungs.

Son: I like it here.

Man doesn't answer this, but angrily takes a seat on couch.

Mother guiltily goes and has seat by him.
Man stares at Son with hate, purposely puts arm around Mother, yanks her close and paws her breast, kissing her violently.

Son in throes of pent-up rage springs out of chair zooms all over the room erupting in a violent verbal assault as he throws a flurry of four-letter words at the two.

Man turns but lets Son continue.
Mother looks on, sadly sympathetic to Son.
Son raging impotently, wanting to physicalize his verbal assault, but unable to, and hating himself for that.

When window lights bang on.
Son petrified in tense fear.
Man sees him, sees window light, rushes to.
Mother getting up, Man urging her to stay out of view.
Man hurls shutters open.

*To reveal Military Man-Son embracing naked Monkey, Military Man-Son
naked from waist up.
Monkey tied up by hands, gut wound, dead.
Military Man-Son embracing her corpse.
Suddenly he looks up and out, yellow-eyed.*

Man zooms to window, slams shutters closed, pants in terror.

Decides to exit (upstage right) and check against better judgement.

*Mother now by window tosses a strange look towards entrance (upstage right),
as Son inches forward to her.*

Son sees her look. Tenses.

*Mother is going to, will, does suddenly erupt with one intent to get out.
Ma lunges for exit.
Son holds her, drags downstage left.
Ma turns round in grip, claws eyes, regains freedom, lunges once more.*

*Son lunges after her, grabs her and drags her downstage left again.
Both fall.
Ma gets outa grip.
Lunges over couch.
Son climbs up her, pins her on couch.
Ma kicks Son in guts, rushes off couch.
Son holds her arm.
Ma drags him along, grabs plank, knocks him unconscious as crashes plank on
head.
Ma runs to door.
Stumbles. Falls.
Gets up. Slips. Falls.
Like puddle of oil.
Holds on to couch, trying clamber up, feet slip, slip. slipping.*

*Son coming to very very slowly.
Ma panicky. Son walking to her very very slowly. Real slow.
Like Blob coming near. Ma screams. Son grabs her.
Drags her downstage centre, they fall, he pinning her down, facing downstage
left.
Son trying to placate her, mumbling sweet nothings, reassuring her, trying to
kiss her cheek, caressing her breast, side of body, left thigh, left thigh, left thigh,
lust, revulsion, lust, guilt, reassuring kiss, no more revulsion, lotsa guilt, lotsa
heavy petting.*

*Ma trying to get outa clutches, manages to clamber up.
Son still reassuring, but angry, grabs her, drags her to bedroom and out, in-
sane look in eyes.
Ma fighting.*

Son in helpless clutches of sinful lust.

Empty room.
Pause.
Ma stumbles out dazed.
Seeks solace of wall.
Claws it.
Turns around, feeling cheap, sinful, disgusted.
Hand feels crucifix.
Damnation for certain.
Son slowly enters (downstage left), back to audience, bare-chested, shirt in hand, strutting like proud peacock.
Showily puts shirt on, buttons, looking at Ma suddenly reels round and sinks to knees and to floor and cries in despair, wanting to undo what can never be undone.

Ma bawling rushes to solace of couch.
Son sees her from corner of eye, rises outa dusty misery, tearfully approaches her, holds her tenderly, looking at her lovingly, mumbling some apologies.
Ma is unresponsive.
Son going in for kiss.
When Man enters from upstage right and sees this.
Son quickly jolts back, ready to punch his head in, not able to punch head in, zooms out (downstage right).

Man walks to behind Ma, grabs her threateningly by hair, but Ma hungrily grabs his hand and clenches it tight against her cheek. Encouraged, Man not letting go of hand quickly takes seat on couch and same time, not yet finishing move, zooms left hand to her right breast, pawing pawing away.
Idealistic romantic Ma gets a bit flustered as panting Man feels her up, eyes full of lust, intent on sex, rough sex.

Shocked Ma lets go of his grip as her angry tearful eyes seem to say "what about love, what happened to that?" and ends by window.

Man feels very guilty as he realizes the error of his ways, hating himself for letting his animalism take over.

Apologetic, he goes over to her and mumbles "I'm sorry."

But Ma won't have any of it as she moves away resisting.
Man persists however and Ma sees he is truly sincere.
Ma melts, as her eyes well with sentimental tears.
A tender embrace.

When the window light bangs on.
The two are alarmed as they try to peer through shutters, Man zooms to bedroom and zooms back in. When Military Man-Son creeps in (downstage right), with a funny look on his face.

The two notice him and the Man knows that look of betrayal.

Military Man-Son looks away guiltily.

Ma seems to say "why?" with the eyes as she walks like a zombie to Son who reaches for her but gets slap in face instead. Ma goes and plasters herself against wall.

Man resigned gets ready to open window.

Last look of despair 'tween Ma and Man.

Man gets trembling hand to latch, hurls shutters open.

When Military Man suddenly changes mind and jumps to stop him.

Man hurls him away.

Same split second fires out window.

Same split second outside window the Son in Military Man's army coat fires back, six frenzied shots.

Both shoot each other, the Son going through a spectacular death fall.

Man holding guts slowly turns round, walks forward, sinks to knees, drops gun, rolls to side and suffers unbearable pain.

Ma slowly walks over and kneels by him, trying to comfort him somehow.

When wounded Son reappears outside window, murderous eyes urging trembling gun hand to steady itself.

Ma turns to give Military Man-Son an "I hate you" look when sees Son pointing gun at her.

Ma is petrified, still in horror as she looks on, waiting.

But Son is dead, as the gun falls off hand and he falls out of sight.

Military Man-Son quickly closes window as he looks intently at Mother.

Mother knows life is at stake as she gives quick looks at door (upstage right).

Military Man-Son produces gun outa pocket, warning her not to try.

Mother, scared even more, will not listen to reason, wants out, out.

Military Man-Son's warnings almost begging now, as he tearfully urges her to stay.

Ma decides to take a chance and zooms past him, past his hold, out upstage right.

Son screams out at her to stop, gun pointed after her, ready to fire.

Son tearfully runs out after her.

Pause.

A shot offstage.

Pause.

Tearfully Military Man-Son re-enteres with Other Woman, dragging the dazed woman in and placing her on couch.

He does not have his gun.

Military Man-Son is frantically trying to revive the dazed girl.
He rushes to bathroom, zooms back in with towel, lifts Other Woman to standing position, 'bout to remove slip.
The window light bangs on.

Military Man-Son is terrified as he sees the light and pushes Other Woman absent-mindedly back, letting her fall on couch.

He walks like a zombie to window.
Hurls shutters open.

To reveal the Mother, naked, hands tied up, gut wound, dead.

Horrified Military Man-Son, slams window shut, every inch of his body quivering, about to burst.

Military Man-Son screams a prolonged "Nooo" with all his might, sinks to knees, doubling up, crying his heart out.

As music slowly slowly fades and lights slowly slowly dim, only Military Man-Son's sobs now being heard as he reels forward to armchair, pulling armchair down, crying all over it.

Lights dim dim. Very dim now.

Music slowly faded. Now faded out completely.

A silent pause. The Military Man-Son sobbing meekly.

Music: *Brindle's Place*

Clashing mournful cymbals and drums.

The craziness, the speed of the action all gone now, back to slow slow pace.

Military Man-Son's sobs slowly subsiding.

Other Woman slowly coming to, but remaining on couch.

Man slowly slowly moving, in unbearable pain.

Man very slowly very painfully managing to roll to side, seeing the Other Woman, slowly turning around trying to get up, when he suddenly painfully crashes on belly.

A pause as the Man grits his teeth, waiting for the pain to subside and slowly painfully tries again.

Very slowly manages to crawl over to couch.

The Other Woman looks at him weakly.

The Man cranes his neck to her and slowly attempts to come closer to her.

Come closer to her face, one last kiss.

Other Woman weakly holds his hand and tries to pull him close.

The Man comes forward closer, closer, closer – but not close enough.

He feels his strength running out.

His face, full of pain, despair, needing that last kiss more than anything, yet slowly, slowly falling back, hand slipping out of her hand, slowly reeling back.

When the cymbals crash and the music screams out. The lonely wail of a saxophone saying "Yup this is the way it is." Mourning, self-pitying.

With the cymbal crash the Man suddenly falls flat on his back – stone dead.

Other Woman sadly tries to get up, too weak, her sobs weak pants, stumbles forward to ground, slowly crawls over to him, kneels by his side and weakly caresses his face, slowly closing his open dead eye-lids.

Other Woman can't even cry any more, her face only reading sadness as she wallows in despair on her knees.
She weakly gets to a standing position and dazedly stumbles out (downstage left).

Long pause. Music wailing wailing away.

Military Man-Son now no longer crying but staring sadly, a blank look, out at nothing.

Other Woman dazedly stumbles in again, goes towards exit (upstage right).

She stops as she feels like she's about to faint.

Dazedly looks at aspirin bottle in hand, opens it, is about to swallow pills, when listless Military Man-Son listlessly grabs bottle outa her hands and listlessly tosses it away.

Frustrated Other Woman stands there dazedly sobbing in frustration.

She gives up as she sinks to her knees next to him.

Military Man-Son poutingly sadly tries not to look at her.

Frustration grips Other Woman once more as she listlessly weakly tries to push, hit Military Man-Son, not even looking at him, seeming to say, "Why can't you lemme kill myself?"

A few pushes later, she lets her hand rest on his shoulder.
She listlessly lets it flop against his cheek.
Listlessly caresses his cheek.

Listlessly turns and listlessly sadly looks at him.
He looks at her equally sadly, wanting to cry.
Both wanting to cry as they sadly look at each other, flopped on their knees.
He slowly holding her waist now, drawing himself closer to her. Now both very close, looking deep into each other's sad tearful eyes. The Son grabs her and holds her in a tight embrace. She equally greedily holds him just as tightly.

Both cry and hold on tight to each other.

The wailing music peaks to an abrupt wailing stop.

BLACKOUT.

Rumours of Our Death
A PARABLE IN 25 SCENES
George F. Walker

George F. Walker most prolific and playwrights. His oured with counting four Chalmers' Governor General Drama (for *Crimi-* is one of Canada's widely produced work has been honless awards, including Awards and two al's Awards for *nals in Love* and *Nothing Sacred*). His works have been produced around the world; *Filthy Rich* and *Zastrozzi* have had over 100 productions in the English-speaking world; *Beyond Mozambique, Theatre of the Film Noir*, and *Criminals in Love* have also been translated into French and German; *Nothing Sacred* and *Love and Anger* have met with great success in the United States with major productions in Los Angeles, Seattle, San Francisco, and Chicago. His latest play, *Escape from Happiness*, which received a workshop production at the Powerhouse Theatre in New York, premièred under his own direction at the Factory Theatre in Toronto in February 1992.

Rumours of Our Death was first produced at Factory Theatre Lab on
12 January 1980.

PRODUCTION
Director / **George F. Walker**
Music / **John Roby**
Choreography / **Odette Oliver**
Design / **Brian Arnott, Sylvalya Elchin**

CAST
Peter Blais / The King
Steven Bush / The Farmer
Dianne Heatherington / Maria III
Jake Levesque / The Farmer's Son
Mina E. Mina / Raymond
Susan Purdy / Maria II
Patricia Vanstone / Maria I
Bob White / The Foreigner
Tim Wynne-Jones / The Terrorist

CHARACTERS
King
Queen, Maria I
Raymond, a novelist
Maria III, a cafe owner
Farmer
Son of the farmer
Foreigner, well-dressed*
Terrorist, with hood over his head*
Maria II, daughter of the king
*played by the same actor

SCENE ONE

(*The* King *on his terrace. He is wearing a business suit.*)

King: My people. I have a small favour to ask of you. Since being restored I have done many things for your benefit. A list of these things will be posted in the town square shortly. In the meantime, because I have a favour to ask, I wish to remind you of two of them. First, one for the women. Under the heading of law reform. It is now a criminal offence to rape a woman in public. Now one for the men. Under the heading of law reform also. If a woman cannot bear a man a male offspring, it is no longer necessary for this man to seek a divorce, he may now simply do whatever he feels like. My people I have a favour to ask of you. I am afraid that through no fault of yours, but for reasons that nevertheless are none of your business, we must go to war. War, as we all know, is something to be avoided at all costs.

Blackout

SCENE TWO

(*An outdoor café in the town square.* Maria III, *the owner, is talking to a customer. His name is* Raymond. *He writes novels.*)

Raymond: What did you think of his speech this morning?

Maria III: He moved his lips a bit this time. Often he doesn't move them at all and that gives me a queasy feeling.

Raymond: Have you heard the rumour that the king is not human?

Maria III: I believe it. If you get close enough you can look through his eyes and see little sparkling blue lights.

Raymond: Do you think he is a machine?

Maria III: Personally, no. I think he is from another planet.

Raymond: In my vast experience, I have learned never to listen to rumour except as a source for amusing anecdote.

Maria III: That's all right for you. You write books. But I'm a real person and I know that anything is possible.

Raymond: In his speech, although I wasn't really listening closely, I believe I heard him promise that not one man would be killed in this war.

Maria III: It's possible he said that. I was busy listening to my heart burst. This country is not equipped to fight a war.

Raymond: I think you love this country too much. Do you want some advice from me?

Maria III: No.

Blackout

SCENE THREE

(Farmer *and* Son *in a field. They are farmers. But they are not working.*)

Farmer: News of a certain kind travels faster than death in autumn.

Son: Father, I have to tell you that when you say things like that I never understand them.

Farmer: When you get to be my age it won't matter.

Son: Is it possible to fight a war in which not one man gets killed?

Farmer: Only if all your soldiers are women.

Son: I heard a rumour about a new bomb that only kills machines.

Farmer: I think you and I should concern ourselves with more important matters. We should be thinking about what crops to plant in our fields this year.

Son: I like wheat.

Farmer: On the other hand, if there's going to be a war we shouldn't plant anything. We should burn our fields.

Son: Why?

Farmer: In a war, that's what farmers do. Have you got a match?

Son: Yes.

Farmer: Hold on to it. No, give it to me. I don't trust you. You'll probably lose it. You remind me of your mother. The way you lose things. You know what bothers me the most of all? The king is making speeches again. That bothers me more than anything.

Son: They say he moved his lips a bit this time.

Farmer: I wonder why he did that. That bothers me. I wish you hadn't told me that. I have enough to worry about. On the other hand, when you get to be my age nothing really bothers you all that much. That bomb you were talking about. Is that a rumour or did you read about it?

Son: Yes. Maybe I did.

Farmer: In that magazine. The one that is always publishing the queen's visions.

Son: Yes. Maybe.

Farmer: That magazine is a terrifying thing. It has a very strong influence on our people. It worries and sickens me. Actually I don't feel all that seriously about it at all. (*The* Son *nods*.)

Blackout

SCENE FOUR

(*The* King *on his terrace*.)

King: Good news. The war has been postponed for awhile. My wife, the queen, Maria One, last night had a vision which concerns us all. This vision is published in its entirety in our local magazine and we urge you to read it. As to the war, although it has been postponed it is still impending. Now for another matter closer to home. It has come to my attention that there is a strong possibility of an insurrection in this country. Earlier this morning a small group of heavily armed terrorists kidnapped my daughter, killing all thirty of her bodyguards in the process and shooting her personal tutor in the kneecaps. Although it is slightly premature to say so, we believe these terrorists are sponsored by foreign interests. I have sent a personal message to the head of the church in the hopes that he may send a personal message to the kidnappers to allow my daughter to send a personal message to me. The lines of communication must be opened. I am not an unreasonable man. But unless steps are taken, you, the people of this country, will be forced to pay the ransom for my daughter. Democracy carries a burden equalled only by its own unfathomable nature. If my daughter is listening, I wish to tell her to be brave. Your people are praying for your quick release. Now in the matter of the war as it relates to my wife the queen, and her vision ...

Blackout

SCENE FIVE

(*The café*.)

Maria III: If the king is not human, then can his daughter be human? Why should I give money for the life of a machine?

Raymond: Forty years ago, this country had no problems. Then one day between then and now I can't remember the exact date, it had a great many problems indeed. That's the line of thinking they'd have us follow. In my new book I will expose the stupidity of the government.

Maria III: While you are busy exposing the stupidity of the government, the government is busy exposing the stupidity of the people.

Raymond: Some time ago an independent survey conducted by an international agency concluded that the people of this country are the stupidest on the face of the earth.

Maria III: Talk like that breaks my heart. All my family are buried in this country. My family was one of the first to settle here. Talk like that makes me cry inside. And you're not even a real person. You write books. Now what do you want to eat? This is a restaurant. You just can't sit there all day and not order anything. I have to make money for the ransom.

Raymond: I'll have a coffee.

Maria III: You'll have a full course meal.

(*She leaves.* Raymond *starts to write in his journal. The* King *comes on and sits next to him.*)

King: Excuse me.

Raymond: (*Looks up*) Your majesty!

King: Shush.

Raymond: But –

King: Shush – I've slipped out discreetly to find out what the people think of recent events. Can you keep a secret?

Raymond: Yes. What is it?

King: That was it. So?

Raymond: Yes.

King: What do you think of recent events?

Raymond: Well I ...

King: Do you have any complaints?

Raymond: Well I ...

King: That's all I wanted to know.

(King *leaves.* Maria III *comes back with a cup of coffee.*)

Maria III: I decided I was too harsh with you. You can stay here all day and drink coffee. You add character to the place. That's not my opinion but I've heard the tourists say so to each other.

Raymond: The king was here.

Maria III: You mean he drove by in his sports car?

Raymond: No. Here. Sitting down.

Maria III: Why?

Raymond: He wanted the people's opinion on certain things.

Maria III: Well, I hope you gave him an earful.

Raymond: I was speechless.

Maria III: Of course. It's the respect for the monarchy. It's ruining us all.

Raymond: I was going to say something.

Maria III: But you didn't. It has something to do with their posture I think. The posture is intimidating.

Raymond: I saw the blue lights sparkling inside his head.

Maria III: So it's true.

Raymond: I heard noises. His veins were making scratchy noises.

Maria III: Oh no.

Raymond: He isn't human. Not really.

Blackout

SCENE SIX

(*The King's apartment. The* King *and* Queen *are having tea.*)

King: The people are content.

Queen: It must be difficult for them.

King: We live in very distressing times. I've heard rumours about a new bomb that only kills children under the age of 12. Imagine how that must make them feel. Especially the religious ones.

Queen: You're a great man. To worry about strangers when our own daughter might be dead.

King: I am a king. (*He takes out a cigarette. Lights it.*) My father was also a king. Did you like my father?

Queen: Not much.

King: No one did. That's why we had all that trouble. He annoyed every-one. Politics. Politics are ...

Queen: I wish we'd told Maria more about politics. Then at least she might have some idea why she's in such danger.

King: You're a saint.

Queen: So are you.

King: Although I have been having strange sensations lately. Feeling of hatred and revenge. Not very saintly I'm afraid. Just the opposite. Feelings of hatred. Just little ones mind you. But one wonders.

Queen: I'm going to pray. (*She leaves.*)

King: One wonders if things are as innocent as they appear.

(*Puffs on his cigarette. Brushes an ash from his lap.*)

Blackout

SCENE SEVEN

(*A dark place. And damp. Maria* II *is tied to a chair. Gagged. The hooded* Terrorist *is standing beside her, reading a piece of paper.*)

Terrorist: I, Maria, an enemy of the people, wish to publicly renounce any claim to authority and also condemn my father and mother and call for their immediate abdication (*Unties her.*) Sign it.

Maria II: *shakes her head "No."*

Terrorist: (*Slaps her across the face.*) Sign. Or you die. Now.

Maria II: *shakes her head.*

Terrorist: (*Pulls gun. Puts it to her head.*) Sign.

Maria II: *nods.*

Blackout

SCENE EIGHT

(*The café.* Raymond *and* Maria III. *Maria* III *is reading Raymond's journal.*)

Raymond: The revolution of our country is totally in the hands of foreigners. As far as I know this is an unprecedented situation. We should all be feeling deep national embarrassment.

Maria III: Your book doesn't make any sense. You seem to be wasting your time. You have no talent. Why don't you get a job.

Raymond: I am well respected in other countries.

Maria III: You should get a job. Everyone here thinks you are silly. Except for the tourists, and they are the stupidest people on the face of the earth.

Raymond: If things get any worse I might get a job leading a revolution against the foreign revolutionaries.

Maria III: This morning I had to pay into the ransom fund. What are the foreign revolutionaries going to do about that?

Raymond: Why are you looking to them?

Maria III: Everyone is looking to them. They seem to be the only ones doing anything.

Raymond: Well, who says it was necessary to do anything?

Maria III: They do.

Raymond: But why do you believe them?

Maria III: Because they are also the only ones saying anything.

Raymond: It's true that an extreme silence is more dangerous than anything. I wonder why the king has stopped giving speeches?

Maria III: You were fond of the king's speeches.

Raymond: I didn't listen very closely. But it was somehow comforting to know he was there.

Maria III: He was leading this country to war.

Raymond: I somehow didn't believe that. I thought it was just politics. Politics are ... I wonder where he is?

Maria III: Why should you care? You saw for yourself he wasn't human. Not really.

Raymond: I forgave him for that. Maybe he had his reasons.

Maria III: A rumour has it that a space ship came for him. Took him away. Things were getting out of hand so they removed him.

Raymond: In the most ridiculous rumours often lie a grain of truth. He does appear to have vanished.

Maria III: Then who is in charge? Who has the power?

Raymond: The foreign revolutionaries I suppose.

Maria III: Where are they?

Raymond: I don't know.

Maria III: What do they look like?

Raymond: I don't know. This is intolerable. Why doesn't someone do something?

Maria III: This is frightening.

Raymond: Someone must do something.

Blackout

SCENE NINE

(*The* King *on his terrace.*)

King: My people. It has come to my attention that there is a great panic amongst you. It seems you missed me and worried about your fate. Thinking perhaps that something terrible had happened to me. It was a test. You failed. But I forgive you as is my right. And now to the issues of the day. All civil liberties are revoked. Until further notice. The war still impending has been postponed again. My daughter's fate is still unknown but the kidnappers have demanded a ransom of twice the original size. Please do what you can to appeal to these men before you all approach personal financial ruin. Your fates and the fate of my daughter are irrevocably entwined. As they should be in a society like ours. And now a few words about my wife's latest vision which I think you will all find pertinent in innumerable ways ...

Blackout

SCENE TEN

(*The café.*)

Maria III: The king has developed a serious twitch in his left eye. And the entire bottom half of his face is paralysed.

Raymond: It's a wonder he could talk at all.

Maria III: It's from all those years of talking without moving his lips.

Raymond: Well at least he's still here. I feel better.

Maria III: I had to put more money into the ransom fund.

Raymond: Don't worry. I hear they plan to set up the ransom fund as a non-profit charitable organization. You'll be able to deduct all contributions from your taxes.

Maria III: Well, that's something. How come you don't have to pay?

Raymond: Artists are exempt.

Maria III: Why?

Raymond: They refuse to pay anyway. So they just exempt them. It's less confusing.

(*The* Farmer *and* Son *come on.*)

Son: Have you heard the foreigners have control of the magazine and are censoring the queen's visions?

Farmer: Grave consequences for those who use those visions as a standard for their lives.

Maria III: No, that was a rumour being circulated here last week, since proven untrue. You country people are always behind the times.

Raymond: What are you doing here? You never come to town.

Son: We're moving here.

Farmer: We burned our fields.

Raymond: Why?

Farmer: Because of the war.

Maria III: The war has been postponed.

Farmer: Preposterous. I'll seek compensation.

Raymond: You can't. You have no rights.

Son: What do we do?

Farmer: I don't know.

Son: You must.

Farmer: No. I give up. You're in charge of the family now. You make the decisions. I'll obey.

Son: Very well. Sit down. (Farmer *sits*.) Stand up. (Farmer *stands*.) Sit down. (Farmer *sits*.)

Farmer: Son, what is all this about?

Son: I was just seeing if you meant it. We'll have some coffee. (Maria III *goes inside*.) So we have no rights. So the foreigners have taken over our revolution. So the war is postponed but will probably still happen. Something must be done. I think I'll do something. Yes. Why not?

(Farmer *and* Raymond *look at each other*.)

Blackout

SCENE ELEVEN

(Maria II *tied to a chair*. Terrorist *is spoon-feeding her cold soup*.)

Maria II: This soup is cold.

Terrorist: Don't complain.

Maria II: I hate cold soup. I hate any kind of soup.

Terrorist: You're lucky we feed you at all.

Maria II: You're letting it dribble down my chin.

Terrorist: Stop complaining.

Maria II: But it will stick and harden and make me uncomfortable.

Terrorist: Look at it this way. You're lucky to be alive.

Maria II: I couldn't sleep last night. You and your friends were making too much noise in the next room.

Terrorist: If you want to complain about something complain about something important.

Maria II: You're feeding me too fast.

Terrorist: Complain about your father refusing to pay the ransom. Making the poor people pay it instead. Complain about the stupidity of the people for going along with it. You seem to be the only person in this country who complains about anything even if it is about trivial matters. (*He grabs her hair.*) You make me angry.

Maria II: Are you planning to kill me?

Terrorist: Yes.

Maria II: Tell me about yourself. What you believe in.

Terrorist: Why?

Maria II: I'm genuinely interested.

Blackout

SCENE TWELVE

(*The café. Farmer is sweeping the floor. Maria III comes out with table cloths. Begins to put them on tables.*)

Farmer: The king's daughter has joined the terrorists and can be seen travelling around the country burglarizing the homes of prosperous merchants. The queen has been praying steadily now for five weeks without food or drink and the king is said to be in the middle of a mood so dark that no one can see the blue lights sparkling in his eyes any more. The head of the church has been taken seriously ill but has given the entire country the last rites from his sick bed. The local magazine advises us all to take this as a symbolic gesture only and to proceed with our lives. But many people have given up. Your friend the novelist has formed an ultra-conservative monarchist party which vows to rid the country of the foreign terrorist revolutionaries and then make the king answer to the charge of abandoning human characteristics in times of crisis. I myself feel that since I gave up my health has suffered severely having had two minor heart attacks and losing the ability to hear unless people shout directly into my ears.

Maria III: I'm very depressed.

Farmer: What was that? (*He has a severe heart attack. Sits in one of the chairs. And dies.*)

Maria III: He's dead. God bless him. I couldn't pay him anyway. The government refuses to return money from the ransom fund even though the king's daughter has joined the terrorists. They say they intend to use the money to pay for her lawyers once she is caught. I'm depressed. I have no money. The tourists aren't coming any more because Mr Raymond is not here to add colour to the place. My life is falling apart. And I'm talking a lot to myself. (Raymond *comes on. He has lost an arm and he has a patch over one eye.*) You look wonderful. Not for your own sake perhaps. But for the amount of colour you will bring to the café. Sit down. You can drink coffee all day. (*She goes inside.*)

Raymond: Wait. (*He sits.*) I have learned much over the last little while. I have learned that artists should not get involved in politics. Not really. I have learned that the loss of an arm is a major inconvenience. I have learned – (*Looks around. Looks at the dead Farmer.*) No one is listening to me.

Blackout

SCENE THIRTEEN

(*The King's apartment. The* King *is pacing. The* Queen *is eating a lot of food very quickly.*)

King: The people are talking to themselves. Right now it's only a problem in the cities but as is the trend with everything it will soon reach out into the country. In the country it will do the most damage because there no one will notice the difference.

Queen: Last night I had a vision that made me believe that soon our country will experience great chaos.

King: Your visions are becoming retrospective.

Queen: (*Spitting out food as she talks.*) In a simultaneous vision I saw that someone had invented a new bomb which killed nothing but which caused all the water in the rivers and lakes to evaporate. The painful consequences of this were so hard to imagine that many people stopped using their imaginations.

King: You're making quite a pig of yourself.

Queen: I prayed without food or water for five weeks. You should have stopped me. I almost died.

King: In some ways that would have been preferable. I could have used your death as something to unite the country. You would have been a martyr. We could have told everyone you died praying. The only problem with that is that no one, including me, has ever known what you pray for.

Queen: You're inhuman.

King: You must learn to take criticism a bit better.

Queen: No. Look, you are growing shiny blue hairs on the back of your hands. (*He looks. He is.*)

King: It's just a small lower circuit malfunction.

Queen: Oh God. Oh God. (*She chokes on a piece of food. The* King *appears to find this distasteful.*)

Blackout

SCENE FOURTEEN

(*The café (and) The countryside. At the café* Maria III *and* Raymond *are standing next to the* Farmer *staring at him. In the countryside the* Son *is unloading a huge crate of books.*)

Son: For 17 days and nearly as many nights my father sat in a chair dead. Then suddenly he stood up and walked away. (Farmer *stands up and walks away.* Maria III *and* Raymond *look at each other. Smile.*) At first, people looked at this occurrence as a miracle and took it as a cause for celebration. (Raymond *pinches* Maria III's *behind. She smiles. They go inside.*) Thinking that my father had risen from the dead and was now alive. Soon, however, it became known that he was still dead but that he had the ability to walk around. Nevertheless he was called a prophet and a large crowd attached themselves to him and followed him everywhere he went. (*Darkness at the café.* Son *begins to unpack the crate.*) Meanwhile I had embarked upon a program of self-education. I travelled to other countries and purchased books that were not available here. Thinking that on my return, having long ago become disillusioned with violence, I would work my way into a position to bring about the necessary changes. Unfortunately, I too became afflicted with the new national disease of (*he looks around*) talking to myself.

Blackout

SCENE FIFTEEN

(*A dark place*. Maria II *is addressing the hooded* Terrorist *and the* Farmer. *The* Terrorist *seems distracted*.)

Maria II: I have a lot of complaints to make. Are you listening?

Terrorist: Of course.

Maria II: First, I want to know why you still don't trust me? I've committed myself to this group body and soul.

Terrorist: I do trust you.

Maria II: Then why do you always wear that hood?

Terrorist: I'm very ugly.

Maria II: Physical appearance is not important.

Terrorist: It is to me.

Maria II: We'll discuss that later. In the meantime I want to know what our long range plans are? Or do we have any?

Terrorist: We'll discuss that later. (*Looks at* Farmer.) When we're alone.

Maria II: Oh. Who is he anyway?

Terrorist: They say he is a prophet.

Maria II: Who are 'they'?

Terrorist: All the people outside. A huge crowd. Apparently they follow him everywhere he goes.

Maria II: Interesting.

Blackout

SCENE SIXTEEN

(*The café*. Raymond *is serving* Maria III *a full-course dinner*. Maria III *is reading the local magazine. The* Son *is reading one of his books. Twenty-two seconds of silence*.)

Raymond: The terrorists have a new leader.

Son: Perhaps now they might even decide on a plan of action.

Raymond: Yes. Which is both good and bad.

Son: Good because we'll be able to finally judge their motives. Bad because it has always been obvious that their motives are selfish and now we will be forced to do something about them.

Raymond: Those books you have been reading have done wonders for your analytical powers.

Son: But they have also burdened me with the responsibility of knowledge.

Raymond: Knowledge of a certain kind is more dangerous than dying in autumn.

Son: My father used to say things like that. I never understood him.

Raymond: But you do me?

Son: No. But I know now that it doesn't matter.

Raymond: You see, Maria, what the printed word can accomplish. The boy has been reading books. He's immune.

Maria III: There's an article in the magazine which says that intellectuals and urban dwellers are all expendable, and that only the farmers are of any worth.

Son: Let me see that. (*He takes the magazine from her.*)

Maria III: The quality of that magazine is falling fast. I can barely read the printing. Everything is fading away. Yes that's right. Everything is fading away.

Raymond: It never had that much integrity. I was once going to write a novel exposing it as a monarchist propaganda machine. Then I realized that I myself was a monarchist. One of life's little ironies.

Maria III: Very little.

Raymond: Would you like some coffee with your meal?

Maria III: Later maybe. You know, I'm very curious about where you got the money to buy me out.

Raymond: Let's just say that I got lucky during the counter-revolution.

Maria III: Rumours are that you stole your soldiers' wristwatches while they were in the shower.

Raymond: Some day you will learn as I have to disregard all rumours except those which can be used for a good laugh. Don't worry about it. You have money and I have a business better than writing books that are only well-respected in other countries.

Maria III: I may have money. But I don't have anything to do. I feel useless.

Son: What was that?

Maria III: I feel useless.

Son: Yes. It's because you live in town. The magazine might be right. I predict a new trend towards the joys of agriculture.

Raymond: I think we should all be very wary of being tyrannized by trends.

Son: That's easy for you to say. You have a money-making business. And unusual physical disabilities. Your position is secure.

Maria III: He's right. The rest of us have to be flexible. Even though it's more trouble than it's worth.

Son: I didn't understand that. Not really. But I didn't care.

Maria III: (*To Raymond*) Actually you too should consider the possibilities of becoming flexible. They say there is a foreigner here now who is buying up everything in sight. This could gravely affect your prospects for the future.

Raymond: Yes. There is a big difference between a person with unusual physical disabilities who owns a business and one who just sits around.

Maria III: Especially to the tourists.

Raymond: But why should I be worried? He can't buy what a person does not want to sell.

Maria III: They say this foreigner has an attitude which is impossible for the people of this country to resist.

Raymond: Nonsense. What kind of attitude is there that is impossible to resist?

(*A Foreigner, well-dressed, walks on. Looks around the place.*)

Foreigner: This will do very nicely. I'll take it.

(*Raymond puts his hand over his eye.*)

Blackout

SCENE SEVENTEEN

(King *on the terrace.*)

King: Is everyone listening to me? Yes, I thought so. (*Smile.*) You see, the national disease of talking to yourself has passed. People are now meeting in groups again and exchanging ideas. This is bound to have a positive effect in the long run. However, in the meantime, because things are worse than ever in the areas of finance and political stability, I have been forced to sell our country to foreign interests, with an option to re-buy when things get better. This new development makes the question of the still impending war a very complicated one. For this reason the war has been further postponed but promises now, for reasons too abstract for you to understand, to some day be even more vicious than was originally expected. I ask you all to prepare for this in your hearts. Now here are today's rumours. Someone has invented a bomb which kills nothing and evaporates no water but which causes people to disappear into another dimension. This is either a truly remarkable bomb or a truly remarkable rumour. Either way it shows that our people are no longer afraid to use their imaginations. Next it is said that the foreign terrorist revolutionaries acting under the advice of their new leader who is still dead but becoming quite physically attractive, have all applied for landed immigrant status. Also since my daughter has sworn never to be taken alive, her ransom-defence fund has been turned into a national endowment program for the arts. This is not a rumour. And application forms will be distributed in the town square shortly. And as to the final rumour which maintains that my wife the queen has discovered that I am not human and is seeking a divorce, I have no comment. Please. No flash bulbs or tape recorders allowed. (*The* King *tries unsuccessfully to lick some of the blue hairs off his hands.*)

Blackout

SCENE EIGHTEEN

(*The café.* Maria II, *the* Terrorist, *the* Farmer *are all writing something.*)

Maria II: I don't understand these application forms. Why are some of the questions repeated three times?

Terrorist: Because it's difficult to lie with any consistency.

Maria II: I think it's humiliating to be applying for government assistance for a revolution. And just a touch stupid as well, don't you think?

Terrorist: Our leader's mind seems to work along very unusual lines. For some reason he believes if we call ourselves artists we will get enough money to allow us to carry out a campaign against artists.

Maria II: Is that the long range plan? If so, I think it's stupid. And embarrassing.

Terrorist: Only in part. The campaign against artists will only be used to throw the queen into disfavour, since she has a history of mingling with them and has now transmitted a disease to the king which causes him to lick the backs of his hands in public.

Maria II: She's disgusting. I never liked her.

Terrorist: Odd. On page 12 it asks who to notify in case of death.

Maria II: Skip that one. It's a trick. (*The* Farmer *throws down his pen.*)

Terrorist: Shush. He's going to do something. (*The* Farmer *stands and goes to another table. Sits down. Crosses his arms. Frowns.*)

Maria II: Well, so much for that idea. (Maria II *and* Terrorist *rip up their forms.*) I'm beginning to get a bit impatient with him.

Terrorist: Trust him. He knows something. See. How beautiful he's getting.

Blackout

SCENE NINETEEN

(*The field.* Raymond, *the* Son.)

Son: We live in complex times.

Raymond: Everyone says that. But no one ever asks who is to blame ...

Son: You're no one to talk. Since that foreigner made you sell the cafe you've done nothing except follow me around.

Raymond: I've given up. I've decided to live my life vicariously through you.

(*He grabs* Son's *arm. Holds it tight. Never lets go.* Son *begins to pace. So does* Raymond.)

Son: It doesn't look like it's going to be much of a life for either of us. I don't know what to do. I can't become a farmer again. I find it doesn't satisfy my thirst for knowledge.

Raymond: Can I give us some advice?

Son: I suppose.

Raymond: I think we should just wait.

Son: For what?

Raymond: Well it doesn't matter what, does it? The next trend I suppose.

Son: all right. Why not.

Raymond and **Son:** Sit down. (*They do.*)

Raymond: I miss your father.

Son: I was just thinking that.

Raymond: I know.

Son: I'm not sure I like this arrangement.

(*The* Foreigner *comes on pulling* Maria III *by the hand.*)

Foreigner: Do you know this woman?

Son: Yes. She works for me.

Foreigner: I found her standing out in the field beside a plough. She was crying. She told me she was tired of moving around and decided to give up. Then she fell down into the manure. A minute later she awoke and stood up but wouldn't talk.

(Raymond *and* Son *go over to her.*)

Son: She smells terrible.

Raymond: He said she fell into the manure.

Foreigner: What's wrong with her?

Raymond and **Son:** She's dead.

Blackout

SCENE TWENTY

(King *on the terrace, holding a thick manuscript.*)

(**King:** The people are dying like flies. Literally. And if it keeps up the head of the church cannot be responsible for their souls. Following is the officially recommended procedure for dying in the manner of a human being. (*He flips through the manuscript.*) Well, it goes on for pages. But in essence all it calls for is, a touch of dignity. Pass the word.

Blackout

SCENE TWENTY-ONE

(*The* King's *apartment. The* Queen *is eating. The* King *is ...*)

King: Due to difficult financial circumstances some of the people have decided to save money by merging into one soul.

Queen: (*Eating*) Fascinating.

King: What was that?

Queen: Fascinating. And also imaginative, don't you think?

King: Perhaps. But for some reason I'm beginning to despise them all.

Queen: (*Eating*) Fascinating. Really, merging into one soul. A few months ago it would have sounded impossible. I'm impressed.

King: I gave them a voice. Made them answerable to their own problems and all they've done is create confusion. Nevertheless I don't like these feelings of hatred. They're causing me to have bad dreams. I miss my father.

Queen: Not unusual. It's the new trend. Patriarch lust.

King: Not altogether an accurate term.

Queen: (*Eating*) Perhaps you need a vacation.

King: Perhaps I do. When are you going to stop eating?

Queen: Never.

King: My father would have been able to give me advice.

Queen: Why don't you go visit him in the forest?

King: What was that?

Queen: In the forest. Surely you've heard the rumours that he turned himself into a tree.

King: Vicious gossip. He did no such thing. He vaporized. I was with him when it happened. The pressures of the day just got to him. It was during the time of the first impending war. People were besieging him with contradictory advice. My father began to sweat. He sweated all of one day and part of the next. And eventually he turned into steam.

Queen: Oh yes, I know the official version. But I believe the rumours. I think he's a tree.

King: What kind?

Queen: How should I know?

King: Well, how would I recognize him?

Queen: He's your father.

King: Well, if you think it's worth a try.

Queen: Personally, I don't care one way or the other. My daughter is a terrorist, foreign interests are censoring my visions, the people are laughing at me, and none of my prayers ever get answered.

King: That's still no reason to let yourself go to pot.

Queen: I need something new in my life. An inspiration.

King: Don't I inspire you?

Queen: Not any more. You seem to lack direction.

King: I need a vacation.

Queen: Who will be in charge while you're gone?

King: You.

Queen: No, thank you.

Blackout

SCENE TWENTY-TWO

(*The café:* Maria II, the Terrorist, Raymond/Son, Farmer, Maria III. *Farmer and* Maria II *have their arms crossed and are getting more beautiful. Everyone else is just sitting there. A long silence.*)

Maria II: It's getting kind of crowded here.

(*Everyone looks at her. She lights a cigar. Inhales. A long silence.* Raymond *coughs.* Son *puts a hand over his own mouth. Everyone looks at him. Everyone looks away. A long silence.*)

Blackout

SCENE TWENTY-THREE

(*The King's apartment. The* Queen *and the* Foreigner. *The* Queen *has stopped eating. She is just staring pleasantly at the* Foreigner.)

Queen: So my husband hired you to stand in for him.

Foreigner: Just temporarily.

Queen: What is your official position?

Foreigner: Advisor. Strictly low-profile. Mostly day to day management.

Queen: Odd that he would hire a foreigner.

Foreigner: On the contrary. I'm the only one not suffering from any of the national diseases. Patriarch lust. Soul merging. Talking to yourself. Et cetera.

Queen: The way you explain it, it seems to make sense although that might just be because I'm fascinated by you. Notice that I've stopped eating.

Foreigner: I like this apartment. I like the surroundings, the furniture. Generally speaking I like everything here.

Queen: Then you plan no changes?

Foreigner: Oh, a few.

Queen: Nothing major.

Foreigner: Not really.

Queen: Not really major?

Foreigner: Not really.

Queen: Have you noticed that I've stopped eating?

Foreigner: I'm sure that once you were a vital and attractive woman.

Queen: Once?

Foreigner: Yes, once.

Queen: Not now though?

Foreigner: No. Not really.

Queen: Then you plan to get rid of me?

Foreigner: Yes. I think I do.

Queen: But I am the queen.

Foreigner: Not any more.

Queen: But I can be helpful. I have visions. (*He looks at her.*) Not really. Not any more. No.

(*She dies. He feels her pulse. Smiles. Takes off his jacket. Starts to rearrange the furniture.*)

Blackout

SCENE TWENTY-FOUR

(*The King in the forest. He is holding a broken branch. Looking at it. Silently crying. He rubs his head with the branch. Kisses it. Cradles it. Suddenly he shrugs. Looks around for a comfortable place. Sits down. Lies down. Dies. Twenty seconds of silence. Suddenly he stands up and begins to walk around aimlessly.*)

Blackout

SCENE TWENTY-FIVE

(*The café. Farmer, Maria III, King, Queen, are all sitting with their arms folded. Becoming beautiful. Smiling. Maria II and Terrorist are whispering to each other. Raymond and Son are tapping the table. Drinking coffee.*)

Son: So the king was human after all.

Raymond: We should have given him the benefit of the doubt.

Son: Although looking back he didn't deserve it.

Raymond: Not that it mattered if we gave it to him or not. He was the king after all.

Son: I was just thinking that.

Raymond: I know.

Son: I know that too.

Raymond: So do I.

Maria II: Conditions here are becoming intolerable. Look at this crowd. Why don't we do something?

Terrorist: We're waiting for him to come up with a plan.

Maria II: I'm fed up with waiting for him. Maybe the rumours are true. Maybe he is dead.

Terrorist: Well, we'll just wait a little longer.

Maria II: I'm fed up!

Terrorist: Lower your voice. This is a secret organization.

Maria II: Don't give me orders. I can't stand to be given orders.

Terrorist: Lower your voice! (*They continue to argue in whispers.*)

Raymond: The head of the church has ...

Son: No he hasn't.

Raymond: Oh. That's right.

Son: But there is more news about the war. Any day now. The new king is almost certain.

Raymond: Finally. Although the new king has other problems on his mind. They say he's having trouble getting used to his apartment. It's haunted.

Son: With memories.

Raymond and **Son:** Whose memories?

Raymond: And there is a rumour about a new bomb. (Maria II *looks up.*)

Maria II: What does it do?

Son: No one wants to know.

(*A long silence.* Raymond/Son *scratch* Raymond's *nose. A long silence. The* Farmer *shifts in his chair. Everyone looks at him. Even the dead. Everyone waits. Nothing. Everyone turns away. Sadly.*)

BLACKOUT

Ten Lost Years

Jack Winter and Cedric Smith

During the 1960s  and 1970s Jack Winter wrote stage plays for Toronto Workshop Produc- tions, where he was resident playwright. His works for TWP included *Before Compiègne*, *The Mechanic*, *Hey Rube!*, *The Golem of Venice*, *Letters from the Earth*, *You Can't Get Here from There*, and *Ten Lost Years*. He also wrote freelance plays for specific commissions, including *Party Day*, *The Centre*, *Mr Pickwick*, and *Waiting*. During the same period he wrote more than two dozen radio and television plays and films for cinema, including *Selling Out*, *The Island*, *Golovlovo*, and *Mask of the Bear*, as well as critical articles, prose friction, and several collections of poetry. In 1976 he moved to England where he continues to write for production and publication.

An original member of the folk group Perth County Conspiracy, Cedric Smith has acted and directed in theatres across Canada. His roles have included Mr Horner in *The Country Wife* at Stratford, Richard III for the

Manitoba Theatre Centre, and Billy Bishop in a national tour of *Billy Bishop Goes to War*. He has also written and performed in his solo show *Under the Influence*.

Ten Lost Years opened at Toronto Workshop Productions on 7 February 1974 for a three-month run. From 16 September to 30 November 1974 it toured western Canada before returning to Toronto for a second run. In August 1975 it played for two weeks in Toronto at the St Lawrence Centre before a tour through Atlantic Canada. In 1976 it toured in Europe, and was revived again in 1981 for a three-month run.

PRODUCTION
Director / **George Luscombe**
Playwright / **Jack Winter**
Music / **Cedric Smith**
Designer / **Astrid Janson**
Lighting / **Alec Cooper**
Costumes / **Astrid Janson, Barbara Suarez**
Stage Manager / **Erika Klusch**

CAST
Jackie Burroughs
Diane Douglass
Peter Faulkner
François-Régis Klanfer
Patricia Ludwick
Peter Millard
Dita Paabo
Richard Payne
Ross Skene
Cedric Smith

From the book by Barry Broadfoot

Additional song material contributed by Bob Burchill, Terry Jones, and The Perth County Conspiracy Does Not Exist.

DIRECTOR'S NOTE

The play should be performed with 10 actors – six men and four women. The women have their "homes" on stage that they continue to return to. The men keep moving as they did during the Depression when they travelled back and forth across the country. When we created the "trains" for the men, the women from their homes made the all-important sounds that accompanied the men on their journeys.

SCENE ONE: THE BENNETT BUGGY

Music in. Actors enter as the buggy.

Balladeer: You ask me what a Bennett Buggy was? Well, in the 20s farmers bought automobiles – Chevs, Fords, Hupmobiles – kinds they don't even make any more. Then came the crash and the drought and nobody had any money for gasoline, let alone repairs; and they'd already thrown away all those fine old buggies every farm used to have. So what was left? A horse, pullin' a car, that wouldn't run.

Song: *Bennett Buggy*
Get out the Bennett Buggy,
Let's go for a ride in the lovely countryside,
Two horse power, five miles an hour,
When Dobbin and Dolly get back to work again.

Make your own Bennett Buggy,
Put a tongue into the chassis, you've an oatburner classy
With horses pulling double you'll have no engine trouble,
And you'll get back from town by next Monday night.

SCENE TWO: IN THE SUMMERTIME

Song: *Summertime*
In the good old summer time,
In the good old summer time,
Strolling down a shady lane with your baby mine,
You hold her hand and she holds yours,
And that's a very good sign,
That she's your tootsie-wootsie in
The good old summer time.

Song: *Let me call you sweetheart*
Let me call you sweetheart, I'm in love with you,
Let me hear you whisper that you love me too,
Keep the love-light glowing in your eyes so true,
Let me call you sweetheart, I'm in love with you.

Song: *And the band played on*
Casey would waltz with the strawberry blonde,
And the band played on,
He'd glide across the floor with the girl he adored,
And the band played on,
But his brain was so loaded it nearly exploded,
The poor girl would shake with alarm,
He'd ne'er leave the girl with the strawberry curls,

And the band played on.

Song: *Circle*
Will the circle be unbroken,
By and by, Lord, by and by,
There's a better home a-waitin'
In the sky, O Lord in the sky.

Music continues underneath ...

Farmer: I thought that you might appreciate this little story. It seems that during the Depression, in Canada, if a jack rabbit wanted to travel from Alberta through Saskatchewan into Manitoba he'd have to carry a lunch pail with him 'cause there was nothing to eat in Saskatchewan. They didn't appreciate that story in Saskatchewan.

SCENE THREE: BIBLE BILL

Song: *Circle*
Will the circle be unbroken
By and by, Lord, by and by,
There's a better home a-waitin'
In the sky, O Lord in the sky.

Music continues underneath.

Quiet man: Then along came Bible Bill Aberhart and, sure, he was a phoney, but he was the phoney that people were looking for. They'd have voted for a guy selling snake oil if he could have shown them a way out. That's what Aberhart did. Every Sunday. Religion and politics. Aberhart offered them hope, and spell that in capital letters.

Salesman: The greatest optimist in the world is the farmer. 1932, sold a binder to farmer's wife. Now you gotta understand that the law of the land in 1932 was not – repeat – *not* what it is today. A man was not responsible for anything his wife might sign – a darn good idea too. But a man has his pride, even in hard times, and a farmer always thinks the next crop is gonna be a good one, hah, hah, hah, hah! Mrs Cody, come on out here and see what I put in your front yard – a brand new 1932 John Deere Binder – the Man o' War of Machinery – ain't it a pip?

Quiet woman (Mrs Cody): Oh I'm afraid we can't possibly afford to buy that binder.

Salesman: Well now Mrs Cody, I know that times are hard but I stuck my nose into the barn on the way up here and I got a look at your old binder and it's a wreck. It ain't got a good week left in it – maybe not a day – and this could be a good summer coming.

Quiet woman (Mrs Cody): My husband is away in Moose Jaw and I think I should wait.

Farmer: Something else you oughta know is that the songs and stories you're about to hear are the real stories of the real people all across Canada who survived the Depression. And they're all true.

Salesman: Might say I never took a backward step in my life until that Depression whipped me: took away my wife, my home, a section of good land back in Saskatchewan. Left me with nothing.

Strong woman: My God but we were naïve. Fight the King's wars, trust our politicians, believe that big wheat crops were the economic cornerstone of the nation, and go to church every Sunday. The 30s sure as hell changed all that.

Young man: We had hopes. We had dreams. Certainly. We were the class of '35 in Newcastle and we graduated with the trimmings, and then we were told: right turn, forward march, enter the world!

Farm wife: I've seen clouds of grasshoppers go over like a great storm. They were in the millions, no, tens of millions. I've never seen a more terrifying sight than nature on the loose, gone mad.

Hobo: It seemed every year you'd read that someone at some university had invented a wheat that would resist rust; but someone was inventing a bigger and stronger rust. Must have been.

Quiet woman: We've run from those 10 years. We are ashamed of them, because of what we call the Protestant ethic, of course, which in essence says: "Work your arse off all your life and do what the boss tells you, and the Big Guy in the sky, when your time comes, He'll see you get your reward."

Salesman: Well now Mrs Cody, I understand that you would be reticent to sign anything with your husband away in Moose Jaw. However, allow me to point out that this is absolutely, positively, indubitably the very last binder I have, and if you don't take it I'm gonna have to let it go to your neighbour up the road.

Quiet woman (Mrs Cody): Well, my husband will kill me, but I guess it'll have to be done.

Salesman: Well, ain't you the cat's pajamas. Now you just sign right there. Now this is crazy 'cause I don't know if you have the right to sign.

Quiet woman (Mrs Cody): But how will we ever make the payments?

Salesman: Well now Mrs Cody, don't you worry about a thing. You've signed so I'm going to make sure you make the payments. (*Pause.*) So I'm going down the road and who should I run into but her old man on his tractor.

Quiet man (Mr Cody): What's up, Harold?

Salesman: I'm here to face ya, Mr Cody ... sold that binder to your wife this afternoon and if you're going to get hopping mad I'll rip the contract up.

Quiet man (Mr Cody): You could sell a whale a week to a small town butcher. Got a pen?

Salesman: So he signs the damn thing. That's the way we did business in those days, anything to get a signature on paper. Of course, they never made a goddamn payment anyway; the grasshoppers had cleaned 'em out by June and if they hadn't done it the drought would have. It was crazy country.

Song: Will the circle be unbroken,
By and by, Lord, by and by,
There's a better home a-waitin
In the sky, O Lord, in the sky.

SCENE FOUR: SQUARE DANCE

Music: depressed dance with the ensemble.

Salesman: Into the breadline ... come on back
Tie yourself to the railroad track.
If that don't ease your troubled mind,
It's better than standin' in a relief line.
Grand chain across the land,
Bums and hoboes take a stand,
Ride the freights ... go trek and roam,
'Cause the wind done blown away your home.
And keep on goin' all the way round
The great big ring and come on home;
If you've got nothin' left to eat,
Boil the leather on the children's feet.
Men to the centre with the right hand out,
See that dust blow in and out,
Got no money in the till,
If the dust don't get you then the hoppers will.
Lost the farm ... what'll we do,
It's only 1932;
If the last three years have made you sad,
There's seven more comin', twice as bad.

Bennett swears he prays a lot,
But God ain't listenin' to his rot.
The people haven't got a chance,
And I hope you like this depressed dance.

SCENE FIVE: HOT SUCKING WIND

Farmer: I'll tell you what that Depression was like. It was survival of the fittest and I read my Bible more now than I ever did and I never read of hard times like that.

Quiet man: It was like a war. In 1915 when my battalion went into the trenches we were healthy, fit and alert young Canadians and we were considered trained to fight. Of course we weren't, but that was something you picked up awful fast.

Girl #1: There were 17 in my family, my mother's sister Marie had 21 and they were all alive.

Hobo: I never heard of any Canadian bankers jumping out of tall buildings into the streets of Toronto.

Girl #2: No baby bonus, no help at all.

Farmer: Let me tell you; the wind blew all the time from four corners of the earth. From the east one day, the west the next.

Girl #2: So there were all these babies anyway; long cold nights and no television. That's what I say.

Farmer: Ask my wife, but she's dead now; she said the wind used to make the house vibrate and it was just a small wind, but there, always steady and always hot. A hot sucking wind.

Girl #3: I could never get my laundry white. I'd try and try. The children's things, the curtains and the sheets, why they all looked as grey as that sky out there.

Farmer: I could pick up a clod of dirt as big as this fist. I'd lay it on my hand and you could see the wind picking at it. The dry dust would just float away, like smoke.

Hobo: It was the interest that got us ... nailed us down – them mortgage companies and the banks.

Farmer: I used to say the wind would polish your hand shiny, that is if you left it out long enough.

Hobo: It brought out the worst in a lot of people.

Farmer: You've got to understand, this was no roaring wind. It was just a wind blowing all the time, steady as a rock.

Salesman: Do you wonder why some people are bitter.

Hobo: The big companies took out the Bull Whip; pay up now or we take over.

Farmer: That dirt which blew off my hand? That wasn't dirt. That was my land and it was going north or south or east or west, and it was never coming back.

Quiet man: Some of these big fortunes you see around today were made by ruthless and totally unlikeable men in those years.

Hobo: The little guy went to the wall; thousands of them. But it often wasn't the economy that did it. In those days the law of the jungle was at its height.

Strong woman: Wasn't it Kipling who wrote a poem about how the weak shall perish and the strong will always survive, and how it was a good thing?

Salesman: We were all of us – from R.B. Bennett down to the lowest of the low, some Bo-hunk smelling of garlic – in one gigantic insane asylum.

Farmer: The land just blew away.

SCENE SIX: BACK TO THE OLD WAYS

Quiet woman: One thing, we had to go back to doing things the way our mothers did. The old ways. The old methods. We'd had electricity but the windcharger, it broke down and it broke down again and again and there was no money to fix it, or for new batteries. I remember making butter in a churn John found in our implement shed. When my mother was over one afternoon and we were churning she said. "This is what I used to do 30 years ago. What went wrong?" I said everything. I said since we had no electricity I separated cream by hand, and because we had no money I baked all my bread and John mended his own harness, right there at the kitchen table by lamplight, and if the cultivator shoes broke, he made new ones, and he'd learned to shoe the work horses and I was doing all the laundry by hand because we couldn't afford no gas-operated washer, and Lord God, that was hard work, and I was telling my mother this and she said: "It'll all work out in the end. You'll be a better woman for it." God, I was never closer to killing a person in my life than right then.

Strong woman: The coal killed my man. Just as sure as if he'd been on the field of battle, through shot and shell. He worked for a coal company. You see, you had this truck and you loaded it with these sacks with bulky coal – it would stick out everywhere and push into his back – and then you drove to the house which wanted the coal and you carried each sack to the chute. My man used to say each sack weighed 125 pounds, 16 to the ton. He could count to 16 all right! Home after dark, maybe seven or eight loads on an ordinary day, and he got $2.50 a day. About 60 a month for the hardest work any one man every ordered another man to do. He'd come home and I'd say. "You look like a coal man," because his face would be black with dust and he'd say, if he had the strength, "No, I look like a whipped nigger."

Farm wife: We had a little house, three kids. My husband's health wasn't so good. He'd gone underground, the coal mines at Sydney when he was 14. He signed his death warrant right there. He was, well he couldn't breathe properly and was kept from getting decent work. We managed in a way. There was never a time I felt I can't go on, it's all too much. The mine finally did its work – my husband died. Really there was nothing unusual about us.

Quiet man: I went underground, to the face, at 13. When I was 17 I could lick any man on my shift. That's why the foreman we had was such a big guy. He had to lick them all. I never tackled him although he would have been no match for me, but you see, he was a dictator. You worked if he said so. We were little white mice, happy to be in our little cage.

Strong woman: He would be strong at the start of winter. But you could just see him running down. How many's the time, oh hundreds, he's just lain down on the kitchen floor and I'd be taking off his wool jacket and pants and one of the kids would be working away on his boots. The dinner would be steaming on the table and the dear man would say, "Eat, it'll get cold." Some times he'd have a bowl of vegetable soup and some bread and then go to bed and sleep right through, not a movement, not a whisper until morning. How could there be a man-wife relationship that way? The man never saw his children. He slept all day Sunday, or just stared out the window. He never cursed. By God, I did though. I used to go to church and I'd curse Mr Bennett, the Prime Minister, and then when he was out, I'd curse King, the new one.

Quiet man: Everything got real bad so I said to my mother, make me a lunch, I'm going up to Montreal and I'll be on the train 24 hours. So, I went over to Halifax and got in that train, the first I'd been on, and somewhere down the line the conductor came along and said everybody should shift their watches back one hour. Well right then and there, I said to myself that even if I should make a fortune, I wasn't going to pleasure myself in a place where a man had to live a different time than the next fellow. I stayed one night in Montreal and came right back home. Been here ever since, working on the face until that pit prop split.

Strong woman: In 1939 my man fell and with this load of coal on his back something snapped. They had a name that long – (*She holds her arms out wide*) – for what he had. But that was it. He died the next year. That's how the hard times destroyed my man. And me.

Song: *I Believe*
I believe I saw a ghost with my inner eye,
Passing through the hallway, I felt I heard him cry.

SCENE SEVEN: JUMPING THE FREIGHTS

Hobo: Jesus, boys, I'm here to tell you I think I still hold the world title for hitchhikin' across this land of ours. Vancouver to Halifax in seven and a half days and I even beat the railroad I think. And I had my own gimmick, boys. You see I got this three-gallon gasoline can and I took out the shears and cut a hole in the side and then I tacked her all back together again with leather hinges. And there, you see, I had my own suitcase; and I stuffed in my precious belongings and I'd walk out to the highway, stand there and people thought I was out of gas and needed a ride to get to my car down the road. You see how it worked, boys. Nothing wrong, people just stopped, naturally, friendly. I wasn't a bum or a hobo, I was a fellow motorist in distress. "How far you goin," they'd say, and I'd say, "Halifax." You see, the joke'd be on them. Rides, rides and more rides, right across the country. Oh, people used to invite me into dinner knowing me only an hour. "Stay the night with us," they'd say, and they didn't know me from Adam. Some'd even offer me money. Oh, things was more free and easy then. Now people are more skeptical – always suspicious of the next fellow. You know, somethings' happened to us all. And I don't like it.

Farmer: It was only when I started thinking it all over after so many years that I realized just how terrible things were in the 30s and how it was criminal to be alone and poor and on the roads, when, for most of us, that was the only place we could be.

Salesman: Every morning, I'd cycle down to my land and I had two dogs with me and I'd send them into the barn first thing to rout out any hoboes. You see, the track ran nearly alongside the farm. Well, the dogs would flush out the men, often a dozen or more of them. They were good fellows, just looking for a warm place to sleep in the hay and there wasn't much damage. A broken padlock or something. Only a few, and very few at that, caused any trouble. I remember one fellow was going to come at me with a pitchfork once, but he soon dropped the idea. I couldn't offer them anything but they were welcome to sleep in my barn if they wanted. What never ceased to amaze me were these men, going nowhere up and down the country, riding back and forth. Freight trains, covered with men, going absolutely nowhere.

Song: I believe I saw a ghost, with my inner eye,

Passin' through the hallway, I felt I heard him cry,
Could it be the dear old farmer, who lived here
    40 years ago,
So confused about the changes of the present, he
    can't let his spirit flow?

Please take another look, what history has done,
People in a restless space, and what about our sons;
Good kind people, gentle lovers of the earth,
The truth has long been sold, and greed has taken
    away our mirth.

Quiet woman: I've seen a train passing through Headingly going west and it would be black with men, hundreds of them, all heading west ... looking for work. Just heading west looking for a dollar a day. And that train would pass another ... going east, you understand, and it would be black with men and guess what they were doing? Heading east – looking for work – a dollar a day.

Farmer: She's a sunny morning and we've got our shirts off, sitting on top of a boxcar just east of Calgary and this other freight from Vancouver comes along to go by us and there's my kid brother Billy sitting large as life and twice as ugly not six feet from me. Hi, Billy, how's the folks?

Hobo: I don't know ... haven't seen 'em for some time. Where you headed?

Farmer: Okanagan Valley.

Hobo: I gust came from the coast. It's pretty country through there so I'll go along back with you.

Farmer: You're kidding!

Hobo: Somebody's got to look after you.

(Hobo *leaps across to join the* Farmer.)

Farmer: Tunnel!

Song: *I believe*
Please stop this hurtful madness called progress by mistake,
Identity of forefathers their wisdom lies in the wake;
Oh I'll drink to the people who tried so very hard that they might live,
Who grew the rippled fields of golden grain that they might give,
Yes I'll drink to the people who tried so very hard that they might live.

Farmer: I was poor. I had not yet learned the ropes. The ways of the road, how to sustain oneself in hard times, how to ⁓rsevere and how to succeed. At 14, I rode into Montreal, a fortress commanded by a couple of hundred Englishmen and Scotsmen, to keep about two million Frenchmen in line. I'm half and half, English and Scots. But my sympathies were for Jean Baptiste. They still are.

SCENE EIGHT: MONTREAL FACTORY

Quiet woman: My mother operated a sewing machine in a factory in the east-end of Montreal. They made pants, other things ... and her salary for 5 days a week, 9 hours a day was $3 a week. Oh, and there was a bonus system if you could go over the quota ... There were 120 or so women in that factory and my mother said no woman ever made a bonus. Never, ever. If you went to the bathroom more than twice in a shift you were docked ... and there were just two toilets for those hundred women. They ate lunch at their machines because there was no washroom ... no lunch-room ... no fire-escapes ... no sprinkler ... no ladders ... windows sealed up tight. There was no union. If you even thought union ... it was out ... out ... out. Ask for a raise? Out. Take two days off, sick? Out. Think? Out. The supervisor and the foreman, they were paid to keep those workers down. They were on some sort of bonus to run that place as a sweat shop. Those women didn't speak English, and they didn't understand what was going on ... just those heavy machines going hours on end. Not even look-ing up from their work, making sailor suits for the navy and uniforms for the army and other things for war. It was slave, slave, slave ... taking dirt and eating dirt and if anyone had given them a kind word, those women would have fallen over dead from shock. I know that ... bodies lying all over the factory floor. Somewhere along during the war, the man who owned that factory and his son were given a commendation from the Ca-nadian Government because of their valuable contribution to the nation's war effort.

SCENE NINE: THE PRINCE OF WALES

Strong woman: I only remember one thing: the Prince of Wales when he became King and that Mrs Simpson. What he ever saw in her I'll never know. We all loved the King, and I had pictures from magazines in my room of the young prince, you know, so handsome, riding a horse on his ranch in Alberta, inspecting a regiment, playing polo, and I guess you could say he was the darling of the world. Anyway, the principal, I can't remember his name, announced there would be a special assembly this par-ticular morning in the auditorium, and it was the first time I remember when all the classes were there, from the little ones up to the Grade Nines.

Young man: Good morning, boys and girls.

All: Good morning, Mr McPhee.

Young man: Please be seated. I know your parents have been reading about That Woman from Baltimore. I want to say this: the King is the King and England is England, and thank God for that in these perilous times. We are gathered here to listen to an important transatlantic radio broadcast. Our King whom we all love dearly is today to make an important decision. A decision that will affect us all very deeply.

Salesman (radio): This is the BBC London. Please stay tuned for a frightfully important message from Buckingham Palace.

Strong woman: His voice came over, quite clear. I mean we could hear the words clearly and the way he put it I don't think most of us realized just what he had said.

Salesman (radio): My loyal subjects ... (*static*) ... an important decision which I must ... (*static*) ... the woman I love ... (static) ....

Strong woman: I remember the part about the woman I love, or the woman I must have beside me to help bear the burdens, you know.

Salesman (radio): (*static*) ... THANK YOU!

Strong woman: Then the principal stood up again, explained that we would soon have a new King, that he would be the old King's brother, the younger one. And then he asked us to stand and sing "God Save The King," and we did and I remember crying. Maybe it was because my own class teacher over by the wall, a lovely woman we all loved, she was crying and then about three-quarters of the way through, the teacher who was playing the piano ... she put her head down on the keys and began to cry. I think it was the most dramatic thing that I have ever seen. Looking back on it, I think what a great movie those days would have made.

(*Everybody is crying by now.*)

Young man: Class dismissed!

SCENE TEN: SATURDAY MATINEE

(*Some actors mime a scene from a romantic movie.*)

All: We want Mr Beasley.

Farmer: Robert! Turn off that projector! (*The "romance" freezes.*) If you kids don't stop firing off these cap guns, throwing popcorn up here at the screen, and rolling those pop bottles down the aisles, and stop flushing those damn toilets, I'll turn off the picture and *send you all home*!

(*One actor stomps off amid cheers and "picture" begins again, this time with one actress dancing to the tune of "The Good Ship Lollipop."*)

SCENE ELEVEN: SHIRLEY TEMPLE

Quiet woman: Shirley Temple ... that's what I remember about the 30s ... Shirley Temple dolls. One year, they were all the rage ... everything; everybody was talking about Shirley Temple, going to see her movies, reading stories about her in the newspapers and in the fan magazines. Shirley Temple, Shirley Temple, Shirley Temple. Eaton's used to turn a big part of their store into a toyland at Christmas and that year, the Shirley Temple year, they had these dolls along one end of toyland. There must have been hundreds of these dolls and they weren't cheap. They moved girls from all over the store down to toyland for about six weeks before Christmas, and I was one that year. I never knew a girl who wasn't glad to leave that place. Girls used to marry fellows they didn't even care for, to be free of Eaton's. Oh, yes ... these dolls. I'd stand there and watch the faces of those little girls. Little faces, they needed food. You could see a lot who needed a pint of milk a thousand times more than they needed a Shirley doll. They'd stare for hours. We tried to shush them away but it didn't do any good. One day, I had this crazy notion that I would give Shirley dolls away to those kids – "Here little girl, this one's for you ... and here's one for you and this big one is for you, darling" – that sort of thing. I thought I'd do it until I was caught and then I'd plead insanity. I never did, of course. Those six weeks with those goddamn dolls were the worst I ever put in. I wonder if Shirley Temple ever realized the misery those dolls must have caused children all over the world ... I suppose she never even thought of it.

SCENE TWELVE: EATON'S

Balladeer (Commissioner): Miss Nolan, you were employed by the T. Eaton Company Limited of Toronto?

Farm wife (Nolan): Yes, I was.

Balladeer (Commissioner): And when you first went there, what was the nature of your work?

Farm wife (Nolan): You see, this dress was cotton crepe, and we had to make the blouse with double fronts and a frill in between on the one side and a raglan sleeve; and we had to make that skirt and we had to join it to the blouse, and we had to sew that bow that is on the shoulder but sewn in such a position that the bow could be threaded through a button-hole: and then we had to make the belt loops; and you got a $1.15 a dozen.

Commissioner: How much?

Nolan: $1.15 for that amount of work.

Commissioner: That is about nine and a half cents per dress?

Nolan: For that amount of work.

Commissioner: What does the dress sell for?

Nolan: $1.59 each. It took an ordinary woman five to six hours to make a dozen. So maybe in a day you could make maybe two dollars, but all the time Eaton's said it was paying 12.50 a week, and it was but you'd have to be an octopus to make it. So I went to the Supervisor.

Quiet man (supervisor): Did you make your minimum for the previous week?

Nolan: Of course not.

Supervisor: You go home. Go home and don't come back until I send for you, and we will send for you when we are ready.

Nolan: So I went to the Manager.

Hobo (Manager): That is the new system we are bringing in. Every time a girl falls down on her work, she will get a week's holiday.

Nolan: Now am I going to live that week?

Manager: You can report to our welfare office. We have a generous welfare office, we are known for that. Eaton's takes care of our sick and destitute as any family would.

Balladeer (Announcer): John David Eaton remembers the Depression as a time when his company spent millions to shield its employees from the desperation of unemployment. That was a good time for John David Eaton, and he remembers it with affection.

Salesman (John Eaton): Nobody thought about money in those days, because they never saw any. You could take your girl to a supper dance at the hotel for $10, and that included the bottle and a room for you and your friends to drink it in. I'm glad I grew up then. It was a good time for everybody. People learned what it means to work.

Song: *The Outhouse*

Balladeer:
We only stopped work for an outhouse call,
To sit all alone with some reading,
Then reach for the catalogue hanging on the wall

All: And rip off a page for Eaton's.

Song: *Fred Blake*

Young Fred Blake's father refused the dole,
Hammered on his bible to save his soul,
Come on down and get some relief,

It's the devil's plan to make you feel like a thief.

SCENE THIRTEEN: CITY RELIEF OFFICE

Quiet woman: I worked in the city relief office in Edmonton for a time.

Farmer: If that woman was back in the kitchen then maybe there'd be more jobs for us men.

Quiet woman: It was just part-time. In the 30s, Canadians had their pride. My God, how they had their pride. Men would say that never in the history of their family, never had they had to go on relief. These men ... a few told me ... they had to walk around the block eight or a dozen times before they had the nerve to come in and apply for relief ... as though they were signing away their manhood ... their right to be a husband and sit at the head of the table. It was a very emotional time, that first time, when a man came in and went up to the counter in that awful yellow and green welfare office.

Quiet man (Clerk): Frank Davis. Haven't seen you out curling lately.

Hobo (Frank): No, been busy going belly up. I've tried and I've lost.

Clerk: So you expect the government to look after you.

Frank: Well, I figure some of that tax money I've been paying should start working for me.

Clerk: All right, I'll put you on the relief list. For you, your wife and how many kids have you still got around?

Frank: Just the two at home. Two boys on the road and the daughter's married off.

Clerk: Right, that'll give you $19 a month.

Frank: We'll live on that. It'll be tight but the wife's pretty canny.

Clerk: Frank, I'm afraid I'll have to ask for your liquor permit.

Frank: What the hell for?

Clerk: Nobody on relief can have a permit. I don't make the rules, Frank, it's just one that's there.

Frank: You know I'm not a drinker.

Clerk: Of course, so you shouldn't mind partin' with it.

Frank: Well, I'm not a goddamn kindergarten kid either.

Clerk: Another thing. I'm not sure this is a regulation but the district office says we got to tell you. You or anybody. Beer. If you're seen in the beer parlour and somebody squawks, then your relief can be cut off just like that.

Frank: Applying for the dole is bad enough but when you treat a man like a criminal –

Clerk: I know, Frank, and when I walk into that beer parlour, I'm as blind as a bat but some ain't. There are people in this town who would just like to squeal on you or the next guy. Just a meanful nature, hoping to make it hard on you. Three families already cut off. One fellow was drinkin' hell and gone over towards Regina when he was spotted.

Quiet woman: It's left its mark on many a good man today, let me tell you. And the worst part of it all was this; the worst part of it all was that they didn't know what was happening to them. They just did not understand it at all. Some still don't. I'm not sure I do.

Quiet man: It got so I hated those people coming to our office for the pogey. It was the way they had lost their spirit, almost their will to survive. They'd come shuffling into that office and ask for something more and sometimes I'd scream at them, "Get the hell out of here. Go down to False Creek and drown yourself. There's the way, right down the hill, go on now, beat it." They'd just stand there and take it.

Farmer: My wife has pleurisy and the doctor won't come to see us.

Young man: The kids need shoes to go to school.

Quiet man: I know what it was doing to these fellows, and I know that even without a Depression, most of them had been in a pretty lousy economic box even before. Talk about your Roaring 20s! Roaring in New York, maybe, or roaring in the slick magazines, but in Canada it was just a lot of whimpering. But back to me. I didn't like what was happening to me. In that office I could see the rottenness of the relief system, what it did to people, the graft – oh yes, there was plenty of that – and the phoney contracts and the phoney people and especially the politicians. You know, there is something about politics that brings out the very worst in people. So I'd blow up and after, I'd apologize, and they would usually just look at me with those goddamned eyes they had. They didn't hate me. Can't even give them that much credit. I found myself turning into a hateful person, spiteful, taking it out on some person when it really couldn't have been his fault. Yelling at my wife, cuffing my kids, snarling at my neighbours, and why? Why? Because I knew I was part of a system which was wrong, and it was turning me wrong, and to protect my wife and kids I had to keep going wrong, and more wrong, just like you can't be a little pregnant.

Strong woman: We lived on Lind Street in Toronto and I think everybody but my Dad was out of work on our block. In the summer they'd just sit on their porches, arms folded, and wait for something to happen but nothing ever did. There was this little man living a few doors down the street from us. You'd have to say he was a nothing, the type that never said anything much. You know. It was six miles downtown to where the unemployment offices were and you had to get there about six in the morning to have any chance of a job, so this guy would get up about 4:30, winter or summer, and down he'd trudge, day after day, but it seemed he never could get a job. Then he'd walk home.

Farm wife: So, you walk into this office in the basement of the firehall downtown. That's where they pass out the vouchers. There was one line for married men and women, and another for the single guys. Don't ask me why. Don't ask me about anything in those days. Everyone is waiting in line and at noon the boss, this little jerk, slaps his hand down.

Quiet man: All right, lunch time. Come back at 1:30.

Farm wife: These women have been standing in line for three hours with their kids crying.

Quiet man: Too bad, but these are the hours.

Farm wife: Where's your assistant, the guy who handles the other line?

Quiet man: I fired him yesterday because there isn't enough work for two around here. And what goddamn business is it of yours, anyway?

Farm wife: Listen, you little creep, it is my goddamn business! There's enough work here for two guys, even four guys, so you're going to stay in line and look after these women until you're finished.

Quiet man: I'll miss my lunch.

Farm wife: Then you can just go piss up a rope! And every time I wanted to make my point I jerks up on his tie and bounces my fist off his chin. I asked him if he understood. You're goddamn right he understood.

Quiet man: I'll call the police!

Farm wife: Then you'd better call a goddamned ambulance too!

Quiet man: I'm going to report you. I'll pull you off the dole. I know who you are.

Farm wife: And I know who these women are and their husbands and when I tell them what is happening down here, they are going to come down with me this time next week and when we walk through that door you're going to have my voucher ready and you'll be serving these poor starving women, and if you call in every cop in Cape Breton, it still won't matter a bit to you because you'll look like an alley cat that's been hit by a mainline locomotive.

Music: "Skipping and Jumpin," underneath.

Strong woman: One day he came home about 7:30 at night, walking as usual, but somehow he'd got a job. He'd made five dollars that day and he let everybody know it. I guess you could say he was the proudest man in Toronto that day, and he sent his girl, about 10 or so, down to the nearest store to buy two quarts of ice cream and some other small stuff. There was going to be a celebration.

Music up.

Farm wife (Mother): Here's you new boots, Jamie.

Hobo (Jamie): They're awful.

Farm wife: They're what we were given for you.

Hobo: Bright red ...?!

Salesman (Father): Well, the boys'll see you coming won't they?

Hobo: With white stitching!

Salesman: Try them on, son.

Farm wife: You can't wear those canvas and rubber things for the winter.

Hobo: Can't walk in them.

Salesman: They're just stiff cause they're new.

Farmer: Come on out, Jamie.

Hobo: I'm staying in.

Farm wife: Jamie, go out now and play.

Hobo: I don't want to.

Salesman: Son, you've got to go out and face them some time. (*He plays a bit of hockey with boys who snigger, "santa claus shoes," "Little Abner boots," then the chant "Jamie's got relief boots." One by one* Jamie *kicks them in shins.*)

Hobo: Don't laugh at my boots any more. Stop laughing at my boots!

Strong woman: But somehow, on the way back between the store and the house, she lost the change. Don't ask me how it could happen. She just lost the change. You could see it in ... in pantomime, her father gesturing on the front walk and the girl going through the little pockets of her dress and looking into the bag, but the money was gone. Now here's a man who apparently never got mad, but he lost his cool. He started to thrash that kid right on the front yard. Hit her, push her, hit her again, screaming all the time, and the girl just stood there and took it. Finally, the guy threw himself full length on the steps and started to cry. Sobbing. Hard. The first time he'd made any money by his own labour in maybe three or four years and it was gone. He cried, big sobs. And you know who went to comfort him? The little girl. She went over and sat beside him and spoke to him and put her hand on his shoulder. Mercy, you don't know whether to laugh or cry.

Song: *Fred Blake*

Young Fred Blake's father refused the dole,
Hammered on his bible to save his soul,
Some went crazy, just had to go
Others stayed home with the radio ... the
radio ... yodel adio ... the radio ...

SCENE FOURTEEN: THE GENERAL STORE

Farmer: Howdy, Jim.

Quiet man: Don't see much of you since you got your radio.

Hobo: How is the old whistler and his dog?

Farmer: What do you fellas remember about last night?

Quiet man: It was cold.

Farmer: But it was clear and just guess what I picked up?

Hobo: The flu?

Farmer: Damn sight better.

Hobo: Ottawa?

Farmer: Got that plenty of times.

Quiet man: Cleveland?

Farmer: Always get that!

Hobo: Then what?

Farmer: WGN.

Hobo: New York!

Quiet man: You didn't!

Farmer: Yup, clear as a bell.

Hobo: Christ! and I still have to depend on my kid's crystal set.

Farmer: They're hopeless.

Quiet man: Oh, if you get one rigged out right you might pick up something.

Farmer: Yeh, if the broadcasting station is in the hay field next to you!

Quiet man: Say, did you hear about Vance?

Farmer: What, is he dead?

Quiet man: No. ...

Farmer: He got a job?

Hobo: No. ...

Quiet man: He just went out and bought himself a deForest Crosley!

Farmer: No!

Farm wife: $300.

Farmer: Christ! Where the devil did he get the cash?

Quiet man: He and the Lord only knows but there it is in his tiny living room, a monster.

Farm wife: It's like one of them opera singers.

Quiet man: He turned it up full blast to show it off, and the panes in the windows actually shook. Vibrated.

Farm wife: They got these little shelves along the walls with chinaware on it and each piece would go into a little dance.

Quiet man: You wouldn't believe it. People will be coming all the way from Pembroke just to listen.

Hobo: There's short wave.

Young girl: That's something.

Young man: Ships at sea –

Quiet man: A ship approaching the Strait of Belle Isle in the fog, asking for a position; now that's really something.

Farmer: You're better off with a small one. Those big buggers really slurp up the juice.

Quiet man: Vance's wind charger has had a hernia already.

Hobo: I'll stick with the kid's crystal set, but I think I might visit Vance Tuesday night.

Farmer: Would that be by any chance the night Joe Louis is fighting?

Hobo: Well, it's a chance to visit Vance and see how Joe handles his latest Bum of the month.

Farmer: Radio drew people together, families together.

Young man: There was good music.

Salesman: Jack Benny, Fibber McGee and Molly were funny.

Balladeer: But the funniest of all was Fred Allen. There was a man who was just naturally funny!

Quiet man: Everybody in town could say, "there's a fellow in our town who has sense of humour like that."

Farm wife: One I never liked one iota was Bob Hope. Thought he tried too hard.

SCENE FIFTEEN: THE RADIO

Song: *Fantasy Radio*

Men: Hey, hey it's fantasy radio hour,
Time to wipe those tears away,
We'll help you smile, laugh and forget
That this week you worked for a smaller paycheck.

Women: Hey, hey it's fantasy radio time,
Come on and drift away and dream,
It's just temporary trouble, don't adjust your set,
The best is coming soon and you ain't seen it yet.

1. Say, remember that Indian kid they hanged out at Headingly?

2. Can't remember the crime.

1. Murder.

2. Of course, but what kind?

1. I believe he was the one who opened his brother-in-law up with an axe from throat to crotch.

2. The condemned man gets his wish for his last meal?

1. Anything he wants!

3. You mean if he wants a roasted 15-pound turkey and everything, just like Christmas?

1. Yeah, that's what he gets!

2. An old English custom.

1. Anyway this kid was off a reserve somewhere up between the lakes.

3. Everybody was poor up there in those days.

2. If you were an Indian you had nothing –

3. Nothing was what they expected –

1. So when his time comes, the deputy warden goes down to see him and asks him what he wants.

2. I want boiled whitefish.

3. Christ, even in jail the grub is 10 times better than that.

2. I want boiled whitefish.

3. Anything else?

2. Yes, boiled tea with lots of sugar.

3. That all?

2. Yes, just boiled whitefish and tea.

1. They say he made a grand meal of it.

Farmer (Listener): Poor bugger.

1. All he'd known growing up all those years was fish and tea.

3. And that tells you something about how we've treated these people.

1. They always had their own Depression all their lives.

2. Whitefish and tea.

1. He was 19, I think.

Woman 1: Dozens of men are working for wages which will provide only the bare essentials for themselves and their families.

Woman 2: Their earnings will not permit the purchase of necessary clothing.

Woman 1: Help a needy fellow citizen through the rigours of a Canadian winter!

Woman 2: Buy yourself a smart new suit!

Woman 1: And donate your old one to some needy man!

Woman 1: Here's the sort of neighbourliness we've all dreamed about.

Woman 2: The sort that will cost you next to nothing.

Woman 2: This public service announcement has been brought to you by courtesy of the Robert Simpson Company of Montreal.

Balladeer: Ladies and gentlemen! Please stay tuned for an important message from the Prime Minister of Canada, the Right Honourable R.B. Bennett.

Hobo: Bennett! When they made him, they threw away the mould.

Quiet man: A fat, sleek, contented bowler-hatted toad!

Farmer: He was a corporation lawyer, you know. A lawyer, God knows, is bad enough; but a corporation lawyer is pure dynamite. He'd steal the pennies off a dead man's eyes and swear because they weren't quarters!

Balladeer: Ladies and gentlemen: the Prime Minister!

Salesman (Bennett): The difficulty about these matters is that too much reliance is being placed upon the Government. The people are not bearing their share of the load. Half a century ago people would work their way out of their difficulties rather than look to a government to take care of them. The fibre of some of our people has grown softer and they are not willing to turn in and save themselves. They now complain because they have no money. When they were earning money, many of them spent it in speculation and in luxury. "Luxury" means anything a man has not an immediate need for, having regard to his financial position. I do not know what the result of the present movement may be, but unless it induces men and women to think in terms of honest toil rather than in terms of bewilderment because of conditions which they helped to create, the end of organized society is not far distant.

Strong woman: Change it over!

Farm wife: Here we are ladies with household hint number three from Housewife Hilda. First you take an empty flour sack from Maple Leaf Milling Company and wash it out well, bleach out the lettering, turn it upside down; cut two holes for the arms and one at the top for the neck. Tuck in here, do a little tightening and fixing there, put in a hem and what do you have? A party dress fit for a nine-year-old queen. And now for household hint number four ...

Balladeer: And now we present a real life, true, Canadian drama. "Prairie Winter." Part One.

Salesman: Cold, day after day, around 45 below. The house wasn't that much, no insulation then, fireburner in the kitchen and wood hard to get.

Quiet woman: Just waiting for the next big wind to blow us into the gully.

Balladeer: Anybody home?

(*The cast assume the various characters in the radio play.*)

Husband: Gosh darn, Gavin up from Regina.

Wife: Gavin, how'd you get through in weather like this?

Gavin: We railroad men stop at nothing. Here's some *National Geograph-*

ics for the kids. No sense having them stinky pipes around without something to put in them, Jim.

Husband: Well gosh darn to blankety heck, a whole tinful of the best brand! Thanks.

Wife: Can I take your coat, Gavin?

Gavin: No thanks, Mary; it's a trifle cold. I've spent considerable time in the Arctic but how in the heck do you stand it here?

Wife: I know, Gavin, God didn't ... God never meant people to live like this in the cold.

Husband: Jumpin' Jehosephat, she's never cried in front of the children before.

Wife: Well I am now.

Gavin: I'm sorry, Mary, but it's just I've seen Eskimos in igloos living warmer and cosier than this. How about you, little one; you like to live in an igloo?

Little girl: Oh yes, yes.

Gavin: Come on, then, outside. Now how deep's the snow in this gully?

Husband: Casting an eye I'd say nine feet.

Gavin: Deep enough. She'll do. Start shovelling, mouth faced away from the wind.

Husband: Sounds loony.

Gavin: Have it built in no time.

Wife: Brought some coffee!

Boy: Straw and boards for beds —

Wife: Oil lamps, stove, magazines —

Gavin: How you fixed for food?

Husband: Just fine. Six dollars a month coming in regular from the Alberta Government.

Neighbour: Well hello there. Where in the heck is everybody?

Husband: Over here in the snowbank, John.

Wife: Yooo Hooo!

Neighbour: Well, cut off my legs and call me shorty. I heard about it but I didn't believe it.

Husband: Come on in John, but you can't share the wife.

Neighbour: Brought some of my homemade singing juice.

Boy: Better watch out, Mr Carver, the police has been around.

Neighbour: Looking for trouble eh?

Husband: No, just curious.

Neighbour: Well, shoot! No wonder. I think you could show an Eskimo a thing or two.

SCENE SIXTEEN: JOE LOUIS AND THE BUM-OF-THE-MONTH CLUB

(*The company becomes listeners in different times and places.*)

Farmer: Radio was the big thing and boxing was radio.

Announcer: Fight #1: Bill Braddock.

Farmer: The sports pages were full of Joe Jouis and what they called his Bum-of-the-month club.

Announcer: Fight #2: Tony Galento.

Farmer: We know now that Joe never threw that many punches, but the announcer threw a lot for him to make the fight more exciting and sell more Gillette Blue Blades.

Announcer: Fight #3: Max Schmelling.

Farmer: Joe wasn't a thinker you know. But he'd been taught well; left hooks, jabs, combinations and he knew how to go in for the kill. But old Tommy Farr baffled him.

Announcer: Farr fight, round #3.

Farmer: In my opinion Farr couldn't hit worth a damn. The thing was, though he wasn't winning, he was still standing up and fighting.

Announcer: Farr fight, round #9.

Farmer: Louis won as he knew he would but Tommy the Welshman sure put up a big fight.

Announcer: Farr fight over – round #15.

SCENE SEVENTEEN: OLD MAN MARSHALL'S

Strong woman: There was this little old man living next door to us named Marshall. He'd been a butcher for a Red and White store and got let go and he had no money put away, none. His wife was dead and he was lonely. He was about 50, I think, but to a kid of 12, well, that's pretty old. One night he came over to play cribbage with my old man and he was feeling low and when he left he said, "Harry, I've been feeling poorly the past while. If you don't see smoke coming out my chimney, would you drop over? See how I'm doing and" – he put his hand up to his heart as if to emphasize his point. My Dad said, "Joe, I never knew you had a bum ticker" and he said, "I haven't. It's just busted right in two." About a month later my mother said she hadn't seen anything doing around the Marshall house for a couple of days and she sent me over. The front and back doors were locked, but there was a basement door and I got in that way. I didn't know where the light switch was and it was black as hell so I started feeling my way up the stairs when I felt two bumps on my chest, as if I'd run into two objects, and you know, I guess my brain wasn't working because it took me a few seconds, in fact until I felt the ankles, and then I knew they were shoes. Feet. Old Man Marshall was hanging there. He'd tied a rope around the beam, put the noose over his head, and just jumped into space.

SCENE EIGHTEEN: THE CALL TO OTHER PLACES

Song: *Other Places*

Girls: I love the long whistle of a train at night,
Moving down the valley, a call, to other places where things might be
    right
As I lay in my bed, I loved the sound of that train
Telling me escape, get away through the mountains,
A passenger train, going to Vancouver
Or to Winnipeg, then on to Toronto ...

Young girl: Maybe romance, if you really think so. But to get away. I was 20 and I had teacher's training and I'd have taught for free just to be given the chance, but no, there was dear, sweet Margaret at home again with a family that was dying. I used to think that if the rest of Canada was like us, lost and dying on 320 acres of Saskatchewan land, then Canada was finished. But there was always that train going to Vancouver, through the Rockies and then the Selkirks and the Purcell mountains and then through the Monashee – oh, what a lovely name – and down to the sea and I would take off my shoes and walk along the sand and let every wave wash around me and I would write my sad thoughts with a stick in the sand and the waves would wash away the letters and those sad times would be gone forever.

Girls: I love the long whistle of a train at night going to Vancouver, Telling me escape, get away through the mountains.

Boys: Or to Winnipeg, then on to Toronto.

SCENE NINETEEN: BOX CAR

Quiet man (Bum): If they wanted you to pick fruit in a hurry, you were an economic saviour, the rest of the time you were shit.

(*Sound effect: train.*)

Bum: You didn't just jump on a boxcar and away you went. No sirree, saw too many bodies cut in two, legs off, heads off. You had to run a quarter of the speed of the train on slippery grade, sloping gravel. When you're going your best lick, you figure how fast it's going. One car goes by, get ready for next and then jump for the ladder. Quick up to the top and lie flat, make sure the bulls aren't checking. The cars were full, or empty but locked. Riding on top on a sunny spring day was a real joy; in fall, raining, snow, it was bad. And in winter, there was a quick way to die. You can always tell the professionals: dirty, lice, crabs, fleas, always needed a shave, a three-day beard, never a one-day beard. A young man's business; older men over 40 couldn't stand the gaff. The cold, poor food, the tension; anyone who survived a year riding freights never had much respect for police.

(*Salesman, hobo, farmer and young man run for the boxcar. The quiet man is already riding. Each one in turn joins chain to help next bum onto car. The boxcar door is closed, sound effects stop.*)

Young man: There was this uncle, Dad's brother in Winnipeg, so I thought I'd hop over there. I didn't know where it was, how far, no nothing. But I'll you one thing: I soon found out. Halfway around the world riding in freight cars.

Balladeer: Here's the garage, boy.

Young man: Hm, funny setup ... big cars ... only a driver's side!

Balladeer: No room for passengers. Frank, you think you can handle one of these?

Young man: You've got a Graham Paige engine here big enough to drive the Queen Mary!

Balladeer: Three cars go together and load up the commodity at the warehouse.

Young man: Commodity?

Balladeer: Scotch, Frank, for the Prohibition. You just head for that border 60 miles away and if somebody tries to stop you, you just bang on through. If anyone chases you, just outrun them and if you get caught ... tough luck.

Young man: Farewell, so to speak.

Balladeer: Isn't much chance of being caught cause it ain't the Mounties' business and the Americans are paid off but some times ...

Young man: What do you mean?

Balladeer: Well, some times a cop wants to be a hero. Then it takes a month or so to get him transferred.

Young man: That still sounds risky.

Balladeer: It pays 50 bucks a week, Frank.

Young man: You're on.

(*Sound effects: piano & kazoo car chase begin.*)

Young man: I worked for a year and one month, until they knocked down Prohibition. Until booze became legal again. $50 a week and later $60. I smashed up two cars. I got shot in the leg once. A friend double-crossed me and stole a load and I often wonder what happened to him. I had a girl friend I kept in an apartment in St Boniface and I had another girl friend in Grand Forks, North Dakota. I made three runs a week. I risked my life every trip and I never saved a cent. But I had fun.

(*Sound effects: car chase crossfades to train again.*)

Hobo: I was born on a farm south of Regina in the Maxton area. I don't believe anyone who wasn't there in 1934, 35, 36 can believe how bad it was. The wind blew hurricane force and it was colder each winter than the Yukon. In 1936 I was 16 and there was no point hanging around. I was just another belly to feed and there were three kids younger. I left and worked my way east. Just a dumb farm kid. There were an awful lot of dumb farm kids around those days. I got down into the Niagara Peninsula for the picking but there were no jobs and I decided to turn myself in as a vagrant.

(*Sound effects: cut.*)

Balladeer: "Boondoggles" – that's what the *Chicago Trib* called them – boondoggles, makework projects to justify the dole – like tidying up back lane, picking rocks, digging dandelions. Sure, digging dandelions. Ain't you never heard of the Great Dandelion Offensive of 1931?

Farmer: Men: When we leave here, we're going to walk over to the top of Niagara Street and start cleaning the dandelions off the boulevard. Now, if everybody will co-operate, we'll get along just fine. Nobody expects you to bust a gut on this job but, if you set yourself some kind of a goal, time is bound to go quicker. There's only one rule: you can kneel down, sit down, or lie down; but I don't want you standing up. Standing up will attract the attention of the people on the street and, if they see you standing around doing bugger all, some of these dames will be phoning in to raise hell. Then I get hell and, if I do, then I'll sure as hell dish out some myself.

Balladeer: We kneeled and jabbed dandelions, we sat down and jabbed dandelions, we lolled full length and jabbed dandelions. We sharpened the blades of our knives. We watched housewives going shopping.

Farm wife: By God! This is it. The last outrage.

Quiet woman: Here's what I sweat and slave to pay taxes for.

Young man: To pay all the lazy bums in Winnipeg to sit around on the boulevard.

Strong woman: Well, by God, I've had it! I'm going to the mayor!

Farm wife: I'm going to the newspapers!

Quiet woman: Me, too.

Balladeer: The next thing any of us knew, one of our gang was over by this taxpayer's car, and he had grabbed the taxpayer's tie, and pulled his head out the open window of his car. Their noses were about six inches apart and a dandelion knife was pointed at the taxpayer's chin.

Hobo: I'm not a bum. I am a railroad fireman. But because this country is being run by stupid people like you, I can't hold a wiper's job in the shops. And we are not being paid for this job, not one dime. We take jobs like this because we're afraid of getting cut off the relief. And you are not going to report anyone to anyone. You are going to get the hell off the street. And if you so much as let out a peep to anyone, there are 20 guys here who have your licence number and who have all the spare time required to make you live to regret it.

Balladeer: He released the taxpayer and gave his face a vigorous assist back through the open window. And, as it moved past him, he held the screaming point of his dandelion knife against the side of that taxpayer's car.

(*Sound effects: Boxcar begins again.*)

SCENE TWENTY: THE JUNGLE

Salesman: Boy, you're in for a treat. Other side of town is the Glencoe Country Club of jungles.

Young man: But I want to get off and into town first to get my mail.

Farmer: Well, better teach you a few tricks of the road.

Salesman: You could be in for a rough time if you look like a real bum; dirty, ragged, you know what I mean. Well, a lot of them houses have big dogs.

Farmer: Never try bumming anything within five blocks of the rail yards.

Salesman: Commonsense; these people have had their doors knocked on for years – even before the Depression.

Farmer: Remember, you don't have to commit a criminal act to get into trouble.

Salesman: You just have to be you, without money.

Quiet man: Kid, you jump when I yell three.

Balladeer: What was the jungle like? Well, the jungle was where the hoboes gathered and it was a place where the cops didn't bother you. You'd find them easily at night, spring, fall, summer because of the fires. Cooking fires mainly. There was always a stew pot going – one of those gallon tomato tins.

Young man: I'll tell you about the famous Calgary omelette. I made it myself. There was a cutbank on the Bow River, on a curve, and there was a kind of jungle there. It was about five miles into Calgary and that was one place, Winnipeg and Sioux Lookout and Vancouver were others, where my dear old mother would send me mail, general delivery. So I went in and sure enough, there was a letter and I'll be damned if two $1 bills didn't drop out.

Hobo: Cows we eat. They eat grass, grain, Russian thistle. What's the difference between a gopher and a red squirrel? Squirrels are a delicacy, ain't they? Paris sort of delicacy. You get a casserole dish and you line it and then you lay down about eight strips of gopher because you get two strips of sides and bellymeat off of one of them. Then you lay a thin layer of sliced potatoes and so on, and then you fold the dough over the top and put it in the oven.

Quiet woman: Ever heard of ketchup soup? Or catsup stew? O.K. Well, these here fellows would come into my place ... "Hi Lily," they'd say. "Hi fellows," I'd say. So they'd buy a glass of milk: five cents. Then they'd scoop up a big handful of them oyster biscuits. They're free. They'd go over to the boiling water urn and take a bowl and fill it up. You still with me? There was sort of a cabinet where I kept all the sauces and stuff. They'd grab up a bottle of ketchup and go over there to a booth. Now, here's how you do it. You dump as much ketchup as you figure you can get away with into the hot water, there, then you unload your crackers and you crumple them up, like so, in your hand and let 'em go in the ketchup and water. Then you stir it around, add some salt and pepper and you've got, mister, right there you've got something that tasted pretty damn good in those days.

Young girl: That goddamned cod liver oil my old man, when he wasn't drunk, would brew out of fish guts the captains would give him. If we were acting up, raising hell, my mother would threaten us with another tablespoon of cod liver oil. One thing, though, we were the healthiest kids within twenty miles. Rosy cheeks, bright blue eyes, tough as nails, and stinking of cod liver oil.

Hobo: There's nothing wrong with the meat, it is just the thought of it. But what is wrong with a gopher? Just the thought, that's it.

Salesman: I heard of farm families eating gophers, but I don't believe it. But if you were to eat a barn rat in a stew, unwittingly, now that could be another matter altogether. Those rats are plump and grain-fed around the barn. Why, back in Toronto, they're just about the best-looking livestock they've got around the place.

Farmer: Hey! It's the kid!

Salesman: Been out stealing?

Young man: No, gentlemen, just to the post-office and back.

Salesman: You got all this in the mail?

Young man: No, just a wee tiny letter from me wee tiny mother, with a wee, tiny $2 bill inside.

Farmer: Jesus, it pays to write home.

Young man: So what's the first thing I do?

Salesman: Faint.

Young man: Then what?

Quiet man: Get a couple of drinks.

Young man: Right, four beer to be exact, gentlemen.

Farmer: So now you're tipsy.

Young man: Remember how it feels? So I start for home to be back with you boys, and I pass this farm and there's a sign –

Strong woman: Eggs for Sale! Don't crush them son.

Young man: What else you got around?

Strong woman: Butter? Cheese? Onions and celery.

Young man: Give you 50 cents for the lot.

Strong woman: Sold.

Young man: They jumped at it.

Salesman: Would've give you the farm for the whole $2. Barbecue dinners for them Yankee oil barons will have nothing absolutely goddamned nothing on Rupert Gill's Great Omelette of 1936.

Farm wife: Anybody who says people wasn't going hungry, why he was a little wacky. I come down to Vancouver for December and January and I seen lots of starving. I seen bodies in doorways down on the waterfront, Cordova, Skid Row, east of Main. At the hospital they'd have a fancy name for it, you know, malnutrition, but a dead body was still a dead body.

Farmer: I was not a hobo. A hobo is a regular bum, a professional bum. Hoboism is a state of mind. I was a wanderer. One of the unfortunates. A victim of the economic situation? Perhaps. Certainly, most certainly, a casualty in the battle between ignorant men who were running this country. Once I got 30 days in jail for riding a freight car long ago into a Godforsaken little Saskatchewan city which, thank God, the economic ebbs and flow of the past two decades have served to reduce to a position of impotence. I refer to the metropolis of Moose Jaw. But I do have a criminal record; and to me, as one who survived what we call the Great Depression, that is a badge of honour.

Quiet man: Excuse me, sir, I'm a poor lad from the Minas Basin down in Nova Scotia and my father is a war veteran, and my mother has just written to tell me that he's dying from his old wounds. I wonder, sir, can you help me just a little bit, sir, to get home to stroke that old white head before he passes on? That would have elicited tears from Cathedral Mountain, especially outside the door of a Canadian Legion hall on a Friday night.

Balladeer: Each man had his own nickname and his own set of stories, and they used to tell them around the fires in the jungles, and you knew damn well they had made them up or stolen them from somebody else.

Quiet man: I'd improvise my story, I'd elaborate on parts, I'd turn on the steam.

Quiet woman: He was a great liar. And, as a consequence, he was never short of money.

Quiet man: I never paid for a ride, even a five-cent streetcar ride, to get me out on the highway. I always had a little story, a tale of woe.

Quiet woman: And he had a voice that could sing to the angels.

Quiet man: I never paid for a meal, even in Chinese restaurants with sloping floors and stove-grease caked on the ceilings. Fancy restaurants I'd get taken to by important gentlemen who'd picked me up on the highway. Thank you, sir, thank you.

Balladeer: And I'd think I'd heard that same story in Brandon or Winnipeg or Toronto, and I'd get up and, sure enough, there would be the same hobo telling his same little pack of stories.

Quiet man: I never worked. During the Depression a lovely woman befriended me in her little home in Regina.

Quiet woman: I used to look at his hands and say they were the hands of a concert pianist.

Quiet man: She was a lovely woman, and an excellent cook, and she was sorry to see me go.

Quiet woman: He had blond hair in those days, with big blue eyes and a face as shiny as the polished buttons on a Dutchman's vest and a gift of the gab which would melt the heart of a woman or a man of stone before they were 18 bars into the melody.

Quiet woman & quiet man: "Down With All The Rascals."

Balladeer: In every story the teller was the hero or the big shot. The joke or the trick was never on him. Never.

Quiet man: I did very well, but things were simpler then. I do well today too. I could be living in a fine apartment. I have good clothes stored with friends in Calgary, Vancouver, Winnipeg, Toronto. I can stay with any of them, any time. But I prefer this life of the road. I bum and hobo and tramp, but I am not a bum, a hobo nor a tramp. I am a man highly tuned to his five senses.

SCENE TWENTY-ONE: ONE MAN KILLS ANOTHER

Hobo: I saw one man kill another man one night in a jungle at Kamloops in British Columbia. It wasn't about food or money either, let me tell you. One fellow said Roosevelt was president of the United States and another said no, it was Mr Coolidge. One thing led to another, they always do. The Roosevelt man grabbed the other fellow and threw him.

Girls: Go to sleep you weary hobo ...

Hobo: He fell and his head hit the iron arrangement we had to keep our pots over the fire.

Girls: Let the towns drift slowly by ...

Hobo: It appeared to me the iron point end went into his ear –

Girls: Can't you hear the steel rails humming ...

Hobo: Anyway it killed him or we thought so –

Girls: That's a hobo's lullaby ...

Hobo: Certainly appeared dead to me –

(*Sound effects: train in the distance.*)

Girls: Do not think about tomorrow ...

Hobo: The Roosevelt man took him up to the tracks –

Girls: Let tomorrow come and go ...

Hobo: and soon a freight came along and squished his head to nothing.

Girls: Tonight you're in a nice warm boxcar ...

Hobo: So where was your evidence?

Girls: Safe from all the wind and snow ... so go to sleep you weary hobo ...

Hobo: I reckon 50 men saw that killing, if one saw it –

Girls: Let the towns drift slowly by ...

Hobo: To this day that was a drunk asleep laying his head on the rail.

(*Sound effects: the train arrives and passes.*)

Girls: Don't you hear the steel rails humming, that's a hobo's lullaby ...

Young girl: I remember going to the Moncton Station one night to meet Daddy as he was coming back from somewhere, and there was this freight train coming in, from Montreal, I guess. And these young boys, young men, were jumping off the box cars and running. There was this friend of ours, a neighbour, a very good friend of ours and I always thought the world of him, and there he was chasing these kids, you know, with a great big club and he was a great big brute of a man, but I had only seen the gentle side, and I saw him chasing these kids and really hitting them with this stick, and I just couldn't believe my eyes. You see, he worked for the railway. This was his job. Such a kind and gentle man, with his family, with his neighbourhood, the kids, I can still see this man striking out with that club of his. Like that and that and that. Horrible. I could never understand it, never.

Balladeer: I know the police cause you trouble –
They cause trouble everywhere –
But when you die and go to heaven,
There'll be no policemen there.

Salesman: I wasn't there, but I heard about it plenty. There was this railroad cop missing at Regina, and they got some of the crews out searching the empty cars in the yards. They found him, nailed up just like Christ was, and his own billy club had been rammed up his ass. We often wondered if they did that to him while he was still alive or after he had died. The whole think was hushed up. Let me tell you, there were railroad cops and railroad cops, but some of those guys who worked for the CPR were the meanest bastards on the face of the earth.

All (singing):

Go to sleep you weary hobo,
Let the towns drift slowly by,
Can't you hear the steel rails humming –
That's a hobo's lullaby.

SCENE TWENTY-TWO: THE MISSUS SAID

Farmer: It was after the third bad year
But somehow, we got through that winter and lit out for
The Okanagan Valley in the spring.
Sold what stock we could,
Gave the rest away,
Put two trunks on the car –
You couldn't give the stuff away –
We left everything behind, and yet
The missus she never looked back, just straight ahead
Down the road. ...

Farm wife: Allan, I just want to walk into an orchard and reach up and pick a nice, ripe peach off a branch. And that's all I want.

Farmer (Allan): It was she who gave the orders we're leaving it all,
Didn't even sign the papers at the Bank of Montreal.
We crossed the B.C. border, she up and sang;
She was strong and swore she'd never go back.
This has got to be the promised land.
But after some time gone by
She got thinkin' and lonesome for our old prairie home
And her friends; I said we're here to stay
If you go back it's alone. She stayed, we lived a
Goodly life at home ...

Strong woman: I remember my garden. Every year I tried a garden, radishes, lettuce, beets, peas, the few things a woman puts in. One year it blew, all the time, and when it was not blowing too strongly I'd go out and do some hoeing. I'd put a dish towel soaked in water around my mouth, like I was a bank robber, and then I'd rub vaseline into my nostrils. It was supposed to stop dust pneumonia, stopping the dust from getting into your lungs. That killed people, you know. So there I was, with my Jesse James mask and my nostrils half plugged with vaseline, hoeing away, but it never was any use. Everything just grew a little and then died.

Farmer: But the wife she up and died on me three years ago;
You could say that I miss her.

SCENE TWENTY-THREE: THE POKER GAME

Balladeer: There was sort of an informal group, a bunch of us, management at a lower level than plant superintendent, and we used to meet and drink a bit and play poker, and it was a good bunch to belong to and I enjoyed it.

Salesman: Well, Bert, I'm going to trim off some more fat this week.

Balladeer: That might have been a foundry or a sawmill.

Young man: How many?

Salesman: Ten sawyers and half a dozen sizers.

Young man: Okay, Harry, let me know if there's a ruckus and, if not, I'll wait a week and match you.

Balladeer: I saw maybe 15 or 20 of my good friends dealing in men's lives, and doing it just like they were raising each other at stud poker.

Farmer: I'm asking my shippers to take an eight per cent cut.

Balladeer: He meant he was telling them there would be an eight per cent cut. No ifs, ands, or buts. No union, so bugger you. If it worked out, then the next guy would do it, and in a month the whole industry in southern New Brunswick would have shippers making eight per cent less a shift, and in another month that rate would be standard throughout the Maritimes. See how easy it worked?

Girl: I knew one man, a wholesaler in fruit and vegetables, and he did very well, one of those fellows who'd do well in a roaring blizzard in the Arctic. He just had the knack for it. He threw big parties. This fellow would make his office staff girls come to these parties and act as maids in black dresses with frilly white aprons; and the men, yes, men with families, they had to come and serve as bartenders and waiters. Free. Not a drink for them, only what they could steal, or sneak off. If that party went on until two a.m. then they still had to be at work at eight the next morning, and as I recall the last streetcar stopped running at 1:45 so we had to walk home.

Young man: You got any pacers?

Farmer: I got a beaut, a Swede, no more brains than a keg of nails, but fast! You stay with him or you die.

Young man: Can I borrow him a week? I need a speed-up on the line.

Farmer: Borrow?

Salesman: Sack a foreman so Jack can get him at 10 per cent off.

Farmer: Done?

Young man: Done.

Farmer: Done.

Quiet woman: We moved to Montreal in 1933 and found what we were looking for the first day, a perfectly lovely house in Westmount. There were houses you could buy everywhere. I phoned an employment agency and told them I wanted some staff and told them I knew nothing about running a house, simply nothing. I wanted the best servants they could find. When our furniture moved in, this agency had people for us: The chef got $40 a month and his board and room. My maid got $30 and board and room. The first domestic maid got $25 and the second maid got $15. The gardener, and he was the chauffeur too, got $25. The laundress got $2 a day and she scrubbed by hand and ironed by hand and she lived at home. I paid her carfare too – 10 cents a day. Perfectly ridiculous isn't it? Buying a human being. Nobody thought anything of it.

Balladeer: What about the legal minimum?

Farmer: That's per week. Look, how many hours in a piece of string?

Salesman: 48.

Young man: 60.

Salesman: 80.

Farmer: So what's a week?

Balladeer: What if they take it to the wage board?

Farmer: The board'll make up the difference. It's got to make up the difference otherwise there'll be 30 more of my piece-workers on the dole.

Balladeer: The government subsidizing the shop owner and him still selling his product at the same price, and the customer still buying it at that price and paying taxes to subsidize that shop owner. The whole game was rigged.

Farmer: If you're not screwing the government and the employee and the customer with the same screw, then you're a schmuck.

Balladeer: What's a schmuck?

Young man: A guy who ain't smart.

Salesman: Like us.

Balladeer: Just a bunch of good lads so eager to get ahead that they never thought of the mass misery they were causing. And if I had once said: "You rotten sons of bitches!" then I would have been out, blackballed, out. There was nothing I could do. Tens.

Salesman: Jacks.

Young man: Aces.

Farmer: Full house.

Salesman/Young man: Shit!

SCENE TWENTY-FOUR: THE WAITRESS

Strong woman: There I was, a better cook than most 19-year-olds, fairly pleasant looking and a very, very good Scots name which made me respectable: McIntyre. The owner, he could have been Greek or Syrian, smooth, olive and oily skin, a most objectionable little creep, he lived with his wife and kids in an apartment up above, he hired me on the spot. A dollar a day, my supper, and all the tips I could make. Tips? You gotta be kidding. This was 1934. Anyway, he showed me how to work the till and waved up to where the menu was printed on the wall. The second night he came down at 11:30, checked me out; he even counted the meat patties in the fridge to make sure the day man wouldn't be pulling a fast one. Then he called me into the little storeroom in the back, pushed me up against the wall, lifted my dress, pulled down my panties, and there it was. There, just as calmly as I'm telling you, he shoved it into me. I admit it wasn't my first time but I've never been more surprised in all my life. In fact, since that day I can't say that anything has surprised me all that much. There it was, rape, whichever way you look at it, and I just stood there and took it. That gives you some idea how badly I needed that job. My poor mother – she would've died. Anyway, he was out in a few seconds, over with. He said to get myself decent and walked out, and I followed, and he said, well, that was part of the job. That's what he said, getting screwed was part of the job. Then he took out his wallet, handed me a dollar. Now, I couldn't figure out, was he paying me this dollar for screwing me and I was working for nothing and that made me a whore, or was he paying me this dollar for my seven hours and I was opening up for him for nothing because I thought he was kind and generous, and that made me an idiot. Something to think about.

SCENE TWENTY-FIVE: DOTTIE MCLAREN AND THE BANKS

Young girl: I was a junior teller in a bank in Kingston and my name was Dottie McLaren then. Banks were terrible places to work then. If you know a man today who was a manager or an accountant in a bank in the Hungry 30s, you take a good look at him because he will not be what he seems to be. Underneath whatever he appears to be you will find a cruel man dedicated to a cruel system.

Song:
Cold cold money runs this town and turns everybody around,
Working for their ticket in the sweepstakes.
Every time a man turns round another payment must be found.
And you know he's sworn and bound to be a law-abiding man.
What do you think it is keeps him going?
What do you think it is keeps him going?

Quiet woman: Any one of us would have said we had socialist leanings, if not outright communist sympathies. We were young and élite ... the chosen few who could go to university ... and believe me there were bloody few of us in those days. Far into the night, until dawn we'd talk, talk, talk ... tea and cinnamon toast ... taking the world apart and putting it together. God, but we were sweet, young people, so naïve, beautiful in our simplicity. Even our stupidity was something very clean and appealing. We were that fortunate part of the generation between 18 and 25. And there was, for us, no Depression in Canada, no Indian problem, no French problem. We would graduate with honours *and* go into the best universities *and* take our rightful place *in* Canada. I realize that only people around 40 or 50 – say 50 – and only those of that class (that upper middle class we belonged to) will understand what it is I'm saying. Probably, my own little group from those late, pre-war years at the University of Toronto will not even recognize themselves now. Occasionally, I see one ... a couple of women keep popping up in the society pages ... on committees. Do you see what I mean?

Song:
It was just the other day
I heard an old hobo say
Anyone who thinks it's fun ain't been a farmer.
What do you think it is keeps him going?
What do you think it is keeps him going?

Hobo: Various agencies, church groups and the like treated Saskatchewan like a disaster area, which it was, and they used to gather together car loads of food and clothing in Ontario and ship it west. Well, one day, this carload of dried codfish came in. Ever seen the stuff? Well, this was tied together with twine in stacks, like shingles. 'Fact some folks said it looked like shingles. 'Fact there was a story around that old Jack McCormick had actually tried to shingle his outhouse with this codfish; but the nails bent. Anyway, it was a good laugh.

Song:
What do you think it is keeps him going?
What do you think it is keeps him going?

SCENE TWENTY-SIX: THE COUTEAUS

Farm wife: I knew this one family who lived across the street from us, the Couteaus. And their children would just walk into our house, and we'd do the same. The Couteaus, they were good to me. I was like one of their own. And they were good to each other, too, always smiling privately like they enjoyed one another. Of course, my family knew the Couteaus were in trouble. But still Mrs Couteau always had plenty of cookies on hand, and she'd give us milk and cookies, and sit with us and sip her tea – how she loved her tea. And then there was always Mr Couteau teasing us and smoking his pipe and joking as if he hadn't a care in the world. I liked going to that house. But this one day I walked in, the Couteau kids were all in the kitchen, kind of huddled there not saying anything, and out of the bedroom were coming the sounds of the most terrible fight.

Quiet woman (Mrs Couteau): No! I will not understand! How could you? How could you do it?

Farmer (Mr Couteau): I did it, that's all!

Mrs Couteau: How dare you!

Mr Couteau: Mind your own business!

Mrs Couteau: It is my business! Mine and the children!

Mr Couteau: Ten cents.

Mrs Couteau: Milk is 10 cents! Cod liver oil is 10 cents! But, tobacco –

Mr Couteau: It's my goddamn tobacco!

Mrs Couteau: Pig!

Mr Couteau: Go to hell!

Farm wife: Mr. Couteau had done the shopping and that day and he had bought himself a package of tobacco. Ten cents. That was the argument.

Mrs. Couteau: Here we are taking money from the county and everyone on the street knows it and you go out and buy tobacco!

Farm wife: That was what it was: they were on the dole, and that was the most terrible and humiliating experience of all. Trying to live on the few cents a day they were given and still keep up a front of being one of the town's most important families.

Mr Couteau: All right. I'll never buy tobacco again as long as I live!

Mrs Couteau: You'd better not!

Mr Couteau: But I won't buy tea, either!

Mrs Couteau: My tea!

Mr Couteau: My tobacco, your tea! Not one dime's worth.

Farm wife: That's what I remember about the Depression: two lovely people at each other's throats.

Young girl: I came home from school one day and told my mother that a little Italian girl in my class couldn't hold her pencil right because her knuckles were split and bleeding because of the cold. No mitts, you see, Connie has no mitts.

Strong woman: Give her your mitts.

Young girl: What about me?

Strong woman: Give that poor child your mitts. Leave them in her desk, if you have to.

Young girl: That's when my mother started knitting mitts, unravelling old sweaters, anything woollen, rewinding that wool and knitting mitts: big ones, small ones, and I gave them out. Mother, I can see her yet sitting by the radiator and knitting away. She did a pair of mitts a day and eventually it got so that every poor kid in our district had some, but mother just kept on knitting. She did it till the year of her death: 15 years later! You see, it had become an obsession.

Hobo: The day of the funeral, in fact when nobody was at home because they were all at the funeral, I saw a man go up the walk of that house and stand there, pretending to ring the doorbell. He looked around and didn't see me, and then he took the black wreath off that front door and slipped it under his coat and walked away. I followed him on my bike, and he went over a couple of blocks and into a house, and then he came out with a hammer and a nail, and he hung that wreath on his own front door. I told my dad and he checked and found out that that man's wife died the night before.

Young man: I was walking back after trying to find some sort of work, and I saw a woman get out of this big car and stuff a lot of letters into a mailbox. I walked up to it, propped open the slot with a chunk of ice, lit my hankie with a wooden match and, when it was going good, I stuffed it into the mailbox and walked away. Nobody saw me do it. I didn't feel any better. I was just as cold and hungry as ever. But I had dropped a blazing hankie in among His Majesty's mail, and that is a serious federal offence, and I could have gone to the penitentiary for a long time. Why did I do it? To this day I really don't know.

Song:
Take me somewhere far away from this madness,
To a place where the sun stays as well as the moon;
Bright jewelled eyes laugh at my madness,
This no-promise living it still makes her blue.
Oh the sadness of parting we all know in our hearts,
The absence of touching that seldom seems to show in the dark,
And all these deep water feelings still spinning me silently upward ...

SCENE TWENTY-SEVEN: THE RELIEF HOME

Young girl: We were in what was called a "relief house," everybody was destitute, and your examiner or inspector or relief officer or whatever he was called usually came about every six months. Not so with Mum.

Farm wife (Mum): Joan.

Young girl (Joan): Yes, Mum.

Mum: You take your homework to the library and stay for about an hour and a half.

Joan: Our relief officer came every month and sometimes every two or three weeks.

Mum: Joan.

Joan: Yes, Mum.

Mum: Here's a nickel for the show. You can sit through it twice.

Joan: He was short and had a belly and, oh God!, he was enough to put a woman off men for life. When I'd come home from school or when my sister Eva would come back from looking for a job, he'd be there. It got so he'd be there a lot.

Mum: Eva.

Strong woman (Eva): Yes, Mum.

Mum: Take Joan with you, please.

Eva: But, Mum –

Mum: Please.

Joan: When I needed a winter coat and galoshes, he signed the chit without a word, and we got other things too. A special allowance of milk, I think, and lots of clothes, and extra food, and this man arranged so that Eva and I could go to a Fresh-Air Camp at the Lake.

Song:
Oh the sadness of parting we all know in our hearts,
And the absence of touching that seldom seems to show in the dark ...

Eva: Joan?

Joan: Yes.

Eva: You asleep?

Joan: Are you?

Eva: Joan?

Joan: Yes.

Eva: I'm a grown woman now.

Joan: Sixteen ain't grown.

Eva: It's enough, Joan?

Joan: Yes.

Eva: Why don't he try for me?

Joan: Do you want him to?

Eva: I'd do it.

Joan: He smells.

Eva: I'd do it, though.

Joan: Why?

Eva: To help Mum; give her a rest.

Joan: We ought to write a letter.

Eva: Who to?

Joan: To the relief people. To tell them what that man's doing because what he's doing is again the law and it's wrong.

Eva: So's what we're doing.

Joan: What are we doing?

Eva: If what he's doing is against the law then taking his stuff, that's against the law.

Joan: Is it wrong?

Eva: It's right, but it's against the law.

Song:
Take me somewhere far away from his madness,

To a place where the sun stays as well as the moon,
A place where the sun stays as well as the moon,
A place where the sun stays as well as the moon. ...

SCENE TWENTY-EIGHT: FRONTYARD AUCTION

Song:
Come to the auction sale,
You cannot possibly fail
To find a bargain
When a man's life is sold
For 25 cents, a box of books
He never did get to read.

Hobo: Ever hear of front yard auctions? I don't think they're legal now.

Song: Come to the auction sale ...

Hobo: When a family was evicted, the landlord had the right to sell their possessions to get his back rent and, boy, some of those landlords didn't have any scruples. It was murder.

Young man: That night a bunch of the boys went around to this man's house on the edge of town, a big house with trees all around and when he came to the door nobody said anything. They just grabbed him and dragged him down his driveway to where the tar was. Hot, but not burning hot. And they tore off his clothes, and over him from head to foot went that tar. By the way, nobody was drunk, not one. I said tar and feathering, but it was really tar and gravelling. One lad put a rope around this bastard's feet and another under his arms and they rolled him back and forth, pulled him up and down in the loose gravel and dust of his own lane. You never, never saw such a mess! Then I got down on one knee and said real close to this bastard's face: don't you raise that widow's rent one red cent. He never did.

Salesman: No, we never thought of the poor people. The reliefers. We'd see them on these make-work jobs, cleaning up back lanes, digging dandelions, hauling coal. I never thought to pity them or help them. Far as I knew, nobody did. They were just there. I can't remember ever asking myself what made such poverty, such conditions. I was up and they were down. No, I can't really say that I had a social conscience. Of course, you must realize that such a phrase had not even been invented then.

Song:
Think of all the money made in lumber,
Think of all the tears that once were shed,
Think of who got gold and count the number,
Of people whose own lives they never led.

When the union's strong – it won't take long –
We ride the tide of time;
I don't want to hear your lie,
Oh no, no, no, no,
I don't want to hear your lie.

SCENE TWENTY-NINE: THE RELIEF CAMP

Quiet man: I am one who is clothed and fed and housed by the Government. I am wondering what the world is doing. I am one apart and I am one of many.

Hobo: These federal camps were voluntary, you didn't have to go, but if you didn't like starving and being hammered about by every cop from Kingston, Ontario, to Vancouver Island, you went. A lot did.

Farmer: Across the country, most mostly in the West, there were 10 or 15,000 men in these camps.

Young man: I read once that they figured about 200,000 men were in them, all told, in five years.

Salesman: That's 200,000 young men who were really pissed off at society, the Government, the politicians, the army way of doing things.

Quiet man: Who am I? My name is William George Rundle. I am a university graduate. On all sides of me are men from every walk of life. The creeds and beliefs and religions of all the nations, all the professions, all the trades, all the labouring classes are gathered here. We are complete.

Hobo: They had turned the running of these camps over to the Department of National Defence and, while the guys in charge weren't army, they had been in the last war. And let me tell you, a guy who has been a captain or a sergeant-major has a hell of a time forgetting he was a captain or a sergeant-major.

Farmer: We were paid 20 cents a day. 20 cents a day. I've told this to people today and they always say, "You mean 20 cents an hour, don't you?" and I'd say no, 20 goddamned cents a goddamned day!

Young man: There was one guy in charge at that Hope camp who used to call us slaves. "OK, slaves, off your arses! We're going to cut trail today!" he'd say, and that was really what we were.

Salesman: The 20 cents a day was an insult. It was the worst part of it. But you forget that quickly. I only think of it four or five times a day now.

Quiet man: In our tent city set off in the Saskatchewan prairie, we are a community to ourselves. We could cook, we could tailor, we could teach, we could fashion our own tools, we could design our own power plant and we could build it. And we do none of these things. We sit in the prairie, unused, alone, hidden.

Hobo: It was the monotony, the jail of it all.

Farmer: It was a jail. What else could you call it? Sure, all the fresh air and sunshine you could stand, but no women, no music, no streets, no people, no place to buy anything, no sound of streetcars or kids playing.

Quiet man: We rise and work and eat and receive hospital treatment and retire to the sound of the bugle. Is it an irony in our camp that the Last Post is played instead of Lights Out? The last note floats high into the air and dies in the hills. The prairie folds over us. Every man lies awake and stares into the night. Oh God, what next?

SCENE THIRTY: NASTURTIUMS

Strong woman: I see a rutted road between two hills, leading to a cattle gate into a barnyard littered with rusting equipment. There is a house, unpainted the way they always were, and a barn whose boards have bleached in the sun. But on the sheltered side of the house, there were the nasturtiums. Blazing with colour. That's the farm at Crestwynd in Saskatchewan which was home to my sister and her husband, three nephews and two nieces until my sister died of tuberculosis. From overwork. She died years ahead of her time. And when she went, the nasturtiums didn't get tended and watered again and the dust moved in and buried what was left and the family just moved out and left that whole section of land to the grasshoppers.

Song:
Well the grasshoppers had nothing left to eat,
So the buggers ate the cushions off the tractor seat.
Mother tried hard but couldn't understand
How a good God could lay such a curse on the land.

Well the dry dust blew all the hoppers away
And I'll never forget that dirty day
The duststorm left a gopher in the sky,
Still digging a hole in the clouds so dry.
Yup some went crazy, were bound to go,
While others stayed home with the radio.

SCENE THIRTY-ONE: GO NORTH! THE MOSQUITOES

Salesman: Northern Alberta! Free land! Rich land! Land so rich it'll grow country gravel!

Hobo: Of course it was good land. It still is good land. But, what kind of sappy government, or the land agents in it, would tell people to go up into that country?

Salesman: Farmers! Immigrants! Why stick around on burnt-out prairie farms? In Northern Alberta there is deep loam and sunshine and rain when you need it! Good land! Free land!

All: *Go North!*

Hobo: Mister, that was pretty powerful bait. In the land office a clerk just looked at the wife and me –

Balladeer: Alberta.

Hobo: Yes.

Balladeer: Land?

Quiet woman: Yes.

Balladeer: It's not my job to tell you to turn around and go back home please, because where your home is ain't no more, probably. So here it is: Northern Alberta. All this area was taken up long ago. All this is open. Take your pick.

Hobo: Now I ask you: how the heck are you going to pick out a farm by pointing and saying "there"? But that's the way it seemed to be done.

Balladeer: OK, I'll give you a break. A fellow was in here yesterday and he's packing and leaving this area. He's leaving a house and a barn and you might find a few pieces of equipment he didn't unload.

Hobo: We'll take it.

Balladeer: She's yours.

Quiet woman: Why'd that man leave his homestead?

Balladeer: Wasn't tough enough. Didn't have enough money. Didn't know how to farm that kind of country. Just lost heart. A few other reasons. Do you want it?

Quiet woman: Looks like your dad is back from town. All right, set the table.

Hobo: You better get young Jim and the girls and the whole family, for it's time we held a council of war. Now, foreclosure is coming on awful quickly and the government says there's good land up north, so ...

Quiet woman: ... We'd better go.

Young man: Can't be rougher than here.

Quiet man: Well, I've really got to like this district ... it's my life ... So we head north. How?

Hobo: Wagon travel.

Song:
Mama said we can't stay no more
Got to leave the land, close and lock the door,
Leave our friends, pack and move away
Maybe we can all come back some day.
Sally, Ray and June rode in the cab
Me and Arthur huddled in the back ...

Hobo: If you were charitable you could call these Goddamn things roads! Freeze in winter, and in summer ... muskeg.

Song:
The only time I heard my mama cry,
The only time since my daddy died,
As we drove away in the pouring rain
Oh sad and sorry day to be pushed to move away ...

Quiet woman: Another wagon up ahead –

Young man: They've pulled off the road –

Hobo: Howdy, can we give you a hand?

Farmer: No, we've quit, had enough. Sell you the whole outfit – horses and all – for $10.

Hobo: Well, I'm afraid the team is in no better shape than ours.

Farmer: Well, go ahead. It's not the muskeg that gets you, but the critters that live in it.

Hobo: Goddamn mosquitoes!

Farmer: They're God's punishment.

Song:
My dad had said when I leave this earth
This farm is ours you know we give it birth;
Please never let this old place come to harm
John, keep the land son, for Lord's sake keep the farm ...

Young man: They're having the blood sucked right out of them, Dad.

Quiet woman: They're too thin.

Hobo: Can't afford to give them grain.

Quiet woman: We've already dumped off the cream separator, a chest of drawers, a few sacks of coal and other things ...

Young man: All the mosquitoes in the world are always right where we are.

Hobo: Don't worry. They're as bad a few hundred yards away. Whoa Daisy!

Young man: You crazy bitch ... she's gone insane.

Hobo: Black with skeeters and red with blood. We're not going to make it. The horses just don't have it in them.

Quiet woman: We can camp here a few days. There's pea vine and vetch for fodder and that creek over there is probably boiling with hungry jack-fish.

Farmer: Smudge fires for the horses, boys –

Young man: We'll slather then with mud to protect 'em too; feed them up with some oats – they'll be OK.

Quiet woman: They're not diseased. Just loss of blood and not enough to eat.

Hobo: No, mother, I just figure both them horses have decided to die. Lost the will to live, and it's the mosquitoes doing it.

Farmer: How do you know?

Hobo: 'Cause it ain't difficult to feel the same way.

Song:
The only time I heard my daddy cry,
The only time since his own daddy died –

Quiet woman: The breeze is up now, Dad, it'll blow the insects away and make it easier. We'll go on.

Hobo: Well, it's three days they've had the mud, the smoke, and the wind; and most of our grain. Time to move.

Young man: But they're still down.

Hobo: I'm gonna boot your Goddamn rumps from here to the Great Slave Lake, but you're gonna get movin. Daisy! ... Christ, she's dead.

Young man: So's the gelding.

Quiet woman: On the same day. It's like being stranded on a rock in the ocean, a bare rock, and watching the last ship in the world sail away.

Hobo: Old girl, that ends it. We come into this world with nothing and at 44 years old, you're back to nothing.

Quiet woman: We'll pack some pots, pans, food, clothes and the rifle and leave the whole kit and kaboodle at the side of the road.

Song:
The Sheriff's men had a paper law
Signed and sealed by our own banker's claw,
Said that we, we had to move along,
Mama needed help, she didn't feel too strong,
And all the children's sadness it just seemed so wrong.

Salesman: Jesus Christ, you been walking 17 days? God you were way off the main road. Miles off, shooting off to a place nobody goes.

Hobo: My fault, should've read the sun.

Balladeer: If you'd waited 'till winter, some lumberjacks with sleighs would have come along.

Hobo: You mean that was a logging road?

Farmer: No farm land up that way at all.

Salesman: I suppose you can't find that a laugh.

Hobo: No, I lost two good horses and all my patience finding out. But I'll tell ya from now on, I'll kill every mosquito that lands within half a mile of me. I'm pure hell on skeeters.

Song:
The only time I heard my mama cry,
The only time since my daddy died,
As we drove away in the pouring rain
Oh sad and sorry day to be pushed to move away ...

Farmer: Me? I'm a Métis: French-Canadian grandfather, Cree-woman grandmother. I'm half-breed: my kids, my grandchildren, all born shit. Everybody north of Prince Albert is Métis. Portuguese on the railway gangs, they're darker than we are but they don't take this shit. Yah, the Dirty 30s. Indians, they hate us; white guys, they hate us. Those days everybody had to have somebody to hate, and we were it. Same today. Us? We didn't hate nobody. Same today. So I hope those Red Power guys sure beat the shit out of those government guys, the bunch of rotten bastards!

Strong woman: R.B. Bennett said nobody in Canada was dying of starvation and if he meant like Biafra kids with bloated bellies, no, not that kind of starvation. But I know one family which lost three children from hunger. Lack of food, malnutrition, then diarrhea which they couldn't fight because they were so weak – and that to me is dying of starvation. They were my sister's kids, and every day if Bennett is in hell I curse him a thousand times, even today, and if he is in heaven, I curse him a thousand times and wish he was in hell. I will do it until I die.

Song: *Bennett Buggy*
Get out the Bennett Buggy,
Let's go for a ride in the lovely countryside,
Two horsepower, five miles an hour
When Dobbin and Dolly get back to work again.

Make your own Bennett Buggy,
Put a tongue into the chassis, you've an oatburner classy,
With horses pulling double you'll have no engine trouble,
And you'll get back from town by next Monday night
Oh ... you don't need no gas ...
Just slap that horse's ass, R.B.

SCENE THIRTY-TWO: OTTAWA TREK

Farmer or Balladeer: I can't remember exactly why we left that relief camp and went on strike in Vancouver, but it had something to do with chicken-shit regulations.

Young man: I've never considered the Regina Riots and the box car march anything more than a skirmish.

Farmer or Balladeer: We met Art Evans. He was a real hard nut, but he could organize. And he was doing something, and that was more than anybody else was doing.

Young man: The communists thought they had everything going for them and really they had nothing.

Farmer or Balladeer: He said: the only way to get anything done was to go down to Ottawa and see R.B. Bennett.

Young man: Most of the Reds were Ukrainians and Jews.

Farmer/Balladeer: So, about a thousand of us left Vancouver, and another thousand or so joined us along the way.

Young man: They could change their names all they liked, but they couldn't change the shape of their heads.

Farmer/Balladeer: We spent one day in Kamloops, got a soup kitchen set up and tobacco passed out and it went OK.

Young man: There were Jews, Kikes, Yids, Hunkies, Bohunks, Hoonyaks, Ukranskes, call them anything you like. They could be spotted a mile away.

Farmer/Balladeer: We spent another day in Golden, a divisional point and the people were really nice.

Young man: No damn bohunk is going to tell me to salute the Red Flag and sing the Internationale.

Farm/Balladeer: Calgary was OK too. In fact, things were just going along just like free beer out of a spigot until the CPR announced they weren't going to let us ride their freights any more.

Young man: No Montreal Jew is going to push me around and say I have to spit on the Union Jack.

Farmer/Balladeer: That was a laugh. Look, look at it this way. We were disciplined. Art Evans told us it had to be that way: that being polite and organized and neat even in our old duds was the way to gain public support. So I always figured the Regina Riot was what today you would call a snow job. A police riot and against us, the trekkers.

Quiet man: I'm sorry the policeman was killed and some of our boys got arrested, and it made a lot of noise across the country, but it was a snow job. Old R.B. Bennett wanted a showdown and he got it. Guns were firing. Guess who had the guns? He wanted to discredit the trek and he did. Oh, yes, he succeeded. We were just a bunch of Reds, carrying the card. It wasn't like that at all. We were just a bunch of ordinary guys, but Bennett stuck the label on us and it stuck. He did a lot of harm that day, that guy.

Farmer/Balladeer: So the next year, along with dozens of boys from the Trek, I joined the Mackenzie-Papineau Battalion that went to aid the Spanish Republic. Why not? Bennett had already taught us all we needed to know about fascism.

Hobo: Too much has been spoken and written about us, and not enough, if you get what I mean. We were just a bunch of guys who got caught in the middle: the wrong war, no bands played for us. People got up in Parliament and called us Communists. Bolsheviks. One fellow said we had gone to Spain to fight for the Red Army, and Canada was best rid of us. Now, there were some Communists in with us, sure, nobody will deny that. But there were a lot, too, who just joined up for the hell of it. They were tired of bumming around the country without a bean in their pockets. But, if you take the lot of us, if there ever was a bunch in Canada at that time that had a social conscience, a unity of purpose, a sense of what was right and what had to be done to defeat wrong, then we were it. There's no sense talking about it. Nobody remembers and I forget a lot. I remember a few names, the battles, and I remember we were treated like shit when we did get home. Here was a bunch of guys in 1939 who were the only soldiers in Canada, the only battle-tested men under modern conditions. Here we were in 1939, we were tough and we knew all the tricks, but they didn't want us in the army, the Canadian army. We were subversives. Like the guy said in Parliament, we fought in the Red Army. That is pure bull. We were treated like rats. But we died like men.

Salesman: Start soccer leagues right across Canada. That will get the young men out of the jungles and off the streets where they look bad for business. Get the lads out playing soccer. Then they won't go round talking revolution.

Strong woman: The Depression. William Lyon Mackenzie King. Sure I remember. They called him the father of Modern Canada. William Lyon Mackenzie King. Well I thought he was a rat. R.A.T.! I've never trusted a politician since – and I'm 85.

Quiet man: Then there was this fellow going around Ontario with this economic theory that, if every family spent half a dollar a day more, then Canada would be able to spend its way out of the Depression. They booed him in Toronto, and threw tomatoes at him in Hamilton, and somebody threw a dead cat at him in Windsor. They sure were waiting for him in Windsor.

Don't rush, lads! There's room for all of you! The army will get you off the street.

Farm wife: There was every type. There were men out of the jungles. There was men in business suits and college kids. There was old guys just itching to get in, guys from the last war, and they was the ones who made sense. They knew how to carry out orders, how to form lines, and already they had a new look to them, straighter backs, you might say.

Salesman (*Singing:*) Come on boys and join the army ...

Farmer (*Singing:*) I just want to get away from the wife

Salesman (*Singing:*) Three square meals a day ...

Young man (*Singing:*) And that lousy job.

Salesman (*Singing:*) No need to worry, nothing to pay ...

Hobo (*Singing:*) That shit of a boss.

Salesman (*Singing:*) And some time tomorrow, we're sending you away ...

Quiet man: I ain't patriotic. I just want some good clothes and a hot shower and three decent meals a day and a few dollars for tobacco and beer, and that's all I want.

Salesman: For the war is sure to come ...

Farm wife: One college kid wanted to impress his girl and he was the biggest fool of all.

Salesman: Bringing work for everyone ...

Farm wife: Who will fight the hun, hun, hun, hun.
That morning there must have been 500 men or 1,000 lined up about three blocks of curbs away from the armoury, we housewives looked out

our windows, and delivery men came and went while photographers took pictures and the men just sat in the sun, and talked. It was September.

SCENE THIRTY-THREE: LINE UP FOR THE MAN

Quiet man: I remember that line. We didn't do much talking about the war and, if we had known what it was going to be like, I guess, we'd have taken off down that street like a cut cat. I remember how some of the city guys just couldn't believe that we could live like we did on the road, in the jungles.

Young man: Everybody got a ticket with a number on it so there'd be no muscling in on the line; you know, get in first, get the best seat, that sort of thing. If we'd only known, we would have waited a couple of years and some of us would have missed that Hong Kong business, for sure, and Dieppe too.

Farmer: I remember the little girls in their frilly little dresses, and the little boys too, as they went down the street past us guys to their first classes of the year at the school. And one of the guys down the line said to me ...

Hobo: They're starting out on a new life, and so are we.

Farmer: I remember that.

Hobo: It was funny: lining up to get into a war to get yourself killed ...

Farm wife: Anybody who says the war wasn't the end of the Depression just doesn't know what he is talking about, because it was.

Song:
Come on boys and join the army,
Three square meals a day,
No need to worry, nothing to pay.
And some time tomorrow we're sending you away.
For the war has surely come,
Bringing work for everyone,
Who will fight the hun – honey in the hive,
A job for anyone – who's still alive.

Song: *Memories*
Memory stains the pages
Calling out the ages
Time will not leave us alone.

SCENE THIRTY-FOUR: MY SON RAOUL

Quiet woman or Farm wife: My son Raoul came out of school in 1932 when he was 18, and that spring he sat on the verandah where we had a big swing, and I'd hear that swing going creak-creak-creak until it used to drive me mad. Raoul did that for five years, until he was a man of 23, and all the time there was no work. I don't think he ever had a girl. I don't know what he did. He was handsome as Jean Beliveau, and he did nothing. He was a vegetable. That's what his sister called him, and it broke my heart. The ninth of September 1939 he joined the Canadian army. He was killed at Dieppe, the summer of 1942. He was a wonderful soldier, a very good soldier. You see, somebody wanted him. There was something for him to do.

THE END

Jennie's Story

Betty Lambert

Born in Calgary in 1933, Betty Lambert moved to Vancouver to study at the University of British Columbia, and until her death in 1983 taught at Simon Fraser University. She was a prolific writer, whose work includes 75 plays for stage, radio and television. Her work expressed her passionate devotion to women's issues and political justice, focusing on such topics as rape, abortion, and (in *Jennie's Story*) forced sterilization. Her other works for the stage include the comedies *Sqrieux-de-Dieu, Clouds of Glory*, the widely produced children's play *The Riddle Machine*, and a harrowing drama about sexual abuse of children, *Under the Skin*, which was produced posthumously to widespread critical acclaim. *Jennie's Story* was short-listed for the Governor-General's Award for Drama in 1983, and her play *Grasshopper Hill* won the ACTRA Nellie award for best radio drama in 1980.

Jennie's Story was first produced by the New Play Centre at the Canadian Theatre Today Conference in Saskatoon in October 1981.

PRODUCTION
Director / **Jace van der Veen**
Stage Manager / **Paddy McEntee**

CAST
Sherry Bie / Jennie McGrane
Pierre Tetrault / Harry McGrane
Lillian Carlson / Edna Delevault
David Ferry / Father Fabrizeau
Laura Bruneau / Molly Dorval

The CentreStage Company's production of *Jennie's Story* at Toronto's St Lawrence Centre, April–May 1983, featured the following cast:
Nora McLellan / Jennie McGrane
Michael Hogan / Harry McGrane
Clare Coulter / Edna Delevault
William Mockridge / Father Fabrizeau
Denise Naples / Molly Dorval

Director / **Bill Glassco**
Stage Manager / **Sue LePage**

CHARACTERS
Jennie McGrane, about 20 or 21
Harry McGrane, about 35 to 39
Father Edward Fabrizeau, about 35 to 39
Mrs Edna Delevault, Jennie's mother, about 48
Molly Dorval, 15

PLAYWRIGHT'S NOTES
For the legal background for this play, see the Sexual Sterilization Act (Alberta, 1928), especially Section 5, which concerns "multiplication of the evil by the transmission of the disability to progeny." In 1937, just before the time of the play, an amendment was passed, making it possible to sterilize a person without his or her consent, provided consent was given by the appropriate relative or, if the appropriate relative did not exist or was not a resident in Alberta, by the Minister of Health. This law was repealed in 1971.

A similar law existed in British Columbia from 1928 to 1973. Also, sterilization is apparently still being performed in the United Kingdom on the "socially unfit" (see *The Observer*, 15 April 1981, page 6, "The Victims of Britain's Secret Sterilisations").

See also the 1972 white paper on "Protection of Life," working paper 24, chairman Francis C. Muldoon.

The author of the poetry used in the play is Gerard Manley Hopkins.

On page 217, the characters use a "waxing brick." This is a brick wrapped in flannel, used as a buffer.

The "Indian rings" referred to in the play are found in southern Alberta, and also in Saskatchewan, along the river, on buttes. As Harry says in the play, they are often found one day's canoe trip apart. Archaeologists guess the age of the circles to be perhaps 100,000 years, and, because of the placement of larger boulders, that they were used as an almanac of some kind.

Betty Lambert

THE PLACE

The McGrane farm, in the house. There is a kitchen, a porch, an upstairs bedroom. There is a door to the porch, and one to the pantry. A hallway leads to the upstairs and the front room.

THE TIME
1938-9

ACT ONE, SCENE ONE

We first see the bedroom. Jennie *is lighting a kerosene lamp. She stretches like a cat. She gets out of bed unhurriedly, putting on Harry's slippers. Then she puts on Harry's kimono, which is much too large for her. Her hair hangs loose about her head. It is fiery, almost red, and curly; tendrils escape like halo flashes. Although her hair spreads about her face like a halo, there is nothing of the madonna in Jennie – everything she does is sensuous. She is a woman at one with her body. Now she smells the kimono, the smell of Harry. She straightens the bed covers, spreading and then folding back the quilt, ready for Harry in case he should come back to bed. Now she takes the kerosene lamp and comes down into the hall and then into the kitchen. At the entrance to the kitchen she looks at the electric switch, and then up to the bulb hanging from the middle of the ceiling. Emboldened, mischievous, she almost switches it on, then, scared, does not. She puts the kerosene lamp on the table, goes to the first of the two doors, opens it, and looks out toward the bunkhouse. Now she comes back to the range and moves the kettle to the hot part of the top. The range dominates the kitchen. It is big and black and shiny with stove blacking. It is always on. In general, the kitchen has a sense of sparse, spare, house-proud prosperity. There is a sink with a pump attached – very advanced for this time. There are electric wires running up and down the walls – hence the electric light. There is a wooden table, scrubbed bone-white. There is a big leather armchair, placed so Harry can look out the door. A book rack is beside it, with a very few old leather books. The door has two doors – in winter there is a storm door and in summer there is a screen door.* Jennie *lays a starched embroidered table cloth on the table. Now she goes to the pantry and brings back a tray with teacups, saucers, plates, etc. – the best china. She starts to go back to the pantry for the pie but then stops. Billy White has just died.*

Jennie: Domine Jesu Christem Rex gloriae, libera anima omnium fidelium defunctorum de paenis inferni and from the deep pit. Deliver him from the lion's mouth, that Hell may not swallow him up and may he not fall into darkness, but may the holy standard-bearer, Michael, lead him into the holy light ... Poor old Billy.

(*Now* Jennie *goes into the pantry to get the pie, heavy cream, sugar, etc., all quite casually, in spite of the prayer she has just said for the dead. As she comes back, she thinks of Billy's old dog.*)

Jennie: Poor Tuffy, poor old thing.

(Offstage, two men are heard coming up to the porch – Harry McGrane and Father Edward Fabrizeau. The Father is in a navy blue heavy wool overcoat, black suit, and a collar. He wears slip-on rubbers over oxford shoes. Harry is wearing jeans, plaid shirt, a windbreaker, a farmer's cap, and wellington rubbers, which he carefully wipes on a boot scraper outside the door. As Harry comes in he takes off the wellingtons and stands them on a piece of paper. The Father, however, goes to the table and sits. Harry peels off his windbreaker. The Father stays hot and sweaty in his overcoat.)

Harry: *(over the above)* Didn't I say she'd be ready? *(laughs)* Didn't I say she'd know? Jennie always knows. She's like an old pagan lady, my Jennie. I bet she knew before Tuffy did, didn't you, Jennie?

(Jennie is getting the tea ready. No sense of urgency. For instance, she warms the teapot against her own body, liking the feel of the heat, before she empties the pot and puts tea leaves in. Now she gets a bucket from the cupboard under the sink, pours some lye in, gets a rag from under the sink.)

Harry: Oh oh, here she comes with her lye'n water, goingta wipe up your footprints, Father. Should'a warned you, take off your rubbers you enter Jennie's kingdom.

(Jennie wipes up the wet marks from the Father's rubbers.)

Jennie: *(pleased)* Oh, Harry.

Harry: No, she knew before Tuffy did even. Like a cat. Cats know first, Father. Then dogs. I said to the Father, here, you watch now, Jennie'll have something on the table for us, soon's we come in, didn't I, Father?

Father: What's that smell?

Harry: That's Jennie an' her damn lye water, always cleaning. I bet I've got the cleanest outhouse the whole parish.

Father: It must burn the hands.

Jennie: *(wrings out the cloth, puts bucket back under sink, hangs cloth up)* Would you like some pie then?

Father: Like a hospital. It smells like a hospital in here.

Harry: *(sits down at his place at the table)* Pie'd do good. Don't sit there in your coat, Father, you'll get all hot and sweaty and catch your death your way home.

(Harry gets up again, helps the Father out of his coat, and hangs it on back of the third chair. He blows out expansively as he sits down – a long hard night over at last. Jennie starts to cut the pie, then pours milk into the Father's cup.)

Father: I don't take milk any more.

Jennie: Oh, sorry. You allus took milk in first before.

Father: I don't now.

Jennie: (*picks up teacup*) Well, I kin throw it out.

Harry: I'll take it, Jen, not to waste it.

Jennie: No, I'll throw it out. You got your own cup.

(Jennie *takes the* Father's *cup to the sink, pours it out, rinses it in water, dries it on a tea towel. comes back, pours tea into it. Then, she pours milk in* Harry's *cup, then tea. Everything is done with a slowness and a sureness –* Harry *enjoys watching her. The* Father *watches her with frustration and exasperation.*)

Harry: Won't hafta wait anyways.

Jennie: No, that's right. Won't have to wait. (*serves* Harry *a piece of pie*)

Harry: That's one good thing, Father. Won't hafta wait if the Chinook holds. 'D never feel right going in fer Communion knowin' ol' Billy's out back in the woodshed waitin' for the thaw. (*laughs.* Father *looks down and cannot speak.*) Aw, come on, Father. Old Billy was ready to go.

Jennie: (*hovering at the pie plate, ready to serve* Father *a slice if he indicates he wants one*) He was eighty-six, Father.

Harry: 'N if he wasn't ready, he shoulda bin! (*laughs, starts to eat his pie*)

Jennie: (*indicating big stoneware jug with a wooden spoon standing up in it*) There's heavy cream.

Harry: Heavy cream'd go nice, heavy cream'd go good.

(Jennie *ladles the cream onto* Harry's *pie. He indicates more. They laugh at each other for their gluttony.* Jennie *and* Harry *never overtly touch in this scene, but, in their laughter, we know how alive each is to the other.*)

Father: Why was he so afraid to die? He'd done nothin', nothin'!

Harry: (*eating*) May be that's why. I mean, look at it this way, Father, imagine goin' an' nothin' on yer conscience. (*laughs,* Father *looks away.*) I mean, what'd there be to talk about! Father, a man without sin ain't human. Isn't that right?

Jennie: He wasn't scared this afternoon. I played Hearts with him all afternoon.

Harry: Eat some pie, Father. Sit down with us, Jen go on.

Jennie: No, my mother never sat down with her men, and I'll not start. I'll see to my dough.

(Jennie *goes to the warming oven, takes out a bowl of dough, takes it to the*

kneading table, sprinkles flour, kneads and pokes dough, etc. When she is
through, she covers it with a clean tea cloth and puts it back in the warming
oven. Conversation continues through the above actions.)

Harry: 'N they say Black Irish is bad. In my house, Jennie, you can sit
with the men! God, these Frenchies! I will speak with your mother,
Jennie.

Jennie: She never sat down with her men.

Harry: Have some pie. Father, you got a long drive back. (*pause*) I'll clean
him up for you first. (*to* Jennie) You got boiler water hot?

Jennie: Yes.

Harry: (*helps* Father *to a slice of the pie*) Eat up, Father. Drink your tea.
(*pause*) Come to think of it, old Billy had lots on his conscience.

Father: Nothin' venial. Nothin' mortal.

Harry: You call his singing in choir nothin' venial, Father? I call old
Billy's voice in choir venial, Father, venial at the least. (Jennie *chuckles. An*
edge of steel in Harry's *voice*) Drink up your tea, Father, while it's still hot.

Father: You find everythin' amusin', Harry.

Harry: And you take things too serious, Eddie Fabrizeau, and allus did.
(*pause*) Sorry. I mean, *Father.* Father, old Billy was old and he was tired
and he was bored. It was time.

Father: He died afraid on me!

Harry: (*pause*) You had to give him his last rites. That's your job. When a
man hears the last rites, he's bound to get scared. For a bit. It's nothing
you can help.

Father: But just before, he was jokin' with you, laughin' with you.

Harry: Hell, Father, I'm Irish. Here, Jennie, why'n't you turn on the light.
(*gets up, goes to switch beside door to hallway, turns on electric light bulb*)
Here, Father, look at this. (*turns it off, turns it on again*) Jennie won't
touch it. Scared to get a shock.

Father: Electricity? You got electricity in, Harry?

Harry: Damn right. And it's indoor plumbing next. I got it in upstairs too,
in our bedroom, and the small room. For when it's needed. (Harry *looks at*
Jennie. *She smiles, looks down.*) I meant to string it out to the bunkhouse,
fer old Billy. But he come in yesterday. I carried him in. He saw it.

Jennie: Oh, he got such a kick, Father. He lay there like a big baby in
Harry's arms. And he did it hisself, he turned it on, he turned it off. He
was *laughin'*! Fit to beat the band.

Harry: He never let up about it all night neither. He kept sayin', "Where's the light, Harry?" 'cause see (*to* Father) I'd promised him electricity out to the bunkhouse and, jeez, he never forgot nothin', old Billy. "Where's the light, Harry?" (*laughs*)

Father: "Where's the light." Yes. I heard him. I thought he meant somethin' else.

Harry: No! He was holdin' me to my word, see. 'Cause I said I'd string out a wire ta the bunkhouse, "Where's the light. Harry?" (*laughs*) Hell, I'll hafta put a light bulb in the coffin, just for him, he'll curse me from the grave else. (*comes back to the table.* Jennie *pours more tea.* Harry *turns the kerosene lamp down, then blows it out.*) Don't need no kerosene no more, Jen. (*pause*) Here, give us some more a that pie. Nothin' like a dyin' to give a man an appetite! (Father *puts his face in his hands.* Harry, *with embarrassment, tinged with disgust*) Git the man a handkerchief, Jen.

(Jennie *goes into the pantry where the laundry basket is kept, comes back with unironed handkerchief and gives it to the* Father.)

Jennie: It's not ironed. I'm sorry.

(Father *puts handkerchief to his face, tries to control himself.*)

Harry: We kin bury him Wednesday.

Jennie: Yes, and if the Chinook holds, we can get in too, this time. I got a new hat.

Father: (*viciously*) You got a new hat!

Harry: Here, Father.

Father: And you got electricity. And indoor plumbing next. You've done well for yourself, Jennie Delevault.

Harry: Yes, we've done good, Father, ever since you married us. Jennie McGrane and me.

Father: Billy White just died in your bunkhouse. I should think you'd have a prayer to say for his soul.

Jennie: Oh I did it already.

Father: (*pause*) What?

Jennie: I said it already, before I got the pie out.

Father: But you didn't know then.

Harry: Jennie knew. (*reminding her*) I'll have some more a that pie, Jen.

(Jennie *cuts more pie, ladles cream, but she is rattled.*)

Father: How could she know?

Jennie: Old Billy, he liked the electric light. He said it was warm. He said he could feel it warming his bones. He hated the cold. He was allus so cold, this last winter. I don't like to think of him in the ground. Will you really, Harry?

Harry: Yes.

Jennie: I mean promise not teasin'.

Harry: I will put a light bulb in Billy's coffin. (*sideways grin at the* Father) When no one's lookin'.

Father: (*pause*) The whole district hailed out last summer except for you. The whole country in a black depression and you get a new truck and electricity and you (*to* Jennie) get a new hat. (*suddenly laughs*)

Harry: That's right, ever since you married us, Jennie's brought me nothin' but luck.

Father: The ony luck is the Devil's luck! The grace a God is not luck, Harry.

Harry: Well, you know, Father, it is a funny thing all right. We're ony farm you didn't bless crop on, and we're ony farm doesn't get hailed out. Maybe you're a hoodoo.

Father: What?

Jennie: He's ony teasin', Father. Harry teases somethin' awful.

Harry: (*eating his pie*) No, but it's true all the same. Give us another dollop that heavy cream, Jen. There you tuk off, up to that retreat you went to, soon's you married me and Jennie, and you never gave my crop the blessing. Give ever'body's else the blessing but not mine. And here I stand, hailstorm all around me, grace a God shinin' down, right along the concession line. I mean, true to God, Father, you never saw nothin' like. Old Bailey's farm? Right acrost barbed wire? Big dark purple clouds. Hailstones big as baseballs, whole wheat field bent flat. I could see it, but my section, sun shinin' away, grasshoppers hoppin', birds singin', like a door in the sky opened up and God said, "save the McGrane place", and all else damn them to Hell. Good thing I'm not an ignorant Black Irish Catholic, Father, or I'd think you're a hoodoo.

Father: That's blasphemy, Harry McGrane, you'll confess to blasphemy Friday night. For Easter.

Harry: That's teasin', Eddie Fabrizeau, that's teasin' get you outa bad mood. (*pause*) Look, sorry. Father, I *mean* to say Father. Billy White just died. It's true he died hard. Sometimes men die hard. But now, look at it this way, old Billy's gone to heaven, a good man and a good Catholic, but a bad bass, never sang a clear note in church, but bound for the heavenly choir, good pitch and true voice at last!

Jennie: And now poor Tuffy'll die too.

Father: What?

Harry: His dog. Billy's dog.

Jennie: Now he'll die. He'll mourn and he'll die.

Harry: (*getting up*) Well, I guess it's time. You get the wash basin, girl. (Jennie *goes and gets a big wash basin and ladles out the hot water from the boiler in the range. She gets soap and a towel.*) Don't give me nothin' good, you want to use later. Billy wouldn't mind.

Jennie: Harry! I'd never.

(Harry *puts on his windbreaker and boots as* Jennie *hands him the basin.*)

Harry: You di'n't put none a yer lye in this, did ya?

Jennie: (*laughs*) Oh, *Harry*.

Harry: Wouldn't want old Bill's skin burnt off *afore* he gets to the Judgment Seat. I mean, might prejudice the case, might predetermine the jury.

Jennie: Oh, you're awful.

Harry: "Here, Billy," says God, "what'd ya do, take a detour on yer way up? Devil singe yer butt?"

(Jennie *and* Harry *laugh together, a gentle, sad laugh.*)

Father: I'll help you. (*does not move from his chair*)

Harry: No ... you anointed him. Now I'll wash him. You stay and eat yer pie. Jennie makes a good pie. You eat up, Father.

(Harry *turns and goes out. He stands for a moment on the porch, not looking back. Now we see how tired he is and how aware of the two people he has left alone in the room behind him. Now he leaves for the bunkhouse.* Jennie *and the* Father *are quiet.*)

Jennie: It's the thought a the grave, I think. So dark and lonesome. And cold. Why he was scared. Sometimes even animals get scared at the end, Father.

Father: We are not animals.

Jennie: (*pause*) Harry says the best a us got some animal in us somewheres. I'd be scared too. I mean, it's a dark'n empty hole, in't it? I wouldn't like it neither, not without Harry.

Father: You said a prayer before you *knew*? (*pause*) What prayer?

Jennie: Oh Father, I'll get it all wrong, front of you.

Father: *What prayer!*

Jennie: Domine Jesu Christe, Rex gloriaem libera animas omnium fidelium defunctorum ...

(Jennie *continues the speech, the same as before until the* Father *cuts her off.*)

Father: Close yer robe, woman! (*pause*) That lye is ruinin' yer hands. They're all red 'n cracked.

Jennie: I use vaseline.

Father: They all die afraid on me. And nobody wants me to do the blessing. I never blessed Harry's crop an' Harry's ony one doesn't get hailed out. It's a blasphemy. A priest can't be a hoodoo.

Father: Harry's only teasin', Father. Harry's against superstition.

Father: Harry's Black Irish, all Black Irish are superstitious. It's Harry's been spreadin' I'm a hoodoo.

Jennie: No. No, truly, Father. No ... Harry ony says yer a scourge.

Father: What?

Jennie: It's a good word, i'n't it? Harry knows lots of good words. (*tastes the word*) A scourge. A *scourge.* It's what I say now, I go to clean the outhouse. "I'll scourge *you,*" I say. (*tries a chuckle; pause*) See, old Billy didn't want you, it's true. But Harry stuck up for you, he says, "No, Billy, we need the priest for dyin' and bornin' and marryin' even if he's a scourge." So you see? Harry sticks up for you. Please eat somethin', Father, you look so peaked.

Father: You poor simple woman.

Jennie: Please, Father, I worry for you, you look so kinda shadowy now. I worry for you without me to do for you.

Father: Mrs Day does perfectly well for me.

Jennie: Mrs Day! Mrs Day's past her prime, Mrs Day can't see dirt in *front* of her, everybody knows Mrs Day's not clean.

Father: Clean? You dare to talk to me about *clean?* Close your robe! (*pause*) Mrs Day does me fine. She's a good woman.

Jennie: Well, her pastry's never nothin' like mine. Go on, eat up. I worry for you.

Father: Your hair's down.

Jennie: (*starts to braid her hair in one long braid*) Well, I allus took it out at night, Father. 'N I allus braids it up hard'n tight in the mornin', ony, it gets out, it escapes me, n'matter what I do. Harry says it's just my nature, my hair leaps out like shining. (*small laugh*) There. It's back proper now.

Father: I'm a bad priest an' all for your sake.

Jennie: But that's all over now, Father. (*pause*) You said that was all over. I confessed and did my penance, so that's all over. Harry says you got to trust to God's infinite mercy.

Father: Yes. (*pause*) You swore you'd never tell. You *swore*.

Jennie: 'N I never! Ony, at first, you see, I was ascared a bit. I mean, when it was Harry an' me, it seemed to come over me again, all what'd happened, so I cried at first, and that's not in my nature, Father. Cryin' is not in my nature, as you well know.

Father: You was allus singin'.

Jennie: Well, I never knew then, did I?

Father: That terrible winter. I had to make a tunnel to the church. Like an underground cave. I'd go into the church and lie on the cold stone, my arms stretched out like my Blessed Lord on the cross, and through the cave of snow to the rectory, I would hear you. Singin'.

Jennie: So one day, Harry takes me on his knee and he says, "What's this then, Jen?" an' I never said nothin', only what I *did* say was, I wished I was dead. So Harry hit me.

Father: Hit you?

Jennie: Harry says that was the worst thing a person could ever say and I was never to say it again, it was despair, and that's the worst sin of all of them. And then (*smiles*) he said some poem about cows. Just to make me laugh.

Father: God forgive you.

Jennie: Oh he has, Father, and God has too. Well, anyways, what he did was, see, he picked me up and he carried me right out there to the porch. (*crosses to the door, looks out toward bunkhouse*) An' he says this poem about *cows*. (*laughs*) I kin say part a it, too. See, he picks me up in his arms – good thing Harry's a big strong man! – an' he takes me to the door and he kicks open the door – it was spring then, seeding time, so we ony had screen door on – and he says, "Glory be to God for dappled things." (*laughs*) Fer skies as cupple coloured as a brinded cow. That's a Jersey, I think, Father. A brinded cow's like a Jersey, the kind they got over to Dora's Bob's place. So anyways. *I* can't help laughin' an' I says. "What kind of a poem is that anyways, Harry McGrane, a poem about cows?!" An' Harry says, "It's the best kind a poem and I was not ever again to

worry no more about sin because what we did together wasn't no sin and
God had blessed our bodies and we was goingta make skies as cupple coloured as a brinded cow together, an' if he ever heard me measlin' on
again, he'd give me another'd send me to Lumbreck and right over the
Crow's Nest." 'N he meant it too. (*pause*) So, anyways I gave it up. I
mean, I gave up measlin', and took back my own nature.

Father: It's a poem by a priest.

Jennie: Is it? I never knew that. I never knew a priest knew nothin' about
cows.

Father: My father had range cattle. I was born a farm boy. I'd had my
dad's place by now, up to the Porcupines.

(Jennie *clears away the* Father's *untouched pie and other things. She goes to
the pantry, and comes back.*)

Jennie: (*nervously*) Father? The thing is, I done my penance, and I do trust
to God's infinite mercy, ony nothin's still happening. So, now I got you
here, could I ask, Father, if you wouldn't mind, I beg your pardon, but
see, Father, it's been a whole year we're married, Harry 'n me, and nothin'
happenin' still, and see, I understood, like, when I was doin' fer you at the
rectory, but now it's Harry, see, and Harry's my husband. And so, Father,
what I got to know is, have you confessed?

Father: What do you mean, you "understand" how it was at the rectory?

Jennie: Well, how nothin' ever happened. I mean, that was God's mercy,
wa'n't it?

Father: (*bitter laugh*) You don't realize what you've done to me, you poor
stupid woman. (*pause*) When I was a boy the priest who came to the Porcupines was like a prince. He came only twice a year. He was like a
prince of the Church, like a king. My mother cried when I went away to
the seminary. I said, "Don't cry, Ma, I'll crown your head with glory."
But Harry's right. I'm just an old plowhorse, takin' them down inta death
or up inta life, or to the marriage bed. A gelding. My people despise me.

Jennie: But Father, Harry 'n me ...

Father: Harry and you, Harry and you!

Jennie: (*stubbornly*) 'N nothing happenin' yet!

Father: (*furious with her*) Even our Lord lost his temper once! Even Jesus
blasted the fig tree!

Jennie: Father?

Father: Harry *knows*! Harry knows and he's destroyed me with my own
people.

Jennie: But I never told him. Father, never.

Father: Ahhhh. You told him, Jennie.

Jennie: No, I never! I never! 'N I kin prove it too!

Father: It's quite clear Harry knows.

Jennie: No. Because if Harry knew ...

Father: (*cuts her off*) He knows, whatever you swear, and the oath of an imbecile is worth nothin'. I knew that, God help me, I knew that.

Jennie: (*simply*) I kin prove Harry don't know, Father. Because if Harry did know, he'd kill you.

(Harry *comes back to the porch. He puts the basin, soap, and dirty towelling down. He looks to the east, stretches, and yawns. Now he scrapes off his wellingtons, and comes in. He takes off his boots, windbreaker, etc., and hangs his windbreaker and cap on a wooden peg behind the door. He walks over to his place by the table.* Jennie *makes a gesture with the teapot as if to ask, "More tea?," but he shakes his head. A small, awkward silence.*)

Harry: Well, Billy White's in back a yer Dodge, Father. Took me longer'n I thought. He'd leaked a bit. (Harry *looks from* Jennie's *suffused face to the* Father's *apoplectic one. He is sizing up what must have been going on.*) Well, he's clean as a baby now. Should be okay 'til ya get him back in the woodshed. Got quite a smile on his face now, if you want to take a look. 'Course that's the stiffenin'. (*pause*) Still, we kin allus pretend, can't we?

(*The* Father *pushes back his chair, gets up, and starts for the door. He turns back, gets his coat from the other chair, and struggles into it.* Harry *does not help him.*)

Jennie: (*finally*) Let me help you, Father ...

Father: (*cuts her off in mid-sentence*) No!

Harry: Anyways, Father, do me a favour. Don't fergit ta close old Bailey's gate top a the pasture. You forgot ta close the cattle gate th'other day, his cows was all down my side there, old Bailey was madder'n hell.

Father: I did not forget to close Joe Bailey's gate. I'm a farmer's son. I never forget to close a cattle gate.

Harry: Whatever you say, Father, ony you was last out, and the cows got out, all down my side, and ol' Bailey, he was fit to be tied.

Father: I'll set the funeral for Wednesday.

Harry: We'll be there. If the weather holds.

Father: (*turns back from the door*) I will bless this house. (Jennie *and*

Harry *suddenly become still.*) I will bless this house, or are you an ignorant Black Irish Catholic, Harry McGrane, believing in hoodoos?

Harry: (*pause*) Right, Father, right. You bless our house. Put yer back inta her.

(Harry *and* Jennie *kneel. The* Father *places a hand on each head.*)

Father: Denedicat vos omnipotens, Deus, Pater et Filius et Spiritus Sanctus. Amen. (*makes the sign of the cross*)

Jennie: (*frightened*) Amen.

Harry: Amen.

Father: And I'll see you both for Easter Confession. Friday.

Harry: If the weather still holds.

(Harry *holds the door open for the* Father. *The* Father *goes out, crosses the porch, and exits.*)

Harry: (*calling out after him*) Listen! If old Billy sits up back a the seat while you're drivin' home, don't worry! It's only nature! (Harry *laughs. He steps out onto the porch, breathing in the soft morning air.*) "... The Holy Ghost over the bent world broods with warm breast and with ah! bright wings." (*pause*) There, that should take the curse off. There's nothin' like a good Chinook. Whole world smells good. (*pause*) We got us a whole half hour to kill. (Jennie *laughs.* Harry *comes back in and shuts the door.*) Well, there it is, Jen, here we got us a whole half hour ta do with and nothin' ta do with ourselves. God's given us a whole half hour holiday between work and sunup.

Jennie: (*mock innocent*) I could get my bread in.

(Harry *chases her.* Jennie *pretends to run away. Finally he pulls her up and around his body and carries her into the hallway and up into the bedroom.*)

ACT ONE, SCENE TWO

Harvest time. Now there is a screen door on the kitchen doorway leading to the porch. It is about nine o'clock in the morning. Edna Delevault *is scouring pots and pans at the sink, although they do not need scouring. She is a brisk, round woman. She wears a starched house dress that crackles and snaps, and, on top of this, a brightly patterned, highly starched bib apron that ties at the back. Her braided hair is in a net. She wears lisle stockings and proper black lace-up shoes. Edna is in a mood of surface frustration as she bangs the pots about, but underneath she is afraid. It is threshing time, and the kitchen should have the appearance of lavish preparation of food: pies, muffins, vegetables, roasting pans. The range is red hot.* Jennie *comes in from the hallway, dressed to go to town. Her hair is braided in two braids and is coiled at the back of her head, but those tendrils escape and frame her face. Jennie too is wearing highly polished oxford lace-ups, but also silk stockings and a two-piece suit, very neat, but somehow sensual as well. She carries a hat box, a pair of gloves, and a black patent leather purse. She is wearing pearls. She sets the box down and puts on some clip-on pearl earrings.*

Edna: You're ready then.

Jennie: Almost.

Edna: Takin' time from Harry's work.

Jennie: It ony takes Harry n'hour to drive me to the train. With the new truck.

Edna: Threshing time.

(*Edna is banging away at the pots, pans, and muffin tins.*)

Jennie: There's never a *good* time, Ma. 'N this way I won't get snowed in. Best time to go *is* winter but the train could get snowed in and I'd be away for weeks, months, like it happened last year.

Edna: (*stops her pot-banging; grumpily*) How long it'll take then.

Jennie: Well, I figure only two days. Then I'll be back. (*Edna comes over, starts to fix Jennie's hair, to push back the fly-away strands.*) Day to go, day to see the doctor, day to visit with Mrs Finlay, and do a bit of shopping – Harry's got me a list – and a day to come back.

Edna: That's four days. I make that four days.

Jennie: Well, I meant ony two days *there*, Ma.

Edna: Puttin' Mrs Finlay out.

Jennie: Mrs Finlay don't mind.

Edna: How you had the gall, write to Mrs Finlay and her United Church.

Jennie: I did fer her first. Ma, and you was pleased enough about it at the time, United 'r not.

Edna: (*slightly mollifed*) I trained you right, it's true. Mrs. Finlay said she never had a cleaner girl do for her. (*pause*) It's not in yer nature to do this, Jennie. Not in yer nature. In threshin time. You was also so ... biddable. But now you get this bit in yer teeth and it's all self self self. I don't know you any more.

Jennie: The doctor said, "Come now," so I'm comin' now.

Edna: Don't think I'm touchin' that electricity. Never mind, maybe you got some sort a shock, that's what I think, playin' with nature like that.

Yes, that's what I think, you got some sorta shock from all the electricity Harry's puttin' in. Machines ta milk cows, what next, they'll all go up in smoke, you'll see. (*begins to scour another pot*)

Jennie: (*mildly*) You needn't do that, Ma. Harry's bringin' the Dorval girl.

Edna: Never mind about no Dorval girl. The Dorvals were never clean.

Jennie: Oh Ma! (*laughs*) Lucy Dorval, she come to the rectory once, run her finger on plate ledge to see if I'd dusted. Wearing white gloves, mind. It's her girl Harry's bringin'.

Edna: (*pause*) I hope you'd dusted it.

Jennie: Only fifteen, but a willin' worker, Harry says. Oh yeah, it was clean. White gloves. Was *she* disappointed. (*laughs*)

Edna: Well, *I* never asked for no Dorval girl. I cooked for threshers before.

Jennie: Unh uh, now Ma, you went on enough about it when I asked you in the first place. So Harry says, we'll get in the Dorval girl, so that's an end to that.

Edna: (*suddenly putting her face in her apron and almost beginning to cry*) Oh Jennie.

Jennie: (*frightened*) Ma? Ma, what is it? (*does not move toward* Edna, *as if contact would change her mind*) I got to go, Ma, don't make me cry, Ma. The doctor's going ta fix ever'thin'.

Edna: (*controls herself, blows her nose*) I don't hold with no doctors pokin'.

Jennie: He saved my life that time.

Edna: You never had no appendix.

Jennie: Oh Ma! ... Ever'body's got appendix.

Edna: Not you. I never held with that. Tearin' off to that place, tearin' off for *appendix*.

(Jennie *takes her hat out of the hat box. It is a straw with a ribbon, very chic for the time. She puts it on, with a hat pin, and looks over* Edna's *shoulder into the mirror above the sink.*)

Jennie: The doctor's ony goingta *look*, Ma, and he's the same doctor was there then, is why I wrote to him first place.

Edna: Well, do what you want. You will anyhow. But it's not like you, Jennie, that's all I will say. It's all self self self with you now.

Jennie: Oh Ma. (*pauses, turning*) Well? What about the hat then?

Edna: It's all right.

Jennie: All right!

Edna: What did that set Harry back?

Jennie: (*proud, knowing the shock this will cause*) Four dollars ...

Edna: Four ... dollars ...

Jennie: ... an' fifty cents! (*looks at herself again in the mirror*)

Edna: You oughta be ashamed of yourself. Four dollars and ... four dollars and fifty cents. It's ony a bit of straw and a bit of veil, I could'a made it for nothin'.

Jennie: Harry says you pay for the style.

Edna: Harry spoils you. He spoils you rotten. (*pause*) Four dollars and fifty cents. And payin' that Dorval girl what?

Jennie: Dollar a day.

Edna: Dollar a day *and* all found? Dollar a day and all *found*?! (*pause*) Did ya get it at Mademoiselle Rose's?

Jennie: Ummmm Hmm.

Edna: (*awed*) I never bin in Mademoiselle Rose's.

Jennie: 'N after harvest, Harry's takin' me back, get a new winter coat with a fox fur collar. And a muff!

Edna: At Mademoiselle Rose's?

Jennie: MMM mmm.

Edna: I'd be scared to go inside Mademoiselle Rose's.

Jennie: Harry says they don't care who comes in, they got money to pay. Come in in your apron.

Edna: (*laughs*) It does look nice though, I have to admit it. (*pause*) Oh, Jennie, it's just, I lost five children before they was a year, and then my Ben. Now there's ony you.

Jennie: (*moves to her, takes her hand*) The doctor's not goingta kill me, Ma. He's ony goingta look.

Edna: It's God's will, Jennie.

Jennie: (*becoming exasperated, pauses*) There's Harry at the bridge now.

Edna: If she don't use lye with her scrub water, she's outa this place.

(Jennie'*s gift for hearing things is so common,* Edna *doesn't even bother to comment on the fact that the bridge is some distance away.*)

Jennie: I got good soap, Ma. Lye's hard on the skin. It burns yer hands.

Edna: I knew I couldn't find it. I looked ever'where!

Jennie: I gave up lye in the spring.

Edna: (*shocked*) You don't have lye in this place?

Jennie: Not since the spring. I give it up. Makes place smell like hospital.

Edna: Lye burns away the filth – Harry'll hafta go into Gifford's he's in town, I'll never feel safe else.

Jennie: You won't find no dirt, Ma.

Edna: I'll find it. (*pause*) Does she dry iron? I won't have a girl doesn't dry iron.

Jennie: Ma, I don't dry iron no more. It's easier sprinkle.

Edna: You don't get to glory on easy. A good housewife uses lye in her scrub water to burn away the filth.

Jennie: Oh Ma.

Edna: It's God's will, yer goin' against God's will!

Jennie: (*finally blazes at her*) God's will? How can it be God's will I don't have a baby?

Edna: Oh!

(Edna *is near tears.* Jennie *has never spoken to her like this before.*)

Jennie: Here's Harry now. I'm sorry, Ma, but you go on. (Jennie *goes to the screen door and waves. Then she goes out to the porch. She calls back, softly*) And the Dorval girl, Ma. My, she's a pretty one.

Harry: (*off*) We're here.

Jennie: (*coming down to the front of the porch*) Hello, hello! Hello, Molly!

(Harry *and* Molly *come up on the porch.* Harry *carries* Molly's *cardboard valise for her.*)

Harry: Here's Miss Molly Dorval come to save the homestead!

(Molly *giggles.* Harry *has been making her laugh all the ten miles from the Dorval place. They come into the kitchen,* Jennie *following.*)

Edna: You use lye in yer scrub water?

(Molly *bursts into laughter.*)

Harry: (*taking valise into the hallway*) I said you'd say that. Mother, right off, first thing didn't I, Molly!

Edna: Well, I don't hold with a lick'n a polish.

Harry: (*coming back into kitchen*) Give the girl a chance, Mother, she just got in.

Edna: Do you dry iron?

(Molly *is holding herself in.* Harry *has been predicting all these interrogations.*)

Molly: My mother makes me dry iron, Mrs Delevault. (*a quick conspiratorial glance at* Harry; *a smothered laugh*)

(Jennie, *at the door, notes this, and is slightly disturbed.*)

Edna: (*grumpily, not satisfied*) Does she. Good fer yer mother. What about lye in yer scrub water? Harry? You get me lye to Gifford's you take Jennie in, they'll be open still, you get me a big can a lye to Gifford's ... (Jennie *casts her eyes heavenwards.*) ... charge it to *my* bill.

Molly: My ma puts lye in the outhouse.

Edna: We put it in scrub water.

Molly: I got soft skin, Mrs Delevault, it blisters real easy.

(Edna *and* Molly *give each other a look now.* Molly *is not going to be a meek slave.* Edna *grudgingly likes her for it.*)

Jennie: (*bursts out*) Makes house smell like hospital!

(*An awkward silence, awkward for everyone.*)

Harry: I'll just get my good jacket then. (*goes out the door to the hallway*)

Edna: I trained my Jennie to do for people and I never had no complaints. My Jennie, she did for the United Church even, Mrs Finlay up to Lumbreck. Mrs Finlay said she never had such a clean girl do for her. Here, you want to be useful, you can do these spuds.

(Edna *hands* Molly *a basin, a bucket of potatoes, and a paring knife.* Molly *sits down at the table and starts in.* Harry *comes back in his other, better, windbreaker, carrying* Jennie's *two-piece leather luggage set.*)

Harry: Got you to work already, has she? Yer a slavedriver, Mother. (*Molly giggles*) But her bite's much worse'n her bark, so stay away from her teeth. (*Molly laughs outright.*)

Jennie: We got to *go*, Harry.

Edna: And them's new too.

Harry: This'n's called "overnight" bag, and this here's fer cosmetics.

Edna: Jennie don't need no "cosmetics."

Harry: Mmm, it's on her list, it's on her list.

Jennie: Harry.

Molly: That's a real nice hat, you get that in Lethbridge? Mr McGrane says yer goingta Calgary. I never even bin to Lethbridge. I never bin farrer'n Lumbreck, 'n Porcupine Hills. They don't count though.

Edna: Yer not being paid for conversation, Miss. Mind how yer goin' – that slice was this thick.

Jennie: Why don't it count, Porcupine Hills, why don't Porcupine Hills count, it's farrer'n Lethbridge?

Molly: Oh that's my uncle's place, Charle Fabrizeau's? It don't count you go to yer relatives, does it? I mean, it's not romantic nor nothin', just goingta yer relatives.

Edna: Romantic!

Jennie: That's right. Yer cousins to the Fabrizeaus.

Molly: Yeah, we're all related on my ma's side, my ma's a Fabrizeau.

Jennie: Yer cousin to our priest.

Molly: Second cousin, once removed. We used to be in his parish too, but my ma won't go to him now, she says she'll never go to Father Fabrizeau, because he's cursed. This okay? (*holds potato up to* Edna *for inspection*)

Jennie: Why is he cursed?

Edna: We don't hold with gossip this house.

(Molly *senses she may have overstepped. She looks from* Edna's *face to* Jennie's, *then to* Harry's. Harry *has turned away from her, and stands stiffly at the door.*)

Molly: I don't know.

Jennie: No, yer ma says Father Fabrizeau is cursed, why is he cursed?

Molly: (*a bit frightened at* Jennie's *intensity*) I really don't know, Miz McGrane.

Harry: We got to go, make that train.

Jennie: Then why does yer ma say that?

Molly: I don't really know, Miz McGrane, all I know is ...

Edna: You better go, you want to catch yer train.

Jennie: Be quiet, Ma.

Molly: (*lays down paring knife*) I shouldn'ha been listenin'. I was supposed to be in bed, but you can hear through floor. (*pause*) Well. My ma says it's because he didn't go to confession one winter. It was one winter he was snowed in. But he heard confession and he gave the mass. An' he was in mortal sin. (*pause*) That's what she said, Miz McGrane. But my da says it's just spite ... he never married *her*, my da says Father Fabrizeau was real nice lookin' when he was young, and he says it's just spite, he married the Church instead of *her*. (*starts to laugh, then stops*) He's a tease, my da. Like Mister McGrane.

Edna: I'll finish up them spuds. You kin go out'n take in the wash. (*Molly gets up obediently*. Edna *hands her the wicker basket from the pantry*.) Mind pegs go in peg bag. (*The peg bag would be on the line outside. Molly goes out. She is on the porch for a brief moment as she looks about her at the neat clean prosperous farm, and is pleased to be here. She exits. Pause*) I don't want you to go, Jennie. Five babies I had, and all dead in the first year. And then Ben in the mine. You're all I have left.

Jennie: Ma, don't start again.

Edna: Mrs Bailey, they cut her open, and she died.

Jennie: You keep talkin' cuttin'.

Edna: Riddled right through!

Jennie: Mrs Bailey had cancer, Ma.

Edna: Holy Mary, Mother of God, don't send my Jennie to no doctor.

Harry: Mother, they're not going to cut ...

Jennie: She keeps talkin' cuttin', why does she keep talkin' cuttin'?

Harry: Mother, would I let anybody hurt our Jen?

Jennie: It's the same doctor saved my *life*! You signed the paper.

(Edna *slaps* Jennie's *face*. Jennie *is astounded*.)

Harry: Here now, you'll be spankin' my woman next. Way you two carry on, a person'd think *you* was Black Irish. Mother? (*goes up to* Edna, *puts his arm around her*) Mother? Now, the doctor's ony goingta look at Jennie, see why she don't start up. Now, don't blush. Mother, a woman with seven children and you kin still blush. I swear, I think a woman gets a virgin every mornin' a her life.

(Harry *has misread* Edna. She *is hopeless now*. Jennie *will know what her mother did that spring*.)

Edna: Oh Harry.

Harry: Now, you want a nice baby to nag and scold and bully, don't you? 'N you know no doctor can do anythin' without I sign a paper.

(Edna *blows her nose. She tries to pull herself back into some reasonable world, a world in which she never signed a paper.*)

Edna: It's a wonder ya don't try fixin' her up yourself, Harry McGrane, you and yer electricity!

Harry: (*laughs*) Mother Delevault! Ah, now that's somethin' not even a Black Irish can fix! Soo now, soo. (Harry *is still holding* Edna, *and she allows herself to be comforted.*) Now, Mother, soo. Would I do something to hurt our Jen? (Edna *shakes her head against his chest.*) Then trust to God, Mother Delevault. And if you can't trust to God, trust to me. (*laughs*)

Edna: (*pushes* Harry *away*) Well, go on then, but don't expect me ta touch them lights. It's kerosene fer me 'til the day you git back, Jennie.

Harry: (*picks up* Jennie's *luggage*) Mmmm ... mmm ... you wait'n see what Jen has fer you she comes home. I'll convert you ta electricity yet!

Edna: What? What infernity're you plannin' now, Harry?

Harry: (*moves to porch*) ... You wait'n see.

Edna: (*moves toward* Jennie) Now don't you go throwin' away Harry's money.

Jennie: (*forgives her – this is the mother she recognizes*) Oh, Ma.

Harry: Don't say nothin', Jen. Let her be surprised. Give her somethin' to chew on stead a Molly Dorval, poor girl. (*laughs*)

(Harry *and* Jennie *move out onto the porch.*)

Jennie: 'Bye, Ma. God bless.

Edna: God bless, Jennie.

(Harry *and* Jennie *exit*)

Molly: (*off*) 'Bye, Miz McGrane, 'bye, Mister McGrane! 'Bye! (Edna *stands very still for a moment. She closes her eyes, and crosses herself.* Molly *comes onto the porch with neatly folded laundry in the wicker basket. She comes into the kitchen, sets the basket down, and goes to the pantry door.*) Iron in here?

Edna: Yes. In pantry. Where else should it be? (Molly *starts to go into the pantry.*) No. Wait. No, it's on back a stove. I put it there myself. I'll lose my head next. It's ready, back a stove, hot. Ironin' *board*'s in pantry. (Molly *goes into the pantry, comes out with the ironing board, sees the light bulb, and then the switch.*)

Molly: Gee! Mister McGrane's got electricity! Gee. (*goes to light switch*)

Edna: Here, you leave that be.

Molly: (*switches lights on, off, on, off*) Gee! Look at that!

Edna: (*not said with the usual asperity*) That's enough a that, you want to wear it out? (*eyes Molly closely*) You call that folded? I don't call them sheets folded.

(Edna *rips out a sheet and* Molly *gets on the other end, and they perform the age-old ballet of women folding sheets.* Molly *is expected to dry iron the sheets once they are folded properly. Over the next they work through sheets, table cloths.* Edna *refolds tea towels, pillow cases, napkins.*)

Molly: Mmm. I love the smell a fresh sheets. Like sunshine. Gee, this is a nice kitchen. Some day I'm goingta have a kitchen just like this. (*pause*) Now they got electric irons even. You just plug them in. We'll, anyways, it won't be hard to dry iron these sheets.

(Molly *sets up one sheet on the ironing board, and goes to get the iron from the back of the stove. There should be two irons on the stove, one to use when the first gets cold.*)

Edna: And tea towels.

Molly: You dry iron tea towels too?

Edna: This house, we do.

Molly: (*impressed*) Gee, even my ma don't dry iron tea towels.

Edna: We don't hold with sprinkle.

Molly: No more does Ma.

Edna: If you dry iron right off, fresh from the line, it's not so bad.

Molly: No.

Edna: It's lazy housewives hafta sprinkle, 'cause they let ironing pile up. Do a job right away, you don't hafta sprinkle. (Molly *tests the iron with spit, then irons the first sheet.*) Do your work as it comes up, you won't go wrong. (*Molly continues ironing.* Edna *folds one last tea towel.*) How far gone're ya?

Molly: (*startled, and then, in a moment, knows it's true*) Oh.

Edna: Careful. You'll burn that sheet. (*takes the iron from* Molly, *puts it back on iron rack on stove.*) Better sit down. (Molly *goes to the table, pulls out a chair, and sits down.*) Didn't ya know? (Molly *shakes her head, no.*)

Edna: I'll make us a nice hot cup of tea. (*puts kettle over the hot part of the range, waits for it to boil.*) You never knew then.

Molly: No. Not 'til you said it. Then I knew.

Edna: You can fool yourself but you can't fool me. I'd say you were about four months gone. (*The kettle boils. During the following dialogue,* Edna *pours water into the teapot, rinses it out, pours it into the sink. She then puts a teaspoonful of tea into the pot, and pours hot water in. She brings some old mugs to the table, along with cream and sugar. Meanwhile,* Molly *bursts into tears.*) Cryin' won't help. Will the boy marry you?

Molly: He's a Doukhobour!

Edna: Oh Lord.

Molly: Come to help with the seedin'. In spring.

Edna: Then marriage is out. Doukhobours's bad as Protestants.

Molly: Da'll kill me.

Edna: You've been a fool, that's certain. You want milk in first?

Molly: You got any cream?

Edna: We got heavy cream. (Molly *starts to ladle sugar into her cup. Like* Harry, *she takes a lot.*) You want a sugar baby? I'll get the heavy cream. (*goes to pantry*)

Molly: Oh boy, Da'll kill me.

Edna: (*coming back with jug*) There. A spoon'll stand up in that. Help yourself. (Molly *helps herself, again abundantly.*) I don't know how you kin drink it that way. (Edna *sits down, pours her own tea, milk in first, one teaspoon of sugar.*)

Molly: How could you tell, Mrs Delevault?

Edna: I kin tell.

Molly: (*drinks tea*) Well, I guess I'll hafta kill myself.

Edna: (*pause*) Fine idea. Don't be a stupid girl, suicide's a sin, and you know it, yer a good Catholic. If you're a bad girl, yer still a good Catholic. (*pause*) Let's think it out. You leave it to me. God works in mysterious ways. There's a way outa anything, if you don't let go. (*pause*) How old're you, Molly?

Molly: 'N I only did it the once! (*pause*) Fifteen.

Edna: Once is enough. (*pause*) All right, you have your tea then. Like a piece of pie? With heavy cream? Go good.

Molly: Yes please.

Edna: All right then, you have your tea. And maybe after, I'll let you sprinkle.

ACT ONE, SCENE THREE

Bring up lights, dim, on bedroom upstairs. Molly is in bed. Edna is already asleep on the other side of the bed. Molly trying to keep quiet, but now and then she sobs. Harry stands at the door, switches on the overhead light.

Harry: Well, now, what's this, Miss Molly Dorval? Homesick first night?

Molly: Oh, you gotta light in here too!

Harry: Sure I do. See? (*turns it off, then on, off, then on.* Molly *laughs*) So? I don't want no measlin' girls around this place.

Molly: It's not that.

Harry: First night away from home.

Molly: (*shakes her head*) Not that.

Harry: Mother Delevault worked you too hard — you did fine job tonight, with supper. With washin' up. Fine job. 'N you just see what Miz Mc-Grane brings back with her from Calgary.

Molly: What?

Harry: Mmmm mmm. Spoil surprises, tell them.

Molly: I'm not homesick. I like it better'n home. But I can't tell.

Harry: (*crosses to her bed, sits on it*) Well, you tell me a story then.

Molly: Me tell you a story?

Harry: Mmmm. I need a bedtime story. Tell me ... best time you ever had, your whole life. (Molly *laughs*) I'm serious, Miss Molly. I want bedtime story. (*leans back comfortably against foot of bed*)

Molly: Oh Mister McGrane! (*shushes him with her finger, indicating* Edna, *who turns and mutters in her sleep.*)

Harry: I'm waitin'. Stay here 'til sunup hafta.

Molly: (*laughs*) Well. *You* won't think it's best time.

Harry: You might be surprised.

Molly: Well. Up at my uncle's place, Charlie Fabrizeau's? Porcupine Hills? They got a hot spring. My Uncle Charlie, he's got it all wired off so's us kids won't get at it. But we do anyways. It's lovely and hot and it smells like old eggs the hen hid and then forgot where she put 'em. (Harry *smiles, his eyes closed.* Molly *is encouraged*) My Uncle Charlie, he says that's the smell a the fiery pit, that's the smell a fire 'n brimstone and the Devil's goingta drag us down by our heels, but that's just ta scare us off.

Harry: But you aren't scared off.

Molly: Naw! See, it's ony an underground river feeds that spring, deep under ground, down near the centre a the world, and it's boiling away down there and it comes up all bubbly and hot and steamy. My cousins 'n me, we used to sneak up early mornings ... (*snuggled down now; sleepily*) One time, one time we was there fer first snow, and we snuck up then too, and it was really somethin'. The snow comin' down and there we was, naked, with icicles hangin' from our hair 'n our eyelashes, and Jack's nose had this long icicle! (*small laugh*) An' all around us, the snow was fallin' and everythin' was so quiet an' still and we was warm. Naked 'n warm. ... I think my Uncle Charlie? He knew. I jest think he never really wanted to catch us. I think he'd done it too, he was young ... (*drowsy, dropping off*) Snow fallin' down and everythin' so quiet and still and us, all warm and naked.

(Harry *waits a moment. He gets up, goes to her and looks at her. He covers her with the quilt. He bends down, and kisses her forehead. In that moment, he knows he feels more than fatherly interest for* Molly. *Slight reaction, then he laughs at himself.*)

Harry: God bless, Molly.

He goes out and shuts off the light.

ACT ONE, SCENE FOUR

The day of Jennie's *return.* Molly *comes into the kitchen with fresh flowers – Tiger Lilies, Brown-eyed Susans. She puts them on the side of the sink, and pumps water into a jam jar.* Edna *is on her knees with a waxing brick, giving a last polish to the linoleum.*

Edna: Wasting good well water?

Molly: Ony a bit. Fer th' flowers. (*puts jar of flowers on the kitchen table*) There, that looks nice. She'll like them flowers. I went all the way up to th'Indian rings for them Tiger Lilies. (*pause*) I'll put the kettle on.

Edna: They won't be here for ages yet.

Molly: On no, truck just come over bridge.

Edna: (*on her heels*) You heard truck come over bridge?

Molly: Just now. (*moves kettle to hot part of range*)

Edna: Bridge's a good piece away.

Molly: Oh I got good ears. My Da says I can hear grass grow.

Edna: (*speaks as if* Jennie *were dead*) My Jennie used to hear things. I better get away this waxing brick then. (*gets up stiffly*) Yes, my Jennie was like that. My Jennie could allus hear things. (*pause*) Well, at least th' floor's done.

Molly: Everythin's done! My goodness, Miz McGrane's goingta drop dead, everythin' done and eighteen threshers fed mornin' noon 'n night. I never worked so hard my whole entire life, an' nothin' dirty to start with!

(Edna *gives her a look to quell.*)

Molly: But it looks real nice, Miz Delevault. She'll like it.

Edna: It needed reddin' out.

Molly: I think everything looks real nice. There, that's them comin' down the coulee now.

Edna: I still don't hear nothin'.

Molly: I'll get the tea things.

Edna: Not them old things. Jennie says use best for Harry.

Molly: Them ones in th' china cabinet?

Edna: Yes.

Molly: Fer ever'day?

Edna: It's her house. She's got her own way a doin' things.

Molly: Oh, I like them dishes. (*goes into pantry*)

Edna: (*alone, crosses herself*) Hail Mary, full of Grace, the Lord is with Thee, Blessed art Thou amongst women, and blessed is the fruit of Thy womb, Jesus Christ. Holy Mary, Mother of God, pray for us sinners now and at the hour of our death. Amen. (*crosses self again*)

Molly: (*comes back with tray and good dishes*) Gee, they're just so pretty. I want a pattern just like this, I get married. (*pause*) Mrs Delevault? You all right? (*sets tray on table*)

Edna: Put on table cloth, girl!

Molly: Oh!

(Molly *goes back into the pantry, brings back a starched, embroidered, lace-edged table cloth, and places it on the table. She then sets out the tea things.*)

Edna: You start tea then.

Molly: (*starts tea, kettle, etc., looks out door*) They're here then. (*pause*) Not gettin' out. (*pause*) You want I should put away the waxin' brick?

Edna: Yes.

(Molly *picks up the waxing brick and can of wax, and takes them to the pantry. Just before she goes into the pantry, she pauses.*)

Molly: I think maybe you done too much, Mrs Delevault.

(Edna *stands stock still and waits.* Harry *and* Jennie *move onto porch.* Harry *is carrying* Jennie's *luggage. They are moving rather slowly.* Jennie *seems a different person – frozen, preternaturally quiet.* Harry *scrapes his boots on the scraper and then opens the screen door for* Jennie, *who goes to the centre of the room.*)

Harry: I'll just put these upstairs then.

Edna: You're back then. (*pause, then to* Jennie) Wipe yer shoes, I taught you better'n that.

Harry: (*comes back in*) Too dry fer dust, Mother. Don't start minute she gets in door.

Edna: (*starts to arrange teacups, etc., on table*) How's Mrs Finlay?

Harry: (*after a second's pause, when* Jennie *does not answer*) Fine. Jennie says she's fine.

Edna: And the kids?

Jennie: (*her first words, and bitter*) They're grown now. They got kids a' their own.

Harry: You've been turnin' things out.

Molly: (*comes back from pantry with ironed napkins; very proudly*) Yes 'n we have too! Pantry 'n all! 'N upstairs too! 'N front room. Wait 'til you see, I never worked so hard my whole entire life.

Jennie: Flowers is nice.

Molly: I picked them. I went all the way up to th'Indian rings for them Tiger Lilies.

(*Everything is strained and silent.*)

Harry: (*making conversation*) They're not Indian rings, Molly.

Molly: Ever'body says so, for the teepees.

Harry: You ever seen a teepee that big around? No, they're old, them stones. Older'n Blackfoot or Peigan or Blood, older'n you, Miss Molly.

Molly: Who made 'em then, fairies? (*laughs*)

Harry: Old old people. You wouldn't remember.

Jennie: You told me they was Fire People. (*pause, then to* Molly) Ma shouldn't ha worked you so hard, you was just for the threshers.

Harry: 'N she didn't fergit yer surprise, Mother. It's out in th' truck. I'll get it. Just give me half a shake. (*goes out to the porch and exits*)

Jennie: You bin doin' too much, Ma. You shouldn't ha.

Edna: Have some tea. (*pause*) Jennie, sit down, have a cup of tea. (*pours some milk in a cup, then pours tea*) Look, I've poured it out for you, way you like it. I've put milk in first.

(Harry *comes back in with a wooden crate. He sets it down on the middle of the floor, goes out to the porch again, exits.* Edna *looks at* Jennie, *who doesn't move.*)

Molly: Oooooh.

Harry: (*comes back with tire jack*) Here we are! Now, Mother, it'll be no use over ta yer sister Dora's place, 'cause Bob's so backwards lookin', but this is fer you you come here. 'Course I don't expect I'll ever git a lick a work outa you again, you'll be at this mornin' noon an' night.

(Harry *starts to pry out the nails, causing much screeching in the terrible silence of the room.*)

Molly: Oh what is it, Mister McGrane?

Harry: Wait 'n see, wait 'n see, jeez, we got excitable women this house, a man can't think. See, I thought maybe we'd put it right here in th' kitchen, over there maybe, so's everybody's got a chance at it. (*almost manic now, talks to fill the silence*) I thought, see, right over there, over by that big chair, but it's up to you, Mother it's yer present. You say where.

Edna: I poured you yer tea, Jennie! Sit down, sit down and drink yer tea!

Harry: (*last screech as last nail lifts out, and he takes a wooden radio from the crate.*) There she is. (*sets it down*)

Molly: (*awed*) A radio.

Harry: All I gotta do is string out over there 'n put a plug in an' ya kin hear London. Paris. San Francisco.

Edna: Oh Harry, you got me a radio.

(Jennie *moves to the table but does not sit down.*)

Harry: It was on Jennie's list, so she got it, and they shipped it out, same train she come on. Today. This mornin'. I'll fix it up tonight, you kin hear ... Why'n't ya take off yer coat and hat, Jen?

Jennie: I don't want to. The whole house smells like a hospital.

Harry: (*pause*) I guess I better get up to the north section, see how they've been slackin' off without me. (*pause*) So I'll just change my things. (*goes out into hallway and up to the bedroom*)

Edna: (*calls after Harry*) It's real nice, Harry.

Harry: (*calling back*) But you'll never touch knobs, *I* know!

Molly: *I* will! I can't wait!

Edna: (*quietly*) You take out chicken can, Molly.

Molly: Yes, Miz Delevault.

(Molly *gets a pan from under the sink and goes out. On the porch, she looks back through the screen door, puzzled, and exits.* Jennie *lifts her teacup and drinks standing up.*)

Edna: Won't you sit down, Jennie, and have yer tea proper? I made pie.

Jennie: I'll stand.

Edna: Let me heat it up fer you then.

Jennie: No. That was enough. I was dry.

Edna: Let me take yer hat and coat.

Jennie: No.

(Edna *sits down heavily at the table. She speaks downwards as* Jennie *stands before her. It is a confession. She cannot look at* Jennie *until just toward the end.*)

Edna: Jennie, you got to try to understand. It was a terrible year. A bad terrible year. First yer dad died. In the spring. But I bore up, because there was you and Ben. An' had ta bear up. You kin bear up when you got to. But then we lost the farm. It broke Ben's heart ta lose the farm. (*pause*) That's the worst thing for a farmer, to lose the land. And Ben went inta the mines. Ben was a farmer, like Harry's a farmer. Ben could stand on a piece of land, and Ben could *know*. What it was for. Oats or barley or wheat or time to summer fallow. Your dad used to say Ben could smell land through his feet. (*pause*) Like you kin hear things. My children were gifted! But then we lost the farm and Ben had ta go inta the ground. And then they come to tell me. He hated it so, down there in the dark (Edna *looks up at* Jennie, *holding out her hand for* Jennie *to take. After a moment,* Jennie *takes the hand.*) You and I, we waited it out then, you and I, Jennie. How long was he there, breathing and breathing and watching the light go out, then not using candles for fear a usin' up the air. It was eight days and nights before they found him, but how long did he wait, Jennie, down there in the dark. (*pause*) I wasn't in my right mind that year. And then come the winter an' I couldn't do for the Father. I couldn't. I couldn't.

Jennie: So you sent me in yer stead.

Edna: So I sent you in my stead.

Jennie: It was like the whole world froze that winter. The snow come and covered the church and the rectory so we had to dig a little tunnel to go back and forth. But I kept the stove goin' in the church and the range goin' in the rectory, and the Father kept the light on the altar goin', but nobody came.

Edna: I couldn't come to you.

Jennie: I liked the rectory first time you took me. I love Aunt Dora, but she keeps a cold house. But I liked the rectory. It was like livin' in a cave. And sometimes, when my work was done, I'd go through the tunnel to the church and I'd pray to the little light, and it seemed like you was there, Ma.

Edna: There was no way to get in or out, the whole world was buried.

Jennie: (*insistent*) You was there, Ma.

Edna: Well, I never wanted to live with Dora, we never got along. It's true she keeps a cold house. (*pause*) Well, it's past and done with now and no use cryin'. Jennie? Jennie? Maybe it's too soon to say what I got to say, but, never leave off a job needs doin', do it right away, you can't suffer, and here it is, see, what I've thought out, like God answered a prayer. See, the Dorvals is good stock, Jennie, French way back like us, 'n Catholic, an' the boy ... Well, the truth is, the boy's a Doukhobour. So see, what I was thinking, oh I forgot, you don't know how it stands with Molly. She's in the family way. (Edna *waits, as if expecting an interruption.* Jennie *has gradually, with growing horror, pulled her hand away, and moved back into the centre of the room.*) 'N you' 'n Harry, you could adopt ... Molly's ... baby. (*pause*) I was prayin', prayin' for an answer. And in comes Molly. I could see at a glance. Four months gone if she's a day. Anybody with an eye could see. It's a wonder her own mother never ... but a mother never sees ... so they don't even know yet. The Dorvals.

Jennie: (*in horror*) You knew all along. That's why you never wanted me to go to the doctor. The doctor said you knew. The doctor said you signed the paper.

Edna: (*denying*) I never knew what it was for!

Jennie: It was a paper to have me cut. And you knew. I said to the doctor, "That's a lie, my ma'd never!"

Edna: I never!

Jennie: You knew. 'N you got it all worked out, even 'fore I got home, how I kin adopt Molly Dorval's bastard.

Edna: I wasn't in my right mind! (Jennie *continues to stare at her. Pause*) I swear, Jennie, I never understood what I was signin'. (*knows now that she cannot convince* Jennie.) All right. All right. But you was in that place. I would've done anything to get you outa that place. (Jennie *continues to stare at her. Pause*) He said it was for yer own protection!

Jennie: The doctor read it to me. He cut me to stop the transmission of evil. (*terrible humour*) You allus said God couldn't blame me fer the way I was made. I'm not the way God made me, Ma. (*small laugh*) I still can't take it in. Maybe it's true I'm not bright. It must be true fer people ta sign papers 'n do that to me. Maybe I'm not bright. But I'm not the other ... You were my mother!

Edna: Oh dear God, blessed Jesus, he was the priest, Jennie!

Jennie: 'N you knew that too.

(Jennie *takes off her hat, which is attached to her coiled hair with a hat pin. She goes to the range. She lifts a lid with the lid lifter. She puts the hat in the fire, and then stares into the fire as it burns. Then she throws the hat pin in as well. She replaces the lid.* Harry *comes back into the kitchen in work clothes. He has been sitting upstairs, waiting for the women to say whatever it is that has to be said.*)

Edna: (*over his entrance*) On Jennie, Jennie, you burnt your beautiful hat. Harry, Jennie's just burnt her hat.

Jennie: Harry, you kin take Ma back to Dora's Bob's place now.

Harry: (*pause*) She ain't heard the radio ...

Jennie: It's time! She's done too much.

Edna: She burnt her new hat you bought her to Lethbridge.

Harry: She has ta get her things together, Jennie.

Jennie: Take her now, Harry. You kin take her things tomorra.

Harry: (*goes to screen door, opens it*) Come on, then, Mother.

Edna: (*starts toward door, stops, looks back at* Jennie) Jennie.

Jennie: Go, Ma. Please. Go. Harry, get her outa here.

(Harry *and* Edna *go out screen door. He puts up his hand to help her off the porch, and they exit.* Jennie *stands stock still in her kitchen.* Molly *comes up on the porch carrying an empty chicken can, and goes into the kitchen.*)

Molly: Is yer ma goin' already? Ain't she goingta stay 'n hear radio? (*pause*) 'N she never tuk her things.

Jennie: She says yer in the family way.

Molly: Oh jeez, Miz McGrane, and she's never let up on it since I got here.

Jennie: What's it like?

(Molly *doesn't quite know what to do. She washes out the chicken can, then later starts to clear the tea things away.* Jennie *watches this girl taking over her kitchen.*)

Molly: Well, most a the time it's not like anything. I don't even think about it ... I ony did it the once.

Jennie: That easy.

Molly: Well, it ain't so easy fer me, I kin tell you. My da'll kill me.

Jennie: Stop doing that ... I mean, stop rushing around. Sit down. (*pause*) Sit down, Molly. Here. You've been worked off yer feet last four days.

Molly: (*sits at the table*) Ooof! Have I ever! Yer ma, she's a slave driver.

Jennie: Have yer tea. (Molly *helps herself in her usual gluttonous way.* Jennie *sits down at the table, very carefully, as if she feels she will break.*) What's it like.

Molly: Well, it's sort a like ... a little fish ... in a underground river. Ever' so often you can feel its little tail go flip flup! (*laughs*) But most a the time I don't think about it (*adds more cream, sugar to her tea*).

Jennie: You don't feel sick or nothin'?

Molly: Me? Naw! I'm healthy's a horse. See, if I don't think about it, or I don't get this little fish tail in the river feelin', I don't worry. It just seems like any other day.

Jennie: Yes.

Molly: On first night here, I thought about it. After I got inta bed. Then I thought about it. Oh jeez! Well, I said, it's just the end a the world, that's all. (*laughs*) Then Mister McGrane come in and turned on the light for me, and that made me feel better.

Jennie: Harry came into your room?

Molly: Yeah, come in, turned on the light, said, tell *him* a bedtime story, so I did, next thing I knew, I was dead ta the world. (*laughs*)

Jennie: Where was my mother?

Molly: Side me, in bed wore out, dead ta the world. (*pause*) I guess you think I'm a bad girl now though.

Jennie: Maybe you couldn't help yourself, 'cause yer not too bright!

Molly: (*defensively*) I passed my junior matric! I got confirmed!

Jennie: *I* got confirmed.

Molly: I am too bright!

Jennie: People allus said I wasn't too bright.

Molly: You!

(Molly *laughs at the absurdity of this.* Jennie *tries to normalize this new reality, tries to make it seem possible.*)

Jennie: Well, I never even got my grade seven. My dad started to get sick and I was taken outa school and went ta work for Mrs Finlay up to Lumbreck. But I didn't mind because my teacher? ... Mrs Williston? ... (Molly *grimaces. She too has had Mrs Williston.*) She said I wasn't too bright anyways. My ma allus said that was the way God made me ... and I wasn't to blame. Even ... even Harry jokes me sometimes. He says I got brains else. I kin hear things. When people die. Or a car comes 'cross the bridge. Or someone needs me. And Harry allus said it never made no mind 'cause I had brains else, but I never got my grade seven. (*pause; with great pain*) I shoulda got my grade seven. (Molly *doesn't understand what* Jennie *is saying, but she understands that something is terribly wrong,*) I better go get changed now, the men'll be in soon fer their supper.

Molly: Oh jeez.

(Molly *jumps up, starts to clear the table. She starts to lay out the table with plates. She checks the range, checks the vegetables. In other words, she takes over.* Jennie *gets up and starts toward the door.*)

Molly: 'N it's th' last night too! Tomorra they'll be done. Mister McGrane's been lucky! He's got his whole crop in and still not a cloud in the sky. Miz McGrane? Do you think Mister McGrane's goingta fix up that radio tonight for sure? I'd sure like to hear that radio.

Jennie: You ask him.

Molly: Ony, he should never leave it in here, Miz McGrane. I mean, it's more a front room lookin' sort a piece of furniture, isn't it?

Jennie: Maybe.

Molly: Oh yes, a radio's more a front room sort a thing. Ony, winters, you'd hafta leave stove on in there.

Jennie: (*pause*) I'm sorry I said that, Molly, about yer not bein' bright. I'm just a little tired.

Molly: Oh that's all right, Miz McGrane. I guess I was a bit dumb, I mean, even if I did do it ony the once. (*pause*) Why don't you go on up and lie down fer a bit. I can handle everything down here.

(Jennie *looks at* Molly *and acknowledges this truth. She goes out into the hallway and we see her go into the bedroom. She stands there, a woman with nothing to do.*)

ACT ONE, SCENE FIVE

The next evening. Outside a heavy rain is falling. We can hear it, and we can see that the porch is wet. A real summer rain. Thunder. Lightning. From off, inside the house, we can faintly hear the sound of the radio in the front room, and, sometimes, Molly's laughter. Jennie *stands on the porch, looking out at the rain.* Harry *comes onto the porch, shakes off his hat and jacket, and hangs them on pegs outside the door. He wipes his head and neck with a kerchief.*

Harry: I put milk in separator shed. (*pause*) Poor ol' Bailey, his whole quarter section got hailed out.

Jennie: And you just done yestiddy.

Harry: Yeah. Mine's all in. All in yestiddy. I think it hit Waterson's place too. I could see that big purple cloud movin' over that way. Hunh. Molly sure likes that radio.

Jennie: Maybe you should keep her.

Harry: If you want. She'd be company fer you. (*Awkward pause. They haven't talked, so this is the moment for it.*) Well, men're happy anyways, all paid off, so that's done. Take wheat inta town tomorror. Nice to have them gone though. Even when they're out there in the bunkhouse, ya know they're out there. Nice to be alone. (*The radio is heard, faintly.*)

Jennie: Except for Molly. (*pause*) It's clearin'.

Harry: Yeah, them hard rains, they clear up quick. Do their damage and turn soft.

Jennie: (*doesn't turn to look at* Harry) I guess you want to ask me.

Harry: Well, I guessed it wasn't good news. I figured you'd tell me you was ready. (*pause*) I don't see why you tuk against yer mother though.

Jennie: You didn't sleep much last night.

Harry: No more'n you, seems.

Jennie: It's clearin'.

(*The rain stops. Music from the front room, faintly.*)

Harry: You don't hafta tell me, you don't want to. It comes to same thing.

Jennie: No it doesn't.

Harry: Well, there's things, Jen, I never told you.

Jennie: It's bin a whole day 'n a whole night 'n another whole day 'n another whole night and everythin' seems just the same.

Harry: When I was out at the Coast, I got inta trouble ... I was in prison

... That's why I was away so long. Why I never come home my father died. For funeral.

Jennie: Prison? You was in prison?

Harry: I told you, you'd have married me?

Jennie: I wish you'd told me.

Harry: You'd'a married me, I told you?

Jennie: Yes.

Harry: (*tries to make this a joke*) Well, then, I didn't hafta tell ya, did I?

Jennie: Have you known about it all along?

Harry: Jen, we don't hafta talk about it.

Jennie: We do, oh God, Harry, I wish we didn't, but we do, we hafta talk about it. And I don't know how. I don't have words ta talk about it. You don't know, you don't know.

Harry: I know some'v it. People said things. When I come back and you was workin' there, at the rectory. 'N I started courtin' you. People said things. Bill Jackson said something, down at Feed Store, so I just took him out back a Feed Store 'n talked to him a bit. I didn't touch him, I ony talked to him. I said "Spew it out, Bill Jackson, 'cause the banns're called two weeks now, and after next Sunday's bann's called, I am marryin' me Jennie Delevault in the sight a' God 'n Man, and I'll hear nothin' agin my wife that day forward."

Jennie: Then you knew. An' Ma knew. Ony you don't know. Not all'v it. An' Ma, she had it all worked out, ta take Molly's baby. (*laughs*)

Harry: (*not understanding*) Take Molly's baby?

Jennie: Harry. (*pause*) That doctor cut me. All that time ago. When the Father tuk me to that place. It wasn't no regular hospital. They sat me down and asked me questions, only I'd sworn not to say, 'n they said I wasn't too bright. They said – they was four a them – they said I was feeble-minded. I never had no appendix.

Harry: Were you in the family way?

Jennie: (*shocked*) No! Oh no. No, he'd'v never done it *then*. No. Oh if I'd been late, it would've been a sign, it would've been a punishment, he'd've never gone against God like that. No. They just cut me.

Harry: Where? What place? What hospital was it?

Jennie: Ponoka. 'N it wasn't just feeble-minded they said.

Harry: (*carefully, very quiet*) Who took you.

Jennie: See, I was sixteen, and so they had ta get ... Ma had to sign the paper ... See, Harry, when I wrote the letter to that doctor, the one who done it, he said he didn't know what to think. That's why he wrote back so fast, come up to see him in Calgary. He's in private practice now. He was just startin' out then, ony job he could get. Anyways, he said, he said, he said ... he didn't have no idea I could write a word of English. (*tries to laugh, numb with shock*) See there's this law, Harry. Against "the transmission of evil." And they said I wasn't too ... No, they said I was feeble-minded. 'N the other.

Harry: What other?

Jennie: I was evil.

Harry: (*almost laughs*) Who said.

Jennie: The people in that room. Who asked me the questions. There was four a them, three men an' a lady. 'N they asked me questions. But see, I swore'n oath to say nothin, 'n I never. (*pause*) That's funny. Everybody knew. That's funny, Harry. But I never said. 'N the doctor, he's in private practice now, oh I told you that already, the doctor said, "Mrs McGrane, I don't know what to say. I didn't know you could write a word of English." He said I wrote him, he was dumbfounded. See, if someone signs a paper, they can cut you out. And Ma, she signed it.

Harry: Who took her the paper? (*pause*) Who took you to that place?

Jennie: (*in spite of everything, still feels she cannot betray her word.*) The doctor said, he can't fix me back again, Harry. I don't seem to be able to take it in. I don't feel anythin'. It's like my body don't belong to me no more. You got your whole crop in, Harry. Look how clear it is.

Harry: Who took you there? Who took yer ma the paper to sign.

Jennie: Ah. He did.

Harry: I want you to say it. Say his name.

Jennie: See, they didn't even hafta tell me or nothin' because I was a minor! See how clear it is, Harry! "Look at the stars! Look, look up at the skies! Oh look at all the fire-folk sittn' in the air!" If I was feeble-minded, how could I remember the words you taught me?

Harry: Say his name.

Jennie: Father Edward Fabrizeau. (*pause*) There. Now I've told, and you can kill me. (*pause*) Only when I go, Harry don't put me in the ground, I want to go like the fire-folk, burnin', burnin', like those old Fire People made the rings up on the butte. (*laughs with the relief of it*) Take me down ta the river and cut me some kindlin', and let me go up inta the sky like fire-folk. (*laughs*)

Father: I'm not goingta kill you, Jennie.

Jennie: Haven't you heard what I've bin tellin' you? You got to kill me, Harry. An' then him, you got ta kill him too. I swore I'd never tell, an' now I did, and I told him you'd kill him.

Harry: (*pause*) I kill ya tomorra. (*pause*) Right now, you go up, get you some rest.

(Jennie *goes into the kitchen, gets the kerosene lamp from the top of the shelf beside the sink, and lights it.*)

Jennie: Oh! I did it again. You see what I did? I'm just not too bright, it's true, Harry. Molly, she's not ascared a bit. I don't know why, everythin' strikes me funny. Mr Bailey gets hailed out and you don't. Luck a the Irish. (*tries to laugh, turns to hallway. The sound of radio music, faint. Laughter*) She'll stay up all night, listenin' ta the ends a the world.

Harry: Go to bed now, Jennie.

Jennie: Yes. Yes, I'm tired out. Good night, Harry. (*exits into hall*)

Harry: Good night, girl. (Jennie *enters the bedroom and places the lamp on the bedside table. The light on the bedroom dims. Now we see only* Harry. Harry *comes into the kitchen. He has been holding himself in. He goes to the range, lifts a lid, puts in more kindling, replaces lid.*) Oh Jesus!

(*He places his right hand down, hard, on the hottest part of the range.*)

ACT TWO, SCENE ONE

The bedroom, two nights later. Molly *is finishing her tidying in the kitchen. The bedroom is dimly lit.* Molly *takes her apron off, looks around with satisfaction, and goes into the front room, turning off the light. The radio flares up, then becomes subdued, and then silent.* Harry *comes in from outside, wiping his boots on the scraper. He goes to turn on the light, then doesn't. He takes off his jacket painfully. We can see the bandage about his right hand. He goes upstairs to the bedroom, enteres, then hesitates.*

Harry: It's been two days you stayed in bed, Jen. It's not good for you. (*cradles the burnt hand with his other hand*) I know you're not sleeping. Nobody could sleep so many hours and days away. You're not asleep. (*turns on the light*)

Jennie: Don't do that!

Harry: Come downstairs, Jennie.

Jennie: Things're gettin' done, aren't they?

Harry: I didn't mean that.

Jennie: She's takin' care of things, isn't she?

Harry: Jennie, it's no use, you can't hide yourself away from it. (Harry *sits on the bed.* Jennie *moves away from him*) Something bad happened to you.

Jennie: It happened, so it happened, forget it.

Harry: (*pause*) No, you don't forget something like that. But you can't brood on it. You can't just lie up here and brood on it.

Jennie: I want to die.

Harry: (*angrily*) Don't talk like that! (*pause*) Things happen to people. Bad things. You can't give in. You got to keep your hope.

Jennie: (*turns, sits up, faces him, accusingly*) How'd you burn your hand, Harry.

Harry: You're not the only one things happen to. When I went into that place and I heard that gate go clang behind me, I thought I'd never make it, all those years without sky or dirt or to hear the river or the birds ... God help me, I love the world, Jennie. I love the world. I love it all, the way the thunderhead comes up all dark and purple and the still before it breaks, everything holding its breath, I love it though it'll flatten my field.

Jennie: I hate the world.

Harry: Don't say that!

Jennie: I was your gift, Harry, I brought you luck. But he told you, the ony luck is the devil's luck.

Harry: We can make our own luck. We can make a life.

Jennie: How did you burn your hand, Harry.

Harry: I know how it is, at first. Black despair. Alone in a cage. Some old guy there, he said, first day, "You can do your time easy or you can do it hard. But whatever way you choose, you'll do your time." I'd'a been like you maybe, nobody got me up and out to march around the yard half hour a day. I hated that half hour at first. It was too little and too much. I wanted to go inside myself and never come out.

Jennie: Yes.

Harry: Jen.

Jennie: I feel so dirty.

Harry: (*reaches out and puts his bandaged hand on her*) Jen, come back.

Jennie: (*grabs his bandaged hand and hurts it, so that he pulls away*) Why'd you burn your hand, Harry? So you'd never have to touch me again! That's it, i'n't, Harry, so you never have to touch me any more.

Harry: No no no. Listen to me. Listen. Try to understand.

Jennie: I can't understand, remember? I'm not too bright.

Harry: It's *I* can't understand it. It's me, I can't understand how it could happen. What happened at first, it's ony nature. The Church says it's bad, but it's ony nature. But what happened after, what he did to you, I can't understand how he did that. It's even against the Church.

Jennie: And you forgive him, you're that good a Christian, you forgive him?

Harry: I can't understand him! I'm not God, to punish him! ... I think I can't be a Christian at all sometimes, I love the world too much.

Jennie: Oh no, you're a big Christian, you forgive him, you forgive me. You burnt your hand you wouldn't have to touch me. No ... No, you burnt your hand you wouldn't have to kill me ...

Harry: (*takes her by the shoulders and shakes her*) Damn it, Jennie, you're alive and life's a miracle! The rest we can swallow.

Jennie: No no, so you wouldn't have to kill him ... That's it, isn't it, so you wouldn't have to kill him!

Harry: (*stops holding her*) I think you should come downstairs now, Jennie.

Jennie: You coward.

Harry: Come downstairs now.

Jennie: What was you in prison for?

Harry: ... You got to come downstairs again.

Jennie: I could start getting up half hour a day, march around ...

Harry: If that's all you can manage. You can't stay up here forever.

Jennie: (*pause*) All right. I'll get up like a prisoner, march around half hour a day. What did you do, Harry? What was *you* in prison for?

Harry: I'll tell you one day.

Jennie: Lie down beside me, Harry. I'm so cold. (Harry *lies down beside* Jennie.) ... I'm no good for anything.

Harry: Shh shh.

(Jennie *puts her arms round him, then crawls over him, rubbing herself like an animal against his body.* Harry *tries to respond but can't.*)

Jennie: You see? You can't make love to me any more, Harry. I'm not a woman to you now.

Harry: It's not that.

Jennie: I was your gift. But you're cursed now, Harry. I'm your hoodoo. (*a long wail of pain*)

ACT TWO, SCENE TWO

Winter, just before Christmas. Harry sits in the armchair, staring out the storm door. The inner door is open, so he can see through the glassed outer door. He has a rifle beside him, leaning against the chair. A cold late blue afternoon coming on to evening. Molly comes in, dragging a pine tree, just chopped. She is very pregnant and somewhat awkward.

Molly: I got a tree. Fer Christmas. Thought I'd put it up.

Harry: Wondered where ya got to.

Molly: I strung berries too, see? (Molly *shows him the dried berries strung for the tree, then starts to take off her outer clothing – boots, coat, leggings, toque, scarf, mittens.*) Thought I'd better, before it really blows.

Harry: Yeah, she's goingta turn tonight. Get real cold.

Molly: Yeah. (*turns to the sink, sees the supper tray untouched; disgustedly*) She didn't eat nothin' again? (*scrapes the supper plate into the chicken can*) Well, pigs eat good here. Chickens eat good this place! (*pause*) Ben Collette cleared road down.

Harry: Hunh. That's Ben Collette all over, clear road down afore the big snow comes. (*pause*) Miss the bridge again?

Molly: (*small laugh*) No, he cleared it down to the gate, right down, he didn't hit the bridge this time. But it's comin' all right, you kin feel it. (*shivers, puts kindling into stove part of the range*)

Harry: Trust Ben Collette to clear road down just before Hell freezes over.

Molly: Yeah, we're goingta be snowed in all right. (*goes to the box of kindling beside the door*)

Harry: Don't stand in my way, Molly! I see that bastard I might shoot you instead!

Molly: Oh Mister McGrane. (*Sits down at the kitchen table and begins to pick at the wood with her fingers.*)

Harry: Oh go listen to radio, Molly. Don't pick at the table. You picked that table inta slivers.

Molly: You're always after me! An' I got th' tree fer Christmas an' every-thin'! (*pause*) It's like livin' in a tomb!

Harry: (*pause*) Sorry. Go listen to the radio, Molly.

Molly: I thought maybe we could decorate the tree together. I found the ornaments from last year.

Harry: I got to watch fer that coyote. Maybe later.

Molly: Ony, I couldn't find the little stand, fer the tree ...

Harry: I'll get it.

Molly: It's drippin' there.

(Molly *indicates the tree. Harry* looks at her. She sighs, gets up, goes into the hall and exits. After a while, faintly, we hear Christmas carols, but they fade out almost immediately. Jennie *turns up the kerosene lamp in the bedroom. Her hair is all about her face, wild. She is in a dirty flannelette nightgown, and the buttons are undone between her breasts. She doesn't put on slippers. She takes the lamp and comes downstairs. She stands in the doorway for a moment and then puts the lamp on the side of the sink. Harry is aware of her presence but does not look back at her.*)

Jennie: What's that drippin' all over my clean floor!

Harry: It's Christmas tree. Molly brung it in.

Jennie: Drippin' all over my clean floor.

(Jennie *goes into the pantry and brings back a bucket, a cloth and a can of Arm and Hammer lye. She fills the bucket with hot water from the boiler part of the stove, and pours lye into the bucket. She dips a cloth in and wrings it out. It must be very hot and very painful, but she does not wince. She washes up around the tree.*)

Jennie: Rubbish – she's always bringin' in rubbish! Rubbish. Filthy rub-bish. I don't want that girl here no more, Harry. She brings in filth.

Harry: She's a good worker.

Jennie: I don't want that girl here. She's not clean.

Harry: Ony tryin' ta brighten things up. Fer Christmas.

Jennie: Whole Dorval family, it's not clean. (*stands up*) What're you readin? (*scornfully*) 'Nother poem?

Harry: No. I'm keepin' eye out fer that coyote's been pickin' off my chickens.

Jennie: I see the rifle, Harry. I know what the rifle's for. (*scornfully*) But I see the book too. Read me a poem, or am I too stupid to understand?

Harry: (*takes the book from beside him, and reads*) "The world is charged with the grandeur of God. It will flame out, like shining from shook foil ..."

Jennie: That's stupid. Shining from shook foil. That don't mean nothin'. That priest wrote that too, didn't he?

Harry: I think it's like, you know, the tin foil you get when you get a new tractor part ... and you know ... when you shake it off ... and it shines ... we got some in th' pantry, we could make a star a it, fer tree ... I don't understand it myself, Jennie, I just like the sound of it.

Jennie: (*back at the sink with the bucket, bangs the supper tray and plate*) She calls that supper? I call that pigs' slop.

Harry: If you want I kin take her home. But I better do it now, the road's still clear.

Jennie: That's what I want. I'm better now. I kin come back downstairs now. I kin run yer house. I kin clean yer place. I kin cook yer food. I'm bright enough fer that!

Harry: Jennie, ever' night you come down, you say the same thing.

Jennie: Ever' night I got to come down and clean up filth!

Harry: Then come downstairs and take care a things yourself!

Jennie: Why won't you kill me. (Harry *sighs, turns away to look out the door.*) Yer hand's better now. So kill me.

Harry: 'N have you on my conscience too?

Jennie: That's more important, isn't it? To be right with God. You wouldn't like ta hafta confess that, would you? That'd be a big penance, wouldn't it? That might take a whole long winter ta get through. (*laughs*)

Harry: I think it would be better you come downstairs again.

Jennie: (*takes the bucket up and scrubs again at the floor where the tree is still dripping*) Oh, I'll come downstairs agin. I'll do it. I can do it. I did fer Mrs Finlay at th' United Church and she said I was th' best girl she ever had. And the Father. No one heard any complaints. Plate ledge clean. Run her finger over it, white glove 'n all. Not a speck.

Harry: We bin over it and over it.

Jennie: Then shoot me. You got yer rifle. Shoot me.

Harry: I'm waitin' fer that coyote. He's bin pickin' off my chickens. An' not just the soup hens, the layin' hens. I think it's not just a coyote. I think it's half ol' Boulanger's Sandy, half coyote. People say they can't breed, dogs and coyotes, but that damned bugger, he comes right up, he's got a layin' hen right in his teeth, squawkin'! And he gives me a grin, right 'round hen, gives me a grin just like ol' Boulanger's Sandy. Coyote's not that bold. I'd bet on it.

Jennie: Kill me and marry Molly, why not. That'd suit you. You could have yer baby then. Not *yer* baby, but a baby. A bastard's better'n nothin'.

Harry: (*tiredly*) We could both have Molly's baby. I told you.

Jennie: You told Molly?

Harry: What's she goingta do, a girl fifteen with a baby.

Jennie: She's goingta sit naked ina underground river, with icicles in her eyes 'n hair and laugh 'n sing, though the snows come. (*laughs*)

Harry: She told you that story, did she?

Jennie: Yes. She told me that story. Too.

Harry: I went to her room that night, she was scared. First night away from her ma. An' she'd just found out. She wouldn't say what it was, I just thought she was homesick. I never bin in her room since.

Jennie: That slut's scared a nothin'.

Harry: Ever'body's scared.

Jennie: And Molly kin have more, after this one. And you like her. I kin tell. She's like a pig, a big fat pig. I'm not stupid, you know, I can see what I can see.

Harry: That wasn't me said you were stupid!

Jennie: (*overlaps the above*) You allus said I was stupid!

Harry: (*overlaps*) That wasn't me!

Jennie: I can't kill myself because you made me swear. All the men I ever knew made me swear. Take care a yer ma. Take care a Ben. Take care a th' farm, don't lose the farm. Be a good girl. Swear. Never tell. Swear. Don't kill thyself, swear, that's despair, that's a sin, that's the worst sin. (*laughs*)

Harry: Stop it, you'll make me hate you.

Jennie: He doesn't know, that's what I said. He doesn't know, I said. Because if Harry knew, he'd kill you. That's what I told him. Harry would kill you.

Harry: He's just a man.

Jennie: I want you to kill him.

Harry: That's what you want.

Jennie: Yes. That's what I want.

Harry: That'll make us a baby.

Jennie: Here, give it to me! (*grabs the rifle from him*)

Harry: You do it, you do it right. You got to cock it first. (*cocks it for her*) Then look through that little "v" on the top. Don't close yer eyes, 'n hold tight to yer shoulder. No, ya got ta sight it with yer eye through that little "v" an' aim fer here. (*Points to his heart.* Jennie, *in self-disgust, pushes the rifle back at him. He takes it casually, and leans it against the chair.*)

Harry: I never meant to come back to this place. This wasn't a happy place. My old man, he was a bully. He beat Jamie so bad, Jamie was never right in the head. Irish temper, they said, as if it was somethin' ta be proud of. Like luck. But it's the prettiest place the whole river valley. 'N th' Indian rings. Funny. Even I call them that 'n know better. No, they was people livin' this place hundreds a thousands a years ago maybe. Before the Blackfoot, before the Peigan, before the Blood. Older people. The ones done them stone drawings down on Milk River. You take a canoe and come down Milk River and you make it a day's trip, every night fall, up on the butte, there's Indian rings. One day's journey by canoe. I made it three days once and every time I found them. I always had it in mind, I'd do the whole river. They was some kinda calendar, or almanac, I think. Sometimes I think a them people layin' out the stones ta tell time with. People living here in this river valley. Lookin' up at the stars. Waitin' out the cold. Waitin' fer the spring break-up. Buildin' fires ta keep warm. One day I had those damn cows a Bailey's over my side and I goes ta drive them back, and they're there, right in the middle a th'Indian rings. It's early on, just afore sunup, and it's spring. It's the first day a spring, and I'm in there, in the middle, lined up with one a them big stones, you know how they's four big stones placed just so, north, south, east, west? Anyways, I'm lined up, and the sun starts ta come up, and God! Jennie! The sun was lined up right over that damn big stone! I could see it comin' all around that stone, like rays. Like hair on fire. An' the stone, big an' black, holdin' it back, right in the centre a the sun. It was like lookin' inta the heart a the sun.

Jennie: Where'd they go, those old people.

Harry: (*shakes his head*) I figure it must happen four times a year like that. I always meant to do that too, go back, in the summer, 'n the fall, 'n the deep a winter. Now. Tomorrow. (*pause*) I killed a man once. I done it already. That's what I was put in prison for. It's easy to kill a man. We can make a life. We can still make a life. (*pause*) I like it you let your hair go loose like that.

Jennie: I got long hair. I never once cut my hair.

Harry: First think I ever noticed saw you in church that Sunday. Never mind how she's braided it tight 'round her head, I says, never mind, that girl's got lots a hair and it escapes her, no matter what.

Jennie: I allus braided it to keep myself tidy.

Harry: But it allus gets away on you. It's not in yer nature ta braid your hair so tight. (*pause*) Ah! There he is.

(Harry *goes easily and quietly out to the porch, carrying the rifle. He lifts the rifle to his shoulder, fires, and waits a moment. Then he goes out to fire another shot, offstage. As* Harry *fires,* Jennie *holds her hands to her ears. The interval between the first and second shots is terrible for her.* Harry *comes back up on the porch, scrapes his boots on the scraper, and comes in. He puts the rifle up on the wall, and takes off his jacket. He starts to close the door.*)

Harry: S'car comin' down the road.

Jennie: I never heard it. I never heard no car. (*with wonder*) I never heard no car comin'! Harry!

Harry: They better be quick about it, whoever, snow's comin'.

Molly: (*enters*) Father's car comin' down the road. It's th' Father's Dodge comin' down coulee now.

(Jennie *turns and goes to the hallway and up to the bedroom. She does not take the lamp; she goes up in darkness.*)

Harry: Put th' kettle on fer tea, Molly.

Molly: You got that coyote then.

Harry: Yeah, I'll take care of him tomorra. Got the tail anyways, they pay quarter fer the tail. Bugger, I didn't get him first time neither, and he just grinned at me. I hate it I don't get them th' first time. Had to shoot him twice ta finish it.

(Molly *bustles about the kitchen, gettings things ready. She goes to the door as the car pulls up.*)

Molly: Gee, he's got Miz Delevault with him.

(Father *and* Edna *come onto the porch.* Edna *scrapes her overshoes against the scraper.* Harry *opens the storm door and lets them in. He helps* Edna *off with her coat, hat, gloves and scarf. She sits to take off her overshoes. She is carrying a parcel, wrapped in white tissue, which she places on the table.*)

Father: Harry.

Harry: Father.

(Harry *does not take the proffered hand to shake it.*)

Edna: I made him bring me, Harry, afore you was snowed in. It's Christmas. I brought her a present. (*pause*) It can't go on this way, Harry.

Harry: She's not feeling well. Molly, see if Miz McGrane kin come down fer visitors.

Edna: Harry, I'm no visitor.

Molly: (*helping* Edna *off with her overshoes*) Miz Delevault! The radio's workin'! I got Paris last night.

Harry: Go up and see if Miz McGrane'll come down.

Molly: 'N she makes me use lye in scrub water again!

Edna: It looks real nice, Molly. That a tree you got fer Christmas?

Molly: Yeah, ony Mister McGrane, he has ta find the thing ya stand it up in. (*to* Harry) I'm goin', I'm goin'! (*goes into hall and upstairs*)

(Father *takes off his coat and hat. He hangs them on the back of a chair.*)

Edna: Harry, I can't stay to Dora's anymore. We had a terrible row. I'm not sayin' it's all Dora's fault, I'm not sayin' it's all my fault, but we're sisters in blood only, not by nature. Dora keeps a cold house.

Molly: (*knocks on bedroom door*) Miz McGrane. (*over the conversation downstairs*) Miz McGrane? Mister McGrane says will you come down, it's yer ma and the Father.

Father: She's got to see her mother.

Harry: She's not got to do nothin'.

Father: An' you've not been to Confession neither, Harry. Not you nor Jennie, and Christmas almost here.

Edna: She burnt her hat. I knew what it was then. She's never goin' back to the Church, I said. I knew it right then. (*pause*) I brought her a present. (*pause*) That was the hat you bought her to Lethbridge at Mademoiselle Rose's. Four dollars and fifty cents. And she put it in the fire right there.

Harry: These things take time.

Edna: All these months, Harry, 'n you never come to get me.

Father: How will you take Communion Christmas night?

Harry: We'll be snowed in Christmas night. Can't you smell it? You, a farmer's son?

Edna: I bin goin' outa my mind, Harry. It's not right she should hold such bitterness against her own mother.

Molly: (*knocks again*) Miz McGrane?

(Edna *starts to cry.*)

Father: Jennie's in danger of her immortal soul, Harry.

Molly: Miz McGrane?

Jennie: Tell them, yes, I'll come down.

Molly: O.K. (*Turns, comes back downstairs, into hallway, and into kitchen*)

Father: In danger of her immortal soul, Harry.

Harry: *Jennie* is!

Molly: She's comin'.

(Jennie *appears behind* Molly. *She is wearing a new flannelette nightgown, buttoned to the neck, long sleeves. Her feet are bare, her hair is cropped off, and in her hands she holds a long fiery-red braid of hair.*)

Jennie: Merry Christmas, Mother.

Edna: Oh Jennie.

Jennie: 'N you've brought me somethin'! Let me see. (*takes the tissue-wrapped package and rips it open*) You don't mind I don't wait fer Christmas? Look, Harry, it's a scarf set. Look, a pretty scarf set, in white angora, with little gloves. (*puts the scarf around her neck so it hangs like a vestment*) I allus wanted one a those scarf sets.

Edna: I made it myself, from Dora's Bob's Angora rabbits, 'fore they died off. Took me ages. Spin it right.

Jennie: 'N I got somethin' fer you. Mother. (*lays her braid of hair in* Edna's *lap*) Merry Christmas. I braided it first, nice 'n tight, so it'll be easy ta carry.

Molly: Miz McGrane, you cut off yer hair ...

Jennie: (*going right up close*) How are you, Father? (*stares at him but speaks to* Edna) Don't mind, Mother, it's ony what they do to nuns.

Father: Jennie, you got to come back to the church. You got to forgive yer mother.

Jennie: (*bitter, ironic*) I forgive my mother. There. All better now. I give her my hair, all braided neat and nice 'n tight, like she taught me, to be neat, to be tidy, to be clean.

Father: Your heart is full a black hatred. Your mother cries all the time.

Jennie: Do you cry all the time, Mother? Never mind. I'll take it away then. (Jennie *takes the braid of hair from* Enda's *lap*. Edna *has not been able to touch it*. Jennie *takes the braid to the stove and lifts the lid. She throws the* *braid into the fire and watches it burn. She replaces the lid.*) There. All gone now.

Edna: Jennie, I swear I ...

Jennie: (*turns and quells her with a look of pure fury*) There'll be no more swearin' in this place. I know what you was goingta swear. You never knew what it was you signed. You never knew. That's all right, then, isn't it? If you're not too bright, God can't blame you. If you can't read a piece of paper someone brings ya ta sign, God can't blame you.

Edna: Dear God, Jennie, I couldn't let you have a baby by *him*!

Jennie: I forgive you, Mother. I forgive you, Father. (*makes the sign of the cross twice*) Ego te absolvo a peccatis tuis, in nomine Patris et Filii et Spiritus Sancti. Amen. There. All better now.

(Father *crosses to* Jennie, *spins her around, holds her by the arms, and shakes her.*)

Father: What are you doing?

Jennie: I'm forgiving you, Father.

Father: You can't do that!

Harry: (*moves in*) Stop that. Take your hands off her.

Jennie: (*pulls away*) Well, if I can't forgive you, Harry will. Let Harry go to Confession and *you* forgive Harry and then *Harry*'ll forgive you. Harry's a good Catholic. I guess that's men's business. I was always too stupid.

Father: It's not Harry's business to forgive. Nor yours.

Jennie: But he does it all the same, don't you, Harry? He forgives you ever'day, on his knees. Look, he burnt that hand to forgive you. On top of range. He burnt his right hand he couldn't shoot you ... on top of range. You kin still see burn scar. Go on, look.

Father: (*not looking at* Harry) God forgives me.

Jennie: Well, that's God's job, i'n't it?

Father: I will not go down on my knees to *you*, Jennie Delevault!

Jennie: Will you not.

Harry: Jennie, for God's sake ...

Jennie: No, Harry, not fer God's sake nor fer yours. Didn't you send Molly upstairs just now and get her to tell me, "Miz McGrane, yer mother's here and the Father's here and you should come downstairs?" Didn't you send her up just now, just a moment ago? Didn't you? Well, I'm

downstairs now. It's the dead a winter now. If we all went out to the Indian rings and built a fire in the centre, and we stayed up all night, we
could turn to the east and there it'd be, the sun behind a stone, lined up,
lined right up. We could look inta the heart a the sun, isn't that right,
Harry? We could all go out and worship when the sun comes up.

Father: You are falling into despair. That's the worst sin for a Catholic.

Jennie: Despair? No. I thought it all out, Father. No, I'm not fallen into
despair. No, it's come to me. That's why I cut off my hair. I got the answer now.

Edna: Oh Blessed Jesus, oh Mary, Mother of God.

Jennie: Shh, Ma, shh! I want you ta hear this. You see, Ma, I've got it all
worked out. (*pause*) Harry can annul me. And I kin go be a nun. (*pause*)
Harry *can* annul me, can't he, Father? I mean, the marriage was blessed
and it couldn't *be* blessed, could it? I bin workin' it out. It can't be a true
marriage the priest lies, can it.

Father: It was a true marriage.

Jennie: No, if the priest lies, it can't be a true marriage.

Father: If the wife lies or the husband lies, it's not a true marriage. But a
priest is a priest.

Jennie: Ah ... That's the way it works, is it. That's the way men work it
out together. If I knew and *I* lied, then Harry could annul me. And if
Harry lied, I could annul Harry. But if you know and you lie, and Harry
finds out, he can't do nothin' 'cause you're a priest and a priest is a priest.

Father: I was not in mortal sin when I married you. I had bin absolved.

Jennie: You'd bin absolved.

Father: You must trust to God's mercy.

Jennie: I spit on God's mercy.

Edna: Jennie, yer talkin' crazy!

Jennie: (*close to Father and speaking at him, though to* Edna) I bin talkin'
crazy since Harvest. I was talkin' crazy just a bit ago. With Harry. I was
talkin', Harry, go shoot him or shoot me, 'n all kinds a crazy talk, Ma, 'd
bring Harry to eternal perdition and everlastin' fire, but now I don't feel
crazy. Cuttin' off my hair did it, I think. My head feels light now. I feel
free 'n I can think, and what I think is, it was an untrue blessing, and
Harry can annul me. You said (*to* Father) God ordained the increase of
mankind, and you blessed our union and called it holy. But you knew. So
Harry can annul me and marry Molly Dorval. (*turns and goes to* Molly)
Molly Dorval, may your union be holy. (*turns* Molly *to* Edna) Molly Dor-

val, I give you to my mother who will have no more children and you kin be hers, reborn, in the fire 'n the spirit. Amen.

Father: You must not speak in such a manner!

Jennie: (*turns to* Father) It's true, I'm just sayin' what's true.

Father: I am not here to ask your forgiveness. This is between me and my blessed Lord.

Jennie: (*crosses him*) No. This is between you and me, Father.

Father: No. You must go to God.

Jennie: Through you.

Father: Yes. Through me.

Jennie: Ah, but I allus did, Father. I thought you *was* God!

Harry: ... Jennie, let me take you up to bed.

Jennie: No. Nobody'll touch me. You said, "Come downstairs," now I'm downstairs. (*calmly to the* Father)
You came to my bed.
I was fifteen.
A man of God.
And one day you took me to a place.
A place called Ponoka.
And they asked me questions there.
Four people in a room, they asked me questions.
Three men and a woman.
But you swore me to silence, and I said nothing.
And then they wrote you.
And they sent you a letter.
And a paper to sign.
And you took that paper to my ma to sign.
And then you come back, and you said, "Jennie, they're goingta fix your appendix and when that's fixed, you can come home. I'll be here you wake up." An' then they put me to sleep.
And you was, you was there I woke up.
And then you went away again.
And then you come to take me home.
And you told me, Jennie, what we've bin doin' is a moral sin, an' we must confess to God, and we got to stop.

Father: Yes.

Jennie: I got it right then, what happened.

Father: Yes.

Jennie: Sometimes I think I can't've got it right.

Father: That is what happened.

Jennie: An' you lied to me.

Father: Yes.

Jennie: It wasn't no appendix.

Father: No.

Jennie: I got to go to God through you.

Father: Yes.

Jennie: Ony here's where I think what I remember can't be true, Father. Here's where I think what I think can't be so, Father. When we got back home, to the rectory I mean. I did my confession and you gave me my penance, and you absolved me. (*pause*) Then you came to my bed again. That can't be true, can it?
That can not be true.
Tell me I don't remember it right, Father, 'cause I'm not too bright!

Father: Yes. That happened.

Jennie: Even when Harry come courtin' me. Even after that. The week before you married us. After you'd called the banns twice!

Edna: Jennie!

Harry: Let her finish.

Father: Yes. (*turns to* Harry) I thought it would stop. I thought I wouldn't want to any more. After they did that. (*to* Edna *and* Harry) But at first, when I took her to Ponoka, I never meant that. It was just, to get her away! (*pause*) And then, they wrote me and they said she was feeble-minded and they did domestics often, and she was promiscuous, and if they did the operation, she could come back home, back to me, and be safe. And it seemed like an answer to a prayer. I though it would stop the occasion of my sin.

Harry: You did that to stop ... the occasion ... of your sin?

Father: She was like an animal! Rubbing up against me. Singin'. Allus singin'. She gave off ... an odour. I couldn't get away from it, even in church! I've confessed. I've done penance. God is merciful. I confessed to Father Ogilvie before I wed you, Harry.

Harry: They asked you, was she promiscuous?

Father: Yes.

Harry: And what did you tell them?

Father: Well, she *was!*

Harry: (*turns from* Father *in disgust*) Ah, get out of my sight.

Father: (*to* Edna) I prayed to our dear Lord Jesus Christ for a miracle. The day I married them. I went into retreat, and I prayed for a miracle. (Edna *turns away.*) God is merciful.

Jennie: But I am not.

Father: (*tries to avoid looking at* Jennie) I trust to God's Infinite Mercy. I do not despair.

Jennie: They spayed me.

Father: I will not despair.

Jennie: He does not turn His face from you.

Father: No. no.

Jennie: 'N there is nothin' I could do to your God to make Him turn His face from you. 'N you do not despair.

Father: (*frantically, to* Harry) I despaired that winter. That black winter. I did terrible things. Terrible things. (Harry *refuses to look at* Father.) Sometimes, not very often, someone'd manage to get in, and I would say Mass. I gave Communion. I heard Confession. In mortal sin. I despaired then.

Jennie: That was the worst?

Father: For a priest it's the worst! It's not what I did to you, Jennie Delevault, it's what I did to God! Can't you understand?

(Father *is speaking directly to* Jennie *now, and she has him.*)

Jennie: Cuttin' me out and makin' me say it was sin, that wasn't the worst?

Father: They were terrible sins, but not the worst, no.

Jennie: (*close to* Father) Why have you come for me?

Father: (*kneels before her*) I have come to struggle for your soul. (*tries to pray*)

Jennie: Get up, Father. I won't have you kneel down for my soul. (*furiously*) No, I won't have you kneel down to me, Father, not for my soul. Kneel down for my body! (*presses his face against her belly*) There, there come to me, poor Eddie. Come to me and I will give you peace. Come to me, poor little Eddie Fabrizeau, never could learn to shut a cattle gate. Come to me. Come to me. Come to me. (Father's *arms come up and he clasps her to him.* Jennie *shoots a glance of fiery triumph at* Harry. *Now she turns to the* Father, *and pulls his head back by the hair, so that she is speaking* *to him face to face.*) Damn you to Hell, Edward Fabrizeau, damn you and damn your god too, and may your soul freeze in everlastin' zero at the centre of the world. There's nothin' terrible enough I can do, is there? Except that. Not to let you have my soul. I smell, do I? Yes. Smell me now. (*pulls his head against her, and moves against him violently*) Smell me now, Edward Fabrizeau. Dead flesh. Dead woman flesh. Dead fish in a dead river. Smell me now, Edward Fabrizeau, bad man and bad priest. (Jennie *pushes him away from her, not violently but almost gently, and he falls sobbing to the floor.*) That's enough now. (Jennie *goes to the sink. She pumps water, washes her face. She picks up the water she has used before, takes a can of lye and goes into the pantry.*)

Harry: (*to* Father) Get up. Get up an' go. Don't make me touch you. I touch you I'll kill you this time. (Father *continues to sob*) Make him stop, Mother.

Edna: (*goes to* Father *but cannot touch him*) Hush, Father, hush.

Father: But what can I do, what can I do! (Edna *helps him to his feet. To* Harry) What can I do.

Harry: You can live and do yer job an' make the best of it. Molly will have her baby and we'll take it. An' you'll do the christenin' and you'll give the baby my name an' anoint it. You're a priest. You're a bad priest but you're our priest. So, bless this place and go.

Father: I can't.

Harry: Damn you, Eddie, be a priest!

(Father *straightens and raises his hand.* Harry *kneels.* Molly *kneels.* Edna *turns her back and does not kneel until almost the end of the prayer.*)

Father: (*makes the sign of the cross*) Benedic, Domine, et respice de caelis super hanc conjunctionem; et sicut misisti sanctum Angelum tuum Raphael pacificum ad Tobiam et Saram, filiam Raguelis ita digneris, Domine, mittere benedictionem permaneant, in tue voluntate persistant, et in tuo amore vivant. Per Christum Domine nostrum. Amen. (*makes the sign of the cross*)

(Harry, Edna, *and then* Molly *cross themselves.*)

Harry: What was that.

Father: It's a blessing on marriage, when there's no nuptial mass.

Harry: (*near to tears, near to laughter*) Go on, go on, get out.

Father: (*puts on his coat, takes his hat*) Did the dog die?

Harry: What?

Father: It was the last time I seen her, she said old Bill's dog would die. Mourn and die.

Edna: (*realizes and wails*) Jennie!

(Harry *turns and looks toward the pantry door and suddenly, he also knows. He races toward the pantry. Everyone stands frozen. Harry returns with Jennie's body in his arms. He takes her to the table, his head bent over her face, and lays her body on the table. Everyone is frozen for a moment. Edna goes to the water boiler at the side of the range and begins to ladle hot water into the basin – the same basin that was used to wash* Billy's *body*.)

Harry: No.

Edna: I'll wash her, Harry. I'm her mother. You get out of here now, Harry.

(Harry *goes out onto the porch*. Father *follows him*.)

Father: She's damned herself, Harry. She took the lye and she damned herself. I cannot bury her in consecrated ground. (Harry *is very still. He shivers in the cold*.) We can talk to Johnston, United Church ...

Harry: I'll take her down to the river, under the butte. I'll take her down to the river, 'n I'll cut her some kindling. And I'll make her a pyre, like they did for the old pagans.

Father: You do that, they'll have the law on you.

Harry: I'll not put you underground dark and lonely and cold. So when yer ma's made you ready, I'll burn you. 'N I'll do it when the sun comes up. And I'll stay and watch you go like fire-folk. Into the skies.

ACT TWO, SCENE THREE

Spring. Molly *enters with a basket. She puts it on the table. She is wearing a new dress, and her hair is loose. She peers into the basket, proud.* Edna *comes in from the porch with crocuses.*

Edna: I thought they'd be nice, for the table. (Molly *takes the crocuses and goes to the sink, pumps water into a jam jar. She puts the crocuses on the table.*) Aren't ya going ta fix yer hair?

Molly: It's fixed, Mother Delevault.

Edna: Yes. Yes, you look nice. Molly. (*looks into the basket, tearfully scolds* Molly) Now don't you go pickin' him up, he don't need pickin' up, he's sleeping. (Molly *looks at* Edna, *smiles*.) Well, everythin's ready. Harry should be here any minute. I'll never forgive yer ma, her not comin' to the weddin' tomorra.

Molly: Oh she'll come. Never mind, she wouldn't miss it. (*pause*) They say prison changes a man.

Edna: Not Harry. They won't beat Harry down, with their judges and their jails, and their 'desecration of the dead.' (*tearfully*) We gotta put that all behind us now.

(Molly *comes to* Edna *and puts her arms around her.* Edna *almost breaks down, then steels herself.*)

Edna: I'll hold Ben, fer the ceremony.

Molly: Yes. (*half-laugh*)

(Edna *holds* Molly *close, kisses her.* Harry *comes up on porch with a suitcase. He is dressed in a suit. He scrapes his boots automatically on the scraper, opens the screen door and comes in.*)

Molly: Mister McGrane! I never heard no truck.

Harry: I hitched a ride with Ben Collette, he let me off up at the gate. (*pauses, moves to table*) Is that him then?

Molly: Yes. That's Ben.

Edna: She spoils him rotten. He doesn't get a chance to give a cry, she's unbuttoned already. If she never gives him a chance to cry, how's he goingta get lungs? (Edna *is very close to tears. She looks to* Harry, *then to* Molly.) I'll take him in front room, listen to radio. (*takes the baby in the basket to the front room*)

Molly: (*puts the kettle on the hot part of the range*) Sit down then. I'll make some tea. (Harry, *bone tired, sits at his old place at the table.*) I'm sorry they wouldn't let you have yer books.

Harry: Oh, I forgot to take off my boots. (*starts to rise*)

Molly: Oh Mister McGrane, you leave your boots on.

Harry: Those books. A man gave me those books when I was in prison before. (Molly *looks at him, pulls out a chair and sits down.*) I was in prison before. I killed a man.

Molly: (*pause*) I mem'rized somethin' you was gone, outa yer books. 'Cause they wouldn't let them come through. (*pause*) You like ta hear it?

Harry: Yeah. I'd like to hear it.

Molly: I'm a bit nervous.

Harry: (*with great effort*) Tell you what, Miss Molly, a man comes home from prison, he oughta get a piece a pie anyway.

Molly: (*hurt, gets up*) There's pie! I was just goingta wait fer the tea!

Harry: So, you get me a piece a yer pie, 'n you tell me yer poem. If th' poem don't give me indigestion, th' pie will. And if the pie don't give me indigestion, the poem will. Can't win 'em all, Molly. Luck a the Irish.

(Molly *realizes he's trying to joke with her. She goes to the pantry, comes back with pie, plate, fork, heavy cream. She cuts it and serves it to him.*)

Molly: *My* pie won't give you indigestion, Mister McGrane. (*clears her throat*) The world ... the world ...
The world is charged with a grandeur a God ...
It flames out ... no, it will flame out like a shining of shook foil.
It gathers to a greatness, like the ooze a oil
Crushed.
An' all ... Oh jeez, Harry, oh jeez, I fergit the words.
But I *know* them, just you wait ... Somethin' somethin' ...
but anyways, for alla this, nature is never spent.
There lives the dearest freshness deep down things.
And 'though the last light a the Black West went
Oh Morning!
At the brown brink eastward springs!
Because the Holy Ghost over the bent world broods
With warm breast and with ah! bright wings. (Harry *has not touched the pie. He raises his head now.*) Did I do that right, Mist ... Harry?

Harry: Yeah, you did that just fine, Molly.

THE END

This is for You, Anna
A SPECTACLE OF REVENGE
The Anna Project

The Anna Project: Suzanne Odette Khuri is an actor, writer, teacher, and voyager, founder of Ad Astra Productions in Brooklyn, New York. Ann-Marie MacDonald is a Toronto-based writer and actor. Her play *Good Night Desdemona, Good Morning Juliet* won the Governor-General's Award for Drama in 1990.

Baṇuta Rubess directs, writes, and teaches in English and Latvian.

Maureen White is a founding member of Nightwood Theatre, and is a director and teacher in Ireland and Canada.

Early incarnations of *This is for You, Anna* benefited from the work of Patricia Nichols and Aida Jordao.

(LEFT TO RIGHT) PATRICIA NICHOLS, BAṆUTA RUBESS, SUZANNE ODETTE KHURI, ANN-MARIE MACDONALD, MAUREEN WHITE

This is for You, Anna was initially performed in a 20-minute version in
1983 as part of the Women's Perspective Festival. Special thanks to
Nightwood Theatre for its initial and on-going support. Further workshop
productions were sponsored by Factory Theatre Lab and Playwrights Workshop Montreal. The 1984 production was funded by Canada Council Ex-
plorations, the Ontario Arts Council, and the Floyd S. Chalmers Fund.
The play was performed at community centres, women's shelters, a prison,
law schools, and various theatres.

PRODUCTION
Stage Manager / **Tori Smith**
Administrator / **Barb Taylor**
Design / **Tanuj Kohli**
Sound Design / **Peter Chapman**
Graphic Design / **Balvis Rubess**

CAST (1985 version)
Maureen White / Marianne 1, Mother, Amaranta, Victim 1, Friend
(last section), Woman 2.
Suzanne Odette Khuri / Marianne 2, Accordionist, Arabella, Maria,
Victim 2, Woman 4
Baņuta Rubess / Marianne 3, Narrator, Allegra, Eena, Interviewer,
Woman 1
Ann-Marie MacDonald / Marianne 4, Daughter, Friend (first section),
Alicia, Jenny, Victim 3, Woman 3

This is for You, Anna is a performance piece for four actors. The four actors change roles continuously. The most frequent role played is that of Marianne Bachmeier, indicated as *Marianne 1, Marianne 2*, etc. The white set consists of various levels containing: a refrigerator; a laundry line; a white suitcase; a white hamper; an accordion; four red chairs. The women are well dressed in black, red, and white.

PROLOGUE

The actors assume the following positions on stage: Marianne 1 [M.1] *and* Marianne 2 [M.2] *facing each other on the downstage corners.* Marianne 3 [M.3] *stands at the downstage edge of the stage facing the fridge.* Marianne 4 [M.4] *sits in a chair at stage left of the fridge, holding the picture of Anna. When the lights go up,* M.3 *walks up to the fridge and places her hand on the door handle.* M.1 *and* M.2 *complete a gesture in slow motion of pulling a gun from their pocket, aiming it, and then pushing it out of reach. When the gesture is complete,* M.1 *begins to speak.*

M.1: What happened? Do you remember?

M.2: Give me time. Give me time. It was a sunny day. I walked up to the courtroom. I opened the door.

(M.3 *opens the fridge and pours a glass of milk.*)

M.4: No interviews!

M.1 and M.2: It was a sunny day.

M.1: It was a sunny day. I walked up to the courtroom. I opened the door ... No. I must have dreamt it.

M.2: Yes, it was a dream.

M.1: I'm glad I did it.

M.3: (*offering the glass of milk*) This is for you, Anna. (*She returns milk to fridge and shuts the door.*)

THE STORY OF AGATE

(*The scene changes to that of a surreal bedtime story.* Anna's *photo is set on top of the fridge.* The Mother *covers* The Daughter *with a gauze sheet, downstage right holding the* Daughter's *head in her lap.* The Accordionist *picks up her instrument, downstage left.* The Narrator *picks up her black cloth and her fistful of nails, and listens to the story in the chair stage left of the fridge. In the background, the strains of yodelling music.*)

Mother: Want a story?

Daughter: Yeah.

Mother: This is a story about revenge. It's about a very old woman named Agate. She was blind.

Daughter: Why?

Mother: Ssh, listen. She was blind. She used to crawl through the bushes on her hands and knees talking to herself. But of course, she wasn't always old. Once she was young and beautiful. She lived in the village by the castle and fell in love with the young baron. He was tall and handsome and they were very much in love. But then he married a woman of his own class, a rich woman, and Agate was left all alone. She used to follow him everywhere. One night, she went to the gardens of the castle where she watched the beautiful ladies and gentlemen dancing in the ballroom. She cried and wailed, she felt so alone. Finally she fell asleep and the gardener found her there the next morning. When the baron discovered that Agate had been following him, he was so angry, that he called all his guardsmen and told them to ...

Daughter: No!

Mother: He told them to put out her eyes. Now go to sleep.

(Mother *tucks* The Daughter *in.*)

Accordionist: (*pumping the accordion, which makes a breathing sound*)

There was a little girl
Who had a little curl
Right down the middle of her forehead.
When she was good, she was very,
   very good,
But when she was bad, she was horrid.
(singing) Curlilocks, curlilocks,
Wilt thou be mine?
Thou shalt not wash dishes,
Nor yet feed the swine,
But sit on a cushion,
And sew a fine seam,
And feed upon strawberries,
Sugar and cream.

(Mother *uncovers* The Daughter.)

Daughter: But Agate never stopped thinking of a way to punish the baron. (*She screams like a witch and speaks in an Agate voice*) "Revenge! I will have my revenge!" (*Normal voice*) One day, Agate told her daughter the true story of how she had lost her eyes, and she vowed that her daughter would never suffer such a fate. (*Agate voice*) "Once upon a time, I was in love with a nobleman. He was tall and handsome, like a prince in a fairy tale. But he betrayed me, and not only that, he ..." (*Normal voice*) And with that, Agate snatched up a burning torch. (*Agate's daughter's voice*) "Mother, no, revenge can only lead to sorrow!" (*Normal voice*) It was too late. Half mad with fury, Agate had already vanished into the night. She reached the castle, and stumbled through its halls, searching for the baron. And when she found him, she clutched his throat, she raised her flaming torch, and –

Mother: Stop.

(The Daughter *gets up and goes to the fridge, opens the door.*)

Accordionist: (*pumping wildly*)

Agate was blind and out of her mind
She burned down the castle with glee
He poked out her eyes
She stifled her cries
A bloody revenge set her free.

(*pause. Pumping more slowly*)

Strychnine in his coffee
Arsenic in his tea
Knife upon the cutting board
Will you marry me?
A poker would have done
Or if she had a gun
Or if he had a child –

(The Daughter *slams the door, turns to Accordionist.*)

Daughter: No.

(The Narrator *rises.* The Mother *and* The Accordionist *leave the stage.* The Daughter *remains at the fridge with her back to the audience – transforming into an image of Marianne Bachmeier.*)

THE STORY OF MARIANNE BACHMEIER

(The Narrator *lays down a rectangular black cloth. She holds 31 nails in her hands. With each line, directed to a member of the audience, she lays down a nail, forming a circle on the floor.*)

A thousand sins, a thousand tragedies. (*offering the nails*)
Marianne Bachmeier is born in 1950, in Lübeck, Germany.
Such a pretty girl!
She cries too much at night.

Her father is an alcoholic.
She is sent to a children's home. So was Marilyn Monroe, wasn't she?
She is encouraged not to get an education.
Isn't she a bit young to have a boyfriend?
At the age of sixteen she tries to get an abortion.
She almost goes to India.
She wears her skirts awfully short, but so did everyone in those days.
She is pregnant at the time of her second rape. Who's the father?
Some women get puffy and ugly when pregnant, but not Marianne!
She never does kill herself. Unlike Marilyn Monroe.
She decides to keep the child.
She decides to keep the child.
Her daughter Anna is just like her mother.
She was really beautiful.
Marianne is rarely at home.
She asks her girlfriend to be a mother to Anna.
A man called Grabowski strangles Anna when she visits him in his room.
Marianne is away, driving around town.
He tells the court that Anna flirted with him.
Anna was seven years old.
Marianne walks into the courtroom and shoots him seven times. (*Narrator drops seven nails*)
There was spontaneous applause. (*no nail*)
She came to the trial with her new boyfriend.
A thousand tragedies, a thousand sins. (*with empty hands*)

(The Narrator *slowly folds up the cloth of nails. It turns into a bundle. She cradles it like an infant, and walks off stage, counting under her breath.* Marianne 4 [*previously* The Daughter] *turns around from the fridge, counting as in hide and seek.*)

M.4: 47, 48, 49, 50 ... Ready or not, here I come, Anna!

(*She walks off stage. Her voice continues to be heard. While* M.2 *walks on stage, pacing, waiting for Anna, holding a cigarette.*)

M.4: (*voice off*) Anna ... are you ... behind the door? Are you ... under the table? I'm coming up the stairs, Anna! I'm on the first step ... I'm on the second step, and I bet you're ... under the bed!

M.2: (*angrily, as if she's finally come home*) Anna! (*Exits.*)

M.4: (*voice off*) Anna! What a great place to hide!

M.1: (*entering with an armful of colourful clothing which she flings in the air*) Anna! Anna banana! We're going to Spain! Either you go out and play or stay and help me pack, Anna! We're going to the beaches! (*She picks up a wild skirt, holds it up.*) Don't you think Mummy will look nice in this,

with a flower in her hair? (*She stamps her feet like a flamenco dancer.*)
We've got to hurry, Peter will be here in a minute. Get your swimsuit,
Anna. And four dresses, I don't care which ones. Not that one, Anna,
that's a winter dress. (*Packing haphazardly.*) We're going swimming. Anna,
I'll teach you how. And we'll lie in the sun, and eat lots of ice cream. And
we'll go dancing ... not you, Anna. OK, well, maybe – we'll see. (*Stops
packing.*) Oh, Anna. Look at your hair, it's all in your eyes. Fish don't have
hair in their eyes, how are you going to swim? (M.3 *enters.*) Quick, let's
go cut it right now. (M.1 *exits.*)

(M.3 *walks up briskly to the fridge, Marianne as The Barmaid.*)

M.3: (*looking in the fridge*) OK: Carlsberg, Carlsberg light ... Henninger –
we need more Henninger! ... Amstel, Beck, Löwenbräu ... Löwenbräu –
dark and light! ... Kronenbourg, Meisterpils – I don't know why we stock
that stuff, nobody drinks it. Lemons, limes and ice, – and I need more
float! (*to imaginary customer*) We're not open yet. We're not open yet.
(*slams fridge*) Oh, shit! I completely forgot! Greta, ... Greta, could you
pick up Anna from school for me today? Greta

(*As* M.3 *exits,* M.2 *enters, again waiting. She sits and waits for a bit. As*
M.2 *exits,* M.4 *enters angrily as Marianne the Teenager.*)

M.4: (*flings a piece of clothing on the stage*) Ok, here! Take it! Take it, I
don't need your lousy stuff, man! Here, you bought me this and this nice
thing and this. (*Flings clothing about.*) I'm gonna grow out of these clothes
anyway because I'm PREGNANT! (*Stomping around.*) I'll look after the kid
myself. OK, so I'm 17. But I bet I know a lot more about bringing up a
kid than you do, that's obvious. Don't worry, I'm getting my own place.
I'm gonna move in with Herman. (*Stomps around.*) And then, I'm gonna
stand outside here with a big sign, that says "Marianne Bachmeier's Pregnant with Your Bastard Grandchild!" But it won't even be true, because
you're not my real father anyway, *are you*!

(M.4 *wheels off the stage, and remains visible, standing stage right.* M.1 *enters and walks up to the laundry line, hangs up a white sheet, talking to
Anna.*)

M.1: You're a good helper, Anna. When I was a little girl, I used to help
my mother. My special job was to be a messenger. Not everyone had a
phone in those days so people would send each other notes. I used to pretend that the war was still on and I was on a secret mission, and I had to
sneak through the alleys and hide behind garbage cans. And every other
day my mother would send me down to the pub with a note for my dad
along with a fresh pack of cigarettes – and he'd let me try his beer and
give me money for the jukebox so I could play our favourite songs. And
I'd play a game of crazy eights with his friends and then we'd go home
and I'd get to stay outside and play until after dark, while my mom and

dad had a private talk. They were always having a private talk. And the yard was just like this one, Anna, (M.3 *enters*) with old tires and all kinds of interesting stuff. (*stays at the line*)

(M.3 *enters by placing her shoes on stage, then stepping into them. Marianne tired and hungover, talking to her current man.*)

M.3: I'm still tired. ... What time is it? Look, it's already dark outside. Did you make any coffee? ... Why not? ... (*Stretches and yawns*) What are you looking at? Are you looking at me? Is there something wrong with me? You're not so hot, baby. ... Look at this mess! (*She kicks some clothing into the suitcase*) ... Why don't you clean up sometimes, help out now and then. ... All I want is a little security for me and for Anna, and believe me, buddy, you're not it. (*Crosses up to fridge, casting a hostile glance at the man.*)

(M.2 *enters, carrying her shoes in her hand and a teddy bear. Marianne leaving Ralph in the middle of the night.*)

M.2: Ssssh. Now we've got to be very very quiet Anna. ... (*Goes to pack suitcase.*) If Ralph wakes up, I'll be very upset ... pick out all your favourite dresses. And all your sweaters, it's cold out tonight. This is our little game, Anna. ... It's like hide and seek ... Ralph is going to wake up and we'll be gone, and then he'll come look for us, but he's not going to find us, not if I can help it. ... No, Anna, we can't take the sofa!

(M.3 *jerks the fridge door open.*)

M.2: Ssssh. Anna, Anna ... you won't have to go to school tomorrow. We'll go far, far away, and I'll tell you lots and lots of stories. Now ... let's pack your fluffy bear. (*She kisses the bear and packs it, shuts the suitcase.*) Sssh.

(M.3 *slams the fridge door. All Mariannes turn their heads stage right.*)

All: Anna?

M.1 and M.4: Did you hurt yourself?

(M.3 *takes Anna's photo and poses with it. The slide projector light comes on. As the slide projector clicks ahead. M.3 pose five times with the photo. The other Mariannes turn their heads as in mug shot.*)

M.2: Anna ...

M.1, M.3 and M.4: No interviews! (*the slide light goes out.*)

M.2: Did you hurt yourself? Come here, and I'll kiss the hurt and blow it away. See – it's flying up there – see – there it goes. Watch – ah – the window's open and – oh – it flew out the window! And it's going to fly far, far away – maybe all the way to China. But we won't go to China, Anna, we'll go to India.

(M.2 *exits with the suitcase.* M.3 *sits down in stage left chair next to fridge, reads newspaper.* M.1 *takes a newspaper and talks to the audience, walking downstage.*)

M.1: It says here I left the court without a flicker of emotion. What did they expect? All I could think of was Anna. Did they want a picture of me crying and tearing out my hair? I'm not that type.

M.4: (*sitting up on stage right*) I never have been.

M.3: "She left the court without a flicker of emotion." "He wrapped the little girl up like a parcel."

M.1: This is me after. This picture has been all around the world. I get fan mail from everywhere. Mostly mothers. This one's my favourite. It's from a woman in Mainz. "Dear Marianne. My daughter's name is Anna. We hope your trial goes well. You are a true mother. My God bless you and protect you." You should have seen the handwriting.

M.3: It's a really pretty picture.

M.2: (*crossing up to fridge*) They got me to pose with a picture of Anna.

M.4: (*crossing up to laundry line*) It's true Anna wasn't my only child but I had to give up the first one.

M.1: (*crossing to stage right downstage chair*) We lived in fifteen cities in two months.

M.2: (*indicating Ann's photo*) She's only four here. It's in Ibiza, Spain. She'd never seen the ocean. And she's just like me – once she gets an idea in her head ... In three days she was swimming. She takes to the water like a fish.

M.3: (*to M.1, who is also reading the paper*) Do you have the entertainment section?

M.2: (*angrily*) OK, Anna, you want a story, I'll give you a story. Once upon a time a little girl was born and made her mother miserable. (*Turns her back to the audience.*)

M.4: (*having taken down the sheet and packed it in the hamper*) The first time I was pregnant, I tried all the things you hear about. You know, diet pills, hot baths, all that. Nothing worked. Herman's parents wouldn't let us get married and I was out to here – here. But that didn't mean I was going to miss my graduation. I had top marks. You should have seen their faces when I went up to get my diploma. (*Promenades proudly over to M.1.*) My Math teacher said to me, "Marianne, you look like an Amazon." I never flinched.

(M.1 *and* M.3 *fold up their newspapers.*)

M.3: I didn't talk to anyone for four weeks after it happened. I didn't want to talk to anyone. Then the interviews started and they offered me the cover of *Stern* magazine. I thought, it's the least I can do for Anna. I thought, I want the whole world to know about this. (*She puts away the paper.*)

(M.1 *and* M.4 *transform into Marianne and her friend.*)

M.1: Thanks for coming. (*The friend touches her shoulder and holds her hand, a gesture repeated by* M.2 *and* M.3 *by the fridge.*)

Friend: You don't have to thank me. I'm your best friend. (*Goes to sit upstage left, behind* M.1) Did you get some sleep?

M.1: How could I? All I could think of was Anna ... and the trial tomorrow. I keep thinking I'm going to have to look him in the face.

Friend: Have you seen the letters?

M.1: They're hard to miss. They're piling up all over the place. What did you think?

Friend: I loved the ones from all the guys who want to marry you and take care of you for the rest of your life.

M.1: How about the one from the eighty-year-old woman who says she'd like to chop him up into little bits?

Friend: Or that man who wants to soak him in gasoline and set his clothes on fire.

M.1: There's hundreds of them that say he should be hung.

Friend: What about the one from the chartered accountant who says ...

M.1: Stop.

Friend: Can I ask you something?

M.1: Sure.

Friend: How do you feel when you read those letters?

M.1: I feel sick. And I just wish Anna wasn't dead.

(M.3 *gets up and opens the fridge. Everyone on stage is Marianne.* M.3 *takes the glass of milk. When she shuts the fridge, everyone paces.* M.2 *lights a cigarette.*)

M.3: No, Anna – you're not sick. (*Pacing*) Anna, the teacher isn't sick. The school didn't burn down, Anna. (*Angrily.*) Anna! (*All other Mariannes turn their heads. She returns the milk to the fridge. Crouching.*) No, Anna, I'm not mad at you.

(*The other Mariannes continue pacing until they speak.*)

M.2: No, Anna, I'm not mad. I love you. (*Crouches*) I love you, Chris loves you, sofa loves you, chair loves you, vacuum cleaner loves you, carpet loves you, lamp loves you, everybody loves you.

M.1: (*crouching*) Anna, you could be whatever you want to be. Maybe you could be a teacher ... or a doctor ... or a computer scientist ... (*She continues quietly under the others, improvising.*)

M.4: (*crouching*) Anna – did you know I used to work in a champagne bar? *The other Mariannes stand up. M.2 stands stage left of fridge, M.3 poses at fridge with back to audience.*) We drank pink champagne all the time.

M.3: Carlsberg!

M.4: (*stands*) That was a real low point for me.

M.3: We're not open yet.

M.4: When I told my friend Henry I felt worthless – I was asking him for advice –

M.3: We're not open yet.

M.4: – he said, "So what? Instead, you are the fairest in all the land. Take it easy, chérie."

M.2: Mother always said, beauty is your downfall.

M.1: Or maybe you could be a – zebra, Anna! Or you could be – a mountain climber – or (*continues sotto voce*)

M.3: (*sitting down in the chair stage right of fridge*) It's funny how you remember your first job. It was in Hanover, I was working at a switchboard and I finally had some money of my own. I spent it all on clothes and makeup.

M.3, M.2 and M.4: I had a great time!

(M.4 *exits*.)

M.1: Or maybe you could be a movie star. Anna, you can be whatever you want to be.

M.2: I could have been a model, you know. I could have gone to India.

M.1: All right Anna, once upon a time there was a little girl who pulled the covers over her head and went to sleep.

M.2: A girl I went to school with is a model now. She makes a lot of money and she wasn't even that pretty. You don't know what money is, Anna, but money is good. (*She exits*.)

M.1: I'm sorry, Anna. Look, tomorrow, we'll go for a walk and see that restaurant with the fish tank in the window. The fish are so big, they look like sharks.

M.3: Okay, Anna, wanna story?

(The story she tells is largely improvised, but an outline is given. While the story is told the other actors set up for the next scene, but they also respond to the more scary bits.)

M.3: Once upon a time there was a little girl just like you, Anna – how many fingers, that's right – five! And one day when she came home from school, there in the yard was her mommy and her daddy and her sister and her brother and a great big alligator called Herman, Anna! Oh, the alligator he looked so mean! And the little girl, she reached into her pocket and she pulled out – a candy, Anna, a piece of candy! And she gave it to the alligator, and he was real happy, and she tied a pink ribbon around his mouth. They they all went into the house, her mommy and daddy and sister and brother and Herman the alligator – and ... it was her birthday, Anna, and she had a beautiful cake with pink and blue icing and everybody sat down when suddenly! THE LIGHTS WENT OUT! OK, Anna, the lights didn't go out, they didn't go out, they didn't go out ... everybody was very happy and singing Happy Birthday to you, when all of a sudden! there was a knock on the door. And everybody froze. And only the little girl she got up and walked up to the door and – Oh, Anna, I'm sorry. OK, I'll tell you a different story. It won't be scary this time. I'll tell you a beautiful story. The story of Lucretia.

THE STORY OF LUCRETIA

(The scene assembles to the strains of "Carmen." Each actor stands with back to audience in front of her chair and slowly dresses. Four women: Arabella *in gold shawl, with gold rose in hair, holding a tea cup – also at her place, a small book and another gold rose;* Amaranta *in floppy black hat, wearing one white glove and holding a small gold purse;* Allegra *in black hat with veil, wearing one white glove – also at her place, a small basket filled with chocolates wrapped in gold foil;* Alicia *in gold jacket, with white handkerchief, holding a tea cup – also at her place, a bouquet of gold roses. It is like some delicate tea party. The line-up is, from stage left,* Arabella, Amaranta, Allegra, *and* Alicia. *Each turns on her first line and sits.)*

Arabella: *(sits down, stirs tea cup, sighs)* Amour.

Allegra: *(turns)* Enchantée!

Amaranta: *(sings a scale, sighs.)*

Alicia: *(stirs tea cup)* I love him .. I love him not ...

Allegra: Chocolate!

Amaranta: (*sings a scale.*)

Allegra: (*pulls a hatpin from her hat. The others move suddenly with small sharp gestures at designated places.*) I am certain that there are plenty of beautiful women who are virtuous / and chaste / and who know how to protect / themselves well / from the entrapments of deceitful men.

Amaranta: (*hums the first two phrases of "La donna è mobile"*)

Arabella: (*starts passing gold rose down line to Alicia as all say "Lucretia is dead."*)

(*Silence. All simultaneously improvise something about Lucretia; out of it emerges Arabella's voice.*)

Arabella: Lucretia was an example to all women. She always knew the right thing to do.

Alicia: It's my favourite Roman legend. 180 A.D.

Arabella: She was so in love.

Alicia: She was radiant.

Arabella: Her husband built her a jewelled palace and she was the most gracious hostess in Rome.

Alicia: Cicero quotes her in his table talk.

Allegra and Amaranta: It's very hot.

(*All sigh.*)

Arabella: The most frequent guest was Prince Tarquin.

Alicia: She was polite to him, even when the rumours began to spread and the gossips curled up like smoke in the corners of her salon.

Arabella: He was her husband's best friend.

Alicia: That was a ruse.

Allegra: What is a woman's most precious jewel?

Amaranta: Her emerald eyes?

Allegra: No.

Amaranta: Her ruby lips?

Allegra: No, it is her virtue (*Arabella begins*), which she wears upon her aspect like the most precious pearls.

Arabella: Was it a ruse, or was he invited? I can't remember. Lots of men liked Lucretia.

Alicia: It's debatable.

Arabella: Hmmmmmm.

Alicia: It's debatable. He broke her heart, she killed herself.

Arabella: Not because of him, because she was raped.

Alicia: Oh, come on!

Amaranta: Bonjour monsieur.

Allegra: Comment ça va? Non, je suis seule, mon mari n'est pas ici.

(Amaranta *and* Allegra *mime welcoming a gentleman and repulsing his caresses.*)

Amaranta: Qu'est-ce que tu fais? Monsieur? Monsieur? Excusez-moi!

Alicia: It's very hot.

(*All the ladies sigh.*)

Arabella: it's true!

Alicia: She accepted all his gifts.

Arabella: Oh, the gifts, I forgot the gifts! There was the box of chocolates wrapped in gold foil, and the book of poetry with the red silk cover ...

Alicia: How dare he!

Arabella: And there was something else ... He knew so many jokes. He was a prince. He was her husband's best friend.

Alicia: The three of them were inseparable. She accepted all his gifts.

Allegra: And, unwittingly, tormented him with fine words.

Amaranta: Poetry? I'd love to ...

(*As the music of Debussy plays, this sequence is an improvised illustration of the gifts and the "torment."* Amaranta *pulls out bits of poetry from her purse,* Alicia *compliments him on his piano playing and offers him tea,* Arabella *pulls out a small book and recites French words for love,* Allegra *enjoys his chocolates and giggles.*)

Amaranta: Her husband was away. Prince Tarquin came to call. She greeted him as usual, but he forced himself upon her. She said, "I'd rather die than consent." And so he blackmailed her. And so she endured the outrage. You see, her reputation was most important.

Alicia: (*jumps to her feet*) But the next day, Lucretia surprised Prince Tarquin in his sleep, and poked out his eyes!

Arabella: (*jumps up*) No, no, she killed herself.

Alicia: I don't feel well.

Arabella: Want another story?

Alicia: No. Let's finish this one.

(*Silence.*)

Arabella: It's stifling. Could you open a window please?

(*Silence.*)

Allegra: My stomach doth turn against kissing extremely. There was an old judge laid me over the face last night, and did so squeeze his grisly bristles through my lips, I'd as lief as kissed a row of pins with the points turned to me. And yet I was forced to take it, take it with a curtsy, too!

Amaranta: I'd as lief they should belch in my face. And yet I like kissing, too, if I may choose my man and place.

Allegra: Fie, fie, if anyone should hear ye.

Amaranta: Well, I'd rather be a wanton than a fool.

Alicia: Let me see – where was her husband?

(*Schmaltzy music from* Ben Hur.)

Arabella: (*melodramatic, on her knees*) On that day, her husband was not at home. Entertaining no thoughts of treachery to come, he had left Lucretia, his most prized possession, in the safety of their bejewelled palace. Trapped within her own bedchamber, Lucretia struggled to preserve her virtue. Prince Tarquin fell into a passion, drew his sword, and cried, "You will not escape me!" And Lucretia replied, "Kill me then, for I would rather die than consent."

Allegra: What is better than an eye for an eye?

Amaranta: A tooth for a tooth.

Allegra: Yes.

Alicia: She had no choice. She had to give in when he threatened to spread his filthy lies. Once rumours have started ... After all, he was the prince. Everyone would believe him.

Arabella: He concocted a great malice, saying he would publicly declare that he had found her with one of his sergeants.

Alicia: She was so scared that she suffered his rape. What else could she do?

Allegra: (*getting up*) Last night, I had a dream. It was midnight. He was waiting for me at the airport. And when he saw me, he said, "Darling!

What's wrong? You look as if you'd like to kill me!" And I said, "Oh no. I'd rather kill myself." BANG!

Amaranta: You mean you shot him? You didn't shoot yourself? That wasn't very nice. What if you had missed and hit someone else?

Allegra: Oh, dear. I'm sorry.

Amaranta: That's all right. It was just a dream.

Arabella: The next day, she called her entire family. She called her father, she called her mother, she called her cousins ...

Allegra and Amaranta: (*whisper, prompting her*) Her husband!

Arabella: She called her father, she called her mother ... she called her husband.

Alicia: And she called Prince Tarquin and poked out his eyes!

Arabella: (*jumps to her feet*) No, no, no, she was a virtuous woman. She took the dagger from the folds of her dress ...

Alicia: (*jumps up*) And stabbed him seven times!

Arabella: No, she was a noble woman!

Alicia: She called the police?

Arabella: No! Tell the story.

Alicia: She took ... She took ... (*She stops, unable to finish.*)

Allegra: She took the dagger from the folds of her dress and allowed it to plunge deeply into her own breast.

Alicia: I don't feel well.

Arabella: And Lucretia said, "This is how I absolve myself of shame and show my innocence." (*Pause.*) Now go to sleep.

(*During the following story the four women clear away the* Lucretia *props and prepare for the next scene as they tell* Anna *a story.*)

M.2: Anna, I just told you a story.

M.1: One story is enough, Anna.

M.4: Anna, it's very late.

M.3: Anna!

(M.1 *is caught in slide light beside fridge.*)

M.1: My name is Marianne Bachmeier.

(*She turns away from the slide light, slide light goes out.*)

M.1: All right Anna – just one more story.

M.3: But it's a sad story.

M.1: It's the story of a princess. She was the fairest in the land.

M.4: She had the freshest mouth in town.

M.1: One day a handsome prince took her as his bride. His cheeks were apple red and his hair was black as night.

M.2: They lived in a castle made of chocolate and they dined on peach pie day and night.

M.1: But then the prince fell under an evil spell and turned into a wild beast. The princess lost her appetite and locked herself in her room. She could hear him growling and snarling outside her door. She was trapped inside forever and she cried day after day after day ...

A MARIANNE INTERLUDE

Eena: Is this the face of a murderess?

(*The women freeze, looking out at audience.*)

Maria: Is this the face of a murderess?

(*The women move in a box step, in unison, then stop.*)

Jenny: Is this the face of a murderess?

(Jenny *claps. As she claps, the women turn their heads as in mug shots. The clapping speeds up and the turns become uncontrolled. They stop and then begin the box step again in unison. It continues through the following lines.*)

Eena: (*putting on sunglasses*) Last night I overheard my husband joking with his friends. He calls me the mattress. Imagine ...

M.1: (*lighting cigarette*) When we lived in Hanover his favourite game was to lock me out of the house in my negligée.

Jenny: (*putting on sunglasses*) Once he drove me out to Etobicoke at three a.m. and told me to find my own way home.

Maria: (*inarticulate, putting on sunglasses*) Well ... um ... you see ... he ...

Jenny: He never uses the front door. He likes to startle me at the window.

Eena: He's so funny. He says I have one breast the size of a lemon and the other the size of a grapefruit.

M.1: He loves secret codes and at dinner one tap means coffee and two taps mean tea.

Maria: Well, you see, last night he tugged at the sleeve of my bathrobe and ripped it.

(*The women freeze. Then* Jenny *and* Eena *take off their sunglasses and turn to the audience for the following joke.*)

Eena: Madge, what can I do about my hands?

Jenny: They look as if they've been through the blender.

Eena: Madge, I'm always locking myself in the bathroom. How can I get rid of him?

Jenny: Hydrochloric acid?

Eena: Is it strong?

Jenny: You're soaking in it.

(M.1 *breaks away and moves downstage and sits beside a lunch bag and an ashtray. She begins talking to Chris.*)

M.1: (*holding ashtray*) Chris, your lunch is ready. I have two salami sandwiches, an apple, an orange and your favourite chocolate bar. (*She puts out cigarette and reaches for the lunch bag. She looks in the bag and then at* Chris.) Two salami sandwiches, an apple, an orange ... an apple, and your favourite chocolate bar ... your favourite chocolate bar. (*She packs and repacks the lunch trying to get it right for* Chris. *She polishes and polishes the apple. The feeling is that the harder she tries to please him the angrier he becomes.*)

Eena: (*interrupts lunch*) Is this the face of a murderess?

(Eena, Jenny *and* Maria *all come together and start to boxstep in unison. They are all wearing their sunglasses. They boxstep through the following lines.*)

Eena: Jenny's real sweet, but I wouldn't want to meet her boyfriend in a dark alley.

Maria: (*hesitantly*) Have you told anyone?

Jenny: It's like this. Either Eena stays or she has to live on welfare. Who wants to live on welfare with three kids? Who wants to live on welfare?

Eena: I'd drive Jenny to the shelter, but I think she's afraid they have a long waiting list. But they don't turn anyone away in an emergency.

Maria: The kids ... the kids need their father.

Eena: She says she fell down the stairs. That's the eighth time this month she's fallen down the stairs.

Jenny: She lives in a bungalow.

Jenny: Well ... um ... was it an accident?

Jenny: If I were Maria I'd leave him on the spot. But she doesn't believe in divorce.

(*A short silence and then they all start to talk at once. The lines are improvised. For example:* "YOU HAVE TO TAKE THE GOOD WITH THE BAD." "I ASKED HIM TO GET HELP." "I CALLED THE SHELTER YESTERDAY ..." *They stop suddenly and look around embarrassed. They start again, then stop. Pause.*)

Eena: It's not going to happen again. He promised.

Jenny: I love him and that's that.

Maria: Nothing has happened.

(*They stop the box step.* Eena *and* Jenny *move to the clothesline singing the first lines of the song "I Can't Stop Loving You".* Jenny *sits in chair by the laundry line and reads a paper.* Eena *hangs up signs with clothes pins. The signs are:* GET OUT / NO / I'D RATHER / CRY / DRINK / EAT / WATCH TV / SHOP / KILL / MYSELF. *The signs are winched out in this order as* Jenny *reads newspaper headlines. During this sequence,* Maria *continues a very small box step.*)

Jenny: "When Love Turns To Bloody Murder. The Story of Colin Thatcher ..." "Reagan Presses Plan For Space Defence. Kremlin Doubtful On Talks ..." "Dr Morgentaler Doused With Ketchup. Crown Presses Appeal ..." "Abused Wife Refuses To Testify Against Husband. 93% never press charges. See Page 7."

Maria: (*removes sunglasses and takes a music box from her apron pocket. She opens the music box, which plays "The Impossible Dream" as she speaks.* Eena *does a tiny box step.*) September ... October ... November ... December ... January. Applied for a job. February. Started work at Eaton's. Verbal threats. March. Billy's tonsils. April ... May. Promotion. Black eye. June. Bruised thigh. July. Vacation in Muskoka. Broken nose, no charges. August. Birthday party. Surprise attack. Nose, cheek, stomach, thigh, pelvis, arm. A week indoors. September ... October ... November ... (*She closes music box and returns it to apron pocket.* M.1 *begins pacing at the end of* Maria's *speech. When she stops and turns to look at the fridge* Maria *is silent.* Marianne *walks slowly up to the fridge and puts her hand to the door as if to open it.* Jenny *and* Eena *turn and look at her. She doesn't open the door. She backs away from it. Turns around and is caught in a light. She sits down and addresses the audience.*)

M.1: Chris and I are having this ongoing fight. We're into day four of the trial and he says it's just like a Sam Peckinpah film. I think it's more like Bergman. There's no violence in the courtroom. It just reminds me of a high school auditorium, and everybody's glad that nobody's looking at them. The judge is up there like the principal laying down the law and you don't have any say and you're sure he knows something you don't want him to know ... Every time I walk into the courtroom everybody turns to look at me. I tell you I've never gotten so much mileage out of a suede skirt ... You know it's funny though, when I look at him – Grabowski – I don't see him at all. I see Anna. And then the next moment I zoom in on his chin and I'm, wondering, did he cut himself shaving? ... It's just like a movie.

Maria: (*starting to box step slowly*) Before I was married, I had a clerical job. But then Frank really wanted to move to Toronto. I didn't mind leaving my job but I really missed my family. (*She turns to look at* M.1 *and inches towards her in box-step rhythm.*)

M.1: (*Starting a box step*) Before I lived in Hanover, I was miles away from where I worked – but I always managed. Hans had a red sports car and usually drove me everywhere.

Maria: Before I met Frank, I never read the Sports section. Now we fight for it every Sunday.

M.1: (*continuing a box step*) I'm not overly paranoid. I didn't go around expecting it to happen to me. I think that kind of attitude brings on bad stuff.

Maria: I couldn't wait to have a baby, but every time I mentioned it, Frank got upset. But then he got a raise. (*M.1 and* Maria *move away from each other in box step rhythm.* M.1 *moves stage left and* Maria *moves stage right.*)

M.1: After I found a flat I could afford, I started working at The Diamond. It was OK – a real quiet time for us – just me and Anna. I sort of wanted to stay in one place.

Maria: (*taking bigger box steps and moving downstage*) After his promotion, we moved into a bigger house, bought a new car, and the kids were getting settled into a new school. He was under a lot of pressure. The mortgage was so heavy, I started looking for work again.

M.1: Look, it's crazy to blame yourself. I hadn't been seeing anyone for three months. And who comes in just as we're closing? ... So I let Hans drive me home.

Maria: (*stops box step*) I would have loved a job in a chocolate shop, but I ended up at Eaton's. I blew my first paycheque on everybody's favourite foods. But when I came home, he had that funny look on his face. I ran up to the bathroom.

M.1: After he raped me, I went home and I thought I'll just wash myself thoroughly and forget the whole thing. I was just about to step into the shower (*stops box step*) when I changed my mind and called the police. I got all dressed up for the courtroom. He got a year and six months.

Maria: Nothing has happened.

(Maria *sits down in chair stage right, puts on her sunglasses.* M.1 *sits in chair stage right of fridge.* Jenny *and* Eena *resume humming, "I Can't Stop Loving You," while* Jenny *reads the paper,* Eena *takes down the laundry, leaving* "KILL" *and* "GET OUT" *up on the line till the last, then taking down* "KILL" *but leaving* "GET OUT" *up.*)

Jenny: One out of five Canadian murders due to wife assault, says government commission. Ann Landers says women prefer cuddling. Hemlines plummet in Paris fashion show. Victim strikes back. Murder or self-defence? See page 4.

M.1: Last night I had a dream. I walked up to the courtroom: Anna wasn't there. It was a sunny day.

(*The lighting has changed to a dream-like blue.* Eena *is slowly winching the* "GET OUT" *sign towards herself.* Jenny *takes off her sunglasses and begins to speak. As she does so,* Eena *talks improvisationally underneath her, about the same topic.* M.1 *improvises moments from her own world – "I walked into the courtroom" etc.*)

Jenny: Well, you know what happened to me last night? Gord was watching TV. I was bored. (Eena *improvises underneath – e.g. "He never talks to me while he's watching TV, so I'm bored out of my skull, right?" etc. non-stop.*) He wouldn't talk to me. So I went to the kitchen to heat up some peach pie. When I came back to the living room, I thought I saw a little halo around his head. But then I realized it was just the blue glow of the TV. Then I noticed that instead of pie, somehow I was holding the heavy no-stick frying pan. (Eena: " *... holding the poker in my hands ... "*) And as I raised it above his head, I said: "Honey?"

(Eena, Jenny *and* Maria *all raise their hands above their heads in a striking gesture.* Eena *and* Maria *echo* Jenny's *"Honey?"* M.1 *lifts her arm in a shooting gesture. They hold a moment of tension.*)

Jenny: Honey? (*pause*) Would you like some eggs? But he was asleep.

Marianne: It was just a dream.

(Eena *rips down the* "GET OUT" *sign.* Maria *takes centre stage.*)

Maria: Last night, I had a dream. Everything is reversed. (*Increasingly in the voice of a B-movie gangster.*) He's really scared this time. He runs up the stairs and locks himself in the bathroom. I take the lock off the door. I can hear him crying in the tub. And I say, "All right, sweetheart, now it's my turn. I've had enough of having my face shoved into dirt." Bang!

Jenny: Is this the face of a murderess?

(*All women gather downstage in a clump, and resume the box step.*)

Eena: You know what happened to me last night? I went to take the garbage out and just kept walking and walking towards the bus depot, without my purse or anything. Imagine. So there I was in the middle of Bloor Street without a cent. So I went home.

Maria: Last night during a commercial I just picked up the phone and for no reason at all I was suddenly dialling my mother's number. When she answered, I didn't have anything to say. So I hung up.

M.1: After Chris hit me, I just laughed in his face. I said, "Can't you hit me harder?" The love of my life. The next time he did it, I threw a beer glass at his head. Now he thinks twice.

Jenny: Do you know what happened to me last night? Last night, he threw the sugar bowl at the wall. It just missed my head. And this morning he asked for sugar in his coffee. (*Laughs.*) I never laughed so hard in all my life.

(*Pause. Then* Jenny, Maria *and* M.1 *begin to speak in low voices simultaneously. Improvised e.g.* M.1 *"Then there was the time with the ashtray ..."*; Maria: *"You have to take the good with the bad"*; Jenny: *"It's hard to make a decision."*)

Eena: (*stops moving, pulls down her sunglasses a bit*) Now go to sleep.

(*The lights slowly fade to blackout, with the three women still moving and speaking.*)

HOW TO BE A VICTIM

(*This scene is one of organized mayhem, much of it improvised, all of it humorous. The performers give each other names such as "Evangeline" or "Roberta" each night, as fancy strikes them. Here, they will be described as* Victim 1, Victim 2, *and* Victim 3. *The fourth performer makes her way off stage and returns as the interviewer later. In the darkness, the beginning of the Mary Poppins' song "Spoonful of Sugar" plays.* Victim 3 *calls out:* "How to be a victim!" *Lights up. The actors are caught in some awkward position moving about on stage.*)

Victim 1: "How to be a victim." This scene may be offensive to some. Please don't watch this scene.

(*The other actors chime in, saying "Please don't watch this scene," as they clean up from the previous scene and get their props. Each victim has her own character: in this production,* Victim 1 *whined and complained about every-*

thing she had to do at this particular moment, while Victim 2 *was overeager and extremely naïve, and* Victim 3 *was a perfect young lady.* Victim 1 *appears on stage seemingly balancing an apple on her head and talking about the importance of posture; as she bends over to scratch her leg, it turns out the apple is attached to her head with a rubber band.* Victim 2 *commences to cross the stage on doilies, improvising lines on her doily-walking technique.* Victim 3 *appears with a red purse on one arm, pulling a toy dinosaur perched on a toy car on a leash. She meets* Victim 2 *in the middle of the stage.*)

Victim 3: Say hello to the lady.

Victim 2: (*screams*)

(Victim 2 *gets to her chair.* Victim 1 *is sorting photographs.* Victim 3 *gets up on her chair and strikes a pose of screaming in fright, as in the proverbial woman frightened by mouse. She then matter-of-factly puts the dinosaur in her purse.*)

Victim 2: (*sitting down, to* Victim 1) I got here.

Victim 1: I know.

Victim 2: And you know what – I saw a dinosaur!

Victim 1: It was fake.

Victim 2: I thought they were extinct.

Victim 1: They are.

(Victim 3 *squeaks her dinosaur and pops it back into her purse. The beginning of a teach-yourself-typing tape clicks in. A male voice booms:* "How's your posture? Are you ready? Type! K-I-J-Y, etc. Victim 1 *shows* Victim 2 *various photographs and gives her instructions.* Victim 2 *assumes various cheesecake positions according to instructions.* Victim 3, *sitting apart, applies lipstick over and over again to her mouth, smearing it liberally.*)

Victim 1: All right, now look at this photograph. Memorize that pose. Ready? Take brown ground wire and connect to point B1 behind head. Take blue wire with spiked ends and connect it to point B1. Run the 2 millimetre socket from point A1 to A2 across foot. And smile. Good! Try this one. Reverse point 2 back to point A1. Bring point B1 down to point C. Good. Lean forward, twist and smile. Good. All right, try this one without me.

(Victim 2 *goes through various poses, quoting the stock market. This in interspersed with quotations from movies, spoken by* Victim 3. Victim 1 *tosses the photos onto the floor, one by one.*)

Victim 2: Pan Am, up 2.

Victim 3: Darling, you're beautiful when you're angry.

Victim 2: General Electric, down one.

Victim 3: Rhett, Rhett, don't leave me, Rhett.

Victim 2: Exxon, up 10.

Victim 3: There's no place like home.

Victim 1: 2: Kelloggs, down two.

Victim 3: You know how to whistle, don't ya?

Victim 2: Amoco, up four.

Victim 3: (*takes out a newspaper clipping. The typing tape stops. Reading in a loud, careful and neutral voice.*) Dear Ann Landers: I never thought I would credit herpes with giving new life to my marriage but it did. Here is my story. Recently, a friend of ours caught herpes from his girlfriend. He gave it to his unsuspecting wife. When the doctor told her what she had she went crazy. That night, while he was asleep, she beat his head in with a tire wrench. He is in the hospital with a fractured skull. Ever since that happened, my husband treats me like a piece of Dresden china.

(*The Interviewer enters, standing behind the audience, sometimes walking up and down the aisle. Although there is a set list of questions, The Interviewer may improvise, as may those answering. The answers should be improvised as much as possible. To indicate the humorous nature of the responses, some of them are recorded here in brackets.*)

Interviewer: Are you ready? Are you comfortable? What's your name? Speak up, please! You over there – how old are you? Do you have any children? How many? What did your father do? Do you really like yourself? Do you work at all? What is your worst quality? (**Victim 1:** Eat too much!) What are you afraid of? (**Victim 2:** Dinosaurs!) Have you ever been in a fight? Who started it? Where are your children now? What are your qualifications? (**Victim 2:** I'm a nice person!) How do you make a car? How do you get a mortgage? (**Victim 3:** My uncle is a lawyer and you ...) How do you rob a bank? (*totally exasperated*) How do you toss a salad? (*All victims make wild tossing gesture*) What are you doing here? Do you drink? (**Victim 1:** Socially.) Do you smoke? (**Victim 1:** Socially.) Are you happy? (**Victim 1:** Socially.) State your weight ... (**Victim 2:** 135 pounds!) ... in kilograms! (**Victim 2:** I'm too fat!) Do you cry? Often? Is it a hobby? What are you afraid of? (**Victim 2:** Dinosaurs!) Who do you hate ... the most? (**Victim 1:** Jane Fonda! **Other Victims:** You don't hate Jane Fonda. **Victim 1:** The workout, I hate the workout.) Would you do a thing like that? (**To Victim 3**) Fix your makeup when you talk to me! (**To Victim 2**) Push back your hair! (**To Victim 1**) You over there – can you dance? CAN YOU DANCE!

(*Victim 1 sheepishly takes centre stage. She dances a few modest steps, and ends with a small flourish, to the sound of the typing instructions.*)

Interviewer: Dance!

(Victim 1 *begins to dance again, as the typing tape is overlaid with a disco beat. She dances the twist, the swim, with the encouragement of the other victims.*)

Interviewer: (*interrupting her*) Dance! (Victim 3 *desperately begins to dance with her feet only, still seated.*)

Interviewer: Dance!

(*The victims exchange secretive glances.* Victim 2 *reaches for a photograph of a young girl dressed up for the prom.* Victim 3 *takes a razor from her purse, rolling her eyes at the audience.* Victim 1 *dances over to* Victim 3, *gets the razor.* Victim 3 *taps out a drum roll with her feet.* Victim 2 *walks to centre stage displaying the photo.* Victim 1 *defiantly slices it in half. The victims giggle in complicity.*)

Interviewer: That's not very funny!

(*All the victims apologize profusely as they clean up the stage. The interviewer walks down to the stage. When everything is ready for the next scene,* Victim 1 *looks at the audience.*)

Victim 1: I told you not to watch this scene.

(*The lights change for the last scene.*)

THE STORY OF MARIANNE BACHMEIER

(*Briefly all Mariannes pace back and forth.* M.3 *swiftly climbs up on stage and walks up to the refrigerator. When she begins to speak, the other Mariannes get into place:* M.4 *far stage right,* M.1 *close to her,* M.2 *seated by the accordion downstage left.*)

M.3: This is a story of revenge. It's about a beautiful woman named Marianne. The Avenging Mother. *Die Rachemutter.*

Accordionist: (*sitting on floor behind accordion*) Revenge. Revenge. Beware you terrible man. You won't escape me. Even if an entire world stood between us I'd crawl up to you on all fours, feeling for each step with my hands. I will catch up to you and then ... (*pause*)

Curlilocks, curlilocks,
What did you do?
Your nest is so empty,
Your fingers are blue.
You are the fairest in all of the land.
Rockabye, rockabye,
Fly away home.

(The Accordionist – M.1 – *gets up, and walks to stand beside the fridge, stage left. M.3 stands with her back to the audience, leaning on the fridge, staring at Anna's photo.*)

M.4: (*physically restrained by* M.1) My name is Marianne Bachmeier. (M.3 *opens the fridge door and gently swings with it.*) I'm 30. I have a wonderful daughter, Anna. She was seven years old. On that day, I was out in my van. Everyone knows my van, it's brightly painted with flowers. I can't keep my eye on Anna all the time. I'm always at the bar. I work there. I thought Chris was at home. I'm not married, there was never any reason. Anyway, I'm not seeing him now. That has nothing to do with it.

(M.2 *lights a cigarette.*)

M.1: (*restrained by* M.4) They say I got off easy. But I think six years is long enough. After all, it wasn't planned. Although it's hard to make people believe it. Sometimes I don't believe it myself ... It was well hidden. I let my hand glide over the pistol ... What seems to bother people is that I was armed and he wasn't. But that's hardly the point, is it?

M.2: Anna?

M.3: (*shuts fridge, turns to look in the light*) Of course I remember the day. It was a Wednesday. (*Gets a cigarette.*) I saw Anna in the morning before she went off to school. She was making her favourite sandwiches for lunch. She was quite grown up in a lot of ways. (*Lights cigarette.*) Most of the time I gave her some money and she'd eat at the place on the corner. I had lunch with her sometimes – well, it's breakfast for me. Anna was very important to me and I don't see how all this has anything to do with it.

(*The slide projector clicks on catching* M.2 *in a square of light. All Mariannes move their heads as in mug shots, while the projector clicks away. Centre-right-centre-left-centre-centre-centre.* M.2 *remains staring into the white light.*)

M.2: Could you stop that please? (*The light goes out.*) I would like to ask the jury, what did you think I was – hysterical? (*She takes a short puff from her cigarette.*)

(*The second scene with* Marianne *and her friend, this time in prison. The blocking is identical to the previous scene, except that the actress who played the friend now plays* Marianne *and vice versa.*)

M.4: Thanks for coming.

Friend: You don't have to thank me. I'm your best friend. I'm going to visit all the time.

M.4: Every week?

Friend: As often as they'll let me.

M.4: What if I get a life sentence?

Friend: Oh come on, you won't be in that long.

M.4: Did you see the papers?

Friend: Of course. They're hard to miss.

M.4: What did you think?

Friend: Well, so far everyone seems to be on your side.

M.4: I think it's great. The day Anna was killed I thought: the whole world has to know about this.

Friend: What the whole world knows is that you shot him at his own trial.

M.4: Anna was on trial there. Not him.

Friend: What's it like here? Do they treat you well?

M.4: Well, It's not the Riviera. The guard is nice though. She worries that I smoke too much.

(*Pause.*)

Friend: Can I ask you something?

M.4: Sure.

Friend: How did you feel when you shot him?

M.4: It felt all right.

Friend: But how did you feel?

M.4: I felt OK.

Friend: Oh come on.

M.4: No, I was fine ... Oh, I don't know ... I'm just sorry I didn't get him in the face ... and they took my pistol away from me.

(M.2 *and* M.3 *have watched this scene, smoking.* M.2 *puts out her cigarette.* M.3 *crouches down.*)

M.3: All right, Anna. You want a story? I'll tell you a story. Once upon a time there was a little girl and she was born and her mother was miserable.

(*All* Mariannes *begin to pace again.* M.3 *puts out her cigarette and paces as well.* M.2 *gets a glass of milk. As she speaks to Anna, the other* Mariannes *take the shooting gesture through a series of starts and stops with each new sentence.*)

M.2: Anna, don't eat that! Careful of the cars! Now you come straight home from school. Anna, I told you not to talk to strange men. (*She sips milk as other* Mariannes *bring down a pointing gun.*) Anna ...

(*Other* Mariannes *relax the gesture and say softly:* "Anna?")

M.2: (*laughing*) ... you're such a clown!

(M.2 *returns the milk to the fridge.*)

THE JURY SCENE

(*The actors walk into the area stage left.*)

Woman 1: Is that the judge?

Woman 2: No, no – that's his lawyer. And there's Grabowski.

Woman 3: He looks like a murderer.

Woman 2: There's his fiancée.

Woman 4: I wish I could see her face. She's wearing a veil.

Woman 3: Well, no wonder. Wouldn't you?

Woman 2: I don't know.

Woman 4: He's still engaged?

Woman 1: Yes. You know, he's divorced. He has two children.

Woman 4: I don't believe that stuff about Anna. It's filthy.

Woman 1: He's a sick man.

Woman 2: He has a filthy mind.

Woman 3: He's lucky he's in jail. Otherwise he'd be lynched.

Woman 1: There she is.

All others: Marianne?

Woman 1: At the door.

Woman 4: This must be so hard for her to listen to.

Woman 3: Tragedy. It marks the face.

Woman 4: No one knows how a mother feels. She's so sad. It breaks my heart.

Woman 1: Here she comes. She's walking to her place.

(Woman 3 *starts a slow clap.*)

Woman 4: What was that?

Woman 3: Oh my God.

(*The clapping increases, also on tape. Everyone improvises on these lines, as they rush forward, run away, applaud:* "She shot him. He's dead. She shot him. I don't believe it. Bravo. Bravo. Bravo." *When the clapping has died down,* The Fiancée *begins to speak. She stands stock still, upstage right. The two remaining members of the jury return to their seats.*)

Fiancée: Yes yes yes, of course the death of a child is a terrible thing and I share her mother's grief. But you cannot expect me to sympathize with Marianne Bachmeier. Klaus was my ... Klaus Grabowski was my fiancé ... I wish people would think of him sometimes. He hadn't had a job in months. He had nothing to do all day. He was a severely depressed man. Pretty little Anna comes knocking on his door. She didn't have to. He didn't force her to come there. He lets her in, he gets her some pop, some licorice ... This is not a nice story. But he said in the courtroom that little Anna threatened to tell her parents that he'd touched her. And he swore in the courtroom that Anna said her father touched her there. Her father. And that her father paid her for it. He said it under oath. Look, I know him. He did not mean to, he just lost control. And he was sorry. (M.1 *appears behind* The Fiancée, *holding a glass of milk.*) He was sorry for Anna's parents. He was terribly shocked by what he'd done. But Marianne? She knew what she was doing. She shot him in the back. And she wasn't sorry. She didn't care that he was dead. All she cared for was the loss of her gun.

(M.1 *takes a few steps forward, while* The Fiancée *turns away.*)

Woman 3: She'll get life for this.

Woman 4: She doesn't look like a murderer. If it had been me, I would have ...

Woman 3: Maybe she was hysterical.

Woman 4: My mother sent her flowers.

Woman 3: She shouldn't get away with this. The law is there for a reason.

Woman 4: I don't feel well. I don't feel well at all.

Woman 3: God never sends us more than we can bear.

Woman 4: She's been through a lot. But at least she's not alone – no one seems to know his name though – the new one?

Woman 3: (*pause*) He's a Turk. (*Pause.*) Apparently he's a regular at the bar where she works. What a sleazy life.

Woman 4: I really sympathize with her. If it had been me, I would have ...

Woman 3: She was hysterical.

Woman 4: Apparently she works night and day.

Woman 3: Abortions, rapes. These things don't happen to just anyone.

Woman 4: She wanted Anna to have a beautiful future.

Woman 3: And why did pretty little Anna have to dawdle about the streets like a little whore? Because her mother didn't give her lunch.

Woman 4: She was just a little girl.

Woman 3: She was just a little whore.

Woman 4: If it had been me, I would have ...

M.1: (*coming forward*) I could have put strychnine in his coffee. I could have put arsenic in his soap. If I had a knife ... I could have hit him with my van ... or if he had a child ...

Fiancée: No.

M.1: No. (*Opens the fridge.*)

Woman 4: If it had been me, I would have chopped him up into little bits.

Woman 3: (*starts to slash the air with her red purse*) Chopped him up into little bits, chopped him up into little bits, chopped him up into little bits ...

M.1: (*sotto voce*) I could have put arsenic in his soup ... (*Continues to improvise underneath.*)

Woman 3: (*leaps up*) She shot him.

Fiancée: In the back.

Woman 3: She shot him!

Fiancée: In the back.

Woman 3: She shot him!!

Fiancée: In the back!

Woman 3: Bravo!

Fiancée: No.

Woman 3: Bravo!

Fiancée: No.

Woman 3: Bravo!!

Fiancée: No!

Woman 4: She was just a little girl.

(*M.1 slams the fridge,* Woman 4 *stands up and as she does so her white purse opens and spills out a mess of nails on the floor,* Woman 3 *drops her red purse in the middle of the nails. Everybody freezes on stage. Then without taking their eyes off the nails, they gingerly make their way back to their final positions – as Mariannes. M.1 and M.2 stand on the downstage edges of the stage as in the beginning. M.4 sits in the chair stage left of the fridge and smokes a cigarette. M.3 stands behind her, at a slight angle. They get into place with great difficulty – one woman crawls up the stage, another creeps across the fridge, for example. When everyone is in place:*)

M.3: (*as Anna*) Mami, du bist zu spät gekommen. (Mummy, you came too late.)

(M.4 *turns her head irritably and says "tsk!"*)

M.1: You're smoking too much.

M.4: Tsk!

M.3: Mami, warum bist du so spät gekommen? (Mummy, why did you come so late?)

M.4: Tsk!

M.2: You should get more sleep.

M.4: Tsk!

M.3: Mami, du sollst nicht spät sein. (Mummy, you musn't be late.)

M.4: Tsk!

M.1: I think I'll read Anna a story tonight.

M.3: Mami –

M.4: (*angrily*) Anna!

(*The slide projector comes on.*)

M.4: It's crazy to blame yourself.

M.3: When I think about Anna, I think about the beautiful things. Even her funeral was beautiful, I made sure of that. She wore a pretty skirt and bracelets, and I put flowers and stars in her hair. And we played her favourite music – Pink Floyd.

M.4: I considered Anna a human being, not my property. I didn't want her to be dependent on me, and I didn't want to be dependent on her. It's like this: Anna wasn't planned for, so when she came along, she just had to hang in there. And she did, she always did.

M.3: Anna's childhood was ten times better than my own. She had a dog.

She flew to Ibiza, Spain, countless times. I didn't go anywhere until I was twenty.

M.4: Once, Anna was out skating and I was supposed to pick her up, but I got delayed. When I finally arrived, she was frozen stiff, with blue lips and everything. And all she said to me was, "Mummy, you came too late. Don't come late next time, Mummy." That was it. No tears, nothing.

M.3: That's what Anna was like.

M.4: No interviews.

(*The slide projector goes out.*)

(*An improvised dialogue takes place between* M.1 *and* M.2, *during which* M.1 *and* M.4 *occasionally perform a moving gesture – leaning forward and walking into the courtroom, a small movement. The following is an approximation of the dialogue between* M.1 *and* M.2. *The major agreements are content and the first and last lines.*)

M.1: What happened? Do you remember?

M.2: Give me time. Give me time. It was a sunny day. I walked up to the courtroom, I opened the door.

M.1: It was a sunny day. I walked into the courtroom.

M.2: Did they search you? Why didn't they search you?

M.1: I let my hand glide over the pistol. It was well hidden.

M.2: It was a sunny day.

M.1: It was a Wednesday.

M.2: It was a Wednesday. I remember the day.

M.1: I saw his back. What if it hadn't been him?

M.2: I saw his back. It was only afterwards I thought – what if it hadn't been him? What if it had been someone else?

M.1: I let my hand glide over the pistol. How many times did you shoot him?

M.2: How many times did you shoot him?

M.1: Seven times, they said you shot him seven times.

M.2: Seven times, no, I couldn't shoot someone even once. It was a sunny day.

M.1: I saw his back. How did you feel?

M.2: I felt fine.

M.1: All I could think of was Anna.

M.2: I'm not sorry he's dead.

M.4: I would not do it again today.

M.3: I'm glad I did it.

M.4: Simply because it is wrong to kill another human being. I don't wish that he could be alive again.

M.3: I'm glad he's dead.

M.4: I only wish I hadn't done this myself.

(M.3 *steps forward, walks down a few steps, then turns to face the fridge. As she walks up to the fridge, the lights dim. She opens the door. Yodelling music begins. She turns and pours a glass of milk. She pours and pours. The milk splatters over her hand and onto the floor.*)

M.1 and M.2: (*very softly*) I did it for you, Anna.

(M.3 *offers the milk to Anna. She puts the glass back inside the fridge and shuts the door.*)

Blackout

THE END

Love is Strange

Paul Ledoux and David Young

Paul Ledoux was born in Halifax, Nova Scotia. He began writing for the theatre in Mont- real, where his play *The Electrical Man* won the Dominion Drama Festival's award for best play in 1975. Since that time he has had twenty-six plays pro- duced, including *Honky Tonk Angels* with Ferne Downey, *Judy!*, *Children of the Night*, and two collaborations with David Young: *Love is Strange* and *Fire*, which won both the Dora Mavor Moore and Chalmers awards for best musical play.

David Young has been active in a wide variety of literary and dramatic pursuits. He is the author of two books of fictions (*Agent Provocateur* and *Incognito*) and is President of the Coach House Press. In addition to his collaborations with Paul Ledoux on *Love is Strange* and *Fire*, he has written extensively for television and is the recipient of the York Trillium Award for his film script *The Suspect*. Currently he is working with Paul Ledoux on a play about Glenn Gould.

DAVID YOUNG (LEFT), PAUL LEDOUX (RIGHT)
PHOTO CREDIT: DAVID HYLINSKI

Love is Strange was first produced at Magnus Theatre in Thunder Bay on 5 April 1984, under the title *I Love You Anne Murray*. It was work-shopped at Factory Theatre in Toronto, Ontario, in March 1984.

PRODUCTION
Director / **Brian Richmond**
Musical Director / **Michael Taylor**
Design / **John Dinning**
Lighting / **Bryan Francis**
Choreography / **Ilsa Maguire**

CAST
David Conner / Franz Jacob Colby
Anne Wright / Linda Barrie, Edna Little, Kimberly Downey
Peter Zednick, Jerry Franken / The Crown, Larry, Chuck Edwards, Cop, keyboards
Brian Kennington / Dr Rand, Jones, Ted, Rick, Cord, Sandy, Reporter, bass guitar
Rennie Heard / The Judge
Michael Taylor / Priest, Cop, Clerk, Reporter, guitars

The show with its new title, *Love is Strange*, opened on 1 January 1985 at Centaur Theatre in Montreal, Quebec. The play was developed with the assistance of the Ontario Arts Council and the Nova Scotia Department of Culture, Recreation and Fitness.

PRODUCTION
Director / **Brian Richmond**
Musical Director / **Michael Taylor**
Set and Costume Design / **John Dinning**
Lighting / **Peter Smith**

CAST
David Conner / Franz Jacob Colby
Anne Wright / Linda Barrie, Edna Little, Kimberly Downey
Ross Douglas / The Crown, Larry, Chuck Edwards, Cop, keyboards
Brian Kennington / Dr Rand, Jones, Ted, Rick, Cord, Sandy, Reporter, bass guitar
Barney O'Sullivan / The Judge
Michael Taylor / Priest, Cop, Clerk, Reporter, guitars
Peter Zednick / Keyboards

CHARACTERS
With the exception of The Judge and Colby all performers play multiple roles and perform the music. Towards this end, a synthesizer is built into The Crown's bench playing area.

Franz Jacob Colby, an articulate, highly intelligent wheat farmer in his early 40s
Linda Barrie, a beautiful, wholesome pop superstar in her mid-30s
The Crown, a slightly pompous, ambitious prosecutor
The Judge, a crotchety old geezer with a wry sense of humour
Dr D.F. Rand, a middle-aged psychiatrist with the emotional maturity of a smiley-button
Sgt Jones, a cop with a notebook where his heart should be
Edna Little, a myopic personal secretary
Ted, a bum with a sense of romance
Chuck Edwards, Linda's husband/producer, a slick record producer with some rough edges
Rick Phillips, a speedy little autograph hound
Cord, a disturbed Springsteen fiend
Kim Downey, a young psychiatrist with a social conscience
Sandy, a gravedigger who hates his job
Cops, a court clerk, a priest, and reporters

PLAYWRIGHTS' NOTES
It can be argued that most modern love songs derive from a romantic tradition which goes back to the poetry of twelfth-century France. *Love is Strange* examines the way this tradition has been transformed by the electronic age. From Michael Jackson's glitter glove to Princess Di's hair, our contemporary understanding of love is shaped in the image of shared public fantasies. But how far into the communal fantasy is a citizen allowed to go before society deems him dangerous or insane?

In the beginning we were inspired by the complex and compelling story behind the headline-making trials of Robert Charles Kieling – a man who challenged the boundaries of convention in search of unity and personal completion. In the 18 months the three of us worked together on this project we found ourselves drawn deeper and deeper into the many questions raised by the case and our fictional retelling of it. Our conversations ranged over the true nature of love, romantic obsession, the way our system of justice deals with the mentally ill, the cult of celebrity, and the concept of freedom of the imagination. We were drawn to the humanity of the situation because, like most people, we've loved and been loved, fantasized about the "perfect mate," and experienced rejection. On another level we realize that we are plugged into the same network of public fantasy which delivered the message of love to Mr Kieling.

At bottom the character at the centre of our play is an explorer – a man lost in the grid of image and fantasy that drives our culture. We think his journey speaks volumes about who we are and how we live.

Paul Ledoux, Brian Richmond, David Young

SET

The action of the play takes place in three distinct manners: *Colby* speaks directly to the audience; defends himself in court; and tries to reconstruct the details of his relationship with *Linda Barrie* in a series of "memory scenes." The part of the play that takes place in *Colby*'s memory shifts locations; his tractor, clubs, arenas, back-stage, at dressing room doors, in his kitchen, at a funeral, in a hospital for the criminally insane, and inside the music of *Linda Barrie*.

As can be imagined the set must be very flexible indeed. What follows is a description of the original set design by John Dinning.

The back of the stage is a cyclorama, with the floor curving up to meet it. The floor is a highly reflective black, broken into squares by a white grid pattern. Downstage of the cyclorama is a platform for members of the band. This area is visible only when lit, the major image of the set being a series of reflective mylar panels that surround an abstract courtroom setting. Upstage centre is a platform, connecting with the band area. A stair unit leads to the main playing space. Stage right of the stair unit is an entrance, to the right of the entrance a small platform. On the platform sits a swivel chair used by the accused, *Colby*. Stage left of the stair unit is a black box, set on a small platform that functions as the witness box. Stage left of the box is the *Judge*'s bench, and beside it the bench of *The Crown*. Downstage of these set elements is an open playing area. The entire set is painted to blend with the floor.

SONGS

The play makes use of pop music from the repertory of a number of contemporary female singers.

Act One:
Stardust (Mitchell Parish and Hoagie Carmichael) Belwin Mills Co.
Snowbird (Gene MacLellan) Beechwood Music
Together Again (Buck Owens) Central Songs Inc.
In Dreams (Roy Orbison) Acuff Rose Publications
Stand By Me (Ben E. King, Leiber & Stoller) Trio Music Co.
Farewell to Nova Scotia (Trad.)

Act Two:
Heart Like a Wheel (Anna McGarrigle) Garden Court Music
Daydream (John Sebastien) Trio Music
That's Not the Way (It's S'posed to Be) (A. Goldmark & P. Gladston)
   Non Pareil Music and Kazzoom Music
You Needed Me (Charles R. Goodrum) Chappel & Co. Inc.

ACT ONE

The house system is playing the love songs of Schubert.

The Crown Prosecutor *enters with a court brief. He puts it down and calls for the ASM who wheels on a TV. He turns on the TV and an interview with* Linda Barrie *comes on the screen. At first the sound is inaudible, but after a moment* The Crown *turns up the sound. The house lights dim. The play begins.*

As the interview continues Jacob Colby *enters from the audience. He carries a briefcase and is dressed for court. He stands watching the interview for a few moments then takes his place and unpacks his briefcase, preparing for his trial.*

(Tape interview:)

Linda: The funny thing is I never really thought I'd end up in show business at this point in my life. You know, I'd be a housewife, raising my kids somewhere down home. That's all I ever really wanted, but ... I guess things never really turn out how you expect them to.

Larry: I guess not. I mean who'd ever believe a little girl from Mount Stewart, P.E.I. would end up a superstar, winner of every major music award. Boy, it must be tough.

Linda: *(laughing)* It's awful! Sometimes I worry about it, but I think I've struck a decent balance between home and the road. And the kids are doing fine.

Larry: Would you like them to get into the business?

Linda: No. It's too tough.

Larry: What's the hardest thing about being a star?

Linda: The lack of privacy.

Larry: Yeah, I heard one guy actually showed up at your father's funeral.

Linda: It was dreadful. Fortunately, the number of people who do that kind of thing is small.

Larry: But you've had your troubles ...

Linda: I guess it goes with the territory.

Larry: Since the John Lennon thing a lot of entertainers are very paranoid. Do you have those kinds of fears?

Linda: Oh yes, it's very frightening. Some nights I'm out on stage and I think there could be someone out there who ... it's usually only a flash. I don't even like to think about it.

Larry: Has Linda Barrie changed much over the years?

Linda: (*smiling*) She's not nearly as vulnerable as she used to be ... then again, none of us are.

Larry: How about a song?

(*On tape* Linda *gets up and walks into a performance area. The Band begins to play the intro to "Stardust."*)

Announcer: (*off*) Ladies and gentlemen ... Let's have a warm round of applause for three-time Grammy Award winner Miss Linda Barrie ...

(Linda *sings on TV and "live" on the upstage platform. As she sings the TV is wheeled off.*

A note on "Stardust": The lyrics of this standard deal with love in terms of dreams and memory. "The memory of love's refrain" is conjured up by the singer as she stands in a garden looking up at the stars.

During a musical bridge in the song the Court Clerk *speaks*)

Clerk: All rise in court.

(The Judge *enters and takes his place, and the song continues to its conclusion.* Linda Barrie *exits. There is a sudden light change which shifts us to court.* Colby *stands and is charged.*)

The Judge: Franz Jacob Colby you are charged with a breach of probation in that on or about the 19th day of October 1983 in the Municipality of Metropolitan Toronto you did willfully violate a probation order of the Provincial Court of Ontario. To wit, not to attend at the offices of Linda Barrie. How do you plead to the charge?

Colby: I plead not guilty.

The Judge: Be seated. The Crown may proceed.

The Crown: Thank you. Your Honour, the accused Franz Jacob Colby suffers, for lack of a better word, from an on-going 'infatuation' with Linda Barrie.

(*As* The Crown *speaks we hear the sound of a jet roaring overhead.* Colby *looks up. The lights shift. Guitar underscoring. The Judge and* The Crown *speak in an altered, slow-motion manner.*)

Colby: Snowbirds.

The Crown: As a result of this infatuation, he's been in and out of court for the past three years.

Colby: Even after all this time I can't hear a plane go overhead without thinking of her ... and snowbirds.

The Judge: Yes, I have the arrest record before me.

Colby: I've been arrested eight times for being in love with Linda Barrie.

The Judge: All of these charges relate to this ... Miss Barrie?

The Crown: It's Linda Barrie, Your Honour ... (*no reaction from* the Judge) of singing fame.

The Judge: Linda Barrie, of course.

Colby: It's true ... I love her.

The Crown: I think his record pretty much establishes the fact that Mr Colby has a habit of ignoring court orders on this matter.

Colby: If she were here she could clear this whole thing up in about three seconds flat, but she isn't. That's not her way. It never has been. It's crazy, but who knows, maybe everybody who falls in love is just a little bit crazy. See, when two people are in love they're in each other's heads all day long, no matter what kind of distance is between them! Love arcs like electricity ... across a city ... across a country ... like a halo around the world.

The Judge: Yes. Interesting. Let's go the charge at hand.

Colby: Now, here's what I don't understand ... For nearly 10 years I wrote to Linda, sent her presents, saw her whenever I could. For 10 years she welcomed, even encouraged my interest. Then one day, out of the blue, I'm arrested and thrown into jail. I was 40 years old and had never so much as picked up a parking ticket. Suddenly, I was trapped in a legal revolving door. I reach out towards Linda and I'm arrested. The same charge. The same arresting officer. Even the same prosecutor – Mr C.G. Broilman, a classic publicity-grubbing Toronto fool. And he calls his buddy Dr Rand, an ambulance-chasing psychiatrist who specializes in spewing narrow-minded notions about Linda and I for public consumption. Of course, the press loves it.

And the result of this circus? I end up in Canada's most famous prison for the criminally insane – Willowood Mental Health Centre, Maximum Security Unit. For doing what? For writing a girl a love letter.

(*The lights shift, action in court becomes "real" again.*)

The Crown: The substance of this charge is simple, Your Honour. On October the 19th 1983, Mr Colby went to Linda Barrie's office and left her a letter. This in violation of an order prohibiting Mr Colby from communicating with Miss Barrie in any way or attending at the homes or offices of herself, her family, or her employees. Mrs Edna Little, Miss Barrie's assistant, took the letter and called the police. Mr Colby was arrested at the Toronto International Airport. When he was arrested Mr

Colby told the arresting officer: "When it comes to my relationship with Linda Barrie, the police and most of the general public are full of cow-flop."

Colby: I object, Your Honour!

The Judge: One moment. Mr Colby?

Colby: I would just like to inform the Court that my statement grew out of an exchange of insults between myself and the arresting officer – a Sergeant Jones. He called me a pea-brained idiot. I was simply responding in kind.

The Judge: You don't need to worry, Mr Colby. Saying an officer is full of cowflop is not likely to affect my judgment. Mr Colby, do you have counsel?

Colby: I'm defending myself, Your Honour.

The Judge: You realize the seriousness of this matter, Mr Colby?

Colby: Yes, Your Honour.

The Judge: You are facing a jail sentence here.

Colby: For personal reasons I prefer to defend myself.

The Judge: Just so long as you know a lawyer can be made available to you.

Colby: Yes, thank you, Your Honour. Based on my previous encounters with Mr Broilman I should do just fine.

The Judge: Good ... you have everything you need for your defence?

Colby: Yes, Your Honour.

The Judge: Let's proceed.

The Crown: Yes, Your Honour, it's my intention to ...

Colby: Your Honour, if I might add ...

The Judge: Yes Mr Colby?

Colby: Yes, I just want to add, about this cowflop incident, that generally I'm very sympathetic towards police officers. My difficulties with the police are part of an ongoing situation which I will bring to the Court's attention in due course.

The Judge: Very well, thank you, Mr Colby.

Colby: Yes, Your Honour. It's just that there is a very good case to be made for the idea that I'm on trial for being in love with Linda Barrie.

The Judge: Let me assure you that is not how the charge reads. Mr Broilman?

The Crown: Thank you, Your Honour. Mr Colby's remarks have brought us very nicely to my first, and I hope only, witness in these proceedings. I would like to call Dr C.G. Rand.

Colby: I object, Your Honour.

The Crown: It is my belief that Dr Rand will be able to show the court that there is every reason to believe Mr Colby is insane.

The Judge: Do you understand Mr Rand's role in these proceedings, Mr Colby?

Colby: All too well, Your Honour. I've been through all of this before. Last year on the basis of Dr Rand's testimony I was committed to The Willows, the hospital for the criminally insane where Dr Rand works. After some months of incarceration my appeal on his committal came before the Provincial Mental Health Review Board and I was released on my own recognizance. In its decision the Board contradicted Dr Rand's diagnosis and that fact makes his presence here irrelevant.

The Crown: Your Honour, while it is true that the Board of Review did decertify Mr Colby that does not mean that in the Board's opinion he is a sane man.

Colby: Then, Your Honour, I wonder if Mr Broilman could explain what it does mean?

The Crown: It means that, in their opinion, the severity or type of mental illness present at that time was not sufficient to warrant further hospitalization.

Colby: So I was crazy, but I wasn't crazy enough to be locked up?

The Judge: In essence, I believe that's what the Crown is suggesting.

Colby: Sounds like a description of half the people in Toronto.

The Crown: Your Honour, I'm sure Dr Rand could illuminate this issue for us all.

The Judge: Mr Colby, at this stage of the proceedings the Crown has the right to raise this matter, however, you will be given every opportunity to cross-examine the doctor.

Colby: Thank you, Your Honour.

The Crown: Dr C.G. Rand, please.

Clerk: Dr C.G. Rand.

(*Underscoring as* Doctor Rand *takes the stand. We follow the proceedings as he is sworn in. But listen to* Colby.)

Colby: Here we go again. This gentleman has a mind like a cookie cutter and the emotional maturity of a smiley-button. He's got one answer for anything that has to do with the workings of the heart ... look it up in the book. Pin that complex emotion down on the page like a butterfly ... and then write something underneath it in Latin script.

The Crown: Dr Rand, are you able to tell the Court what, in your view, Mr Colby is suffering from?

Rand: Mr Colby suffers from a classic case of Erotic Paranoia.

(The Judge *looks up. He's been reading a report.*)

The Judge: What? What was that?

The Crown: Erotic, that's E-R-O-T-I-C. Paranoia, P- ...

The Judge: You may proceed, Dr Rand.

Rand: It's a textbook case, really. Here's a description of the condition I've copied from *Modern Clinical Psychiatry* by Kolb ...

The Judge: By who?

The Crown: Kolb. K-O- ...

Rand: It's a standard psychiatric text. (*Reads*) "The patient believes that some woman of wealth whom he may have casually seen or met is in love with him. He writes her affectionate letters and perhaps poems. Her failure to respond in kind is intended solely to test his love."

(Colby *moves away from the courtroom action.*)

Colby: Did you see the way everybody perked up when he said the magic word? E-R-O-T-I-C. I looked it up in the dictionary – it's from the Greek, eros, meaning: "the drive toward higher forms of being and relationship."

But just listen to them ... like a bunch of adolescent boys clamouring over a girlie book in the back corner of a schoolyard. They turn me into whatever it is they fear inside themselves.

The fact is, this whole business began in about as down to earth a way as you can imagine ... it was my thirty-third birthday ...

(*Underscoring begins. Lights fade,* Colby *pulls a baseball hat from his briefcase and walks to the upstage platform. He sits on a stool in a tight spotlight.*)

Colby: Eight a.m. and still next to pitch black, the way it is in the middle of February, in the middle of Alberta. It had snowed a lot during the night and I'm out plowing the road up to the house ... it's funny, I can still remember the smell of Aqua Velva, a little present I brought for myself in town ... and with that aroma the exact thought I have as I reach up to turn on the radio ... (Colby *reaches up to turn on his radio. He snaps his fingers. We hear radio static.*) I'm thinking about my place in the world. Thirty-three years old what am I? A single man ... on an 800-acre family farm ... alone ... (*The sound of a jet.* Colby *looks up.*) A plane roars overhead. I look up into the darkness ... and strangely ... it's as if I'm up there on that plane. I look out and see myself, a tiny detail in an aerial photograph, a little blob of light on a lonely road. A man in a glass box with waves of snow shooting up all around. (Colby *tunes in a station.*)

Announcer: And across Canada it looks like more snow.

Colby: This is how it's going to be for me. Trapped in a pattern that's entirely governed by the tilt of the earth on its axis. Six months of light and warmth where you struggle to bring in a decent crop ... (Colby *changes stations again.*)

Announcer: Six killed in Cambodia ...

Colby: Then she tilts back the other way ... it gets darker and colder ... until everything dies except for what's inside the little circle you draw around yourself. And then you vanish ... become part of a big silence. (Colby *changes stations again. We hear the last chords of a song.*)

Disc Jockey: And that was Miss Tammy Wynette singing "He's Gone." Now here's a new release from a little lady from P.E.I. who is rising fast on the country charts in the U.S. of A no less. Here's Linda Barrie with a Canadian classic.

(*Soft lights up on the lower playing area.* Linda Barrie *is standing in front of a mike, playing guitar and singing "Snowbird." She's dressed simply. This is the very beginning of her career.*

The lyric of "Snowbird" deals with images of winter and spring. A tiny bird struggles against the wind as the singer dreams of a peaceful country setting.

Colby *listens to the song intently. When it ends he looks down at* Linda *and speaks to her, although she can't hear him.*)

Colby: See ... sitting there, listening to you, it was like I was stepping away from myself. I wasn't much different from a lot of guys I knew. My Dad had passed on. Mom was in a nursing home in Red Deer, and my brother, well he never much cared for farming. So there I was; "stuck with the farm." But I never saw it that way. No, I wanted that farm. I plunged right into it, tried to create my own little 800-acre universe.

What I couldn't afford to buy, I'd build. What I couldn't find, I'd invent. I put up a new barn, and a windmill. I ran a model operation ... but ... it didn't matter. I still felt like nothing. Jacob Colby, going through the motions of working a deserted family farm.

Then that dawn, listening to you ... it was like something opened in my heart and let in a burst of pure colour. Suddenly that old song I'd heard a million times seemed to make sense out of life, and the feelings I was trying to control. Both of us were caught in the same cycle of death and rebirth ... in a world where love had been lost. But ... a little bird was struggling against the winter wind, flying away to ... the land of gentle breezes where the peaceful waters flow. A land of love.

But ... what did I know about love? A dozen dates with women who didn't understand half of the things I said to them. But there you were. The radio. A voice ... the simple, clear voice of a country girl who took my feelings and turned them into poetry. I think I fell for you that very moment and I didn't want to be alone any more.

(*Underscoring out.* Colby *walks downstage. Jet roar. Lights shift back into court.*)

The Crown: So, in summing up you would say that Mr Colby's condition must inevitably deteriorate?

Rand: Without treatment, yes. I have no idea what he may do next.

The Crown: No further questions, Your Honour.

The Judge: Mr Colby, you may cross-examine Dr Rand.

Colby: Thank you, Your Honour. Dr Rand it would seem that crucial to your whole argument is the delusional aspect of my mental state. Is that right?

Rand: That is the primary symptom, yes.

Colby: What am I deluded about?

Rand: That this relationship between you and Linda Barrie exists.

Colby: I see. And what constitutes a relationship between two people, Dr Rand?

Rand: Well, I would guess a mutual acceptance of the fact that a relationship exists.

Colby: You mean, I would have to be asked if I believe there is a relationship between Linda Barrie and myself, and then she would have to be asked.

Rand: That's the problem, Jacob. There has been no mutual response on her part.

Colby: You know that isn't true, Clarence. You know from previous appearances that I have produced proof of her response ... for instance, this letter and picture sent to me by Linda Barrie. (Colby *takes the picture and* *gives it to* Rand.) Could you please read the inscription on the photo for the Court.

Rand: But, a person in her position probably gets letters from a large number of ...

The Judge: The inscription please, Dr Rand.

Rand: "Keep in touch, Linda." But this is the kind of picture Ms Barrie would send out to all her fans. Does that mean she has a "close" relationship with each and every person she responds to?

Colby: Dr Rand, I would suggest that she does indeed have a relationship with those people. However, I would note that you have added the word "close" to our discussion.

Rand: Those are your words, not mine.

Colby: I would point out to the Court that Dr Rand has been the only one to use the word "close" during this cross-examination.

Rand: You have always insisted that the relationship is intimate.

Colby: Oh, so now your are adding "intimacy" to our relationship.

Rand: All I'm trying to say is ...

Colby: You don't suggest my delusional system was based on intimacy when I asked you to define your terms, Dr Rand. Why are you trying to confuse the issue now?

Rand: I am not trying to confuse the issue. All I am saying is that your relationship with Ms Barrie is the same kind of relationship she has with thousands of other fans who correspond with her ...

Colby: Your Honour, a moment ago Dr Rand claimed I should be committed to a hospital for the criminally insane because I am deluded in my belief that I have a relationship with Linda Barrie. He now admits that, in fact, I have had a relationship – perhaps casual, perhaps not – but nevertheless, a relationship. Having lost that point he then falls back on innuendo, suggesting I believe I have an "intimate" relationship with Linda, when in fact I have suggested no such thing in Court today. Clearly, Dr Rand is contradicting himself and, in view of the decision by the Review Board that I'm as safe to walk the streets as the next fellow, I ask the Court to find that I am fit to stand trial.

The Judge: Well, Mr Colby, you may or may not be deluded, but it clearly doesn't affect your ability to defend yourself. No more questions, Dr Rand.

The Crown: But Your Honour ... Mr Colby has in the past freely admitted that he believes Linda Barrie is madly in love with him!

Colby: Your Honour, I'm on trial for breaking probation. My dramatically publicized "love" for Linda Barrie is not the real issue here.

The Judge: Quite so, Mr Colby. Dr Rand may step down, but at any time during this trial if I decide that the issue of your mental health is substantive I may recall the doctor.

Colby: Yes. Thank you, Your Honour.

The Judge: Let us proceed.

The Crown: Miss Edna Little, please.

Clerk: Miss Edna Little.

(Little *comes on and is sworn in. She then takes her seat.*)

Colby: Edna Little has been with Linda almost since the beginning. For years I thought she was one of the nicest people I'd ever talked to. I remember the first time I phoned Linda's office. "Call Me" had just been released. It was on the radio all the time and I just couldn't get Linda out of my mind ... and here was her framed picture hung up there over the fridge saying "Keep in touch." Well, one day I just picked up the phone and called.

(Colby *pulls out a telephone and dials. Lights down on court, and up on the band platform where a party is in progress. Lots of riotous singing. A phone rings.* Edna *leaves the party and comes downstage to answer it.*)

Little: Fellas! Can you keep it down a bit! Wylde Rose Limited. Edna Little speaking. Can I help you?

Colby: Ah ... yes ... This is Jacob Colby from Red Deer, Alberta, well from just outside Red Deer actually ... ah ... I wrote Linda a little while ago and she wrote me back and so I thought ... that, you know, maybe I should phone and see how she's doing.

(*The dynamic of the noise goes up.* Edwards *enters. He's a bit drunk.*)

Edwards: Hey Edna, where's the ice?

Little: She's doing just fine, Mr Colby. Thanks for the call.

Colby: Is she ... is she there?

Little: No, I'm sorry she's gone ... to rehearsal. But she'll be sorry she missed you.

Edwards: Business, Edna old girl?

Little: Just a fan.

Edwards: Well Lord-liftin'-Jesus let's see this fan club you're always talking about in action – where's the file card? (Edna *points to a file box*. Edwards *looks through it*.) What's the name?

Colby: Hello?

Little: Yes, she'll be very sorry she missed you, Mr Colby.

(Edwards *flips through the rollodex and pulls out a card*.)

Colby: She sent me a couple of lovely notes in response to my letters.

Little: Yes, I think I remember. You're the ...

Edwards: The wheat farmer.

Little: Wheat farmer.

Colby: Why, yes I am.

Edwards: Let's see that sales pitch in action, girl.

Little: Yes. Linda just loves wheat.

Colby: Well, gosh, I'll send her some.

(Edwards *laughs and heads back to the party. The band is playing "I's the B'y."*)

Little: Oh, I wouldn't go to any trouble, you know. (*to* Edwards) He wants to send Linda some wheat!

(Edwards *laughs, joins the singing of "I's the B'y," making up the lyric below*.)

Edwards: Colby's the b'y that sells the wheat to buy the records that Linda sings!

Colby: Gee, sounds like you're having a party over there.

Little: Yes, well, it's just a little bon voyage party. Linda is going out on tour next week.

Colby: Really? Well, my call is opportune!

Edwards: Is he coming to the show? Maybe we could get some publicity stills. Linda standing on this pile of wheat with an adoring farmer in the background.

Little: Maybe you can make one of the shows. She'd love to see you.

Edwards: That's what we need for the cover of her next album! Linda with a farmer and ... and a cow! Does he have a cow?

Little: Do you have a cow?

Colby: I beg your pardon?

Little: You know, a cow. All farmers have cows, right?

Colby: I'm a wheat farmer.

Little: No cow.

Colby: So ... ah ... I guess Linda won't be coming to Red Deer.

Little: No, but she's playing Vancouver next week.

Colby: Vancouver. Well, that's a ways from here. I'd have to fly to get there.

Little: You sure as heck couldn't walk. This is getting boring, Chuck. (Edwards *listens in.*)

Colby: I guess some people would think nothing of flying to Vancouver to see Linda ...

Little: Oh yes, some of Linda's fans love her so much that they'd probably ...

Edwards: Wax feathers to their arms and fly over the Rockies solo ...

Colby: I beg your pardon?

Little: Chuck.

Edwards: You're right, this is boring! Let's boogie!

(Edwards *tickles* Little. *She fights him off, laughing.*)

Little: I'm sorry, Mr Colby. The office help is getting out of hand. Look, I've got to go. I've ... I've got a call on the other line. Remember ... keep in touch.

Colby: Oh I will ... in fact, I might even make that concert ...

(*The line goes dead.*)

Colby: ... in Vancouver.

Edwards: Hey Jack! Know anybody with a cow?

(Edwards *runs back up to the party. The band reprises "I's the B'y." Colby hangs up the phone. Little takes the stand. The lights shift back to court as the music ends.*)

Little: Edna Little. Wylde Rose Limited.

The Judge: How is that spelled?

The Crown: I believe it's W-I-L-D-E.

Little: No, it's W-Y-L-D-E.

The Judge: Thank you.

The Crown: Now, Miss Little, you are employed by Wylde Rose Limited, Miss Barrie's personal management company. You were on the Wylde Rose premises on October 19 1983, is that correct?

Little: Yes, I was walking through the reception area and looked up and saw Mr Colby standing by the office door.

The Crown: Yes. And how were you able to see him?

Little: The door is made out of smoked glass.

The Crown: All right. And what did you do after you saw him?

Little: Well, I was frightened at first, but finally I went to the door, opened it and Mr Colby ... he spoke first, said: "I'd like to leave a personal message for Miss Barrie." And I said: "Fine," accepted the envelope from him, closed the door, and telephoned the police.

The Crown: Good. Now, Miss Little, can you identify this object for the Court?

Little: (*Taking an envelope*) Yes. That's the letter Mr Colby gave me. See, it says right here: Linda Barrie, Personal.

The Crown: I would like this to be made an exhibit, Your Honour.

The Judge: Very well. Exhibit One.

(*They begin to go through the laborious business of making the letter an exhibit. Lights shift. A Muzak underscoring begins.* Colby *walks to the upstage stair unit, sits and pulls out a letter.*)

Colby: Exhibit One. I wrote that letter on a concrete bench in the Toronto International Airport. Letters have played a special part in our relationship – Linda always used to answer them. I mean, what's a phone call? Five minutes of embarrassed small talk that disappears as soon as you hang up. But a letter ... a letter has substance. (*A jet roars overhead.* Colby *reads what he's been writing.*) Dear Linda: I've made a reservation for you on flight #153, leaving Toronto at 7:10 p.m. for Calgary under the name of Miss A. Avena – Avena is Linda's first name ... she was named after her Grandmother – (*romantic tone*) I'll meet you, wait for you, near the flight monitors in front of the Western Airlines Ticket counter.
    Practicality is both my greatest virtue ... and the curse of my existence. I start out trying to sound like Errol Flynn ... and end up sounding like a farmer. (*He chuckles, then writes again. As he writes* Ted *enters, slightly rumpled, maybe a little drunk and eating a hot dog. He tries to read the letter over* Colby's *shoulder.*) I won't buy your ticket until I meet you. I think I have enough money, but you might bring along the last money order I sent you if you've still got it.

Ted: It's with a "Y".

Colby: Pardon?

Ted: It's B-A-R-R-Y. Not I-E.

Colby: Well, it's "I-E" in this particular case.

Ted: You sure?

Colby: I've been corresponding with this lady for ten years now. I think I should know how her name's spelled.

Ted: Ten years. Wow. I thought it was a love letter.

Colby: It really isn't any of your business what it is.

Ted: Sure thing, but, you know, I just thought like you looked like you were writing a love letter, ya know? Had kind of a far away look in your eye. But it couldn't be a love letter, right? I mean, you don't write a chick you've known for 10 years a love letter, right?

Colby: Why not?

Ted: Well, you know ... 10 years ... the embers must be burning kind of low, eh?

Colby: The trouble with people like you is you're in love with the sizzle, not the steak. Well, it's not like that. Real love is something you grow. It takes time, patience, devotion. Ten years goes by in a flash if you're really in love.

Ted: Hey, heavy stuff. That's beautiful! I mean, this is not like going for a chick we are talking about here, that's for sure. You are really in L-U-V, love. (*Sings*) All you need is love rah-ta-da-ta-da!!

Colby: It hasn't been easy ... the way the world works today ...

Ted: Never mind the world, man! Ten years of writing love letters? Fantastic! Go for it! Ah ... say ... you couldn't spare a quarter, could you? I want to get a coffee to wash down this ...

Colby: Go away.

Ted: Right. Got ya ...

(*A jet roars overhead. Underscoring starts to fade.* Ted *exits.* Colby *finishes writing his letter. As he writes he conjures up an image of* Linda, *as he once saw her on TV.* Linda *comes on and performs "Together Again," she is in her 70s country period, well dressed, but with a down-home image. The growth of her professionalism is clear, and at one point during a musical break in the song she walks into the audience.*)

Linda: Hi, what's your name? (*The audience member gives name.*) Thanks for coming. Remember, "Keep in touch." (Linda *continues the song till the end, playing the last verse to* Colby. *She exits.* Colby *finishes the letter.*)

Colby: I can't see why you wouldn't come. (*pause*) I hope you're fine ... Jacob.

(*Action shifts back to the court.*)

The Judge: Any questions, Mr Colby?

Colby: Yes, Your Honour, thank you. Miss Little, you've said I frighten you.

Little: Yes. That is correct.

Colby: Why? Have I ever done anything that has caused you to be afraid of me?

Little: I'm frightened when you come to the office.

Colby: Yes. I understand. But ... why?

Little: Because you keep on coming back regardless of court orders.

Colby: But, aside from the issue of court orders, what personal conduct have I displayed that causes you to be afraid of me.

The Judge: Excuse me, Mr Colby. I'm having trouble following your argument. "Personal conduct?" How does this relate to the case?

Colby: I'm trying to establish two things, Your Honour. First, that there has never been any indication that any of my actions gave anybody cause to be afraid of me. Second, that there has never been any representation made by any office staff that anything I wished to leave was unacceptable.

The Judge: I see. Well, because you are defending yourself, I will allow you some latitude.

Colby: Thank you, Your Honour. I would like to ask the witness if she has ever personally declined a message to Linda.

Little: I have never personally declined a message from you, Mr Colby. I'd be afraid to.

Colby: But why?

Little: Because I think you're crazy.

Colby: I'm crazy? So, you saw this crazy man you were afraid of lurking out in the hall. Between you and him there was a locked door, but instead of phoning the police you go to the door, unlock it, take a letter from this very frightening madman and say: "She's in."

Little: I didn't say that, Mr Colby.

Colby: Was she in?

Little: That has nothing to do with ...

Colby: She was in there and the reason that you took that letter from me instead of calling the police was that Linda told you to, didn't she?

Little: The police said we should ...

Colby: The police! the police weren't called until after Linda read my letter and knew I was leaving town, with or without her.

Little: That's not what happened.

Colby: Then why was I arrested at the airport? Could it be because Linda can't get all this public attention focused on her and me if I'm back on the farm?

Little: It's because she's afraid of you!

Colby: Then why doesn't she act like she's afraid of me? Why does she take my letters and tell you to, as it were, "Let down the drawbridge"?

Little: You have no idea what it's like to be afraid of someone, Mr Colby.

(Colby *moves toward the audience.*)

Colby: No further questions.
    (*mocking*) I have no idea what it's like to be afraid of someone! Her testimony is going to send me to the jail or the madhouse! Boy, I'll tell you, the mercy of the Court has taught me a thing or two about fear.
    Of course, all of this is peanuts compared to how I felt the first time I went to see Linda. I was scared to death! Tours! Parties in the afternoon! Was I ready to pursue that kind of relationship? A thousand goodbye scenes played out in airport waiting rooms? That's what a courtship with Linda would be ...
    I sat there is the kitchen trying to measure the strength of my feelings. My crop was only half in and there were literally hundreds of things I had to do to get the farm ready for another winter. I sipped my tea ... and looked at Linda's picture smiling down at me from above the fridge ... for an instant it seemed like the only sane thing to do was forget my dreams ... then ... at that precise moment ... there she was on the radio.

(*Music begins to resolve into "In Dreams." Lights shift. Move into next fantasy sequence.*)

Colby: Neither of us came from people who fly halfway across the country to go to a nightclub, she'd have to know how scary that would be for me. I guess I took it as a challenge. In the end I realized that love always tests your faith. If you don't believe in something bigger than yourself ... some thing on a higher plane, you fail. I went down to the bank, took out $800 I didn't have and drove to the airport ...(*Sound effects: Jet flying overhead.*) The next thing I knew, I was in Vancouver sitting in the Cave Theatre and Restaurant. (*Lights come up on* Linda, *still in her folksy period.*

She sings the opening verses of "In Dreams" playing some of the song to Colby. *The song deals with a love between two people being real in the singer's dreams. During the musical bridge in the song* Colby *speaks.*)

Colby: One moment I was just a face in the crowd, then our eyes met ... You see before Linda, I wasn't interested in popular music. I loved the songs of Schubert, but then the words, they were sounds and nothing else. But with Linda ... a whole new world of poetry opened up for me. A world of symbols and sounds. We were together inside the "magic night." The physical distance between us didn't mean a thing. All we had to do was close our eyes and we were walking hand in hand. Together "in dreams."

(*The song ends.* Linda *exits. Underscoring with a slight circus feel comes up.* Colby *stands and pulls out a bouquet of roses. Just then* Linda *enters, and is button-holed by two reporters. The reporters' questions are played on the synth and* Linda *responds.*)

Linda: The L.A. cancellation? No, it doesn't bother me. All in all, the tour is doing great. (*question*) I've been dreaming about this moment for years. (*question*) Blue jeans? Well, I prefer something a little more romantic, like ... (*She turns and sees* Colby. *He holds out his bouquet*) ... roses.

Colby: Fresh-cut roses. I picked them right out of my own garden in "Wild Rose Country."

(Linda *looks at* Colby *and smiles.*)

Linda: Roses. I love roses.

(Colby *hands them to her.*)

Colby: From a hay baler to a herring choker.

Linda: My garden back home is full of roses. Some nights it used to feel like paradise out there. (*she sighs*) But that was long ago.

Colby: Is something wrong?

Linda: No, it's just that sometimes – things are going so fast – sometimes all I seem to have to keep me going are my dreams.

Colby: I know what you mean. My dreams are full of roses. And you.

Linda: That's sweet. I love to dream ...

Colby: To spread your wings and drift away into the magic night ...

Linda: Maybe nothing else matters ...

Together: (*sung*) "Nothing else matters, cause we're together again." (Linda *smiles and squeezes his hand.*)

Linda: You know what? You're really great. (*She gives him a kiss. It's a* *magic moment.* Linda *is gone, leaving* Colby *touching his lips in amazement. He calls after her.*) Keep in touch.

Colby: I'll send the wheat!

(*Underscoring out. Lighting shifts. We're back in court.* Colby *is staring off into space.*)

The Judge: Mr Colby?

(Colby *snaps back into reality.*)

Colby: Your Honour, I would just like to point out that Miss Little has admitted she opened a locked door to take my letter. No one in Linda's office has ever refused my letters or indicated by their behaviour they were afraid of me. To my way of thinking, this amounts to an implicit encouragement of my actions.

The Judge: Very well. Next witness.

The Crown: Sergeant Jones, please.

The Clerk: Sergeant William Jones, please.

(Jones *enters.*)

The Clerk: Hi, Bill.

Jones: Hi, Len. (Jones *is sworn in.*)

Colby: Jones is one of those men who automatically assumes that anyone who falls in love with "a star" must be a pea-brained idiot. 'Course, the only thing he's in love with is his uniform.

(Jones *takes the stand.*)

The Crown: Sergeant Jones, you are the officer in charge of the Colby investigation?

Jones: I am, sir.

Colby: Everything is black and white for Jones because he lacks the heart to see in colour.

The Crown: And on October 19, 1983, you were assigned to go to the Toronto International Airport to pick him up. Is that correct?

Jones: Ah ... with the Court's permission, I'd like to refer to my notebook ... for the exact times.

The Judge: When did you make these notes?

Jones: During my investigation of Mr Colby.

The Judge: Have you changed them since?

Jones: Of course not. I just scribbled them down.

The Judge: (*to* Colby) Do you have any objection to the witness referring to his notebook?

Colby: No, Your Honour. (*to audience*) At least he'll lie in complete sentences.

The Judge: Very well, you may use your notes to refresh your memory.

Jones: Thank you, You Honour. (*He reads quickly*) My partner and I arrived at the Toronto International Airport at 5:02 p.m. Parked on the Arrivals Level, Terminal Two. We found the accused adjacent to the Air Canada ticket counter. Suspect was very angry when we approached him. He called me a ...

The Judge: Excuse me, Sergeant Jones. I said use the notes to refresh your memory. Do not give a recitation from your notes. You're testifying, not reading us a novel.

Jones: Yes, Your Honour.

The Crown: And is the man you arrested in court today?

Jones: Yes, That's him (*indicating the accused*).

The Crown: That is the substance of my case, Your Honour. Colby presented his letter to Miss Little at the Wylde Rose office. Miss Little took it and telephoned the police. The call was answered by Sergeant Jones. As Mr Colby was in breach of probation the officer went to the airport and arrested him. He has now identified Mr Colby in court today.

The Judge: You have no further questions?

The Crown: No, Your Honour. I've made my case.

The Judge: Mr Colby?

Colby: Sergeant Jones, do you recall the first arrest you made in regard to this matter of my attention towards Linda Barrie?

Jones: (*checks notes*) April 16th 1980. Yes, I have it here in my notes.

Colby: What was the charge?

Jones: Intimidation.

Colby: Is that a serious charge?

Jones: Of course it's serious. People were frightened.

Colby: Well, if it was a serious charge, didn't it warrant a serious investigation?

Jones: It received a serious investigation.

Colby: Who was I supposed to have intimidated?

Jones: Linda Barrie.

Colby: And what did Miss Barrie say when she was questioned?

Jones: You know I had no opportunity to talk to her personally.

Colby: So I was charged with a serious crime on the basis of hearsay evidence? Is that standard police procedure?

Jones: No. But ...

The Crown: Your Honour, I can't see what this line of questioning has to do with the case at hand.

Colby: Your Honour, I wish to petition the Court during summation that, in fact, my probation is unlawful, based on bias and incompetent police investigation.

The Crown: Your Honour, this is an absurd charge.

The Judge: Yes, but it is an interesting defence.

Colby: If I could cite a number of instances. I was originally charged with intimidation, even though the person I was said to have intimidated was never even questioned by the police. This charge was dismissed, but led to the original probation order against me. Subsequently I was charged for violation of probation on a number of occasions. This amounted to virtual harassment.

The Crown: Your Honour, there have been no instances of harassment against Mr Colby.

Colby: Last year, on February 17, I was acquitted on two charges and when I walked out of court ... right outside these very doors, Your Honour, Sergeant Jones arrested me again!

Jones: Now hold on there ... I ...

Colby: Apparently I had broken probation merely by thinking of Linda, because she sure as heck wasn't in the court.

Jones: The charges had been relaid, Your Honour.

The Judge: And why had they been dismissed, Sergeant Jones?

Jones: I don't know the wording of the documents of the court, so I couldn't say.

Colby: Isn't it a fact that the cases were dismissed because you were so gung ho to arrest me that I was charged on a probation order that didn't even exist?

Jones: It existed. Well, a new one existed. All I did was charge you under the old probation order that was no longer in effect.

Colby: Which is typical of the slipshod, biased work Sergeant Jones has done on this case from the word go.

The Crown: Your Honour, surely you aren't going to let the accused turn a single instance of confused paperwork into a charge of police harassment.

Colby: That isn't the only piece of confused paperwork we're looking at, is it, Mr Broilman?

The Crown: Just what are you getting at?

Colby: To bring matters up to date, Your Honour – after this last arrest I went before Judge Richmond for a bail hearing. After three days of testimony the judge spent three more days in sober deliberation of the facts, he then gave me bail so I could go home and harvest my crop. The Crown then appealed my release, knowing full well I would be in Red Deer and unable to defend myself at the hearing. Sergeant Jones, how long did that second bail hearing last?

Jones: I don't know.

The Judge: Well, then look it up. I'm sure you've got it somewhere.

(Jones *checks his notes.*)

Jones: 25 minutes.

Colby: Twenty-five minutes to overturn a decision that took the first learned Judge six full days to render! I just wonder what the crown prosecutor had to tell that Judge to get me slapped back in jail.

The Crown: What I had to tell the Judge is a matter of record, Your Honour. Essentially, I demonstrated that Judge Richmond had made an error in releasing Mr Colby and as a result a warrant was issued for his re-arrest!

Colby: Right, a warrant with a phoney charge pencilled in.

The Judge: A what?

Colby: The warrant that I was arrested on said I was wanted on an indictable offence. Both the Crown and Sergeant Jones knew the charge against me was a summary conviction.

The Crown: Your Honour, I don't see how the charge on the warrant, even if it was mistaken, could possibly be seen as an example of harassment. There was a warrant for his re-arrest. It was served. He was returned to custody in Toronto by the RCMP.

Colby: I think Sergeant Jones could help clarify the advantages inherent in sending out a warrant on an indicatable offence, can't you, Sergeant Jones?

Jones: There's no advantage.

Colby: Oh, come on, Jones. You get two warrants, one for bank robbery and one for parking violations – which do you act on?

Jones: The robbery.

Colby: And the parking tickets?

Jones: I don't do parking tickets.

Colby: But if you did ... ?

Jones: I'd get around to it.

Colby: Exactly, you'd get around to it. What makes you think the RCMP in Red Deer would be any different? They get a warrant to pick up an indicted criminal and they move on it .. but to arrest a farmer in the middle of harvest over a minor probation violation ... well, in your own words, "They'd get around to it."

Jones: Your case is different than a warrant out on some guy who's dodging parking tickets.

Colby: Not by much. You knew if the warrant read summary conviction it would go on the back burner and you couldn't stand that, could you?

Jones: Are you saying I somehow faked that warrant so ...

Colby: I'm saying that the RCMP dragged me out of my home in handcuffs. I'm saying half my crop was left in open bins and it got wet. It froze. I'm saying that "confused paperwork" cost me half my crop. We're talking about big money here! We're talking about my life! But you and Broilman couldn't leave it alone, could you? You couldn't just let me bring in my crop and prepare for my trial. No, you had to have me re-arrested so I wouldn't bother a women who was living two thousand miles away! When I look at the way I've been treated only one word comes to mind: harassment. I call it harassment.

Jones: And I call it getting a dangerous nutcase off the streets. I don't want another Mark Chapman on my hands.

The Judge: Sergeant Jones, are you admitting that a warrant was purposely falsified?

The Crown: Of course he isn't! Your Honour, while Sergeant Jones perhaps overstates his case I feel that we must all understand his concern. Nevertheless, let me assure you that the natural worry over the safety of Ms Barrie has never overshadowed our sense of justice.

The Judge: Yes, well, obviously Mr Colby doesn't agree.

Colby: I certainly don't. My life is being wrecked, though it's clear I am not the one to blame in the case. It is Linda Barrie who is creating the public mischief.

The Judge: Linda Barrie?

Colby: It's obvious, Your Honour. The Crown speaks of Linda Barrie of singing fame. Jones draws a parallel between myself and the man who shot John Lennon. Clearly Linda is receiving proportional favouritism at the hands of the court. To put it simply, her fame prejudices my case, and that is a fundamental violation of the principles of justice.

The Crown: Should Linda Barrie not have access to the protection of the courts simply because she is famous? Would that be Mr Colby's version of justice?

Colby: You don't care about justice, Broilman. All you are concerned about is the prominent place this case has in the public eye.

The Judge: Now Mr Colby ... .

Colby: The fact is that my conviction, or better yet my committal will boost your public image!

The Crown: Your Honour I have had just about enough of Mr Colby's slanderous ...

The Judge: OK, that's enough. Both of you take your seats. Are there any more questions for Sergeant Jones?

The Crown: Sergeant Jones, did you have anything to do with the warrant that was made out for the re-arrest of Mr Colby?

Jones: No sir, I did not.

The Judge: Thank you Sergeant Jones, you may step down. (Jones *exits*.) Well things have certainly warmed up. Mr Broilman, what have you to say about Mr Colby's charges?

The Crown: I think there is only one comment worth making under the circumstances, Your Honour. Mr Colby is deluded.

Colby: Mr Broilman is making my case for me. Your Honour, he assumes I am insane because of my alleged "delusions" about Linda Barrie but as I have pointed out again and again Linda Barrie has never been questioned. How does he know I am deluded?

The Crown: Your Honour, while it is true that Ms Barrie has never been questioned personally, it is a patent falsehood to state that the police have not verified the charges against Mr Colby. I have spoken to Ms Barrie's husband many times. He is eloquent in his description of the problems Mr Colby's delusion has created over the last few years. He would be happy to testify.

Colby: I object!

(*Lighting change. Underscoring begins, an intro to "Stand By Me."*)

Colby: Chuck Edwards. I ask for the queen and they send me her coachman. I mean, we all knew that he'd produced her records ... but when the papers announced that they'd been married ... I felt like I'd been run through a baling machine. How could it be possible? For five years I'd been following Linda's every move. I'd kept in touch, and so had she. And then, from out of the blue, Chuck Edwards. It didn't make any sense. Nobody really believed they could be in love. I couldn't understand it. I was lost. I had to talk to her. She ... she was playing in Vancouver again ... so I took another plane. (*A jet roars overhead. The band enters behind* Colby *during the speech, playing the intro to a hard-rocking version of "Stand By Me." They are all dressed as cops, and bar the way between* Colby *and a new* Linda Barrie, *dressed in leather, singing rock. As she sings the song* Colby *tries to reach her, but again and again he is blocked, until finally he slips through the cops and holds up a handful of roses.* Linda *takes them, and sings the song to him. The song ends.* Colby *is suddenly alone on stage.*) The song was like a bombshell. The first verse described our situation perfectly, the night, the moon, the strength I felt knowing she was beside me ... but then ... then images of dissolution ... the sky, our relationship, falling like a star into the sea, and one phrase repeating again and again ... "Whenever I'm in trouble ... stand by me!" (Colby *turns up his collar and, holding a program, runs across the stage. Underscoring music from within. We are outside a stage door.* Colby *is standing outside the door, program in hand.* Rick *enters. He's an autograph hunter in a long greasy trench coat.*)

Rick: Nice weather for July, eh?

Colby: I suppose. (*pause*) Ah ... say, this is the stage door isn't it?

Rick: You kidding? Would I be standing here if it wasn't?

Colby: I don't know.

Rick: No way, man. Rick Phillips doesn't stand around in the deluge unless he can cop some penmanship, right?

Colby: If you say so ...

Rick: Say so, man, I know so. You got any traders?

Colby: Got what?

Rick: Autographs. For swapping.

Colby: I don't collect autographs.

Rick: Then why are you out here in the rain, bub? What are you, a duck?

Colby: I'm waiting to see Linda, she ...

(*Sound of applause up and out.* Linda *and* Chuck *enter, moving fast.* Rick *rushes towards her.*)

Rick: Miss Barrie! Miss Barrie, could you sign ...

(Chuck Edwards *moves between* Rick *and* Linda, *moving him offstage.* Linda *pauses for a second. She seems shaken, looks at* Colby, *then away as she walks by him.* Colby *steps toward her.*)

Chuck: Sorry pal, Linda's really in a hurry. We've got a plane to catch.

Rick: Aw come on. All I want is an autograph ... (*fade under*)

Colby: Linda!

Linda: Hi, did you see the show?

Colby: You know I was there.

Linda: Imagine, me doing a rock song. I was scared to death. (*Pause.*)

Colby: You don't have to be afraid. Linda, I'll stand by you.

Linda: I wasn't really scared, you know, I just meant ...

Colby: It's your career isn't it? The road ... you're being pulled away from your feelings ... your dreams ...

Linda: No, it's great. I'm rolling.

Colby: Then why did you sing that song?

Linda: I ...

Chuck: There's the limo, honey.

Linda: Okay. (*She takes* Colby's *program and signs it.*) Thanks for coming. It means a lot to me.

(Linda *starts to go.* Colby *grabs her wrist.*)

Colby: No, wait. The wedding. You didn't really ...

Chuck: Cool your jets, friend. (*He takes* Linda's *arm away.* Rick *comes up behind him.*)

Linda: It's okay, Chuck.

Colby: I just wanted to ...

Chuck: Get into the limo, Linda. (*to* Colby) You shouldn't grab at people, you know.

Linda: He didn't mean anything, Bill.

Colby: Take your hands off me.

Rick: Hey man, leave the guy alone.

Chuck: Linda, will you get into the goddamn car?

(Linda *exits*.)

Rick: Ya jerk.

(Chuck *pushes past*.)

Chuck: Why in the hell can't you treat her like a human being.

Rick: Oh boy, yeah, isn't that typical, eh? Once they start making it big they bring in the goons. Heaven forbid somebody should "Touch the star." The dirtbag wouldn't even let me have her autograph. I should have listened to my mother and stayed out of showbiz.

(Colby *ignores all this. He is totally absorbed by* Linda's *autograph on his program*.)

Rick: Say, did you get her? (*He looks over* Colby's *shoulder and reads*.) "I love you, Linda Barrie." Hey, beauty! give you five bucks for it.

Colby: What?

Rick: Five bucks. I'll give you five bucks. What do you say?

Colby: Don't be ridiculous.

Rick: It's a fair price. I mean, we're not talking about Streisand ...

Colby: Linda wrote this to me.

Rick: OK, OK. I'll trade you. What do you want, Sammy Davis, Jr?

Colby: Sammy who?

Rick: OK, OK. I'll throw in Lightfoot ... what do you say?

Colby: I told you, I don't collect autographs.

Rick: All right, autographed glossies then! Take your pick. Gump Worsley?

Colby: You don't understand. I'm in love with her. I wouldn't part with this picture for .. for my life.

Rick: Oh, I got you. You're a Linda Barrie freak.

Colby: I'm not a freak. I love her.

Rick: Oh, right, and obviously the feeling is mutual.

Colby: Of course it's mutual. Don't you even listen to her songs? Look: "I love you." That's what she wrote.

Rick: Yeah, right. That's why she just married that Edwards dude. What do you think that means?

Colby: How could she possibly be married to him and still write that to me?

Rick: You sayin' he's a beard?

Colby: A what?

Rick: A beard ... it's a showbiz term. If, you know, you're seeing someone and you don't want anyone to know, you get this other guy to pretend like he's going out with you. He's your disguise. Your beard.

Colby: Yes ... that ... that must be it.

Rick: Fat chance, fella. Later.

(Rick *exits*. Colby *stares after him. Lights shift. We're back in court.*)

The Judge: Mr Colby?

Colby: What?

The Judge: Mr Colby, do you object to calling Linda Barrie's husband to the stand?

Colby: What? Yes, I would object. Edwards' testimony is of no more substance than that of Miss Little or any other of Miss Barrie's employees.

The Crown: He is her husband, Your Honour.

Colby: Her alleged husband.

The Judge: Her alleged husband?

The Crown: This is typical of his thinking, Your Honour. He claims they aren't married.

Colby: I have reason to believe they are not married.

The Judge: Why do you say they aren't married, Mr Colby.

Colby: Your Honour, there are certain private elements of my relationship with Linda Barrie which don't have any place in a court of law.

The Judge: (*to* The Crown) Do you wish to call Mr Edwards?

Colby: Your Honour, it's Linda who needs to be brought before this court, not that man.

The Judge: Nevertheless, Mr Edwards is ...

Colby: He's a puppet. Nothing but a ...

The Crown: Your Honour, I would ask: Why is Mr Colby so afraid of confronting Charles Edwards on this matter?

Colby: I'm not afraid of that.

The Crown: It's because his whole, sick delusion would come crumbling down around him when Mr Edwards testified about Colby's visit to Mount Stewart and the ...

Colby: That son of a bitch would lie about the funeral! He's a big pile of shit plopped between Linda and me and I'll be damned if ...

The Judge: Mr Colby! Order! I won't tolerate that kind of language in my court!

The Crown: You see what we're afraid of here, Your Honour. This is why Dr Rand's testimony is ...

Colby: Let's not get into that again, Rand is a ...

The Judge: Stop right there, Mr Colby, before I cite you for contempt.

Colby: I'm sorry, Your Honour, but it's my life that's at stake here.

The Judge: I am aware of that. I have been bending over backwards because you have chosen to proceed without counsel, but there are times when I've felt like you aren't quite with us. I'm afraid I'm going to have to allow Dr Rand to testify again.

Colby: Your Honour, he's plainly biased in his testimony!

The Judge: And I will arrange for a second opinion.

Colby: I am not insane!

The Judge: I don't know if that's true, Mr Colby. It's my job to see that if you need help you get it.

Colby: I'll be happy to have Mr Edwards testify, if that's the matter of concern.

The Judge: And I'll be happy to hear what he has to say about ... the funeral? ... after we've heard from the doctors. We'll adjourn until Monday. Mr Broilman, you will arrange for another psychiatrist to talk with Mr Colby in the interval and ...

(*Their voices fade out. Special light on* Colby. *He gets out a portable tape recorder.*)

Colby: With Edwards at the helm, Linda's career took off like a sky rocket. As her fame grew I felt that she was moving further and further away from me, like a late-night radio station drifting in and out, getting fainter and fainter until I began to wonder if I was really hearing anything at all ...

Then, that day ... that day the dawn broke with the roar of jet engines. Planes soaring over my house, all day coming together, almost touching the ground and then soaring up, trailing streams of silver and gold.

I couldn't work with those planes stunt flying over the farm. I sat in the kitchen, all day, playing her songs.

(Colby *starts and stops the tape on his machine, listening to fragment of songs as he speaks.*)

Listening to those messages of love. Over and over, looking for ... I didn't know what. The light faded. I gave up. (Colby *stops the tape and switches the tapedeck to the radio mode.*) I didn't know what any of it meant any more. I switched on the radio and stood at the window, watching the last jet barrel-roll off into the sunset. Then. Linda's voice drifted through the twilight. (*On the radio we hear* Micky *and* Sylvia*'s version of "Love is Strange."*)I leaned exhausted, head against the window pane, looking out at those long empty fields. The song ended. The D.J. spoke softly ...

Disc Jockey: Ladies and gentlemen, for all of you who are fans of Linda Barrie we have some sad news. Linda's father, the Right Honourable Joseph Barrie passed away today in Mount Stewart, P.E.I.

(Colby *shuts off the radio. A solid, musical scream comes from an off-stage chorus, like the drone of a bagpipe.*)

Colby: The words rushed through me like ... like a scream of anguish from half-way round the world. And I knew ... I knew she was calling out to me. I knew ... she needed me. The night had come, she needed someone to stand by her. I had to go. I knew I had to, I was the only man on earth who could bring her home again.

(*Underscoring begins, an a cappella bagpipe drone from the chorus, based on "Farewell to Nova Scotia."* Colby *walks up the stairs to the platform.* Linda, Edwards, Sandy, *and a* priest *wheel on a coffin.*)

Colby: Barrington Passage, Nova Scotia. Snow thick on the ground. A little graveyard on the hill. Breath hanging still in cold winter light. The long black hearse taking Linda's daddy home to be buried where he had been born. And Linda standing by the coffin. Like a lost little girl.

Linda: The sun was setting in the West. The birds were singing on every tree
All nature seemed inclined for a rest, but still there was no rest for me
So farewell to Nova Scotia the seabound coast
Let your mountains dark and dreary be
For when I am far away on the briny ocean tossed
Will you ever heave a sigh and wish for me

Grieve to leave my native home
I grieve to leave my comrades all
But my captain calls and I must obey
So it's early in the morning
And I am bound far away.

(Colby *speaks over the verse of the song.*)

Colby: Linda and I had come full-circle. I had been lost in a cold and empty world ... her song lifted me up ... up onto a higher plane. And now the wheel of life had turned carrying her into the shadows.

   She had forgotten that beyond winter lies spring, beyond grief, hope. I could return to her the love she had given me ... lift her up into the light ... with love ... love flowing like a river from one human heart to another ... and I knew ... I knew I could give her back her soul!

Linda: For it's early in the morning I am bound far away.

(*Lights fade to black.*)

ACT TWO

At rise we are in a holding cell in the Willows Hospital for the criminally insane. Colby sits alone, writing in his notebook. As he speaks Rand appears as a memory in a dim glow on the upstage platform.

Colby: Well Linda, here I am sitting in an empty room waiting to try and convince a total stranger that there really is something going on between us. God, what kind of chance do I have? I remember trying to explain it to Rand that first time at Willowood. I said to him: "Love is like a revolution in the mind." He smiled and made a note. "Look at it as a cascade of neuro-chemical reactions that make you see sudden pictures of a perfect world." He wrote a whole sentence. "When you're in love you lose that huge separation between yourself and everything around you. Your senses expand to fill every available space!" And he looked up from his notebook and said ...

Colby and Rand: "Mr Colby, you have just given me a textbook definition of schizophrenia."

(*Underscoring begins. Rand fades out.*)

Colby: Saint Paul can be hit by a bolt of lightning on the road to Damascus. Edgar Cayce can cure hundreds of people he's never even seen and twenty million people a day can base their lives on what Jeanne Dixon writes in an astrology column, but if I say "Our spirits have touched" then I'm mad.

(Linda *appears where* Rand *had stood.* Colby *remembers her music and dreams she is with him.* Linda *sings "Heart Like A Wheel," a song about lost love and broken hearts. As the song is sung.* Linda *comes down the stairs, she and* Colby *almost touch but the image fades. She disappears; and as the song ends* Colby *is alone, back in his cell.*

A cop and Cord *enter.* Cord *is handcuffed. The* cop *chains him to a chair near* Colby.)

Cord: Take you stinking hands off me, you doorknob's arsehole!

The Cop: Will you keep it down?

Cord: Not much to get it up for in The Willows, is there, chumbly?

The Cop: That's your problem, not mine.

Cord: I am not nuts!

The Cop: You're about as smart as a toaster.

Cord: You're all walking stiffs. Ya can't believe in anything anymore!

The Cop: You're pathetic.

(*He exists.*)

Cord: Jesus, Jesus, those monkey-headed bastards ... you scum bucket! (*to* Colby) Well, what are you looking at? (Colby *looks away*) Oh, sorry to disturb your meditation, man. Just ignore me. I'm just another poor slob being run down in the street. The shrink in there just shoved my dink in a light socket and flipped the switch, but what's it mean to you, right?

Colby: Who was it?

Cord: Eh?

Colby: What was the psychiatrist's name?

Cord: C.G. Rand. What's it to you anyway ... say ... I know you. Jake Colby, right? Wow, I don't believe it. I got your picture from the paper pinned on my wall. Man, like, you're a folk hero, right?

Colby: What are you talking about?

Cord: Linda Barrie, man. That's huntin' for bear. You really love her, right? (*pause*) Hey, what's the matter? You deaf? You love Linda Barrie, right?

Colby: I'm facing a stretch in the Willows myself, because of her. You might say the romance is at a low ebb.

Cord: A breakdown on the rocky road of love, right? Quelle drag. (*pause*) I mean, you gotta prove your love, right? That's what it's all about! You're like a knight or something ... like that guy in the Monty Python and the Holy Grail. You know the one I mean?

Colby: No.

Cord: Oh it's great! There's this Sir Lancelot-guy, see, and this note comes fluttering down from the tower saying 'Rescue Me!' and – shunk – out comes the old sword-a-rooney and he charges up into the castle carvin' his way up this winding staircase, blood and arms and heads flying all over the place! And he kicks down the tower door and inside is this real wimpy little fruit! (*He loses himself in laughter for a moment, then is suddenly serious.*) See, that's what worries me. I mean, how do you know for sure? How can you ever really know if someone loves you?

Colby: I don't know.

Cord: I was working at this Chrysler dealership in Windsor, see, washing out the cars on the lot ... and the guy who owned the place had a daughter. Seventeen. Hair down to here. (*pause*) From the first time I saw her I knew ... but who was I to be messing with the boss' daughter, right? I mean, this guy's precious little idol and me – a car jockey with bad skin and a wop name. But none of that mattered 'cause Cathy and me, right from the word go, we connected. Bang. Electricity. First time her old man saw us talking he knew ... fired me right off the lot. But that didn't stop me. I followed her to school. Hung out at the variety store across the street. Called her on her private phone. I was in love, man, you know like nothing else mattered. I kept chipping away at her until that night. I stole the best car right off that sucker's lot. A big black LeBaron with a four-eighty under the hood! And we took off ... like something off a Springsteen album. Gino and Cathy peel off into the night.

Colby: She loved you?

Cord: It was heaven, man. We were gonna roar down that road till we hit the tip of South America. We'd build a shack on the beach, live off black marlin I speared from my boat. Make babies. It was going to be perfect.

Colby: Well ... what ... what happened?

Cord: I'm asleep in the back of the car. Wake up beside this fly-speckled garage on the side of the road in Nevada. She's gone. I get out of the car and find her inside the diner. She's on the phone to her Goddamn father! Goddamn women, man. I hit her. Just once. Open palm. Okay, more than once but open palm, see ... oh God, I hit her too hard ... I ... blood, cops. (*pause*) They say I'm crazy but I'm not. I'm just like you. I did it all for love.

Colby: You ... you hurt that girl ... you can't ... you never, ever hurt someone you love, Gino. You ...

Cord: Don't you call me Gino, you son of a bitch! That's our name! I ain't no wop! I'm Cord, see? Cord!

The Cop: (*enters*) Hey, what in hell ... (Cop *sees* Cord *is getting violent; he drags him off.*)

Cord: That bitch ... she loves me. She loves me and she calls her old man, the rotten little ...

Colby: For God's sake, get this pathetic little animal out of here!

Cord: Pathetic? I'm just like you, Colby! And you know it! Just like you! Just like you!

(Cord *disappears. His words hang in the air for a moment.* Colby *reels back in shock. After a beat* Downey *enters.*)

Downey: Mr Colby, I'm Kim Downey, the shrink the court wants you to talk to. (*She holds out her hand.*) Call me Kim, okay? (Colby *doesn't respond.*) Look, I know you must be frightened but you've got to believe I'm on your side. (*pause*) All I want to do is help you. (*pause*) Jake, are you okay?

Colby: I don't know.

Downey: What's the matter? (*pause*) Look, Jake, I can't help you if you won't talk to me.

Colby: Jacob.

Downey: Pardon?

Colby: My name is Jacob.

Downey: Okay, Jacob. Listen, we don't have a whole lot of time. If you want me to help you get out of this jam, then you've got to help me. (*pause*) I've ... I've been looking through your file and I don't think what they've done to you is fair ... I mean ... Dr Rand has certainly put together a neat little package here. (*indicating one of her files*) I've never seen such a pack of half-baked assumptions in my life.

Colby: You don't think I'm ... ?

Downey: Schizophrenic? I can't see much evidence of it. Looks to me like the last time you were committed you behaved pretty sensibly. You sold the Review Board, that's for sure. (*pause*) In fact, Jacob, I think you must be a pretty stable guy to keep your head together out in that zoo.

Colby: Iatrogenesis.

Downey: Iatrogenesis?

Colby: An illness arising during the treatment of another malady. Being in the Willows can drive you crazy.

Downey: Right. That's pretty high-flown talk for a farmer from Alberta.

Colby: The hayseed gets in your boots, not your brain. Why are you so gung ho to help me, Dr Downey?

Downey: Kim. The Crown has Dr Rand. I'm the psychiatrist for the defence. (*pause*) Look Jacob, I don't like the idea of somebody like you going to the Willows on a Lieutenant-Governor's warrant, okay?

Colby: I can't take another stretch out there. Your every waking moment is spent in the company of sick, dangerous men.

Downey: Yeah, and then there are the patients. (*They laugh together.*) We've only got one real problem in this case, Jacob.

Colby: What's that?

Downey: You think that you and Linda Barrie are in love. It's pretty hard to argue a guy's total sanity when he's making a claim like that.

Colby: I just don't understand what's so darn hard to believe.

Downey: (*checking her files*) Well, according to Rand you believe she sends you messages over the radio.

Colby: Look at it this way, Doctor, I become an admirer of Linda Barrie's and join her fan club. Then about a month later a radio ratings company starts sending me surveys. They want to know my listening habits. Why me? How did they get my address? Maybe Linda gave it to them. Maybe she had access to the forms I filled out.

Downey: Go on.

Colby: If Linda phoned Peter Gzowski and asked him to play one of her songs on ... say ... a Tuesday morning, do you think he'd do it?

Downey: Sure. Why not?

Colby: And on my rating card I said I always listen to *Morningside* on Tuesdays.

Downey: How about this one? "Mr. Colby claims I had his teeth removed because he refused medication."

Colby: A simple statement of fact. I refused to take drugs so Rand took my false teeth away and locked me in solitary.

Downey: Okay, I've got one more for you. According to your files you think Linda Barrie has little birds whispering messages in your ear.

Colby: The Snowbirds.

Downey: Right, snowbirds.

Colby: Not snowbirds. *The* Snowbirds. The Canadian Forces aerobatic team. They're stationed about a hundred miles from my place in Red Deer.

Suggesting somebody might get a pilot to fly over my house isn't exactly behaving like I think I'm Saint Francis Assisi.

Downey: Are you telling me you think that Linda Barrie can affect the flight plans of Canadian Forces jet fighters?

Colby: They named the squadron in her honour, why wouldn't they do her a little favour?

Downey: Oh, come on, Jacob!

Colby: Okay, I know how it sounds, but God, you hear stranger things on the news every night!

Downey: Yeah, but the newscaster doesn't face a fitness hearing that could put him in the Willows.

Colby: Look Kim, do you believe in love?

Downey: Sometimes.

Colby: Do you remember what it was like the first time. Thinking about the other person all day long. And maybe there's a song ... your song, and every time you turn on the radio they seem to be playing it ... and you know how sometimes you just pick up the phone on a whim and call and that other person says: "I was just thinking about you."

(Downey *smiles*.)

Colby: You know what I'm talking about.

Downey: Yeah. I've been in love.

Colby: When those little magic moments come along you don't say: "My, what a bizarre coincidence." You sit back and you think: "That's beautiful."

Downey: Damn, Jacob, people just won't buy it.

Colby: And that's the problem with the world today.

Downey: Jacob, a nice little metaphor about the synchronicity of love isn't going to carry your case in court. You'd make my job a hell of a lot easier if you'd just go in there and admit the error of your ways.

Colby: I will never deny my love for Linda.

Downey: Why can't you just give it up? You're an attractive man. Why can't you just forget her, go home, and find somebody else?

Colby: There's no one like Linda back home, Kim.

Downey: Well ... I guess I'll have to concentrate on convincing them you just aren't "mean" enough to be locked up.

Colby: If I was a schizophrenic what would be the best indicator that I would become dangerous?

Downey: A past history of violence.

Colby: My past history of violence amounts to a schoolyard fistfight when I was 12. I lost.

Downey: Okay, I'll do my best. See ya in court.

(Downey *shakes* Colby's *hand and exits.* Colby *picks up his notebook. Lights fade to a spot on* Colby. *He writes.*)

Colby: Love is a revolution in the mind ...

(*Suddenly the band and* Linda *pop onto the stage, dressed in court robes and wigs.*)

All: Hi Jake!

(Linda *and the band sing* "Daydream," *a song in praise of daydreams about love.* Colby *finds it very funny, especially when they change the lyric to sing:* "Colby you are not insane, maybe just a bit deranged." *The song ends with a whistled verse.* Linda *and the band back out, and* The Judge *enters. Lights shift. We are back in court.*)

The Clerk: All rise.

(Dr Rand *takes the stand.*)

The Crown: Dr Rand, would it be fair to say Mr Colby may be suffering from schizophrenia?

Rand: The existence of paranoia without the presence of schizophrenia is quite rare. In the case of an encapsulated delusional system like Mr Colby's the patient may at first only suffer from the delusion itself, but usually a schizophrenic element develops. Given similar cases, one would expect Mr Colby's condition to deteriorate. He is involved in very stressful situations – prison, a failing ability to run his farm due to court appearances ... and of course, his frustration over the unresponsiveness of Linda Barrie.

The Crown: And what would be the result of this deterioration?

Rand: Well, almost anything could happen. He could become unpredictable, perhaps violent.

The Crown: Your experience with Mr Colby does lead you to believe he is deteriorating?

Rand: Yes. The delusion seems to have expanded to include the court and during the course of his last stay in Willowood his illness had clearly come to encompass our attempts at treatment.

The Crown: Dr Rand, do you feel that Mr Colby is fit to stand trial?

Rand: No sir, I do not.

The Crown: Thank you.

The Judge: Mr Colby?

Colby: Thank you, Your Honour. Dr Downey is going to be called in this matter?

The Judge: Yes, she is.

Colby: In that case I have no further questions for Dr Rand. I would prefer to have my mental state assessed by a more impartial authority.

The Judge: You may step down, Dr Rand.

The Crown: Dr Downey, please.

The Clerk: Dr Kimberly Downey.

(Downey *enters and is sworn in. She takes the stand.*)

The Crown: Dr Downey, have you had a chance to speak with the accused?

Downey: Yes, I have.

The Crown: Would you concur with Dr Rand's opinion that Mr Colby is unfit to stand trial?

Downey: No sir, I would not. His capacity to function in areas not related to his delusional system is not impaired at this point.

The Crown: But, Dr Rand is adamant in his opinion that Mr Colby is slipping into a schizophrenic state.

Downey: I saw no evidence of that.

The Crown: You don't think Mr Colby's condition will worsen?

Downey: I don't think he could go against court orders more than he has. In fact, for the record, the frequency of his violations has decreased. If anything this may indicate an improvement in his condition.

The Crown: Are you saying there is no chance he is a danger to himself or other persons in the community?

Downey: That is a very complex issue. The best predicator of future dangerousness is past dangerousness. Mr Colby appears to be a very gentle man and there is no evidence of violent behaviour in the past.

The Crown: But, Dr Rand had indicated that if ... if delusions expand beyond their encapsulated form, schizophrenic behaviour will begin to occur. I take it we agree that Mr Colby's delusional system is expanding?

Downey: I'm not sure. I don't think so.

The Crown: But his delusion now encompasses the actions of the police and the proceedings of this court.

Downey: At first glance, yes, but from my discussions with him ... when you talk to him about his feelings of harassment he makes sense.

The Crown: What do you mean by that?

Downey: To put it bluntly, I don't think it's particularly insane for Mr Colby to feel he has been victimized.

The Crown: Victimized?

Downey: Mr Colby's case is more interesting than most but it's not uncommon. Yes, he is deluded, but there is no evidence that he is dangerous. This is obviously why the courts have had trouble dealing with him.

The Crown: Your Honour, while I admire Dr Downey's very sympathetic position vis-à-vis the plight of the mentally ill in this province I don't think this is the time or the place for a sociology lesson.

Downey: Your Honour, I think it is reprehensible that someone like Mr Colby who suffers from an essentially harmless delusion can end up in an institution for the criminally insane. We're not talking about a sociology lesson here, we're talking about a human being.

The Crown: A human being indeed. Dr Downey. I wonder how you would feel if you were being bothered by Mr Colby. Would it not be fair to say that you would feel personally violated by his "harmless delusion"?

Downey: As a woman I understand the kind of fears Miss Barrie has. We all have fears and we have to learn to live with them. I think a man should be punished for what he does, not what he thinks.

The Crown: Your Honour, the question at hand is whether Mr Colby is dangerous.

Downey: The question is how long will we continue to allow our system to feed victims into institutions just because we have no place else to put them.

The Judge: The question before this court is neither of the above. I want to know if this man is able to defend himself.

Downey: Your Honour, sending this man to Willowood on a Lieutenant-Governor's warrant is, in my opinion, the worst thing that could happen to him.

The Judge: Dr Downey, this courtroom is not a forum for your social views. You will confine yourself to answering the Crown's questions.

Downey: But, Your Honour ...

The Judge: Do you have any more questions for the witness, Mr Broilman?

The Crown: Thank you, Your Honour. Dr Downey, in your opinion is Mr Colby capable of defending himself?

Downey: He is a highly intelligent and articulate man. It's obvious that he understands court procedure.

The Crown: Dr Downey, if His Honour were to rule that Mr Colby's defence bears no relationship to the case, how would that affect your opinion of his fitness to defend himself?

Downey: It wouldn't lead me to say categorically that he was unfit.

The Crown: Well, I say his defence is poppycock in so far as the issue before this court is quite simply whether or not he broke probation by taking a letter to Ms Barrie's office. (*pause*) Dr Downey, do you have any doubts about Mr Colby's ability to stand trial?

Downey: Psychiatry is not a precise science. There are always doubts ... but ...

The Crown: You do have doubts then.

Downey: Yes, but ...

The Crown: And do you also have doubts about whether or not Mr Colby will become a dangerous schizophrenic?

Downey: You can't commit a man for what he may or may not become.

The Crown: Dr Downey, can you categorically deny the possibility that Mr Colby may in the future deteriorate into a violent schizophrenic state?

Downey: No, but ...

The Crown: And what, clinically speaking, might push him over the edge?

Downey: As Dr Rand suggests, stress but ...

The Crown: The stress of repeated court appearances?

Downey: Perhaps.

The Crown: The stress of losing a whole wheat crop?

Downey: Well, maybe ... but ...

The Crown: And above all, the stress of his continued rejection by Linda Barrie?

Downey: No, above all the stress of being locked up in a hospital for the criminally insane.

The Crown: Where he would receive treatment. No further questions, Your Honour.

The Judge: Do you have any questions for Dr Downey?

Colby: No, Your Honour ... if I might ... if I might just make a statement.

The Judge: Certainly. You may step down, Dr Downey. Mr Colby?

Colby: Your Honour, there seems to be some indication that you are about to find my arguments before this Court irrelevant to my case. Before you take that position, I would just like to point out one more time that there has been no real attempt to discover the true facts behind my case. Linda Barrie has never been questioned.

The Judge: Mr Colby, if you'll recall there was an attempt to look into your allegations. Mr Edwards is willing to testify to your behaviour. Upon this suggestion you became irrational in your objections.

Colby: Linda is the only one who can explain what's going on.

The Judge: The Crown claims Mr Edwards can be of assistance.

Colby: Look, Your Honour, if it will prevent you from ruling against me I'll talk to the man, but it won't solve anything.

Voice: Call Charles Edwards!

(*Music underscore: "Farewell to Nova Scotia," hummed by cast in a bagpipe drone. Lights shift; we leave the courtroom and go again to the fantasy sequence funeral. The* Priest, Linda, Edwards *and* Sandy *enter.* Colby *walks upstage and observes the action.* Sandy *stands near* Colby, *sneaks a drink;* Colby *notices.* Sandy *notices him.*)

Sandy: Cold enough to freeze the best bits off a brass monkey.

Colby: Do you think drinking is appropriate today?

Sandy: Nobody up here to see it but you. (*pause*) It's just that I can't stand funerals. Scare me to death, the way everything suddenly gets so permanent.

Colby: Well, if you don't like it why did you come?

Sandy: I'm the gravedigger.

Colby: Oh.

Sandy: I mean, it's a steady job, right? I can't be complaining ... but I just don't understand why people put themselves through all this malarky. I mean, it doesn't do the guy in the box any good now, does it?

Colby: The funeral isn't for the deceased. It's a time for the living to gather strength from each other.

Sandy: You sound like a funeral director.

Colby: I hate funerals. But it will help Linda.

Sandy: She's a friend of yours?

Colby: Look at her down there. Like a little bird brought to ground.

Sandy: You from T.O.? You work with Linda or something? Hey buddy!

Colby: Why don't you just watch the funeral?

Sandy: You know, if you're such a friend how come you aren't with the funeral party?

Colby: I'll go to her when the time is right.

Sandy: You're weird, buddy.

(Sandy *walks down to* Edwards *and whispers in his ear.* Edwards *leaves the party at graveside and walks up to* Colby.)

Edwards: Jacob Colby, right? The love letters, the cans of wheat, the airplane tickets ... Jake Colby?

Colby: It's none of your business who I am.

Edwards: Would you mind telling me what in hell you're doing here?

Colby: I think I have a right to share in Linda's grief.

Edwards: Look down there. They are putting her father in the ground. You have no rights here.

Colby: Linda wants me to be here.

Edwards: Linda doesn't know you from Adam.

Colby: You know that's not true.

Edwards: Isn't it? Then why did she send me up here to get rid of you?

Colby: You're always in the way, Edwards. Filling Linda's mind with lies, pulling her away from the reality in her songs.

Edwards: The reality in her songs? Damn, Colby, this isn't some dream world conjured up off the radio! This is reality! Linda's father is dead and you can't do a damn thing to help her. You can only hurt her by being here.

Colby: Don't you think I know how desperate and lonely she is? Can't you hear what she's singing about? No, I guess you're so in love with the sound of cash registers that you can't hear anything else.

Edwards: Man, you're the one who can't hear anything. She doesn't want you here. Just pack it in, okay?

Colby: I think I'd better talk to Linda.

Edwards: Fine. Come on down the hill. Quote her a lyric. You'll get a real good dose of reality when you see what's in her eyes when she looks at you.

Colby: With you hovering over the proceedings like a vulture?

Edwards: Don't worry. I'll give you all the room you need to ruin her father's funeral.

Colby: You just go about your business, Edwards. And I'll go about mine.

Edwards: You're afraid of confronting her, aren't you? You're afraid because way down deep you know she doesn't give a shit about you. And you can't do a damn thing to help her.

Colby: That's a bloody lie!

(*Humming stops.* Linda *looks up at* Colby *and* Edwards, *then away.*)

Edwards: I think you'd better go before I call the police.

Colby: I don't think Linda lets her domestic help make those kinds of decisions for her.

Edwards: I've had enough of this crap? Move it!

Colby: You're nothing but a sleazy showbiz hustler sucking Linda's blood and ...

Edwards: That's it. Move it or I'm going to pop you one. No joke.

(*Humming picks up again.*)

Colby: Then who'd be ruining the funeral?

Edwards: You would, Mr Colby. Now move it, because if you don't things are going to get very messy, very fast. I said, MOVE IT!

(*Music out. Lighting change. Quick exit by all but* Colby *and* Edwards, *who takes the witness stand. We're back in court.*)

Edwards: After the business at the funeral, well things just seemed to be getting out of hand. The harassment of Linda just had to stop. So we took the necessary steps. We've put about a hundred thousand dollars into various security systems in the last two years. And as far as Mr Colby goes, well, he'd come to the house in Mount Stewart as I've said so the next time he came to the office we phoned the police. It's beyond me how he can say Linda's never discouraged him. If I'd been dragged through the courts the number of times he has I'd sure feel discouraged. And that's about it.

The Judge: Very well. Mr Colby, do you have any questions?

Colby: Yes, Your Honour. Mr Edwards you claim your worry over my attentions to Miss Barrie has led to the installation of expensive security systems. Is it unusual for a performer of Miss Barrie's public stature to be highly security conscious?

Edwards: Mick Jagger carries a hand-gun. We haven't gone that far yet, but sure, once a career gets to a certain point a performer has to be protected from guys like you.

Colby: I see, then you would have installed security systems regardless of my involvement with Miss Barrie. Now, you testified that I came to the house in Mount Stewart, is that correct?

Edwards: Yes, that is correct.

Colby: Mr Edwards, isn't it a fact that I did not go to the Barrie home in P.E.I. I attended the funeral in Barrington Passage, N.S.

Edwards: The funeral?

Colby: Of Miss Barrie's father.

Edwards: You weren't at the funeral.

Colby: You just testified that I came to the ...

Edwards: I just testified that this other guy showed up at the funeral. That made us decide we had to stop all the people who were harassing Linda. You aren't the only guy we have trouble with, you know.

Colby: You claim I didn't come to the funeral?

Edwards: I just told the court. You came to the house at Christmas. I invited you in to try and reach some understanding about this whole situation. We had words and you left. You didn't show up at the funeral.

Colby: Then ... why ... why was I arrested after the funeral?

Edwards: Didn't you hear a word I said? You weren't there.

Colby: It was up on the hill ... in the graveyard. We almost came to blows.

Edwards: The graveyard isn't on a hill, not the Catholic one, anyway.

Colby: Why ... why would I lie about something like that? It's here ... it was even in the paper ... here in my ... my scrapbook ... (*He leafs through his scrapbook.*) Here ... it's "Linda Barrie Tops Billboard Chart" ... No, "Barrie plays the Cave ... ," "Triumph at the Orpheum ... ," "Still a Down-Home Girl ... " no, it's ... "Psychiatrist Claims Ardent Fan Mentally Ill ... " no ... yes ... yes ... here it is? "The Price of Fame": "An unwelcome guest lent a sour note to the funeral of Linda Barrie's father in

Barrington Passage yesterday. The would-be songwriter approached Miss Barrie during the burial service and ... "

Edwards: Mr Colby, you aren't a songwriter.

(*Synth tone.* Colby *realizes he's way off base.*)

Colby: Well I ... I wanted to be at the funeral ... I ... I knew Linda would need someone to stand by her. But ... but ... when I thought about the reporters, Edwards, all the people who wouldn't know me, and what was going on I ... I ... I was there with her in spirit. (*pause*) I failed Linda, didn't I? That's why she's doing this.

The Judge: Mr Colby, are you all right?

(*Long pause.*)

Colby: Your Honour, I ... I realize that I have made a mistake here. My ... the pressure of the trial has led me to mistake the occasion to which Mr. Edwards was referring. He is correct in saying that I ... I did visit at Christmas. But Your Honour, this mistake on my part in no way alters the fact that ... Your Honour, despite the many attempts of the Crown to have a finding of mental incompetence brought against me by the Court I find at this time that I must once again point out that Linda Barrie has never been questioned in this matter, even though I have proved beyond a doubt that we do, in fact, have a long-standing relationship. The facts are on the record. I have sent Linda Barrie over a hundred separate items, including two items of wheat. She has never returned one of them, yet I am to be found insane because I believe she encourages my attentions.

In North American society the man is encouraged to play the role of pursuer in male/female relationships. In most situations the fact that I am pursuing a women would not be considered insane, especially since I have never forced my attentions on Linda. My great crime, remember, is bringing her a love letter. That's all, but because of Linda Barrie's fame I have been brutalized by the court process and committed by a doctor who obviously bears me malice. My God, when I try and point out the fact that my Constitutional rights are being abused the court calls me deluded and suggest further psychiatric imprisonment.

The Judge: Mr Colby, this isn't Russia. The issue here is not imprisonment. It's treatment. The issue is whether or not you require psychiatric help.

Colby: The Review Board doesn't think I need help.

The Judge: I'll decide if you need help.

Colby: She's using the courts. She's manipulating the proceedings. This is her little playhouse and she's the puppeteer. She's arranging us like furniture.

The Judge: Mr Colby, I am not a piece of furniture.

Colby: Your Honour, although my case may be incredible, unique, even bizarre, the fact still remains that to date there is no real proof that Linda Barrie hasn't done what I claim she has done. Say it any way you choose, but there is no arguing that the spirit of Linda Barrie hovers over these proceedings. If it didn't, then why are there reporters off in the corner taking such voracious notes? I say, Linda Barrie's behaviour in this matter is reprehensible and that she is indeed creating a public nuisance. If the Court wishes to prove me deluded in this matter it is a simple thing to do. Have Linda Barrie come in here and deny what I'm saying. Have Linda Barrie come in here and say she is afraid of me, that she feels endangered by me, that she personally does not want me to ever write to her again. Have her return my mail and tell me to go away. Then if I persist in my behaviour then maybe your doubts about my mental competence may have some basis in fact, but until the court takes this step then I am a victim of abuse in these proceedings.

Edwards: Your Honour, if I can interrupt here, we have had enough of Mr Colby's implications that somehow Linda is pushing him around. She's taping a TV show just down the street, I'll go get her. Let's lay this whole thing to rest once and for all.

The Judge: Miss Barrie would agree to testify?

Colby: That's all I'm asking for.

The Judge: Well then, call Linda Barrie.

(*The roar of a jet overhead. Dramatic lighting shift.* Linda *appears on the up-stage platform in silhouette as the musical intro to "That's Not The Way (It's S'posed To Be)" begins. A followspot hits her. She's dressed in an ultra-sophisticated sparkling black dress. She sings the song to* Colby. *The lyric deals with hidden love, suppressed anger, and confusion over the singer's emotional relationship with the man it is address to. The song ends. Lights shift. The ASM comes on and drapes an expensive white fur over* Linda's *shoulders. We are back in court, and she is talking to* The Judge.)

The Judge: Would you like to be seated, Miss Barrie?

Linda: Yes, I would. I'm sorry about the way I'm dressed but I just completed a taping.

The Judge: It's quite all right. You look ... lovely. Mr Broilman?

The Crown: Miss Barrie, how long have you known the accused?

Linda: I would say approximately seven or eight years.

The Crown: Mr Colby claims there is a relationship between the two of you.

Linda: There is no relationship. The first time I became aware of him, he sent me a letter that had some kind of wheat in it, and it was a very nice letter and I wrote him back thanking him for the wheat and the letter and then he started showing up at concerts and so on, and it just went from there until he started to visit us in Mount Stewart. At that point I had the office phone the police to see if they could help keep Mr Colby away.

The Crown: Yet, Mr Colby claims you encourage his attentions. Through letters, songs, and so on.

Linda: I do not encourage Mr Colby's attentions.

The Crown: What is your position today regarding Mr Colby?

Linda: Well, I am just frightened of him a little. He shows up at Mount Stewart. We have to deal with him at the office. He seems to have no regard for the people around me and I am very concerned about what might happen to someone, that's my position.

The Judge: Mr Colby, do you have any questions to ask the witness?

(*A pause. Then* Colby *decides to go for it.*)

Colby: Yes, Your Honour, I do. Do you recall when you appeared in Vancouver at the Cave Theatre and Restaurant?

Linda: Yes.

Colby: Do you recall meeting me on that occasion?

Linda: Not particularly.

Colby: You don't remember me giving you some flowers and saying from a hay baler to a herring choker?

Linda: No, I don't.

Colby: On the back of that album, the title of which I told you I didn't like, there was a picture of you taken at Red Hill Pioneer Village, do you recall it?

Linda: On the back of *The Secret*? Yes, I recall it.

Colby: There is no association between what I said to you backstage in Vancouver and that picture on the back of the album showing you and a farmer with a background of baled hay ... baled hay as I recall it, is it not?

Linda: I'm feeding a goat or something.

Colby: No, a cow.

Linda: Oh, whatever ...

Colby: Could I add also ... were you not wearing a cape of herring-bone design in this photograph, a garment that is often worn by Maritime people?

Linda: It was just a red wool cape.

Colby: You deny that there is an association between my phrase: "From a hay baler to a herring choker" and that photograph?

Linda: The album covers are designed by a firm in the States who are paid to do that sort of thing. My only involvement in the whole process is to have my picture taken, and that's it.

Colby: You're trying to tell me that that picture isn't symbolic of our meeting backstage at the Cave Theatre and Restaurant?

Linda: I'm afraid I don't know what you're talking about.

Colby: Don't you see the contradiction in claiming you won't see me and then sending me that kind of symbolic message?

The Judge: Mr Colby, it is clear that your interpretation of Miss Barrie's symbolic communications is incorrect. Can we go on to something more concrete?

Colby: What about the letters, Your Honour? She's never returned any of my letters.

Linda: My office staff reads all the letters. The only one I read from you was the one where you sent me the wheat and told me how to make chewing gum out of it.

Colby: And that was the time you wrote back and thanked me? In 1973?

Linda: Yes.

Colby: You're going to contradict yourself. The wheat you just described ... the chewing-gum wheat, I sent you that batch in 1976.

Linda: The wheat that you've just described is the wheat I thought arrived in 1973. I don't remember, that's the wheat I remember. The stuff you wanted me to chew.

Colby: There's a three-year separation. You must have read at least two of my letters. Both times I sent you wheat.

Linda: I only remember one time.

Colby: Don't you realize that those two parcels were separated by three years?

Linda: Do you realize how much mail I receive?

Colby: Insignificant mail that doesn't require a personal response?

Linda: Yes.

Colby: But on two occasions you admit taking my letters seriously enough to reply personally. Isn't it possible that you wrote more letters which you have now conveniently forgotten?

Linda: I didn't write any more letters.

Colby: Did you have someone write letters?

Linda: No.

Colby: Did you dictate letters over the phone?

Linda: I did not.

Colby: Did you cause letters to be written to me?

Linda: No.

Colby: Come on, Linda. Of course you did. Whose office did the letters come from? Whose publicity machine have I supposedly confused with the real person? Who is responsible for all the encouragement I've received over the years? Who is responsible, Linda? (*pause*) You are responsible.

The Judge: Is that all, Mr Colby?

Colby: I have just one more question, Your Honour. Is the snowbird having a lark with the schizophrenic jailbird? Is this a simple case of a cuckoo and a canary?

The Judge: Can you answer that question?

Linda: No.

(*A pause, then the tone on the synth, lights begin to shift. Once again we are moving into* Colby's *fantasy.*)

Linda: Your Honour, I wonder if I might speak to Mr Colby in private for a few moments.

The Judge: If the Crown does not object ... .

The Crown: No, Your Honour.

The Judge: Mr Colby?

Colby: Your Honour, that is what I have wanted all along.

The Judge: We will adjourn for a few moments. There will be a guard at the door, Miss Barrie.

(*All exit but* Linda *and* Colby. *Long pause.* Colby *doesn't move. He is utterly transfixed.*)

Linda: Look, Mr Colby ...

Colby: Jacob, please. There's no one here but us.

Linda: Mr Colby, listen, I sing songs for a living. They're not symbolic for me. They're just good songs. I ...

Colby: Don't be afraid of your feelings, Linda – just because people in the courtroom don't understand.

Linda: You're in great danger, Mr Colby. Do you understand that? This is not a relationship. It's a legal proceeding in a court of law. The judge has the power to institutionalize you. Maybe for the rest of your life.

Colby: Now don't you go worrying about that, Linda.

Linda: How am I supposed to "not worry"? I'm a human being, not a machine. A minute ago you said I was responsible for all this trouble you're in.

Colby: I know you were angry, that you felt I failed you, but Linda ... I ...

Linda: Listen to me. I am trying to help you. You're got to come back to reality. Get a lawyer. Defend yourself. Let the case run its course. They might even let you go.

Colby: They have to let me go, Linda.

Linda: You're not above the law, Mr Colby.

Colby: I'm innocent. What crime have I committed?

Linda: You stole something.

Colby: I never stole anything in my life.

Linda: Look, I was born with a gift, OK? I can use my music to touch people, and I've spent my life learning how to use that gift. When I stand in front of a crowd, or one of my songs is played on the radio, well, I help everybody share feelings ... sometimes feelings about love. That's what a performer does. When you snatch that feeling out of the air and say, "This belongs to me," well, you're a thief. You're stealing something from everybody I'm trying to share those feelings with.

Colby: No, Linda. Our love exists on a higher plane. It's more pure and meaningful than anything they'll ever understand. Maybe ... maybe they'll drag us down forever, but I know our love ...

Linda: Stop it, Mr Colby. Just stop it. (*pause*) You are in love with something that doesn't exist.

(Colby *shakes his head.*)

Colby: Linda, you exist.

Linda: I'm a married woman. I have two children and I'm very happy ...

Colby: Come on Linda, you know those children are symbolic. You know they are ...

Linda: My children are not symbols! They are flesh and blood and I love them and I am terrified when I hear you talk about them like that!

Colby: Why are you pretending to be afraid of me?

Linda: I *am* afraid of you! You make me afraid to walk down the street! You make me afraid to meet people after a show? (*pause*) You make me afraid to sing.

Colby: You're not being fair, Linda.

Linda: Fair? You come in here and talk about me and my family as if we're all some kind of projection. We aren't. We are real. We have feelings.

Colby: I HAVE FEELINGS TOO! (*pause*) I ... I'm sorry ... I didn't mean to ...

Linda: I know you have feelings, Jacob. That's why I'm here.

Colby: I love you, Linda.

Linda: Look, Jacob ... if you really love me, then you've got to believe me when I tell you the truth.

Colby: I will.

Linda: Well the truth is: I do not love you, Jacob Colby ... I'm sorry you got hurt.

(*There is a pause. Lights fade on* Linda, *leaving* Colby *alone, sitting in a spot. As he speaks* Linda *stands and very slowly walks away, back up the stairs to the upstage platform. Underscoring begins, an intro to "You Needed Me."*)

Colby: My heart can't be broken any more. It really is over. The thing is, she's just not the same girl I fell in love with. And that's sad. The saddest truth of the whole affair, cause ... they change her in the end. She just got too big to touch the ground. And her heart, her heart just flew away. Still she's really not to blame. It's hard to keep your perspective when you've been up so high for so long. After a while nothing looks real anymore. There's nothing you can dig your fist into like a clod of farm dirt.

No real sounds or smells ... just light ... and clouds ... and way down below ... maybe a glimpse of a ... a checkerboard of land where there's some little man working. Everything drowned in distance, and the whoosh of the jetstream. A little thing like love ... it can disappear.

(Linda *begins to sing "You Needed Me," she stands in a spotlight high above* Colby, *and he looks up at her as she sings the song, full of love, distance, and a promise she will never leave. Slowly* Colby *packs up his briefcase and leaves, the way he entered the theatre, through the crowd.* Linda *finishes the song. Lights fade to black.*)

THE END

A Woman from the Sea

Cindy Cowan

Cindy Cowan lives with her family in the small Inuit community of Pangnirtung, Baffin Island, where she works as an adult educator for Arctic College. She has been an active member of the Mulgrave Road Co-op Theatre in Nova Scotia for over ten years, working as an actor and playwright. In addition to writing *A Woman from the Sea*, she has completed three other plays. The most recent, *Honey and White Blood*, was produced by the National Arts Centre in 1989.

A Woman from the Sea was first produced by the Mulgrave Road Co-op Theatre on 18 February 1986, in the Guysborough Masonic Hall, Guysborough, Nova Scotia.

PRODUCTION
Director / **Joanna Mercer**
Sets and Costumes / **Gillian McCulloch**
Music and Soundscape / **Bob Atkinson, Kurt Hagen**
Stage Manager / **Gary Vermier**

CAST
Wanda Graham / Almira
John Dartt / George
Mary-Colin Chisholm / Sedna

A Woman from the Sea was developed with the assistance of the Canada Council, the Nova Scotia Department of Culture, Recreation and Fitness, and the Banff Playwrights' Colony. It was also workshopped by the Mulgrave Road Co-op Theatre in May 1985. Most importantly the author is grateful to Johanna Mercer, Wanda Graham, John Dartt, Mary-Colin Chisholm, Gillian McCulloch, and Ed McKenna for their vision, patience, and faith in this play.

PLAYWRIGHT'S NOTES

When my daughter Meghan was born, the first emotion I experienced, after relief, was that of utter astonishment. Lying on the table, between my shaking legs, was a living human being. This was power. Real power! Like wind and water and fire. What had this to do with those frothy, baby doll maternity clothes? Why didn't women look like Amazons when they were pregnant? Why had I never seen a pregnant woman swagger? Why hadn't I?

Then, from the introduction to Germaine Greer's *Sex and Destiny*, came the words ... "madness ... living inside a body ... a body that creates life but cannot control the fate of that creation."

As I lifted my eyes to the sea that forever surrounds me in Nova Scotia I started to hear a story. One of destruction and birth and the endurance and power of women's love. A love which must be far greater than the megatons of destruction released by a single nuclear explosion. And riding the crests and troughs were the women of Greenham Common. They waved. And I tried to wave back.

Cindy Cowan

SET AND SOUND

The real time is afternoon and evening, in February 1986, at a deserted fish shack on a cliff overlooking Chedabucto Bay in northeastern Nova Scotia. However, there is another time and place, that of the Floating Island, which exists simultaneously to the physical reality of the beach, cliff, and shack.

The only requirement of the set is that it encompass these realities and allow the characters to remain on stage at all times. In the original production there was a downstage-right sand dune which secretly held Sedna's props, ie., the kimono, the tea-tray, the combat helmets, etc.

When a character is not actually involved in a scene, she or he remains onstage and continues to underscore the local scene with business: George looks through his binoculars, Almira sleeps, Sedna waits or drinks from her wineskin, does yoga, and at times seems to be simply a seal basking in the sun.

George can occupy different space and time to Sedna and Almira. He doesn't hear what Almira hears, nor does he see or hear Sedna except for the exchange at the end of scene 8. Sedna appears to George either as a rotting seal corpse or an old woman, as at the top of the play.

The sound and music were written as a fourth character: the environment. They are also the greater expression of Sedna's being. In the original production musical themes were written for all the characters which underscored their "realities" or emotional turmoil. Sedna had many themes but they were all encompassed by one overall sound quality which I called Sound of the Sea/Music.

The booms are menacing and disturbing. They are both the approaching presence of Sedna and the disintegration of Almira's grasp on reality. George hears only one boom, that at the end of scene 8.

The poem used in scenes 9 and 10 is by George Barlow and is entitled "The Soul."

Love is the moving energy of life. It is both blindly erotic and deeply
personal, a passionate, prideful, powerful caring for oneself and others. It
is the law of the goddess and the essence of magic.
— Starhawk, *The Spiritual dance*

PROLOGUE

The repetitive cries of the gulls fade to the sound of the sea.
   As the lights come up, a beach strewn with large white bones is revealed.
*The bleached ribs and vertebrae are ghostly against the blues and greys and
pinks of a North Atlantic winter's day.*
   *There is also a fish shack which appears to be balanced on an outcropping of
rock.*
   And crouched on the beach is Sedna. *She is a Selkie, a creature who is capable of being both a woman and a seal. Sedna and the actress playing her may
transform at will from woman to seal by slipping in and out of her seal tail
which is detachable at the waist. On Sedna's upper body she wears a coat. The
glory she once possessed as a goddess of the sea is reflected in the coat's remaining tatters and skins. Worn with the tail it reinforces the transformation to a
seal. Worn alone, it gives the impression of someone regal having fallen in the
gutter. Finally, Sedna wears a head-dress that serves as a seal mask when she
lowers her head as she does now.*
   *Sedna is on the beach in her human form. Her hands, which are swaddled
in torn black bandages, gently caress her seal body as she holds it in her lap.*
   *After some time Sedna lifts to her lips a conch shell. From it is emitted one
long, sweet note, a lament, recalling a distant memory of the first sounds ever
heard. Setting down the conch the sound repeats itself at Sedna's bidding.*

Sedna: Caw!! Caw!! (*Her cries to the birds echo on the empty beach. Returning her attention to the seal tail, she stops, alert and animalistic.*)

(*A loud boom.*)

Sedna: They're here! (*Sound of human voices.*) It took you long enough!
(Sedna *freezes, gazing out to sea.*)

(George *and* Almira *enter.*
The most notable thing about Almira, *other than her wild and unruly hair, is
the dark sunglasses she wears.* George *is appealingly "6os" with long hair, a
beard, and wire-rimmed glasses. He begins the ritual of unpacking from his
knapsack a notebook, an eversharp, toilet paper, and a pair of high-powered binoculars.* Almira *stands thunderstruck holding a grocery bag and her purse.*)

Sedna: (*hastily hiding her tail*) Company at last.

Almira: A fish shack?

George: I knew you'd love it as soon as you saw it!

Almira: It's full of feathers and mouse droppings. George, this place hasn't been lived in for years ...

George: (*exiting to the outside*) Look at the view!

(*Again the boom*)

Sedna: (*whispering*) Allmmiiraaa?

(Almira *stops*)

Sedna: (*waving*) Almira!

(Almira *turns toward the call, straining to identify where it is coming from.*)

Sedna: (*raising a wineskin*) ... To you, Almira. A toast! Death to our best friend.

(*The sounds of the sea / music rise as* Sedna *wraps an old shawl around her head and huddles down onto the beach. Above her is* George *on a rock watching through the binoculars.*)

ACT ONE

SCENE ONE

George: Hellooo! (*He slowly lowers the binoculars and descends to the beach.*)

Sedna: Not from around here?

George: No. We're spending the day in the old fish store up top there.

Sedna: Murdoch. Mr and Mrs?

George: Right!

Sedna: Hhhmm.

(*Silence.*)

George: Do you know anyone with a boat I might borrow?

Sedna: My father. He was a fisherman.

George: I'd just putter in along the shore.

Sedna: No tellin' what a person might find.

George: You ever see anything unusual out in the bay?

Sedna: My father he saw somethin'. Lifted its head right out of the water and waved. (*Turning, she looks directly into* George's *face.*) Waved ... Last time he ever set foot in a boat on that bay! (*Pause*) I guess I can't help you.

George: Thanks anyway.

Sedna: Ahuh.

George: See you ...

Sedna: Ahuh.

(*Sounds of the sea.* Sedna *enters her sealskins.*)

SCENE TWO

George: Almira!!

Almira: (*startled*) Oh! (*Surprised.*) It's you!

George: You were expecting someone else.

Almira: No. It's just ...

George: What?

Almira: I was dreaming, I guess. You were gone a long time.

George: I met this fantastic old woman down on the beach. Look, you can see her. (*George has a look.*) She's gone ... But listen to this. I was right. This is the place. Her father saw something out in that bay. The story is something waved at him. What do you suppose he saw!

Almira: Something out of a bottle of Hermits.

George: I believe her.

Almira: A monster from the sea?

George: It could have been a Hood seal! There hasn't been a confirmed sighting of one of those babies this far south since 1953. What a coup! You wouldn't have caught me rowing away.

Almira: Even after it waved at you?

George: (*lying on the cot*) Hah! I bet that old guy never did set foot on water again. (Almira *has picked up the binoculars and stares out to sea.*)

George: If there is a big mother of a sea tusker out there I want to meet it. (*Pause. He watches* Almira.) What are you staring at?

Almira: Fog.

George: Fine friggin' weather for a holiday.

Almira: I like the fog. (*Soft.*) Death to our best friends.

George: Been out sealing?

Almira: No.

George: That's from an old sealing song.
"Talking of death brings me in mind
O' a toast which seemed tae be unkind.
But an explanation makes amends,
'Twas only, Death to our best friends."

Almira: I've never heard it before.

George: You must have.

Almira: I haven't.

George: You wouldn't know the words.

Almira: I don't.

George: Almira! You're giving me the creeps.

Almira: The song just popped into my head!

George: Why are you acting so weird?

Almira: (*finally lowering the glasses*) I'm sick to death of seals.

George: Let's do something normal!

Almira: What?

George: Let's eat. I am starving!

Almira: In the brown paper bag.

George: (*searching*) ... Today is going to be good for us.

Almira: Under the cot.

George: This place is great! Am I right? (Almira *turns away, removing her hiking boots.*) Right! (*Horrified.*) This isn't food.

Almira: What is it?

George: I can't eat junk.

Almira: I can.

George: (*wailing*) I can't eat this. Chips, popcorn, fritos. Pink popcorn?

Almira: Chemicals stay down. Anything else ... (*She mimes vomiting.*)

George: (*eating a chip*) It's so unhealthy.

Almira: Who cares?

(*The boom.* Sedna *sits up listening.*)

Almira: (*listening*) What's the point in being healthy?

George: Discipline!

Almira: Superman.

George: Combat discipline. To fight the enemy. Stroke, angina, coronary, high blood pressure, enlarged prostate lurk around every corner.

Almira: You'll make a pretty corpse.

George: (*imitating* Almira) Running is joy! Pure joy!!

Almira: You can run for the both of us. (*Watching* George *she enjoys letting him continue running.*) Oh stop it, George. I'm exhausted just looking at you.

George: Come on. Get your shoes on. We'll go for a run together.

Almira: I didn't bring them.

George: You didn't bring them! You'll gain weight.

Almira: It doesn't matter, George.

George: Your heart rate.

Almira: It doesn't matter, George.

George: It doesn't matter?!

Almira: Trust me, George. You used to trust me.

George: I trust you. Or I used to trust you. Junk food? No jogging?

(*Pause.*)

Almira: When I was running all I could hear was my own heartbeat.

George: There's nothing wrong with that! It's the blood circulating in the brain. It's normal.

Almira: It got too loud.

George: Your heartbeat got too loud?

Almira: I got too attached to my heartbeat.

George: That's crazy!

Almira: I was afraid it might stop.

George: Don't be so emotional!

Almira: I am not emotional!

(*Silence*)

George: (*realizing his mistake*) Wrong. Wrong. We're going to take things calmly.

Almira: You just said that because I'm a woman and because I'm ... (Almira *stops*.)

George: What's got into you lately?

Almira: You. (*Pause.*) Nothing. That's what I like about the fog. The simplicity of nothingness.

George: This isn't like you.

Almira: (*curious*) What am I like?

George: Melodramatic!

(Almira *tosses to* George *a stack of postcards with seal pups on them.*)

Almira: There's melodrama. These stupid postcards you brought down here. Look at the itsy, bitsy seal pups ...

George: If you want someone to listen, grab them where it hurts. (Almira *reaches out for* George's *groin.*)

George: Hey! don't attack me!

Almira: I'm not attacking you.

George: You're attacking my work.

Almira: Your work?

George: No. Your work! I'm not a fund-raiser. You're the suit-and-tie lobbyist. I'd much rather be out on the ice floes.

Almira: No battles are won on the ice floes anymore. It all happens in government offices.

George: Is that why you quit?

Almira: I've had it up to here with the seal hunt. I don't want to talk about petitions and numbers and depleted species.

George: The postcard mail-out was your idea.

Almira: (*bundling herself in an old quilt*) I'm retreating from society.

George: Sure. I'd forgotten. (*Pause.*) You can't stop caring.

Almira: Not caring feels very, very good.

George: You should jog. It'll help you get on top again. (*He picks up the binoculars.*)

(*The boom.*)

Almira: Do you smell something peculiar?

George: No.

Almira: Are you sure?

George: Wait just a minute ...

Almira: (*uneasy*) It's revolting.

(*The sounds of distant crying.*)

George: There's something out on the bay!

Almira: Like something dead. This place stinks! (George *grabs his coat.*) George?

George: I'll be right back.

Almira: Don't leave.

George: I'm just going out ... jogging.

(Almira *curls up under the quilt. George exits to the beach where he discovers* Sedna. *To George she appears to be a rotting seal corpse. Revolted he struggles to put it out to sea. The sound of the cries moves closer and can be identified as a herd of baying seals.*)

SCENE THREE

(*As* George *turns away.* Sedna *rolls once more onto the beach. With each roll she moves further up the beach and the cries and* Almira's *nightmare intensify.*)

Sedna: Look at me.

Almira: (*tossing*) No ... no ...

Sedna: Look at me.

Almira: No ...

Sedna: Thick, crimson blood.

Almira: No ... no ... no-o ...

Sedna: Arms rising and falling.

(George *enters.*)

George: Wake up, Allie. Honey, wake up.

(*Silence.*)

George: You were dreaming.

Almira: I was drowning. Down ... down ... down.

George: (*holding her*) It was only a dream.

Almira: I'm swimming and on the beach.

George: (*startled*) On the beach!

Almira: As far as the eye can see ...

George: What did you find?

Almira: Oh George.

George: Ssh. Almira, ssh.

Almira: The blood and the smell ...

George: It's all right. On the beach ...

Almira: It's still here. Can you smell it?

George: Listen to me, Almira! (George *is frantically removing his sweater, fearing that the smell from the seal corpse is on it.*)

Almira: It won't go away. (*She grabs from her purse a bottle of perfume.*)

George: Will you just listen to me. I got rid of it.

Almira: (*splashing her body with the scent*) It's me. It's me. It's me ...

George: Almira! Jesus! (*Taking the bottle from her.*) Everything is going to be fine.

Almira: (*suddenly Almira stops. Composing herself.*) I'm all right. (*Slowly she eats a chip.*)

(*Silence.*)

George: Would you like to hear the text I've written for the postcards?

Almira: I don't think so.

George: Remember when we used to do everything together?

Almira: No. (*Softer.*) Yes.

George: It's only rough.

Almira: Go ahead.

George: Dear Friend of Animals, Despite last year's decision by the European Parliament to ban the import of seal products with the resultant drop in the commercial value of the pelt, the killing continues. Forty thousand kills last year alone.

Almira: They don't care.

George: Who?

Almira: Great Britain boycotts our fish because of the cruelty of the seal hunt! But at the same time they support the slaughter of sea turtles for a bloody bowl of soup!

George: That's politics.

Almira: Hypocrites.

George: Life is about compromise.

Almira: Life is about death.

George: The whole world's idiotic. We go on!!!

Almira: Finish your letter.

George: It is very important, at this time, that the federal government be aware of the desire ...

Almira: Desire?

George: ... that this slaughter of marine life be ended.

Almira: I have forgotten desire.

Sedna: You have forgotten more than that!

George: ... If we try hard enough this year could perhaps see the end.

(*The boom.*)

Almira: I see the end.

Sedna: You have forgotten our bond.

George: These animals surely deserve to be left in peace.

Almira: (*crossing herself*) In nomini patri, et filii, et spiritu sanctu.

Sedna: (*at the same time*) In the name of the mother, the daughter, and the Holy Ghost.

Almira: On behalf of the seals we thank you. No postage necessary for federal politicians.

Sedna: Well, well, well.

(George *stares at* Almira.)

Almira: It's fine.

George: How about punch?

Almira: I liked "deserve to rest in peace."

George: Left in peace. I said "left in peace."

Almira: It would be nice to rest in peace.

Almira: Words. Words. Words.

George: What was I reading to you?

Almira: Words. Words. Words.

George: You weren't listening to me!

(*The boom. Both* Almira *and* Sedna *sit up alert.*)

Almira: I'm listening.

George: Be honest.

Almira: What do you think that fisherman saw out there?

George: A rare Hood seal.

Almira: No more seals.

George: No more seals. (*Pause.*) The line has to be drawn somewhere. We are guilty for so much killing. I know you don't agree with the seal issue. I'm sorry the fishermen were used to stop the destruction.

Almira: George? I'm frightened. There's something going on and it's far more insidious than the seals and the fishermen. It's sneaky. The last memo I received I had to read it over a few times. Then I caught it. Most of the sea turtles killed are nesting females. Pregnant turtles lumber up onto the beach, to lay their eggs ... then calipee hunters flip them over and with machetes hack off their belly plates. Getting inside to the precious calipee. Turtle soup won't thicken without the calipee. Then they are left mutilated, gutted, lying in the sun till dogs and pigs, or gulls ... (Almira *gags*. George *tries to hold her*.) Vomiting develops the stomach muscles. You think I've taken leave of my senses! Slipped over the edge.

George: You're not eating properly.

Almira: I've got a morbid preoccupation with death because I'm vitamin deficient!

George: You're a good fund-raiser. You got too close, that's all. You need a break.

Almira: Listen to me! The seals slaughtered on the ice floes? Nesting females! The annihilation of the penguins, gannets, spearbills, swiftwings ... How was it accomplished?

George: By eggers. Allie ... lie down.

Almira: I'm not finished! Nesting females have their eggs smashed because, fools that they are, they just keep laying more eggs ensuring freshness.

George: I'll take care of you.

Almira: You don't really understand.

George: I'm trying.

Almira: It doesn't pay to be female and pregnant. (*Pausing.*) That stench ...

George: I can't smell it. (*Grabbing the binoculars he looks for the dead seal corpse.*)

Almira: It's back again. That same smell.

George: Some fishguts. That's what it is ... (*He stops. Silence.*)

Almira: What's on the beach?

George: (*lowered the glasses. Relieved.*) Nothing.

(Almira *lies on the cot pulling the quilt up to her chin. She also wears her dark glasses. George steps outside. After a few breaths of air he re-enters.*)

SCENE FOUR

George: I spy! (*Removing* Almira's *glasses.*) I spy!

Almira: Oh George.

George: When was the last time? You can't remember.

Almira: Last summer ... in the park. Pip. Pip. Pip.

George: That's right! We were watching the snipes on Cavendish Beach. Inside or outside?

Almira: Outside.

George: I see a jay.

Almira: (*looking.*) Sorry.

George: I see a ... fish jump!

Almira: I see a fish jump. (*Her turn.*) I see a Javex bottle.

George: Go on. Where?

Almira: Not really.

George: This place is right for us! (*Pause.*) Why don't we stay!

Almira: What?

George: Let's move here.

Almira: For how long?

George: Forever!

Almira: Too long.

George: This is a great site you know. Gravity feed, wind power, tidal power, solar ...

Almira: Power!

(*The boom*)

George: Peace.

Almira: Our own CMHC-approved family bunker.

George: A bunker? Sure! Why not be prepared.

Almira: You're amazing.

George: I am?

Almira: George, this place barely has walls!

George: I could fix it up!

Almira: You and your tool bag. A hammer, a tape measure, and four nails.

George: So I'm not Mr Fix-it.

Almira: Always when something needs fixing you say you'll do it.

George: So.

Almira: Then you get out your tool bag.

George: So?

Almira: Then I fix it.

George: So what?

Almira: Why do we pretend that you do it?

George: Because it's no big deal.

Almira: It is a big deal!!! (*Silence.*) You're obsessed with survival.

George: I certainly don't want to die.

Almira: Don't you?

George: Look out the window. I see a gull.

Almira: I see a gull.

George: I'm happy we both see a gull. Now you.

Almira: (*explaining*) I also see a dragger. But it isn't just scraping the bottom of the ocean. It's inside me.

(*The boom.*)

George: There is life in everything outside that window only it's secret and quiet. On a day like today you can feel it. Walking, collecting stones, letting the old grey matter unravel. Nature is very subtle.

Almira: It's so darn fragile I have to hold my breath.

George: Actually it can't be that subtle. People haven't stopped having babies.

Almira: Maybe we should.

George: You want to have a baby!

Almira: I'm not sure.

George: We talked about it.

Almira: We had a fight.

George: It didn't seem natural.

Almira: That's what's wrong!

Sedna: Life didn't seem natural?

Almira: Life doesn't seem natural.

George: It didn't seem natural to plan it. It should just happen. You say ... "Guess what, George?"

Almira: I'm pregnant.

George: I'm pregnant. Right! Then I'd be a father.

Almira: You'd hand out cigars.

George: It wouldn't work.

Almira: I'd be a terrible mother.

George: Neither of us are really prepared for such a big change.

Almira: You have to get up early.

George: (*stunned*) Allie? You are pregnant.

Almira: Me. Us. Together?

George: I guess not. (*Pause.*) It's been a long time, hasn't it. If you felt ...

Almira: (*cutting him off.*) Nine months is a long time to be up. You know what I mean?

George: For you it certainly is.

Almira: I could say something.

George: Sorry. (*He picks up the binoculars.*)

Almira: Would my being a mother mean anything to you?

George: (*not looking at her*) You'd be a mother. Would my being a father mean anything to you?

Almira: You'd be a father. (*The boom. It continues to rumble in the distance.*) After the successful explosion of the first atomic bomb, the National Baby Association named Robert Oppenheimer its "Father of the Year."

Sedna: If he was the father and the bomb was his baby ... who was the mother?

Almira: Eve! She was the first.

George: Pardon.

Almira: Eve was pregnant.

George: Almira! She was not.

Almira: Eve ate from the tree of knowledge and put two and two together. She produced life!

Sedna: Eve rejoiced more for the coming of her child than all the trappings of Paradise!

George: She didn't.

Almira: (*grinding her hips*) A fusion ... a fusion ... But that wasn't enough. We took two-and-two apart.

(*The boom increases into a long slow explosion.*)

Almira: The knowledge of life required the knowledge of death. A fission. A fission. We all fall down. (*Leaping onto the fishcrate.*) Hallelujah! Death worshippers unite! (*The boom reverberates into a dark mushrooming cloud.*) A baby is born! Bearers of life know thy enemy.

George: I am not your enemy.

Almira: (*leaping onto the cot*) Every human being including myself is my enemy. (*Sedna sits up. In a very high sound she hums the tune of ring-a-ring-a-rosies.*) Ring a ring a neutron, a pocket full of positrons, Ashes, ashes, we all fall down. (*All sound stops.*) What are we doing holed up in this shack hanging off a cliff half into the sea? Tell me!!

Sedna: Waiting.

Almira: Waiting?

Sedna: It's very hard waiting for that moment when a baby is born.

Almira: I'm so tired. Honestly, I feel like God's grandmother.

(George *helps* Almira *to the cot.*)

George: Come and lie down.

Almira: There'll be no more babies. Woman won't be able to have them. We'll keep getting bigger and rounder only there's nothing inside. Nothing! Only some grey mushrooming gas that bloats us. But there can be no baby ...

Sedna: We'll see, Almira. I have other plans.

(George *wraps* Almira *in the quilt.*)

Almira: Oh George. Please, oh please ...

George: (*stroking her hair*) I would like to have a baby. My mother had 12 and after each one she said, "A baby brings love into the world."

Almira: Please don't touch me.

George: Let me kiss you.

Almira: I don't want you to.

George: (*teasing*) Then you kiss me.

Almira: No. It's sad without love.

George: You love me.

Almira: I don't love. I don't hate. Don't!

George: I can touch you, for cripes sake.

Almira: I just want to keep dissolving.

George: You can't. (*Softly touching her.*) You're in a body that's healthy, and round, and soft.

(Sedna *stealthfully slips from her tail.*)

Almira: I'm not soft.

George: Look at me, Almira.

Almira: Be aware of desire.

George: Look into my eyes.

Almira: You have black eyes.

George: (*slowly lowering* Almira *to the floor*) I love you.

Almira: Leaden lovers living love lower me to my grave.

George: (*on top of* Almira) A baby brings love into the world ... (*As* George *kisses* Almira *ever so slowly* Sedna *rises from behind the fish shack.*

Playfully she tosses a piece of musket shot ... A gentle sound of wind chimes is heard. It continues until Sedna stops it by placing the musket shot down near Almira.)

Almira: There it is again.

George: What?

Almira: The smell!

George: There is no smell.

Almira: Get ... it ... out ... of ... here!

George: There is nothing here.

Almira: (*beginning to gag*) Take it away ... take it away ...

Sedna: (*picking up the musket ball* Sedna *returns to the beach*) It stinks of fear.

(*The sounds of* George's *theme music. It is soothing and comforting for both* Almira *and* George. George *wipes* Alimira's *face. Places her on the cot. Slowly wipes clean the floor where* Almira *has vomited.*)

SCENE FIVE

(Almira *is asleep.* George *sits beside her. His arm around* Almira *echoes that of* Sedna *around her tail. Downstage right.*)

George: There aren't enough temptations in my life. You're the only one. I should leave. Right now.

Almira: (*opening her eyes sleepily*) ... George?

George: You were sick.

Almira: I don't remember.

George: I scratched your back. I stroked your hair. I held your hand. All the time you lay with your eyes closed so you couldn't see who it was ...

Almira: I knew.

George: Go back to sleep. Sleep Almira. I won't leave you. Who would hear your whimpers ... who would hold you in the dark? Me! And in the morning you will have forgotten.
What am I saying! (*Picking up the binoculars.*) People close their eyes when they're being sick. This place is getting to me! (*Watching.*) Nothing! Not even a buoy. Fog and water. Water and fog. Where the hell are all the gulls!? (*Grabbing his notebook and the sick towel he exits tossing the towel outside.*)

(Sedna *gives a gull-like movement ... screams of gulls ... circling ghostlike.* Sedna *slips into her tail.*)

SCENE SIX

(Almira *opens the crate and discovers the plunger and child's plastic pail, a tattered old man's sweater, and a pair of rubber boots. She decides to plunge for clams.*)

Sedna: (*A soft whistle.* Almira *stops. Another whistle.*)

Almira: Go away. (Sedna *moves closer to* Almira, *creeping out from her hiding place behind the sand dune.*)

Almira: I want to be alone. (*Another whistle. Turning.*) ... I mean it. (Sedna *slithers towards* Almira.) Trick or treat George. (Sedna *lifts her head and waves, echoing the old woman in scene 1.*)

Sedna: George?

Almira: George?

Sedna: What's a George?

Almira: My husband.

Sedna: Oh. Yes. Him.

Almira: You're not George. (*She returns to plunging with quiet determination.*) I've had too much fog!

Sedna: That's no way to forage for clams.

Almira: This is a very sensible way to pick clams.

Sedna: Tusks are far superior!

Almira: (*desperate*) It sucks the clams right out of the sand. (*Unfortunately it doesn't.*)

Sedna: Too much effort.

Almira: I couldn't find a shovel.

Sedna: Humans are peculiar.

Almira: Haven't you ever had a craving for clams?

Sedna: Often.

Almira: I'm hallucinating. Or dreaming. (*She inverts the plunger and sits.*) Allie. Get it together. You're talking to yourself!

Sedna: There's nothing wrong with dreaming.

Almira: Oh yeah. Since George dragged me down here I've been having some really peculiar dreams.

Sedna: You take yourself too seriously. What you need is to loosen up ... have a few laughs.

Almira: Ahah! Ahah!

Sedna: (*thinking* Almira *is barking at her. She barks back.*) Arhuh! Arhuh!

Almira: Almira!

Sedna: That is your name?

Almira: How do you know my name?

Sedna: (*playfully she gives a seal-like roll*) Ahruh! I know who you are.

Almira: You are not real. (Almira *takes out a bag of chips from her beach bag.*) My mind has collapsed.

Sedna: It happens to the best of us.

Almira: Only temporarily. (*Watching* Sedna.) You know my name ... what do I call you?

Sedna: Humans can't pronounce my real name. But you may call me Sedna.

Almira: So where do you live?

Sedna: In the mother of us all. She who embraces us, bathes us, and to whom we will return when our time is come. (Almira *doesn't understand.*) The sea!

Almira: (*laughing*) I'm talking to a mermaid.

Sedna: How predictable!

Almira: You don't really look like a mermaid.

Sedna: Oh? Go on ...

Almira: You're very heavy.

Sedna: (*advancing on* Almira) ... And you are so thin I could play chopsticks on your ribs! (Sedna *plays a macabre version of chopsticks on a piece of bleached bone.*) You know nothing about merpersons.

Almira: Oh for heaven's sake! A liberated hallucination.

Sedna: (*shivering with disgust*) Merpersons have fish heads and human legs. They also have a disgusting habit of trapping unsuspecting fishermen.

Almira: Then grant them three wishes ...

Sedna: Actually ... they eat them!

Almira: You're not going to eat me ... (Sedna *chases after* Almira.) Heeelllppp!!!

Sedna: Selkies find humans ... indigestible.

Almira: Selkies?

Sedna: I'm half seal and half ... human.

Almira: Are there more of you?

Sedna: We'll see. How did you like my present?

Almira: Sorry?

Sedna: I thought you might be curious as to where it came from. (Sedna *rolls the musket ball toward* Almira. *Wind chimes are heard.*) I brought you another.

Almira: This afternoon. You were in the fish shack?

Sedna: I am discreet.

Almira: I didn't see you.

Sedna: I left at the appropriate moment ... but ... you did see my little gift. Musket shot!

Almira: I don't want it!

Sedna: No! Humans don't like to be reminded of their responsibilities.

Almira: (*beginning to gag*) Take it away.

Sedna: You ask if there are more of me. You with your muskets, and knives and axes and clubs and harpoons! We have been wiped out forever. Too often we selkies have been mistaken for seals. Then you humans had the nerve to lament our loss from the world in poetry and songs of mermaids ... pushing those left into the mists of legend. (*Softly.*) "Death to our best friends."

Almira: My dream.

Sedna: My dream.

Almira: You?

Sedna: What do you recognize now, Almira?

Almira: You're in my dream?

Sedna: Night after night.

Almira: But it's daylight!

Sedna: I could make it night.

Almira: Leave me alone.

Sedna: When you decide to leave the Earth alone.

Almira: Stop tormenting me!

Sedna: (*blowing into the conch shell. Again the sound continues at her bidding, growing darker to accompany the nightmare.*) This could be my dream.

Almira: It isn't like this. My dream is always the same.

Sedna: What is your dream? (Sedna *summons the sounds of the sea.*)

Almira: I'm in the sea.

Sedna: I'm in the sea.

Almira: There are waves.

Sedna: Lots of blue waves.

Almira: I'm swimming on the beach, as far as the eye can see ...

Sedna: People are watching.

Almira: I can hardly see them.

Sedna: Black silhouettes shimmering in the glare of the ice.

Almira: They laugh and say I am beautiful.

Sedna: Swinging their arms up and down ...

Almira: They wave ... floating, my hair is like seaweed. Dead seaweed. Only dead seaweed is free. They wave again ...

Sedna: Thump!

(*The sound reverberates into the cries of seals baying. It is eerie and barely perceptible as a "real" sound.*)

Almira: Red! Blood! In my eyes. All around me ... thuck ... thuck ... thuck ...

Sedna: (*simultaneously*) Hold on ... hold on ...

Almira: Arms rising and falling. Cry out loud ...

Sedna: Father!!!

Almira: Not my baby!! Not while it still suckles. Scream.

Sedna: I'm going to die.

Almira: I'm alive. Underwater it is quiet. So quiet it hurts. Softly ... boomp ... boomp.

Sedna: (*overtop*) Wwwwwhhhhyyyy?

Almira: My heart mingles with the streaming blood and milk.

Sedna: I was your daughter, father.

Almira: I have to breathe.

Sedna: I'm too tired to breathe.

Almira: Maybe on the bottom I'll breathe ...

Sedna: Why did you throw me away? I loved you ...

Almira: Down ... down ... down ... down ...

(*Together they gasp for air.*)

Sedna: Wake up!

Almira: It's not my dream. I've been dreaming your dream. Why?

Sedna: Because you care.

Almira: A long time ago.

Sedna: Not so long ago.

Almira: Perhaps that was a dream too.

Sedna: Once you fought passionately for the great creatures of the sea.

Almira: I can do nothing ... I've tried.

Sedna: I know how you feel.

Almira: And just how do I feel?

Sedna: Trapped! By something you can't change.

Almira: I can.

Sedna: Will you?

Almira: Watch me.

Sedna: Almira, the mystery of your womb makes you more powerful than that!

Almira: There's no baby.

Sedna: You always feel that way with the first.

Almira: I'm tired.

Sedna: Me too.

Almira: Too tired to have a baby.

Sedna: I'm tired of my world being a place of depleted things made up of stories of what never was ...

Almira: Who are you?

Sedna: (*sound of the sea and* Sedna's *music*) When I was born, the sea held many marvellous creatures and nowhere was there a place more mysterious or a greater haven of life! And dotted throughout the seas were pools of shimmering sand, milky white crescents, where the creatures came for rest, and to feed upon sweet dewy grasses, and mate; listening to the heavy grey roll of the sea. So many worlds there were! For three million years I have travelled and I have slept in a hundred islands. Islands appearing and disappearing ... Now there is but one left. After that is gone there will be none.

Almira: I need some rest. That's why I'm here for some peace and rest.

Sedna: Come with me.

Almira: I can't.

Sedna: Fight with me! (*Pause.*) What has happened to you?

Almira: I'm an observer. I watch and wait.

(George *stands and circles the horizon with the glasses.*)

Sedna: You don't know what it is to watch the bitter barren days pass one after the other; day after day; watching and feeling the end close in, knowing I am the last!

Almira: Be quiet.

Sedna: You need me. I need you ... And the child.

Almira: (*Picking up the plunger*) There is no baby.

(*Distant sound of a heartbeat.*)

Sedna: Come with me, Allie ...

Almira: (*swinging the plunger*) Stay away.

Sedna: You are powerless to make me do anything.

Almira: I am human.

Sedna: You pathetic creature.

Almira: You're some hallucination. (*She clubs Sedna.*)

Sedna: You're hurting me.

Almira: Or some screw loose in my head.

Sedna: Don't!

Almira: (*tugging on* Sedna's *body*) Let's see who's in whose skin ...

(*The cries of baying seals join the heartbeat.*)

Almira: (*with one last yank she pulls off* Sedna's *head-dress.*) You're a woman.

Sedna: And sometimes a seal.

George: Almira! (*He is looking for her in the shack. Then calls outside.*) Aaaaallllllllliiiiiiieee!

Almira: There's George.

Sedna: (*Helpless without her skins* Sedna *can barely walk. Desperately she tries to retrieve her head-dress.*) Life is precious to me ... it once was to you.

George: Where are you?

Almira: On the beach.

George: Hurry! The sun is going down.

Almira: I should go to George.

Sedna: No ...

George: It's getting dark.

Almira: It's getting dark.

Sedna: You let your eyes be closed in darkness.

George: You won't be able to see.

Sedna: A darkness from which no light will be emitted ever!

Almira: George needs me.

Sedna: I need you.

Almira: He can't light a lamp.

George: Aaaallllliiieeeee!

(Almira *turns towards* George's *cry.* Sedna *lunges and retrieves her head-dress.*)

Sedna: Lice! Earth's cockroach! (*Within the sound are the cries of distant wailing voices.*) I am not an hallucination! I am a selkie!! (*Slowly she climbs up onto the upstage rock.*) You think you have power because you are human? You whose stay on this Earth has been so short! All you have done is increase the power of death! Can you understand the language of the birds and animals? NO! For it you did you would hear how their sweet cries mock you. You know nothing! Watch! What do you see? Now a porpoise, now a raven or dog, fish, or ... (Sedna *stands with arms outs-tretched. In one is an axe, in the other the headpiece.*) ... perhaps a rare Hood seal! While in the heavens the moon, stars, sun, hasten to my call. Clouds! Quickly now! (*The sky darkens with her call.*)

Sedna: (*descending from the rock, she puts on her head-dress*) I am not a bare-breasted manifestation of a sex-starved fisherman. Mermaids indeed!

Almira: Stay away.

Sedna: (*as Almira cowers she advances with the axe upraised*) Here comes your darkness to cower and hide in. Run to George. Run from the sick-ness of men. But you cannot run from me! Each creature that lives in this sea, each boat that travels her waves and the people on board, of them, I know when they will live and when they will die!! (*Blackout.*)

Almira: NNNOOOOOOO!!!!

George: Aallllmmmmiiirrraaa!

ACT TWO

SCENE SEVEN

(*On the beach. There is no sign of* Sedna *or her tail.*)

Almira: George?

George: Almira!

Almira: What are you doing here!

George: What are you doing here?

Almira: I'm confused.

George: You fell asleep. I decided to go for a walk.

Almira: That's right. I woke up. You were gone!

George: When I went back up you were gone.

Almira: I was hungry.

George: Didn't you hear me?

Almira: I heard you. "It's getting dark."

George: Dark? Blackout! Just like that! One big cloud drifted right over top of us. I couldn't see to put one foot in front of the other ... (*Pause.*) I looked everywhere for you!

Almira: And ...

George: Nothing.

Almira: Nothing?

George: I swear. Sixty seconds ago you weren't on this beach. We got to get away from here.

Almira: You go!

George: And leave you alone?

Almira: Just for a few days.

George: It's too isolated.

Almira: It's familiar.

George: You expect me to leave you alone here when you say ... it's familiar.

Almira: It's as if I had lived here before.

George: This place is weird. I've been taking notes. This place is empty!! No ducks, no squirrels, no shags, no gulls, no fish! Not even a clam to be found.

Almira: (*remembering*) Clams! I was on the beach.

George: You weren't.

Almira: I was plunging for clams. George is here. I'm here ...

George: Somewhat.

Almira: Where is she?

George: Stop it, Almira.

Almira: Oh boy. Get out your book and sharpen your pencils ...

George: You're frightening me!

Almira: I'm frightening me. (*Pause.*) That old fisherman. Blasted on Hermits? He was right.

George: Tell me exactly what you saw.

Almira: (*whispered*) A 3000 pound seal.

George: A Hood seal is only a half tonne.

Almira: I was talking to her. (*Shouting.*) Sedna!

(Sedna *pops up from behind the fish shack.*)

George: Sedna?

Almira: That's her name.

George: The seal has a name?

Almira: It's not her real name.

George: Of course not.

Almira: Where could she be hiding?

(Sedna *plays hide and seek with* Almira.)

George: A 3000 pound seal ...

Almira: Well, around that.

George: That narrows places down. (*Pause.*) In the sea.

Almira: Of course.

George: Come off it, Allie!

Almira: It was so obvious.

George: You don't seriously expect me to believe you were talking to a seal.

Almira: Actually Sedna is a selkie.

George: Almira! there is no such thing as a selkie. Dugongs! Fishermen thought dugongs and manatees were mermaids.

Almira: No they're not. They're half human and half seal.

George: (*moving into the shack*) We're getting out of here.

Almira: Sedna needs our help.

George: We need help!

Almira: That nightmare where I'm swimming away from the blood ... it's not my dream!

George: Whose is it?

Almira: Sedna's!

George: This is a nightmare.

Almira: (*grabbing* George's *pencil and notebook*) Endangered ... the selkie ... who is our ... our ... dream.

George: You're trying to save a hallucination.

(Sedna *begins to slowly circle the shack to the faint rhythm of a drumbeat.*)

Sedna: There was a time when the Earth's spirit was the spirit of everything that walked and crawled and swam on her surface.

Almira: Pardon?

George: I am talking to you.

Sedna: I am not a hallucination.

Almira: In a second.

Sedna: I am not a merperson.

George: It's too late.

Sedna: I am a selkie.

Almira: By donating your time and money, we can ensure that selkies continues to live on this planet. No postage required for federal politicians. (*She looks at* George, *triumphant.*)

George: We could have stayed here forever.

Almira: I'm serious, George.

George: So am I.

Almira: This is something I could fight for again.

George: Deadly serious.

Almira: Sign this letter with me.

George: No way will I sign that letter.

Almira: We promised to work together! Love each other!

George: I remember! But there is nothing to share in this fucking insanity! SAVE A SELKIE? There is something out there! And it stinks. It's a putrid, rotting ...

Almira: Stop!!

(*Sensing what is occurring* Sedna *slips from her tail and leaves it on the beach. On it she places the axe.*)

George: I know what's upsetting you.

Almira: All that is upsetting me is you.

George: I'm gone.

(Sedna *perches on the large outcropping of rock behind the shack.*)

Almira: (*crumpling the letter*) Somebody help me.

SCENE EIGHT

(*George does not hear* Sedna *until the last exchange.*)

George: (*throwing stones*) Damn. Goddamn. Talking to a selkie. (*Shouting up to the shack.*) You want me to leave?

Sedna: Definitely.

George: I won't leave.

Sedna: Well, I won't leave.

George: I'm pathetic.

Sedna: Poor pathetic creature.

George: I can't leave (*Noticing the seal corpse.*) What the fuck is going on?

Sedna: Trick or treat!

George: (*gagging as he goes nearer*) I got rid of you!

Sedna: Are all humans cowards?

George: It's this place. This beautiful ... empty place. Nothing here ... except a stinking rotten corpse.

Sedna: Flattery will get you everywhere.

George: (*picking up the axe ... dreamlike*) I'll get rid of you.

Sedna: I'm not going anywhere!!

George: Then everything will be all right.

Sedna: I want to keep things as they are for awhile.

George: I'll cut it into pieces.

Sedna: Don't touch me.

George: If the tide brings it back again no one will recognize it ... Cut it up!

Sedna: Don't you dare touch me.

George: I'll fix it, Almira. There'll be no more seals.

Sedna: The mighty protector of his family.

George: (*kicking the corpse*) Go away!

Sedna: (*whispered*) Father ...

George: Close your eyes. (*Paralysed.*) Do it!

Sedna: (*coming down behind George*) May the dogs eat your hands and feet.

George: (*closing his eyes*) I love ... (*On the first blow* Sedna *cries out in anguish. She is joined by the baying seals. On each cry Almira tosses in a nightmare.*)

Sedna: No!

George: Love!

Sedna: No!

George: Love!

Sedna: No!

George: Love!

Sedna: No!

George: Love you ... (*Silence.*) Oh sweet mother of God ... what have I done?

Sedna: I loved you, Father. Long ago ... (George *crouches rocking. His head between his knees.* Sedna *cradles her seal tail.*)

Sedna: You cursed me. Half human, half seal. Each part of me hating the other. You owe me ...

George: It should be simple. You and me.

Sedna: You owe me a child.

George: A child ... Almira? A child. (*The boom.* George *hears it.* Sedna *lifts her face to* George.)

George: (*recognizing the face of the old woman*) You?

Sedna: I shall get it?

(*The boom.*)

George: Nooooooo!!!

SCENE NINE

(*Sounds of* Sedna's *music. Gently* Sedna *places her tail into the sea.*)

Sedna: The soul shall burst her fetters
    At last and shall be free.
    As the sun, as the wind, as the night,
    As the stars, as the sea.

(*A faint heartbeat.* Almira *steps from the fish shack walking slowly towards the sea ... *)

Almira: I used to run. As I ran all I could hear was my own heartbeat ... boomp, boomp, boomp, thudding over and over. Maybe it'll stop right now.

Sedna: Close your eyes. Open your ears. Listen. Just wave after wave, swelling, shattering, returning to the sea once again. Soothing isn't it?

Almira: I don't want to hope. But I do. I don't want to love. But I do ...

Sedna: The soul shall be crowned and calm ...

Almira: I don't want to be afraid.

Sedna: ... eyes fearless and she ...

Almira: But I am. Any minute now there'll be nothing but dead silence. No petitions! No seals! No beaches! No George! No baby! No me!

Sedna: No anger. No loneliness. No fear. Only the wind and the waves and the sounds of the sea forever.

Almira: (*stepping into the water*) Forever is too long.

Sedna: Don't do it, Almira!

Almira: What am I doing?

Sedna: I'm not a fool.

Almira: George thinks I'm crazy.

Sedna: Then trust me.

Almira: Trust you?

Sedna: I trust you.

Almira: (*stepping out further*) The whole world is dying ... (*With a gesture* Sedna *stops her. With another the sound of* Almira's *frightened heartbeat fades and* Sedna's *music becomes stronger. With a final gesture the lights shift to deep pinks letting us sink just below the surface of the sea as the floating island is revealed. The floating island is* Sedna's *home and a place for nurturing and magic. It could also be a ghost of all the great breeding grounds that were once dotted throughout the Atlantic.*

Sedna *draws a silk kimono from the sand dune. It is a precious and sensual detail from her past, giving the impression of a wedding dress that has never left its trousseau. When the kimono is unravelled, dried rose petals drop from it. Its movement is evocative of the sea.* Sedna *wraps* Almira *in the kimono.*)

Sedna: The soul shall burst her fetters
At last and shall be free
As the stars, as the wind, as the night.
As the sun, as the sea.

(Sedna *sets a garland of seaflowers on* Almira's *head.*)

The soul shall struggle and stand
In the end swift and free
As the stars, as the wind, as the night.
As the sun, as the sea.

(*They dance a courtly dance.*)

> The soul shall be crowned and calm
> Eyes fearless and she
> Shall be queen of the wind and the night
> Stars, sun, and sea.

(*From amongst her skins* Sedna *takes out a small mirror. Chimes are heard. They continue softly, sporadically throughout the scene.*)

Sedna: Look into the mirror.

Almira: No!

Sedna: Just a quick glance.

Almira: NO ...

Sedna: There's nothing to be afraid of.

Almira: There's the dark ... ghosts ... senility ... losing someone ...

Sedna: (*persisting*) Look into the mirror, Allie.

Almira: (*transfixed*) Friends. (*Looking away.*) I'm afraid of making friends.

Sedna: That's just a little one. (*Again she places the mirror in front of* Almira.)

Almira: I'm afraid of dreaming. I'm afraid of tomorrow and tomorrow and tomorrow. I'm losing my mind! (Sedna *forces* Almira *to look in the mirror.*) I don't want to be alone.

Sedna: Excellent. That's that then! Let's eat. (*Pausing.*) I forgot. Kneel on the cushion.

Almira: (*dismayed*) I don't see any cushion.

Sedna: I'm getting too old for this. (*From the dune she pulls a pink brocade shell-shaped cushion.*) Kneel! Almira Murdoch, I christen thee Pearl.

Almira: What's wrong with Almira?

Sedna: Don't interrupt.

Almira: I like my name.

Sedna: Here you take a new name. It's part of the ritual. Like the mirror.

Almira: Why?

Sedna: Who remembers after three million years? Now you've made me lose track ...

Almira: And where are we?

Sedna: (*getting out a silver tea tray. On it are teacups, a pot, sugar, milk, honey cakes, and asparagus tips.*) A floating island. Somewhere between the sea and the shore.

Almira: In Japan they have whole districts devoted to beauty and pleasure. They are called floating islands as well. (*Pause.*) It's a glorified red light district really.

(*The boom.*)

Sedna: (*Diving behind the dune she rolls infantry style and returns to* Almira *with two World War II combat helmets.*) You better keep these handy. (*The boom.*) During the time when man fought man it wasn't so bad for us selkies. You left us to bear and rear our pups in peace. (*The boom. Then the sounds of whales singing.*)

Sedna: Oh, that's just the whales. They get melancholy and start remembering. (*Both women listen to the sounds of the great creatures' songs.*)

Almira: What do they remember that's so beautiful?

Sedna: In the war ... the one you call the second ... their songs were mistaken for the sound of submarine sonar ... (*The boom.*)

Sedna: Pow! No more whales. (*Silence.*) But they still sing. And like myself they still return for whelping.

Almira: Whelping?

Sedna: It's February.

Almira: February.

Sedna: Why else would we be here?

Almira: Something happens in February.

Sedna: This is the time when we selkies take our positions for lying in.

Almira: There are no other selkies here.

Sedna: It wasn't always like this. It's an old habit. (*Looking around the island she notices how empty it is.*) Without much meaning I suppose ... seeing there's only one island and myself and the ghosts ... (*Pause.*) And you!

Almira: Don't look at me! I can't help you.

Sedna: Milk? Sugar?

Almira: Milk. (*Noticing that the tea is blue.*) No. Yes. Sugar.

Sedna: This is a party!

Almira: A wake.

Sedna: New life is a wonder. And should be celebrated. A baby brings love into the world.

Almira: Oh no.

Sedna: After all it's February. Selkies love to party.

Almira: I don't believe it.

Sedna: What? What? What?

Almira: This is a baby shower!

Sedna: Go on. A baby shower?

Almira: Yes, a baby shower.

Sedna: What a wonderful idea. A fallout of babies!

Almira: No, a baby shower.

Sedna: What is this wonderful thing I've never heard of before?

Almira: A bunch of women get together and by devious means trap an un-suspecting woman ...

Sedna: (*fearful*) ... Go on ...

Almira: They make you open presents.

Sedna: Presents? (*Laughing.*) Tell me more.

Almira: As you open each gift you have to stick the bows on your head. Good friends only put one bow on their present. After that ...

Sedna: There's more?

Almira: ... Everyone takes off her wedding ring. Puts it on a thread and holds the ring over their bellys. Back and forth means a boy ... a circle a girl.

(*As she speaks* Sedna *circles* Almira's *belly with her finger.*)

Almira: (*abrupt*) Then they drink lots and lots of tea!

Sedna: Remarkable.

Almira: I'm not finished. Have you ever tried to see how many clothes-pins you can hold in one hand while flipping wet clothes onto your shoul-der with your feet?

Sedna: Couldn't you just pick them up?

Almira: Not with another baby on your hip! (*Pause.*) Sixteen is the highest I've ever seen. Then you play Bingo. (Sedna *shouts "Bingo" as if she has played.*)

Almira: Most likely, though, you'll drink more tea and eat some lighthouses.

Sedna: That's what's happened to all the lighthouses!

Almira: You don't know what a lighthouse is? Lighthouses are a dessert made with a Ritz cracker, a layer of jam, a marshmallow, and a cherry on top. And that is a baby shower!

Sedna: I am amazed.

Almira: Wait till George hears this.

Sedna: So we keep the same rituals still.

Almira: (*realizing her predicament*) What if I never see George again?

Sedna: (*offering the honey cakes*) Try one of these little cakes.

Almira: No thanks.

Sedna: Honey cakes are always eaten at whelping.

Almira: No poison?

Sedna: (*eating one*) Delicious. (Almira *takes one and nibbles.*) Women of the sea believe that this is a time for rejoicing.

Almira: And sorrow.

Sedna: That too.

Almira: For what?

Sedna: For the great mystery that is ours. (*Pause.*) You like them?

Almira: They stay down!

Sedna: More tea?

Almira: A woman has to be careful about food. (*Pause.*) Myself sometimes I'll be cooking up a pan of mushrooms and this thought will just jump into my head. I think, someone has just rounded up the dearest, sweetest, little cock tips, and here they are sautéeing in my pan of butter. Puts me right off.

Sedna: (*fanning herself*) Warm isn't it?

Almira: George doesn't understand. I know it's crazy. But you watch for it. I haven't touched a mushroom since. ... It shouldn't run your life. But it does. Food, I mean.

Sedna: At whelping parties it's important to eat foods that represent the forces that fertilize. (Almira, *giggling, waves a piece of asparagus.*)

Sedna: A reminder of our humble beginnings.

Almira: Lust! (Almira *chomps the asparagus.*) George's smell use to drive me crazy. I loved it. Heavy with oils. As if I were in a foreign market filled with unknown and forbidden scents. One whiff and my stomach would flip. What a wonderful sensation ... desire. Beware of desire and the lunacy of love. Look where it got me.

Sedna: I envy you.

Almira: Don't be foolish.

Sedna: Oh Almira, most of the real pleasure in the world for men and women is still provided by children.

Almira: (*sighing*) And the burden.

Sedna: The work's in raising the husband, not the children.

Almira: I've been through the 60s. George and I are equal. Just because he's useless with cars, and doesn't know the first thing about nailing two planks together. Why should he? I mean ... I know he's helpless if he cuts his finger, or gets a cold. But that doesn't make him a dependent! For heaven's sake ... I'm a feminist!

Sedna: I had dozens of litters. If I hadn't passed the age for bearing ... Who knows?

Almira: You are crazy!

Sedna: Wanting more?

Almira: Wanting more.

Sedna: (*lying on her back she scratches seal-like*) Young pups are delicious! The bring a lot more pleasure than mates. (Sedna *brings out of the folds of her clothes a wineskin.*)

Almira: I like George.

Sedna: (*drinking*) Then you are twice fortunate.

Almira: I don't understand him, that's all. (*Pause.*) Do selkies marry?

Sedna: We're here to talk about you.

Almira: I only wondered.

Sedna: I am half human. Wine?

Almira: I thought maybe you didn't do that sort of thing.

(*Silence.*)

Sedna: It was a long time ago.

Almira: Ahuh!

Sedna: Ahruh!

Almira: I thought so.

Sedna: I was human. All I could do was marry.

Almira: What happened?

(*Softly* Sedna*'s music enters into the background.*)

Sedna: I refused every male that appeared at my doorstep.

Almira: But not everyone.

Sedna: No. (*Smiling.*) One day a most beautiful man came to my father's doorstep. Such eyes he had. Black as night. He told me he would cherish and honour me with a home and warmth and food. He also promised me a room of my own. So I married.

Almira: And lived happily ever after.

Sedna: I murdered him.

Almira: George doesn't know how lucky he is.

Sedna: He lied!

Almira: "'Till death do you part."

Sedna: You should have seen that place! It was worse than a nest; full of feathers and mouse-droppings. Talk about crumbs in the bed!

Sedna: (*Behind* Sedna *the music builds. Layering the many voices of the sea.*) Before the sun had set, my father had heard of the murder and came to take me back to his house. Suddenly, while crossing the water, the sea became fantastic. The wind rose, the waves grew monstrous. My father, thinking that God was angry at my actions, offered me as a sacrifice and tossed me overboard into the sea. (*Shouting.*) Coward! What a coward you were, father!

Almira: He left you to drown?

Sedna: I clung to the gunnels. Taking out a small hunting axe my father hacked at my hands.

Almira: (*taking* Sedna*'s hand in hers*) Oh Sedna ...

Sedna: The first blow tore off the first joints of my fingers. As they dropped into the sea from each was born a dolphin. Do you believe me?

Almira: Of course.

Sedna: On the next were born the seals and the walrus. On the third and final blow I dropped to the ocean floor. Then from all around me, from my flesh and blood, were born the whales. They swam beneath my father's small dory till the sea boiled. ...

Almira: He drowned?

Sedna: I think it's time for more wine.

Almira: I'm sorry.

Sedna: (*bitterly*) I rid myself of a husband who would have all my power drained in preparing his nest, his food, his clothes, and a father who bartered with my life. They prepared the scene for their own finish. (*Pause.*) As we all do.

Almira: So, peace and quiet!

Sedna: What do you think it's like being the very last selkie in the world?

Almira: No past ... no present ... no future. Heaven!

Sedna: Heaven is overrated. My whole race lost forever.

Almira: I wish mine was.

Sedna: You sound very certain. No one to remember you, no future generation to mourn you, no one to miss you. All the good that you have said and done lost forever.

Almira: And the evil. We are a deformed and demented race.

Sedna: Fool!

Almira: (*softly*) You're the murderer.

(*A long silence.*)

Sedna: All right! (*She knocks the garland from* Almira.) I will show you what it is to have all that love would create destroyed in one stupid act.

(*The lights shift as* Sedna *begins to weave her spell.* George *dresses in a wool jacket and watch cap. In one hand is a harpoon, in the other is a small axe.* [*The same one as* Sedna*'s in scene 6.*])

Sedna: Long ago,
The Earth's Spirit was everything
That walked, swam, crawled
On her surface.
That bond is broken.
And once ...

(*Having slipped off the kimono* Sedna *crawls onto* Almira*'s back as she lowers her to the floor. They become one.*)

Sedna: Fishermen and the creatures of the sea

Believed
That the Spirit of Man
And the Spirit of Animal was one.
That bond is more than broken,
It is forgotten.
Why?

(*They both adopt the movements of a seal.*)

Sedna: On the beach, lying and bathing, as far as the eye can see, are the great seal.

George: (*stealthfully he creeps around them*) Look at those mothers.

Sedna: Beautiful mothers.

(Almira *mimes swinging her tusks.*)

George: Careful of the tusks.

Sedna: If we see any man on the shore and catch him ...

George: Careful. (*Nudging with the harpoon*) Careful. You're not going to get this man, big one.

Sedna: We could rend him with our sharp-biting teeth ...

George: Yoh girl. Soft big one.

Sedna: But we use them only to climb ladderlike to the very top of the beach rock. Where tired ...

George: (*caressing the beast*) SSSSHHH! Sleep now. That's right, you sleep.

Sedna: We fall fast asleep.

George: Make haste! Part the hide from the fat ... (*Slicing and pulling the rope through* Sedna. *He wraps the rope around her shoulders. It is attached to the harpoon.*)

George: Into the skin goes strong cord. Tie it to the tree over there.

Sedna: Black silhouettes shimmer in the glare of the ice.

George: This one is near unto 3000 pound.

Sedna: They saw we are beautiful.

George: (*laughing*) Never leave nothing to the devil.

Sedna: Arms rising and falling ...

(*George pulls the rope taut.*)

George: Throw the stone. Now. At the head. The head!!

Sedna: Angry we descend after the attacker ... stripping ... off ... the thick ... skin!!

(Almira*'s body goes rigid as* George *strips away* Sedna*'s skin*)

Almira: AAaaaaaagggggghhhhh!!

Sedna: One slice ...

(*Kicking Almira* over, George *mimes slicing her from belly to chin.*)

Sedna: The seal opens. Her heart quivering and steaming in the cold ... (George *lifts up the axe.*) ... Exhausted, fearful and half-dead the great seal is made rich prey.

(Almira *and* George *stare into each others' eyes as he stands over her. The sounds of the seal baying and the heartbeat and the sea voices all mingle.*)

Almira: George ...

Sedna: My dream is the nightmare you humans have spewed on this earth.

Almira: George, don't!

(*With one swift stroke* Sedna *motions* George *to finish the kill.*

Blackout.

The sounds of the sea rise in a great cacophony of cries and seal baying.)

Almira: NNNNOOOOOOOOOO!!!

(*The cries soften to the ripples of water on sand ... Then silence.*)

SCENE TEN

(*The lights come up very slowly. Very gently.* Almira *and* Sedna *sit on the beach. They are still listening.*)

Sedna: Are you all right?

Almira: No. (*Pause.*) That was quite a show. All for me?

Sedna: Yes.

Almira: Thanks.

Sedna: It was like this after the rains! Only I couldn't stop crying long enough to listen to the silence.

Almira: The rains?

Sedna: Then right away we were called to the nesting grounds. And I went.

Almira: Why?

Sedna: There'd be no more selkies! You have go to on.

Almira: Where'd you find the energy?

Sedna: Where I found the love. Way down inside.

Almira: I would've stayed behind.

Sedna: You and the unicorns.

Almira: And kept right on playing.

Sedna: You don't want to be a legend. I could have shown you the beautiful part of the story too.

Almira: What? Like the waves and 'sweet dewy grasses' and snipes. Pip, pip, pip. You should talk to George.

Sedna: George doesn't need talking to.

Almira: I don't understand why you did that!

Sedna: Don't you?

Almira: I know all about the cruelties you suffer.

Sedna: You write papers.

Almira: It's been my life's work.

Sedna: But you quit.

Almira: I'm tired.

Sedna: Try living three million years. So you quit your job. George isn't what you thought he should be. So you quit him. And now you want to quit on life. Go on then. Ignore what little power you have been given. The power to create life.

Almira: Women have been having babies since forever. We haven't changed one single event because of the birth of our children. All we've done is provide ammunition and victims!

Sedna: What will you change by destroying yourself?

Almira: How dare you talk of life! You murdered! You killed your husband!

Sedna: That's right! You are finally getting it! I killed. I am guilty of becoming what I feared and hated. I tipped the balance of my world into despair.

Almira: If I can't have control over the life I bear then I will take it away any way I can.

(*Pause.*)

Sedna: What would bring you peace?

Almira: I'd like ... I'd like to go out there ... I don't know ... just drift! For a long time ...

Sedna: I can do that for you ... Go on. (*She pushes* Almira *towards the sea. Sounds of the seal music.*) Drift. Dissolve. Disappear. Your body is light as water melting into the sea. Your hair is free. Petitions, numbers, slaughters, seals drain from your mind. Friends, hopes, fears pass from you! No more love! No mate! No baby! You're adrift. Floating. At peace. All colour fades away. No red, no yellow, no green. Or orange, no purple, no blue. The sea whitens and cracks. Laughter shrivels. Words dim. Sound dies.

Sedna: The whole world is arid. With one gust it will vanish. (*The music has become thin and empty.*) It never was, and never will be ... It is gone!

(*Silence.*)

Almira: You can't do that.

Sedna: I did.

Almira: (*placing her hands on her womb*) No you didn't.

Sedna: Yes I did.

Almira: I found something you can't do.

Sedna: I wasn't really trying.

Almira: You can't take my baby.

Sedna: (*smiling*) Why not?

Almira: Because this is mine. (*Pause.*) And because I don't want you to.

Sedna: (*teasing*) You'd be a terrible mother.

Almira: You'll have to help me. After what you just did to me. You owe me. Help me.

Sedna: I'll give her webbed feet!

Almira: All the kids will laugh at her at school!

Sedna: (*barking*) Ahruh! Ahruh!

Almira: (*clapping and barking*) We're mad, mad, mad. Mad!!

Sedna: What'll you tell George?

Almira: Oh ...

Sedna: I'll tell him.

Almira: He'll die.

Sedna: Oh Almira, the sea will give you strength to bear the child. And when the child is born I could raise her with the wild creatures of the sea. She'd accept being a selkie and soon mate. The cycle would begin again!

Almira: Oh God ...

Sedna: Daylight under the sea is beautiful but the nights are magnificent ... (*Realizing what* Almira *just said.*)

Almira: You're serious. Sedna ... I'm so sorry. I can't help you.

Sedna: (*packing her possessions into the sand dune*) I can't think why I wanted to be a mother again.

Almira: You can't leave me! I need your experience.

Sedna: It would seem that I've had enough.

Almira: I need your courage. (*Putting her arms around* Sedna.) ... I would like you to be the child's Godmother.

Sedna: No you don't.

Almira: I do. We could share my child.

Sedna: You and me.

Almira: And George.

Sedna: George isn't so bad.

Almira: Agreed?

Sedna: Agreed! (*They hug each other.*) I'm through with whelping parties.

Almira: I've just begun ...

(*In the shack,* George *finds the crumpled letter as the loons cry.*)

Almira: Loons in love.

Sedna: (*teasing*) Be aware of desire and the lunacy of love.

Almira: Is it true they bond for life?

Sedna: Never leave each other's side!

Almira: Their cries are so lonely.

Sedna: Maybe they recognize something we don't

Almira: What's that?

Sedna: Union is a gift. (*Pause. Starting to move away.*) We are always alone.

Almira: I could stay.

Sedna: Those are roles to which we are not suited.

George: Almiraaaaa!

(*The sound of gulls, wind ... Reality.*)

Almira: That's George! You go tell him, I'll wait here. No ... I want to do it.

Sedna: I could trade places with you ...

(Almira *stops*.)

Sedna: (*shaking her head*) Three million years of pups is enough.

Almira: I don't know how to find you!

Sedna: Floating islands, like sensations; a caress, a sigh, desire ... they are all affected by fear. When we're afraid we simply stop perceiving them.

Almira: I'm not afraid.

Sedna: You'll find me.

Almira: What's next?

Sedna: In the time that I have left ... Maybe I'll travel with the loons. Perhaps they'll help me find forgiveness before my father and I meet again ... Now go on! I almost forgot! (*From around her neck she takes a small skin bag tied with a red ribbon.*) That's for the baby. Just one bow. Open it!

Almira: A pearl! To you, Sedna. A toast. Death to our best friend.

George: Alliee!!

Sedna: You better go now ...

Almira: You go first.

Sedna: Close your eyes and count to three.

(*Chimes.*)

Sedna: (*spinning* Almira) In waking and sleeping dreams, in joy, in love, a seed is planted. Dream us a new dream, Almira. (*Blackout.*)

The soul shall struggle and stand,
In the end swift and free
As the stars, as the wind, as the night.
As the sun, as the sea.

SCENE ELEVEN

(Sedna *and her seal tail are both gone.* Almira *is still in the kimono and spinning.*)

George: Almira!

(*Silence.*)

Almira: (*stopping*) You didn't go home.

George: Someone's got to take care of you.

Almira: I'm glad you stayed.

George: (*noticing the kimono*) Where'd you get this?

Almira: It's a gift from the floating island.

George: You going to take me there?

Almira: You were there.

George: I was?

Almira: Maybe you don't remember.

George: Don't do this, Almira.

Almira: (*pause*) I almost stayed.

George: You're here.

Almira: I kept remembering your smell ... (*She puts her arms around him.*) I couldn't resist ... (*She kisses George.*)

George: Your nose will be the life and death of us.

(*Loon calls.*)

Almira: Loons mate for life.

George: Good for the loons.

Almira: For better or for worse.

George: In lunacy or love.

Almira: I'm not crazy.

George: I know that!

Almira: Neither are you.

George: No? (*Taking from his shirt the crumpled Save-the-Selkie letter.*) I found this. (*Pause.*) There are societies for the preservation of everything on this planet except for selkies and ... ourselves. (*He signs the letter.*) George Murdoch!

George: No, I don't feel crazy when I'm alone.

Almira: Neither do I.

George: Then we're only crazy together. That's all right then!

Almira: Just a pair of loonies. (*Silence.*) George ... we are going to have a baby.

George: A baby? When?

Almira: Four more months.

George: You're five months pregnant and no one knew.

Almira: Four days ago, the doctor, she knew.

George: I couldn't tell.

Almira: Nature is very subtle ... I'm sorry. I should have told you.

George: (*grabbing her*) That's what all this vomiting, and junk food and smells are all about!

Almira: Maybe.

(*The sound of the sea music enters softly. Almira begins to spin.*)

George: A baby! That's wonderful!

(*The kimono fans out, rippling in higher and wider arcs.*)

Almira: Names ... babies need to have names. Dylan for the sea. But it won't be a boy. Morgan or Merriweather. No ... Pearl! Pearl for a girl.

George: A girl? You don't know that.

Almira: Sedna does.

(*Silence.*)

George: Almira ... For an instant ... I might have seen her only ... (*Realizing*) ... the child. She wants our baby!

Almira: She doesn't any more.

George: Almira ...

Almira: She's a friend. (*Pause.*) Hold me, George. (*The music takes on the rhythm of a waltz.*) We have never waltzed.

George: Sure we have.

Almira: We sway together.

George: That isn't dancing?

Almira: Ballroom dancing with hundreds, thousands, millions of other dancers bobbing in those crazy hoops ... 20 feet around.

George: (*twirling Almira around him*) Fifty.

Almira: A hundred.

George: A thousand!

Almira: A million!!

George: We'd all collide. (*They bow.*) Shall we?

Almira: (*dancing*) Look up! What do you see?

George: Clouds.

Almira: Inside!

George: Chandeliers.

Almira: What do you hear?

George: Music.

Almira: The whole room is swaying ...

(*The music swells.*)

George: The chandelier is swaying.

Almira: We can't collide. Keep looking up. And on my breasts is a great big red bow!! (Almira *stops. The music disintegrates.*) Smell ...

George: (*lightly*) I'm not pregnant.

Almira: This is wrong! I smell that stink again. ...

George: Fishguts. ...

Almira: It shouldn't be here.

George: Let's just think about the baby.

(*Silence.*)

Almira: You know what it is.

(*Silence.*)

George: When I saw it through the glasses I knew it was the Hood. A fisherman must have caught it in his nets. I went down to the beach. The entire head was sliced right off! She must have been a beauty but now the hide was burned crisp from the salt and the sun. It was swollen with gas and the stink ... It has been rotting for weeks.

Almira: You should have told me.

George: The smell was upsetting you! I knew it was causing those dreams. I tried to tow it away. Only the tide kept bringing it back! Every time I went down onto the beach there it was!

Almira: (*barely audible*) What did you do?

George: I cut it up. I cut it up into little tiny pieces so that if it came back on the tide again no one would recognize it and the gulls would eat it ... Only there weren't any gulls. I wanted to fix it for you so I cut it up.

Almira: It was Sedna!

George: That's when I saw her ...

Almira: Nnnnoooooooo!!! (Almira's *cry reverberates into silence.*)

George: I wanted to fix it for you ...

Almira: (*very still*) Sssshhh ... (Almira *puts* George's *hand on her womb.*) Feel ...

George: What's wrong?

Almira: The baby. She moved.

George: Where?

Almira: Way down inside ... soft as a sigh. There's nothing to be afraid of. Close your eyes. (*They listen.* Almira *lifts her arm.*) It's still there. The wind, and the waves, and the sounds of the sea.

Almira: (*waves*) Forever ... George?

George: Almira ... I love you.

Almira: I love you. (*They freeze.*)

(*The sound of the sea music.*)

Blackout

THE END

Being at Home with Claude

René-Daniel Dubois
Translation by Linda Gaboriau

Born in Montreal in 1953, René-Daniel Dubois is an actor, director, and playwright. After graduating from École Nationale de Théâtre du Canada in 1976, he studied at the Institut Alain Knapp in Paris. He is the author of seventeen stage plays, including *Ne Blâmez Jamais les Bédouins* (which he originally produced himself in a solo performance, and which has since been translated and published in English as *Don't Blame the Bedouins*), *Being at Home with Claude*, and *"Pericles, Prince of Tyre" by William Shakespeare*, all of which have been successfully produced in English-speaking Canada as well as in Quebec. *Being at Home with Claude* has also been

PHOTO CREDITS: (LEFT) MONIC RICHARD, (RIGHT) GUY BORREMANS

produced in Amsterdam and London. Dubois was named "Grand Montréalais dans le domaine du théâtre" in 1983.

Born in Boston, Linda Gaboriau moved to Montreal in 1963. After completing BA and MA degrees in French Language and Literature at McGill University, she decided to make Montreal her home. As a freelance broadcaster and journalist, she has hosted and produced radio shows for the CBC and Radio Canada networks, was theatre critic for the Montreal *Gazette*, and has contributed to various publications in Canada and the United States. She has been particularly active in Canadian and Quebec theatre. In addition to numerous contracts as a consultant for theatre companies and festivals, for both federal and provincial arts agencies, she has worked as a dramaturge and translator. For several years she was responsible for dramaturgical workshops as well as translation and exchange projects at Montreal's Centre d'essai des auteurs dramatiques. She now devotes most of her time to translation, and has translated more than twenty plays.

Being at Home with Claude was first produced by the Théâtre de quat'sous in Montreal on 13 November 1985.

PRODUCTION
Director / **Daniel Roussel**
Set Design / **Michel Crête**
Lighting / **Claude Accolas**

CAST
Lothaire Bluteau / Him (Yves)
Guy Thauvette / The Inspector (Robert)
Robert Lalonde / The Stenographer (Guy)
André Therien / The Police Officer (Latreille)

CHARACTERS

Him (Yves), early 20s. Slim. Nervous
The Inspector (Robert), late 30s
The Stenographer (Guy), the Inspector's assistant. Late 30s, same as his boss. A chain-smoker
The Police Officer (Latreille), employed as a security guard at the Courthouse. Has no idea what's going on in Judge Delorme's office and couldn't care less

SET

Judge Delorme's office in the Courthouse. A massive oak desk with one of the chairs which usually face the desk placed behind it. The judge's swivel armchair has been pushed to the side. On the desk: blotter, pen set, inkwell, perpetual calendar, ashtray, picture frame, desk lamp, paperweight, books, etc. For the time being, all these props have been pushed to one end of the desk, leaving the top free for the entire interrogation. The second of the two visitors' chairs is taken by Him.

In the middle of the wall stage left: the "side" door, leading to inner chambers, in stained wood.

In the middle of the upstage wall: the "main" door, the official entrance, imposing, upholstered. Him has the keys to this door in his pocket.

A very large map of the Island of Montreal, in colour.

A transom of frosted glass over the door.

A cardtable and a folding chair have been set up near the main door for the Stenographer. On the table: unused rolls of transcription paper and the rolls bearing the transcription of the interrogation; a large ashtray overflowing with cigarette butts; a stenotype machine.

The overall impression should be one of an office which has been set up for such a long time that its usual occupant obviously considers it his "living-room" and it has temporarily become the scene of a barbaric invasion.

Lighting: harsh and naturalistic.

PLAYWRIGHT'S NOTES

1   One of the dangers inherent in this text is the temptation one might feel (and to which one might succumb) to portray Him and the Inspector as merely wanting to give each other "a hard time." In fact, they are simply hoping for a chance, in the case of the former: to sleep a little, while waiting for the judge who, he thinks, at least in the beginning, can help him; and in the case of the latter, to understand what it's all about and how he ended up in this delicate situation where he risks finding himself in big trouble.

2   All of the characters, except for the Police Officer, Latreille, who has just begun his day and who is employed as a security guard at the Courthouse and is not part of the Montreal Police, are exhausted. Nevertheless, the pace is fast. It would be helpful to imagine that this play is the last act of a drama which has been going on for the past 36 hours and of which we will be witness only to the last hour (and a bit). This last hour is however totally autonomous and reaches its own peak which also happens to be the peak of the drama of which it is the final scene. The actors are not, therefore, beginning at "Square One," but rather at "Square 80."

At the moment where the play begins, at 10:30 in the morning on 5 July 1967, the interrogation has been going on since 1:00 o'clock in the morning of 4 July, without interruption. One has the feeling that Him and the police officers are getting nowhere; in Him's case, because he has no intention of telling them any more than what he has already told them a hundred times; and in their case, because they know who, when, and where, but the "why" is missing and there's no one there to help them dig themselves out of this explosive situation.

3   An hour after the beginning of the performance (at precisely 11:30 fictional time), there are three knocks at the main door. The judge has arrived. *No matter at what point this happens, the effect is the same:* the Inspector motions to the Stenographer to go out and ask the judge to wait a few more minutes. Immediately at the sound of the first knock: total silence on stage. The silence of citizens who have been tracked down. The Stenographer exits. Returns. As soon as the Stenographer has gone back to his place, the actors go back to the beginning of the line interrupted by the knocks or they continue where they left off, whichever seems more appropriate.

René-Daniel Dubois

TRANSLATOR'S NOTE

In the original French-language version of *Being at Home with Claude*, René-Daniel Dubois used phonetic spelling and unorthodox punctuation extensively. These effects were not used to create a sense of dialect or social class, but rather to reproduce the sound and the music of the spoken language, as it is spoken daily by "ordinary" people in the street and at home, with all the variations that personality and circumstance bring to bear. The use of phonetic contractions and the frequent dropping of the "g's" throughout the text of this translation are used to achieve the same effect in English. Actors can simply view these spelling eccentricities as an invitation to listen for the sound of the characters' inner and outer voices.

Linda Gaboriau

Being at Home with Claude was originally published in French (under the same title) by Éditions Leméac, 5111, ave Durocher, Outremont, Quebec, H2V 3X7.

Gong. Lights go up. Freeze-frame onstage for three seconds. Gong rings again. The three actors begin to move. Immediately:

Inspector: (*shouting*) And whatabout me? Dontcha think I'd rather be standing in line at the Japanese Pavilion, instead of being stuck here with a trick from Parc Lafontaine who gets off on slitting people's throats? You think I got nothing better to do in life?

(*Beat.*)

Inspector: (*calmer*) Okay. So when you left the park, then where did you go?

Him: Oh, Christ, I told you 10 times already.

Inspector: Tell me again.

(*Beat.*)

Him: All right, listen, I'll tell you again, the whole bit. But this is the last time. Tape it or film it. Mark little x's on the map with a numbered code. Draw pictures for all I care, but ...

Inspector: Hey, watch it, kid. Forget the good advice and answer my questions. You called the cops? ... Well, here I am. I've listened to your half-cocked story. Now you can deliver the goods and let me ...

Him: Don't call me kid.

Inspector: ... and let me do my job. C'mon, shoot. Tell us the story. The real story.

Him: Jeesus, I told you everything. What more do you wanta know?

Inspector: Your name.

Him: ...

(*Beat.*)

Inspector: Start over again.

Him: When I left the park, I went ...

Inspector: From the beginning.

Him: (*sighs*)

(*Pause. Someone knocks at the side door.*)

Inspector: What is it?

(*The* Police Officer *enters.*)

Police Officer: You wanted to know when it was 10:30, well, it's just after. The judge will be here in an hour.

(*The* Police Officer *exits, closing the door behind him.*)

Inspector: Let's go. Shoot.

Him: When I left his place, I took the metro. Got on at Jarry. Must've been around nine. I got off at Bonaventure. And I walked down to the port. When I got there, I headed west. Must've walked for about an hour. Maybe more. I dunno. I don't have a watch. After a while I sorta woke up. I was sitting on a fence in Westmount. I felt like I had a headache. Like I had fallen asleep in the bathtub. Ya know what I mean? You fall asleep, you know you're in the bath, but you dream anyway. So all of a sudden, I woke up, sittin' on a green wood fence, and I realized that all that time I'd known I was walkin' and at the same time, I didn't know. I was just walkin', that's all.

Inspector: You can skip the moods, kid. We got an hour left. Get to the point.

Him: What the hell do you think I'm doin'? I'm tellin' you what happened. I didn't slit his throat for twenty bucks. Or because I didn't like the way he looked at me ...

Inspector: So why did you do it, then?

(*Beat.*)

Him: The whole time, I knew I was walkin', but at the same time, I didn't realize what I was doin'. I even knew why I was walkin', but I didn't want to think about it.

Inspector: What were you thinking about?

Him: About the other times I had been around there.

Inspector: What other times?

Him: Other times. Just walking around. When I feel ... whenever I felt real down, I used go for a long walk. I'd feel just as down afterwards, but at least I'd be tired enough to go to sleep.

(*Beat.*)

Inspector: Then what?

Him: What?

Inspector: We reached the point where you were sitting on the fence.

Him: I felt scared.

Inspector: Scared of what?

Him: Huh?

Inspector: Scared of what? If you were so scared, why didja call the cops?

Why the hell didn't you take off? Why did you call police headquarters to tell us there was a dead body in an apartment on Casgrain? And why did you call back an hour later to tell us you were the one who killed the guy? And if you were so scared, why the whole fuckin' trip on the phone to get us to come here? And how the hell did you get a hold of Judge Delorme's keys anyway? And why did you call the reporter from *Montréal Matin*? Why did it havta be here? And why don't you want to tell us your name?

(*Beat.*)

Inspector: (*calmly*) Okay. Let's get on with the story.

Him: When I woke up, I couldn't believe it. It was like, you know, like when you're with someone and suddenly you feel like you've been there before, in a dream, and you're even sure you've already told the other person about it. You say to him, I dreamt about this situation. Remember? I mentioned it to you once ... And the other person isn't sure. Well, that's the way I felt. I'd been walkin' for more than an hour, I woke up sittin on a fence, and the whole time I was walkin', in the back of my head, there was like the memory of something I wasn't sure I had really done. And when I woke up, the picture was sharper than ever, but it didn't seem possible I'd really done it. Just didn't seem possible. Hey, can't you tell him to get outta here?

Inspector: Why?

Him: I can't stand him anymore. He just sits there writin' everything down and never says a word. Nothin'. Not a sound. 'Cept when he slurps his coffee. You never look at what he writes anyway.

Inspector: If I tell him to leave, are you gonna tell me your name and why you killed that guy? Are you gonna tell me what the fuck we're doin' here? And what it'll take to prevent you from making a scandal when we walk outta here?

(*Beat.* Him *doesn't answer.*)

Inspector: Guy, go get me another coffee. You want one?

Him: No thanks.

Inspector: The joint next door must be open. Then wait outside 'til I call you.

(*The* Stenographer *takes the dollar bill the* Inspector *hands him and exits.*)

Inspector: All right.

Him: There was kinduva cool breeze, you could tell it was gonna rain. Real muggy. I was on I dunno what street ... one of those streets that run off Sherbrooke. I guess I was headed for the mountain when I stopped.

Inspector: Why were you headed there?

Him: Whaddaya mean, why? What do you think? Why do you usually go walkin' on the mountain in the middle of the night in early July?

Inspector: How the hell do I know?

Him: You puttin' me on?

Inspector: C'mon, out with it, for chrissakes, let's get to the point.

Him: Cause you're looking for a good fuck, that's why. Okay? You happy now?

Inspector: Jesus Christ Almighty! Can you please tell me why you went lookin' for a fuck on the mountain an hour-and-a-half after you slit some guy's throat in his own apartment?! ... And why you ended up calling us instead?

Him: I didn't call you.

Inspector: Oh, yeah? So what are we all doing here?

Him: Not right away. I called you later. Two days later. I called his place first.

Inspector: Whose place?

Him: His place.

Inspector: So you're really not gonna tell us his name?

Him: (mum)

Inspector: Why didja call him? You knew he was dead. You're the one who killed him.

Him: I thought it was a dream.

Inspector: Okay. Okay. So you thought it was a dream. So you called him.

Him: Not right away.

Inspector: When?

Him: I was sittin' on the fence. I sat there for a while, starin' at the houses. I like the houses in Westmount. Always wanted to be rich. My father, when he was little, his family was rich. He used to tell me stories about when he was rich. My grandparents, my father's parents, they used to tell me about it when we went to their house for dinner at Christmas and Easter. They had a tiny apartment, full of Louis XIV furniture. It was my grandfather who built the building for my grandmother's father. Then when they lost all their money, they moved into the second floor. It looked like Ali Baba's cave. There was too much stuff. Paintings ... silverware ... china ...

Inspector: Westmount.

Him: Yeah. They lived in Westmount. Before they lost their money.

Inspector: You were sitting on a fence in Westmount.

Him: Right. You could see the light inside the house flickerin' through the blinds. People must've been watchin' television.

Inspector: So why did you call his place?

Him: Huh?

Inspector: The guy ... (*He leans over to read a file on the desk.*)

Him: Hey! Don't!

Inspector: What? Whatsa matter?

Him: Don't say it.

(*Beat.*)

Inspector: So you called his place ...

Him: Yeah.

Inspector: Then what?

Him: I told you a thousand times already: when I left his place I went for a walk.

Inspector: You took the metro.

Him: Right. I took the metro, then I went for a walk and I ended up sitting on a fence ... There's where I woke up. Then ... I took off down the hill, running like crazy. All the way to the Forum. Running like there was no tomorrow. Like I thought I could prevent somethin' terrible from happening.

Inspector: All the way to the Forum?

Him: Yeah.

Inspector: What did the street look like? The street where you ended up on the fence?

Him: uhhh ...

Inspector: Did it go straight up? Tell me about the street. Not the houses, the street.

Him: It went uphill.

Inspector: The cars were going uphill? Were you above Sherbrooke?

Him: Yes.

Inspector: You said there were cars goin' by ...

Him: Yeah. I remember this one big white Chrysler that went by real slow. The guy inside was lookin' for an address. He had the light on. The interior was bright red.

Inspector: Which side of the street was he on? Was he going up the hill or headed down towards Sherbrooke? Or were there cars in both directions?

Him: He was headed up the hill. But it was a two-way street.

Inspector: Lansdowne. (*He writes it down on a piece of paper.*)

Him: What?

Inspector: Forget it.

(Inspector *goes over and puts the paper on the* Stenographer*'s table.*)

Inspector: So then what happened?

Him: I ran to the Forum.

Inspector: That's quite a ways.

Him: Maybe.

Inspector: You run the whole way?

Him: Yes.

Inspector: How many blocks?

Him: I dunno.

Inspector: You run along Sherbrooke?

Him: Probably.

Inspector: Did you or didn't you?

Him: Why the hell do you care if I ran along the Metropolitan Boulevard, along Sherbrooke or down the middle of Saint Catherine Street?

Inspector: Never mind why I care, just answer the question. Look at me. Look me in the eye. (*He glances at his watch.*) It's quarter to eleven. Monday morning. I been here with you since one a.m. Sunday. And here it is Monday, for Chrissakes, and we're gettin' nowhere fast. You set it up so we had to come and meet you here, right? And you're the one who baited the fuckin' reporters who are standing outside that door waiting for a scoop. Right? You're the one who told them that some heavy shit was gonna go down at the Courthouse. Well, listen, kid, you're the one who's in deep shit now. Stuck in your own shit. Right up to the neck. And now it's my turn to make a move. You're the one who called us to tell us to check out an apartment ...

(*Someone knocks at the side door.*)

Inspector: Yeah?

(*The side door opens. The* Stenographer *enters and hands the* Inspector *a small file of documents.*)

Stenographer: This just came in. I'm gonna go getcha coffee.

(*The* Stenographer *exits, closing the door behind him. Pause. The* Inspector *leafs through the documents.*)

Inspector: It's gonna be your birthday soon.

(*Beat.*)

Him: How do you know?

Inspector: Nice name ... Yves.

(Him *stands up.*)

Inspector: Sit down!

(*Pause. The* Inspector *is reading.*)

Inspector: Does your sister know you work Dominion Square?

(Him *sits there, frozen.*)

Inspector: You think we're a bunch of idiots? Did you really think we were gonna sit around and twiddle our thumbs while you gave us the runaround in this office? Did you think we were gonna sit around and wait for you to decide to tell us your name and why you want to get the whole fuckin' city out to watch you wash your dirty laundry?

Him: I'm not givin' you the runaround. I killed a guy. I told you I did it and I turned myself in. Here I am.

Inspector: So?

Him: So what more do you want?

Inspector: The autopsy shows he died between 9 and 11, July 1st. You called us in the middle of the night, July 3rd. I wanta know where you were in between.

Him: That's what ...

Inspector: Shut up. I wanta know where you were and what you did. I wanta know why you killed him. I wanta know who you are. Where you come from and what you do in life. And all I can get outta you is a bunch of half-assed stories that don't fit together and make no goddam sense at all. I'm beginning to feel like you've been laughing in my face for the last 36 hours. And I hate that feeling. You hear me? I hate it.

(*He turns abruptly, goes over to the* Stenographer's *table, picks up the transcription and begin to read some random excerpts out loud.*)

Question: Name? Answer: Forget it. Question: Your first name? Answer: Forget it. Age? None of your business. Here I am. I'm the one who killed him. What more do you want? Give me a break. If you want to know anything else, call Judge Delorme. (*Skips several excerpts.*) How did you get in here? Answer: Figure it out. That's your job, not mine. (*Further on.*) Question: What do you do for a living? Answer: I fuck. For money? A guy's gotta earn a living. Where do you hang out? Answer: hesitates, then: in the park. Parc Lafontaine? No answer. And now we find out that you work Dominion Square. If you don't call that laughing in my face, what the fuck is it?

Him: And why the hell do you care where I come from?

Inspector: (*waving one of the documents at him*) You didn't even want to tell us his name. You take us for a bunch of jackasses? Everything was right there in the apartment: his passport, his social insurance card, his lease. You think we were gonna tiptoe in, pick up the body, wash the floor and leave, lockin' the door behind us? Who the fuck do you think you are? James Bond? Let's cut the shit now. C'mon, out with it. What do you want? (*He goes back to the desk and picks up the rest of the file.*) He didn't have a police record. Neither do you.

Him: What makes you so sure?

Inspector: Next time you leave a cup on someone's desk, if you don't want anyone to check your fingerprints, make sure there's no pig around picking up after you, wise guy ... No sign of dope or alcohol in his blood. No trace of nothing in the apartment. But ... (*Looks up at the ceiling*) ... he died screwing. With a guy. And it wasn't rape cause he came too. And his clothes weren't torn. They were all over the kitchen floor but all in one piece. Your fingerprints were all around the apartment, except on the handle of the knife that was used to slit his throat. A steak knife with a fuckin' imitation hickory plastic handle. Impossible to get any prints off it ... Maybe he was one of your customers. Your "colleagues" in the Square say you're okay ... just a bit loose sometimes. Couple of them don't have much good to say about you ...

Him: My colleagues? You don't even know where I work.

Inspector: Listen, kid. You want some cheap advice? Next time you decide to kill someone, make sure he's not a lit major who writes in his diary every day and talks about you, saying how weird it is to sleep with a "pro." Once you got that straight and you decide to set up a meeting with the cops in some judge's office in the middle of the night, during Confederation Day weekend, with a quarter of a million tourists in town for Expo ... just remember not to leave your jean jacket hanging on a chair beside the door with AVAILABLE embroidered on the back in day-glo orange beads. And don't spend 36 hours sitting next to a window when you're not sure who can look in and see you ... What kinduva weirdo are you anyway? How long did you know him? And why did you slit his throat in the middle of his kitchen floor?

Him: I thought it was all written in his diary?

Inspector: No. He doesn't say much about his love life. All we know is that it's been at least a month.

Him: A month?

Inspector: Yeah. In the last month, he wrote about you on almost every page.

Him: Ah.

Inspector: Surprised?

Him: No.

Inspector: Holy Jesus! ... Okay ... Let's start over again. And let's make it fast, okay? Your name is Yves. His name was Claude. In the evening of the 1st of July, last Thursday, you left the Square, all alone, around six-thirty, seven o'clock and apparently no one knows why you left. There were lotsa prospects hangin' around ... Maybe you had an appointment or maybe you were off on a house call. Then nobody sees hide nor hair of you 'til around midnight. After midnight, people remember seeing you at the Lorelei, at Bud's, at the Tropicana, the Taureau and then at the Rocambole. But you weren't talkin' to nobody. Some of the girls figured you just struck it rich, or maybe you dropped some acid or some five-star mescaline. Seems like you were so hyper, people were afraid you'd fall over if they blew on you too hard. Then you left for the Square. No one seems to know if you scored or not, cause they all left when it started to rain. You claim you scored twice ... Then no news 'til Saturday night. Patrick, one of your regular lays – not a customer, another hustler – he says he tried to call you at least 20 times but there was never any answer. He went by your place Saturday morning, not a sound. He can't figure out where you disappeared and he never heard of the other guy, Claude. Nobody ever heard of him.

Saturday night, at 11:30, someone calls police headquarters and says there's a guy dead at 8544 Casgrain. We get there and there's this guy, stretched out on his back, bareass, in the middle of the kitchen floor, with his throat slit wide open. There are two plates and two wine glasses on the table, with an unopened bottle of $15 wine. People who aren't too crazy about you say you're kinda cheap. The meat and vegetables in the plates are covered with blood. The guys at the lab say the meat was already cold when the blood hit it. Your fingerprints are everywhere. He was 22 years old and he came from Sainte-Foy. Came to Montreal two years ago to study literature at the University of Montreal. Lived alone. A card-carrying separatist ... member of the R.I.N. His girlfriend ...

Him: What?

Inspector: ... works with them full-time. She almost fainted when we showed up.

Him: His what?

Inspector: His girlfriend.

Him: It's not true. You're just sayin' that to get a rise outta me.

Inspector: We don't all get off on telling stories and playing games, smart ass. You don't want to talk. Tough shit. I'll just finish my little run-through and we can pack it up and take care of the formalities at my office. I've had it.

Him: It's not true. Admit it's not true.

Inspector: Get a hold on yourself, for chrissakes. He's not the first guy in town to have a girlfriend. When we took the fingerprints, there were his, and two other people's – his girlfriend's and yours. She let us take hers. She says the guy who did it is sick. I'm not about to contradict her. And I don't recommend you try it either. We took your prints off the first cup of coffee your lordship ordered.

Him: What's her name?

Inspector: Whose name?

Him: The girlfriend.

Inspector: On no you don't, junior. You don't get to ask any more questions. From now on in you can start answering. Otherwise, just shut your trap and listen to what the grownups have to say.

Him: How ...

Inspector: Shut up! That means you didn't know him well enough to know he had a girlfriend. Don't tell me we're making some progress here! Let's keep it up. At 12:45 the same night, the same person who called to report the dead guy calls back. That's you. You tell us you're calling from Judge Delorme's office at the Courthouse. You say you're the one who killed the guy and you're waiting here for us, but we shouldn't try to force you outta here cause you've told the police reporter from *Montréal Matin*

your story and he's agreed to sit on it as long as no one tries to get you
outta here by force. And if anything does happen to you, the Judge is up
shit's creek.

(*Beat.*)

So here we'are 36 hours later. We don't know how you got your hands
on the keys to let yourself in, but you did. If we try to clamp down on the
reporter and his fuckin' photographer, everyone's gonna accuse us of police brutality. And we don't want any of that, with all those tourists in
town. Fuck! Did you work all that out by yourself? We got 'til 5 o'clock
this afternoon to come up with a good explanation. With all the goings-on
this weekend, they had their headlines for today. But now the party's over
and they're lookin' for something juicy to dress up tomorrow's front page.
A judge is damn tempting. I gotta hand it to you. You got a great sense of
timing. (*Sighs.*) Okay. We been here since the wee small hours of the
morning yesterday. And the only thing I managed to find out is that someone tore the doorbell and the phone off the wall at your place. You live in
a slum on Saint-Dominique, between de Montigny and Ontario. You called
us from your neighbour's and before you left her place you managed to get
her stoned outta her head. You left her with enough shit to keep her blind
'til Christmas. She could hardly remember her name. (*Shouts.*) What the
hell are you after anyway?

Him: The judge knows. Ask him.

Inspector: If you tell me that once more, just once more, I'm gonna knock
your head off. (*Beat.*) I don't know why you wanted to wipe out your
writer friend. I can't figure out what you had against him. Or what he had
against you. I don't get it. I don't see where you could've met, except
maybe on the corner of Saint Catherine and Peel at rush hour. He was
good-looking. Educated. I don't know what he could've seen in an asshole
like you. He didn't take dope. Drank good wine. Didn't hang out in the
bars from what we can tell. His neighbours fuckin' flipped when they saw
us arrive with an ambulance and carry him out in a body bag. What the
hell were you doing having supper on Confederation Day with a guy who
used to take three hot meals a week to the old lady who lives downstairs?!
Sonofabitch ...

All we know is you'd been seeing each other for at least a month, but
we can't really tell why, cause his diary is written in code, with references
to more goddam books and novels than you can name. We'd have to go
through half the public library to decipher a quarter of a page. The only
thing we're sure of is that beginning the first ...

(*The side door opens. The* Stenographer *enters with a paper bag. He puts it
down on the desk and takes out a little container of cream, sugar and a styro-
foam cup. He's about to take the lid off the coffee to add the cream for his boss*

when the Inspector *motions to him to leave immediately. The* Stenographer *goes out, closing the door quietly behind him.*)

Inspector: All we know is that your name never showed up in his diary before June 1st. Around that time, the name Yves starts appearing in every line, almost.

Him: A while ago you said "every page" ...

(*Beat.*)

Inspector: What difference does it make? Who was that guy to you? Did he wanta write a book about you?

(*Pause.* Him *remains silent.*)

Inspector: The inspector who went to see the girlfriend asked her if she thought her friend had ever slept with another guy. She screamed so loud he thought her jaw was gonna come unhinged. He decided not to insist ...
   Your friend kept all the letters he received and copies of the ones he sent. He even kept a notebook with all his debts, and the names of everyone who owed him money. Even his girlfriend is in it. But not you ...

(*Pause.*)

Inspector: (*calls*) Latreille!

(*The side door opens. The* Police officer *enters and closes the door behind him.*)

Inspector: (*pointing to* Him) He has to piss. Bring him back here after.

Him: Huh? I don't ...

Inspector: Get going.

(Him *and the* Police officer *go to exit.*)

Inspector: (*just before they exit*) Send Guy in. Wait a minute ...

Police officer: Yeah?

Inspector: (*pointing to the phone*) Do you havta dial 9?

Police officer: Yes.

(Him *and the* Police officer *exit. The door closes behind them. The* Inspector *remains seated for a second. Then he gets up suddenly and goes over to the window and opens it wide. He leans on the windowsill. After a moment he comes back to the desk, picks up the phone and dials a number. At the beginning of his conversation he mixes his coffee, sitting on the corner of the desk. Then he starts looking at the room around him as if he was just beginning to realize where he was. Then he gets up from the desk and sits down on the chair.*)

Inspector: (*on the phone*) Hullo. ... Dead. How 'bout you? ... Sure I am. ... Sure. Who got in touch with you? Dupras? ... Uh huh. ... Oh, I dunno. ... I guess I'll know better around 5 how long it's gonna take. ... I know, I know. Why don't you go by yourself. I'm too tired anyway, haven't slept a wink. ... I'll tell you about it later. ... No, no. No big problem. ... Don't worry. ... Sure. ... Sure. ... No. ... Yeah, but I just as soon forget it. If it's not too late when we finish here, I'll give you a call before I leave. ... No. I can't. ... It's not my usual number and you havta go through an operator. ... Of course, I'm in Montreal, whaddaya think? ... Okay, okay. ... Well ... Guess the best thing would be to call Dupras or his replacement. They'll know how to get in touch with me. ... 'Bye.

(*The* Inspector *hangs up. During the call the* Stenographer *enters. He's standing behind* Him's *chair. The* Inspector *goes back over to the window, leans on the sill for a second and goes back over to his chair.*)

Stenographer: So?

Inspector: So? So, nothing. It's getting worse instead of better. I don't understand fuck all. Anything new?

Stenographer: Janine has just about finished studyin' the notebook with his accounts. He wrote down every penny he spent in the last year. Looks like he had started to have money troubles. He was keepin' careful track. There's a letter from his mother where she talks about some crisis. There's no copy of his answer. It's not clear what it's all about, but it seems like the folks started tightening the purse-strings around that time. Anyway, since the end of last summer, his finances seem to balance real tight. There's no way he could've paid our friend (*Points towards the door.*) for as many times as he shows up in the diary. He had about three thou in the bank. Plus some bonds his parents bought him. He had over 100 bucks cash in his pants pocket. And if I hocked the watch he was wearin' I could pay six months rent. That's about it.

(*Beat.*)

Inspector: What time is it?

Stenographer: Going on 10 to.

Inspector: What about his sister?

Stenographer: Nothing much. She's been livin' with some guy in Montreal North for the last three years. Four years older than him. The mother died in '57. She was a fashion model. She died in an office at CBC in the middle of the night, a Friday night. Cleaning lady found her on Saturday morning. In one of the big bosses' offices. No details. There were orders from Ottawa to keep it hush-hush. The newspapers said she died of a heart attack. Problem is, she was only 36 years old. With no history of heart trouble. But an alcoholic. Seems like she wasn't alone in the office. They had been drinking and she fell and hit her head. Guy must've panicked and took off. Died of a hemorrhage

Inspector: The father?

Stenographer: Cancer. Two years ago.

Inspector: (*sighs*) That's it?

Stenographer: Just about. He was an engineer. Some kinda consultant. A big spender. Lotsa connections. Friends in high places, in Quebec City, mostly with the Liberals. He had been sick for a long time.

Inspector: Did you reach the sister?

Stenographer: She's away on vacation. No one knows where.

Inspector: Do you think he knows?

Stenographer: No idea. But her neighbours don't know him. They knew she had a brother but they don't remember ever seein' him. They don't recognize the picture.

Inspector: Anyone else? Friends? Other relatives?

Stenographer: A few, but they don't know nothing. His father's parents are still alive but he hasn't spoken to them since his father died. Same goes for the uncles and aunts. Nobody's seen him for over two years. His mother's father died in '56. She was in the middle of a family feud when she died. Some deal about the will. The last time the grandmother saw him was at her daughter's funeral.

Inspector: No friends, no girlfriend?

Stenographer: Just the guy from the Square. Period. The only other possibility is the neighbour, but she claims she doesn't know a thing.

Inspector: Who spoke to her?

Stenographer: Dupras.

Inspector: What does he think? Is it worth pushing?

Stenographer: He doesn't know. But he's got the feeling he's the kinda guy who never makes the first move. You gotta call him, he won't call you, type thing. Dupras doesn't think we're gonna find out much, unless he decides to talk.

Inspector: Okay. I get the picture. What about the other guy? Besides the dough?

Stenographer: His parents?

Inspector: Yeah.

Stenographer: We haven't gotten back in touch with them. They're in a state of shock. They don't believe us. Real big wigs. He's in the pulp and paper business. And trucking. Doubled his fortune with the dam at Mani-couagan. And she's from an old Quebec City family, real blue-blood. Something tells me we better leave well enough alone.

Inspector: Go tell that to the guys from *Montréal Matin*. Or the judge. How's he doin'?

Stenographer: No news. He's not answerin' his phone. His wife neither. His secretary tells us his plans are still the same, he'll be here at 11:30, as scheduled.

Inspector: You weren't able to reach him.

Stenographer: Impossible. Apparently he's just gonna sit back and let the shit hit the fan. But ...

Inspector: But what? What's the matter?

Stenographer: The Minister called. He doesn't want anything to get out. Nothin'. Dupras got a real earful. He was still shakin' when I saw him. Apparently whatshisface lit into him the minute he picked up the phone. Didn't even have time to say he wasn't you. Seems like he rolled out every threat in the hook.

Inspector: Christ. Why didn't you tell me before?

Stenographer: He called while I went to get the coffee.

(*Beat.*)

Inspector: And what about the vultures outside the door? Anything we can feed them in exchange?

Stenographer: No. I tried. I told the office to let us know if there's anything we can pass on as a scoop. But so far, there's fuck all. A few minor accidents. Some woman who got ...

Inspector: Okay. Okay ...

Stenographer: Anyway it would havta be one helluva story to take their minds off a murder, a judge and a male prostitute all rolled up in one. Don't think they'd settle for much less than a bomb at Expo.

Inspector: ...

Stenographer: Nobody at *Montréal Matin* has made a peep. They don't wanta get their story stolen out from under them. We warned the others to keep the lid on it. *La Presse* and most of the radio stations are willing to co-operate as long as nobody gets hurt. Their attitude seems to be, if we can find a way to bury the whole thing, good for us. But if we get heavy with our friends from *Montréal Matin*, they're gonna raise a stink.

Inspector: Happy birthday.

Stenographer: Pardon me?

Inspector: Forget it. Oh, by the way, the street with the fence ... from what he says, it must be Lansdowne. Go send someone to check if there's a green picket fence somewhere between Sherbrooke and the roundabout at Côte Saint-Antoine. It should be on the east side.

Stenographer: Right away.

(*The* Inspector *gets up and goes over to the map on the wall.*)

Inspector: Doesn't make sense.

Stenographer: What?

Inspector: If you wanted to call someone in the middle of the night and you were on Lansdowne north of Sherbrooke, would you decide to run all the way to the Forum to find a phone booth?

Stenographer: Not in the middle of summer.

Inspector: Huh?

Stenographer: In the winter, if that was the closest place I knew ... maybe. But not in the middle of summer. I'd take it easy and try to find one closer by, cause I know the Forum's closed at that hour anyway.

Inspector: (*turns away from the map*) Right.

(Inspector *goes back over to his chair, slowly. The* Stenographer *watches him.*)

(*Beat.*)

Inspector: So you wanta know where things stand? We're stuck between a rock and a hard place, that's where. Between a judge who doesn't give a shit and who's fallin' apart at the seams; a minister who doesn't want a word of this to get out, in order to preserve the name of Justice; a mad dog who's lookin' for his bone; a separatist girlfriend who's not gonna believe any story we come up with, who's gonna make a scandal, who's gonna rant and rave and claim it's not true, her boyfriend wasn't queer, and it's all a frame-up; and the guy's parents who don't want a word to get out, in order to preserve the family name. Hot enough for you? (*Beat.*) Okay. Keep on top of the reporters. Make sure they've all been warned. And send someone out to check the fence. Then ...

Stenographer: Yeah?

Inspector: Nothing. Forget it. I thought I had an idea but I lost it. Better get going.

(*The* Stenographer *exits, closing the side door behind him. The* Inspector *re-*

mains still briefly then goes back over to lean on the windowsill. The side door opens. Him enters and goes back to his chair. The door closes. Brief pause. The Inspector straightens up, closes the window and turns back towards the room. Notices the kid. Returns to sit on the corner of the desk.)

Inspector: *(while heading towards the desk)* You been back long?

Him: Just got back.

Inspector: Why did you tear the doorbell and the phone out?

Him: I didn't want to be disturbed.

Inspector: Figured as much. But why? Did you do it as soon as you got home?

Him: No.

Inspector: So when did you do it?

Him: Friday morning.

Inspector: At what time?

Him: I don't remember.

Inspector: Do you remember why?

Him: It's kinda vague.

Inspector: Try.

Him: I woke up around nine, quarter past nine, and ...

Inspector: What time did you get home?

Him: Around five-thirty, six o'clock.

Inspector: Did you come right home?

Him: What do you mean, right home?

Inspector: You didn't stop anywhere to eat?

Him: No. I wasn't hungry.

Inspector: You walk home?

Him: Yes.

Inspector: How come your customer didn't give you a ride home? Was it the first time?

Him: It's not his style. As soon as he comes, he feels ashamed. And he gets mad. Especially when he's drunk. He gets all red in the face when he comes and he stays that way after, cause he's so mad. He usually throws the money on top of my clothes and throws me out the door.

Inspector: How long did it take you to get home?

Him: I dunno, maybe 15 minutes.

Inspector: You must've been pretty tired by then ...

Him: No, not too bad. But I had a terrible headache.

Inspector: (*looking at the map*) Do you walk fast?

Him: Average.

Inspector: A fifteen-minute radius from your place ... that brings us where?

Him: Forget it. You'll never figure it out and I'm not telling you.

Inspector: (*to himself*) That's none of my business either?

Him: I got to my place around 5:30. It had rained all night so it was nice 'n' cool. The sky was clear. It was nice out.

Inspector: Did you go right to bed?

Him: Yes.

Inspector: Were you stoned?

Him: Stoned? Why?

Inspector: Forget why. Just answer, okay?

Him: N ... No. I wasn't stoned.

Inspector: Did you fall asleep right away?

Him: No.

Inspector: How long did it take?

Him: I dunno. Maybe half an hour, maybe more.

Inspector: And you woke up around nine.

Him: Maybe nine-thirty. I didn't notice. My clock is fast anyway and I can never remember when I set it at the right time. So I never look at the minute hand. Just the hour hand and I figure the rest out approximately.

Inspector: Okay ... So you woke up between nine, nine-thirty. Nine, nine-thirty in the morning?

Him: Yeah, whaddaya think?

Inspector: You sure?

Him: Of course, I'm sure.

Inspector: What time did you get up the day before?

Him: Around noon.

Inspector: So between noon Thursday and six o'clock Friday morning you hadn't slept at all?

Him: ...

Inspector: I'm talking to you, buster.

Him: Huh?

Inspector: I want to know if you slept between the time you got up Thursday morning and the time you went to bed Friday morning.

Him: Not to speak of.

Inspector: What does that mean, not to speak of?

Him: No, I didn't sleep.

Inspector: And you went to bed at six and you didn't fall asleep 'til six-thirty, seven?

Him: That's right. It happens to me a lot. Especially in the summertime. Can't sleep cause of the light. I don't have any curtains. I hate curtains. That's why I live on the third floor, with no neighbours out front, no neighbours out back. Across the street, there's the Dozois housing project. And out back, it's the rear end of one of those warehouses on the Main.

Inspector: What do you do when you can't fall asleep? Smoke a little joint?

Him: Sometimes. But not this time.

Inspector: How come?

Him: Cause I didn't feel like it. That's all. I splashed some cold water on my face and went back to bed.

Inspector: That's it?

Him: Yeah. No ... I read for a while.

Inspector: What didja read?

Him: A ... a book one of my friends lent me. But I was too tired to understand what I was reading so I put it down and counted sheep.

Inspector: And then you fell asleep?

Him: Yeah. It didn't take long ...

Inspector: What was the book about? Do you remember the title?

Him: No. I only read a few pages. Couldn't understand a thing. I just told you that.

Inspector: And you woke up around nine?

Him: (*sighs*) Right.

Inspector: That's not much sleep for a guy who was too tired at seven o'clock to understand what he was reading and who hadn't slept for the past 18 hours. What woke you up? Did the phone ring?

Him: No. I just woke up. I already told you all this last night.

Inspector: You told us you didn't sleep long, but you didn't tell us you'd torn your doorbell and your phone off the wall. We never would've found out if we hadn't gone over to your place.

Him: I woke up because I had a stomach ache.

Inspector: What kinduva stomach ache?

Him: I had like a brick in my stomach, right around the belly button. It hurt. I woke up cause I must've rolled over onto my belly in my sleep and it hurt. And I was too hot ... it was like I hadn't slept at all ... like I was more tired than when I fell asleep. I was drooling. Don't ask me why. I felt really sick. I couldn't focus on anything. All sorts a pictures floatin' around in my head ... but I'm not crazy.

Inspector: Relax. I didn't say a thing.

Him: No, you didn't say anything. But you're goin' outta your skull lookin' for some reason to prove to the reporters that I'm crazy. And ... and ...

Inspector: And what?

Him: I dunno. I'm too tired to think ...

Inspector: Do you still have a stomach ache?

Him: It's almost gone.

Inspector: Okay. So you ripped out the wires when you woke up?

Him: No. I managed to go back to sleep. But it was the same kinda sleep as before I woke up. Made me feel more exhausted than anything else. I kept waking up, moaning.

Inspector: Whaddaya mean?

Him: I don't know how to describe it. I'd wake up and I couldn't tell if I was awake or still asleep, or maybe I had been awake before and now I was asleep. And my stomach ache was gettin' worse. At one point I got up to piss. That's when I thought about the phone. I called his place.

Inspector: Whose place?

Him: *His* place.

Inspector: Did you know his number by heart or did you have it written down somewhere?

Him: There was no answer. Made me really mad, so I tore out the wire. As soon as I did it, I realized I didn't want to be there for anyone. Didn't want anyone to get in touch with me. Just wanted to disappear. Without even thinking, I went 'n' ripped out the doorbell. Wasn't very solid. I installed it myself when I moved in there. Then I unplugged the TV and the radio ... . Then I went back to bed and I slept a little better.

Inspector: Then what?

Him: Then what? Nothing. I slept. I got up. I went back to bed. I slept. I woke up. I slept some more. Till Saturday evening.

Inspector: What time Saturday?

Him: I dunno. My clock had stopped. I forgot to wind it. I didn't even know what day it was and I couldn't've cared less.

Inspector: But you looked at the clock 'cause you noticed it had stopped.

Him: Yeah, but much later. Around 11 o'clock.

Inspector: And you didn't leave the house at all between Friday morning and Saturday night?

Him: No.

Inspector: Didn't eat?

Him: Maybe I ate something at my place.

Inspector: Yesterday afternoon you told us you didn't mind eating sandwiches, you were used to it, you never eat at home, and when you don't have much money that's what you eat.

Him: Yeah, but this time maybe I had somethin' in the house ...

Inspector: Listen, don't start in again. Okay? There's nothing in your fridge, nothing in the garbage pail except dirty kleenex, torn up envelopes and some crumpled up flyers, and ...

Him: No. I didn't eat. And I wasn't hungry. I told you, I had a stomach ache.

Inspector: Still no dope?

Him: No.

Inspector: What do you think made you sick?

Him: I dunno.

Inspector: Okay. So what happened at 11 o'clock?

Him: I decided I'd had enough. That I had to get outta there. I took a shower and went out to get a couple of hot dogs. Then I came back and I called you. I called the reporter at home, but he had left. I called the newspaper. I told him my story. I came here. I let him and his photographer in and then I called you back.

Inspector: You had his home number?

Him: Yeah.

Inspector: How did you get it?

Him: You really think I'm gonna answer that question?

Inspector: And you had his number at the paper too? He's not too shy, eh?

Him: The phone book wasn't invented to wipe your ass with. I know how to read.

Inspector: How come you don't want a lawyer?

Him: I don't need one.

Inspector: What makes you so sure the judge is gonna be able to bury this story? What makes you so sure he even wants to?

Him: I never said he could ...

Inspector: I know, I know. All you said was, you killed the guy on Casgrain. You wanted to turn yourself in but we had to come and get you here. And you wouldn't walk outta here till the judge agreed to meet you. The reporter is just here as a guarantee. That's all. And anyone who thinks that sounds like blackmail has a twisted mind ... right?

Him: Why do you insist on puttin' all the pieces together? Somebody was killed. It's your job to find the murderer? You got him. What more do you want?

Inspector: Are you as thick as you seem or have you decided to give me a hard time, just for the hell of it?

Him: Just wait till the judge shows up, then we'll see ...

Inspector: I've heard some weird stories in my time, but this one takes the cake. A guy turns himself in, even tho' the cops never could've found him cause no one ever would've connected him with the victim, but instead of keepin' his trap shut, he turns the fuckin' city upside down and blackmails a judge so the judge can find him innocent ... when he's the one who turned himself in.

Him: You don't ...

Inspector: And to top it all off ... he had no reason to kill the guy. He didn't take his money. He didn't take nothin'. He kills him then he goes downtown for a few drinks. At one point, he even considers going to check out the action on the mountain. Then he disappears and the next thing we know he's waiting for us at the Courthouse. And he gives us the runaround for 36 hours while we wait for the judge to show up. He doesn't want us to know his name. Doesn't want us to mention the name of the guy he killed. And he doesn't even want to tell us why. Holy Christ. And you're trying to tell me there's nothing wrong with you? Maybe I'm the one who's crazy? Give me a break. I'm supposed to leave on vacation tonight, not get fired ... . Let's start all over again.

Him: Oh, no. Not again.

Inspector: Let's go.

Him: Listen ...

Inspector: I said: let's go. Left his place around ...

Him: Nine o'clock.

Inspector: Then what?

Him: I took the metro to Bonaventure. Then I took a walk. I walked all the way to Westmount.

Inspector: And from there?

Him: I ran.

Inspector: Where to?

Him: Uuh ... to the Forum.

Inspector: What did you wanta do at the Forum, in the middle of summer, at 10:30 at night on Confederation Day?

Him: Make a phone call.

Inspector: You trying to make me believe you ran all that way in the heat just for the thrill of using a phone at the Forum, when you must've passed about forty phone booths during your little sprint?

Him: Yes. No. I dunno. That's what I did. The way you tell it, it doesn't make any sense, but it made sense at the time.

Inspector: You bet! ... All right, so you finally reached the Forum?

Him: Yeah, but it was locked up tight. I went over to the Alexis Nihon Plaza. I called his place. There was no answer. I thought I dialled the wrong number. I hung up and called back. No answer.

Inspector: What's his number?

Him: You know it as well as I do.

Inspector: Tell me again.

Him: Then I walked out onto Saint Catherine. The wind was gettin' stronger and there were lotsa people. Laughin' and havin' a good time. They were comin' out of the metro, wavin' little Canadian flags. I didn't feel like talking. I felt the way I feel when I come out of a good movie: the movie stays clear in my head until I start to talk about it. I know that if I talk about it, and I always do, I'm gonna lose the sense of it. But this wasn't even a good movie. It was a cop movie and the worst scene was stuck in my head. Anyway, I did what I always do, when I come out of the movies at Alexis Nihon Plaza, I headed east along Saint Catherine.

Inspector: Okay. And while you were walking, before and after the phone call, did you hear anything? Did you notice any particular noises?

Him: No.

Inspector: You didn't hear any cannon shots?

Him: This guy is a real pain. You keep askin' me the same fuckin' question and I keep givin' you the same fuckin' answer: No. I didn't hear any cannon shots. No jet planes. No bombs. No military parades. And I didn't find any grenades on the sidewalk.

Inspector: Don't get wise. On the night of the 1st of July, there were fireworks on Saint Helen's Island. The people with the flags were coming back from there. You could hear them right up to Metropolitan Boulevard. So can you explain how you managed to take a walk along the harbour-front without hearing them?

Him: No. ... I thought maybe he had gone out. We met at the Love Bar ...

Inspector: (*shouts*) You don't say! It's about time! They met at the Love Bar. As simple as that. So you knew the guy?

Him: Yes.

Inspector: We're finally gettin' somewhere. When did you meet at the Love Bar? The day before the 1st of June?

Him: ...

Inspector: Are you the Yves he talks about in his diary?

Him: ...

Inspector: Great. Here we go again. He's pressed the Off button again. So you met at the Love Bar. Then what?

Him: There's where we met. And I thought maybe he'd gone out. So I went to see if he was there. He wasn't. I checked out all the other bars. He wasn't there.

Inspector: Did you meet anyone you know?

Him: At least 40 people.

Inspector: Where did you go afterwards?

Him: To the Square. I'd told him ...

Inspector: What? What did you tell him? When?

Him: I'd told him I was gonna work that night.

Inspector: When did you tell him that?

(*Beat.*)

Him: That afternoon, on the phone.

Inspector: (*relieved*) Phew.

Him: Whatsa matter?

Inspector: Nothing. Go on.

Him: I told him there were so many tourists in town it was worth workin' two shifts a day. He didn't think it was very funny.

Inspector: Why not?

Him: Well ...

Inspector: Was he jealous?

Him: No. It was just a stupid joke, that's all.

Inspector: Were you seeing each other regularly?

Him: You should know. You said you read his diary.

Inspector: Cut the shit and answer me ... were you seeing each other regularly.

Him: Yes.

Inspector: You have a fight?

Him: No.

Inspector: So why did you kill him?

Him: When he wasn't at home, I thought maybe he'd gone lookin' for me in the Square.

Inspector: Had he ever gone looking for you in the Square?

Him: No.

Inspector: Why not? 'Cause he hated that scene?

Him: No, no. You got it all wrong.

Inspector: If you made more sense, maybe I wouldn't get so confused. What time was it when you arrived in the square?

Him: I was still around for the first last call at the Taureau ... I left right after ... Some guy, a customer, asked me where I was going. I told him. He said: Don't bother, how much? I took off anyway. He started after me, but he fell down the last seven or eight steps. Too pissed to hurt himself ... I dunno, the time it takes to walk there ... maybe it was ten to three.

Inspector: What were you thinking about?

Him: I told you. I was thinkin' I must've missed him. We must've been in the wrong bars at the wrong times. And he'd come and meet me in the square. I'd told him I was gonna be there.

Inspector: You really thought he was still alive?

Him: Yes. When I got there and saw everyone drinkin' and laughin', talkin' and cruisin', tokin' up and necking ... it kind of erased the picture. And I couldn't hear the ... (*He stops suddenly.*)

Inspector: You couldn't hear what?

(*Beat.*)

Inspector: (*louder*) What couldn't you hear?

Him: There was quite a crowd in the square ...

Inspector: (*interrupts him*) What couldn't you hear?

Him: Huh?

Inspector: Don't give me a hard time. You started to say something. You were saying that when you saw everyone in the bars having a good time, you couldn't hear ... you couldn't hear WHAT?

Him: All I meant was, the music and seeing all those people made it seem impossible that he was gone. All those people who had been there the day before, and the day before that, and ever since I been going to those bars. Before I even knew him. Seemed impossible that they could still be around and him gone. Everything seemed too real. So the picture in my head was like ... erased.

(*Pause.*)

Inspector: (*takes a deep breath, then*) What would you say if I told you your sister was waiting outside that door?

(*Beat.*)

Him: (*stunned at first, then relaxes*) I'd laugh in your face.

Inspector: Oh yeah?

Him: It takes three days by car to get where she goes on vacation. And mountain climbers don't carry phones in their knapsacks.

(*Beat.*)

Inspector: Okay. So you had reached the square.

Him: You try to pull any other ones like that?

Inspector: You reached the square.

Him: Hold on.

Inspector: Too late. Should've thought of that earlier. The square.

Him: The bit about the diary ... was it true?

Inspector: (*goes to take a sip of the coffee he hasn't touched since he called his wife but it's cold*)

Him: And the bit about his girlfriend?

Inspector: Whatcha got against that girl?

(*Beat.*)

Inspector: Let's get on with it. You reached the square. What time did you get there?

Him: I told you five minutes ago. The time it took to hear the first last call at the Taureau, go out the door, down the stairs and walk over to the square.

Inspector: You didn't stop anywhere on the way?

Him: No.

Inspector: Didn't meet anyone you knew?

Him: No.

Inspector: Okay. So you reached the square. Then what?

Him: I sat down on a bench, over by the caleches.

Inspector: In the park?

Him: Yeah. Along the walk that leads to Peel.

Inspector: The first bench on the walk?

Him: Yeah.

Inspector: How come your friends didn't see you?

Him: Who says my friends didn't see me? Maybe that's another one of your stories ...

Inspector: If you had talked to your friends, you'd know I was lying. I could only be making it up if you didn't talk to them. Are you sure you went to the square?

Him: Yes.

Inspector: So how come your friends didn't see you?

Him: 'Cause I usually move around. And I hang out around the statue.

Inspector: How come you didn't go there this time?

Him: I didn't feel like it.

Inspector: Why didn't you feel like it?

Him: 'Cause I felt like bein' alone. That's why.

Inspector: So why did you go to the square?

Him: 'Cause I didn't feel like stayin' at the Taureau for the parade, and I felt ...

Inspector: Parade? What parade?

Him: The game. When everyone knows the last call is comin' up, they go to the john and comb their hair, splash some water on their face and then they line up as close to the door as possible, so they can't miss anyone who's leavin' on his own. I call it the parade. I didn't feel like watchin' it that night and I didn't feel like goin' home either. I wasn't sleepy. So I went over to the square before everyone else and I didn't go to my usual spot. That's why nobody saw me. I was sittin' on a bench facing Peel.

Inspector: For how long?

Him: Not long.

Inspector: You sure?

Him: Yeah, 'cause I left before the whole gang started to arrive.

Inspector: How long?

Him: The time it takes to walk outta Pepe's and cross half the park, lengthwise.

Inspector: Huh?

Him: I'd just sat down when I heard someone shouting in the middle of Peel Street. I stood up. At first I thought someone got hit by a car ... but it was just a bunch of Americans comin' outta Pepe's. Having a good time. They stopped the traffic to cross Peel and they came into the park 'n' went over to take a look at the statue. Then they headed towards me.

Inspector: To talk to you?

Him: No. They wanted to go for a caleche ride. I'd sat back down on the back of the bench. They walked right by me. There was one good-lookin' one in the gang but he was the drunkest. They all looked at me when they walked by. The good-lookin' one stopped and gave me a big smile ... then he went and caught up with the others. They were talking with one of the caleche drivers. Then they went over to another one. None of the drivers wanted to take them cause they all wanted to go in the same caleche and they were too pissed. All of a sudden the good-lookin' guy covered his face with his hands for a second, then looked up at the sky. Then he turned around slowly and he saw me. Another big grin. And he came over and sat down beside me. On the seat of the bench, not on the back. He muttered something. I think he was apologizing for being too drunk to keep his balance on the back of the bench. Then he asked me to get down 'n' sit beside him. So I did. He asked me if I wanted to go home with him. I told him it would cost him. He asked me how much. I told him and he gave it to me right away. He put his hand on my neck to get me to stand up. He shouted "bye" to his friends and we headed towards Peel to grab a cab. His friends shouted something at him. We took a cab to the corner of Pine and Aylmer. It had started to rain. He was staying in a flat there with his friends. It belonged to one of them who's studying at McGill. He said we'd have plenty of time before they got back. But he didn't touch me. Usually I can't stand customers who beat around the bush. I like it short and sweet. Don't like hangin' around for an hour waiting for something to happen. But he didn't touch me and I didn't mind. He took out a map of the city and started askin' me different things. Where was the Wax Museum, stuff like that. I told him. He was really pissed and he started to make a speech. Couldn't understand much of it, but I think he was talking about one-night stands and people who hang out in bars checking each other out for hours, without ever saying a word. People who don't wanta talk, they just wanta fuck. He seemed fed up. Then he finally said, all right, let's go to bed. We went into the bedroom, he threw himself on the bed and fell asleep on the spot. I undressed him tucked him in. He was sound asleep. I looked at him lying there sleeping. Then I turned out the lights and left ... (*Beat.*) ... I left his money on the table ... (*Beat.*) ... First time I ever did that. I always figured, once they get me there, what the fuck do I care if anything happens or not. Like at the dentist's. You got an appointment. They charge you whether you come or not. But this time, it just didn't seem ... Something ... When I got outside, it had almost stopped raining. I walked back to the square. I knew there was something waiting for me there. I didn't know what. But I had to go see ... Anyway, it was there in the bedroom with the surfer ... that I realized that I wasn't gonna be anyone's chicken anymore.

Inspector: ...

Him: It's got nothing to do with how old you are. Chicken is a way of life. A way of looking at life. It means going through life with a little smirk on your face, a smirk that says everything's gonna be fine, even if you're up to your eyebrows in shit. A smirk most people don't even notice. When it works, you stretch out naked on the bearskin rug and strut your stuff. And when it doesn't, you take off, on your tiptoes, the way you sneak away from some customer's house, at five in the morning while he's sound asleep. Saying to yourself, that guy was really cheap, but there'll be others. And you take off with his watch if you feel like he took more than he gave.

(*Pause.*)

Inspector: Finished?

Him: (*he nods yes.*)

Inspector: My turn now. Now that you've told me everything that crossed your mind. I'm surprised we didn't get to hear about your ancestors and when they first arrived from Brittany. And I still don't know any more than I did at one o'clock yesterday morning. You want me to tell you what I think of your story? Eh? Want me to tell you what I think you're after?

Him: (*doesn't budge*)

Inspector: Stop looking at me like I was dogshit. I wasn't born wearing a uniform. But I'm not about to tell you my life story just to make you cry. Your friend there ... Thursday night ... when you went to see him, I think you were stoned. Stoned outta your mind. I think you got into a fight cause he lives on Casgrain while you work the square for money, and the mountain for fun. I think you got into a fight and you lost control. I think you went nuts cause he wanted to kick you out. I think you killed him without realizing what you were doing. Then you went home and hid. And when you came down off your high, you were scared shitless. And you made up this whole friggin' story, just hoping you could pass for crazy. Right? Called the reporters. Arranged to steal Judge Delorme's keys. Where did you get them? Huh? Forget it. Don't bother. I know. In his pants pocket. Perfect set-up for blackmail, right? Did you steal them before you killed your boyfriend or after?

Him: After.

Inspector: That's right. What could he do about it? If he calls the cops, he's cooked, right? And all you had to do is call him and tell him: keep this case outta the papers or I call the reporters, or your wife, or the provincial police and I show them the keys ... Am I right or not?

Him: No.

Inspector: No? No, what? When are you gonna come out with it, for the love of Christ? Why did you take them? And when did you change your mind? And why? Listen. I've met hundreds of smartass kids like you. Ten a day, every day, for the past five years. I've seen all kinds. Some get into it cause they need the money to pay for university, and when they've got enough money, they stop. Some of them start one night when they're high on acid and they never come down. Others it's just too much beer. Some of them do it 'cause they're starving to death. Some come down from Out-remont, just for the trip. They come in all shapes and sizes. Tall and short, fat or skinny as a toothpick. I've seen some with faces that look like they been carved with a tomahawk. And others with real babyfaces. It's the 50-year-old ones that scare the shit outta you. Sometimes I wake up in a cold sweat in the middle of the night, thinking I can smell their perfume ... I'm not stupid. I know chickens aren't just something you eat for Sunday dinner. I knew it before you were even born. And your profound observations on the subject aren't teaching me a thing. Nothing! So drop the pretty speeches and deliver the goods.

Him: (*stares at the* Inspector *without blinking. Makes no move to respond. Pause.*)

Inspector: Okay. So let me tell you something else. Something you can call my wife and tell her when you get outta jail, or if they give you one last wish. Something I've never told anyone. There are times when I'm sitting at my desk and they're sitting there across from me and I look at them and I feel like crying my eyes out. Sometimes, if Guy wasn't there to transcribe what they're saying, I wouldn't be able to remember what they said for two, three, maybe ten minutes. I don't hear a thing. Nothing. They could be speaking Hebrew or Arabic, for all I understand. And it takes every last bit of strength I got not to tell Guy to leave. Not to get up and go over to them and take them in my arms. Okay? (*Beat.*) I've seen all kinds. You name it. But I hope I'll never see another one like you as long as I fuckin' live. I hope you're the only one of your kind. 'Cause your little trip is the lousiest, the sickest trip I've ever seen.

(*Pause.*)

Inspector: (*slowly, deliberately*) I don't know how I'm gonna prevent you from getting what you want. But you can be sure, I'm gonna do everything I can. I dunno how I'm gonna prove you stole those keys. I dunno know if I'm gonna have to commit perjury, but I'm gonna prevent you from implicating the judge. Not because he's a buddy. Not because there's anything in it for me. Not even to save my job; I've had tougher nuts to crack. I'm gonna do it just for the pleasure of shutting you up and taking you out of circulation. And for that pleasure, I'm willing to do anything. You hear me? Anything. I'm gonna get you. You can count on it. (*Beat.*) And for starters, I got a big disappointment for you. Your reporter friends aren't even gonna get to see you walk outta here. (*Shouts.*) Guy!

(*The* Stenographer *opens the side door and looks in. The* Inspector *motions him to come in and shut the door.*)

Inspectors: Have the reporters taken out to the lobby.

Stenographer: Okay.

(*The* Stenographer *opens the door.*)

Inspector: Wait.

(*The* Stenographer *closes the door and waits.*)

Inspector: Get instructions to Judge Delorme to come in through the back door of the courthouse. And make sure the photographer doesn't see him arrive. Then come back here.

Stenographer: Okay.

(*The* Stenographer *exits, closing the door gently behind him.*)

Inspector: (*brief pause*) Maybe it won't do any good. I'm too tired to think. But I'm gonna find a way, you can count on it.

Him: (*after a pause equivalent to the time it takes to count from 1,000 to 1,030, without looking at the* Inspector) I wasn't stoned. It was worse than that. I was in love. I never been in such a state in my life. I never been so out of it. I'd called him from the Peel metro station, to tell him I was on my way. I was feelin' good cause I'd had a good day and I wanted to invite him out for supper. Nothing fancy. Maybe at the Saint-Denis or Gabrielli's. Afterwards, we would've gone back to his place and made love. I called it recharging my batteries. Everytime I spent two hours in his arms, I felt like nothing bad could ever happen to me again. You're right – he lived on Casgrain Street and I work the square. But he never talked about it. And it's true that I sometimes went up on the mountain right after I left him. I'm an addict. Understand? You capable of understanding that? Sure you are. But you don't feel like it. If you let yourself understand that, how could you continue doing your job? You see, I'm capable of understanding things too. (*To himself again.*)

It's not true that doing it for money, or getting off on the mountain five nights a week and being in love is all the same thing. It's easier to believe that. But it's not true ... there are some things you're just born with, you don't get to choose. Your ass is no different from your head. Some people can't do any better than the quiz shows on Channel 10. And even that's an effort. Others, they write. They don't do it to put other people down ... but it just comes out beautiful. Fucking is the same thing. It's a gift. Either you got it or you don't. You do it well or you don't. Either you like it or you don't. I like it. Any old way. Doing it for money is just a job. I don't even want most of them to touch me. Some of them I do. Why some and not others? I dunno. I never bothered to ask myself the question. It's not necessarily the good-lookin' ones or the nice ones. It's sure not the rich ones. Some customers, I'll giv'em whatever they want as long as I don't havta take my clothes off. Others, I'll spend the night with them for the same price. But they're all just customers. I never forget there's cash at the end of the line. Even when they're really nice.

(*The* Stenographer *comes back in and closes the door behind him, silently. The* Inspector *motions to him to start transcribing.*)

Him: On the mountain, it's a whole other trip. I get to choose. And if I get fed up, I can drop it right there. And it's outside. Sometimes, just before dawn, when the birds first begin to sing, it's something else. It's so quiet. Almost everyone's gone home to bed. And the ones who are still around are finishin' up fast. It's always a real gang bang just before daylight. Then there's hardly anyone left on the trails. Sometimes I go there without lookin' for anything special. Just cause I know I'll be with other guys like me. All lookin' for the same thing: somebody to fool around with, have some fun, maybe get a bit of pleasure out of it, you never know. No more, no less. Sometimes I'm lucky and I pick up a couple of customers early at the square; when I figure I've made enough money and it's still early, one o'clock maybe, I go up on the mountain, don't even havta be stoned, and I spend the whole night walkin' around all by myself, playin' games. Sometimes it's Cowboys and Indians. Or Robin Hood. Sometimes I play war, I'm in enemy territory, the last survivor of a commando unit, and I practise walkin' around without makin' any noise. Can't let anyone see me or hear me. Sometimes it turns into a horror movie. I brace myself against a tree and let the spooks roll by. Until I can't stand it anymore ... that's usually when I imagine this ... guy, about 30-35, with a plaid shirt, fat, bald, and he's got a ... a knife. (*Beat.*) I don't even know where Brittany is.

(*The* Stenographer *looks up from his work, glances at the* Inspector. *But the* Inspector *is looking out the window.*)

Him: Anyway, if there's anyone who didn't care about my workin' the square, it was him. He was another one capable of understanding. He didn't mind my talkin' about it. Sometimes, when we spent the night together, just before I'd fall asleep I'd feel like this wave of disgust and I'd ask him to kill me to prevent me from going back. And he'd just take me in his arms and hold me so tight I couldn't breathe, and he'd whisper, shhhh, shhhhh. But I tried not to say things like that to him, even when I felt them, cause sometimes it made him cry. And I could take anything but that ... (*To the* Inspector.) To see a man come, any man, is the most beautiful thing I've ever seen in my life. Even if he's ugly. But with him, it was more than that. It was like the first sunrise. But I can't stand seein' a guy cry. I never know what to do. And when he cried, especially because of me, it was the end of the world. I'd rather disintegrate than make him cry. (*Back to himself.*) Sometimes he told me stories. Any old story. Hansel and Gretel. Little Red Riding Hood. He had a voice ... like ... made me feel ... I dunno ... just fine. He could've told me his carrot cake recipe with that voice and it would've had the same effect on me. Once he read to me out of a book by Claudel. The book was beside his bed. "Wait a minute, I'm going to read you something." He managed to get an arm free. He picked up the book. "Hold on, I can't read like this." I was sorta lyin' on top of him and he rolled me over on my back. He propped the book up on my chest and started lookin' for the page. When he found it, he moved up and kissed me. He said "Goodnight." And he moved back down and started to read. I can't remember what it was about. But I remember it's the only time in my life I ever fell asleep on my back. Like on an air mattress in the middle of a lake. He lent me the book. It's over at my place. I never managed to get beyond the part he read to me.

When I arrived at his place, he was cookin' supper. He'd bought some wine and he'd run me a bath. Stupid, huh? But that's all it took. When I saw the bath full of bubbles – I'd gone rushin' into the bathroom cause I had to pee bad – and when he came in behind me and put his arm around my chest and kissed me on the neck ... I stopped breathing on the spot. It wasn't ... how can I say it? ... it wasn't anything like the lovin' wife greetin' the husband when he gets home from a hard day at the office. It wasn't like the mother in "Father Knows Best." He was the one who joked about it afterwards. But it wasn't like that. He was a guy. A boy, I mean. And it was simple. Perfectly natural. It was like ... like ... suddenly I was at home. And I wanted so bad to make him as happy as he'd just made me. And the great thing was: I knew how. For the first time in my life, I was sure I understood how someone else's head worked. It was easy. So easy. All I had to do was ask myself what I felt, what I wanted, what would make me happiest in the whole world, and then do it for him. The way he'd just done for me. That's all. (*To the* Inspector *without looking at him.*) You fed up?

(Inspector *has his back to him, motions no. Pause.* Him, *without even looking at the* Inspector.)

Him: It won't be long now.

(Him *turns around to look at the* Stenographer *for a second then goes back to his previous position.*)

Him: We kissed for about a half-an-hour. Then I took my bath. Lukewarm. When I got out, supper was ready. There were two candles on the table. I lit them and I went to turn out the lights, but I stopped and asked him: "I like the candles, but I feel like seein' you, as clear as possible. Can we leave the candles *and* the lights on, or do you think I'm being silly?" He looked really surprised. He put the plates down on the table. I was still standin' over by the light switch. I felt pretty silly. I dunno why, when I feel really comfortable with someone, it makes me feel really silly. With him it was ridiculous. He came over and put his hands on either side of my neck. He took his time before answering. Then he said: "Yes, I think you're being silly. And I never knew anyone, with his head screwed on as tight as yours, who could be so silly. That might not be why I love you, but I think it's why I love you as much as I do. Just before you got here ... " Yeah, that's when he mentioned the bath. "Before you got here, just a few seconds before you came rushing in yelling 'Yoohoo, it's me, be right there' and went charging into the bathroom, I almost emptied the tub. I was afraid you'd think I was trying to play the loving wife. And I knew you wouldn't like it. The only role I want to play with you is that of your brother." His eyes were all watery. I kissed him before it got any worse. "If you'd arrived five minutes later, the tub would've been empty. So you can stop feeling silly."

By the time we remembered the food, everything was cold. And the candles had burned halfway down. Had to heat everything up again. At one point the phone rang. Some friends who were calling to get him to go to Expo and boo during the Confederation Day fireworks. Were part of some separatist group. Some nights when I went over to his place, he'd come home late, all excited. All heated up. Not drunk, but like he had a fever. Would take a while before I felt he was really there with me. Sometimes, in the beginning, when we hardly knew each other, he'd even try to tell me about their discussions. But it wasn't really him talkin' about that. Not the same guy I slept with anyway. In the beginning, the only reason I kept goin' back was to fuck with him. 'Cause as soon as one of us opened our trap, we were sure to have a fight. But once he threw his roommate out, all that changed. I know he still kept goin' to the meetings, but he didn't try to talk to me about it. (*Pause.* Him *sighs. Pause.*) When you're fed up, or when Guy runs outta paper, let me know and I'll shut up. (*Pause.*) Anyway, that night, when he hung up the phone, he hadn't changed. It was the opposite of what usually happened. I think that for a few seconds, a few minutes even, for the first time, it wasn't the dream his friends stood for that won out, it was the dream I stood for. Instead of changing scenes, while he was on the phone, he stayed there with me. I don't mean there in the kitchen, that's obvious, That's where the phone is. I mean he stayed there with me in his head. So he didn't have to shift back to me, like usual, like a stranger who had to get used to me all over again. It was just the opposite. He talked to them like he was talkin' to me. He told them he had somethin' real urgent to do, and he was looking right at me. I felt hot. I was shivering. Didn't know what to do. He told them he'd call them back the next morning. I think it had all been arranged in advance. Guess he figured we would've finished supper by then and he'd told them to call. And he changed his mind somewhere along the way. Anyway, it sounded like the girl on the phone was madder than hell with him.

When he hung up, he asked me if I intended to introduce him to my friends some day. I said I'd never thought about it. But it wasn't true and he could tell. I'd never thought about introducing him to my friends 'cause I never thought it would last. Even tho' we had been together for almost four months. The first time I ever dared believe it could last was while he was talkin' on the phone. Because of his voice and his hands. And his skin. His eyes. But he understood. He said that it was the same for him. That he didn't feel like mixin' up things that didn't go together. And that he knew that he'd probably have to choose. And that he thought he'd just made his choice.

I don't know how to explain it, but ... you don't havta believe me, but I'd like you to understand ... when he said that, he wasn't asking me to choose. He wasn't asking me to do anything. He just wanted me to know. That's all. We started to kiss again. And to make love. I think it's the only time in my life I ever really made love ...

You know those corny stories: I am him and he is me? Well, it's true. It exists. I dunno how to explain it. But that's the way it is. I didn't feel like I was holdin' someone in my arms. It was like there was no difference between him and me. I know that sounds corny and it pisses me off. It's like the words ... the words ... refuse ... Just hot air. Empty. There's no way you can put it into words ... I don't even think he could've done it. Anyway. That's the way it was. I don't remember thinkin', I should do this to him, I should do that to him. I wasn't thinking. It was just happening. We weren't on the floor anymore, between the fridge and the table. We were somewhere else ...

(*Angry.*) You see what I mean? Ya see? No way. How come there are no words for it? How come? You're supposed to be able to put everything into words. That's what they taught us in school, right? A word for everything. Everything has a name. Right? Just learn your irregular verbs and there's nothin' to it. Just learn to tell the subject from the object and where to put the adjective and you're home-free. No problem. All you have to do is say it and everyone will understand. Right? Forget those weirdos who spend their lives writing. They're sickies. Make a big deal outta nothin'. Got something to say? Say it. It's easy. So what the fuck is wrong with me? It's so simple. I know what I mean, so how come you don't understand? How come it doesn't come out right? When I try to talk about it, it sounds like some weird trip, but it was no trip. It was true. I was stone sober. We didn't even open the bottle of wine. I hadn't smoked a thing since noon.

We were holding each other. Rolling around. Moaning. Was it him or me? I dunno. I was like a yoyo. Like ... like ... What can I say? I felt like I was being turned inside out. Just when I was gonna come and him too, we'd stop and burst out laughin'. Then we'd hug each other even harder and flip over like pancakes. You name it, we did it. Then all of a sudden ... all of a sudden ...

(*Pause.*)

I don't know what happened. I guess we knocked the table too hard. I dunno. Anyway, stuff fell off the table. On the other side, a glass fell and broke. Maybe it was a plate. No. It was a glass. The plates stayed on the table. Then a knife fell, right in front of me. Right beside his head. We were on our way. We were gonna come together. For sure. For sure. I could feel it in every part of my body. And I could feel it dead centre. I thought I was gonna explode. And I know it was the same for him. Then ... Then ... I dunno. I could feel all that but at the same time, there was these other pictures going through my mind. And they felt as real as his skin, as our noises. As real as my hands, as the sound of the glass hittin' the floor ... It was all happening at once. Not over it or under it, but right there. You know how they say you see your whole life pass by just before you die? Well, it was just the opposite. I wasn't dying, I was being born. So I wasn't looking back. What I saw was ahead of me. Like realizing you're alive in the middle of an earthquake.

(Him *stands up*.)

He was so beautiful. So tall. So everything. He was all ... fur and flesh ... all rock. And he made me feel as beautiful as him. He. He. He went right through me. Understand? Eh? It was like nothin' I ever knew. I didn't know if I was coming or going. On my belly or flat on my back. Then a second later: Pow. Just when the knife hit the floor, in the time it took for the sound to register, we came. Together. Not him. Not me. Both of us. And suddenly I saw us. Me leavin' to meet my customers, or havin' to decide not to. And him, having to argue with his friends. How long could we have stuck it out? Eh? How long?

(*To the* Inspector.)

A while ago, you called me an asshole. Do you think I feel insulted? Dontcha think I know why you said that? Dontcha think I know how you wanted to make me feel? Do you think it's the first time?

Do you know how it feels to screw some guy, about this high and this wide? With a bald spot the size of a dinner plate? All pimply. With a purple nose. And you can tell he was good-lookin' when he was young and you know it wasn't just age that wrecked him. Married. With kids. A job. And you're afraid he's gonna have a stroke before he can say "take your pants off." Jumps on you like a tiger. Huffin'. Puffin'. Snortin'. Sweatin'. But he looks like a kid who's seen Santa Claus and can't believe it. He wants more. Lots more. But he comes after two minutes. And then he gets scared. Scared he's gonna get caught. His job. The wife. The kids. The pension. Labelled a FAG for the rest of his life. And while I go to take a piss (*He points to the side door.*) he has time to pull himself together. And he fuckin' flips out. Doesn't know where to hide. He wants to pull up his pants but he's forgotten how to do up his fly. His shirt half-buttoned. That's when his so-called real life takes over again. 'Cause what he just did was nothin' but a passing weakness. No doubt about it. Look, he's got a wife and a good job. Kids. Two cottages. A big car. He almost offered you all of it, just before he told you to take your pants down. But that's all over now. Now he feels like he had an epilepsy attack. Now that he's come, it's a whole other scene. He doesn't think about the fact that tomorrow morning he's gonna start all over again. He doesn't think about nothin'. He just throws your clothes on the floor beside the door and kicks your sneakers on top of the pile. Then he comes over to the bathroom door and starts screamin' and yellin': "Get outta here. Get out! Scram! Beat it. You hear me? Trash. Get out, I said. Out!" But that's nothing. If you're dumb enough to tell someone about it, one of your friends, and you tell him that while you were pissin', you thought to yourself, maybe this time he's gonna be all right. Cause you know he's gonna start all over again tomorrow. And you know he knows. You know that if you told anyone that you were ready, if he didn't have his usual fit, to give him a kiss and go for a walk with him. The one think he didn't dare hope for in his life, you were gonna offer it to him. You know that if you're dumb enough to tell that to anyone, they're gonna tell you you're stupid. Naïve.

How come people can spend ten minutes making love with someone, just once, and not know what he's dying of? How can you go through five guys a day and not wanta get involved? Eh? Can you tell me? How? That's my job, goddammit, to get involved. In the only way I know how. With my ass. I got nothing but my ass? So what the fuck, I havta use my ass to get involved.

With him. With ... with ... Claude. I saw it in his eyes. I saw everything shake, and I saw what he understood, all of a sudden. That's why we kept stoppin' just before we came. That's why we stopped 15 times. And every time, it started up again, stronger than ever ...

And the second the glass hit the floor, I knew I had to make a move. I knew we'd never be able to walk outta that apartment like nothing happened. We couldn't, shouldn't. We shouldn't even try to act like nothin' happened. The only thing that's real is him, screaming. Crying for joy, in my arms. I felt like we were drowning. I felt like we had almost drowned and suddenly it's all over, we're not in the water any more and we're breathing for the first time. I was drowning with him, in him. And there was the rest of the world. The opposite of what was happening to us. I know. I know real life means being able to handle both. I know. I know you gotta take the bad with the good. I know there's lotsa shit in life. I learned the hard way. You don't havta draw me any pictures. But right then and there, I wasn't thinking. Nothing else seemed real. Nothing. But we couldn't stay locked up, like monks, with the blinds down, living the love of our lives. And we couldn't relive what was happening then, just a few minutes a month, and spend the rest of the time dealing with everyone else. So all I remember is, suddenly I had the steak knife in my hand.

And I could feel it coming over me. I could feel it. I could feel myself taking off. Head first. Feet first. Spinning and exploding Then I heard our cry. Then ... then. All of a sudden. We were drowning. Then I heard crying again. Then I heard bubbles. Bubbles. Like in a milkshake. And then. Then. At the same time I could feel myself exploding. Drowning. And I could see us never leaving his place. Never getting up. And I could feel his sex, like a tree, exploding. Then already, I didn't have the knife in my hand anymore. And I was screaming. And he ... He ... His throat was bleeding. He was coming and at the same time his blood was spurting all over the place. On the windows. The fridge. The stove. The table. Then I was kissing him all over. Everywhere. Everywhere. On his wound. I was drinking his blood. I had it all over me. And he was still throbbing. And his body was still arching, and trembling. Just like mine.

Then, I guess I fell asleep. On top of him. Couldn't have lasted more than a few minutes. Something had changed. I think first thing I realized was that his heart wasn't beating anymore. Before I even opened my eyes. Before I really woke up. You know, on TV, when you see those guys, those runners, who fall on the ground as soon as they've crossed the finish line? I guess that's how they must feel – empty. That's all – empty.

Something had changed – everything.

I didn't look at him. I kept my eyes closed. I kissed him. He was still warm. I kissed him. All over.

I pulled myself away from him. Slowly.

Real slowly.

And I walked outta the kitchen without lookin'. I turned off the light. I took a shower. I think it was the best shower I ever took in my life. I went back into the kitchen and got dressed. That's when I looked at him. (*Beat*. Him *looks at* Inspector. *Looks away*.)

You know what? (*Beat*.) He was beautiful.

He wasn't even holdin' onto his throat. For a minute I was afraid it had hurt. But I'm sure it didn't. No. He was smiling. Lying there with his arms spread wide open. It's true, he couldn't have held on to his throat, he was holding on to me. I just hope. Just hope he didn't see the same pictures as me. I just hope he was born, without seeing what was ahead. Without seeing the other side of the coin first. I closed his eyes. I wasn't even able to do that for my father, cause I wasn't there when he died. My mother neither, cause she was alone when she died. But him, my brother, my twin, my reflection, him, yes, I closed his eyes. And he died of pleasure. Without seeing his life go to ratshit.

I love him.

When I left his body ...

I told you the rest ...

Later on, down by the port ...

I dunno ...

The second one who picked me up, in the square ... I thought about my sister ... I knew I had to call you, cause just the thought of ... rotting...
I give up.

(*Pause.*)

(*There are three loud knocks at the main door. The* Stenographer *gets up. The* Inspector *motions to him to take his things and leave with* Him *by the side door. The* Stenographer *picks up his things and goes over to* Him. Him *stands up, takes a small key case out of one of the front pockets of his jeans and throws the keys on the desk in front of the* Inspector. *The* Stenographer *goes over and opens the side door. Waits. Outside, the* Police Officer *is waiting in the doorway. The* Stenographer *walks out. The* Inspector *and* Him *exchange a long look.* Him *turns away and walks out slowly. The* Inspector *gets up and picks up the keys from the desk. Hesitates briefly, wondering whether he should clean up the judge's desk. Decides not to.*)

Gong.

Blackout.

THE END

Zero Hour

Arthur Milner

Arthur Milner has been resident playwright at The Great Canadian Theatre Company in Ottawa since 1983. He is the author of many plays for children and adults, including *Shanty Lake*, *Home Sweet Home*, *Robin Hood's Latest Adventure men of Cache* (with Greg Tuck), *1997*, *Cheap Thrill*, *Zero Hour*, *Learning to Live with Personal Growth*, *The City*, *Masada*, and *Sisters in the Great Day Care War*. He has also been involved as the writer on two GCTC collective creations, *Sandinista!* and *Red Tape, Running Shoes and Razzamattazz*. In 1992 Arthur Milner was appointed Artistic Director of GCTC.

Zero Hour was first produced by The Great Canadian Theatre Company in Ottawa on 14 May 1986.

PRODUCTION
Director / **Patrick McDonald**
Sets and Lighting Design / **Peter Gahlinger, Larry Laxdal**
Costume Design / **Sheila Singhal**
Music and Sound Effects / **Ian Tamblyn**
Stange Manager / **Season Osborne**

CAST
Robert Bockstael / Ross
James Bradford / Harlan
John Koensgen / Wade

Zero Hour was workshopped by the National Arts Centre English Theatre Playwright's Circle in March 1986, under the direction of David McIlwraith with Maureen LaBonté as dramaturge, and the following cast:

Robert Bockstael / Ross
Michael Hogan / Harlan
Tom MacBeath / Wade

SET
November 1985. San José, Costa Rica. A cell. A bunk bed, a toilet. A metal door with a small barred window.

CHARACTERS
Harlan Cole, 48 years old. He chose to do a doctorate in economics instead of playing professional football
Wade Sinclair, 38 years old, maybe from Texas. He is typical CIA material: well-built, well-educated, gregarious, and ambitious
Ross Gibson, a 22-year-old working-class kid from New Jersey, in good shape but smaller than Harlan or Wade

SCENE ONE

(As the lights come up, Ross *is sleeping.* Harlan *has just entered and is standing in front of the closed door. It's late afternoon.* Harlan *notices* Ross, *and looks over the cell. He moves to* Ross. Ross *opens his eyes.)*

Harlan: Buenos tardes.

(Ross *jumps away, scared, ready to fight.)*

Been here long?

Ross: Who're you?

Harlan: Harlan Cole.

Ross: What are you doing here?

Harlan: What are you doing here?

Ross: Where are we?

Harlan: Costa Rica.

Ross: I mean here.

Harlan: Looks like a jail cell.

Ross: You a lawyer?

Harlan: You need a lawyer?

Ross: You from the embassy?

Harlan: You need someone from the embassy?

Ross: Hey, what the fuck, man?

Harlan: What are you charged with?

Ross: I don't know.

Harlan: They didn't tell you?

Ross: No.

Harlan: But you were arrested.

Ross: No one said anything, man.

Harlan: You think you were arrested?

Ross: I don't know.

Harlan: Why do you think you were arrested?

Ross: Hey, I don't fuckin' know, all right?

Harlan: Sorry.

Ross: Fuck.

Harlan: What are you doing here? In Costa Rica?

Ross: I'm a tourist.

Harlan: Yeah.

Ross: Yeah, I'm just visiting.

Harlan: The border maybe? (Harlan *stands and moves towards the door.* Ross *freaks and jumps.* Harlan *calms him quickly and moves past him to check the door.*) They feeding you?

Ross: Fuck all.

Harlan: Nothing?

Ross: Rice and fucking beans.

Harlan: They hit you? (Harlan *is checking out the door.*)

Ross: Door's solid, man. Whole place is solid.

Harlan: They hit you?

Ross: No. You from the embassy?

Harlan: Have you been interrogated?

Ross: You're the first.

Harlan: You talk to anyone?

Ross: I haven't seen anyone.

Harlan: (*pointing at lightbulb*) All the time?

Ross: No. Who the fuck are you?

Harlan: Harlan Cole.

Ross: Were you arrested?

Harlan: No.

Ross: You here to help me?

Harlan: Yes. What are you doing in Costa Rica?

Ross: I'm a tourist.

Harlan: Sure.

(*Pause. The lights fade.*)

SCENE TWO

(Ross *is sitting on the floor. Prison sounds.* Harlan *goes to the door.*)

Harlan: (*into the hall*) Hey. Quiero ver el gerente. (*He paces. To* Ross.) What are you doing in San José?

Ross: I told you, man.

Harlan: Visiting. But what are you doing? Where are you staying?

Ross: A hotel.

Harlan: Nice hotel?

Ross: Yeah.

Harlan: What's it called?

Ross: The San José Hotel.

Harlan: Luxury hotel.

Ross: So?

Harlan: Very expensive.

Ross: I got money.

Harlan: They've got a great bar.

Ross: Yeah.

Harlan: I go there myself sometimes.

Ross: Yeah?

Harlan: You ever talk to the bartender, what's his name, Pedro?

Ross: No, man.

Harlan: That aquarium they've got, it's beautiful.

Ross: Oh yeah.

Harlan: Nicest angel fish I've ever seen. (*Pause*) The strippers are pretty good, too.

Ross: Yeah.

Harlan: There's no San José Hotel.

Ross: You don't know all the hotels, man.

Harlan: I know the big ones.

Ross: Yeah, well, this one's new.

Harlan: Where is it? At the border?

(Ross *gives up*)

You know Jim Kemp?

Ross: Who?

Harlan: Jim Kemp.

Ross: Never heard of him.

Harlan: How long've you been in here?

Ross: Four days.

Harlan: Long time.

Ross: Yeah.

Harlan: How are you feeling?

Ross: Bored out of my fuckin' mind.

Harlan: No, I mean ... let's see your eyes.

(Harlan *moves to* Ross, *slowly and cautiously. He looks closely at* Ross *and checks his eyes.*)

Ross: You a doctor or something?

Harlan: (*He stands.*) You're all right.

(Harlan *slams* Ross *with the back of his hand and sends him sprawling off the bench.*)

Ross: (*He smiles.*) Hey, you are from the embassy.

Harlan: I want to know what you're doing in Costa Rica.

Ross: I'm not scared of you, man.

Harlan: Good.

Ross: I'll tell you 'cause I know you're from the embassy.

Harlan: Start.

Ross: I could beat the shit out of you if I wanted to.

Harlan: I know.

Ross: Hey, I don't know why they picked me up.

Harlan: Who?

Ross: Hey, I'm a friend, right?

Harlan: Who?

Ross: The fucking Costa Rican government. They got to come down on someone, they take me. Big show, everyone's happy, right? Am I right?

Harlan: Who picked you up?

Ross: The Civil Guard.

Harlan: Where?

Ross: Zapote.

Harlan: What were you doing there? (Ross *doesn't answer.*) Look, if you want me to help you get out of here ...

Ross: (*pause*) Jim Kemp sent me to pick something up. He says someone's gonna meet me where the boat docks, right, but there's no one there. So I start walking to Zapote, these two guys stop me, take me back up river to where their car is ...

Harlan: You said Kemp wanted something picked up.

Ross: Yeah, they had a package with them.

Harlan: What was it?

Ross: I figured it was C-4 plastic and that's why they're coming with, cause of what happened with the last plastic.

Harlan: What happened?

Ross: To the plastic?

Harlan: Yes.

Ross: Which time?

Harlan: The first time. Before you went to Zapote.

Ross: Jim Kemp brought in six charges, right, and he tells ...

Harlan: When?

Ross: Three weeks ago.

Harlan: So ... Kemp brought in six charges ...

Ross: Yeah, and he tells Vega to stash them. Later on he says go pick 'em up and Vega comes back and ... you know Ricardo Vega?

Harlan: Yes.

Ross: Well, Vega comes back, he's only got one charge, right? He says I can't find the other five, I buried 'em, can't remember where. Jim Kemp was real pissed off but he sends us across the border with the one charge and when ...

Harlan: You crossed the border?

Ross: (*pause*) Yeah.

Harlan: Jim Kemp send you across?

Ross: No.

Harlan: Did he know?

Ross: Fuck man, I came to fight, not to be a fucking gopher for Jim Kemp.

Harlan: Did Kemp know?

Ross: No.

Harlan: Go on.

Ross: We cross the border into Nicaragua to set the last charge, right, but there's fuckin' Nica soldiers everywhere so we go back to Amparo. Then Vega sells the last charge to some guys from Costa Rica Libre. And those fuckers blow up a power line to Nicaragua, only it turns out that the power isn't going to Nicaragua, it's going to fuckin' Amparo. They blacked out Amparo and Jim Kemp's farm too. That was real funny, cause, you know, you look at the wires and, fuck, how's Costa Rica Libre supposed to know which way the power's going? Jim Kemp was real pissed off.

Harlan: Did you have much contact with Costa Rica Libre?

Ross: Hey, man, when I got here I heard Costa Rica Libre this, Costa Rica Libre that, I thought they were fucking communists. Who'd think they'd have a name like that and be on our side, right?

Harlan: Did you see them much?

Ross: I saw them. They talked a lot with the contras, and Vega, he'd slip 'em guns and ammo, and even some plastic sometimes. Or they'd be at the farm, they were cool, but I couldn't always tell if I was talking to one of them or to a Cuban or a contra. Or a fuckin' Civil Guard. Fuck the Civil Guard though. I mean, we helped those fuckers. They knew fuck all about guns, I showed 'em how to clean 'em, how to strip 'em, even how to fuckin' shoot 'em. We'd go drinking together in Amparo, then they fuckin' arrest me.

Harlan: So the two Civil Guard put you in their car ...

Ross: Yeah, a Toyota, you know, a jeep.

Harlan: Yeah.

Ross: Yeah, and we drive, and when we get to the cut-off to Jim Kemp's farm they go right by. I go to say something, the one guy, he puts his M16 in my nose. They put a hood over my head, tie me up and make me lie down in the back. We drove for a couple of hours, we spend a while in the car just sitting there, then we drove for another hour and they put me in this place.

Harlan: They say anything?

Ross: To me?

Harlan: Yes.

Ross: Just what I told you, man.

Harlan: They didn't tell you you were under arrest?

Ross: No.

Harlan: They talk to each other?

Ross: Yeah.

Harlan: What about?

Ross: I don't speak Spanish.

Harlan: But they spoke English.

Ross: Yeah, one of them.

Harlan: Good English?

Ross: Yeah.

Harlan: Accent?

Ross: Yeah.

Harlan: Did he speak good English or not? Was it a strong accent or not?

Ross: I don't know, he didn't say that much. Look, it was the fuckin' Guard, man.

Harlan: Maybe.

Ross: It was them.

Harlan: How do you know?

Ross: Million fuckin' spics runnin' around in camouflage, how you supposed to tell 'em apart.

Harlan: What if it wasn't the Guard?

Ross: Then who?

Harlan: You tell me.

Ross: No, it was them, man.

Harlan: If it wasn't?

Ross: Then you wouldn't be here.

Harlan: What's your name?

Ross: Ross.

Harlan: How old are you?

Ross: Twenty-two.

Harlan: Why did you come to Costa Rica?

Ross: To fight communism.

Harlan: That the best work you could get? ... What job did you quit to come fight communism in Costa Rica? You come to Costa Rica and get your head blown off or maybe you don't. What do you do next?

Ross: Vega said he'd look after me, maybe get me work in a training camp in Florida.

Harlan: Good job.

Ross: Hey man, I came down to fight communism, that's what I'm doing here. If we don't stop them in Nicaragua they'll be in Salvador and Costa Rica and then all over Central America. That's the plan, don't you know that? Jim Kemp says when Mexico goes communist there's gonna be five million refugees crossing into the U.S. and that'll wreck the U.S. without the Russians even firing one single shot. It's guys like me and Vega and Jim Kemp that are the ones putting our asses on the line. You guys, you sit in your fucking air-conditioned rooms at the embassy and you move your little papers around. You think that's gonna beat the communists? Fuck that.

Harlan: Jim Kemp say that too?

Ross: No, man, that's what I say.

Harlan: How did you meet Kemp?

Ross: Vega brought me.

Harlan: How did you meet Vega?

Ross: In Miami.

Harlan: What was he doing there?

Ross: Hey, I thought you knew him, man.

Harlan: I don't know him, I just heard of him.

Ross: He lives in Miami.

Harlan: So he's Cuban.

Ross: He's a Cuban-American.

Harlan: Who set it up for you to meet him?

Ross: There's a difference, you know.

Harlan: Okay.

Ross: His old man was at the Bay of Pigs thing in Cuba.

Harlan: Yeah.

Ross: Yeah, he died on the beach there 'cause Kennedy wouldn't give them air support even though the CIA planned the whole fuckin' operation. That Kennedy was a communist.

Harlan: How did you meet Vega?

Ross: You think Kennedy was a communist?

Harlan: How did you meet Vega?

Ross: Do you?

Harlan: Yes. How did you meet him?

Ross: I answered an ad in *The Defender* magazine. Someone called me up and asked me what I could do, and they said okay.

Harlan: What can you do?

Ross: I can fly backwards.

Harlan: (*pause*) Then what?

Ross: I took the fuckin', twenty-six hours on the fuckin' bus to Miami. Vega met me in this restaurant, Los something, really fancy, right. I even met the guy that owns it, uh, shit, I forget his name and some guys who were soldiers in Nicaragua before the communists took over.

Harlan: Did Vega tell you he was acting officially?

Ross: Oh yeah, he was.

Harlan: How do you know?

Ross: Well, he was always with Stassen and Martin Holme. You know them?

Harlan: No.

Ross: Oh, well, Martin Holme, he's from *The Defender*. And Stassen, he's real high up in the American Council for Freedom. I met all those guys, man. Stassen even had a letter from the President.

Harlan: From Reagan.

Ross: Yeah. I saw it, man, the fuckin' seal and everything. He said he read it out loud at an American Council for Freedom dinner.

Harlan: Did you read it?

Ross: He read it to us at the restaurant. It said "Dear Bob ..." It said Stassen was doing God's work and that Reagan personally thanked him for everything he did. And, oh, Stassen told me about all these guys who had lots of money in Nicaragua, and then when Vega took me to the airport this guy took our bags, right, and Vega was joking with him in Spanish and then Vega says to me, you know that porter I was talking to, that man owned a fuckin' castle in Nicaragua, he was a colonel in the National Guard and he had four sons and, get this, each son had a Mercedes fuckin' Benz. Now his wife makes tamales at home and the sons sell them on the street in Miami. That's what the reds did to them.

Harlan: So Stassen had a letter from Reagan.

Ross: Yeah.

Harlan: That's it?

Ross: That's what?

Harlan: Vega's official connection. Stassen's letter from the President.

Ross: You don't think a letter from the President's good enough?

Harlan: It doesn't prove he's acting officially.

Ross: Come on, man, no one moves in Miami without the CIA sanctions it. They're all the time bitching about it, too. Vega doesn't trust the U.S. this much 'cause of what they did to his old man, shit, he didn't like taking orders from the CIA, but he fuckin' took 'em.

Harlan: Why did Vega meet with Holme and Stassen?

Ross: Holme and Stassen raise money for guns. Vega moves 'em.

Harlan: Why did he take you?

Ross: Because he wanted me to meet these people.

Harlan: Why?

Ross: Just to see them.

Harlan: Twenty-two-year-old kid comes down from ...

Ross: ... New Jersey ...

Harlan: ... to fight communism. Now why does he take you with him?

Ross: C'mon, man, he just took me with, all right?

Harlan: How long were you in Miami?

Ross: Six days.

Harlan: Did they train you?

Ross: Vega took me to see one of the training camps but he said I already knew enough.

Harlan: About what? ... Look, I have to know about this. You want me to help or not?

Ross: Explosives.

Harlan: Where'd you learn that?

Ross: On my own. I got a feel for it.

Harlan: Yeah?

Ross: They didn't believe me neither.

Harlan: So they checked you out.

Ross: Yeah.

Harlan: But they didn't want you to teach in the camps.

Ross: Vega said they needed me in Costa Rica.

Harlan: For what?

Ross: I don't know.

Harlan: Ross ...

Ross: I don't know, man.

Harlan: Did you ask?

Ross: He just said don't worry.

Harlan: And when you got to Costa Rica, he didn't tell you what he needed you for?

Ross: No.

Harlan: Did you ask?

Ross: Fuck, man, I told ya.

Harlan: Vega tells you in Miami they want you for something special. But he doesn't tell you what. He doesn't get you to teach the contras in Miami how to use explosives. And then you get to Costa Rica and he still doesn't tell you what he wants you for.

Ross: Yeah.

Harlan: And you're pissed off because no one'll let you fight.

Ross: Yeah.

Harlan: But you didn't ask him.

Ross: He never said.

Harlan: You want me to help you?

Ross: Fuck, man, I told you.

Harlan: How did you get into Costa Rica?

Ross: Just walked off the plane.

Harlan: Sure.

Ross: This guy in a blue uniform meets us and we walk right in, didn't check our papers or nothing. Someone's waiting for us, he takes us to San José. Then another guy takes us to Jim Kemp's farm. And then Jim Kemp checked me out, said if there was anything I needed, to clear it with him.

Harlan: He was in charge.

Ross: Yeah, he's the CIA liaison.

Harlan: How do you know that?

Ross: He told me.

Harlan: Hi, I work for the CIA.

Ross: Pretty near. He said he's the CIA liaison and he's the fuckin' contra liaison too. He said it like it's secret, right, but he was always joking about it, like this one time he said that every month the U.S. government puts ten thousand bucks into his Miami bank account, and then, then he said, God help me if the revenue people find out about it.

Harlan: What did you do there?

Ross: At the farm?

Harlan: Yes.

Ross: Hung around. We'd off-load planes that'd land on his strip. Go to Amparo and get pissed. Then the contras'd come, and Jim Kemp and Vega and them'd talk, and I'd bring 'em coffee.

Harlan: Did they let you listen?

Ross: If I looked like I was interested they'd ask me to leave. They talked mostly in Spanish anyway. Fuck, man, I was getting really pissed off 'cause I expected to see some action and I talked to Vega about it. And then when he went to set that charge that time after Jim Kemp chewed him out, he said to me do you wanna come.

Harlan: Vega crossed the border, too?

Ross: Yeah.

Harlan: He's pretty high up.

Ross: Well, he knew Stassen and Martin Holme. And those guys treat him with respect.

Harlan: But he crossed the border.

Ross: Yeah, he wanted to fight too, man.

Harlan: And he sold the plastic.

Ross: Yeah, but it was to either Costa Rica Libre or the Civil Guard. Vega's always moving, making deals, making friends. And Costa Rica Libre can do things we can't, they got friends high up in San José.

Harlan: Who?

Ross: Some guy in the government. The guy that runs the police.

Harlan: Minister of the Interior.

Ross: Yeah, the interior, what the fuck's the interior, anyway?

Harlan: The guy that runs the police.

Ross: Yeah, right, thanks man.

Harlan: You think Vega set you up?

Ross: Fuck, man, I got no grief with Vega.

Harlan: Maybe he told Kemp you crossed the border.

Ross: He wouldn't do that.

Harlan: So why did Kemp set you up?

Ross: He didn't know I crossed.

Harlan: Maybe he did.

Ross: No way.

Harlan: Maybe he had some other reason to set you up.

Ross: I wouldn't know.

Harlan: Looks like someone set you up.

Ross: Yeah.

Harlan: I think you're right.

Ross: 'bout what?

Harlan: You're in prison because they have to come down on someone. Big show. Everyone's happy.

Ross: Can you get me out?

Harlan: No.

Ross: I'm a U.S. citizen.

Harlan: That doesn't matter.

Ross: What's the embassy for?

Harlan: The embassy didn't ask you to come to Costa Rica.

Ross: Fuck, what do you do at the embassy, anyway?

Harlan: I work with the cultural attaché.

Ross: You came to get me out, right?

Harlan: (*pause*) No.

Ross: Then why'd they send you?

Harlan: To pass the time, I guess.

Ross: What're you doing here?

Harlan: I don't know.

Ross: Fuck, man, I been straight with you.

Harlan: I don't know why I'm here.

Ross: Who sent you?

Harlan: I was getting into my car, two guys point guns at my head.

Ross: But you're from the embassy.

Harlan: Yeah.

Ross: Holy fuck.

Harlan: Yeah.

Ross: Holy fuck. (*pause*) Going into the embassy, that's fuckin' serious, man. You must be in real shit. I come down here to fight communism and you're from the embassy, and they fuckin' arrest us. Why would they do that? You gotta have some idea, right? Maybe they don't trust you or something. You selling embassy secrets? It's gotta be something pretty heavy for them to go into the embassy. ... This is really, really fucked. You know, man, sometimes I wonder what I'm doing down here. You ever think about that?

(*Prison noises off stage. Then the lights fade.*)

SCENE THREE

(*As the lights come up* Harlan *is seated and* Ross *is doing push-ups.*)

Ross: You should be doing something to keep in shape. We could be in here a long time. ... You wanna do some with me? ... Fuck, man, I wish a had a gun. (*He mimes firing a pistol.*) You don't shoot every day, you lose the edge. It's something you gotta do every day.

Harlan: Like playing the violin.

Ross: Yeah, right. Hey, you know the Beretta 92SB dash F?

Harlan: No.

Ross: It's the new standard army pistol. Short recoil, semi-automatic. Mean nine-calibre piece, man. I got the 92SB. Same thing as the dash F but, no way was I gonna pay fifty bucks extra for a few fuckin' fluorescent dots on the sights, then I read in *The Defender* that in a stress situation the dots'd just confuse you anyway. Six hundred bucks apiece. I got one at home, couldn't bring it with me, right? You shoot much?

Harlan: No.

Ross: Cultural attaché, huh?

Harlan: Assistant to the. (*Prison sounds*)

Ross: I guess you don't need guns for that, huh? ... Don't you carry a gun?

(*The door opens,* Wade *comes flying in, blindfolded. The door closes behind him.* Harlan *removes* Wade's *blindfold.*)

Wade: Harlan, what are you doing here? ... What's going on?

Ross: Who're you?

Wade: What's going on?

Ross: We don't know.

Harlan: They arrest you?

Wade: No one said I was under arrest. Two Civil Guard ...

Ross: You sure?

Wade: Por favor, señor Sinclair. Lo siento, señor Sinclair, take me to their car, put this (*blindfold*) on me.

Harlan: The Costa Rican government does not arrest embassy people.

Ross: Maybe they started.

Harlan: Who're they gonna bring in next, the ambassador?

Wade: I hope so.

Ross: Maybe they're picking up Americans all over Costa Rica.

Harlan: This isn't Lebanon, Wade.

Wade: Shit, Harlan, we're here, ain't we?

Harlan: So what's going on?

Wade: How the hell do I know? You got any ideas?

Harlan: (*pause*) He's been at the farm.

Wade: With Jimbo?

Ross: Yeah.

Wade: Welcome to the fifty-first state ... Tico-land? Costa Rica? Wade Sinclair, son. (*offers his hand*)

Ross: Ross Gibson Jr.

(Ross *and* Wade *shake hands.*)

Wade: Imagine them spics treatin' us like this. Even odds we bought them this place, and their shiny weapons too. How long have you been here, Harlan?

Harlan: A few hours.

Wade: (*to* Ross) You?

Ross: Four days.

Wade: Have they been ... cruel?

Ross: Fuck man, I haven't even seen anybody.

Wade: They feed you?

Ross: Yeah.

Wade: Thank god for that. It's some mistake, Harl. (*He pounds on the door.*) Come on you friendly Ticos. I'm the first secretary at your favourite embassy, I demand to be interrogated. Stupid spics. (*to* Ross) You know they call Costa Rica the Switzerland of Central America? Truth is it's the Puerto Rico of Central America.

Ross: No way they're gonna arrest people from the embassy.

Wade: Yeah, well maybe we're hostages. Let's think. Who'd want us? And what the fuck for? ... You start, Harlan. This is more or less your field. ... I'll start you off. The Ticos, I mean the government of Costa Rica, acting in an official capacity. Why? Wait. This place wired?

Ross: It's all right, man, I checked it out.

Wade: Good. Okay Harlan, the friendly Ticos. Why?

Harlan: For show.

Wade: If it was for show, they'd pick up some merc like ...

Ross: I'm not a mercenary.

Wade: Well, what are you, then?

Ross: I'm an adventurist.

Wade: They'd arrest an adventurist like Ross, here, and make a speech about Costa Rican neutrality. They wouldn't touch the embassy.

Ross: Not unless it's sanctioned.

Wade: Big word. By who?

Ross: The CIA.

Wade: Why?

Ross: Kill us, blame it on the Sandinistas.

Wade: CIA do a lot of that? ... Who's next?

Ross: The contras.

Wade: Why?

Ross: Same reason. But they wouldn't go near the embassy either, unless it was sanctioned. They'd want the okay from Jim Kemp.

Wade: Jimbo.

Ross: Costa Rica Libre might do it.

Wade: Smart kid.

Ross: They could even do it without Jim Kemp.

Harlan: ARDE (*AR-day*), FDN, MDN, UNO (*OO-Noh*), you know this shit, Wade, some of them like us, some of them hate us, doesn't matter, there'll be a new one tomorrow.

Wade: That don't stop any of them from wanting us dead.

Harlan: Us. (Harlan *and* Wade) Then why's he (*Ross*) here?

Wade: (*to* Ross) Harlan's very important. He's assistant to the cultural attaché. That means he's in charge of Coke sales here in Costa Rica, the drink, not the drug. Maybe the mothers of kids with cavities are out to get you, Harl. (*pause*) What about the Company, Harlan? What do you think?

(*pause*) C'mon, Harlan. This is too important for the usual rules of secrecy.

Harlan: If the Company's involved, you know about it.

Wade: I know you mean that as a compliment, but I want to think it through. If the Company's involved, I know about it. That means either the Company isn't involved, or else I know what's going on. I don't know what's going on. So the Company must not be involved. But that doesn't satisfy me. If there's one thing I've learned in this business it's that no one's safe. Someone might not like the colour of my eyes.

Harlan: So we're hostages.

Wade: Whose?

Ross: Hostages are for trading. I'm not worth trading. And I got nothing to hide, not from our people. I've been in here four days, I haven't seen anybody, no one's asked me a thing. They slip food in under the door. It's like they don't want to be bothered.

Wade: I think there's a lot in what the boy says, Harlan. If ARDE's got us, well they might wanna trade for CIA money. But you couldn't trade the kid for a tortilla. Maybe the Ticos are trying to make a point but we're big fish, Harlan, too big for the friendly Ticos.

Harlan: You're going in circles.

Ross: What about the Sandinistas?

Wade: What about 'em?

Ross: They're communists.

Wade: Yeah.

Ross: Yeah, well, maybe they got the order from the Soviets. And they're pickin' up Americans all over and making a move into Costa Rica.

Wade: Call in the marines!

Harlan: Something unusual is happening, Wade.

Wade: You think Nicaragua's invaded Costa Rica?

Ross: There's a fucking war.

Wade: What are they gonna do?

Ross: They're gonna kill us.

Wade: Here in Tico-land?

Ross: Anywhere.

Wade: They do that kind of thing?

Ross: Yeah.

Wade: Really?

Ross: Yeah. Those two Civil Guards.

Wade: On the border.

Ross: Yeah.

Wade: That's the border.

Ross: So?

Wade: Take it, Harl ... (*looking at* Harlan) Someone, I don't know who, fires across the border. The Sandinistas shoot back, they hit a couple of guards. How are the Sandinistas supposed to know they were friendly Ticos? (*To* Harlan) Did I get it right?

Ross: Why are you defending them, man?

Wade: I'm just telling you what happened. Don't quote me.

Harlan: What ...

Ross: Jim Kemp says the Sandinistas are gonna invade Costa Rica and it's only 'cause we're keeping them pinned down inside Nicaragua that they don't.

Wade: Right, let's keep 'em there. Now, back to the Company.

Harlan: What are you doing, Wade?

Wade: I'm just ...

Harlan: We get picked up in the middle of San José and you act like you're on a game show. Except that within two minutes of walking in here you announce to the world that we're ... CIA.

Wade: Ross here isn't stupid. He's figured out for himself that the cultural attaché doesn't need an assistant. I'm just trying to figure out what's going on, and I want to know what you think. That make you uncomfortable, Harl? Ross isn't uncomfortable, he isn't hiding anything, are you Ross? I got nothing to hide, from friends. But I'm glad you let me know you're upset, Harl, this is a good place to get things off our chests. What about you, son, you upset too?

Ross: About being in here?

Wade: Well, Harlan says I'm upsetting him. Am I doing anything that upsets you?

Ross: No.

Wade: See, Harlan. (*pause*) No air conditioning. I'm gonna have to talk to the ambassador about that.

Harlan: Ross crossed the border.

Wade: Into Nicaragua?

Ross: No, into fuckin' Afghanistan.

Wade: Good work, Harlan, what else you find out?

Harlan: He's lying about something.

Wade: 'bout what?

Harlan: I don't know.

Wade: You keeping secrets from us, Ross? (Ross *doesn't answer.*) So, you crossed the border. Jimbo send you across?

Ross: Man, I came down here to see some action, I spent a thousand bucks of my own money to come ...

Wade: Did Kemp send you?

Ross: No.

Wade: You just went.

Ross: Fuck.

Wade: By yourself.

Ross: No.

Wade: With who?

Ross: Some people.

Wade: Name one.

Ross: Ricardo Vega.

Wade: Richard Vega took you.

Ross: Yeah.

Wade: You like Vega?

Ross: Yeah.

Wade: You trust him?

Ross: Yeah.

Wade: Did Jimbo explain why you couldn't cross the border?

Ross: Yeah.

Wade: Jimbo's very sensible. Jimbo's the salt of the earth. You should listen to him. Did he tell you about his neighbour Bruce?

Ross: Yeah.

Wade: Did he show you those pictures in *Life* magazine? Bruce with the wife and kids in the friendly Tico sunset? Bruce charging through the trees in camouflage, Bruce with twenty contra up to their pits in water, their M16's held high over their heads. That stream runs through Bruce's farm and it's this high (*half metre*) and they're on their asses to make it look deep. I love Bruce. Salt of the earth that man. Bruce was a poet too. "Just a little piece now and a little piece later, until we're all gobbled up by the Red Alligator. Remember, you can't play good guy with murderers and thugs ...

Ross: ... or shake off their threat with handshakes and hugs."

Wade: Too bad the friendly Ticos had to kick him out of Tico-land. What did Jimbo say when you asked why you couldn't fight in Nicaragua? ... Tell us.

Ross: Why doesn't the fuckin' army just invade!

Wade: What did Kemp say?

Ross: He said they don't want U.S. citizens caught in Nicaragua.

Wade: Jimbo's a very sensible man.

Ross: (*pause*) You gonna tell him I crossed?

Wade: I don't know.

Ross: Come on, man, don't tell him, all right?

Wade: (*to* Harlan) What do you think?

Harlan: Get him (*Ross*) out of Costa Rica.

Wade: That's kind of extreme, Harl.

Harlan: There's no controls. It makes the Company vulnerable.

Wade: They're doing things for us, they're risking their lives.

Harlan: There's procedures, Wade.

Wade: Sometimes you got to compromise.

Harlan: There's rules.

Wade: That's funny, you talking about rules.

Harlan: The border's a zoo.

Wade: Aw, they're just taking a little initiative, Harlan. Anyway, it's none of your fucking business.

Harlan: You asked what I thought.

Wade: Did I?

(*Pause. The lights fade.*)

SCENE FOUR

(*Lights come up. Middle of the night, no one can sleep.* Wade *is hitting the bench with his fingertips.*)

Harlan: Wade. (Wade *continues.*) Hey!

Wade: (*He stops.*) Fuckin' Tambs.

Harlan: Something bothering you?

Wade: I like it here. The quiet, the home cooking. (*pause*) This wouldn't have happened with Windsor.

Harlan: What wouldn't happen?

Wade: This.

Harlan: What's this?

Wade: Us. Here.

Ross: Who's Windsor?

Harlan: Ambassador before Tambs.

Ross: You don't like Tambs?

Harlan: He's not very popular.

Ross: What's wrong with him?

Wade: Noting a brain couldn't fix. (Ross *laughs.*) They threw him out of Colombia.

Ross: Yeah, I knew that.

Wade: He fucks up there, they send him here.

Ross: Why would they do something like that?

Wade: Same reason they do anything. He's got friends.

Ross: Jim Kemp says he's all right.

Harlan: Kemp likes anyone that hates Reds.

Ross: Yeah.

Harlan: Tamb's got the speech down and it's the same speech Kemp makes, only Kemp put it together himself and it took him twenty years to write. He doesn't know you learn that speech the first day of ambassador school.

Wade: Ooo, I don't know if you should be talking about a U.S. ambassador like that, Harl. Besides, I thought you liked him, I thought he was your kind of man.

Ross: Vega doesn't like him either.

Wade: Yeah.

Ross: He said Tambs came down hard on drug traffic in Colombia, now he's doing it here. He said how do they expect the contras to raise money.

Wade: I thought you liked Tambs, Harlan.

Harlan: Why?

Wade: You didn't like Windsor.

Harlan: He was ineffective.

Wade: I thought Windsor put forward the U.S. position very well. Costa Rica should have an army. And shove neutrality up their ass.

Harlan: And Costa Rica threw him out.

Wade: That's not true, Harlan.

Harlan: They asked the U.S. government to remove him.

Wade: We should've refused. The U.S. gives the Ticos a few hundred million dollars every year. You'd think it'd buy us something.

Harlan: He's a diplomat, Wade. He's supposed to be diplomatic.

Wade: You're so traditional.

Harlan: (*pause*) We've been in here too long. The embassy knows we're missing now.

Wade: Relax.

Harlan: Like you?

Wade: You want me to bite my nails?

Harlan: You're too calm.

Wade: Look at the kid. He's been here four days.

Harlan: You throw fits when you run out of staples.

Wade: My mother was like that. My brother was dying of cancer, you've never seen anyone as calm. But when she burned the toast, she cried for an hour. She said some things are God's will. Burning the toast isn't.

Harlan: That's not good enough.

Wade: The truth is, Harlan, I set this up. I wanted a chance for us to talk. You know what a pain in the ass you've been, I thought we could have it out. (*pause*) Actually Ross and I set this up. (*pause*) Maybe Ross set this up.

Ross: Fuck.

Wade: Maybe he's an undercover Sandinista. You a communist, Ross?

Ross: Man, you fuck right off.

Wade: What do you think, Harlan? (Wade *threatens* Ross.) He's the one that said the Sandinistas set this up. You think he's trying to throw us off? (*to* Ross) Who you working for, kid? How many times you been to Nicaragua? You can't fool us. (Ross *is very confused.*) Look at him. You think he's just pretending to be confused? ... You're no fun, Harl.

(*The lights fade to black.*)

SCENE FIVE

(*Lights come up.* Ross *and* Wade *are doing push-ups.*)

Wade: One, two, three, seven. One, two, three, eight. One, two, three, one. One, two, three, two. One, two, three, three. (Wade *stops, exhausted.* Ross *continues.*) All right, you're making me feel bad. I can't even count any more.

Ross: (*He continues, then stops.*) I don't have a passport.

Wade: What?

Ross: I don't have a passport. How'm I going to get home without a passport?

Wade: What the fuck you do with it?

Ross: I gave it to Vega.

Wade: We'll get Tambs working on it. Where you from, Ross?

Ross: Newbury.

Wade: Where's that?

Ross: North end of New Jersey.

Wade: What do people do in Newbury, New Jersey?

Ross: Nothing.

Wade: What's your dad do?

Ross: He works for Goodyear.

Wade: Yeah.

Ross: Yeah, he worked there thirty years.

Wade: Long time to work for one company. (*to* Harlan) Don't you think that's a long time, Harl? (*to* Ross) You want to work there, too?

Ross: My brother tried to, right? My old man figured after working there so long they could get his son a job, specially since Brady's a vet. Goodyear said they had to go through the union, union said he was way down on the list.

Wade: What about you, what were you doing before you came here?

Ross: I was gonna go in for electronics after high school, but ... I sold magazines for a while, then I was picked up for, I ripped off a car. So, then, well my brother was in Vietnam and I was pissed that I didn't get to go.

Wade: That why you came to Costa Rica?

Ross: I didn't care where much, I just wanted to see some action. I was in Junior ROTC and the Civil Air Patrol. I been reading *The Defender* for years, man, training myself.

Wade: Did you try to enlist?

Ross: No.

Wade: They train you.

Ross: I'm trained, man, I want to see action.

Wade: You sorry you came?

Ross: You could spend your whole life in Newbury and not meet the people I've met or learn the things I've seen. Like Jim Kemp, I never met anybody like him in Newbury.

Wade: It's warm here, too.

Ross: Beats the hell out of winter in New Jersey.

Wade: ¿Aprendes español?

Ross: I don't think I'm much good at languages.

Wade: What's Jim Kemp like?

Ross: You don't know him?

Wade: What do you think of him?

Ross: He's doing what he wants to do, he's good at it. I don't know. This one time, this contra came in, right, with his whole fuckin' leg blown right off. Jim Kemp, he bandaged him up, himself, and sent him off to the hospital in San José. After he left, Jim Kemp said he's gonna lose his other leg too and you could see he had tears in his eyes, that's the kind of guy he was. Sometimes late at night we'd just sit and talk, just him and me. Like he'd explain about communists in Congress, he even knew their names. He's got one of them dish antennas and we'd watch TV, he used to watch those preachers, just like my old man. Fuck, he was really good at explaining things, like these people from the U.S.'d come, newspaper people, and like one time, you could tell she was a communist, you know, like from the questions she was asking, but Jim Kemp, he'd explain things real calm and real straight.

Wade: Harlan tell you he used to play pro football?

Ross: Who for?

Harlan: I didn't.

Wade: I thought you did.

Harlan: I could have played, I didn't.

Wade: But you were all-American, right? The Forty-niners wanted to sign you.

Harlan: The Rams.

Wade: You should have signed.

Ross: Why didn't you, man?

Harlan: I wanted an M.B.A.

Ross: What's that?

Harlan: Master of business administration.

Ross: Fuck. You guys got any kids?

Wade: A boy and two girls.

Ross: What do they do?

Wade: They're in school.

Ross: (*to* Harlan) You got kids? (Harlan *isn't paying attention.*) Yo! Harl!

Harlan: One's an architect, my daughter's in medical school.

Ross: How did you get to work for the ... Company?

Wade: You looking for a job?

Harlan: They asked me.

Ross: Just like that.

Harlan: I was doing a Ph.D. in economics and my uncle asked if I would put my education at the service of my country.

Wade: You should've said no. You ever wonder about that, Harl? You got all this education and you're still a fuckin' operative. I don't have a Ph.D. and I'm ten years younger than you. You ever wonder why my career has taken off and yours is still in first gear? I think it's a question of attitude. (*pause*) So, you want to work for the Company, son?

Ross: Yeah.

Wade: You wanna help the contras?

Ross: Yeah.

Wade: You know much about 'em?

Ross: I know that they're fighting for freedom.

Wade: Sort of.

Ross: Meaning?

Wade: Well, Harlan could tell you some stories that'd curdle your blood. Harlan doesn't pretty things up, he's got a mind that sees things the way they are. ... But today, I don't know why, he's holding back. See ... (*to* Harlan) I want you to listen to this, Harl, I want you to tell me if I got it right ... (*to* Ross) now the contras fight two ways. In the first, hit and run, they attack farms, health centres, schools. They blow up the buildings, kill whoever's handy. Sometimes they rape, sometimes they mutilate.

Ross: I don't believe that.

Wade: Ask Harlan.

Ross: That's communist disinformation. That's what Jim Kemp says.

Wade: I've said that too. I'm saying this just for you and Harlan. Now the second way they fight is called take and hold. Three hundred contras sweep into a town and hold it. They make speeches, execute some Sandinistas. We like it when the contras take territory. We like it because it makes them look like a real army and people in Congress like that. But when the Nica army finds out where the contras are, they wait with those new helicopters they got from the Soviets, and rat-ta-tat-ta-tat. So before Congressional votes we got to convince the contra commanders to order take and holds. Now they're sitting in hotel swimming pools in Honduras and Miami so they don't mind take and holds. But your actual man on the ground, he prefers hit and run.

Ross: Shit.

Wade: Pardon.

Ross: I talked to contras, man, they're just ordinary guys fighting for their country.

Wade: Guys like Krill, you know Krill?

Ross: No.

Wade: He worked with Suicida, out of Honduras. An ordinary guy, an ordinary soldier in the Guard, but when be became a contra, he changed. He turned into a natural leader of men. Strict, mind you. I understand he's killed at least forty of his own men, some, I've heard, for being late. But mostly he was a quiet, thoughtful guy. He liked to go off by himself and fire his machine gun into the hills.

Ross: I don't know what the fuck you're doing, man, you got some really strange things going on inside your head.

Wade: As God is my witness.

Ross: How come you're putting down the contras?

Wade: You want to fight, I'm just telling you ...

Ross: No, you're putting them down. You're saying the same thing as the communists ...

Wade: Help me, Harl.

Harlan: Leave him alone.

Wade: You're always goin' on about how we gotta know the truth. Ross is one of us, isn't he?

Harlan: What do you want?

Wade: Stick up for me.

Harlan: (*to* Ross) He's right.

Ross: Fuck.

Wade: Give him some detail. Matiguas. Do it.

Harlan: Shy?

Wade: Trust me.

Harlan: Matiguas. June nineteenth, 1985. A wedding party. Seven males, nine females ambushed by contra under the command of Oswaldo Lopez. Discovered by a Dutch television crew. The men and older women appeared to have thirty to fifty rounds each fired into them at close range. The girls were raped and strangled.

Wade: Or strangled and raped. What kind of weapons did the wedding party have?

Harlan: They were unarmed.

Wade: And where is Oswaldo Lopez now?

Harlan: He commands a contra camp in Honduras.

Wade: What was the name of the guy in Matagalpa? ... Harlan.

Harlan: Gustavo Romualdi owned a coffee plantation. President of the Nicaraguan Association of Coffee Growers. Abducted from his home August nineteenth. Found dead in Matagalpa eight days later.

Wade: Don't hold back, Harl.

Harlan: His arms, legs, and head were missing.

Wade: His dick, too. But we didn't just sit on our behinds. Now follow me here. We found out that Romualdi voted against the Sandinistas in the election. We said the Sandinistas killed Romualdi and that we had very convincing evidence they'd started a highly secret campaign to exterminate businessmen. The Sandinistas censored the story in *La Prensa*, but they couldn't bury it. Papers in Costa Rica and Colombia picked it up. So did the *Times* in Washington. You know what happened then? Contra radio broadcast a warning from Honduras. They said, I'm translating here, "Coffee production in Nicaragua must be stopped. Anyone that cooperates with the communists will be dealt with. Gustavo Romualdi is an example of what will happen." They ran that broadcast four times, and the *Times* in New York picked it up before we killed it. I just want you to understand, son. I know Rambo and John Wayne don't rape and mutilate. But that's the kind of war we got. You still want to fight? ... Once you understood how important burning schools and mutilating corpses was in the fight against communism, shit, you'd jump right in. Death is pretty much the same from one round in the gut or fifty. So I've heard, anyway.

Harlan: Why are you doing this, Wade?

Wade: For you, Harlan. I'm trying to show you I know the difference between the lies and the truth. I know how important that is to you.

Harlan: Why're you doing this now?

Wade: ... Mid-life crisis.

(*Lights fade.*)

SCENE SIX

(*As the lights come up,* Wade *is standing in front of the door with a tray of food in his hands.*)

Wade: (*He looks at the food.*) Where do you think we are, Nicaragua? (*He laughs.*) Cigarettes! (*He opens a pack of cigarettes.*) You smoke, Ross?

Ross: No.

Wade: Good for you, (*He lights one.*) See, you light the end with the brand name on it. That way, when they find the butt, they can't tell what brand it was so they don't know who smoked it. It's an old spy trick. You hungry? (Wade *offers the food to* Ross. Ross *shakes his head.*) Have some, keep your strength up. You know, when I was your age, no, I might've been a bit older, I was at university. There was the moratorium and every-one was skipping class to protest the war in Vietnam. My father came to school and sat with me. For two hours we sat all alone. No students, no teacher. One day I got a letter asking me if I was interested in an impor-tant government position. The duties included foreign travel and it would be like working for the State Department. When I was in training there was a party one night and this guy asks me what I'm doing in Washing-ton. He was real persistent but I kept giving him the cover story, some shit about working for the Department of Agriculture. Then he went to talk to someone else. The next day there were a few of us missing from class and the same guy was there to talk to us about communism. He told us it was real important to watch who we talked to. He said the Soviets were recruiting agents all over the U.S. He said they prey on shy, lonely outcasts and recruit them into the American Communist Party. These peo-ple have no friends, no links to decent society. The Soviets brainwash and exploit these sad people to the point where they're willing to violently overthrow our government. He told us some of them have made it into high positions in the government, even into the CIA. He said to us, you people are not going to let that happen. We used to sing the national an-them before classes then, every morning, we'd stand up and I'd close my eyes and I'd just sing. Jesus, I loved to sing it. Now the Company's differ-ent. People fuck around. All they care about is better postings and more money. The spirit's not the same. ... We need more people like you, Ross, people with the right spirit, the right commitment ... You got the makings, son.

Harlan: For Christ's sake, Wade.

Wade: I'm serious. Why he's typical Company material. He's E-R-A, ex-trovert, regulated, adaptable. Mesomorphic body type. Magnetic, charming and captivating, just like you and me, Harlan. Not everyone gets recruited out of university, we still hire a few Neanderthals. You know what a Neanderthal is, son? That's what we call the recruits that come up through the military side. Demolition, explosives, underwater techniques. The Company pays well, and they never fire you, no matter how bad you fuck up. Sometimes they even give you a family sometimes. The Company brought a whole bunch a new men into Costa Rica and they set 'em up in

real nice houses in the suburbs. Two months later they decide these men'd
fit in better with the neighbours if they had families. They did that for
Harlan here. They moved in a Tico woman and her Tico kids. Can you
believe it? Whoever did that one up Harl, must be either really stupid or a
great sense of humour. You know what I want to know, Harl? Are you
poking her? Was that part of the deal? Are you? ... What's with you,
Harl? You've got no sense of humour any more. I noticed that. You know
what your colleagues are saying about you, don't you? You're drinking too
much, you're hostile, keeping to yourself, not part of the team, and no
sense of humour. That's in your file, too.

(*Pause. Lights fade.*)

SCENE SEVEN

(Ross *is gone. Footsteps off-stage.* Ross *yells* "No." *A gun shot. Then* Ross
yells "Jesus Christ.")

Wade: Something bothering you, Harl?

Harlan: Why him?

Wade: Why not him?

Harlan: Why not you or me?

Wade: It's random.

Harlan: Come on.

Wade: Who knows what the fuck they're doing?

Harlan: Two Company officers with embassy cover and they go for the
22-year-old kid from New Jersey?

Wade: It's random.

Harlan: It's absurd.

Wade: Take it easy, Harlan.

Harlan: They took that kid out of here and ... you're not even thinking
about it. Your mind a little foggy today? ... What's going on, Wade?

Wade: You wondering about me, Harlan? That's good. Sometimes I wonder about you, do you know that? Do you know what I wonder about,
Harlan? C'mon, take a guess. ... Go on, Harlan. ... I wonder about your
loyalty, yeah, that's right, Harlan. I know you been with the Company for
fucking ever, how long, eighteen years? And a year and a half in Costa
Rica. I know you got a fine evaluation for the time you were in Jamaica,
same thing for the work you did in Chile with, what's that newspaper

called, the *El Mercurio*? You won a fucking merit award. Course they're a dime a dozen, but still, for eighteen years no one's ever had a reason to question your loyalty.

Harlan: Loyalty to what?

Wade: To the Company. To the United States of America.

Harlan: You got something on me, let's see it.

Wade: What do you want, photographs, taped conversations with Soviet agents?

Harlan: You're saying I'm compromised?

Wade: We'll have to do a series of lie detector tests. Just routine, but we are very concerned.

Harlan: About what, exactly?

Wade: The questions you been asking about Company activity get out, it could blow six years of hard work.

Harlan: Is there a leak?

Wade: There could be.

Harlan: There could be?

Wade: Yeah.

Harlan: Do you mean you think there is one or do you mean everything is possible?

Wade: I say a simple thing, you argue. You see what I mean?

Harlan: You're accusing me of ...

Wade: It's not just me, Harlan. If it was just me ...

Harlan: Who else?

Wade: The deputy director has expressed his concern.

Harlan: I'm concerned too.

Wade: Good.

Harlan: Why're you pushing this now?

Wade: What's your classification?

Harlan: Why now, Wade?

Wade: What are you supposed to be doing in Costa Rica?

Harlan: Data collection.

Wade: What have you found?

Harlan: You've seen it.

Wade: It's not very much.

Harlan: It's what I've found.

Wade: But there's no shortage of data.

Harlan: Some of it doesn't stand up.

Wade: Analysis isn't your job.

Harlan: What's bugging you, Wade? Your wife screwing around again?

Wade: The U.S. Citizens Committee in San José.

Harlan: I watched her the other night at the Swiss embassy. She was all over the Argentinian trade commissioner.

Wade: The U.S. Citizens Committee isn't mentioned in your last report.

Harlan: I think she's hot on me too.

Wade: She never had any taste.

Harlan: The U.S. Citizens Committee is not communist.

Wade: They sit in downtown San José and they publish stuff about contra camps in Costa Rica. According to our government, and the government of Costa Rica, those camps don't exist.

Harlan: But they do.

Wade: That's not the point.

Harlan: I ran a check on the leadership.

Wade: What do you want, red flags?

Harlan: I've got someone at the meetings.

Wade: That's analysis.

Harlan: I don't think so.

Wade: What is it then?

Harlan: As I understand it, I am supposed to collect evidence of communist activity in Costa Rica ... If I'm collecting rocks for a geological survey, before I send off a sample I make sure it's a rock. I do this to avoid wasting time on tennis balls and potatoes. Is that simple enough for you? What do you want, Wade? Every time a Russian or Cuban sets foot in the country, I report it. There's statistics on land expropriation, state ownership, rationing, tax increases, export controls. What the fuck do you want?

Wade: You attached news clippings of Nicaragua border violations to a memo saying you want information about their origin and you sent the memo to our offices in Managua, Guatemala, Honduras ...

Harlan: Salvador, Bolivia and Chile.

Wade: And Langley, Harlan, don't forget Langley, Virginia. What were you doing exactly?

Harlan: Verifying the authenticity of the reports.

Wade: Why?

Harlan: To verify the authenticity of the reports.

Wade: Why is that any business of yours?

Harlan: I'm trying to separate rocks from potatoes.

Wade: And I'm trying to separate good old boys from communists.

Harlan: Look, Wade. Listen to me. When I was in Jamaica, when I was in Chile, it was my job to fabricate reports. I made things up. A bomb'd go off somewhere, we call the local paper and claim responsibility in the name of some left-wing group. I'd fake a story that there were 3000 Cuban military advisers and plans for a Soviet air base. We'd surface the stories through agents in Venezuela or Colombia. If we worked it right they'd show up in the NBC news. But that's not my job here. Here in Costa Rica I'm supposed to gather information about communist strength, activity, that kind of thing. No disinformation, but information. You with me so far?

Wade: One hundred per cent.

Harlan: Now here, in Costa Rica, I'm taking this slow, step by step so you'll understand, somebody else does for Nicaragua what I used to do in Chile and Jamaica, right? They fake that information if necessary but they get it circulated. I've got no trouble with that but it's not my job. My job is to do research. So. One day I'm sitting in my office, cutting out clippings to send to Langley, and I say to myself, I know this style, I recognize this. This is just like what I used to write. I thought it was funny. Here I am sending off evidence of communist activity and it's probably the operative in the office next to mine that made it up. I thought this is not good research. So I started to make sure that I only sent in actual intelligence.

Wade: You missed the whole point.

Harlan: I'm talking about good intelligence.

Wade: What about direct orders? Does it matter to you that you've been told more than once, by more people than me, to stop separating rocks from potatoes?

Harlan: Yeah, it matters to me.

Wade: That you went over my head.

Harlan: It matters a lot to me.

Wade: Yeah?

Harlan: I was sure I'd find support up the line.

Wade: How high?

Harlan: Anywhere. Christ, Wade, I would have been happy with you, I wanted you to understand. I am saying that I don't mind us making up shit. I used to do it and I did it well. But isn't it important that we know the difference between intelligence and disinformation? We said that the Sandinistas were responsible for the attack on Pastora. Good. But we believed it. We listed the Corinto bombings as a contra operation. There it was, the one biggest operation of the war. We're telling each other, three months, six at the most, we'll be celebrating in Managua. Then we find out, the whole fucking world finds out, it was a Company operation, planned and executed by us. If we want to win this we should know what they are really doing. If I send in phoney data, it gets analysed, the conclusions are wrong because the data is wrong, and Langley, never mind Langley, the State Department starts making policy based on completely wrong assumptions about communist strength and strategy.

Wade: So what's the truth?

Harlan: What do you mean?

Wade: What's lies, what isn't?

Harlan: Go on.

Wade: Where's it end, Harlan? Nicaragua some nice little country? We making a mistake here?

Harlan: You've been through my files.

Wade: Yeah.

Harlan: It's all there.

Wade: Yeah, When I was a kid, my father used to make me hunt cougar with him. One time, I was fourteen, it was almost summer but in the mountains there was still snow. It was cold and wet, and I noticed the sound my boots made coming out the mud. I started running, just to hear the sound, and feel the pull of the mud on my boots. I ran past my father and the dogs took off ahead of me. Christ I ran. Over fallen trees, through creeks, jumping over boulders, I just ran. I wasn't tired or feeling that pain under my ribs. I just felt the cold air sting my skin. I was running through this gully and there was a ridge on my right. It got bigger and steeper until it was like a wall. Then I saw the dogs. They were barking at a patch of trees by the ridge. I moved closer and I saw a big cougar, trying to get a foothold in the rock, but it was too steep. She moved towards us, the dogs barked, and she'd try the ridge again. My father caught up to us. He said, "She's a big one." He said, "She's yours. Go ahead." He shoved me with his rifle butt. "Shoot. Shoot." I lifted the rifle and aimed. The cougar just stood there, looking right at me. I squeezed the trigger. She fell. (Wade *goes and knocks on the door.*) See, I liked the mountains. I liked running. But before that, I didn't like the kill. I know you find part of your work distasteful. But you can't say "I like this, I don't like that." It's all part of the hunt.

(*Prison sounds. The door opens and* Ross *is thrown in. His wrists are tied and he's been beaten.*)

Ross: (*to* Wade) What the fuck's going on, man? I thought you were running this thing. You never fuckin' told me, what the fuck they beat me up for? I thought I was coming in here to get him to talk, then you give me this communist bullshit and I get the piss taken out of me. Why don't they beat him up, he's the fuckin' traitor.

Wade: You should sit down.

Ross: I'll fuckin' stand.

(Wade *throws* Ross *down.* Wade's *violence is always clean and precise. Like a torturer, he is neither obsessed nor appalled.*)

Wade: You got a big secret, Ross. I want to know what it is.

Ross: I don't know what you're talking about.

Wade: Yes you do.

Ross: You never told me about this. This wasn't part of the plan. (Wade *hits* Ross.) I don't know anything.

Wade: I'll start you off. You were in on a plan to hit the embassy.

Ross: I don't ...

Wade: I want to know about it.

Ross: (*to* Harlan) He set this whole thing up, man, to trap you.

(Wade *hits him.*)

Wade: Tell me.

Ross: You're crazy.

Wade: I don't have time. (Wade *hits him again, then* Harlan *gets in* Wade*'s way.* Wade *pushes* Harlan *away,* Ross *jumps* Wade, Wade *kicks* Ross.) (*to* Harlan) I want you to listen to this. (*He moves to* Ross *and makes him sit up.*) You want to go back to the States, you start talking now. The plan to hit the embassy. Who was in on it? The Civil Guard?

Ross: No.

Wade: Costa Rica Libre.

Ross: I don't know.

Wade: Who? ... I'll smash your fucking head in.

Ross: Fuck, man.

Wade: Who? (*He hits him.*)

Ross: I'll tell you. I'll tell you.

Wade: Who?

Ross: Vega.

Wade: Who else?

Ross: Stassen. Holme.

Wade: In Miami.

Ross: I wouldn't do it.

Wade: Whose idea was it?

Ross: I wouldn't go along with it.

Wade: Whose idea was it?

Ross: Stassen said it came from upstairs.

Wade: From who? (*another threat*)

Ross: Maybe Bush.

Wade: Vice-President Bush?

Ross: Yeah.

Wade: Did Stassen say the order came from Bush?

Ross: He said Bush knew about it. And Vernon something.

Wade: Vernon Walters?

Ross: Yeah. Stassen talked to him on the phone.

Wade: You heard him.

Ross: I was in the room, man.

Wade: Did Reagan know?

Ross: No one said.

Wade: Did they mention Tambs?

Ross: Yeah.

Wade: What about him?

Ross: He was the fuckin' target, man.

Wade: (*pause*) You're sure?

Ross: That was the whole plan. We blow up Tambs, the Sandinistas take the rap, we send in the Marines. (*pause*)

Harlan: They talked about this, in front of you.

Ross: Fuck, they had maps of the embassy and everything, I swear it. I didn't believe it neither, you ask them what's this about, what's this mean, they say you don't need to know. You sit quiet, you hear it all.

Wade: Did they say when they wanted to do it?

Ross: No.

Wade: What else?

Ross: That's it. That's the last I heard about it.

Wade: No one ever mentioned it to you on Kemp's farm?

Ross: No.

Wade: Jim Kemp never talked about it?

Ross: I swear.

Wade: You're sure?

Ross: I swear.

Wade: (Wade *hits him.*) Look, son. I don't want to hit you again. I'll just tell you what I'm asking is for the good of your country. I know you want to protect him. I know he's your friend. But it's very important that we know if he knew about the plan.

Ross: (*pause*) We were at this sawmill ...

Wade: When?

Ross: A month ago, maybe more.

Wade: Where?

Ross: Near the border. There was stuff stashed there. We went to pick up some shit for the contras. I grabbed some M79 grenades and some Claymore mines. Jim Kemp said to leave 'em. He said, "We may need 'em to do an embassy later on."

Wade: That's it?

Ross: I swear, I'll never fucking forget it.

Wade: That wasn't very hard, was it? What do you think, Harl?

Harlan: Other sources?

Wade: One.

Harlan: Vega.

Wade: Yeah.

Harlan: Very reliable.

Wade: He's okay.

Harlan: And Bush is in on it?

Wade: Vega said the same thing.

Harlan: Bomb the embassy, kill the ambassador.

Wade: There were fucking phone calls ...

Harlan: To Vernon Walters. Maybe.

Wade: Why wouldn't Bush be in on it? We're losing. We fucked Nicaragua, people make more money selling oranges in the street than they do working in factories and there's fucking food shortages but you can count contra supporters on one hand. Nicaragua isn't gonna attack anyone. If we want to invade, we're gonna have to make our own reason. So okay, Bush isn't in on it, let's say. But Kemp's in on it and Kemp don't jack off without word from higher up. I didn't believe Vega either. He told me about the kid, (*Ross*) said ask the kid. You think he's lying?

Harlan: No.

Wade: No.

Harlan: (*pause*) So you want to hit Tambs.

Wade: Yeah.

Ross: Fuck!

Harlan: You're serious.

Wade: One hundred per cent.

Ross: No fuckin' way am I gonna kill Americans.

Wade: You think the U.S. should invade?

Ross: Yeah.

Wade: So who's gonna die if we invade? Americans. Kids like you. Maybe ambassadors should get to die, too.

Ross: And CIA assholes like you.

Wade: I don't mind. (*to* Harlan) What do you think, Harlan?

Harlan: It got stopped.

Wade: We hit the embassy, we set the whole thing in motion.

Harlan: Maybe they had a reason to stop it.

Wade: Some of them are soft, some of them are scared. They're afraid it'll come out. You worried about that? It came out in Chile, a few people got transferred. But Chile's ours now, that's what counts.

Harlan: What if you hit Tambs, and the U.S. doesn't invade?

Wade: Americans might be getting soft but things aren't so bad that we'll sit back and watch the communists kill U.S. ambassadors.

Harlan: What do you want me to do?

Wade: We'll need information ready to go, Harlan, and you know how to do it. The best agents you've found in eighteen years, AP, Reuters (ROY-*ters*), UPI, all gotta be primed. We can't let 'em know what's up, but they gotta be primed.

Harlan: You hit Tambs, it'll get headlines without me.

Wade: No, I've thought this through. If it hadn't been stopped, Nicaragua'd be surrounded by U.S. troops on manoeuvres, everything'd be ready. But when we hit Tambs it'll be a surprise, they won't be ready. It'd take, I figure, minimum 36 hours, maximum 72 to invade. For 72 hours we've got to flood it. Headlines won't be enough. We'll need hard evidence that the Sandinistas did it, not the Libyans, not the Ayatollah, not the, we'll need editorials, backgrounders, analysis, all that in-depth stuff you're so good at. ... What do you say, Harlan? You're the only one that can do it right, you got years of contacts. (*pause*) I need you, Harlan. There's no one else in Costa Rica.

Harlan: What if I say no?

Wade: It's easy. It's all set up. We get to do for them what they already wanted to do. We lost Cuba, Harlan. We don't want any more communists on our turf.

Harlan: Christ, you talk about following orders, about the team. Where are the orders for this? Where's the team when ...

Wade: Don't you remember how a team works, Harlan? If you got the right attitude, if you know what direction you're moving in, you don't need orders, you know what's right for the team. We're not talking details here, forget the details, look at the whole picture. What's the team trying to do? That's all you gotta know. ... It's a war, Harlan, all over the world. It's freedom against communism, we gotta take action, and all I'm asking you is to make it possible for that to happen.

Harlan: I can't.

Wade: I knew it wouldn't be easy for you.

Harlan: No one knows what's going on any more ...

Wade: Fuck, you and I know. Ross knows.

Harlan: No one knows what's lies, what isn't ...

Wade: Everyone's got doubts, but that's small shit. You look at anything hard enough, it starts to look funny.

Harlan: There's too many lies.

Wade: We're here to lie. That's what our job is, to clear the way for what has to be done. And we know what we want to do, we don't need your research to tell us what we want to do. Forget this lie shit. The bottom line is Nicaragua's communist. We'll bomb the fucking embassy and we will prove to the people of America and to our government that the Sandinistas did it. They will want to hear lies and we will give them lies. It'll be for the good of the U.S.A., and I have no trouble living with that.

Harlan: I can't.

Wade: Fuck, Harlan, in Washington, they got to worry about politics. What do you expect, a letter from the president, "Dear Harlan. Bomb the fucking embassy. Sincerely, Ron." It don't happen like that. And that's what makes us different. We can take action. And there's people in Washington that understand that. There's people there that want it.

Harlan: What are you saying?

Wade: Harlan.

Harlan: What are you saying?

Wade: Just what I said.

Harlan: Are you saying there's authorization for this?

Wade: I didn't say that.

Harlan: But I'm supposed to believe it.

Wade: Believe whatever the fuck you want.

Harlan: I need time to think, I don't know who to talk to, I don't know what to do.

Wade: Harlan.

Wade: I can't do it. ... I can't do it.

Wade: All right, Harlan. You cut your own throat a long time ago. I gave you another chance. You're gonna be all alone. You're gonna find out what a lonely place the Company can be. ... You're real good at explaining things, Harl. You can explain this to yourself any fucking way you want. But this is war. And you let down your country.

(Wade *exits, leaves door open.* Harlan *looks at the door but stays. The lights fade.*)

THE END

Boom, Baby, Boom!

Baņuta Rubess

Baņuta Rubess is an award-winning playwright and director whose work has travelled to such places as England, Latvia, and Newfoundland. Her plays range from the comedy *Pope Joan*, to the drama *Smoke Damage, A Story of the Witch Hunts*, to the jazz play *Boom, Baby, Boom!* She directed the première production of *Goodnight Desdemona, Good Morning Juliet* by Ann-Marie MacDonald, with whom she began collaborating when they were members of the collective that created *This is for You, Anna*. She has created non-traditional theatre for teenagers, such as the multi-media meditation on suicide *Horror High*, and a drama about date rape, *Thin Ice*, co-written with Beverley Cooper. Baņuta Rubess also writes and directs for a third audience, a Latvian one. In 1989 her musical play *Tango Lugano* toured to Latvia with an emigré cast; in 1991 she co-directed, with Neil Bartlett of England, *The Avenging Woman* by Aspazija for the Kabata Theatre in Riga.

Boom, Baby, Boom!, a jazz play set in Toronto in 1959, was first produced at the du Maurier World Stage Festival at Harbourfront in Toronto, 15–18 June 1988.

PRODUCTION
Director / **Baņuta Rubess**
Movement / **Susan McKenzie**
Set Design / **Marilyn Bercovich**
Costume Design / **Reg Bronskill**
Stage Manager / **Cheryl Landy**
Music / **Nic Gotham**

CAST
David Bolt / Clem Hambourg
Cynthia Eastman / Laila Ozols (*née* Mednis)
Martin Julien / Jekyll
Vieslav Kyrstyan / Aivars Pūtvējiņš
Kate Lynch / Ruthie Hambourg
Ann-Marie MacDonald / Austra Mednis

THE BAND
Richard Bannard / Babe – drums
Victor Bateman / Herbie Durbie – bass
Allen Cole / Allen Kennedy – piano
Nic Gotham / Black Hat – saxophone

CHARACTERS

The Club:
Clem Hambourg, a real character, a minor legend in the Toronto jazz scene. Born a Russian Jew in London, England at the turn of the century; moved to Toronto in 1910 where his father established the Hambourg Conservatory of Music. Belonged to the upper-class set of Toronto. His brother Mark – 19 years his senior – was a child prodigy of the piano whose lessons were paid for by Paderewski. His brother Jan lived in Paris with his wife, the daughter of Lord Muir and close chum of Willa Cather. His brother Boris played with the Hart House Quartet and ran the Conservatory in Toronto until his death in 1952. Clem was trained as a concert pianist but rarely played. The story of his life previous to the House of Hambourg is murky. He was an eccentric who ambled through life with a bowler on his head, a cigar between his teeth, and a chihuahua on his elbow. After the demise of his club, he played piano at restaurants and did some extra work for the CBC.
Ruthie Hambourg, Clem's wife, a real character, somewhat fictionalized. Slaved in the kitchen of the House of Hambourg and sewed costumes for

the Victory Burlesque for extra income. Also belonged to a mystical Order which communed with the spirits of the dead. Allowed their apartment to be overrun by some 18 cats and conducted fierce quarrels with Clem.
Jekyll, in his mid or late twenties, an aspiring poet-cum-artist-cum-musician. Bound to be working for an institution in his forties.
Musicians: Black Hat, Kennedy, Herbie, Babe.

The Latvians:
Austra Mednis, later **Shirley,** a spunky, yet haunted aspiring beatnik with a faint European accent. Latvian. She became a refugee at the age of 6 and arrived in Canada at the age of 13. Now she is 21 and testing her limits.
Laila Mednis, Austra's sister, 7 years her elder. By 1959 she has two children. Her husband Gunars travels selling life insurance. Laila believes her older culture to be superior to the barbaric Canadian one.
Aivars Pūtvēgiņš, Austra's fiancé. Aspiring to upward mobility, and in 1959, reaching it. Sober, nationalistic, he desperately wants a cultured wife and a growing family.

Sundry cameo appearances of Toronto's community:
Dr Roy Milford, mental health expert
A Latvian policeman
Radio announcements
Miss Toronto
TV ads
Wanda
Several sections throughout the play suggest action, music and imagery. The specific nature of these scenes must be developed via improvisation with actors and work with a musical director.

In scenes among the Latvians, text in brackets should be spoken in Latvian. It is not my intention to provide employment only for Latvian actors. These parts could be played by any actors with an Eastern European background, or by anyone with the willingness to learn a foreign language.

The New Canadians must not be played by any other ethnic group or as any other ethnic group than East European. Bulgarians, Hungarians, Poles, Ukrainians, Lithuanians, Estonians, Byelorussians, Serbs, Croatians, and Czechs may harbour reasonable fears as regards an invasion by Russians. Italians or Germans do not share the same historical experience.

INTRODUCTION
Boom, Baby, Boom! is a study of how people confront a painful past and an ominous future.
Clem Hambourg, age 59 or 66 at the time of the play, runs an after-hours jazz club and is considered a patron saint of the growing Toronto scene. Few of his patrons realize that he comes from a family of world-renowned classical musicians. Clem is an oddball, considered a profligate black sheep

by the old society of pre-war Toronto. The club – The House of Hambourg – is his pride and joy, and its impending closure an unmitigated disaster.

One night, a young woman clambers through the window of the club. She calls herself **Shirley** but her real name is **Austra Mednis**, a Latvian immigrant or "New Canadian." Since her arrival in Toronto in 1951, memories of the war are constantly kept alive by her family and friends. She is convinced that either the bomb will drop or the Russians will invade very soon – either way the world is about to end. In the meantime, she wants to live it up, do it all. She runs away from her engagement party into the underbelly of Toronto, and behaves as outrageously as she imagines a proper Bohemian should.

It is 1959 in Toronto. The world of jazz has lost Lester Young and is about to lose Billie Holiday. Buddy Holly dies earlier in the year. The Cuban missile crisis is down the road. Nixon is visiting Khrushchev. The papers are full of news about fallout shelters and heroin addiction in Hogtown. It is also a time of optimism and excitement – the world is just discovering Kerouac and flower power will soon flex its muscle. **Austra** and **Clem** have an adventure.

FIRST SET

SCENE ONE

(*The club. An empty space. A piano on stage. Darkness.* Ruthie *stands in the darkness with her back to the audience, holding an empty picture frame.* Clement Hambourg *is seated at the piano with his back to the audience, smoking a cigar, blowing rings in the air. He starts to play* The Moonlight Sonata *with a great flourish. Puts cigar down. Squints at the audience.*)

Clem: I remember you ... welcome, welcome back to the House of Hambourg. We've missed your esteemed company, old man – haven't seen you since we had the club on Bay Street, – no, Bloor Street! Bloor Street – yes they're building the new emporium there now, the Madame Host Renfrooze where squares croon the blues while trying on shoes. – it's taken you five years to get back to my conservatory – where have you been, Korea? Oh, much has happened, much, very much. Yes, I'm still married to Ruthie, she's sewing for the Victory Burlesque, and ... petit point and ... You're not a real estate agent, now, are you? No? Oh good good good. Listen to this. (*Pulls some doggerel out of jacket pocket*)
Give me your tired, your beat,
Your cool subterraneans yearning to breathe free,
The wretched hipsters of your teeming shore –
Send these, the homeless, tempest-tost to me.
I lift my lamp beside the golden door.

(*During this roll call, three* Musicians *appear and take poses behind the gilt frame.*)

Toscanini? Present.
Rubinstein? Present.
Ravel? Present.

(*The musicians take a bead on* Clem *and start to move towards him, slowly.*)

Clem: Chaliapin? Present. Stravinsky present Michael Mark Jan Boris and *Clement* Hambourg present Austra Mednis.

(Austra *enters and grasps* Clem *by the arm. The musicians return to their portrait image.*)

Clem: Present.

Austra: I could hear you from the attic. I even unplugged the fridge so I could hear better.

Clem: But you haven't even arrived yet.

Austra: I have read Henry Miller (*Musicians applaud after names*) and Jack Kerouac and Allen Ginsberg and Jean-Paul Sartre. And I am an atheist. And I don't care if I'm a virgin.

Clem: (*To* Austra) Welcome. (*To* Kennedy) Welcome.

(*Image changes to surreal club.* Austra *sits down at the table.* Kennedy *strides to the piano, the frame disappears, the musicians take off their formal clothing.* "*Moonlight Sonata.*")

Clem: Hey, Herbie Durbie, how're ya doin, and Babe, nice to see ya, (*To audience*) damn fine drummer that – he looks like a missionary –

(*All other cast appear. They seat themselves and echo the movements of the pianist precisely with their torsos and their heads. Even the drummer echoes him.*)

Clem: (*Going out into audience*) Welcome, welcome to the House of Hambourg. Clement Hambourg, I'm delighted to, etc. (*Comment on appearance*) That's Allen Kennedy playing and Babe and Herbie Durbie, keep an eye on them, they're going to be famous those boys (*listens and we watch*) and later we'll have Black Hat and maybe Sarah Vaughan or Louis Armstrong, he's in Burlington tonight, they all come here to jam and – that where you've been? ... oh and you must re-visit one of Ruthie's pizzas, she makes them herself and you don't have to drive all the way to Buffalo to try one ... Come in, come in ... (*Pointing at pianist*) Does that look like a beatnik to you? Are you hep? Are you hip? Do you dig? Are You Enlightened? Eh, plus ça change ... Jack Kerouac's 37 today ... the old get younger all the time.

(*All watch pianist, until he turns to* Clem.)

Clem: I dig! Bloody excellent! Okay-erooni, you can come any time, but not this Sunday, Monday, Tuesday and Wednesday we are closed, Toronto doesn't swing until 11 p.m. next Thursday, see! you! then!

Black Hat: (*From audience*) Two-three-four!

(*Scene erupts into strong and emphatic jazz.*)

SCENE TWO: TORONTO, HECK

(*Sax starts to play.* "Jekyll" *theme.* Austra *and* Clem *leap to their feet and stride in the manner of* Black Hat *the sax player.*

Black Hat *the sax leaps up on stage and leads all others except* Laila *and* Aivars *in this movement.*

Each character has an instrument which determines their actions: Austra – *piano and drums,* Clem – *piano,* Aivars *and* Laila – *bass,* Jekyll – *sax,* Ruthie – *bass.*

Jekyll *peruses the crowd, asks them for money – hey, I'm an artist.* Austra *is wandering through the city using movements: crouch, lean, pivot, and leap.*

Laila *sniffs about looking for* Austra. *It is 6 a.m. Aivars, in his black hat, is wandering through town, looking for* Austra. *Diagonal movement. He has a photograph of* Austra *in his hand. Wherever he stops, he asks "Have you seen* Austra Mednis – *my fiancée?" Finally he asks that of the moon.*

N.B. *Lines printed in square brackets are spoken in Latvian or the appropriate other language.*

At the end of the music there is a cacophony of sound. Ruthie *appears at the top of the stairs, wielding a broom.*)

Ruthie: What's all this ruckus, Clemmie!? I'm trying to concentrate up here on a fitting, it's impossible, and it's the Divine Delilah with her pink spangles and all. You promised that Allen Kennedy was never to play here again, he pumps the piano so hard, we have to re-tune it every time, I won't have it, we're poor as church mice, you tell him that.

Clem: Yes, Ruthie, my dear.

Jekyll: "Howl." By Allen Ginsberg. "I saw the best minds of my generation destroyed by madness, starving hysterical naked, ... angelheaded hipsters burning for the ancient heavenly connection to the starry dynamo in the machinery of night"

Ruthie: (*Interrupting*) I thought you were going to get that student, that Hagood Hardy, now there's a *nice* boy, a real musician, and he has a very deep soul, I can see that.

Clem: Yes, Ruthie.

(Jekyll *exits.* Aivars *falling asleep,* Laila *shaking him.*)

Laila: *Neguli, neguli* [Don't sleep, don't sleep]. (*He slumps forward*) She comes home. I kill her. I kill her. (*Laila gets more and more drowsy, as her anger turns to anguish and falls asleep*)

Clem: When everyone has dispersed, Clem likes to play Beethoven with his eyes closed. (Kennedy *begins to play Beethoven.*)

Clem: Beethoven, what a champ. Stone deaf and dying of liver disease, he cooks up the Missa Solemnis. Man, that's hot! (Clem *starts singing some Beethoven, conducting.* Austra *leaps into centre stage.*)

Austra: Mr Hambourg. I could hear you from Cumberland Street. I even climbed through the window to hear better.

Clem: But we haven't been introduced.

Austra: Oh, I like windows. Sometimes I climb out of my bedroom window at night. There is a magnolia tree which always hits me in the face. Once in the war I pushed through a window on a train because a man looked hard at me and said "devuchka" which is Russian for "girl" but really it means I'll huff and I'll puff and I'll

Clem: Blow your house down.

(*Spotlight on the cameo appearance of the real live* Dr Roy Milford, *Toronto mental health expert. He is a man with a cigarette glued to his lips, darkened glasses and a clipped moustache.*)

Dr Milford: Dr Roy Milford, Toronto mental health expert. As a mental health expert, I know that music can have a soothing effect. For instance: when I play jazz recordings for my patients prior to shock treatments, I find their fears and apprehensions diminished greatly. My favourites are Ron Collier and Dave Brubeck. Guy Lombardo, no. Oh, you'd rather have some benzedrine. Hey, no panic. In this age of the H-bomb, we've all got our problems. (Laila *wakes up, cries out "Austra!"*)

(*"Swinging Shepherd Blues" by Moe Koffman. Movement sequence,* Clem *and* Jekyll *hiding* Austra. Clem *turns around,* Austra *is gone. During this sequence,* Aivars *wakes up, looks at a newspaper, simultaneous with* Ruthie *doing the same.* Laila *pacing.*)

Laila: Hello, Mount Sinai hospital? yes, I am looking for my sister, she has disappeared. A-u-s-t-r-a M-e-d-n-i-s. *Mama, es esmu pie telefona!* [Mama, I'm on the phone!] She is just 21 years old, a baby, an A-student ... Nothing happened, we had a party, she was ... *Aivar, kā saka līgava?* [Aivar, how do you say "bride"?] ... fiancée, fiancée ... (Ruthie, Musicians, Aivars, *are all looking at the newspaper:*)

Ruthie: (*Picks up newspaper*) July 10, 1959. Your stars today: (*Sundry lean in to look at paper*)

Aivars: "Staggering girl tells of buying dope in restaurant." Norrrm's Grrill ... Norm's Grill ...

Laila: (*To phone*) thank you. *Mama!*

Herbie: Norm hates bad press. (Clem *suddenly tears open the door, as if to catch sight of* Austra. *Nothing there.*)

(*Scene changes to* Norm's Grill. *Sleazy music – on* AM *radio. Image à la Edward Hopper. A nylonclad leg belonging to* Wanda *dangles through a picture frame. The musicians hang out at the grill.* Ruthie *wanders in and out of the scene in a trance.*)

Jekyll: The heat was on in Toronto's jungle last night and the inhabitants walked warily.

Black Hat: (*To the nylon leg*) Hey, Wanda, your "uncle" says better go out and make some loot.

Herbie: He said: your "uncle."

Other men: Hey, Wanda!

Wanda: (*Played by* Laila) Aw, shut up! (Wanda *gradually exits.*)

Jekyll: It was in Norm's Grill at Carlton and Jarvis. One of those fetid Friday nights at Norm's Grill. When the good of Toronto was sleeping tight. Norm curled up around his cash register like a stinking sock, sucking up the pennies from heaven and the dollars from hell. Hey, it's a thirty dollar a day habit, and it's a seller's market. An attractive 17-year-old blonde wearing a light blue skirt spilled her coffee while haggling for a fix. She was lucky she wasn't sold to the white slave trade.

Ruthie: It was one of those swampy Toronto nights, the kind of night when you brush against someone on the street and they scream because you don't give them enough space, their head is too crowded. (Austra *appears, having run away from her engagement party. She wears a print dress with a full skirt, and glasses. She is in the wrong place at the wrong time.*)

Austra: I'd like to speak to Mr Norman, please. I am looking for employment.

Kennedy: At two o'clock in the morning?

Herbie: Get lost, kid, go back to mommy.

Austra: *Tu esi riebīgs un nosprāgsi ellē.* [You are disgusting and will perish in hell.] (*Population of Norm's Grill laughs.*)

Black Hat: You know what makes Norm sick. Sputniks. Beatniks. And ethnics.

Babe: You ever waitressed before?

Herbie: Norm don't need no waitress, kid.

Ruthie: This is a rough town. It only looks nice compared to where you came from.

Jekyll: Let me show you something. Over there, in that booth. Count 'em – five, five females. It's two o'clock in the morning on a Friday night – what are they doin' out here at Norm's. Look at the one with the duck haircut oiled to her head. I don't think she's my mother's daughter. And the one with the sharp sports shirt and the stripes and the spick and span shoes. *Men*'s shoes. I'm tellin' you, mister, it gives me the creeps. What's wrong with a toasted Danish at Fran's. Let 'em go there.

Austra: I will take any job. – I would like to join the white slave trade.

Black Hat: Where do you think this is –

Black Hat, Herbie & Kennedy: Detroit?

Austra: I would like to join the white slave trade.

Black Hat: Where do you think this is –

Black Hat & Babe: Moscow?

Austra: I would like to join the white slave trade.

Ruthie & Jekyll: Can you type?!!

Austra: I'm not going home.

Clem: Welcome. (Austra *runs away*. Aivars *arrives on Norm's Grill scene just as everyone is leaving and the bar gets pushed away.*)

Aivars: Excuse me, there is a question I have. You have seen – (*No one is there,* Aivars *has to leave. Norm's Grill disappears.*)

SCENE SIX: THE HOUSE OF HAMBOURG, CLOSING TIME

(*Band starts to play jazz standard* "So What?" Jekyll *is trying to sell a poem to a customer for a quarter.* Clem *either helps convince the customer to buy it, or makes* Jekyll *leave them alone.*)

Jekyll: (*Either sarcastically or gratefully*) Thanks a lot. Clem, old timer, I really needed the money.

Clem: Money, money, money in the carpet, money in the brain, money sonny no funny. Jekyll, if you're an artist, you must learn to live on air.

Jekyll: Keerist man, let me live in the sewer, in your attic, in the gutter-snipe's garter buckles, throw me to the rooms you keep locked from public sight, because I'm writing it all down, Clement, all down, this is *it*, it has it, it means it, it says *it*, *it*. *BLOW MAN BLOW.* Writing it down and I will splash it out word-made-flesh *ON A MAJOR* canvas here on the venerable venerated Rintin-tintinnabulating House of Hambourg walls. A one-man show, friend, whaddya say.

Clem: If these bills keep coming in, there won't be a House of Hambourg. I'll be playing dining room piano at the King Eddy and my wife Ruthie and her cats will be out washing cars.

Jekyll: Sharks! sharks! – will you listen to that! (*Referring to the music*) – so get one of your rich family to buy the place.

Clem: What rich family?

Jekyll: Clement, BABY, I hear you come from the most lah-de-dah scene in town.

Clem: You know what Clem says. Clem says don't ask questions and there will never be lies.

Jekyll: Never look back, never! thus spoke the sage. Our Clem is a visionary. He could sell a few dreams. If Dr Jekyll gave him the dust dreams are made of.

Clem: My dear McJello. Clem does not want in the first place any merchandise and in the second place he is too old for such shenanigans and in the third place this is not Morocco or Charlie Parker's vestibule this is Toronto.

(*Jekyll waves a packet of heroin at him.*)

Jekyll: Consider it a donation. (Clem *does not take the packet.*)

Clem: It's closing time, Jekyll esteemed Hyde. (Clem *turns on his heel, waving* Jekyll *away. Starts to put sheets of classical music on the piano.*)

Jekyll: (*Singing along*) So what? (Jekyll *exits.*)

SCENE SEVEN: IN THE WEE HOURS

(Herbie *still perches on his stool, picking a string now and then, but above all listening to his own internal music.* Ruthie *works at her sewing machine.*)

Clem: In this North America, you are nobody until you're dead. Then you're the greatest. Billie Holiday for example – they're all just waiting for her to drop, then she'll be the singer of the century. (Clem *goes to count the take, wearily, chomping on a cigar.*)

Clem: We're closed now, Herbie.

Herbie: (*Without opening his eyes*) That's right, man. Closed.

Ruthie: (*Barely turning around*) How much did we make?

Clem: Barely enough to keep us in cat food, I'm afraid, dear Ruthie.

Ruthie: I've made enough G-strings to last a hundred years. Maybe if we hadn't expanded to three floors we might be able to save a penny or two.

Clem: I'm a visionary, not a businessman. Just think of it – everyone who wants to play can play. Everyone who needs to listen, can listen. Everyone who wants to dream – can dream.

Ruthie: I dreamt about Dr Rubinstein again last night. He threw me down into an enormous root canal. If we don't pay him soon –

Clem: She dreamt about Dr Rubinstein again last night.

Ruthie: He thinks we make money if we ask for two cents from some darn university student I told him ask for more but he won't listen and now they're opening up clubs all over town he'll die if they close the club he'll have a heart attack and I'll be left alone on this wretched globe I'll be playing with the Salvation Army like going to afternoon concerts in the park. (*Ad lib continuation as* Ruthie *walks out of theatre.*)

Clem: She dreams of our dentist, I dream of Schönberg. (Kennedy *appears as Schönberg and begins to play. Apparition of concert audience in frame in far upstage corner.*)

Clem: Schönberg. Ah! It's 1911. We've just come to Toronto. My father has an opening gala for the Hambourg conservatory. A concert of Schönberg. Schönberg is there. The shocked audience pelts him with eggs. This of course would never happen in Toronto, but in the Toronto of my dreams. Schönberg sits down in his chair, but I'm sitting in it. He sits in my lap. He doesn't notice me. I'm not very comfortable, but I like the smell of eggs. I like the smell of eggs! (Ruthie *returns, nattering about the state of their financial affairs.*)

Ruthie: The club was my idea, I know, but I said a club, not this three ring circus. And tonight – Freddie comes in and all he plays is two notes over and over again because he's meditating.

Clem: Ah, Ruthie, we've had three House of Hambourgs, Ruthie, we'll have a fourth one. Something will happen. This town needs me, why – they'd all be crying in their soup if I pulled up my stakes. Boris won't lend me any money. Anyway Boris is dead.

Ruthie: Ask him anyway. (Ruthie *begins to raise the dead with her broom.*)

Ruthie: Boris. Boris. (*She sees* Boris.) Present.

Clem: Boris! Listen, old chap, I need seven thousand dollars and – (Boris *disappears.*)

Clem: Paderewski.

Ruthie: Present.

Clem: I need – (Paderewski *disappears.*)

Clem: Lady Eaton.

Ruthie: Present.

Clem: Sorry to be asking you this, but I need seven th – Paganini. (Clem *and* Ruthie *scream when they catch sight of him and shoo him away.*)

Ruthie: They can't help.

Clem: (*Mournfully*) The Bird is dead. Bix Beiderbecke is dead. Arturo Toscanini is dead. All the masters are dead.

Ruthie: Someone is coming. Someone is coming for you. There is a window. (Austra *falls into the room. Freeze.*)

SCENE EIGHT: HOME

("Windows" *music begins.* Austra *climbs through a tableau of her window at home made up by the rest of the ensemble. Tree hits her, window comes crashing down.* Austra *has arrived at home through the window, very late, after sneaking out with* Aivars. Laila *has been waiting up for her.*)

Laila: *Nu tā. Beidzot mūsu princesīte ieradās.* [Well, there. Finally, our little princess arrives.] Twenty-one years old and she still goes climbing through windows.

Austra: I like windows.

Laila: (*Sarcastically*) *Un Aivars? Vinš arī mīl logus?* [And Aivars? He loves windows too?]

Austra: I wasn't out with Aivars. I went to the kino. By myself.

Laila: *Tu melo.* [You're lying.]

Austra: I saw Audrey Hepburn.

Laila: *Tu melo.* [You're lying.]

Austra: She's very beautiful. She's very delicate. She's very deep.

Laila: You are lying. Why do you keep sneaking out of your room? Kicks, it's kicks? One day I will barricade the windows and you will never get in again.

Austra: *Laila, izbeidz.* [Laila, stop it.] (*Pause.*)

Laila: *Kāpēc tu are mammu runāji angliski? Kāpēc?* [Why did you talk English to Mama? Why?]

Austra: Why shouldn't I talk English to Mama? We're in Canada now, right? (*Pause*) *Man ļoti žēl.* [I'm sorry]

Laila: *Mamma raud un raud un raud.* [Mama cries and cries and cries.]

Austra: OK, I said I'm sorry, I don't know what came over me. OK. *Es tūlīt iešu augšā un atvainošos.* [I'll go up and apologize right now.]

Laila: *Šā vai tā mamma ar tevi nerunās.* [Mama won't talk to you anyway.]

Austra: Oh it's the corpse routine. Oh boy, *Es drīz būšu debesīs, bērņini. Neņemiet mani vērā. Esmu redzējusi trīs karus un divas kāzas un nu ir laiks mirt.* ["I'm going to heaven soon, children. Don't mind me. I've seen three wars and two weddings and now I'm going to die."] Death, death, death.

Laila: It's fifteen years ago and you don't remember a thing.

Austra: I do remember so there I remember everything. I remember the soldiers and the donkey and the ration cards and Kalna kundze dying and under the bridge and all of it. It's over now. It's 1959. And I don't think it's fair if Mama keeps saying she's going to die.

Laila: Hurry up and get married before she does die, Austra. *Vai tu saproti? Ap-pre-cies.* [Do you understand? Get married.] Why should Aivars marry a monkey like you, anyway, climbing out of windows in the middle of the night –

Austra: – it's only ten o'clock –

Laila: – *viņš grib kārtīgu latviešu meiteni, tas ir ko viņš grib* [– he wants a proper Latvian girl, that's what he wants.]

Austra: Oh, Aivars wants a proper Latvian girl. I sing in the choir. I go to the folk dancing. I read Latvian newspapers. I – oh, are you still – I am not going to Latvian Girl Guides tomorrow, and that's that. They're all babies. (*Sound of baby crying.*)

Laila: (*Exiting*) And there goes another baby. And you're the biggest baby of them all.

Austra: Why should I teach them the stupid granny or grandfather knot anyway, what do they think, they're going to go sailing when the bomb is going to drop and there won't be any Great Lakes anyway, (Musicians *cheer her on*) get married! why should I go picking out china as if any of us will be here to eat off the plates in ten years time, I'm sorry about Mama, I just won't speak, OK, I will never speak again – (*Picks up the paper.*)

Austra: Hey, Laila, "Be a Walter Thornton Model. (*Tableau of window changes to group of models and starts to move towards her*) Whatever your ambition ... Model ... Secretary ... Career Woman ... Or Homemaker, there is a course for you. Walter Thornton training will pay you dividends for life. Only 37 dollars and fifty cents for a three week course." Hey, Laila ...

SCENE NINE: WINDOWS

(Austra *climbs through several windows again, made up by the rest of the ensemble.* "Windows" *theme plays. Bedroom window* – Laila *calls for her train*

— *Chorus of* "Devuchka, Devuchka" *like train wheels. Wall she climbs over pushing into full club — empty club.*)

Clem: What have you got to say for yourself? (Austra *runs away.*)

SCENE TEN: DR HAMBOURG, I PRESUME

(Clem *hears a sound at the window and grabs a chianti bottle candleholder with which to brain the burglar.* Austra *comes through the window, still wearing the same clothes, as if she came upon the House of Hambourg while wandering back from Norm's Grill. She is very tired and a little surprised at what she has done. She moves around the club. She touches the instruments. She goes to the table with the money.*)

Clem: What do you want? Is it money? Do you want money? You're so thin. Take it, take it. You're not the first junkie to drop in here. (*Grabbing her tight by the arm*) Let me see.

Austra: I'm afraid sir that you will discover that I am not afraid of anything so if it is your intention to hurt me, twist my arm, I won't give you the pleasure of screaming.

Clem: Do you mind if I scream just a little? After all, I am the one who is surprised.

Austra: Please, I am very tired. I have just turned 21 and being of age appears to be more difficult than I ever imagined. I have been looking for employment for the last 24 hours and I am very tired and I'm not going home.

(*Freeze. Both move to table, both smoking cigars.*)

Clem: So you are a runaway.

Austra: You could call me a refugee. (*Looking around*) Is this a place of ill repute? This must be a place of ill repute.

Clem: Yes, it's an after-hours jazz club. Nasty business. But you will find the patrons to be very polite.

Austra: Are you the owner?

Clem: Well, I ain't Glenn Gould.

Austra: I am not Doris Day. Please let me work for you, sir. I will work very hard.

Clem: Do you have any experience?

Austra: An unhappy childhood.

Clem: Funny, so did I. Clem failed to be a child prodigy and so ate a heap of beets. Beets were the punishment for whenever I didn't play the piano so well especially that damned adagio. Beets for breakfast, beets for lunch, beets, beets, beets.

Austra: Mr Owner. Give me a job. (*Bullshitting*) I love jazz music with all my heart.

(Clem *pulls a chair around.*)

Clem: Who's your favourite? The Bird? The Pres? The Skunk? Or are you a fan of Mr T-H-E-ELONIOUS Monk? (*The Bird – Charlie Parker; the Pres – Lester Young; The Skunk – trick question*)

Austra: I cannot tell you, but please don't hold that against me. You see, I was struck by deafness at age of 6. But by laying my hands on the radio, I could perceive the beauty of this music. Simply I could not discern the differences between the players and the instruments – whether it's harp or oboe – but then – shortly before my 21st birthday – during a great great storm the power of hearing was restored to me. It was then I realized that I must work in a jazz club. I came as quickly as I could. (Austra *clambers up on a table.*) Do you think I have an accent?

Clem: Yes. Swiss private school. You're not Hungarian. Or is it Czech.

Austra: Yes. No. I grew up in ... New Guinea, you see. My mother was half-Dutch, half-Persian. A distant relative of Mata Hari. My father was related to the King of India. He lost all his money in a casino. He went on a tiger hunt in order to win back his wealth and unluckily he was eaten. Hearing the news, my mother choked on a silver spoon. I was an orphan. A wealthy dowager took pity on me and I live with her in her summer home in the Muskokas. I come from Haliburton and I'm going straight to hell. You see, Mr Owner, I am 21. The Russians will invade by 1965. There is no future. Please, I am a very good waitress. The customer is always right. I make very good potato salad. The trick is in the herring. Just no sewing, that's all, no sewing.

Clem: And your name is – ?

Austra: Austra.

Clem: Sorry?

Austra: Shirley. Shirley ... Hepburn.

Clem: Clement Hambourg.

(*They shake hands. Freeze. The door opens.* Aivars *appears, hat in hand.*)

Aivars: My name is Aivars Pūtvējiņš. Please call me Harry. I am looking for a young woman called Austra Mednis. She is a sweet young girl with fine features and an excellent education. You may have seen her entering a museum. No? Sorry?

(Aivars *exits.* Austra *and* Clem *are lying on the floor after having smoked a couple of reefers.*)

Austra: I must tell you, Mr Clement. I am being followed. By ... by ... bybyby.

Clem: You are a very good liar, I must say. And so ... athletic ...

Austra: I like your green ... tea ... stuff.

Clem: I was once caught climbing through the window. It was a party, in 1921 ... '22? ... I think it was the Muirs, you know, the house at Castle Frank ... That's right, Caesar Finn was with me. Caesar Finn. He had a very large nose and a very small chin. Everyone was always especially nice to Caesar because he had gonorrhea. And – (*He moves closer to* Austra, *who has fallen asleep*)

I'll tell you a secret.
You see I'm an expatriate too.
From a crystal cut mili-oo [milieu]
Via Voronezh, Moscow and London, England.
I'm a refu-gee.
From my fami-ly.
I have my father's hands.
My father hated Stravinsky. Don't tell anybody.
None of them ever set foot in any one of my clubs. Of course, quite frankly my dear,
I wouldn't hear of it.
But you mustn't tell. Eternal springs one's hope, eh, young Titania?
It's not a bad room, the attic.

(*The musicians return to their instruments wearing pyjamas.* "Ruthie" *theme.* Clem *carries* Austra *upstairs.* Ruthie *enters to clean up, notices* Jekyll *lying behind the piano, carries him out.* Jekyll *stumbles back into the club,* Ruthie *pushes him out.* Clem *enters club,* Ruthie *pushes him out by mistake. They hug, then sit down and watch the sunlight begin to stream in.*

Image of Laila *looking out the window for* Austra, *closing it up.*)

END OF FIRST SET

SECOND SET

SCENE ONE

(House of Hambourg. *Scene begins with dialogue between sewing machine and drums. Other* Musicians *enter. We have an actual jam session.*

As band heats up, they play the theme for "Black Hat." *Austra enters, looking like a beatnik. On a platter, she carries the word* "beat." *She grooves for a while with the sax player, then swooshes over to the piano where she draws a variety of words on paper and shows them to the audience: "bongo," "Apocalyptic," "Cheese Whiz," "Eat Beats," etc.*

Throughout the piece, Jekyll *paints words from the bongo poem on the back wall.*

Austra *is followed by* Clem *who plays the bongo drums and cheers the musicians on.* Austra *exits with her platter.* Aivars *walks through the audience with an identical platter bearing the sign "Austra Mednis."* Austra *returns with some sort of drinks (non-alcoholic champagne substitute) for the musicians. During this section,* Ruthie *serves apple pie to a member of the audience.)*

SCENE TWO

(Clem, *presenting his musicians, but also sounding like a roll call. Assisted by* Austra. Musicians *respond with a bow, or a yeah. During roll call,* Ruthie *comes into the club carrying a fateful letter.)*

Clem: Thank you, thank you, thank you!
Black Hat!
Herrrrbie Durbie!
The serendipitous Babe!
And maestro of the keys, Allen Kennedy!

Ruthie: Maestro, he's no maestro. Where's his left hand? (*To Kennedy*) Where's your left hand? A good pianist should be able to play everything, even Mozart.

Clem: Well, Ruthie, yes, the left hand, but concentrate on his right hand, there are those marvellous Chopinesque stylings in his improvisations, don't you think? Shirley, you agree?

Austra: Maybe he doesn't like Mozart.

Kennedy: I love Mozart.

Ruthie: Of course he loves Mozart, we all love Mozart, Charlie Parker grooved on Mozart. (*Looks at the letter*) I miss Herbie Spanier, you know, Clemmie? His trumpet is really spiritual, it's Buddha. And Freddie Stone, where's Freddie, the dear? Black Hat – your sound – a bit strident tonight –

Clem: But his instrumental mastery is like that of a Paganini –

Austra: And when he blows his ... axe ... all the cats and dolls at their tables are under hypnosis, shall we trance?

Clem: Dig it.

Ruthie: And your serendipitous Babe, how come he only plays in four four when Bela Bartok taps it out in ⅝, ⅞ all the time.

Clem: Babe? But Ruthie dearest, his seraphic syncopations!

Austra: Oh, yeah, to the core: the hidden thing, the subconscious that lies in the body; you feel this, you play this. It is jazz, Ruthie, that's what it is.

Ruthie: I know what jazz is, young lady, I'm talking about genius. Genius on the piano, genius on the harpsichord, music is music, but it's genius I'm talking about.

Clem: And welcome, here it is, right here in our club. Ruthie dearest. Patience! Nature needs nurture: *il faut arroser les fleurs!*

Kennedy: I'm a genius all the time.

Clem: Don't you fret your fugal stretti, Ruthie dearest, they are all tutti musici, tutti orchester, tutti fortissimi pianissimi – look at Herbie here, whose fingers fly across the strings like crazed tarantulas. You know, sometimes, just a little, he reminds me of Boris –

Ruthie: – Boris, now there was a maestro.

Austra: Boris?

Clem: My brother. He played the cello – with the Hart House Quartet –

Ruthie: You should tell them about Boris.

Clem: – but what is Boris to Herbie or Herbie to Boris? (Ruthie *exits up to her sewing machine*) The young ones don't want to hear about the past, the past is boring, they want to crack open the non-alcoholic champagne substitute and burn, burn, burn into the *now*. No-surname Shirley here never talks about the past, she has no past, she was born yesterday. She is of the *now*, the everlasting present, no past, no future, an eternal immediacy in which the musicians of the House of Hambourg play forever.

Ruthie: (*Looking at the fatal letter*) I don't think so.

Clem: Why not? They are happy here, huh, boys?

Black Hat: Not bad, Clement, but how about some dough?

Babe: There's a hole in my shoe.

Herbie: I've been living on hot dogs for two weeks.

Clem: All right, all right (*Paying them*). You see, oh infanta Shirley, we fight for our boys. We tell the CBC again and again – you must play their music! we tell those lousy critics Durov Idiotski at the Globe and Stale: go stuff it in the wazoo! We give tutti musici all their ten dollars tonight, eh Ruthie? so this is the jazz mecca and they will play here for the next hundred years!

Ruthie: I don't think so.

Austra: It's a long time, Mr Clement.

Ruthie: There's a letter here from the city, Clem. The subway is coming through Cumberland Street. The Club will have to move.

Musicians: Again? (*etc*)

Clem: But we can't move, we can't afford to move again.

Ruthie: It's a letter from the city. Clem, we've got to do something.

(*Silence.*)

Clem: I'm a visionary, not a businessman. Black Hat, Herbie, Kennedy, Babe. My dear, dear, dearest boys. You must never give up. No matter what happens, doesn't matter, this club, some other club, the basement of your Aunt Tilly, you must continue. An artist's love of his art must be so big as it will carry him over everything, every mountainous disappointment, like the elephants of Hannibal. Kennedy, son, play something for me?

Kennedy: You play something, Clem.

(Clem *hesitates, all* Musicians *urge him on.*)

Kennedy: C'mon play something.

Clem: Rachmaninoff's C sharp minor prelude, perhaps.

(Musicians *stare at the floor, cough, etc.*)

Clem: No, my fingers are stiff today, the weather, go ahead Kennedy, and watch that left hand, all right? (*As* Kennedy *plays*) It's very interesting, very interesting. Not the sort of thing I would play of course. Don't have the knack, really. In my youth, Debussy was ugly; Ravel was ugly; Stravinsky was ugly; Schönberg was worse than ugly. These boys are cherubim. (*Emphatically*) We are spreading the gospel of music.

(Clem *exits.* Austra *follows him, but he stops her with a look.*)

SCENE THREE

Ruthie: It's a letter from the city.

Austra: Money. Money, money, money.

Musicians: (*Echo:*) Money, money, money.

Austra: A hundred bucks in your back pocket. (*Starts to talk into* Babe's *ear, who responds with drumming*)

Herbie: We'll just have to play somewhere else.

Kennedy: So go to the Park Plaza or something.

(Herbie *and* Kennedy *exit. Black Hat stays glumly put. Babe's drumming becomes a duet with* Ruthie.)

Ruthie: The mail I bring the mail, read it Clem, look at it? NO and who would but we've got to do something we've got to sell something what is there to sell, our couch is too old. The sheriff will come and take it all away. Someone is coming here to get *something* I can see that I've got the sacred premonition. You boys going to help? You love him but do you respect him? You'd respect him sure if he played for you he doesn't play enough for you I've told him that (*To* Black Hat) You hungry? (*Pulls a sandwich from her pocket*) Go get yourself some milk. I'm supposed to be practical I'm not practical, I just look practical because I worry. Sewing costumes, making pies, I've gone through all my savings, Clem has spent some $30,000 of his own, there's nothing left.

(*End of drumming.*)

Austra: Money falling from airplanes in the sky.

Ruthie: You do something you worry with me Shirley, you worry you look for signs in your dreams. Turn around. (*Making* Austra *model for her*)

Austra: I should worry? would Sartre worry? No. Dig the spendour of being. But when the being becomes nothingness? When the splendour is gone? I should worry? *C'est une question de perception.*

Ruthie: How long are you planning to stay? Shush. It will be raining and you will be under a bridge. That's not so long, I don't mind. Eat all the pie you like. There's one room. It's off limits. It's Clement's room. It's locked.

Austra: I don't understand what you are saying.

Ruthie: Of course you do, you understand everything. You're not some baton twirler. Why are you wearing black? Don't be so silly. Look, I know about you. I know about most people. Everyone has secrets. Souls travel, you know. Take this soul. Once it was a fish. Now it's a drummer in a jazz club. Once it was a Sumerian slave driver. Now it's Miss Cognac at the Victory. Shirley. You're no Shirley. Your eyes are too old. You've seen something.

(Clement *enters wearing aviator suit and eating spaghetti.*)

Clem: Cheer up!

Ruthie: (*To* Clem) See this costume? It slips off in seconds! (*To* Austra) Go ahead and worry. And there's a pizza in the oven from two days ago. (Ruthie *exits.*)

SCENE FOUR: JEKYLL POEM

(*Drum roll. Showtime.*)

Clem: Welcome, welcome, welcome. Tonight we have a very interesting line-up and whenever I think of where it is going, I'm reminded of Paderewski when he – or maybe it was Hindemith. Now there was a fellow. You all have tried Ruthie's sandwiches I hope and next week we will experiment with potato salad. Yes indeedy. Clem has had some crazy news, crazy. Subway subterrane-ay, House of Hambourg no delay. So what. But now! I give you the Saint Incarnate of Our Sewers, the Archangel Resident Poet of Our Troubled Establishments, do not heckle our Mister Zoot Jekyll.

(Jekyll *takes the stage for a dramatic reading of a poem accompanied by sunglasses, bongo drums and sax.*)

Jekyll: Hi you cool cats and chicks. I was down in The Village the other day, took in the Cafe Bizaaarre. Saw Allen

Clem: Ginsberg

Jekyll: and Jack

Clem: Kerouac.

Jekyll: and all those guys. Saints. And they inspired me to – (*Groans for a long time*) This here from a cat called Delacroix (*Reads from a scrap of paper*) "If you have not sufficient skill to make a sketch of a man throwing himself out of a window, in the time that it takes him to fall from the fourth floor to the ground, you will never be capable of producing great machines." Great machines ... (*He reads the poem (ec)statically, and moves in unison with bongo player and sax,* Babe *and* Black Hat *respectively. Bongo bongo bongo.* Jekyll *keens.*)

Jekyll: The symptoms of nerve-gas poisoning.
    (*Neutral voice*)
    A concrete poem transcribed from the manual.
    (*Dramatically*)
    Runny nose. Tight chest. Dim vision. Pinpoint pupils.
    Laboured breath. Drooling, spittle, saliva, guck.
    Ex
    ce
    ssive
    sweat SWEAT.
    (*bongo bongo bongo*)
    Bang in the guts. Boom in the brains.
    Puke-vomit-puke-vomit-CRAMPS.
    Involuntary shit

Involuntary piss
Twitching jerking staggering Aspirin-g
help
(*Falsetto*) Mom, dad
(*Strong*) Confusion, coma, convulsion, cessation
of breathing.
Death.
(*Bongo*)
Death.
(*Bongo*)
Death.
(*Bongo bongo bongo*)

(Jekyll *falls on the floor.* Babe, Black Hat *and* Jekyll *lie on the floor too long. Silence.*)

SCENE FIVE: BLIND MAN OVER MY DEAD BODY

(Austra *stand up and looks at the "dead" bodies. Cast walks on stage and joins her.* Laila *begins to sing "Lācītis ir bēdigs, kas viņam kaiš?"* ["The little bear is sad, what's wrong with him?"] *Others join in, as do* Jekyll, Babe, Black Hat. *"Lācītis" is the song for a round which has people in the middle of a circle pretending to be weeping bears, crouching with their arms over their heads. During the second verse, they leap up and dance. Then others take their place in the middle. Their positions look like "duck and cover" poses.*

As the dancing continues, the musicians peel off and play a different, haunting melody: "Avotāi guni kura." The dancers change from a happy image to a surreal one of war. First chorus: freeze. Second chorus: circle the other way, Jekyll *peels off and stands at the periphery with the information of watching a bomb attack. Third chorus:* Ruthie *and* Clem *peel off, and stand same as* Jekyll. *Fourth chorus: all are huddled on the ground,* Austra *and* Laila *look up at the sky.* Austra *is having fun.* Laila *tries to make her duck, she won't.* Laila *hits* Austra. *Everyone backs away from* Austra. *As* Austra *continues her dance on her own,* Laila *enters with a baby buggy.*)

Laila: Mommy got a letter, mommy got a letter.

(*She settles down to read the letter. At certain points,* Austra *stops and watches her.*)

Laila: Dear Laila ... We are well. Irina's pregnancy is going well ... The birch tree is also well and sends her love to you, so far away now from our little Latvia ... Is your husband Gunārs still working so hard? Do you look like an American yet? The Ozols next door say that ... The price of eggs has gone up. There is no meat in the market ...

(Herbie *walks over behind* Laila *with his bass. Starts to make insistent sound of planes flying over.* Laila *gets very worried.*)

Laila: It's only an airplane.

Laila: (*Starts to pace*) Austra. Austra! Austra! They are coming! (*She runs to the door. She hides under the table in the same pose as* Austra. *The drone of the bass changes to the drone of an accordion. During the next scene,* Austra *and* Laila *change places.*)

SCENE SIX: HEY MAC!

(Aivars *and* Kennedy, *with an accordion, appear on an upper balcony. Music and text dialogue.*)

Aivars: I hear an airplane and you know what I think, I think: "watch out!" No, no. Joke. I think: here is progress. Here I am Aivars Pūtvējiņš, never gone anywhere, and some day soon, airplanes will be so cheap, I can fly to Paris for lunch. Some day, *ja*. What you need is to always have $100 in your back pocket. They teach me this when I worked as a used car salesman, long time ago. There was this guy, Bob McDuff. Canadian guy. He wears checkered trousers. Drives a sports car. No wife, no family. Always has money. Calls everyone "Mac." "Hey, Mac." I am very bad at selling cars. I make no money. I hate the bastard. One day he looks at me and says "Harry" – my name is Aivars, but he calls me Harry – Harry you need $100 in your back pocket, then you'll sell. I think crazy, $100. Crazy. I make twenty dollars a week. But I do it. I don't eat lunch. I walk home without streetcar. Takes me a few months, but I do it. And you know what. I sell. $100 in my back pocket and I sell. Now I work in a bank. Don't have to sell anything. But there has to be some money in my pocket. There are other things in life. There is the family. There are the millions dying behind the Iron Curtain. There is all that. Last time Austra had a birthday, you know what I gave her? A broom with a red handle. You understand. Next time I give her something special. No money, no object. A television. I can give her a television. We will watch the news together every night! A hundred dollars in the back pocket. What you know, mac.

(*The airplane drone returns.*)

SCENE SEVEN: THE NEWS

(*Ads and newscasts: movement sequence in frames of televisions and radios.* Austra *is crouching under a table in the club.* Clem *bends over her.*)

Ad #1: Tense, anyone? There's so much bad news these days that it's a little trying on the nerves to get it all repeated on the radio, television, everywhere you turn.

News: Plans for a "War Supplies Agency" ready to swing into action in the event of an attack on Canada were announced last night by Prime Minister Diefenbaker.

Ad #1: As a tonic, we prescribe the *Saturday Evening Post*. We think our editorial balance helps *Post* readers keep theirs.

Clem: I've never been afraid. The day I was afraid was when I lost for two minutes my capacity to wonder. I heard Mingus play a honeyed riff and thought so what. So what. Horrors.

Austra: You're afraid they'll close the club.

Clem: Some things you can escape. Others come and get you in the end. Then all you can say is

Austra: Welcome.

(Austra *and* Clem *move with the media frames.*)

Ad #2: Do you realize that if 263 bombs dropped on the United States, the fallout from Maine, Michigan and the American West would knock out Canada's population centres? The trapper, the Eskimo and the farmer are the only men who might survive.

Marlene: I was Miss Toronto this year, and Miss Toronto Maple Leaf the year before, and a few years ago, Posture Queen of Ontario. It's strange.

Ad #2: Ralph Lapp, well known writer on atomic topics, predicts the Russians will be capable of an attack by 1965.

(Austra *and* Clem *at the piano.*)

Austra: Mr Clement, I will serve the club for the rest of my life. I will never be in love. I will play the saxophone.

Clem: You'll blow your mug out of shape.

Journalist #1: Today it is impossible to go anywhere in my city without coming in contact with the foreign born. They work in our banks, our offices, libraries and department stores. They are cultured and educated people.

Austra: Look at Herbie, Black Hat, Kennedy, Babe, Jekyll. Radical independence. In their steps, I will follow.

Clem: Ridiculous! most ridiculous. What is Clement without Ruthie, hm? Human beings weren't made to live alone.

Austra: Then I'm an extra-terrestrial. And the House of Hambourg is the only home I recognize.

Clem: (*Exiting*) You might have chosen something a little more permanent. Something more concrete. A bunker.

(*Slams the door in her face. During next sequence* Austra *and* Clem *change
places so that* Clement *is in the club space and* Austra *is seemingly speaking
through a locked door to* Clement *in the next section.*)

Journalist #2: Many Canadians, raised in the flapjack and maple syrup tradition, are switching to more pungent European foods. The sales of black
olives have increased.

Journalist #3: 300%.

Journalist #2: since 1956. We can sample new specialty cheeses like

Journalist #3: gouda or Edam.

Journalist #2: The imports of exotic spices like

Journalist #3: oregano, basic, chervil,

Journalist #2: fennel,

Journalist #3: rosemary and tarragon,

Journalist #2: have taken off like a rocket.

Ad #2: A shopping list of conserved foods for a crucial fourteen days is
one of many useful tips in his new book, *The Family Fallout Shelter.*

Journalist #1: Thirty years ago, if anybody had told me that today our city
would have a Jewish mayor, Ukrainian and Polish aldermen and foreign-
born policemen, I would have waved them off to the funny farm. Now
you can't walk down the street any more because it is so crowded with
people speaking all different languages. And that's what makes Toronto
the city it is today.

Austra: Clem, many tips. The guy with the art gallery gave me a whole
dollar. Clem, they say Ella Fitzgerald might stop here after the show tonight. (*Silence*) OK. Frank Sinatra, Elvis Presley, and Audrey Hepburn are
all trapped on a hot air balloon. Only one of them can stay. Frank turns to
Elvis and says – OK. Diefenbaker, Khrushchev and Castro are all trapped
on a hot air balloon. Only one of them can stay. Castro looks at Diefenbaker and says – OK.

SCENE EIGHT: LAMENT

Clem: All we'll get is another kick in the face. Tierra del Fuego. Tierra
del Fuego. That's how much love there is in this city for music. Ripping,
soaring, pulsing, wailing, cooking, moving, grooving, crying: music. Just
listen to my boys, MY BOYS, saints! Angels!

("Lament" *music begins, baritone sax and piano.*)

Clem: (*Crooning*) Goodnight, goodnight.
Goodnight, you ladies and gentlemen.
All good things come to a swansong.
All good people to an end.

Take Charlie Parker. There's not a jazzman alive doesn't owe something
to the Bird. This Bird doesn't get the worm, the worm gets the Bird.
Hooks him on heroin at age 14. The Bird wanders around Greenwich Village like an ambulatory trash can. But they love him. They all love him.
Even Baroness Pannonica de Koenigswarter loves him when he collapses
on her doorstep and dies in her guest room watching the Tommy Dorsey
show.

Charlie Parker, dead at 34.
Sonny Berman, 23.
Clifford Brown, 25.
Bob Schilling, 26, remember Bob Schilling?
Bix Beiderbecke, 28.
Fats Navarro, 27.
Chu Berry, 31.
Bunny Berrigan, 33.
Chick Webb, 37, Fats Waller, 39, Bessie Smith, 43, Lester Young, 50.
Miles Davis ain't looking so good.

(*He leaves the stage, music solo. End of music,* Clem *reappears up in the attic.*)

Clem: Jazz fans, I'm talking to you. Schubert took the exit at 30 years of
age. Young Master Mozart didn't last too long. So here is Clem, a hipster
of 59 years. If my music had more whoopee, I might not be around to
play.

Dr Roy Milford: (*Played by* Laila) I have tickets to give away to three
callers for the First Canadian Jazz Festival, sponsored by the Canadian
Mental Health Association.

SCENE NINE: BEATNIK MEETS ETHNIC

("House of Hambourg" *music.* Jekyll *enters and lies on the floor.*)

Jekyll: Hey waitress!

(Austra *enters with a tray and a cup.*)

Jekyll: I didn't order cappuccino. I want it black.

Austra: Oh, I'm very sorry. Your name is Zoot, yes?

Jekyll: Zoot Dr Jekyll of the Potions. Poet, Painter, Man oh Man About Town. Dr Zoot Jekyll, and you?

Austra: I've seen your work, it's good. Van Gogh, like. Paint what you see, colour and line, exactly *fast*.

Jekyll: (*Laughs*) Van Gogh, hey, get hip, sister, like de Kooning is where it's at, and Jackson Pollock down in the Big Apple.

Austra: Yes, de Kooning is quite marvellous, but my father always preferred Van Gogh.

Jekyll: So who's the old man.

(Clement *enters,* Austra *doesn't want him there. Once he goes to the piano, she speaks again.*)

Austra: My father runs an art gallery in Paris.

Jekyll: Oh?

Austra: Yes, I ran away from him. It was too much. But he follows me. If you see a man in a black hat, please warn me. (Austra *exits*)

Jekyll: Sure babe sure.

(*Re-take of scene. Music.* Jekyll *gets up and leans against the piano.* Austra *re-enters, lounges against the door.*)

Jekyll: Hey, miss, I didn't ask for cappuccino, I like it black.

Austra: Hey, bongo man, you're too tense. It's me who should be tense. I am being followed. By a man in a black hat. Call me Shirley.

Jekyll: Shirley. You don't look like a Shirley. Are you the chick who smuggled Ginsberg's *Howl* into Canada? Shirley?

Austra: (*Pauses for quite a while*) I think maybe not that Shirley.

(*Re-take of scene. Music.* Austra *and* Jekyll *sitting at the same table. They do not speak for a long time. They are lost in each other's eyes.* Clem *is discomforted by this attraction, clears his throat.*)

Clem: I never drink cappuccino. I like it black.

Austra: (*Appassionata*) Money is a drag and politics stinks.

Jekyll: Soon we're all going to go pop, man, boom, baby!

Austra: Everyone dies sometimes.

Jekyll: No, doll, I don't mean kicking the individual bucket, I mean the big blast, the ultra-fungoid, the End!

Austra: There is no future. I know that. The world teeters on the edge of a volcano.

Jekyll: Only the consciousness of imminent death can focus your spiritual being. The world is rotting, it's disintegrating, it needs a coup de grace, a heavy stick of dynamite up its arse. The sixties are coming and I am not afraid.

Austra: (*Idly*) Isn't it curious, how the bubbles gather in the corner of your mouth when you talk so much.

Clem: (*Walking over to the two*) So – you like my niece?

Jekyll: She's not your niece.

(*Music resumes.* Jekyll *and* Austra *jump to their feet and dance, joined by* Kennedy *and* Black Hat. *They crowd* Clem *out, stare at him with the last beat of the music. Throughout this scene,* Herbie *twirls his bass and* Babe *plays his sticks on his shoulders. Stylized movement with text.*)

Austra: Black, his mood is very black. It is a catastrophe. This club is the secret heart of Toronto, it beats, it beats, boom, boom, boom. Yes, he is a great mystery. I found a room – upstairs – where the door is locked. And the windows are closed, too.

Jekyll: I tried to paint him once and all I got was a great big laughing skull.

Austra: He is a great man. I can see this right away. He is a great man. We will do it. A bake sale. A special concert. A raffle – the Girl Guides made big bucks with a raffle. In Switzerland. Before my father disowned me. We must sell something.

Jekyll: You could sell a few dreams. If someone gave you the dust dreams are made of.

(*Dangles the heroin in front of her.* Clem *is completely blocked out and exits.*)

Austra: What?

Kennedy: What?

Jekyll: Dream dust for the jazz mecca.

(Austra *does not understand what it is.*)

Austra: Yes?

Black Hat: What?

Jekyll: Norm's Grill at Carlton and Jarvis. 8 o'clock tonight. You wait for a guy to come in with kind of sandy hair and a blank expression. He'll wink at you. Twice. Then you sell him the dust. For (*Whispers the amount*). Come back to the club and presto press the money into Clement's hands. It'll cover the bills, at least. But don't tell him where the dollars came from. Say you got it from ... your uncle.

Austra: I don't know.

Jekyll: You square?

Austra: No.

Jekyll: You scared?

Austra: I'm not scared of anything.

(Jekyll *gives her the heroin*.)

Jekyll: I've done it before. I'd do it again, if the narcs weren't watching me. Itching to empty my unholy pockets. But they'd be crazy to nail an upstart daisy like you.

Austra: For sale.

Jekyll: For Clem.

SCENE TEN: TENSE, ANYONE?

(Jekyll, Black Hat *and* Kennedy *leave* Austra *as she stands alone with the heroin and music for* "Tense, Anyone?" *begins. She makes gestures of decision, trying to throw the heroin away, stuffing it into her coffee cup, pirouetting with the heroin, throwing it on the ground.* Clem *bounds in.* Austra *covers the heroin with her foot.* Clem *forgets what he has to say and bounds out again.* Austra *exits.*)

SCENE ELEVEN

(*Norm's Grill, as before.* Austra *is sitting in a corner, looking nervous, with heroin to sell.* Jekyll *leans nonchalantly at the door, waiting for the customer.*)

Jekyll: The steam was rising from the Jarvis Street manholes while broads in bright dresses lured the unsuspecting to their lairs. Like one-eyed lemmings they came. If you catch my meaning. If you don't, beat it. Flog it to death.

Herbie: Key, Kennedy. Hey, sweetheart. Your fly is open.

Kennedy: What's the world coming to.

Jekyll: It was a tense and trying evening in Toronto and you couldn't resist but kick the tires of every car. Jack be nimble, Jack be quick, Jack jump over the icepick in your head. What a night. Good citizens wrote letters to the *Telegram*. Buns staggered through the alleys. New Canadians huddled in their kitchens and sang strange ballads, barely audible to the human ear. I caught a bat in my kitchen. Stuffed it in a bag and knocked its brains out against the door. It was that kind of night.

(*Silence.* Jekyll *paces. Radio news comes on.*)

Radio: July 17, 1959. The news. Plagued by drugs Billie Holiday dies. The Negro entertainer, called "Lady Day," was arrested on her deathbed for heroin abuse. She died a wasted shadow of the once great blues singer who packed night clubs from coast to coast. She was 44 years old.

(Austra *has a change of heart. She starts to pour the heroin into her coffee.* Jekyll *catches her hand and pushes the sugar container towards her.*)

Jekyll: Norm supplies the sugar here, lady.

(*At this moment, a* Policemen *enters. There is a coffee waiting for him.*)

Cop: So boys, keeping it clean tonight? (*Eyeing* Austra) New girl on the strip? Who does she think she is, Leslie Caron?

Black Hat: Nah, she's some Transylvanian nursing student.

Cop: You speak Russian? *Govorite po-russki* [Do you speak Russian]?

Austra: *Ne, es esmu latviete, tu lielā cūka.* [No, I'm Latvian, you big pig.]

Cop: *Es neesmu liela cūka un kas tu tāda?* [I'm not a stupid pig and who are you?]

Austra: *Ak tu kungs man ļoti žēl. Es domāju, jū esat krievs.* [Oh my God I'm sorry. I thought you were Russian.]

Cop: (*Laughing*) She called me a stupid pig because she thought I was Russian.

Jekyll: Are you Russian?

Cop: You crazy? *Kā tevi sauc, mazā?* [What's your name, little girl?]

Austra: *Mednis. No Liepājas.* [Mednis. From Liepaja.]

Cop: *Mednis – no Liepājas?* [Mednis – from Liepaja?]

Austra: I have a crazy cousin who ran away from home the night of her engagement party.

Cop: That's right, Austra, her name is Austra. They say she's been found in Las Vegas. She's a stripper now. Such a shame.

Black Hat: The night of her engagement party. I ask you what do women want.

Cop: Austra Mednis. The fiancé works in a bank. Nice guy, real nice. *Es atgriezīšos pēc divām stundām ja tev vajag pavadoni.* [I'll come back in two hours if you need an escort.]

Austra: Oh, don't worry about me, my husband will be here any minute. He is a boxer.

Cop: *Kā tu gribi.* [Whatever you say.] Austra Mednis. Such a sad story. Her sister crazy too. Sits in the basement all day, waiting for the bomb to drop. So fellas, see you. And don't do things I would never do. (*Exits.*)

All: Sure, Mac.

(*Norm's Grill disintegrates, while* Ruthie *speaks, in a trance.*)

Ruthie: It was a night like any other night in this our city of slop. Far away on Bloor Street West, five hundred young people listening to rock and roll cracked each other's noses on the lawn. A squirrel was found dead in Queen's Park. Electroshock. Down at Norm's Grill, it was the quiet before the storm. Norm sniffed the air like he'd lost his armpit. There's some bitter people in this town. They don't suck cocktails at Diana Sweets. It's an ugly business. If you can't take it, move your noodle to the fields of North York. Now there's some rolling hills.

SCENE THIRTEEN

(Austra *and* Jekyll *walking down the street.* Austra *crosses to the other side, every time* Jekyll *wants to walk with her. During this scene she changes out of her beatnik clothes and into her engagement party dress.*)

Jekyll: I give you powdered money, You pour it in your java. Now we're playing skip tag from sidewalk to sidewalk. What is this? oral limbo? You have to stoop too low to talk to me?

Austra: Ten cents, you have ten cents for phone?

(*He looks for ten cents, and tempts her with it while he speaks.*)

Jekyll: What happened, was it the radio? Billie Holiday died, so what? Fate, risk, death, that's life. What Swedish Sunday School did you crawl out of? Swedish, yeah, I heard you in there, Shirley. Or is it: Dagmar.

Austra: Just give me ten cents, OK?

Jekyll: I happen to love Clem. I do. Those cool tight-bearded hipsters sitting without moving with their unfriendly girlfriends dressed in black, they might take the GALACTIC liberty of laughing at him now and then, but not Jekyll, I love the old geezer from one end of his Rachminanoff to the other. And you just threw his future, his future, the future of jazz music in this city and probably throughout this great nation of ours, you threw it right down the sink.

Austra: Talk, talk, talk, where's the Gravol. Your goddam dream dust dirt went down the drain, that's all. Mr Clement will be fine. You just wait and see. Give me the ten cents.

Jekyll: Please.

Austra: Heck, please.

Jekyll: Now say it in Swedish.

Austra: Take a short walk on a long pier.

Jekyll: You mean take a long walk on a short pier.

Austra: Oh you artist you smart aleck you beatnik peacenick jelly roll formica top (*She grabs the dime from him*) Scram.

Jekyll: Eternity. You never think of it.

(Jekyll *exits*. Austra *contemplates calling* Aivars.)

Austra: *Sveiks Aivar, vai tu vēl dzīvs.* ("Hello Aivars, are you still alive?" – a colloquialism) *Sveiks Aivar, vai – Aivar. Sveiks.* I do so remember, I remember everything.

(Aivars *leaps into the scene.*)

Aivars: Austra. Austra. I love you.

("Austra Austra I love you" *music and movement – lover's quarrel duet)*

END OF SECOND SET.

THIRD SET

(*Whirr of the sewing machine. No one is there.*)

SCENE ONE: I DO SO REMEMBER EVERYTHING, I DO.

(*Image of* Laila, Aivars *and* Austra, *fresh off the boat.* Aivars *raising a glass; they sing:*)

Lai dzīvo sveiks, lai dzīvo sveiks! Lai dzīvo sveiks, lai dzīvo sveiks! [*A celebration song – "May They Live Well"*]

Aivars: *Mēs, jaunais pāris, mēs būsim maza latviešu sala. Te nav Amērika. Te nav nekāds* melting pot. *Kanada ir viens* – jigsaw puzzle! "I am proud to be – *ne takai* – Canadian *bet* – : a Latvian Canadian. "*Kamēr esam tālumā, tālu no mūsu dargo Latviju, slava mūsu trimdas mājām:* Toronto!

[We, the young couple, will be a little Latvian island. This is not America. There is no melting pot here. Canada is a – jigsaw puzzle! "I am proud to be – not only – a Canadian – but a Latvian Canadian." While we are abroad, far away from our precious Latvia, hail to our home in exile: Toronto!]

(*The three begin the "Walter Thornton" movement, walking like models.*)

Laila: Toh-ronto! Heck! Everything is *so ugly* here, I'll never get used to it. *Kanadiešiem nav kultūras, nav kultūras.* [Canadians have *no culture, no culture.*] Little ugly houses, *ne dārzu, ne stādu, ne klavieres, ne grāmatu, nekā.* [no gardens, no flowers, no pianos, no books, nothing] just Television! We come to Toronto, it is 1951. Haalifaks-Montreal-Toronto. The bread on the train – Canadian bread like *pape!* [cardboard]. (*Searches for the word*) Wood!

Austra: (*Flatly*) Cardboard.

Laila: (*Cheerful*). Yes. We all come, Mama, Papa, my sister, my cousins, and on the ship we meet our neighbour from Liepaja, Aivars Pūtvējiņš, and I, I meet my husband, Gunārs. He is a good man. *Dabū* [He gets a] job *caks* [like that!] [Then I got a] job, *caks* [like that!] (*Snaps her fingers*) Papa, he was a teacher, now he is security guard, what you can do. Twenty-five dollars a week *mazgājot traukus* [washing dishes at] Hospital for Sicks Children. "Good Morning!" *Tad Ozola kungs man atrada* [Then Mr Ozols got me a] job *pakojot zekes* [packing socks at] McGregor's Sock Factory. Spadina Avenue. I'm wearing some right now. (*Points at her foot*) Nice? *Mana mamma un Austra šuva blūzes priekš* [My Mama and Austra sew blouses for] Elite Blouses. Spadina Avenue. We gave all our money to Mama, and she divided it among the family. Austra.

Austra: *Liec mani mierā.* [Leave me alone]

Laila: (*Exasperated*) Mamma always said: the man who marries Austra, he'll end up in the nuthouse.

SCENE TWO

(Clem *and* Kennedy *playing the piano and having a lot of fun. Surrounded by the other* musicians, *they toy with the theme of* "Three Blind Mice, see how they run, oh say can you see." *Hilarity.*)

SCENE THREE: LANGUAGE CLASS

(Austra, Aivars *and* Laila *are reading from Reader's Digest.* Musicians *read along with them, standing at the piano, in the voices of little boys.*)

Aivars: "Yellowknife is not everybody's cup of tea." (*Others repeat sotto voce*) "The natives of Montreal are known for their (*Cautiously misreading*) joie de vivre." (*Others repeat*)

Austra and Aivars: "Halifax is a naval city."

Laila: – is a naval city.

Little Boys: The Calgary stampede draws many a curious visitor.

Laila: Canadians. Funny people. Smile, Candid Camera. God Save the Queen. The customer is always right. I am a new Canadian. Cheeze Whiz.

All: Vancouver is a jewel not to be overlooked.

Austra: I am a new Canadian. My name is Austra Mednis. I was born in Liepaja, Latvia, in 1938.

Aivars: I have a high school diploma from Augustdorf, Germany, where I was in a camp. I speak English and I can type. Career goal: journalist.

Austra: Now I am a student at Harbord Collegiate.

Aivars: I do not play golf or bowling.

All: The merchants of Fredericton are made of sturdy stuff. Whale blubber is a choice commodity for the people of the North.

Austra: I have been in Canada for one year and three days and I am 15 years old almost. My New Year's resolution for 1952 is to make many Canadian friends. My resolution is to tell jokes so they can understand when to laugh. Also I will save up my money and buy a baton. Also I ...

Laila: My boss, he said, what's your name. He said "too hard. I call you Sally." No, no. Laila. Not hard. My boss he says "call me Hirsch." He's OK. He says "Merry Christmas." He says "egg nog." My boss, he gives me a poin-set-ti-ya. Cheers. We are alive.

All: In Winnipeg, the temperature drops far below the freezing point. Spring is greeted with joy by the farmers of Annapolis valley. Yellowknife is not everybody's cup of tea!

SCENE FOUR

(Aivars *jumps up, throwing off his coat. It is 1953. He turns into a boxer, with* Austra *as his coach.*)

Aivars: CBC! *Man ir darbs pie CBC!* [CBC! I have a job at CBC!]

Austra and Laila: CBC!

Aivars: I don't believe it. CBC. I went to Jarvis Street, funny building, like the radio house in Riga, and there at the desk is a pretty lady –

Austra: Oh?

Aivars: For a Canadian. She sits there, nice desk, and I tell her all about myself, how I wrote for the newspaper in camp, and how I know Mr Kalns cousin who is a good friend of Max Ferguson and the lady smiles and gives me an application, and so I write: Aivars Putvejiņs, born in Riga, Latvia, 1929, I speak English and I can type! I give her the application.

She looks at it. Looks at me. Looks at it again. I can see her thinking, thinking. And then she says: "WE'LL CALL YOU!"

Austra and Laila: WE'LL CALL YOU!!

(*Split-second freeze, then realization sinks in.*)

Austra: (*Dejectedly*) We'll call you!???

Aivars: CBC. We'll call you! *Šī stulbā zoss* [This silly goose], this bobby soxer treats me like I have a big gaping hole in my brain!

Austra: I know exactly how you feel. The girl beside me in Harbord Collegiate – she's so stuck-up. And she reads comics.

Aivars: Yeah? (*He looks at* Austra *for the first time as if she's not a child*) *Ak Austra. Tu esi tik jauna. Un skaista.* [Oh, Austra, you are so young and so beautiful.]

Austra: I'm not so young.

(Aivars *touches her knee.* Laila *smiles, standing behind them.*)

Austra: (*Embarrassed*) CBC!

SCENE FIVE

(*Full club.* Herbie *and* Kennedy *play spirited intro.*)

Clem: Radio Slobvia reports from Lemon Krushki, Emperor of Russia, Grand Duke of Siberia and Guardian of Lower Slobovia: Our way of lifeniki, or elsenikoffski. Workers of the world unite, under me! You have nothing to lose but your shoes! Your shirts are at the Chinese laundry.

(*More hilarity.*)

SCENE SIX

(Laila *enters* Austra's *bedroom at night, carrying a candle.* 1955. *While she speaks, we see* Aivars *and* Austra *dancing on another level of the stage.*)

Laila: (*Mischievously*) Austriņa, are you asleep? Peekaboo I see you, the green goblins are coming to get you. (*Listens*) How you can sleep so quietly. I hear Gunārs snoring beside me, and Mamma snoring in the other room, snoring, snoring, it's like the ocean. (*Whispering*) Austra come on, wake up. I'm gonna tickle your toesies. Wanna feel a little kick? This one is going to be a girl, Austra. She's going to be an A-student, just like you. Tūteris' daughter went off to marry some Canadian and be a Mrs Gordon Smith and eat Cheese Whiz and plastic sausages on a table without a tablecloth. But that won't happen to you. I'll betcha you'll wake up if I say somebody's name. (*Teasingly*) Aivars. (*Louder*) Aivars. (*Turns on the light, The room is empty*) Oh! Not again! Climbing out the window! You monkey!

SCENE SEVEN

(*Loud Buddy Holly music, coming from a record player. Club in full force.* Jekyll *rushes in.*)

Jekyll: This Columbia High Fidelity recording is scientifically designed.

(Aivars *and* Austra *enter close to the audience and dance a combination of jive and Latvian folk frolic.*)

Jekyll: If you are the owner of a new stereophonic system, this record will play with brilliant true-to-life fidelity. In short, you can purchase this record with no fear of its becoming obsolete in the future. Kee-rist! who spins this ephemera?!!

(Jekyll *exits.* Austra *and* Aivars *exit.* Jekyll *returns, carrying the record. He breaks it over his knee.*)

SCENE EIGHT

(Laila *typing, wearing glasses, hair pushed up,* 1959.)

Laila: This month it will be eight years we have been here. Gunārs dreams in English sometimes. What's next.

(Austra *enters in her folk costume, carrying a record, looking dejected.*)

Laila: Austriņa, what can I say to our cousins in Latvai.

Austra: Buddy Holly died.

Laila: Buddy Holly? That was in February! They want summer news.

Austra: (*Emphatically*) He died.

Laila: So he died? so what? (Austra *makes a face behind her back.* Laila *makes a face when* Austra *exits without deigning to speak to her*) *Mazā princesīte* [The little princess.] Austra says hi. She is very happy. Right after graduation, she found a job in a movie house box office, and even handed out leaflets as a Leslie Caron look-alike. That is a film star here in a film called *Gigi*. She is saving up money so she can go study to be a nurse, that is a good job. We just celebrated her twenty-first birthday: I gave her ten piano lessons with Zariņš and Aivars gave her a broom with a red handle. I think he wants to tell her something. I don't mean to brag, you know, we are not like Egons Kronbergs who sent a picture of himself to Latvia with the caption: This is me and the fridge.

(Aivars *enters from the direction of* Austra*'s room.*)

Aivars: Austra is crying. I have never seen such tears. And over what, a popular singer.

Austra: (*Offstage*) He was an artist. An artist!

Aivars: Such passion. Such fire. It's wonderful.

Laila: Yes, wonderful, unpredictable, she comes, she goes, and you better marry her before she disappears in the wind, *caks!* [like that!]

Aivars: Marry her? ... (Laila *resumes typing*) Marry her?

Laila: The photograph of the birch tree is on the wall and I smile at it every day.

Aivars: (*Walking towards* Austra*'s room*) Austriņa ...

(Austra *appears in her coat, singing* "Lai dzivo sveiks." Laila *and* Aivars *join her.* Laila *continues singing as* Aivars *speaks and* Austra *creeps away from them.*)

Aivars: We two, as man and wife, we will be a small Latvian island. This isn't America. This isn't some melting pot. I am proud to be not only a Canadian, but also a Latvian Canadian –

(*Club music starts for* Jekyll*'s poem.* Aivars *and* Laila *freeze as they realize* Austra *is gone.* Aivars *puts on his black hat and exits in the opposite direction to* Austra. Laila *watches* Jekyll *and* Herbie, *and as the poem progesses, starts to throw things at them – baby clothes, shoes, socks, whatever. The poem is very beat.*)

Jekyll: Clem's boys
    Blazed
    Away the night,   **Laila:** Shhh!
    And little wet-behind-the-ears
    Cats
    Flew singing
    Off to pads
    With beers and beds.
      The rest of us
    Blew,
    Out of our minds,
    Swinging   **Laila:** Shut up!
    In the cool red morning
    Till the glow went out
    With the street lamps. ("SESSION," "f.a.c." dated 1959)

(*A shower of articles falls on* Jekyll.)

Jekyll: Hey, what's going on!?

Who? –
Lady! Lady!
What is this
Personal
Ambush
when you know the world is going to go –
  look, lady –
POP
  will you put that thing DOWN
lady, what the heck
I live the life that Jack Kerouac imagines he lived
heck
it's a drag to be an artist in this day and age but
we shrug as we look at our TV dinners and

Laila: I live the life that your heckuva Jack or John Wayne or bang bang I live that life of Zhivago but no vodka fun, I tell you, and now I am in this ugly stupid city this *desert* in a basement with canned foods with the jolly green giant, nuclear this, nuclear that, and you, you take my sister and you turn her into a walking nothing, a nothing, an emptiness. Zero. You're so tough. Oyoyoy. Tip top tailors. Eh you are just a school boy in short pants.

(Austra *walks onto the scene.*)

Austra: My name is Austra Mednis. You must excuse me.

(*Light change*, Laila *exits.*)

SCENE NINE

("Nervous" *drums. Everyone is nervous – stylized movement throughout the scene.*)

Clem: A man with a black hat

Austra: The man with the black hat

Jekyll: Watch out for the black hat

Band: Black Hat!

(*Club*, "Nervous" *music. On bass lines of music, all look at door, relieved when the one who enters is* Ruthie, *carrying a part of a splendiferous costume [which she wears in the portrait-selling scene]. When the music ends, the physical rhythm continues.*)

Ruthie: It's like this: there's a man with a black hat. He's coming, he's coming very soon. He will take something away. He's slouching, yes I'm sure he's slouching. (*Asking her spirits*) Could we persuade him to wait a month or two? Of course not. It's like this, Clem: we've got to do something. Something, Clement, something. Sell something, borrow something, dig up some buried treasure. (*To spirits*) Oh don't go away – (*Sigh*) It's a bad connection. Something.

Clem: A man with a black hat. Ruthie said so. A man with a black hat will come and close the club. And I'll be dragged off to debtors' prison. The last of the Hambourgs. Sheriffs and bailiffs with mastiffs trailing, large yellow dogs with pink-rimmed eyes, slavering. Radio Slobovia reports the Decline of the British Empire. They'll take me to a small dark room, I can't see through the windows because of the caked black grime and the red on the floor – aargh!

Jekyll: A man with a black hat following us on the way from Norm's Grill. Was there? A hallucination of mine, the Godhead in the inner city, or perhaps an undercover cop. An innocent passerby. A cop, a member of the morality squad, a squinting squealing SCURVY square. Sheesh those guys they always wear black hats and grey flannel suits and they look like that arsehole whatchamacallit: Nixon.

Austra: Mr Clement, I am expecting a visitor, a man with a black hat. He can be of great help to you, to the club. He is well connected to financial circles, you can tell from his accent. I must confess he is in love with me. We've never met. We must disregard his flights of fancy and ask him for a loan. And then the House of Hambourg will be a new place with beige curtains and smoked mirrors on the wall and windows with light streaming in, windows overlooking the Mediterranean, the Bering Strait, the Red Sea –

Clement: A man with a black hat and a letter from the city to say we must go (*With great dignity*) oh pity us (*anthem starts*) who love the House of Hambourg so

(*All rise to their feet.* "House of Hambourg" *anthem.*)

Kennedy: The House of Hambourg is a beehive of boptivity.

Jekyll: The House of Hambourg is the ultimate fallout shelter.

Ruthie: The House of Hambourg is where people like to come.

Jekyll: The House of Hambourg. So show me another place!

Austra: The House of Hambourg is where a New Canadian goes to feel old.

Clement: The House of Hambourg. A home for black sheep music. Where Clement tells you: welcome.

SCENE TEN

(*Door opens. Silhouette of a man with a black hat* [Aivars]. *No response from crowd. Sax sets a beat. All start simultaneous* "Boptivity," *wild dance movement.* Aivars *enters, looking for* Austra. Austra *keeps eluding him. Frustrated, he throws his hat on the ground and sarcastically mimics the hipsters. Just as he is about to leave, he catches sight of his fiancée. The music stops.* Jekyll *hides, thinking* Aivars *is a narc.*)

Clement: You have come for the House of Hambourg. Welcome, welcome. We have some fine musicians here, fine. The instruments are their own, of course, except the piano. Take the piano, you must do your job. The tablecloths, the chairs, you will want to take them too. Take everything away. We will not tackle you. There is just a matter of some portraits, programs, all framed and signed, I assure you their value is purely sentimental.

Aivars: I do not run an art gallery, mac.

Clem: Welcome, then, welcome. Take your time. Shirley will get you a roast beef sandwich and the boys will play anything you'd like to hear – go, Shirley, quick now –

Aivars: Shirley? Her name is Austra Mednis.

Austra: Mr Clement, this is my cousin. The man in the black hat.

Aivars: I am not her cousin. I am her fiancé.

(Jekyll *pulls* Aivars *aside.*)

Jekyll: Listen, mister, listen, I had nothing to do with it, I found the stuff in my pocket, you hook her up to a lie detector. I'm very busy. (*Exits.*)

Austra: My cousin. He works in a bank. Mr Clement, I called him for you.

Clement: This is a case of mistaken identity. The young lady's name is Shirley. How much money can she possibly owe you. You may confiscate my couch.

Aivars: I don't want your couch. Or your table. Or the piano. A week she has been gone. I had just asked her to marry me. She said Yes. Why did you say yes.

Austra: Okay, swell, he is not my cousin. He asked me to marry him. I said yes. I went for a walk. Mr Clement, I heard your music from Cumberland Street. I climbed through the window.

Clem: How about a nice little tune – "Three Little Words"! They're just itching to play –

(*Suggestions come from the band – e.g.* "Stella by Starlight," "Misty.")

Austra: Aivars. Please. This man is an artist. His club is in danger. You are assistant loans officer, and so I called you —

Aivars: Next time someone asks you, just say no.

Austra: You asked me to marry you. I said yes. You woke everybody up.

Aivars: We were happy.

Austra: I was happy for thirty minutes.

Clem: "Rhapsody in Blue" is *my favourite* piece.

Austra: Then you started to talk about the coming war, world communism, Bumbieris who'd built a fallout shelter at his cottage. I was wondering whether you would like a honeymoon in Tangiers.

Black Hat: "Night in Tunisia"!

Austra: I said I'm going for a walk. I didn't know it would take so long.

Clem: *Blow!*

(Musicians *begin jazz standard, "My Little Suede Shoes," softly.*)

Austra: Welcome to the House of Hambourg. Nothing has ever happened here before. No airplanes, no armies, no camps —

Aivars: No culture. You like this music? It's great music. It's not *your* it's not even *their* music. It's African music. They borrowed it without even asking permission. We have our own music. It is 2,000 years old. (Musicians *stop playing.* Aivars *addresses them*) She wants something new, I buy it for her. She wants music, we go to the symphony. I buy her records, Buddy Holly. She wants poetry, I give her poems. Austra, you know the latest, Sodums in Stockholm has published his translation of *Ulysses.* Ten years it takes him to translate James Joyce into Latvian after work every day. That guy Sodums made his 60-year-old mother type the manuscript from beginning to end three times. It weighs several kilo.

Austra: So, Mr Clement, view the situation. The man with the black hat. A real gone cat with his hands in his pockets. You talk to him, you make a deal.

Clement: Shirley is the best waitress we have ever had.

(*To* Austra's *chagrin,* Clement *exits, refusing to involve himself.*)

Aivars: You want me to arrange a loan for this kind gentleman. Your friend he has been here all his life, and he needs me for a loan? So why does my Austra want to help him so much. Is she a beatnik now?

Austra: I don't want to marry a man who looks like a dentist and have children who will die in the next war.

Aivars: So who looks like a dentist?? (*Pointing at* Herbie) He looks like a dentist. Don't marry him.

Austra: (*Wavering*) Mr Clement is a European, Aivars. You would like him.

Aivars: Listen to me, Austra, I don't care about this Clement. If you want a loan for him – OK I can help. For you. No strings. I will not beg you to come back or offer to play jazz records to our babies. You can phone me at the bank. *Sveiki*. [Bye.]

(Alivars *exits*. Austra *turns and looks at the* Musicians. *They heave a great breath, move as if about to play, but they don't. She slowly goes up the stairs to* Clement's *room*.)

Austra: Mr Clement, I have to talk to you. (*She exits*.)

SCENE ELEVEN

(*The* Musicians *rush to the door. They exit as* Ruthie *enters wearing her fabulous "roaring twenties" style stripper's costume. She sits down at the piano and picks out* "Lullaby of Birdland." Austra *exits from above and runs down the stairs, grabs a coat behind the door, looks around the club as if saying goodbye. Sees* Ruthie)

Austra: I'm just going for a walk.

(Austra *exits*. Ruthie *looks at the audience*.)

Ruthie: Could we talk business for a minute? He's upstairs in his room, we can't go there just now. Looking at them all: the photographs, the posters, the caricatures. Concert programs. Wall to wall, all framed. And autographed. That's right. They used to hang in the front hall of the Conservatory. He's standing there looking right at them. And they're looking right back. (*She looks around at the imaginary room*.) Arturo Toscanini over there. The great Chaliapin there. And Schönberg. What a nice man.

(Ruthie *gets up and* Black Hat *takes over on the piano*.)

Ruthie: The big house in that picture is the Hambourg Conservatory of Music. They came here from Moscow in 1910. In those days, it was like moving to Borneo. There's Catherine, Clem's mother. Michael Hambourg, the pater familias. "We Brought Music to Canada." Look – (*conducting movement*) like Clem, huh? Mark Hambourg, the famous one. Six years old, when he played for the Czar. Clem loved Mark so. "Never Play Down to an Audience!" Jan Hambourg, with his violin, and the red satin jacket. He was a little more relaxed. He had a parrot, Coco, could sing the Kreisler Liebeslied, fancy that. And of course, Boris and his cello and the Hart House Quartet. Boris died five years ago and ... we don't see him much. There's the bunch of them: Mark, Jan and Boris. Clem played with them once – see, in this picture.

Ruthie: He was the youngest. You know what that means. Why can't you be like. Never as good as. They took one look at his red baby face the day he was born and said never as good as. They knew to say that. To look at his pudgy fists and shake their heads. (*Looking down at her dress*) These seams if they're not double-stitched this costume will give right away in the middle of that performance and once it's given away you've given everything. Yes, they're very special pictures. Stravinsky, Ravel, Kreisler, Menuhin. "To Clement Hambourg, my esteemed friend and companion," that's what they say. If the light is right and you squint just a little. Really they're to Michael, to Mark, to Boris. But they should be to Clem. He's one of them. They don't admit it, but he is. He's been a genius all along. He's never played down to an audience. They should be. To Clem, to Clem, to Clem. We could walk in on him right now and he wouldn't even notice. Take a little portrait from the corner – oh say the one from Anna Pavlova's big ballet show in the twenties. I'll make you an offer. Just you. You understand, under the circumstances. You can have it for 500 dollars, it's a deal. The frame alone is a bargain. And you don't have to go to Buffalo to get one.

(Clem *appears at the top of the stairs.*)

Ruthie: Don't be angry.

Clem: She came to the room, Ruthie, the door was unlocked, I spoke sharply, and I frightened her away.

Ruthie: They didn't want to buy it anyway.

(Ruthie *exits.*)

Clem: I'm just going for a walk. (*He pulls on a coat, and exits.*)

SCENE TWELVE

(Austra *is walking through the city, followed by* Black Hat *and* Babe, *who use their instruments – saxophone and mallets – to create a brooding soundscape.* Herbie *and* Kennedy *re-create the airplane drone. Slowly,* Laila *and* Aivars *step into the space, wearing the coats they wore as immigrants.*)

Austra:
One two three four five six count the steps
Don't step on the cracks or you break you mother's back.
Rain rain go away come again another day.
First it's Bloor and then it's Danforth.
First it's Bloor and then it's Danforth.

First it's Bloor and then
(*beat*)
I remember I do too I remember everything.
It was under the bridge. I was six. It was fun,
   I had fun.
Nobody said I couldn't.

Laila: Nobody said we weren't ever coming back.

Austra: Mama buried the jars of jam in our yard. School was over. There wasn't any school. The jam jars would sleep there like bears in winter, Mama said. Laila still made me read every day.

Laila: We're just going on a little trip.

Austra: Mama made us play hide and seek under the haystack.

Laila: So the soldiers couldn't find you.

Austra: When the bombs dropped, we were under the bridge. Mama said don't be scared. They were great big lights. I liked it. But Laila was crying. And Aivars was singing. And Laila hit me.

Laila: It was under the bridge. I was thirteen. It was the end of my life. They had to cancel the spring dance. Mama buried my earrings with the jam jars. Miks was never coming back. I knew we wouldn't come back. Mama told Austra to play hide and seek. I knew it was because if the soldiers found us that was it. I knew it would be bad. Russian, German, American soldiers it didn't matter. The bombs were terrible. I hear them in my sleep. I hear them when my children cry in the park. These people in their big countries they don't care how much they drop. They always have more people left. I wasn't afraid right away. I was always afraid. I saw the soldier crying and then I was really afraid.

Aivars: It was under the bridge. The man across from me looked like my father who had been deported. The girl beside him looked like my sister who had disappeared. The woman next to her looked like my mother. My mother stayed and joined the Party. I didn't know that yet. It wasn't our war, it never is. It was that murderer Franklin Roosevelt and Winston Churchill and Harold Macmillan. They are murderers. They shook hands with the butcher Stalin. I had a trick for when the bombs fell. I like to hum under my breath. This time it didn't work.

(Clem *enters*.)

Clem: It was under the bridge. I knew this was the last good club. I knew all my brothers would be dead soon. I knew I would go on living. I knew Ruthie would never forsake me. It was under the bridge. I found Shirley there. Under the Danforth. The rain was so loud. I kissed her on the cheek. I knew she wasn't called Shirley. I kissed her on the cheek to say goodbye. It was a smooth cheek. Under the bridge.

(Clem, Laila *and* Aivars *exit.*)

Austra: I laughed when the bombs dropped and Laila hit me. And Aivars frowned as he hummed under his breath. They wanted me to be afraid. I don't want to be scared of anything. Canadians are never scared. Canadians are so naïve. My name is Austra Mednis.

(Ruthie *appears.*)

Ruthie: It was under the bridge. I knew it!

SCENE THIRTEEN

(Herbie *hides behind the bass,* Babe *stands by it as if holding the neck,* Kennedy *buries his face in the score.* Jekyll *enters seemingly empty club, wearing a suit and carrying a briefcase.*)

Jekyll: Hey, I got a job with CBC!

(*No one is there, no one responds.*)

Jekyll: CBC!

(*No one answers.* Jekyll *goes over to the drums and plays a little, as he speaks.*)

Jekyll: I got a job at CBC!
    Down in the House on Jarvis Street,
    The chick at the desk was giving me the rumpled
        sheet look.
    As I picked up the Official Application.
    So I told them:
    "Gerald Brown" – my maiden name –
    "born in Lindsay, Ontario, 1933,"
    editor of the high school newspaper, Trinity
        college, all that.
    I couldn't tell them everything.
    They are afraid of knowing everything.
    "Sax lessons in September, Psychoanalysis in
        October," they don't want to know my
        favourite composer.
    Just the meaningless statistucs of your journey
        through life.
    I was empty that day.
    I had no expectations.
    The chick at the desk was waiting.

I handed it to her.
She looked at me.
I looked at her.
She said, "We'll call you."
I said, "Don't make me laugh."
She watched me slide out the door,
And tossed her hair like french fries in oil.

(*Musicians appear*, Jekyll *leaves the drums*.)

Jekyll: Hey, guys, I'm gonna put you guys on the radio!

Herbie: Wow, man, you're breaking my heart. Cheer down, will ya?

(*Sixty seconds of bad music, 'CBC' theme "Meditation."* Jekyll *dances a very funny, flamboyant* CBC *dance. Music ends.*)

Jekyll: Sooooo. Drinks on me, OK? The Park Plaza. The Park Plaza and then down to the Purple Onion and later maybe this new place, the whatchamacallit. I'll be waiting for you. See you then!

(Jekyll *exits.*)

SCENE FOURTEEN: THE LAST OF THE HAMBOURGS

("Clement" *theme plays. We are in Clement's room.* Clement *enters with an empty picture frame, and places it in front of each musician. Image of reverie. He puts the frame on the floor. A knock on the door.*)

Austra: (*Offstage*) Mr Clement, I have to talk to you.

(Clem *hides.* Austra *enters the room.*)

Austra: Mr Clement? Hello? (*Looks around the room*) Toscanini ... To ... someone ... Hambourg! Oh look at this ... Oh Mr Clement! You look so funny with the black tails and ... The Hambourg Trio. To mxflz ... Hambourg ... In friendship ... B ... Bela Bartok?

(Clement *standing above her.*)

Clem: I do not recall asking you to meddle in my personal matters.

Austra: This is a miraculous secret, why do you have this kept secret? and oh ... look ... Happy Birthday from Arnold Schönberg to ... Cl ... B ... Boris ... Boris!? Oh I see and this is Boris and ... Boris and – (*surprised*) They're not to you.

Clem: Mr *Clement* Hambourg may stop liking a certain runaway.

Austra: Mr Clement Hambourg. You will have your new club. My fiancé is happy to get you a loan. To try to get you a loan. To do his best. (*Silence*) Mr Clement, baby, I am talking to you. I am telling you something.

Clem: Yes, Shirley, dear Shirley. Bank managers are very important people to know. As are undertakers, and sellers of encyclopedias. But Clement is a solo artiste. A visionary. Not a businessman.

Austra: I called him here for *you*. New he can send me flowers every day, he can buy me brooms and negligées. Now the worms are out of the can, know what I mean?

Clem: You made sacrifices. Clement did not ask for them. (*Pause*) We can get you married, Shirleykins. We'll find you a nice jazz fan. They're very polite, you know. They don't blow their nose in the tablecloth and they clap just so. We will find you someone polite.

Austra: Mrs Gordon Smith.

Clem: It's a free country.

Austra: Mr Hambourg, please. Please, he will get you the loan.

Clement: A loan, a loan, crazy. How does Shirley think will we pay it back? Perhaps we will sell these treasures. One, two, three, a dozen? All of them? Who's first? Anna Pavlova? Or Toscanini? Mark Hambourg? Who do you think, Shirley, who?

Austra: My name is Austra Mednis.

Clem: No, no, for us you are Shirley, always Shirley. We will not send you back, your are a refugee. We shall be keeping you in chocolates and nylon stockings and American nicknames until you are a proper Canadian girl. Yes, a shiny New Canadian, in *mint* condition, a Shirley to beat all Shirleys.

Austra: My name is Austra Mednis. I was born in Latvia. That is a small country by the Baltic Sea with only a few million people. Something like Switzerland. There are few of us, and we don't make cuckoo clocks.

Clement: My name is Clement Hambourg. Apparently I showed some promise. In the future, I shall try hard to be innocuous. Did you receive an invitation?

Austra: I am going for a walk.

Clem: I won't hear of it. You will get doused. The rain is pounding the sidewalks, why should you?

Austra: A walk!

(*She turns, runs to exit. Clement stands in her way, plays cat and mouse, laughing nervously. She get out, leaving we see her pull on the coat which she wore under the bridge. He turns back to audience.*)

Clem: My doctor says I'm a very high-strung chap. I must absolutely do the least shockable things to myself. I mustn't smoke or drink anything stronger than milk. He says, "If you want to play, baby, eat ice cream and walk the tight rope!" There's not so much whoopee in my playing now. It's too dangerous. I say let the young ones play the jiujitsu music. Tear your lip up. Bruise your knuckles. I like black.

(*He sinks into a chair.* Ruthie *appears.*)

Ruthie: If this club shuts down, he'll get cancer. Clement will draw his last breath, I tell you, an apocalyptic day will dawn the night this club shuts down.

Clem: Well, we'll have to close the club. A man with a black hat will come and close the club down.

(*Knocking on the door. He opens the door. No one is there. The portraits in the room begin to gleam eerily. People are standing behind the frames. The portraits have come alive.*)

Clem: Clement Hambourg!

Ruthie: Present.

Clem: Ruthie Hambourg!

Ruthie: Present.

Clem: Mark Hambourg!

Ruthie: Absent.

Clem: Jan Hambourg?

Ruthie: Absent.

Clem: Boris Ha – ?

Ruthie: Absent.

(*The portrait of the trio has been emptied out.*)

Clem: Catherine Hambourg?

Ruthie: Present!

Clement: (*Horrified*) Present!

(*Two dead mothers begin to speak simultaneously in two picture frames.*)

Dead Mother #1: Clement. Your father and I are rolling in our graves.

Clement: Oh dearie me. (*He starts to dance a defiant boogie woogie.*)

(*Other portraits of musicians lose their subjects, who walk down the aisles reciting,* "Your brother Mark, Your brother Jan, Your brother Boris" *over and over again.*)

Both Dead Mothers: Clement. A seedy nightclub is not the 1812 overture. An after-hours coffee shop on Cumberland Street for various ... characters ... is not Handel's *Messiah*. Is this music? This is noise. Clement, you are a great disappointment to us. And a disgrace ... To the family. And to this city.

Clem: I am not Glenn Gould!

("Dies Irae" *music begins. The demise of the club.* Ruthie *appears in the doorway with her broom.*)

Ruthie: I summon the dead.
        I summon ye spirits of the dead jazzmen.
        I summon ye to save our club.

(*No one answers her.* Clement *staggers across the stage like a broken wind-up toy,* Ruthie *rushes to his support.*)

Clem: Yes, welcome, welcome, oh, how was New York, jolly good, no, and you don't have to drive to Buffalo to get them, no, I'm not really with the Hart House Quartet, that's my brother Boris, no, I never met Paderewski, that's Mark, no he wasn't married to Willa Cather, that was my brother Jan, I mean his wife was her bosom friend –

(Clem *wanders into the audience and continues speaking until he runs down.*)

Clem: No they aren't coming tonight, do sit down, we will have Norm Amadio and Ed Bickert and later Don Francks will present a reading from *The Connection.* They just did it at the Living Theatre you know, that's in New York, too, where is that oh there I'm terribly sorry –

(Austra *has begun to whisper her life story in* Babe's *ear; he plays his drums in response.* Jekyll *and* Aivars *arrive stiffly in their suits and begin to dismantle the club.* Ruthie *tries to make it at least more comfortable for everybody. The drum seems to fly through the air as it is brought to the front of the stage, with* Babe *and* Austra *maintaining contact. The bass is carried across the stage like a coffin, with* Herbie *still playing it. He lies down on his back, still playing until he peters out.* Clem *clambers back up on stage, waving a stash of classical music.*)

Clem: It's closing time. It's closing time. (*He throws the music up in the air and collapses under the sheets.* Kennedy *slowly slithers off his piano bench.* Black Hat *is carried out by the two men, still playing, his sax wailing and wailing.* Ruthie *goes with him.* Austra *stays on stage talking to* Babe.)

Austra: ... under the bridge. And the funny thing is, the sound of the rain was louder than the bombs.

(Babe *slumps over his kit.* Austra *looks up. Light change.*)

CODA

(Ruthie *enters, close to the audience. She looks at them as if they are attending her funeral.*)

Ruthie: Welcome, welcome, welcome. I remember you – you were so hungry all the time. And you – you lived in that nice house on Bridle Path. And you – you were dating that lovely Negro girl from Settlement House. And you. You'd just come here from Newfoundland. You proposed to your girlfriend in the parking lot. And you. You're driving cab now. And you. And you. Who the hell was born in Toronto anyway except for Vincent Massey. And he was born in

(Ruthie *blanks, exits.*)

FINAL IMAGE

(*1963.* Aivars *pushes a baby buggy.* Austra *reads from* Howl *to the baby.* Clem, *his hair ever more wild, sitting alone at the piano. The club has disappeared. It is many years later, when* Clem *is playing piano in a spaghetti restaurant.*)

Clem: I've been fighting for years to find a place like this one as an intermission pianist. The super-Stalinists of the piano who like to listen to their Ferrante and Teicher to drown out the dentist's drill, they would turn their noses up, but I'm very happy. Very happy. Ruthie is my old age pension. I told her to make ties she makes damn good ties. I made an ad for Kleenex. My boys, they played for me. And that waitress in the bunny suit over there – she's a sculptor. Clem is telling you the truth. I want to play the piano for all the spaghetti eaters of this world. I'll play any request. Beethoven with a beat. Berlioz with a bump. Bartok with a boom, baby. The Götterdammerung? Mind if I spice it up?

(*He flexes his fingers to play the first chord.*)

THE END

Lola Starr Builds
Her Dream Home
A TRAVESTY

Sky Gilbert

Playwright, poet, queen extraordinaire, Sky Gilbert is co-founder and Artistic Director of Buddies in Bad Times Theatre in Toronto. He has written and directed numerous plays for Buddies, including *Pasolini/Pelosi, The Dressing Gown, Drag Queens on Trial, Ban This Show, The Postman Rings Once*, and *Capote at Yaddo*, as well as *Lola Starr Builds Her Dream Home*. In keeping with the nature of his work, he has been an outspoken commentator on issues affecting the lesbian and gay communities. He has also been instrumental in nurturing and inspiring young artists through the *Rhubarb!* and *QueerCulture* festivals he initiated at Buddies. Sky Gilbert is the recipient of the Pauline McGibbon Award for directing in 1985, and the Dora Mavor Moore award for his play *The Whore's Revenge* in 1989.

Lola Starr Builds Her Dream Home was first produced by Buddies in Bad
Times Theatre for the Edmonton Fringe on 13 August 1988.

PRODUCTION
Director / **Edward Roy and Sky Gilbert**
Sets and Costume Design / **Leslie Frankish**
Music / **Cathy Nosaty**
Lighting / **Lorne Reid**

CAST
Sky Gilbert / Lola Starr
Debra Kirshenbaum / Tina Starr
Joe Colborne / Eat Me, Decorator
Steven Cumyn / Malcolm Inklepoop, Mover, Cleaner, Reporter
Les Porter / Minoola Grump, Mover, Cleaner, Reporter
Edward Roy / Johnny Bad

CHARACTERS
Lola Starr, a film legend
Tina Starr, her teenage daughter
Eat Me, their dog
Johnny Bad, a no-good bum
Malcolm Inklepoop, an intrepid reporter
Minoola Grump, a busybody neighbour
**Various Reporters, Decorators, Movers, and Members of the Norwich
Junior League,** PTA **Clean Council and 4-H Club**

SETTING
Lola's dream home in Connecticut

NOTE
All characters should be played by men except for Tina, and Johnny and
Malcolm should be played by the same actor.

ACT ONE

SCENE ONE

The set is the bare bones of Lola Starr's *new home in Norwich, Connecticut. The time is the mid-1950s.* Lola *has recently purchased the home which is a large old 1920s vaudeville theatre, in a shambles. The lights come up on a large empty room with cobwebs. In the upper regions of the set we see the vaulted ceiling of the old theatre dimly. The effect is chilling and lonely. We might get the feeling that the theatre is haunted. After a moment or two of this we begin to hear humming noises in the distance. The effect is reminiscent of the approach of the seven dwarfs in* Snow White *singing "Whistle While You Work." The door finally opens and* Lola *appears, resplendent in white furs and sunglasses. She looks around.*

Lola: Oh my ... oh dear ... (*pause*) Oh ... Lord ... this is it ... I can't believe it, my ... new life ... starts here ... oh my ... . (*The clamour of voices outside the door, all the little people.*)

Voices: Can we come in?

Lola: (*breaking out of her hypnotic reverie*) Oh yes of course everyone ... do come in please do ... yes ... I'm sorry I forgot ... yes come along ... . (*the door opens further and light floods the room.* Tina – Lola's *daughter – enters, followed by four movers dressed in mover outfits, and finally, the dog,* Eat Me. *All carry boxes, including the dog. They hum as they come in.* Lola *is being very magnanimous. She reminds us of the Good Witch of the East in* The Wizard of Oz.) Yes ... everyone ... fell free to enter make yourself at home yes please ... go ahead everyone ... yes ... that's it ... lovely yes ... relax make yourself comfortable ... .(*They begin taking things out of boxes and start to sing.*)

All: Busy busy busy busy work work work
It's time to clean and shine
It's busy time
We're moving in.

Lola: Moving in

All: Busy busy busy busy

Lola: Moving in

All: Busy busy busy busy

Lola: Moving in

All: It's furniture that's new
and lights that are bright
it's toil but it's fun
like opening night!

Busy busy busy busy

Lola: Moving in

All: Busy busy busy busy

Lola: It's no sin!

Mover: Here's a lamp

Lola: Put it here

Mover: And what about this box?

Mover: Here's a knick-knack

Lola: Oh I love it

Mover: And what about these sox?

All: Busy busy busy busy

Lola: Moving in

All: Busy busy busy busy

Lola: It's no sin!

All: (*continue underneath the next*) busy busy busy busy

Lola: (*speaks over them*) Moving is such fun ... .new bright spaces, dirty little holes to clean, dark interesting corners that you never thought existed ... cobwebs ... sweep them away ... we've got nothing to hide ... we're starting anew starting afresh with an attitude that's positive and a feeling that's – what the heck!

All: Busy busy busy busy

Lola: Moving in

All: Busy busy busy busy

Lola: It's no sin!

All: We're moving

Mover: Wait I forgot a chair!

All: We're moving

Lola: Wait watch my hair!

All: We're moving

All: Busy busy busy busy
It's no
It's no

It's no
(*a big finish*) SINNNNNNNN! (*The movers continue bringing in furniture and humming.* Tina *and* Eat Me *surround* Lola.)

Lola: Oh Tina Tina Tina and little Eat Me come here ... Eat Me ... (*she giggles*) Oh, Tina darling, whatever possessed you to buy a dog and call him Eat Me?

Tina: (*a tough girl*) I don't know, Mom. But you never know when a brilliant and heroic dog can come in handy!

Lola: Oh, you're so right Tina, life's like a baseball game with many an unexpected fast curve, but remember darling with the right hair and makeup, and if you design your own costumes you can do just about anything your little heart desires!

Tina: I don't have a little heart, Mom. It's a big one!

Lola: Oh Tina. You're such a card. (*music begins*) But we're here Tina, we're finally here ... this is it ... our dream home ... is it as you imagined?

Tina: Just about.

Eat Me: Arf arf!

Lola: Tina ... Eat Me ... it's so idyllic ... (*She goes over to a window*) How lucky we were to find this quaint old vaudeville house ... in rural Connecticut. I know now ... just how our lives shall be ... Tina ... you're going to go to those fabulous Connecticut schools and become a normal, feminine little girl ...

Tina: I'll do my best, mom –

Lola: And you'll forget those horrible fantasies of yours of becoming a horrid prison matron –

Tina: I just want you to be happy, Mom!

Lola: I know. And Eat Me will calm down, and suddenly it will all become clear why we have a dog, and why he is so oddly named.

Eat Me: Arf arf!

Lola: And my life will become placid and unglamorous and I'll join the PTA.

Tina: Aw Mom! The PTA.

Lola: You said it, Tina. Because you're my family, and after all, family is the most important thing in the world. What would we have without family?

Tina: Why gee Mom, without family we'd have to become self-reliant!

Lola: You're so right Tina, and we wouldn't want that, would we?

Eat Me: Arf arf!

Lola: Oh Tina ... everything is so right ... just and joyful, all we need to do now is make it truly clean!

Tina: You don't mean?

Lola: Yes darling ... yes ... I think I'm getting the urge to iron!

Tina: Not you, Mom!

Lola: Yes Tina. Your mother is going to iron. Forget for a moment that she is a famous star who has rubbed noses with the great and near great, a woman who has dined with kings and hurled potatoes at princesses! No that's all in the past now. And I think I'll iron a plain cotton shirt. Do we have one?

Tina: I have one, Mom!

Lola: Oh Tina darling ... somehow I knew you would. I'll just iron and iron and iron. I'll iron all our cares away. I'll iron away the past and I'll iron into the future. Do you suppose I should put it on steam?

Tina: (*getting her stuff*) Gee Mom, if I were you I'd stick with permanent press.

Movers: (*singing still*) Busy busy busy busy work work work

Lola: Oh aren't these movers industrious!

Movers: Busy busy busy busy work work work

Lola: And so musical – Tina you know I so rarely take time to talk to the little people who have made me what I am today ... perhaps I shall begin now in my quiet secluded dream home. Hello ... you ... little person ... come here.

Malcolm: (*dressed as a mover but pulls down his hat to hide his face*) Who ... me?

Lola: Yes you, there, ordinary person. How are you? What is your life like?

Malcolm: Oh ... pretty ordinary.

Lola: That is what I suspected. But it satisfies you, doesn't it?

Malcolm: Ahh ... sure.

Lola: A humdrum routine can be satisfying can't it? You yourself probably have a home and a wife and a dog you can love.

Malcolm: That's right ma'am! Now if you'll excuse me – (*He goes back to moving*)

Lola: Wasn't he quaint wasn't he picturesque and real! Oh I feel somehow I shall love a man like him. One of course who is not himself already married. Tina ... is the iron hot?

Tina: Yea Mom.

Lola: Oh don't say "yea Mom" Tina, certainly you could learn to say "yes Mommy" and giggle like other little girls.

Tina: I don't like giggling.

Lola: Oh you will, dear, once you meet a big strong handsome man and fall in love there will be lots to giggle at.

Movers: Busy busy busy busy work work work

Lola: They're an energetic lot those little movers!

Movers: Busy busy busy busy work work work

Lola: And noisy too ... do you have my apron Tina? I certainly couldn't iron in this ... (*She takes off her fur coat with help from* Eat Me. Tina *brings a sequined apron which* Lola *puts on beneath her rhinestone studded blouse. Her sunglasses remain on.*) Ahh ... now ... where do I begin.

Tina: You could turn the iron on!

Lola: Brilliant Tina. What a marvellous idea. And then ... I suppose I should start ironing like any other wife and mother. Oh it will be idyllic. Now ... where's the switch –

Tina: Here, mom –

Lola: Thanks, Tina. Now all I have to do is actually begin ironing! Which I'm certain to do at any moment. This is quite an historic event, isn't it. If there were reporters here, they would be snapping pictures like nobody's business. But fortunately there are no reporters here.

Tina: That's for sure.

Eat Me: Arf arf arf!

Lola: At any moment now it will be time to iron. In fact I am picking up the iron now. Oooooo ... it's hot.

Tina: Yea, well that's the way irons are, mom.

Lola: And the next step is I suppose to iron.

Tina: You got it, Mom.

Lola: Well ... that's what I shall do then. Immediately if not sooner. (*She stares at the iron idly. The she holds the iron up. Suddenly all the movers whip off their mover outfits and underneath are wearing classic forties reporter out-*

fits. They pick up cameras and snap pictures. Lola *screams*) AHHHH! Oh my God ... Tina! Reporters!

Tina: Oh ... fuck!

Lola: Tina darling ... I told you not to say one of the words you just said and that word's not oh! (*They continue to take pictures*) No ... no, stop this please ... I came to Connecticut to get away ... no more pictures please. Can't you see ... I'm just an ordinary person like you.

Reporter 1: No, you're not, Lola.

Lola: Yes I am ... yes I am!

Reporter 2: No Lola ... for the little people you can never be truly ordinary!

Lola: But ... but ...

Reporter 3: It's true!

Lola: No, it's not true. I came to Connecticut to prove I can have a normal life like any other human being.

Reporter 4: But you're not human, Lola ... you're a star!

Lola: Untrue untrue! False and misrepresented!

Reporter 1: But what about the little people, Lola?

All Reporters: The little people the little people!

Lola: The little people I ... almost forgot about them!

All Reporters: How could you?

Lola: Yes. How could I? To ignore the little people is to ignore life itself.

All Reporters: The little people must know.

Lola: How true. They have a right to know. All right. That decides the matter. I shall give ONE FINAL INTERVIEW.

All Reporters: THE FINAL INTERVIEW! (*All arrange themselves.* Lola *takes the fur coat and arranges it around her. She poses.*)

Reporter 1: How could you do this? How could you leave all your fans and leave Hollywood and the little people who love you?

Lola: But I have not left.

All Reporters: No?

Lola: I've started a new life.

All Reporters: (*scribbling*) A new life.

Lola: Yes I'm still alive, I still laugh and cry, muse and eat dinner, only now I do things for real and not on a silver screen. Everyone needs reality, it's an important part of everyone's life. Except for myself. I have existed in a world of tinsel and sawdust, a mysterious world where anything can happen and often does. The real world is not like that. In the real world there are houses to clean and clothes to iron and lovely giggly feminine daughters and devoted dogs named Eat Me. It is to that mundane, even dull and boring world that I now belong.

All Reporters: But Lola!

Lola: Yes?

All Reporters: How will you survive?

Lola: I often ask myself that.

All Reporters: And how do you answer?

Lola: I answer like any ordinary person.

All Reporters: And what do you say?

Lola: I say, look Lola, you've had it all, the ups and downs, the big moments, the little moments, incredible highs, the huge disappointments. And what does it all boil down to? It boils down to being a wife and mother and having the love of your family. After all ... (*She is almost crying*) What else is there? (*Pause*)

Eat Me: Arf arf!

Lola: Have you got that?

All Reporters: Oh yes Lola yes yes yes!

Lola: Thank you. That's all for now.

All Reporters: But Lola –

Lola: No ... I'm sorry ... no more questions. I must have solitude, quiet, my peaceful, family life –

All Reporters: Please, Lola –

Lola: That is all. The little people will have to make do with that.

Malcolm: (*who also played the mover that* Lola *singled out earlier and is now dressed as a reporter*) Lola –

Lola: I told you I won't answer anymore –

Malcolm: (*breathlessly*) What about ... Johnny Bad!

All Reporters: (*all gasp, as do* Tina *and the dog*) Ooooooohhh!

Lola: Johnny ... who?

Malcolm: Johnny Bad. (*Pause*) Don't pretend that you don't know the name, Lola. After all he's been your lover for the past two years.

Lola: Has he?

Malcolm: (*bravely*) Yes, he has.

Lola: I see. Who told you this?

Malcolm: But everyone knows.

Lola: They do?

Lola: Listen to me. (*A hush falls over the room. All stare at her tensely*) The time I spent with Johnny (*pause*) Bad is over now. And will continue to be over ... forever. To call him my lover is ... (*pause*) inaccurate. We were – very close friends (*They all scribble*) that's all. He was a very close friend of mine who treated me rather miserably. I suppose some would call that ... love. I would not. But all that matters little. He is gone. Johnny Bad is merely a distant, rather repulsive memory. (*They scribble*) I will answer no more questions.

All Reporters: (*mumbling as they leave*) Wow ... that was amazing ... the real truth about Johnny Bad I can't wait to get back to the office and get this one on AP – (*etc.*)

Malcolm: (*remaining behind*) But do you still love him?

All Reporters:/Tina:/Eat Me: (*gasp*) EWWWWWWWW!

Lola: (*weirdly, putting her hands in her hair*) What ... did you say?

Malcolm: I said ... do you still love him?

Lola: Who?

Malcolm: Johnny ... Bad?

Lola: (*screeching*) GET OUT ALL OF YOU GET OUT. YOU PARASITES! MAG-GOTS! FOR CHRIST'S SAKE LEAVE ME ALONE!

All Reporters: All right already, we're going ... wow, she really need the rest ... better leave her alone ... (*Etc. They exit, and only Malcolm, Tina and Eat Me are left*)

Malcolm: (*carefully*) I'm sorry ... Lola –

Lola: (*fiercely*) GET OUT! (Malcolm *leaves*)

Tina: Hey, mom.

Lola: (*quietly, after a pause*) Don't say ... hey, Tina.

Tina: Sorry, Mom.

Lola: And don't say Mom. I'm your ... mother.

Tina: Yes, mother. Hey (*pause*) I mean ... would you like to do some more ... ironing?

Lola: I think, Tina, that your mother has had enough ironing for today.

Tina: Yea?

Lola: Yes. Now ... could you please leave me alone?

Tina: Yea Mom. (Lola *winces*) I mean yes Mother.

Lola: Good. Thank you very much darling. And take that dog with you.

Eat Me: Arf arf!

Tina: I hope you fell better, Mom. (*She leads the dog off*)

Lola: (*Pause. She is alone. She looks around the chaos of her new house, rather forlornly*) How quiet it is. (*pause*) How lonely. (*Pause, then forced cheerful*) Don't be silly Lola once it gets all spruced up with new curtains and some throw cushions it will be just ... LOVELY (*She suddenly breaks down crying and collapses on a couch somewhere in the corner. She cries for a moment and then suddenly a phone rings. The phone is on the opposite side of the room, hidden. She looks up*) The phone (*it rings again*) But how could that be? I have no phone. (*ring*) At least that is, none was installed. (*ring*) Well perhaps it's an old phone. One that should have been disconnected. (*pause*) Well then of course there's no point in me answering then because the call is most probably in fact directed to the former tenants. (*pause*) There ... I don't have to worry. It stopped. Perhaps it was just in my imagination. (*The phone rings*) Perhaps not. (*pause, then ring*) No, there is definitely a phone ringing. Perhaps it would be in my best interests to answer it. (*a ring*) Perhaps it wouldn't. (*pause, a ring*) This is silly Lola. Answer the stupid phone. You've told yourself you've got to grow up to be a human being and deal with the outside world. (*ring*) It's probably one of the decorators, one of those rather effeminate character actors, I mean colour specialists. (*ring*) It's probably one of them. (*pause, ring.*) You're going to go crazy if you don't answer it. ANSWER IT FOR CHRIST SAKES! (*Ring. She goes over to the area where the ring comes from to look*) Where is it? (*ring*) If I was in a movie, the maid would answer it. BEULAH! (*ring*) This isn't a movie, Lola, you said it yourself. It's real life. (*Pause. She picks up the phone, listens, and then gets very tense. Music begins, the stage darkens.*) Oh my god (*Pause, very tense*) How did you get this number? (*pause*) I'm going to hang up I'm going to hang up right now. I will. I mean. I am. (*pause*) No ... it's not true I'm very happy I'm here with Tina and Eat Me and Johnny no. (*pause*) You mustn't. You'll never find me and besides I never want to see you again I told you. Oh Johnny no please ... I can't stand it (*a little voice*) Yes. (*pause*) Tell me again ... what will you do to me? (*pause*) Oh please Johnny ... come soon God Johnny ... how I need you how I miss you ... (*she screams*) AHHHH! (*a shiver of pleasure*) Whatever you say Johnny ... whatever you say ... yes ... I can feel your hands on me now ... yes I still have the marks ... yes ... but promise you won't hit me this time ... do you promise? You always promise (*She rolls around on the couch. Suddenly* Tina *appears at the top of the stairs, dimly viewed, in boy's pajamas with her toy truck.*)

Tina: Mommy?

Lola: Yes dear?

Tina: Are you all right?

Lola: Yes dear, your mother's just fine. Now you go back to bed.

Tina: Are you sure?

Lola: Yes darling. Don't worry. Nighty night.

Tina: Night, Mom. (*She goes part way upstairs but is still glimpsed watching her mother*)

Lola: (*thinking she is gone*) Oh God Johnny ... don't stop Johnny please tell me again what you're going to do to me ... please yes (*She screams*) AHHHH! Oh I miss you ... I can't tell you how much I miss you ... (*Lights dim.*)

SCENE TWO

(*Malcolm, the intrepid reporter is discovered on stage. It is late the next day.* Lola *is not up yet.* Malcolm *creeps in through the front door stealthily and looks around. Then he speaks.*)

Malcolm: (*after a pause he looks around*) Have you ever had a guilty secret? One that you didn't dare tell anyone? Well I have. Yes. I have (*pause*) It's a very horrible secret, so horrible I don't dare tell anyone. (*pause*) And yet the strangest thing is I have a desire to tell everyone, to let everyone know. Even though I know my secret is wrong and the whole world would scorn me. You would scorn me. I know you would. You wouldn't be able to take me seriously as a character or as a human being if I told you this but I have this urge to tell you this urge to tell someone and somehow I think that you would understand me. Because I think everyone has a deep dark secret somewhere. Don't they? Well maybe they won't admit it maybe you won't admit it but you do. You know what. I think that if everyone in the world was willing to come out and talk about their deep dark secret then the world would be a better place. I really do. If people would get together in clubs or something and meet monthly with meetings and points of order and minutes and everything and talk about their guilty secrets then I think everyone would be a lot happier and calmer. At least I would be. And so would you. (*pause*) OK, I've got an idea. I want everyone to close their eyes really hard. Now that's it. No peeking because if one person peeks then they'll be the only one without a guilty secret. Everyone close them. That's right. Now I want you to think about your guiltiest secret the weirdest most perverted thing you've ever wanted to do to anyone but you've never done. Are you thinking about it? Good. Now I want you to tell yourself that that dirty secret is OK. Good. Now open your eyes. There. Wouldn't the world be a better place if we all loved our guilty secrets? I don't know. Sometimes I feel guilty for thinking I shouldn't be guilty. OH! Here she comes. (Lola *enters with two decorators. She is wearing sunglasses and a dressing gown and the two decorators are very effeminate.*)

Lola: Well, here we are.

Decorators: Oh yes.

Lola: Quite a mess isn't it?

Decorators: Oh no ... no ...

Lola: Do you think ... something can be done?

Decorators: Well hmmm ... let me see ...

Lola: You see ... the effect that I want is that everything about this house which is dirty or nasty or secret or in any way disgusting is ... erased.

Decorators: Ahhh.

Lola: I would like everything to be bright and fresh and clean and no ... remembrance of things past.

Decorators: Ahhh ... Proust.

Lola: What?

Decorators: Nothing.

Lola: Do you think you could manage that?

Decorators: It's our specialty.

Lola: Oh ... it is?

Decorators: We're asked to do it all the time.

Lola: Really?

Decorators: Yes.

Lola: I can't imagine what it would be like ... to be an interior decorator.

Is it amusing? (Malcolm *is peering out from under a chair where he is hiding.*)

Decorators: (*sing*)
We
take their little sadnesses
and
hold them in our hands
our sweet and tender nature
makes it easy
makes it grand
we siphon off their silliness
the frothy stuff of dreams
forgive forget
it's gone away
loves like that
so it seems
to decorate
to consecrate
these hallowed old lies
we cover up the past
so they forget why they have cried

Lola: (*slightly perplexed*) What an odd experience. I always imagined that as decorators you were concerned with colours and designs, naturally I assumed your effeminate natures had something to do with your close association with the aesthetic arts.

Decorators: (*they find their note*)

MMMMMMMMMM
Effeminate we are for sure
and of it we are proud
we hate all violent sentiments
things nasty rude or loud
devoted as we are
to deleting memories
a curtain covers up the pain
but our emotions do not freeze
we're sensitive
to past misdeeds
we have some of our own
we help sinners to
start anew
and enjoy their happy homes

Lola: Well, perhaps calling me a sinner is overstating the case but let us just say that I have lived a full life and I want everything in the house to reflect my new positive family-oriented philosophy.

Decorators: We understand. (*They go off, looking at fabrics and humming to themselves.*)

LAAAAAAAA
La la la
la la la la
laaaaaaaaaa (*Etc.*)

Lola: What odd gentlemen. But I'm sure there's a place for them in this world just as there is a place for every one of God's creatures. (*The doorbell rings*) I'll have to answer that. (*She goes to the door and opens it. Music.* Minoola Grump *stands there looking very mean.*)

Minoola: MISS Starr.

Lola: She is I.

Minoola: I'm your neighbour, Minoola Grump.

Lola: Oh Minoola, why I've never actually met you but I've seen you puttering around your immaculate house and garden –

Minoola: There's no use trying to soft-soap me. MAY I come in?

Lola: Why certainly but ...

Minoola: I'm so glad to see that you are not completely moved in. Is there any place for me to sit?

Lola: Why certainly, Miss Grump. (*She gestures to a chair.* Minoola *sits uncomfortably*) would you like some tea or coffee? Or ... perhaps a hot buttered bun?

Minoola: It's no use trying to buy me off with depraved foodstuffs. I know your kind. (Malcolm *is still under the couch where* Lola *is sitting. He peers up from between her legs.*)

Lola: And why Miss Grump ... (*getting a little testy*) what could you possibly mean by that?

Minoola: I'll tell you what I mean. I'll be frank and get to the point. There's no sense in beating around the proverbial bush with women like you. Well, to put it bluntly, Miss Starr, we don't want your kind here.

Lola: And what kind is that?

Minoola: Do I need to tell you?

Lola: (*holding her own*) Yes. I have no idea what you –

Minoola: Don't play innocent with me, missy. How many times is it you've been married?

Lola: Well actually approximately (*screws up her face*) not counting Nicky Tippler who was –

Minoola: You don't even know! You can't even remember how many times you have been married!

Lola: I can too. I just didn't know whether to count Nicky or not because the experience was so short. (*Pause.* Minoola *frowns*) That is, I'm not speaking of Nicky himself I'm speaking of the length of the – oh my – (*Embarrassed*)

Minoola: You just can't stop, can you? Whatever you do filth just spews out of every orifice. Well, Miss Starr, I'm a decent God-fearing woman and I've owned a house in this neighbourhood for twenty years and I don't think I want to see this neighbourhood going to the dogs. (Tina *and* Eat Me *appear on the stairs.*)

Eat Me: Arf arf!

Minoola: You see what I mean?

Lola: Miss Grump.

Minoola: Yes.

Lola: May I have the floor for a moment?

Minoola: Go right ahead. And while you are at it you should wash it. It looks pretty filthy.

Lola: (*coldly*) Thank you. I suppose it has never occurred to you, Miss Grump, that people can change.

Minoola: (*intense*) Oh really, can they?

Lola: I have an intense personal belief in the power of human beings to mend their ways. It's true that in the past I have led an existence which at the very least might be called irresponsible –

Minoola: HAH!

Lola: And at the very most might be called wanton –

Minoola: Fiddlesticks. You're a slut and a harlot!

Lola: No ... it's not true –

Minoola: All you're interested in is sex –

Lola: No ... (*She collapses on the couch*) No ... stop ... please, you're torturing me.

Minoola: (*like a viper*) From what I hear about your sex life you probably wouldn't find that very unpleasant –

Lola: (*screams*) Get out of my house, you dried-up old hag!

Minoola: This isn't a house! It's an ex-pornographic movie theatre.

Minoola: It's not, it's a quaint old historic vaudeville theatre which will soon be my home.

Minoola: But I hold the mortgage!

Lola: But the mortgage is held by sweet old Miss Scroton down the street –

Minoola: She's a front!

Lola: A ... a front –

Minoola: – (*getting up on the couch*) Yes, Miss Starr, I can have you turned out of this smelly smut palace at any moment. And if you don't mend your ways as of this second I'll see you lying in the gutter where you belong! (*She starts to cackle loudly and jump up and down on the couch. Malcolm screams and bounds out.*)

Malcolm: Don't you dare talk to Lola Starr like that!

Lola: Oh my God.

Eat Me: Arf arf!

Minoola: Miss Starr ... who is this man?

Lola: I ... I don't know –

Malcolm: She is a sweet, honest, caring and loving person. She's just had a few bad breaks!

Minoola: Men under the couch! Next thing you know it will be ... communists! That's it! I'm reporting you to the police!

Lola: FOR WHAT?

Minoola: FOR BEING WANTON!

Lola: THAT'S NOT A FELONY!

Minoola: I'LL MAKE IT ONE. MY SON IS THE CHIEF OF POLICE (*She exits cackling.*) AHAHAHAHAHAHAHAHAHAHAHAHAHAHAHHHHH!

Lola: (*collapses crying*) AHHHHHHH!

Eat Me: Arf arf arf.

Tina: (*heroic*) Hey Mom, are you okay?

Malcolm: Don't cry, Lola, please. (*He takes out his camera and snaps a picture of her, crying*)

Lola: What are you doing?

Malcolm: I'm just ... taking a picture –

Lola: Who do you think you are?

Malcolm: My name is Malcolm Inklepoop. I'm a reporter.

Lola: Inklepoop? Your name is Inklepoop?

Malcolm: Yes it is. Oh Lola, you of all people must know what it's like to be saddled with an offensive past –

Lola: What were you doing under my couch?

Malcolm: Well I was ... hiding there because –

Lola: Why?

Malcolm: Because –

Lola: Get down on your knees.

Malcolm: Yes ma'am. (*He does, quivering*) What is it, ma'am?

Lola: Miss Starr to you. Now did I not say no more reporters?

Malcolm: Well, yes you did but –

Lola: And what are you –

Malcolm: Well, I'm more than a reporter, I'm a devoted fan.

Lola: Can't you see what happened? I had the possibility of convincing this witch that I had changed my lifestyle, that at last I had become a decent God-fearing church-going woman and one more minute with her and I would have convinced her but –

Tina: Oh Mom, do you really think you could have convinced her of –

Lola: (*threateningly*) Shut up, Tina. (*pause*) And you ... you ruined everything. My life is ruined. My new life ... my new dream home perhaps I shouldn't have tried to make a home out of a vaudeville theatre, it is such an odd smelling place, though historic ... what has it all come to ... (*Collapses on the couch*) all I wanted was love ... and perhaps a little sex now and then ... but not often and it doesn't have to be good sex that is ... as long as we can go out occasionally to a party ... I like parties and seeing people, trying to have a good time ... that's all I wanted and I was going to try and raise my daughter here like a little lady, and now it's all ruined because of you –

Tina: Oh Mom ... I'm never going to be a lady –

Lola: Shut up, Tina, speak when you're spoken to! (*She starts crying again*) And you ... you little Inkle-what?

Malcolm: Poop.

Lola: You little Inklepoop, you spoiled everything.

Malcolm: I'm sorry, Lola.

Lola: Sorry isn't good enough. Get up. (Malcolm *does*) Promise me you'll never darken my door again.

Malcolm: (*repentant*) I promise.

Lola: Good. Now go away.

Malcolm: Lola.

Lola: MISS Starr.

Malcolm: Miss Starr.

Lola: Yes.

Malcolm: I'm sorry. I worship the ground you walk on.

Lola: I understand. But that's no excuse. (*Pause. He leaves, hanging his head*)

Eat Me: (*whimpers*) Eugh eugh.

Lola: Shut up, Eat Me. (Eat Me *curls up in the corner.*)

Tina: Why did you get so mad at him, Mom?

Lola: Mother, I'm you mother, Tina. Because he is an odious little man and he ruined my tea with the new neighbour.

Tina: The new neighbour already thinks you're a slut –

Lola: Tina, if you don't have anything nice to say then don't open your mouth.

Tina: Well, I kind of like him.

Lola: Who?

Tina: That Inklepoop guy. I think he's neat.

Lola: Neat is not what I'm looking for in a man, Tina. Nicky Tippler has been described as "neat" but he certainly knew nothing about satisfying a woman like myself.

Tina: Mom.

Lola: Yes, Tina.

Tina: Can I ask you something?

Lola: Of course you know I am always open to a frank and caring discussion on any topic as such a discussion may be important to your development as a young woman.

Tina: Yea, but can I ask you something?

Lola: Of course.

Tina: What are you looking for in a man?

Lola: What an odd question to ask your mother.

Tina: Well I just wondered because well ... last night well I may be wrong but I thought I heard the phone ring and so did Eat Me and we got up and I was sitting on the stairs remember and was it him?

Lola: Why, what do you mean, Tina? (*Music*)

Tina: Was it ... Johnny? (*Music*)

Lola: Why, Tina, I told you your mother is not having anything to do with him any more ...

Tina: But Mom, you were acting like you used to ... before and –

Lola: Tina, please. I refuse to talk about this any longer. Your mother is very tired.

Tina: Can I just say one more thing?

Lola: Just one.

Tina: Mom, if he ever tries to hurt you again I would like to kill him.

Lola: Tina! What are you talking about?

Tina: You heard me. I bought this. (*She takes out a gun.*)

Lola: Where did you get that?

Tina: I bought it.

Lola: Tina, give me that gun this minute.

Tina: No, I have a right to protect myself. And you.

Lola: Tina, have you gone crazy? Give me that gun right now.

Tina: I won't. Mom. I love you. And I don't want you to get hurt. It was okay at first because at first with you and Johnny I thought it was like a game. But now I know it's real. That he's really hurting you. And I want it to stop. And I'll do anything to stop it. Anything.

Lola: I'm sorry Tina ... but there are some things that grown-ups do that you don't ... fully understand.

Tina: I understand that people shouldn't want to hurt themselves. That's wrong.

Lola: No, Tina, you don't understand. You don't understand anything. (*She makes a rush for the gun.*)

Tina: Stay away from me – if you don't care about yourself then I do – (*She runs off.* Eat Me *follows.*)

Eat Me: Arf arf –

Lola: Tina, you come back here. Eat Me, you come back here too ... the two of you ... (*She yells out the door.*) Tina, OH ... (*She leaves the door open and goes back to the couch. She stares off. Music. The wind blows and some leaves come in the door. The door swings once or twice. A shadow appears and looms larger.* Johnny Bad *appears finally in silhouette. He stands there looking at her for a moment.* Lola *does not turn around, but she knows he's there. He is smoking a cigarette.*)

Johnny: Hey.

Lola: (*not turning*) Yes?

Johnny: Hey, babe.

Lola: Johnny?

Johnny: Yea?

Lola: Oh, Johnny. (*She turns, slowly*) I told you not to ... come here.

Johnny: Didja?

Lola: Yes –

Johnny: So what.

Lola: Well –

Johnny: That never stopped me before.

Lola: No, I guess it didn't. (*Pause, she moves away*) Oh Johnny, you mustn't, that is I ... I'm starting a new life I have a lovely new home in a lovely neighbourhood and I've started decorating and –

Johnny: Shut up.

Lola: What?

Johnny: I said. Shut up.

Lola: All right.

Johnny: I'll tell you when to open that big mouth of yours and what for.

Johnny: Yes Johnny. (*Pause*)

Johnny: Didja miss me?

Lola: Well actually –

Johnny: (*a hoarse whisper, goading her*) Come on Lola ... tell me, didja miss your Johnny? Eh? Eh?

Lola: Well now you see I've had lots to occupy me what with colour swatches and the new drapes and ironing I've just been ironing endlessly, you haven't lived Johnny until you've discovered the joys of ironing –

Johnny: (*hoarser still*) I said ... didja ... MISS ME? (*Pause*)

Lola: Yes Johnny yes. (*pause*) I missed you.

Johnny: How much.

Lola: Very much.

Johnny: Are you wet for me baby? (*pause*)

Lola: Very ... wet. (*pause*)

Johnny: Come here.

Lola: (*pause*) No.

Johnny: I said ... come here. (*She does. He slaps her.*)

Lola: (*screams*) AHHH!

Johnny: You bitch. What the fuck are you doing? Trying to get away from me –

Lola: But Johnny –

Johnny: (*grabbing her as the lighting and music become very film noir*) Listen to me, you bitch. Don't you ever try and get away from me again. You hear me?

Lola: Yes, Johnny.

Johnny: (*shaking her*) YOU HEAR ME?

Lola: Ow Johnny ... you're hurting me!

Johnny: Oh poor little Lola's getting hurt. (*He throws her down.*)

Lola: AHHHH!

Johnny: And there's more where that came from –

Lola: Johnny ... no –

Johnny: What is it –

Lola: I don't want to do this any more, I can't –

Johnny: That's what you always say. COME HERE –

Lola: No.

Johnny: YES.

Lola: NO – (*He lunges at her, she screams*) AHHHH. Stay away from me –

Johnny: (*yelling*) COME HERE YOU BITCH! (*He lunges at her, grabs her and starts hitting her. She screams.* Tina *appears in the doorway.*)

Lola: Johnny quick go out the back –

Tina: I'm here Mom –

Johnny: What the –

Lola: She's got a gun – quick, that way –

Tina: (*fires the gun*) Hey you – (*A police siren is heard.* Johnny *runs out the back.* Tina *runs in.* Lola *collapses on the couch.*)

Lola: Oh God help me ...

Tina: Mom, are you all right –

Lola: Shut the door.

Tina: But –

Lola: SHUT THE DOOR! (Tina *slams it.*)

Tina: Mom, I told you –

Lola: SHHH. (*A banging on the door. A voice*)

Voice: Open up. It's the police. (*They bang on the door. Music. Tableau of* Lola *terrified as she looks at her daughter who stands over her with the gun. More banging on the door*) Open up. I said OPEN UP!

(*More music. The lights dim.*)

ACT TWO

SCENE ONE

During the intermission the set has changed considerably. Lola *has done quite a bit of cleaning and decorating – with the help of professionals, of course – and the old grimy haunted-looking house has somehow managed to look perky and cheerful with throw cushions and curtains everywhere. Two things are very important, a) that the haunted-house feeling still peeks through the make-over; that there is the subtlest reminder of horror behind it all and b) that everything is spotlessly, obsessively neat and clean.*

Lola *enters. She is wearing a bright polka dot fifties dress, very Lucille Ball or Laura Petrie. She looks like the model of the fifties housewife. She walks in, looks around, sighs. Lovely music. She plumps cushions or something and runs her finger along a table to check for dirt. The doorbell rings.*

Lola: (*singsong*) Oh ... it must be them. (*She checks her watch*) My ... right on time. (*doorbell rings*) Tina, Eat Me! (*sound of dog barking as* Eat Me *rushes in.* Tina *stands at the top of the stairs looking very unhappy in a dress identical to her mother's*).

Tina: Do I have to?

Lola: Yes darling, oh Eat Me ... calm yourself down please, down boy – oh my, some day, dear, you'll explain to me why we have this dog. (*doorbell*) Oh, I'll have to answer that. (*She sails over to the door. Opens it. Three bearded and bespectacled men stand there. They carry note pads and are wearing white gloves. They are played by* Johnny Bad, Malcolm *and the* Police Chief *but are unrecognizable because of beards and spectacles.*) Oh, it is you. (*Smiling*) The gentlemen from the Norwich Junior League and PTA Clean Council and 4-H Club?

Clean Council: That is us.

Lola: Won't you come in?

Clean: Thank you. (*They walk in, look around.*)

Lola: Can I get you anything? Coffee? Tea? (*Pause*) Holy water?

Clean: Not for us, thanks.

Lola: Well then, won't you sit down?

Clean: (*with utmost disdain*) No.

Lola: No? You prefer to remain erect?

Clean: Yes. Thank you.

Lola: Well then ... I hope this meets with your approval, that is, we've been working for months.

Clean: Uh-huh.

Lola: And at last, I think we have gotten the house truly clean.

Clean: We?

Lola: Well I myself and ... I'm sorry, I should have introduced you to my daughter Tina.

Clean: What a cute little girl. (Tina *frowns.*)

Lola: Say hellow, Tina.

Tina: (*after a pause*) Hi.

Lola: Now curtsey.

Tina: Fuck off.

Lola: Tina.

Tina: I will not fucking curtsey.

Lola: Tina darling –

Eat Me: Arf arf.

Lola: Oh and our beloved and faithful dog, Eat Me.

Eat Me: Arf arf!

Clean: (*recoiling*) House-trained?

Lola: Yes, of course. It's not easy keeping a house clean with a rambunctious canine and a daughter who's a bit of a tomboy –

Tina: Fucking right I am, get me out of this stupid –

Lola: But we manage.

Tina: I hate this silly –

Lola: Shh, Tina. (*Pause*) So.

Clean: So.

Lola: So ... the big question ... is it truly ... (*She walks over and poses beside a chair*) clean?

All: The Big Question. (*The look at each other and sing.*)

CLEAN. Is it truly clean
Is it truly clean
We're not being mean
Is it truly clean
Does it really shine
We don't mean to whine
Is it truly clean
Clean ... clean

All: Clean ... clean ... clean
Is it truly clean

Clean: We don't mean to bitch

All: Is it truly clean

Clean: But is it without a hitch

All: Is it truly clean
It's not our desire

Nor do we aspire
To be merely neat
For that's no feat

Lola: No ... not a feat (*Music plays under this, she speaks*) More than clean you mean without a blemish or a mistake you mean good and healthy and right and true, more than clean I think you mean truly honest and caring and loving, after all it's family values we're referring to here, isn't it?

All: Family! So ...
Is it truly clean

Clean: Not a spec of
nasty stuff

All: Is it truly clean

Clean: We panic
If we see dog fluff!

Eat Me: Arf arf!

All: Is it truly clean

Lola/Eat Me: Truly, truly clean!

All: Is it merely clean

Lola/Eat Me: No, truly clean!

All: IS IT TRULY CLEAN
YOU KNOW WHAT WE MEANNNNNNNN!

Lola: (*giggling cutely*) Oh, that was fun. And I do think I know what you mean by clean. And I think you've come to the right place to find true cleanliness. Oh gentlemen, I do so want to get the Norwich Junior League and Clean Council and 4-H Club Seal of Approval. I've had my heart set on it. What do you say?

All: Let's have a look. (*They hummm the clean song as they look around*) La la la la la Clean clean La la la la la Clean clean (*Etc. this goes on for a minute as they take notes, then suddenly they discover something in the corner*) OH NO! (*They all recoil in horror as they pull back some chintz to reveal a large fresh-looking pile of dog poop on the floor.*)

Lola: What is it?

All: It's ... it's ... dog no no.

Lola: Dog no no?

All: Yes.

Lola: I'm sorry, what is that, I don't know what you –

All: THIS. (*They point to dog poop.*)

Lola: (*screams*) AHHHHH! My god, that looks horrible.

All: IT CERTAINLY DOES.

Lola: And it ... smells fresh ... (*She turns suddenly savage*) EAT ME. EAT ME. WHERE ARE YOU, I'll kill you!

Eat Me: (*howling*) ARHGHGHGHGHGH.

Lola: I'll kill you. (*She grabs him and starts to beat him.*) You stupid dog I've always hated you I've never understood why we have you around you're supposed to be heroic but you've never done anything heroic I can't stand it you ruined my life you stupid ugly dog!

Eat Me: (*howling*) ARGHGHGHGHGH.

All: (*embarrassed*) Well, excuse us, yes, we'll just go –

Lola: I'm going to CHOP YOU UP AND HAVE DOG MEAT FOR DINNER FRESH MUTT FOR LUNCH AND WE CAN EAT DOGGIE PIES FOR LEFTOVERS I HATE YOU YOU DISGUSTING MONGREL –

All: Yes. Well, goodbye. Thank you. Nice meeting you (*Etc. They exit.*)

Lola: (Eat Me *bites her.*) Ow ... you bit me ... you stupid mutt I hate you you've ruined my life I had a chance things were going to be different (*She starts to cry, resting her head on the couch.*)

Tina: (*approaching her, tentatively*) Mom, I – (*The doorbell rings.*)

Lola: Oh Tina darling ... could you get that ... I'm having a nervous breakdown at the moment –

Tina: Yea Mom. (*She opens the door and Minoola Grump stands there.*)

Minoola: MISS Starr.

Lola: Oh my god ...

Minoola: And don't try and pretend you're not home ... trying to get the Norwich Junior League Clean Council PTA and 4-H Club Seal of Approval. Well, it's impossible. You'll never get it ... and you know why? Because you're a sleazy disgusting mess, that's why. And your life is a mess and it always will be because you're a slut.

Lola: LEAVE ME ALONE!

Minoola: I won't leave you alone, your house is under police surveillance now you wiggled out of the last one but my son is the chief of police and one wrong move and we'll get you your days are numbered Miss SLUT Lola Starr ... HAhahahahahahahahahaha!

Eat Me: Arf arf.

Minoola: And your little dog too ... (*She cackles wildly and leaves. Pause.* Tina *looks at her mother.*)

Tina: Well, Mom.

Lola: Yes dear. (*Pause*)

Tina: Things aren't going too shit hot for us are they?

Lola: I wish you could learn to express yourself without using expletives, darling.

Tina: I'm sorry, Mom. I really wish I could be the little girl you want me to be but I just can't. I hope you don't mind.

Lola: Well it's just one more hope, one more dream shattered in the –

Tina: You know what, Mom.

Lola: (*sitting on the couch, forlornly*) No, what.

Tina: I think I know what your problem is.

Lola: Well I'd be grateful for any help you could give me, I've been trying to lead a normal life like any other boring little person and it's just not working.

Tina: That's just it, Mom, you're not being normal. During the day you act really normal and put on a silly dress and wash and try to iron –

Lola: That's not fair, Tina, I almost did a blouse yesterday –

Tina: Face it, Mom, you'll NEVER be able to iron. It's just not in you.

Lola: Oh, I know, Tina.

Tina: And at night, well at night ... he comes to visit and beats you up again and you just revert to your old ways –

Lola: Well he promised he wouldn't hit me any more ... that is, not as hard as he used to –

Tina: But he always does, Mom. Now look at me, Mom.

Lola: Yes.

Tina: Do you really love him?

Lola: Well I –

Tina: Or are you just addicted to him?

Lola: Well ... I don't know ...

Tina: You know who I think would be really good for you?

Lola: You mean ... a man?

Tina: Yes.

Lola: Who?

Tina: Malcolm.

Lola: Malcolm? Malcolm who?

Tina: Malcolm Inklewhatever. That little reporter.

Lola: Oh Tina ... you're not serious. He's one of the little people. I couldn't ...

Tina: But he loves you, Mom, I've watched him. He REALLY loves you. I don't think Johnny loves you.

Lola: You don't?

Tina: No. If he loved you then he wouldn't ... hurt you like that.

Lola: Well ... you may be right, Tina –

Tina: It's like ... you've been living a double life ... fake homemaker by day and abused woman by night ...

Lola: But Tina ... I just can't leave him ...

Tina: But ... why?

Lola: You're too young to understand ...

Tina: Then I think we've got to kill him before he kills you.

Lola: But ... Tina I ... can't allow myself to feel such a thing or even think it but Tina I know I've often hoped or wished or just mused over the idea that something might happen to Johnny that he might get in an accident or just die (*Music. They look at each other.*)

Tina: It could be arranged, Mom –

Lola: No ... I won't listen it's horrible and evil and cruel and (*pause*) How?

Tina: Well ... the plan is ... now listen, Mom, I want you to throw out all your preconceptions about right and wrong because I think that's the problem here you have to stop thinking of me as this perfect little girl and start realizing what I am. Mom I'm a ... a tomboy.

Lola: A tomboy? That's not so awful, you'll grow out of –

Tina: Mom, I think I'm a tomboy who will never stop being a tomboy. Do you know what I mean?

Lola: (*staring at her oddly*) I ... think so ...

Tina: I'm not sure I know what it means myself but the point is this Mom

I'm only 17 years old and I'm still a kid according to the law and that means that if I kill Johnny then they'll just send me to reform school for a couple of years and you know how much I've always wanted to grow up to be a prison matron well I don't know how to explain this to you Mom but I've just got this feeling that being in reform school with all those other tomboy type girls would just be a dream come true for me –

Lola: (*talking out a hanky*) But darling ... I wanted so much for you to attend one of those lovely Connecticut boarding schools –

Tina: Those girls are sissies, Mom. I wouldn't be happy there. I need to be around real WOMEN.

Lola: Aren't I a real woman?

Tina: Of course you are, Mom, you're even more of real woman sort of than me, but that's okay, we're just different. I think I'm more like Dad than you.

Lola: Well ... (*She gazes at her*) You always were so much like your father ... by the way ... how is your father?

Tina: He wrote to me about a month ago, he's starting to like Alcatraz. They're letting him keep some birds.

Lola: Oh ... how sweet. (*Pause*)

Tina: Well, what do you say. Are you going to let me take the rap for you and get you out of this stupid mess or what, eh?

Lola: Well, Tina, I ... no ... I won't do it ... I won't be an accomplice to ... murder ...

Tina: Tell me something.

Lola: What.

Tina: You know he's a horrible piece of rotting infected pus, don't you?

Lola: Well –

Tina: Admit it. He's the lowest of lows, he's a crook and I think he hates women –

Lola: But –

Tina: Men who love women don't beat the shit out of them – besides he'll end up killing you, anyways it's almost self defence –

Lola: Oh Tina –

Tina: Look at me, Mom. Why is it? What makes him so special? Is it because he has a ...

Lola: Tina.

Tina: What.

Lola: What are you saying?

Tina: You know what I'm saying, Mom.

Lola: No I don't, of course I don't. (*Pause*)

Tina: A big –

Lola: Don't say it, Tina.

Tina: Well, that's the only thing I can think of. Because I can't see why you –

Lola: Tina, I can't imagine how you could ever think such a disgusting thought and I'm thoroughly annoyed and offended by the mere suggestion of what you (*Sits down, pause, she looks off dreamily*) It's enormous, Tina.

Tina: That's what I thought ... (*pause*)

Lola: You've never in your life seen anything like it. When I first saw it I ... I almost fainted. It's just ... gargantuan, Tina. He's ... ruined me for other men. (*pause*)

Tina: And that's the whole reason? The only reason.

Lola: I ... I'm afraid so, Tina.

Tina: But Mom ... it's not worth it –

Lola: You've never seen –

Tina: Mom, I mean ... you can find another ... thing like that somewhere but what about your self esteem.

Lola: Self esteem –

Tina: Yea ... who's the dog shit, you or him. You know that dog shit you found under the table just now – the reason you got upset and strangled poor Eat Me is because you know what the dog shit in your life is, the dog shit of the world it's Johnny Bad and we've got to kill him –

Lola: Oh Tina ... I can't believe I'm actually imagining we might ... do this ... you know Tina ... it might work ... I mean it seems evil and cruel and wrong but then I have always lived outside society's rules.

Tina: If you're going to live outside society then you REALLY have to do it all the way. Besides, it's society that's made those rules that turned you into this passive woman who accepts that a man has a right to beat on you. And if you don't kill him he'll go on to beat on other women, women who are anaesthetized by society's double standard.

Lola: Tina, your arguments are so terribly eloquent for one so young and living in the 1950s.

Tina: I'm ahead of my time, Mom.

Lola: Let's do it. But what's the plan?

Tina: Well. When are you expecting him?

Lola: Well, I don't know ... he didn't say, that is I ...

Tina: When.

Lola: Well ... any minute, actually.

Tina: Good. Now this is what we do. You get him in here, and when you've got him in a vulnerable position like he's on the couch or something bang on the wall and see and I'll come out to the landing and I'll shoot him.

Tina: Oh, Tina ... do you think it will work?

Tina: I know it will.

Lola: All right. You'd better go up, he'll be here any minute.

Tina: Okay.

Lola: And Tina ... one more thing.

Tina: Yes?

Lola: I love you, darling ... and thank you.

Tina: No problem, Mom. (*She exits upstairs.* Lola *looks around. The room is getting darker. It seems to be dusk. She is alone.*)

Lola: (*music under*) It's so cold. (*pause*) How could I say yes? Am I becoming insane? What did my daughter just ask me, what did she say? (*pause*) And I said yes. Yes was the word I spoke to her. I am complicit. (*pause*) How could I say I would – because I just ... it's true that he attracts me, terribly, and it's true that he is very masterful but sometimes when he hurts me, well, it started out to be a game and then suddenly, he's hitting me and it hurts, it really hurts, and I beg him to stop and I suddenly realize ... he doesn't really care about me – there's so much anger in him and he doesn't care, and then I feel am I worth so little that no one cares about me ... that no one really cares? How can he do that to me? Leave me so alone when I need him? (*pause*) Well I suppose it's important right now for you, the audience the little people ... for I know you're out there the little people I know it's important for you to know something about why, something of my motivation. (*She suddenly gets very teary-eyed.*) I DO love you ... I do love you all, and I know secretly, in your hearts even though I've decided to leave the movies for a few years to get my life in order as it were to pick up the pieces that you know all of you that I am doing this so that some day ... some day I can make a comeback and be with you all again because ... you ... the little people, I need you ... and you need me and perhaps the only real relationship I have is with you. Now I know even though this play is just supposed to be a light commercial comedy and everything it's still murder and I must don't honestly feel as an actress and a human being that I can go on, that I can do this deed if I don't get the encouragement I need from you. So listen to me, all of you, all the little people out there help me ... if you think I should go on living a tragic split-personality existence attached to this horrid piece of pond slime named Johnny Bad who abuses me mercilessly then don't clap now at all but if you believe in your heart of hearts that I have a right to exist to be happy, to make my own life with a man who really loves me even if it means doing away forcibly with a piece of woman hating toad droppings named Johnny Bad if you believe I have such a right as a woman and as a human being but most of all as an actress then give the courage ... don't let me down ... if you believe in all this and yes I will say it I must say it because this is after all a play, theatre magic, if you believe in FAERIES then put your hands together and clap. (*She waits. The audience will burst into spontaneous applause. If they don't then a tape will be played which bursts into spontaneous applause for them. When* Lola *hears it, vindicated, she raises her arms, then bursts into spontaneous tears of joy. Then there is a knock on the door.*) Oh my God. It's him. (*pause*) Can I, will I? Should I? (*pauses*) You've given me permission, you've told me I can. (*Another knock*) Oh no. I'm so frightened suddenly. Why is this house so empty, so lonely? Why can I never make it home? Will I ever have a home? (*Another knock*) Lola ... the only reason this house has never really been truly clean is because you've bothered so much with the externals, you have to do an internal housecleaning before you do an external one. (*Another knock, very loud*) Well then let the real housecleaning now begin. (*She goes to the door and opens it. Johnny stands there. He seems to be wearing a silk scarf made up of different colours.*)

Johnny: Hey Babe.

Lola: Hello, Johnny.

Johnny: You busy?

Lola: Not right now ...

Johnny: Mind if I ... come in?

Lola: No. (*He does. Pause. He looks around*)

Johnny: Hey babe, you fixed up this place real nice. Real nice and cozy.

Lola: We've done our best. (*pause*) But we can do better.

Johnny: Oh yea?

Lola: Yes. This house can be cleaner still.

Johnny: Huh? Well I guess I'll take your word for it. (*He wanders over to a chaise-longue.*) What's this thing?

Lola: It's new, we just bought it.

Johnny: It's neat. I like it.

Lola: Well we think it's lovely and it's just the right colour because –

Johnny: Lie down.

Lola: What?

Johnny: I said ... lie down.

Lola: But Johnny I want to –

Johnny: (*pushing her*) You heard me. Look what I bought you. (*He takes off a scarf.*) What's this?

Lola: A ... scarf?

Johnny: That's right, baby. (*He starts to tie her up.*) A ... silk scarf.

Lola: What are you doing?

Johnny: What do you think I'm doing –

Lola: Tying me up?

Johnny: You got it baby.

Lola: No, Johnny ... don't, please ... I don't want to play this game – (*He slaps her.*)

Johnny: Fuck off, bitch.

Lola: Ow ... no Johnny ...

Johnny: There, it feels nice, doesn't it? (*He has her arms tied.*) Nice and soft and (*he tugs*) gentle.

Lola: (*a gentle cry*) Ahhh! You're hurting me –

Johnny: I guess you haven't quite figured out yet baby, but that's the idea –

Lola: No Johnny ... you mustn't –

Johnny: (*doing her legs*) But I am –

Lola: Not now ... not tonight –

Johnny: Oh yea baby ... tonight's the night ...

Lola: But I don't understand

Johnny: What don't you understand –

Lola: Why you're tying me up –

Johnny: All finished. (*Pause*) You want to know why and you can't figure it out?

Lola: Yes, I want to know because –

Johnny: (*he pulls out a knife. Music. Room gets darker.*) Because of this –

Lola: Oh my God ... you're not going to –

Johnny: Kill you? No ... that would be too easy ... I'm just going to mark you up a bit. (*He draws the knife across her throat.*) Like this ... (*He cuts her slightly.*)

Lola: (*a gentle intake of breath*) Ahhh –

Johnny: Ohhh that's nice ... that's real – oh shit.

Lola: What is it.

Johnny: I gotta that is ... I gotta take a leak. Where's the can?

Lola: It's ... well the new powder room is in there behind the kitchen we had to put in a powder room downstairs because there was none downstairs you know these old theatres need special renovation –

Johnny: Shut up. That way?

Lola: Yes.

Johnny: I'll be right back. Don't you go away. (*He laughs at his own joke.*) That's a good one. Don't go away ... (*He goes off chuckling. Lola is alone.*)

Lola: Now's the time. This is it. I just have to call Tina. Tina? Tina. (*Louder*) TINA? Oh no ... she told me to knock on the wall. She's probably in her room with the door shut because she thinks she can hear me knocking on the wall but I can't knock on the wall because I'm tied up ... oh God ... he'll be back any minute ... he's going to kill me ... I have to get untied Tina Tina TINAAAAAA ... (*The dog suddenly appears.*) EAT ME EAT ME EAT ME. Come here. EAT ME.

Eat Me: Arf.

Lola: Eat Me. Come here, Eat Me. (*He does*) Good boy now Eat Me, come here boy. Chew on the scarves ... come on Eat Me, please ... Eat Me ... (*The dog starts chewing on the scarves.*) good boy ... good boy Eat Me ... good boy yes – oh Eat Me you are a heroic dog! (*She is free. She bangs on the wall three times.* Johnny *enters.*)

Johnny: Sorry I took so long, you know what they say, shake it more than three times and you're playing with it – Hey, what's going on –

Tina: (*at the top of the stairs*) TAKE THAT YOU MISOGYNIST PIG POND SLIME FROM HELL! (*She fires at him. He drops the knife and falls.*)

Johnny: FUCK ... YOU. (*He dies.*)

Lola: AHHHH. Oh my God Tina you did it ... you really did it you my daughter committed murder in my new house. I can't stand it THERE'S BLOOD ON THE FLOOR! (*She picks up the knife and slashes her wrists.*) AHHH.

Tina: Mother, what have you done! (*She collapses. The door opens and the* Police Chief *and* Minoola Grump *come in.*)

Police: You're under arrest. We saw the whole thing.

Minoola: I cut a hole in the hedge for better viewing.

Tina: Arrest for what?

Police: For the murder of Johnny Bad. (*Music. Lights dim on tableau of* Tina *cradling her mother with bleeding wrists. Blackout.*)

SCENE TWO

(*Lights up on* Lola *sitting in a wheelchair. Music. Her wrists are bandaged and she is wearing sunglasses and a white turban and a white blanket is over her. At her feet is her faithful companion* Eat Me *who has a white bow around his neck. Music.* Lola *pats the dog and sighs. The doorbell rings.*)

Lola: Eat Me ... could you get that?

Eat Me: Arf arf!

Lola: There's a good heroic dog. (*He opens the door. Reporters file in, played by all the other actors except* Tina. Malcolm *is of course one of them. They stand around her quite frightened to speak.* Eat Me *closes the door.*)

Malcolm: Excuse us ... (*Louder*) Excuse us ... Lola.

Lola: Yes? (*She shakes her head*) Oh I'm sorry ... who is it ... I can't see you properly ... the light ... and I was just dozing off –

Malcolm: It's us ... the reporters ... the little people.

Lola: Oh yes ... the little people, yes ... I'm so sorry ... I was just you see ... I get so tired these days ... .

Malcolm: We understand. Would you mind if we asked you, just one or two questions, Miss Starr?

Lola: Well ... (*pause*) I suppose ... I could manage one or two, yes, but only that.

All: Oh thank you Miss Starr ... thank you ... we're so grateful yes thanks for your kindness Miss Starr ... thank you –

Malcolm: Well ... what we wanted to ask you about was, if you don't mind ... the accident.

All: Yes, the accident ... the accident ...

Lola: Ah yes, the accident. Hence. These bandages. Yes. Well where do I start. (*Music. Lola speaks over it.*) AHH.
Well ...
It's a story it's a story
It's not long or involved
It's simple yes quite simple
And uncomplicated too

All: Tell us, tell us, tell us do –

Lola: AHH.

Well...
I was standing in the kitchen
In the kitchen in the kitchen
Cutting up zucchini
When the accident occurred

All: Ahh. Ahh. The accident occurred
Was it a big zucchini?
Was it very big?

Lola: AHH.
Well ... (*Pause. The music stops; she speaks without music.*) My memory failed me for a moment, it wasn't in the kitchen at all. Do you mind if I start again?

All: No, not at all, Miss Starr.

Lola: It's a story quite a story
But hard to understand
I almost was near tragedy
But I narrowly escaped

All: Escaped escaped but somehow she escaped

Lola: Yes ...
Well ...
I was sitting in the bathtub
Peeling peaches as is my wont
When I suddenly dropped my knife
And it hit the water font

All: The font the font it hit the water font

Lola: It hit the water font
And bounced onto the floor
I slipped and cut my wrists
And hit my head upon the door
I couldn't call an ambulance
I was so incapacitata
So I actually missed completely
This tragedy involving my daughta

All: She actually missed completely
This tragedy involving her daughta

Lola: Oh yes oh yes I'm sorry to say

All: She missed it missed it
It has all gone away

Lola: Due to an unfortunate accident
It's all gone away!

Malcolm: (*speaks, no music*) But how do you explain the scarves that were found tied to your bloody wrists and ankles?

Lola: The scares. (*Music*) the scarves. (*pause*) I'm sorry. I can't answer any more questions right now. I'd like to ... but I can't.

All: We understand Lola ... we understand. Thank you Miss Starr ... thank you ...

Lola: It's nothing ... any time ... I'd answer more questions if I wasn't ... you know ... recovering ...

All: We understand, goodbye Miss Starr. Goodbye. (*All leave except for* Malcolm *who hides in the corner.*) Thank you. (*After they are gone* Eat Me *closes the door.*)

Lola: Ahh ... they're gone. How quiet it is again. Eat Me ... Eat Me, it's just you and me ... now I understand why my poor unfortunate Tina bought you ... so that I wouldn't be lonely. I worry so about her ... do you suppose she's happy in prison?

Eat Me: Arf arf.

Lola: I suppose you're right. It's where she wanted to go, after all. What do you suppose she meant by always being a tomboy. A tomboy is something you grow out of, isn't it?

Eat Me: (*cryptically*) Arf.

Lola: I suppose you're right ... I wonder if she's happy ... (*She pulls up something hanging from around* Eat Me's *neck.*) What have you got there ...

on my ... a letter from Tina (*She pulls it out and reads it. Lights dim on* Lola *and up on* Tina's *face. She is in prison garb.*)

Tina: Dear Mom ... I am happy. I've worked real hard in reform school, and I got a lot of time off for good behaviour, and I'm going to have the career I wanted, as a prison matron. I can help a lot of these women here, Mom, and they all seem to like me a lot, 'cause a lot of them are tomboys too, what I tell them is, that it's society's fault that most of us are here. And I know that's true, but you know Mom, the more I think about it, the more I think that even though Johnny Bad didn't deserve to live I shouldn't have killed him. No human being should ever kill another one. Sure ... at the time it seemed like self-defence, but now I realize that we were just trapped in our traditional feminine roles, aw Mom, I wish you could break out and realize who you really are. P.S. Don't forget to feed the dog.

Lola: (*speaking to her image as it fades*) But who am I? Who am I? Sometimes even I don't know. Tina ... Tina ... (*The doorbell rings*) Oh dear, not more reporters. Eat Me, darling could you be a dear and tell them to go away?

Eat Me: Arf arf! (*He runs over to the door.* Minoola Grump *comes roaring in.*)

Minoola: Well, Missy, I just came by to see how you were recuperating from your so-called accident.

Lola: Well, I'm as well as can be expected –

Minoola: As well as can be expected for somebody who slit her own wrists after murdering a man so she could escape the electric chair and put all the blame on her defenceless young daughter who is turning into a diesel dyke in prison I can tell you that –

Lola: Why, what do you mean ... what are you talking about ... these false hurtful accusations, why are you hurling them against me –

Minoola: And you, Missy, you know why this all happened don't you it's because of what you've got down there ... (*She points to* Lola's *private parts*) If I had my way women like you would be sewed up at birth –

Lola: Oh get out ... for God's sake can't you leave me alone ... stop torturing me ...

Minoola: No ... I'll never stop torturing you ... for as long as you live in this house. (*She gets up on the couch over* Lola) I'm your conscience, Miss Starr and I'll follow you everywhere and deep down inside you know I'm right –

Lola: Oh please ... leave me alone ... go away I can't stand it any longer this time I really will do it ... end it all –

Minoola: That's it, kill yourself ... you filthy minded slut, I'd love to see you do it but for God's sake don't mess it up like you did the last time. (*She cackles. Suddenly* Malcolm *pops out from behind the couch.*)

Malcolm: Stop!

Minoola: What?

Malcolm: I said stop. You're the filthy minded one.

Lola: Oh my ... it's one of the little people –

Malcolm: Yes, Lola. It's me. You may not remember my name but I'm Malcolm Inklepoop and I may be a little person but my heart is big and full of love. You're the one with the filthy mind, Miss Grump.

Minoola: I? I?

Malcolm: Yes. To the outside world you may appear pious and virtuous but in fact it is you who are diseased and wrongminded. I have spent the last few months in successful psychotherapy, Miss Grump, and I understand that it is wrong to run away from what is natural inside oneself. Sexual desires are not evil, Miss Grump, and Miss Starr is entitled to the full realizations of her sexual self.

Minoola: I don't know what you're talking about but whatever it is it sounds dirty.

Malcolm: Dirty to you, Miss Grump, but holy to me. Now I will have to ask you politely to go and never to darken this door again –

Minoola: All right. But you just wait. I'll get you someday. I'll hunt you down Miss Starr ... in some alleyway in some sleazy bar ... you can't escape from your conscience. – (*She cackles wildly.*)

Malcolm: And stop cackling. (*He pushes her out the door*) God, that woman drives me crazy. (*Pause, he looks at* Lola.)

Lola: She has a similar effect on me. (*Pause.* Lola *looks at him*) Oh Lord I ... (*She suddenly breaks down*) Do you have any Kleenex, Mr Inklepoop? (*He rushes to get some.*)

Malcolm: Here, Miss Starr.

Lola: Thank you ... I don't know what came over me. I ... I've had a rather eventful past month or so ... and well ... what do you think of my new home?

Malcolm: It's lovely, Miss Starr.

Lola: I think so. I wish Tina could be here to see it. She was always so fond of pretty things. (*pause*) No, she wasn't. (*pause*) The lies are over, Mr Inkle – what –

Malcolm: Poop.

Lola: Poop. Unfortunate name – I'm tired of lies. The fact is my daughter always hated pretty things. And she's a ... a tomboy ... and I'm a ... how shall I express it?

Malcolm: A sexual woman with sexual needs?

Lola: Yes. That's what I am and even though I know he was a piece of rat turd that didn't deserve to live ... I still ... miss him.

Malcolm: Johnny?

Lola: Yes ... Johnny ...

Malcolm: Miss Starr –

Lola: No ... hear me out. And I've searched and searched for reasons why I loved him. It certainly wasn't his charm or wit and for a while I thought it was because he had such a large ... that is ... Johnny was deformed ... in a rather attractive way –

Malcolm: I think I understand –

Lola: But now I realize that wasn't it either and I've racked my brain for a reason for the attraction and I've actually discovered that I liked it when he hit me around. Not when he actually hurt me ... but before that ... (*Pause*) There, I said it. (*pause*) And that's what I think I missed.

Malcolm: That's not so awful, Miss Starr.

Lola: It's not?

Malcolm: No. But –

Lola: What –

Malcolm: You see, the problem with Johnny was that he really wanted to hurt you. It wasn't like fun and games.

Lola: Why ... that's what Tina said –

Malcolm: And, well ... it seems to me that ... Lola, you are a very beautiful woman ...

Lola: Some have said that –

Malcolm: And a woman who ... knows what she wants and ... how to get it and ... that is ... if you were to ... tell me what to do then I know that I would obey you, because I'd know that we ... have feelings for each other, that is ... I have feelings for you, and because of those feelings I know, I trust that ... you'd never ever really hurt me, and I'd never really hurt you ... no matter what kind of fun we were ... (*Music comes on – similar to that for* Johnny Bad.)

Lola: Shut up.

Malcolm: What?

Lola: I said ... shut up.

Malcolm: Yes Miss Starr.

Lola: What are you doing?

Malcolm: I'm licking your shoe.

Lola: (*slowly*) Then lick it ... well.

Malcolm: I'm doing my best.

Lola: Good. Now get up.

Malcolm: Yes ma'am. (*He does, looks at her.*)

Lola: (*suddenly vulnerable*) Oh Malcolm ...

Malcolm: Yes darling ...

Lola: Do you think it's possible?

Malcolm: Anything is possible ... (Malcolm *flicks a light on a family portrait to reveal* Tina *as a prison matron,* Eat Me *and* Malcolm *kissing* Lola's *shoes.*) ... ble ...

Lola: (*tears in her eyes*) Kneel, Malcolm.

Malcolm: Yes ma'am. (*He does.*)

Lola: You know ... Malcolm I think I've learned a lesson from all this.

Malcolm: What's that, Lola?

Lola: It's ... well ... I suppose I did build my dream home after all and we have turned out to be one big happy family ... in our own way and ...

Malcolm: Yes Lola.

Lola: Anything is possible ...

Eat Me: Arf arf!
(*Music ... lights dim.*)

THE END

Newhouse

adapted from Tirso de Molina's *Don Juan*
(*The Trickster of Seville*) and Sophocles' *Oedipus Rex*

Richard Rose and D.D. Kugler

The founding director of Necessary Angel Theatre in Toronto, Richard Rose has directed many of the company's productions since 1978, including Chekhov's *The Seagull*, Michael Springate's *Dog and Crow*, Milan Kundera's *Jacques and His Master*, the collective's *Mein* (Dora Mavor Moore Award, 1984) and *Desire*, John Krizanc's *The Half of It* (Chalmers Award, 1989) and the acclaimed productions of Howard Barker's *The Castle*, *The Possibilities*, and *The Europeans*. He has also adapted and directed several other projects, including *Boom* (from Buchner's *Woyzeck*), *Censored* (from

Bulgakov's *A Cabal of Hypocrites*), *Newhouse* (from de Molina's *Don Juan* and Sophocles' *Oedipus Rex*), and *Coming through Slaughter* (based on the novel by Michael Ondaatje). Directing credits for other theatres include Krizanc's *Prague* for Tarragon Theatre, *The Emperor* for Theatre Plus, *Lily*, *Alta* and *The Dreamland* for the Blyth Festival, and *Not Wanted on the Voyage* (based on the novel by Timothy Findley) for the Canadian Stage Company.

Richard Rose's direction of Krizanc's internationally acclaimed *Tamara* won him a Dora Mavor Moore Award in 1982 and the Los Angeles Drama Critics Award.

During his association with Necessary Angel Theatre in Toronto, D.D. Kugler has served as production dramaturge on Howard Barker's *The Castle* and *The Europeans* (in its world première), Michael Springate's *Dog and Crow*, and John Krizanc's *The Half Of It*. He also collaborated with Richard Rose on the adaptations of Michael Ondaatje's *Coming Through Slaughter* and Timothy Findley's *Not Wanted On The Voyage*. As a freelance director and dramaturge, D.D. Kugler both developed and directed the premières of Eugene Strickland's *Darkness on the Edge of Town*, Connie Gault's *The Soft Eclipse*, Keith Dorland's *True North*, Michael Springate's *Consolation of Philosophy*, and the Koprowski/Anderson opera *Dulcitius* (for the Canadian Opera Company).

Newhouse was first produced by the Necessary Angel Theatre Company at the William H. Bolton Arena in Toronto on 19 April 1989.

PRODUCTION
Director / **Richard Rose**
Environment Design / **Graeme S. Thomson**
Costume Design / **Minda Johnson**
Video Design / **Cliff Clifford**
Dramaturge / **D.D. Kugler**
Stage Manager / **Sarah Stanley**
Technical Director / **John-Kelly Cuthbertson**

CAST
Albert Schultz / Newhouse
Melissa Bell / Isabel, Prostitute
David Hughes / President, Doctor
Vanessa Dykun / Ambassador Peters, Anna
Rodger Barton / Prime Minister
Elizabeth Hanna / Prime Minister's Wife
George Merner / Mr Crane, Angus
Mark Christmann / Chambers
Doug Hughes / Baker, Commander Gordon
Stuart Clow / Evangelist, Marcus, Patrick
David Main / Minister of External Affairs
Marguerite Pigott / Amy, Susan Redstone

CHORUS
Rhea Akler, David Caron, Marion de Vries, Rick Little, Kate Main,
Ewan McLaren, Alda Neves, Pierre Toth, Jennifer Tripp, Tanya Walsh

Members of the 1987 Pilot Project *Newhouse* Workshop / **Stewart Arnott, John Evans, Fran Gebhard, Elizabeth Hanna, Michael Kelly, Lorraine Landry, Lynn Woodman**
Stage Manager / **Cheryl Landy**
Design Consultant / **Dorian Clark**

PLAYWRIGHTS' NOTE
Newhouse is a speculation about possible, but avoidable, future events – the political and social effects a sexually transmitted disease, at epidemic levels, could have on the individual and society.

Any plague, but especially a sex plague, is a catalyst for radical change in human behaviour. Unfortunately, the fear and ignorance surrounding such a plague can be manipulated by political parties and religious groups to reshape society. Fortunately, many organizations exist to inform the public, and their efforts not only abate the spread of the disease, but undercut the hysteria.

Our particular disease, while having many similar attributes, is not identified as AIDS. It is simply referred to as the "plague." Research continues, and each day more is known about AIDS, but we have chosen to focus on the effects of the unknown.

Two characters catch the plague from a one-night encounter. While this is suitable for dramatic purposes, in reality the chance of acquiring AIDS in one encounter is highly unlikely, although possible.

The title page lists the two primary sources for this free adaptation, but we also drew on material from Molière's *Don Juan*, Seneca's *Oedipus Rex*, Diderot's *Rameau's Nephew*, and numerous political personalities of the hour.

Special thanks are extended to John Krizanc for his dramaturgical contribution; the Laidlaw Foundation, the George Cedric Metcalf Foundation, and Labatt's Ontario Breweries for taking the risk with us; Libby Appel, Chairman of Theatre, and the cast of the seminal *Newhouse* workshop at California Institute of Arts; members of the 1987 Pilot Project *Newhouse* workshop; and the cast of the first production for their contributions and advice.

This play is for Brian Bailey.

ACT ONE
SCENE ONE

(*Washington. Masked Ball at Canadian Embassy. A bed rolls by.* Newhouse *and* Isabel *making love.*)

SCENE TWO

(*The TV news appears live, the commentator in front of pillars made of TV sets. Underneath the speech a helicopter approaches [sound]. Riot approaches.*)

Commentator (Com):

It is morning –
Grey morning on Parliament Hill.

The seventh day
Begins quietly for this city
After six days of violent battles
On our streets –
Marches by high risk groups,
Counter-protests by Evangelists.

The police
Afraid of infection
Remain behind their barricades.
They who have served us loyally
Abandon us to chaos.
Will the streets remain unruly?
Will government act?
Or has fear paralysed us?

Beyond the violence, the anarchy,
Beyond the stone-throwing and hardened passions,
The list of dead grows longer –
Forgotten in the anger
And the despair.

I have seen the victims.
We all have seen
Their eyes and bodies,
Skin on fleshless bone.
I have seen our hospitals,
Cities of the dead.
I have seen dying worse than death –
The numbering, pounding, swelling, aching,
burning, shouting out for
Death
To come.

SCENE THREE

(Newhouse *and* Isabel *scramble from the bed and dress hurriedly in elaborate costumes.* Newhouse *masked.*)

Isabel: Was someone at the door?

Newhouse: Let's go – there's a way out the back.

Isabel: When can I see you again?

Newhouse: Soon – I promise –

Isabel: – I can't wait – I don't even know your name –

Newhouse: I'll find you.

Isabel: Oh come on, tell me your name.

Newhouse: Do you really need to know who I am?

Isabel: Yes, of course –

Newhouse: – wasn't it delirious – not knowing names –

Isabel: – it was fabulous. But no more games – tell me who you are –

(*Pause*)

Isabel: All right – no names, no past, no future. Let's make love again – now!

(President *enters in a masked costume.*)

President: Who's there?

Isabel: Jesus, it's the President.

President: What is going on here? (*turns on light*) Who are you?

Newhouse: A man and a woman.

(President *leaves.*)

President: Ambassador Peters, there is a man with a woman in your guest room –

Ambassador: (*in costume*) Sir?

President: fucking – you know (*gestures*) – every cock-sucking reporter and his motherfucking brother here – I've got staff up the ying-yang to keep my cherry intact, and I turn my back at this jerk-off Canadian embassy function and take it up the ass – now get your perfumed cunt in there and wipe up the fucking mess.

Ambassador: Yes, Mr President.

(Ambassador *enters room*.)

Ambassador: Whatever you two are doing – I want you to stop.

Newhouse: This is none of your business.

Ambassador: Don't make me call security.

Newhouse: You can't arrest me – Ambassador.

Ambassador: Wait outside for me, Miss. (*to* Newhouse) You stay. (Isabel *exits*)

Ambassador: Who the hell are you?

Newhouse: You know me.

Ambassador: Newhouse – you should know better! Why tonight?

Newhouse: Ambassador Peters, my apologies for disturbing your Masquerade –

Ambassador: – half of the American government, all of the press –

Newhouse: – she's very attractive –

Ambassador: – and you couldn't drive to a motel?

Newhouse: – not so easy – identification, proof of marriage – besides, in this disguise I could remain anonymous.

Ambassador: She doesn't know who you are?

Newhouse: We were both a little too impetuous –

Ambassador: What were you thinking of?

Newhouse: We were trying not to think. Nothing will happen if you don't say anything. The girl doesn't even know my name – she'd barely recognize me.

Ambassador: You disgust me, Newhouse. But this isn't uncommon behaviour for you – is it? I know why your father posted you here – the affair with Commander Gordon's wife –

Newhouse: – "Damage control" –

Ambassador: – he was protecting you.

Newhouse: I won't ask you to protect me. It would be insincere.

Ambassador: Sex is dangerous unless you're tested and registered –

Newhouse: – sex is spontaneous –

Ambassador: – sex is illegal – you've abused your diplomatic immunity –

Newhouse: – but not my sexual immunity –

Ambassador: You're relieved of your post. Get out of Washington. Disappear. You and your assistant.

Newhouse: Advice, or a command?

Ambassador: Both. Leave – out the back!

Newhouse: Is that what the President wants, Ambassador Peters –

Ambassador: Go!

(Newhouse *leaves*. President *joins* Ambassador.)

Ambassador: Mr President, the man disappeared when I went to call security.

President: Fuck! No ... good! Shit, I recognized the slut – Isabel Duke – her father's a congressman – our side. And I know who her horny boyfriend is.

Ambassador: It was her boyfriend?

President: Who the fuck else? Robert Baker – also our side.

Ambassador: Then the less said the better.

President: Except she knows that I know – I'd better give her ass a reaming. Make fucking sure we're not disturbed.

(Ambassador *leaves*. Isabel *joins* President.)

President: Isabel, I am shocked. Your lewd conduct –

Isabel: I didn't –

President: – don't interrupt me! This is an official function of the Canadian government. Your indiscretion is appalling. Imagine the ramifications if this were to get out. Headlines, your picture, Robert's picture –

Isabel: It wasn't Robert.

President: Don't compound my anger by protecting –

Isabel: I don't know who –

President: Have you been tested?

Isabel: No.

President: Are you registered?

Isabel: No, but –

President: You and Robert could be arrested – your father busted his ass pushing the bill through Congress for me, for God's sake. Couldn't you control yourself? Don't you recognize the threat – don't you feel the danger? That law is there to protect you. You want us to build prisons and quarantines – walls to cage people like you who can't control their lust?

Isabel: Robert wasn't here – the Ambassador knows –

President: Robert's career – and your father's – could be finished – destroyed. Out of deference to your families, you have my reluctant silence. I am now indebted to Ambassador Peters for her discretion. You've compromised my government.

Isabel: It wasn't Robert – he's not at fault.

President: Young lady, you will have to be tested. The health of this government takes precedence.

Isabel: Don't turn away sir, let me explain.

President: My back is turned, Miss Duke. You've hurt me.

(President *joins* Ambassador.)

President: Being tested should keep her fucking quiet.

SCENE FOUR

(*A large parade. Helicopter lands, and* Prime Minister *emerges.*)

Prime Minister (PM): Citizens, I know that you have family, friends, and companions who suffer. I suffer with you. I know your anxiety. You are not alone. I am one of you.

Com:
Will you act?

PM: Yes, but our crisis resembles a maze that requires us to examine every possibility, pursue every avenue, before providing an answer.

Com:
When does study end
And action begin?

PM: We have already acted. Our first step was an unprecedented coalition between Mr Crane's Conservatives and my own party. Both of us have put aside partisan politics for the sake of unity in this crisis. After consultation with the assembled field of experts, Mr Crane, as Minister of Health, will propose concrete policy.

Com:
How much longer
Must we wait?

PM: I expect his commission to complete their inquiry some time today. But in this dark hour before solution, we must first seek tolerance. We who do not suffer from the disease must keep our minds, our hearts, open.

(Mr Crane *emerges from a committee room.*)

Crane: After public hearings across the country, we have prepared this proposal. The report is not good news, but good can only come from exacting measures.

Com:
We have a right
To know.

Crane: Our report should first be presented to government, permitting them time to study and respond.

Com:
People are desperate
For answers.

PM: All parties are united in coalition to battle this crisis. Your inquiry affects us all, Mr Crane, and must be openly debated.

Crane: Our principal recommendation is simple. We must test everyone – identify the diseased and the carriers – to contain the spread. Only by isolating the infected from the uninfected, can we inhibit further contagion. Continued research monies may result in a future vaccine or cure. But it would be a misrepresentation, false hope, to assume that we can easily outwit nature. This brief time – when we lived immune to all life-threatening contagion – is over. The disease and its effects are complex. Prevention, through certification and quarantine, may be our only option to preserve the future.

Com:
Will you act immediately
On the commission's recommendations?

PM: We will act, but not thoughtlessly. No "quick-fix" solution will be implemented to appease special interests. Your recommendations, I'm certain, address the effect on civil rights.

Crane: We must identify the endangered with tolerance and acceptance. They are not criminals.

PM: And yet you suggest treating them as criminals.

Crane: The minority discussed this at length, but the majority concluded that public identification is the only effective way to save the country. The number of sick increases every day. But it is more daunting that the disease incubates unseen for as many as seven to ten years. The number of unidentified carriers is estimated at near epidemic levels. We fully expect an exponential increase in hospitalized cases. If we allow, the disease's spread will accelerate with a devastating momentum to destroy every man, woman and child. This nation, in fact the entire human race, could perish.

Com:
You name our unspoken terror.

Crane: It is our moral obligation to act. The commission recommends a hard, but effective, solution – following the lead of other countries. All sexual activity must be authorized through state-issued certificates that require continually updated tests. By monitoring, and licensing, we can guarantee your safety in this sacred human act. The alternative is painfully clear.

PM: Our difference of opinion is also clear, but consensus and conciliation are possible if we honestly debate your proposal. Nature's unsolvable riddle forces us to seek a political answer. Many thanks to your commission for its hard work – and to you for your effort, your guidance, and your loyalty. The citizens will find this government committed to a responsible solution. The disease affects each of us. I protect the whole nation – healthy and diseased – as I would myself.

Com:
Promises of resolve.
Deliverance from our affliction.
Have we waited too long –
Past point of return?
We can only wait – and hope.

SCENE FIVE

(*An office in the White House.*)

Newhouse: Hello, Baker, I came by to pick up those reports I loaned you. Chambers and I have received a new posting.

Baker: Oh really? Where are you going?

Newhouse: South America.

Chambers: Guyana.

Baker: Guyana? What did you do – poke the President's wife? Your daddy doesn't make it easy on you, does he?

Chambers: I think it's the other way around.

Newhouse: Pardon?

Chambers: Nothing.

Baker: Good luck, Newhouse.

Newhouse: You're in early.

Baker: Couldn't sleep – I was up half the night.

Newhouse: Really? I expected you to attend our Masquerade Ball.

Baker: I was there – arrived late – left early. Do you know Isabel Duke?

Newhouse: Isabel Duke ... don't think so ... Congressman Duke's wife?

Baker: Daughter.

Newhouse: Chambers, you know everybody –

Chambers: Congressman Duke did come in with a young lady –

Baker: So she was there! When did you see her?

Chambers: – they both left early I believe.

Baker: That's odd. I called her at home.

Newhouse: Are you in love? –

Baker: – I like her – we're just dating.

Newhouse: (*laughs*) – Baker, you're lying –

Baker: – it's nothing – I find her attractive –

Chambers: – nothing's wrong with that! –

Newhouse: – you've lost your reason to an attraction and your sense to an infatuation. Chambers, I think this is serious. Now, does this Isabel love you?

Baker: It never comes up.

Newhouse: Sounds like that's your problem.

(*Intercom buzz.*)

Baker: Excuse me. Yes. I beg your pardon ... send her in. That's odd. Ambassador Peters is here to see me.

Newhouse: The Dragon Lady – she's the one who transferred me to Guyana. I'm going out the back.

Baker: What would she want with me?

Newhouse: Well, her surprise visits usually mean trouble.

Baker: Trouble?

Newhouse: Maybe she didn't like your costume ... Chambers!

(Newhouse *and* Chambers *exit*.)

Ambassador: You're in early.

Baker: I take great pride in my duties, Madame Ambassador.

Ambassador: Yes. The President said you were a man who takes his responsibilities seriously.

Baker: I try to earn his respect. Can I be of service?

Ambassador: The President thinks that your education might benefit from a posting to Ottawa.

Baker: He does?

Ambassador: Is there a problem?

Baker: Not at all, Ambassador. I just don't understand the reason for his decision, but please, I'm listening.

Ambassador: I'm afraid he's very disappointed with you – at the moment.

Baker: What have I done?

Ambassador: Mr. Baker, the President thinks he caught you making love at our Masquerade Ball.

Baker: What?

Ambassador: Isabel and you –

Baker: It wasn't me – and I know it couldn't have been Isabel. Who identified us?

Ambassador: The President discovered her in a rather compromising position – and he deduced the man was you.

Baker: Oh God – if she was with someone else I want to know who.

Ambassador: Robert, it appears you've been eclipsed.

Baker: This is unbelievable ... I ... to think she – You're absolutely sure – Isabel and this man were –

Ambassador: I don't question the President's eyes.

Baker: And he thinks it's me – Shit, Isabel, we love each other.

Ambassador: The President considered having both of you arrested. Given the climate, her deceit is a tangible threat – personally and politically. I suggested the posting as a remedy, Robert – a little time, a change of place, among friends.

Baker: You have an ally for life, Ambassador. I'm honoured you'd have me. Thank you.

Ambassador: Good.

(Ambassador *exits*)

Baker: Fuck! – Isabel fucking someone – fuck!

SCENE SIX

(*Fundamentalist Gathering. Disabled* Evangelist *prays.*)

Evangelist:
We suffer beyond all telling.
No one weeps as the children die.
No pity for the mother's cry.

Nature surfaces and
Sickness fills our ranks,
Outstripping invention of
Man-made remedy.

Commandments
Warnings years ago
Have been ignored.

There was a natural order.
Sacred love created
Life –
Death followed.

Now order becomes chaos.
Time flows backward and
Death
Precedes conception.

SCENE SEVEN

(*Night. In headlights of limousine.*)

Minister of External Affairs (MEA): So they want to cut a deal, Commander Gordon?

Commander: As you predicted, Mr Newhouse, the Fundamentalists are preparing a smear campaign. At present they are reviewing what can be used – sorting fact, innuendo, hearsay.

MEA: Against who?

Commander: My sources only named minor party officials.

MEA: Then why approach the Minister of External Affairs?

Commander: There will eventually be more prominent targets – possibly the Prime Minister – certainly senior ministers, and members of their families – scandal by association.

MEA: Do they really think we can be intimidated?

Commander: Those inflated disease statistics they published last week have already accelerated the panic. Now they're releasing information, through masked sources, on prominent carriers – some true, some suspected, some manufactured – but all damaging.

MEA: If they start a media battle, I like our chances.

Commander: I'm not so sure. They've been monitoring government members for years – traced a chain of sexual relationships. Should a verifiable carrier appear in the chain, they'll publish their accusations – with a map.

MEA: That's none of their goddamn business.

Commander: But it's more than sexual impropriety. They present it as a public service – identifying carriers in the guise of public safety.

MEA: Safety my ass – they want power.

Commander: Absolutely. These scandals involving political leaders make the ordinary citizens feel vulnerable. The more deaths, the stronger the morality, the greater the need for prohibition. I think they'll succeed.

MEA: Government by tabloid.

Commander: Tabloids are the weather vane of public feeling. They may stir up prejudice, but prejudice is very real.

MEA: There'll be a backlash – people aren't totally stupid.

Commander: The Fundamentalists invested in the media, and placed their people on corporate boards. So they argue not only the need to inform the public, but the profitability of scandal.

MEA: They're already campaigning – and we don't even know there's a fucking election.

Commander: But they want to negotiate – they like you.

MEA: What are they offering?

Commander: In return for leaving you alone –

MEA: – that's no "offer," it's blackmail –

Commander: – in other words no mail blitz, no campaign to discredit you with untoward sexual relations –

MEA: – well, fuck them – rooting around like maggots –

Commander: – you remain neutral on policy concerning the plague.

MEA: How do they expect me to remain neutral – I'm the goddamn Minister of External Affairs – I can't dissociate myself from the Prime Minister –

Commander: They suggest you focus on external affairs and side-step domestic policy – at which they believe you're already quite adept.

MEA: Arrogant bastards.

Commander: They're being flexible, and you've got the manoeuvrability.

MEA: What's your advice?

Commander: If they form a coalition with the Conservatives after the election, and you resign from the Party to sit as an independent – your expertise would be invaluable to them. You might even regain your former ministry.

MEA: Maybe I can temper their policies – save the country from a worse fate. Keep negotiating – see which way the wind blows.

Commander: Good.

MEA: I owe you, Commander –

Commander: I'm honoured to be of service.

MEA: What kind of world are we leaving our kids?

MEA: That's the Fundamentalist's greatest argument – protecting the children.

MEA: What – arranged marriages from birth?

Commander: If Anna and I had children, I know exactly what we'd do. Virginity is a valuable commodity. (*pause*) Some parents know where sexual freedom leads.

MEA: Are you referring to my son, Commander? His indiscretions with your wife were no less compromising to me. But I sent him packing. Any further danger from that affair won't come from him – if you catch my drift.

Commander: If you're suggesting that Anna –

MEA: – I'm suggesting that you keep her locked up when she's in season – much safer for all concerned.

PM: (*Address to the Nation*) Citizens of this great nation, there are those who demand mandatory testing of the entire population, as well as the segregation of plague victims and carriers.

(*Pause*)

I believe we can halt the spread of the disease without such drastic measures. If you act with courage, for the collective health of the nation, we offer a humane remedy to our distress.

Tonight, through the executive powers of the Prime Minister's Office, I announce the establishment of clinics for voluntary testing in every health centre across the nation. Your test results, I guarantee, will remain strictly confidential. Only with complete self-knowledge can each of us act conscientiously and responsibly.

(*Pause*)

Anyone who suspects themselves to be a carrier, anyone living in fear that they have been exposed, I especially urge you to come forward. It will require courage not to go underground, but I implore you to participate willingly.

(*Pause*)

You may suspect a family member, a friend, an associate at work – encourage them to volunteer for the test.

Reassure them that they will face no recrimination. Earn their trust, and you earn the nation's gratitude.

(*Pause*)

Because I ask you to test voluntarily, I will fiercely protect your right to privacy. But I can only defend the freedom of high risk groups if they accept their personal responsibility. (*Pause*)

You all know the radical solutions proposed to cope with the disease. But I reject any proposal that undermines the civil rights of our citizens. We must remove the shame, deny the stigma, and show mercy to those in distress.

(*Pause*)

Only those who knowingly pass on the disease, without informing their partners, deserve prosecution. But I trust people will change their behaviour – act for the common good – if they have self-knowledge.

(*Pause*)

I am your leader. I also have a family – a wife, children. I fight for you as I would fight for them – bringing light to the dark fear in each of us. Fear is our enemy – do not obey it.

I am hopeful. I see a brighter future. We are a great nation. This contagion can not destroy our faith in human nature, or the enduring principles that built this country. Join with me in our continuing pact of courageous democracy.

SCENE NINE

(*Cathedral.* Commander *and* Anna *kneeling in rear pew.* MEA *enters pursued by reporters.*)

MEA: No comment. No comment. The nation's health is not the responsibility of the Minister of External Affairs.

(MEA *kneels in forward pew and is joined by* Commander.)

MEA: Me and my shadows. I feel like a fresh piece of meat.

Commander: We just received a diplomatic pouch from Ambassador Peters. Your son seduced a young lady at our embassy's Masquerade Ball –

MEA: – that sounds like him –

Commander: – it's worse – the President walked in on them –

MEA: Shit! Who was the girl?

Commander: Isabel Duke – daughter of Congressman Duke.

MEA: Oh Christ – the Genghis Khan of Capitol Hill. How could he be so fucking stupid – they could lay charges or expel him –

Commander: Not likely. She claims not to know who she was with –

MEA: – must be love – she's protecting him –

Commander: – but the President thinks it was Robert Baker –

MEA: – Robert Baker? Christ –

Commander: – The President ordered the Duke girl tested, and sent Baker here as a reprimand. He arrived this morning.

MEA: To keep it quiet rather – the Baker family is too important. Where the hell's my son?

Commander: Peters order him to Guyana, but he disappeared –

MEA: – then he'll show up here – for money –

Commander: Minister, I have the highest regard for you, but your son is a prime target for the Fundamentalists –

MEA: It's more complicated than that, Donald –

Commander: – they won't negotiate with you if they know they can eliminate you.

MEA: If they smell blood, they'll come in for the kill. When he gets back, I'll get rid of him. He can go out to the estate and fucking rot.

Commander: He won't stay there – you said yourself he's beyond control –

MEA: If he shows his face I'll tell him he's a carrier –

Commander: – but he's not – is he? –

MEA: I'll tell him I reviewed and altered his medical reports.

Commander: That might slow the little weasel down.

MEA: You better hope it does, Commander – because it might be true.

(MEA *leaves*. Commander *turns to nearby aide*.)

Commander: (*on phone*) I have a bit of a problem. Set up routine surveillance of my home today – you've got the address – no later than 2300 hours. I want a log and video evidence of all traffic – in and out.

(Commander *joins* Anna.)

SCENE TEN

(*The* chorus *responds through phone-in show*.)

1st Chorus: I don't have it – I won't take a test – I know I don't have it – and I've never met anyone who has.

PM: But only by taking the test voluntarily can you be absolutely sure. It's up to you.

2nd Chorus: Force the sick to identify their partners. Find out who's got it by following the links in the chain. Carriers walking our streets should be publicly identified. When it comes to a choice between public safety and human rights, I take the side of safety every time.

PM: I believe private lives must be revealed voluntarily, and with mutual consent. I hope, if we provide the conditions for individual courage, people will come forward on their own. The government can't do it alone. We need your co-operation.

2nd Chorus: Have you spoken to the church?

PM: Yes. Most denominations have been amenable to our proposals, and we have responded to their suggestions. Such church leaders, however, seem more committed to civil unrest than to concrete discussion. Their inflammatory rallies ... disappoint me.

3rd Chorus: Rumours, accusations, lovers informing on lovers – it's the beginning of a police state.

PM: Our proposals are designed precisely to prevent a police state. Paranoia is rampant – eating away at the fabric of society. Confront fear with honesty and responsibility.

3rd Chorus: We already have laws protecting human rights. You're encouraging a climate of mistrust.

PM: There are dangers. But isn't the unknown, the uncertainty, the speculation more dangerous? We eliminate fear with knowledge.

Evangelist: Where do we come from, where are we going, why is there a universe? Are there not limits to what mere humans can know?

PM: We need a lot less mysticism, and a lot more knowledge.

Evangelist: There is a purpose to this disease. It is neither mystical nor arbitrary.

PM: Explain yourself. I welcome this opportunity to challenge your thinking. Enlighten us.

Evangelist: Why do we suffer from the plague? Crimes against nature were committed in arrogance and pride. We assumed an immunity to the enduring laws of nature. Now we must accept the punishment – the suffering. Humble yourself. Acknowledge the limits – to our freedom, to our understanding – and you will have my prayer.

PM: Your prayers ignite the fear that grips us. You conspire with the disease to maximize its lethal effect –

Evangelist: – man no longer has the answers –

PM: – Your words inspire protests, riots, terror –

Evangelist: – now and in the past we challenged nature, ignored the fundamentals, betrayed the larger meanings with a shrug. You too must suffer. You are diseased.

PM: Now they attack me. There are consequences to slanderous accusations.

Evangelist: It is yourself you seek – you who must be tested –

PM: Accuse me again – clearly – leave no room for misconstruing. This is your opportunity.

Evangelist: It only makes sense. We reap what we have sown. Defy His commandments and you suffer the consequences.

PM: – you will regret this –

Evangelist: – like all men who think themselves immortal, you betrayed the sacred union with the one you love. This disease is payment for your past.

PM: Do you think you can malign me – my marriage – so freely?

Evangelist: I do – if truth has any power.

PM: Truth, yes! Not shameless lies. They cannot harm me, or anyone who thinks. Did my political opponents put you up to this?

Evangelist: You are your only enemy.

PM: Must honourable members resort to tabloid tricks – sifting my past to discredit my freely-elected mandate to govern? Reasoned thought, careful analysis and action by consensus are the hallmarks of my government. This is little more than prophecy for profit. Does your holy alliance expect to govern through visions and speculation – by consorting with psychics and gossips? Then allow me a prediction. You will retract your statements, and your cohorts will be exposed. There will be no political gain – only the people's punishment.

Evangelist: You ridicule me, but you fail to see a half century of mis-
guided freedom and arrogant pride – in the guise of civilization.
You think you are immune –
Infallible.
But who have you loved?
How many have you loved?

Now that love becomes a curse:
Your eyes – shall know true darkness;
Your ears – the scream of marriage vows;
And your children, your poor children –

PM: This is intolerable. Your rantings are lunacy.

Evangelist: Your past speaks differently.

PM: What do you know of my past?

Evangelist: Only what I sense.

PM: Oh, intuitions, not intelligence.

Evangelist: You are the famous 'man of reason' – use your reason.

PM: I will – to save this country from you and your kind. Only then will I be satisfied.

Evangelist:
The killer, the disease
Lies dormant
Among your thoughts –
Your base desires.

What you think you see,

Hides truth to be known.

Lover
And killer
Have become one.

(Evangelist *and* Prime Minister *exit*.)

Com:
What will be his fate?
How can we judge?
We must know. We must understand. We must decide.
Not through fervent prophecy,
But through facts and wisdom.

Be wary of words
Until they are as real as things.

SCENE ELEVEN

(Newhouse *and* Baker *meet in Ministry of External Affairs. Hallway*.)

Newhouse: Baker – in my home and native land?

Baker: I thought you were in Guyana?

Newhouse: Family business.

Baker: I'm here ... for a while – re-assignment.

Newhouse: I thought you were more politician than diplomat.

Baker: Negotiations – we're tightening continental immigration.

Newhouse: Let me show you around. To the outsider it's a boring, bureaucratic town, but there's an underside –

Baker: I imagine you know all about it.

Newhouse: My hometown. I'll buy you a drink across the street.

Baker: Later – after my orientation meeting.

Newhouse: Leave the orienting to me, pal.

(*An intercom buzz*.)

MEA: Good. Send him in. I want to welcome him personally.

Baker: I hope I'm not interrupting?

MEA: Not at all.

Baker: I just ran into your son. We're meeting for a drink.

MEA: You know my son?

Baker: We knew each other in Washington. (*pause*) I hadn't expected to see you so quickly.

MEA: We've heard a great deal about you, Robert.

Baker: I understand.

MEA: Excellent reports – from the highest office in your country. I understand you're a natural.

Baker: Is that what the President said?

MEA: We've been informed about the unfortunate incident. Contrary to the President's belief, Ambassador Peters claims you've been wrongly accused. I propose to do everything in my power to minimize the effects on your reputation. You must realize, Robert, that you are presidential material. Why else were you sent here? As punishment? No, to protect you from further tarnishing – away from the media's rather harsh glare. I intend to take good care of you, candidate Baker.

Baker: And I thought this posting was –

MEA: Well, you're not in exile. I want to make absolutely certain that when you do return, you'll think of this country as your second home. We can always use friends like you.

Baker: Thank you for your confidence. Some day your hospitality will be repaid.

MEA: Good. We're having a small reception for you upstairs – I'll introduce you to some of our national treasures.

SCENE TWELVE

(*Parliament. Thumping.*)

Crane: Mr Speaker, Honourable Members, my ministry is paralysed by innuendo. If the Prime Minister, this house, the nation thinks I would subvert our unity in a time of crisis, then let it be said now – before me and the people.

Members: (*loud thumping*)
No to Anger!
No to Confusion!
No to Lies!

Crane: Did you, Prime Minister, accuse me of collusion with the religious radicals?

PM: You violate the solemn agreements of this house – and solely to grasp at power. I only defend myself against you.

Crane: Mr Speaker, we can attack each other, charge and countercharge, but what I have to say in simple, honest, and needs an unbiased ear.

PM: Your malicious actions speak louder than simple words.

Crane: I don't attack you.

PM: Was it not your commission that proposed mandatory testing?

Crane: I would not hesitate to do the same again.

PM: Did you not recommend that test results be made public – that carriers be publicly identified?

Crane: That was my opinion, given the findings.

PM: Opinion? It was a calculated political tactic.

(*Thumping*)

Crane: A tactic – how absurd.

PM: How long did you deliberate before making recommendations?

Crane: Weeks of public hearings with many concerned parties –

PM: Including the churches.

Crane: All denominations were surveyed.

PM: Equal weight was given to all voices.

Crane: Yes, of course.

PM: But beyond the formal inquiry, were there private discussions?

Crane: No, none. Everything was public.

PM: No backroom meetings, no private solicitations, no strategy sessions?

Crane: No.

PM: Then why the sudden attacks on my character? – flimsy accusations? – calls for me to be tested? – a media blitz demanding that my private life become public?

(*Thumping*)

Crane: That has nothing to do with with me. Your questions judge me. May I question you?

PM: The Conservatives recently received substantial contributions from Fundamentalist organizations.

Crane: Am I to ask the affiliation of every citizen who donates a dollar?

(*Thumping*)

PM: You and your evangelical friends conspire to defame me, to dismantle this coalition – to force an election over hearsay.

Crane: I do not bend to their demands, nor submit to their influence. Haven't we agreed to coalition in the crisis?

PM: Yes – we have a written agreement.

(*Thumping*)

Crane: And you gave me a voice in Cabinet affairs?

PM: Your voice has been heard.

Crane: And despite differences of opinion, I united behind your single voice.

PM: Initially – but you unwittingly revealed your party's private agenda and poisoned our trust.

Crane: No. Consider my position rationally. What astute politician would want to be leader? Given the current health crisis – it's political suicide. I had your confidence. My advice was acknowledged, debated, and sifted by your judgement. I enjoyed the privilege of power, without becoming a target.

PM: You try to sidestep blame, but these "anonymous" donations undermine our coalition.

(*Thumping*)

Crane: My offices are open to your inspection. Put me, and all I value, to question, but don't convict me on suspicion. If you purge my voice, you throw away the strength of our unity, and destroy our only hope. I ask you for your trust.

(*Thumping*)

PM: I cannot believe these protestations of innocence. You are baiting and frightening the public with scandals. You call for trust and force an election.

(Crane *leaves.*)

PM: Today I reluctantly dissolve this government. Let the people judge.

(*Thumping*)

SCENE THIRTEEN

(*Ottawa.*)

Newhouse: Baker's been reassigned – demoted to Ottawa. The Dragon Lady fingered him – instead of me – and Pop must know all about it.

Chambers: You're gloating.

Newhouse: And why not – things are working out wonderfully.

Chambers: Don't you have a conscience? You broke the law and you broke Isabel's heart –

Newhouse: Our desire rose from slightly lower.

Chambers: –you abandon her to be punished and betray a friend – you won't get away with it –

Newhouse: Chambers. Chambers. You are dangerously naïve.

Chambers: – and you're a cynic.

Newhouse: – a realist –

Chambers: – you should be punished.

Newhouse: But I am free – even though I was caught breaking an American law by the President of the United States. Chambers, the law, the government – the whole system – needs me. We all know that politics is nothing more than insider information, old-boy favours, and back-room lies – all disguised as good intentions. Well, I oil that machine. I have given the President, my father, and our Dragon Lady a wonderful new relationship – interlocking IOU's – because they serve themselves by conspiring to protect me.

Also I serve the electorate who think they want to love and deify their leaders. But as soon as scandal such as I can offer cracks the reputation of their beloved statesmen, they experience the exquisite joy of watching them crumble. Ah yes, it's the stuff of myth – and it fills their papers, their speakers, their screens. So you see my humble efforts promote the only real passion in the political process.

Chambers: Well ... I just don't like the way you live or anything you say and I should turn you in myself.

Newhouse: And defy the wishes of dear old Dad and the prez? Listen, if they wanted me arrested, they had ample opportunity.

Chambers: Your father's protecting you because he loves you –

Newhouse: Ha!

Chambers: Don't you believe in virtue?

Newhouse: There's only boredom in virtue. Virtue mortifies the flesh and denies every human desire.

Chambers: And what about love?

Newhouse: I didn't love her. She didn't love me. And yet there was a real passion that you'll never feel –

Chambers: Gratuitous excitement. You were strangers – she could be a carrier or you could be a carrier –

Newhouse: Desire is all we have, Chambers. We are desiring machines.

SCENE FOURTEEN

(*Tabloid headlines and simultaneous news conferences*)

Headline: Snap Election Called During Bitter Government Battle.

Prime Minister's Wife (Wife): It's the first I've heard of this. I'm not prepared to comment.

Headline: Conservative-Fundamentalist Conspiracy.

Wife: Of course our family has been deeply hurt by these rumours. When people are dying, how can so-called Christian people add to the misery?

Crane: A coalition government, rife with animosity, cannot govern with the nation's trust and confidence. The Prime Minister created an impossible situation for me and my party.

PM: I recognized the need to co-operate, I initiated a working coalition, and then I was stabbed in the back. The Conservatives plot against the very policies they endorsed.

Crane: Look at our finances. We're not ready for an election, and he knows that. He's simply seeking a majority because he's tired of compromise – tired of listening to people who aren't yes-men.

Headline: PM Accused Plague Carrier.

Wife: Why is the media creating this storm? My husband is being judged without a trial.

Com:
Political battle.
Unwanted election.
We need unity not division.

(*Computerized headlines are projected simultaneously throughout the remaining scene: "Polls Find Election Useless"; "I Made Love to PM"; "Political War of Accusations"; "PM Linked in Plague Chain"; "Christian Party Points Finger"; "Carrier Claims She Loved PM"; "PM's Health?"; "Majority Reject Election"*)

PM: I agree. This is an unwelcome, but necessary, election. You must make a choice. I seek a mandate to govern effectively.

Com:
Heal this rift.

PM: I cannot as long as these lies about my health persist. Only the people's confidence can restore my authority.

Com:
Bound by common dilemma –
Cast aside suspicion and
End this war
Of accusation.

PM: I will not retreat. Crane will do anything to topple me.

Com:
Those were not
His words.

PM: Slander and libel rob me of any ability to lead, and strip me of my rights as an individual. If he would do this to me, when I hold the highest office in the land, what would he do to the sick, the suffering, the powerless.

Crane: Where there is faith, he sees hate; where there is loyalty, he sees betrayal. He yields to these slanderous attacks by calling the vote. He defames himself.

PM: The election date is set.

Crane: This is paranoia. The Prime Minister is not fit to govern.

SCENE FIFTEEN

(*Private.*)

Wife: How can I comfort you?

PM: No comfort until I have destroyed him.

Wife: One injustice will lead to another.

PM: Are you saying I am unjust?

Wife: Yes ... you may be.

PM: I am defending my reputation.

Wife: Enough of this fighting. The country is in torment – and now we are. You must rest.

PM: Rest! – their accusations infuriate me.

Wife: I am not turning against you, I'm here to help. You've given your life to this country – fifteen years. You've done things no other man could do and people still have faith in you. Lead us back to safety and security. That's all I want, they want. Let your anger go.

PM: But these lies about me –

Wife: Ignore the rumours. What do they know ... how do they know? It's gossip – prophecies by a lunatic.

PM: How am I to lead?

Wife: You don't actually think he sees into the future, or conjures up the past.

PM: I can't go on until my name is cleared.

Wife: Prove them wrong. Take the test. Publish the results. This dread disease can't touch us. We've been married for years – in devotion to each other.

PM: I know that. But I can't not think about it.

Wife: They can root through your past, bribe witnesses to make any sort of claim, but don't let them create doubts inside you.

PM: I know I know I know – but I'm obsessed – I just can't help it.

Wife: People indulge and paralyse themselves by thinking endlessly about the disease, and forget the actual sick. You remember my friend Susan Redstone. She knew someone who tested positive, and all she could talk about was herself – whether she had it, how it gets transmitted, and on and on. So little was publicly known about the disease – she was in utter panic. She believed all those myths about dirty taps and toilet seats – worried that it was carried by mosquitoes. I asked about her friend, and she said something about the look on his face – life had left his eyes – and then went right on about herself and her worries that she got it by living next door to him. Her friend Lawrence lived on and went on – knowing he would one day die – living with the terminal. But Susan cut herself off from Lawrence. She started seeing doctors every week. She trapped herself in a state of paranoia – for nothing. Nothing ever happened to her. What do we have to be afraid of? Fear never changes the future, it only destroys the present.

PM: This Lawrence has the disease?

Wife: He died recently.

PM: Who told you? Susan?

Wife: They hadn't seen each other in years. She read about his death in the papers.

PM: When did he find out?

Wife: What's wrong?

PM: When? Tell me?

Wife: Susan told me ... five years ago.

PM: Were they lovers? Did Susan make love to Lawrence?

Wife: I don't think they were lovers – they were friends and neighbours –

PM: – do you know, or don't you –

Wife: Women didn't interest Lawrence except as friends. What's going on?

PM: I should see Susan.

Wife: Why?

PM: My God, I can't believe that ...

Wife: What is it?

PM: If I tell you –

Wife: Tell me.

PM: Seven years ago I slept with – made love to – Susan Redstone. I was on the west coast campaigning for the leadership and we swept the local delegates. There was a celebration. The media was there – the hacks, the bagmen – everybody. But we somehow managed to slip away to her house. I was so scared and so excited. I felt like a kid. It was my reward. That was the only time I have every been unfaithful to you. One night.

Wife: Why are you telling me this now?

PM: About three in the morning, as I was preparing to slip back to the hotel, Susan answered her front door. I overheard what sounded like a lovers' quarrel. I asked her, but she didn't want to talk about it. She said it was her neighbour – they hadn't been getting along – and dismissed it as platonic –

Wife: – I think that's true –

PM: – I didn't believe her. I remember that night very clearly – Susan shouting his name over and over again ... Lawrence ... Lawrence. If they were lovers, then you and I may be linked in a chain –

Wife: You can't allow some incident in the past – whether they made love – to obsess you –

PM: – some absurd modern curse –

Wife: – even if they did, it does not necessarily mean that you are a carrier –

PM: – the consequence of betrayal – a judgment –

Wife: You and I will not be infected.

PM: If I have hurt you – don't let me live to see that day. (*They embrace.*)

Wife: Trust knowledge – only the facts.

PM: I must find her.

Wife: I will call her.

PM: Now. Call her now!

Wife: All right. You should rest.

SCENE SIXTEEN

(*Bar.* Marcus *enters* – *sees* Newhouse.)

Marcus: What are you doing here? I thought you'd been run out of town.

Newhouse: I've returned.

Marcus: And you didn't call me, your old friend!

Newhouse: Perceptive as ever, Marcus. What's new to screw?

Marcus: Nothing.

Newhouse: Yeah, this place is usually packed at this hour.

Marcus: The whole scene has changed, Newhouse.

Newhouse: There's always new hotspots, but where are the ladies?

Marcus: It's a desert. All the regulars have disappeared.

Newhouse: Come on –

Marcus: Jennifer retired – married. Teddie disappeared – rumours of her not feeling well. Caused quite a stir in the circles – that put everyone on their guard. And Muffy's too active. No one will touch her –

Newhouse: Let's check out the Underbelly.

Marcus: That club's crawling with the same old scum, but public sex at arm's-length is the new order of the night. They have these "Lite Your Skirt and Fly" parties. But once the skirt is lifted the rule is – Look But Don't Touch. There's so little sex to go around now that whenever anyone has the nerve, it makes sense to share it with hundreds. Flirting is definitely the end of the line. Sex is dead.

Newhouse: Men like you, Marcus, must still – engage.

Marcus: No – I'm in love –

Newhouse: Marcus, Marcus, you've forsaken me – no more lust among the ruins –

Marcus: – I'm in love –

Newhouse: – you're just going to get married and join the mob.

Marcus: Can't. She already married – to a protégé of your father's –

Newhouse: Who?

Marcus: – Gordon –

Newhouse: – and she loves you?

Marcus: Yes. But she knows about my past, so I'm a risk.

Newhouse: Marcus, you are being strung along.

Marcus: No, Anna loves me, however reluctantly. She's scared and a little guilty. (*pause*) I've been tested and the results are negative. I want to prove my love to her –

Newhouse: – by proving you're negative –

Marcus: Yes. To be tested is to love. Now we will be able to enjoy our love –

Newhouse: – except her husband –

Marcus: – that's why she meets me here –

Newhouse: – sounds paranoid –

Newhouse: – he's a real prick. Order me a drink – I've got to bleed the lizard.

(Marcus *exits*.)

Chambers: You're not going to start this Anna Gordon business – again?

Newhouse: Wipe that look off your face.

Bartender: Where's Marcus? I've got a call –

Newhouse: Is it a woman?

Bartender: Yes, his lady friend.

Newhouse: He's coming right back – I'll hold for him. (*voice*) You try to be faithful, but you can't, can you? Why do you waste yourself on that ridiculous husband? (*laughing*) Anna, relax, it's Newhouse. (*pause*) I was, but I've returned to more familiar pastures. (*pause*) No, no, no, please don't explain. I'm hardly jealous. In fact, I'm glad to be of service. (*waiter's* *voice*) What would you care for this evening? (*pause*) Ah, a rendezvous avec Marcus chez toi? A quelle heure? (*pause*) Ten o'clock. Is the flash-light still your signal? (*pause*) The more things change, the more – yes, yes, your secret is safe. Just leave the sordid details in my capable hands. Ciao. (*hangs up*) Anna. I'd forgotten how desirable you are.

Chambers: You're thinking again – I can see it in your pants.

Newhouse: You know I take great pleasure in playing tricks. We've got a busy night ahead of us, Chambers.

Chambers: Some new perversity.

Newhouse: We are going to pay a visit to my old flame – Anna.

Chambers: I disapprove. You won't get away with this forever.

Newhouse: No more preaching – please –

Chambers: I'm right.

Newhouse: Right is relative. You're my assistant. If you want to continue earning a living, it would be "right" for you to co-operate with my initiatives.

Chambers: All right. I'm at your command – but under threat.

(Marcus *returns*.)

Newhouse: Marcus, she called you at the bar – she wouldn't identify herself – I wanted to get you – but she said it was urgent and she whispered, "Tell him to come to my home – 11:00 p.m. – the flashlight will signal him." It's your lucky night – her husband must be going out of town. I'd avoid being seen by the neighbours – park up the street.

(Minister of External Affairs *enters the bar*.)

Marcus: Isn't that your father?

Newhouse: What's he doing here?

Chambers: Searching for you, I suspect.

Newhouse: Marcus, I'll be right back. Good to see you, Pops – in a place like this.

MEA: What are you doing here?

Newhouse: This isn't the capital of Guyana?

MEA: I cancelled your appointment with Robert Baker.

Newhouse: You're upset with me.

MEA: I heard from Washington – all the sordid details about that woman. I know too much – you'll have to leave the capital.

Newhouse: It's my home.

MEA: It's my home too. Fortunately, the few people who know about your masquerade are discreet. They're protecting me – not you – if that's what you think! Your behaviour threatens my career. If the media vampires find out, they'll suck me dry.

Newhouse: It's my duty to keep you honest, father.

MEA: But you, my son, have much bigger problems. Isabel Duke is going to be tested. What if she's a carrier – what if you are?

Newhouse: I don't give death much consideration – it impedes my performance.

MEA: You'd better. The congressman's daughter will test positive.

Newhouse: How do you know?

MEA: I told you – I know too much.

Newhouse: I don't believe you.

MEA: If you don't believe me – take the test.

(*pause*)

MEA: I won't cut you off if you do exactly as I say. Stay at the estate until we know whether she lays charges.

Newhouse: Whatever happened to diplomatic immunity?

MEA: Grow up. I can stick-handle myself around the law, but the front page – and it's a lot more dangerous – is beyond my control. No one must know of your return – you stay away from Baker – stay in hiding.

(MEA *begins to exit – pauses with* Chambers.)

MEA: I want daily reports by phone – nothing on paper.

(MEA *exits.* Chambers *joins* Newhouse.)

Chambers: Your father's very upset with you.

Newhouse: It suits him. Now we must prepare for what suits me.

Chambers: We are not going ahead with your plan.

Newhouse: One word to my father – and you're out of a job.

Chambers: You're a plague on women. You love and hate them. You seduce and destroy them. You worship and betray them. Men like you are supposed to be dead.

Newhouse: We are an endangered species.

Chambers: And yet like some monster you persist.

Newhouse: It's my destiny.

(Newhouse *joins* Marcus.)

Marcus: Was "Dad" pleased to see you?

Newhouse: Father was quite overcome with emotion – he had so much to tell me. But I prefer to talk of lovers – now this unfaithful married lady – does she –

Marcus: Newhouse, you don't understand women today, they want romance – sex is rarely mentioned. We've gone back to wooing –

Newhouse: I don't mind – actually it presents more challenge to men like us.

Marcus: You're passé, Newhouse, you're a womanizer –

Newhouse: Please, you're not going to tell me that I hate them too –

Marcus: That's obvious –

Newhouse: – not true. I love women. But I love each and every one of them – and there's my problem.

Marcus: Her husband just walked in! Probably traced the call!

Newhouse: Now you're paranoid.

Marcus: You don't know him – the man's a lunatic!

Newhouse: Leave – out the back. Go!

(Marcus *exits*.)

Chambers: She won't think you're Marcus. You can always tell who you're making love with – at least that's what I'm told.

Newhouse: What could the faithful bureaucrat's wife say – and to who? The truth is my disguise.

SCENE SEVENTEEN

(*Psychiatrist's couch.*)

Isabel: I know I could be arrested.

I know I've hurt Robert.

I know the President is furious.

I know my parents would die of shame.

I know it's dangerous. (*pause*) But I don't know who he is. It wasn't important – names weren't necessary. It was just what it was. Spontaneous. Animal. I never knew such intimacy. (*pause*) What do they expect? I spent all my energy, my effort, not sleeping with Robert. All we ever did was talk about it. Talk about waiting for the right time, the right place – the right. Why were we so good, so obedient, so ... afraid of each other? I'm no fool. I'm cautious. I think before I act. I follow the rules. I order my life, I contemplate and temper my needs – but this was different. I just let go – that's all. Released myself. Our eyes met ... across the room. He moved toward me ... and took my hand ... and led me away. He said nothing – we both knew. He knew – exactly how I was feeling – did exactly what I needed – knew me – it was honest – he was honest. (*pause*) How will I find him – warn him? How am I going to say it? I know I must tell him – it's only fair. But who is he?

SCENE EIGHTEEN

(Anna*'s home. Back door.*)

Newhouse: Turn off that flashlight. I prefer darkness.

Anna: You're not Marcus.

Newhouse: No Anna, I'm not Marcus.

Anna: Newhouse ... what are you doing here?

Newhouse: Turn it off!

(Newhouse *grabs flashlight.*)

Anna: You shouldn't be here. What if –

Newhouse: It's early. Marcus isn't expected for another hour.

(*Pause.*)

Anna: Then we have a little time. You look great.

(*Doorbell rings.*)

Commander: Anna! Anna!

Anna: It's my husband.

Commander: Open the front door! Anna – are you there?!

Anna: Newhouse – I'm sorry – I have to do this. Donald! Help!

Newhouse: What are you doing? Don't panic.

Commander: Anna! What the hell is going on?!

Anna: I'm in the back! Help me!

Commander: What's wrong? Who's there? (*enters*) Anna, turn on the lights.

(Newhouse *shines flashlight in* Commander'*s eyes.*)

Commander: What are you doing in my house – with my wife?

Newhouse: I don't want to hurt you.

Commander: So it's you, Newhouse, you little shit. I'm going to enjoy this –

Newhouse: – I'm armed –

Commander: – take care of yourself –

(Newhouse *hits* Commander *with flashlight.*)

Newhouse: I am. (*hits him again*) I do. (*hits him again*)

Chambers: Stop it! You're killing him. Oh God!

Commander: Anna! Anna ...

(Commander Gordon *dies.*)

Chambers: You killed him you killed him you killed him –

Newhouse: He would have died eventually.

Chambers: Let's go – please – your father –

Newhouse: I'm a stranger, Anna. Your husband caught a thief breaking into your house. The thief attacked him. If you identify me to the the police, I'll identify you to the Health Authority. Anna! Do you understand?! (*pause*) Go phone the police. Go!

(Anna *goes inside.* Newhouse *and* Chambers *leave.*)

Chambers: What was that about the Health Authority?

Newhouse: Nothing. It will keep her quiet. I think we should visit the family estate.

Chambers: What do you think I've been saying! I should warn you that I told your father –

(MEA *enters.*)

Newhouse: Oh Christ!

MEA: I told you to get out of town – what are you doing at Gordon's?

Newhouse: Just saying 'au revoir' to an old friend –

MEA: – your brain's in your fucking crotch – what's going on, Chambers? –

Chambers: – well – the Commander met with a slight accident –

Newhouse: – and he seems to be slightly dead –

MEA: – God help us all – who did it?

Newhouse: It could have been anybody – Anna was a very popular lady –

MEA: Get the hell out of my sight – I'll call the estate later and you'd better be there.

(Newhouse *and* Chambers *encounter* Marcus *as he approaches* Anna's *house.* MEA *observes.*)

Marcus: Why doesn't she turn on the light? Where is she? Who's there?

Newhouse: Marcus.

Marcus: Newhouse? Jesus you scared me. What are you doing here?

Newhouse: I'm in trouble with Pops – I need to borrow some money – he's forcing me to leave town again.

Chambers: Can we get out of here?

Marcus: Who's that?

Newhouse: My assistant.

Marcus: What's the problem?

Newhouse: Further intrigues of love. I couldn't help myself. It was sacrifice – or be sacrificed.

(Marcus *gives* Newhouse *money.*)

Marcus: Whatever you're up to, Newhouse, you're on your own – I've got an appointment.

Newhouse: Thanks, friend. Have the best of nights, Marcus –

Chambers: – in jail.

(Marcus *at* Gordon *house. Trips over body, picks up flashlight.* Officer *shines light on* Marcus.)

Officer: Who's there?

Marcus: A friend – a neighbour. What's going on? Where's Anna – Mrs Gordon? I'm going to call the police.

Officer: I think you'd better stay right there, sir – I am the police.

Marcus: Is she all right?

(Anna *appears at doorway*.)

Officer: Don't worry, Mrs Gordon.

Marcus: Anna!

Officer: Everything's under control. I think you should go back inside.

Marcus: Anna!

(MEA *in phone booth*.)

MEA: Gordon's been killed – yes dead – and they're bringing in one Marcus Lavotte. I'll get him a lawyer. He doesn't talk to the detectives, the media leeches – nobody until he's seen this lawyer. (*pause*) Well – just keep it quiet as long as you can. (*pause*) And I need a safe house for Anna Gordon – somewhere the bloodhounds can't find her. Can you do that? (*pause*) My son's involved somehow. (*pause*) No! He didn't kill Gordon! (*pause*) No – she didn't identify him – (*hangs up*) – yet. And I don't know why.

ACT TWO
SCENE NINETEEN

(*Masked Evangelists march.*)

Com:
Political battle
Spawned in Parliament
Spills onto our streets.
Faceless, nameless gangs
Armed with cans of paint
Breed petty tyranny –
As if they were immune – and
Inflict more pain
On those who suffer most.
We turn to leaders in time of crisis.
But can our Prime Minister,
Under slanderous attack,
Survive this campaign of hate,
Endure the challenge to his authority?
Will he show us strength,
Courage and
Tolerance?

SCENE TWENTY

(*Country wedding. Groom* Patrick *and bride* Amy – *showered by confetti – lead a crowd toward the reception. At rear,* Newhouse *and* Chambers *chat with* Angus, *the bride's father.*)

Angus: Oh, it's no intrusion at all!

Newhouse: I'm here for a little rest and relaxation after my last assignment, Angus. When I heard Amy was getting married I just had to express my best wishes.

Angus: There's lots of food – good country cooking. Go ahead, feel like one of the family.

Patrick: (*to* Amy) Just because his family owns half the town – it's our wedding isn't it?

Any: Patrick what are two more guests?

Angus: (*to* Newhouse) I only wish your whole family could be here.

Patrick: He's always had this reputation –

Amy: You're jealous.

Patrick: No – just because he is handsome, wealthy, physically fit – (*they pose for photo*) – it doesn't mean I'm jealous.

Amy: This dress wasn't fitted right.

Patrick: You're not having second thoughts, are you Amy? (Amy *stares at him*.) Just asking – I have to tell you something.

Amy: All right. Say it.

Patrick: I'm not feeling what I'm supposed to be feeling.

Amy: What's wrong?

Patrick: I'm not happy. You make me miserable.

Amy: Sorry.

Patrick: We're married, but I don't think you love me.

Amy: What do you want from me?

Patrick: I want you to love me on our wedding day.

Amy: I have to. I married you.

Patrick: But when you love somebody, you should show it – I should see it.

Amy: That's the woman you're marrying. If I don't suit you, we'll get a divorce.

Patrick: See! Exactly! What did I tell you. If you loved me, you wouldn't say that.

Amy: Maybe if you stopped talking about it, it'll just happen.

Patrick: All right – (*crying*) – just try to love me a little.

Amy: I'll do my best but it's (*turning to him*) you're crying.

(Patrick *exits quickly*.)

Newhouse: You don't look like the happy bride.

Amy: I don't think that's possible.

Newhouse: What would make you happy?

Amy: You're going to make me cry.

Newhouse: Tears can be beautiful.

Amy: No they can't.

Newhouse: You must express your emotions. I imagine your tears are exquisite – always surrender to your feelings.

Amy: I know this is crazy, but I didn't want to marry him.

Newhouse: Then I think you two should talk.

Amy: It just doesn't feel right – I don't know why – I said I'd get married but –

Newhouse: You can't argue with your feelings.

Amy: My father can.

Newhouse: Well, your father didn't have to marry him.

Amy: I feel like I've been coerced into it, but my father says Patrick is a good choice for a husband – he's safe –

Newhouse: – ah yes, safe –

Amy: – he hasn't slept around a lot – been tested – my God, he's probably a virgin –

Newhouse: How quaint.

Amy: Father says happiness comes with time in marriage.

Newhouse: And love?

Amy: He loves me.

Newhouse: And you love him?

(*Pause*. Patrick *enters*.)

Patrick: What are you doing in my chair?

Newhouse: Talking to the bride.

Patrick: You're acting like the bridegroom.

Newhouse: Amy could do worse.

Angus: Mr Newhouse, my new son-in-law, Patrick.

Newhouse: Oh excuse me – it's your seat. (*joins* Chambers) The bride-groom seems perturbed.

Chambers: You're all over his new wife. But who cares – just another innocent victim.

Newhouse: She's not innocent – just lacking experience. Amy, you make a very attractive bride. I'm jealous of your husband.

Amy: You're just flattering me.

Newhouse: But with very good reason.

Patrick: Is the moon full tonight? The wolves are howling.

Angus: Ladies and gentlemen – your seats. Dinner is served.

Newhouse: (*takes her hand*) Are you suddenly shy?

Amy: You're leading me on.

Newhouse: I'm trying to open your eyes.

Amy: Would you marry me?

Newhouse: I'm not the marrying kind.

Amy: Then what would you be?

Newhouse: A friend.

Amy: You want to touch me.

Newhouse: Yes.

Amy: You want to kiss me.

Newhouse: Yes.

(*They kiss*)

Patrick: What do you think you are doing?

Angus: Music please, while we dine.

Newhouse: I forgot to kiss the bride. Congratulations!

(Newhouse *returns to* Chambers.)

Chambers: I'm touched. You normally kiss your women before they know who you are – you've reformed.

Newhouse: It's genetic – I'm the son of a Liberal.

Chambers: But now her husband knows too. If I were you I'd be worried.

Newhouse: She has lovely eyes and lips.

Chambers: This is a wedding party, not a pit stop.

Patrick: This wedding has become my worst nightmare.

Angus: Music! Where is the music!

Patrick: I'm dying.

Amy: Me too.

Chambers: From the way they're staring at us, I thing we should eat what may well be our last supper.

SCENE TWENTY-ONE

(Paparazzi. *En route to Delphic Hospital.*)

Pap #1: Have you read about your husband's womanizing?

Wife: It is very difficult to ignore reports identifying women who claim to have slept with him.

Pap #2: Are you thinking about divorce?

Wife: I have complete faith in my husband – I will not be victimized by innuendo. I trust him, and I trust our marriage.

(Prime Minister *enters press scrum.*)

Pap #1: So why are you being tested?

PM: I voluntarily take the test –

Pap #3: Do you think you're a carrier?

PM: – because I ask the same of my fellow citizens. I am not above them.

Pap #1: Are you worried about your pregnancy?

(*pause*)

Pap #2: Will you release your test results to the public prior to the election?

PM: I think you would agree that I have no right to know your test results. I can also fairly say that the public has no right to know mine. Confidentiality is the central campaign issue.

Pap #2: Polls show the majority supports your efforts to maintain civil rights.

PM: I'm encouraged.

Pap #3: But a high percentage of uncommitted voters say they have the right to know about the health of their leader.

PM: My personal life has become an election issue. But I practise what I preach – unlike certain clergy who sermonize at the expense of others.

Pap #3: You're avoiding the question.

PM: Hardly. People know the difference between "hysteria" politics and "issue-oriented" debate. And I trust the legitimate press will eventually focus on campaign issues rather than character assassination.

Pap #1: But Prime Minister, you are a prime target for leaked test results.

PM: I have faith in the confidentiality of the Health Authority.

Pap #2: Then how are they getting their information?

PM: You are in the business of making surmises. Which hybrid of church and political party advocates the public identification and branding of carriers, as well as quarantine measures?

Evangelist: I only want to protect the innocent – the future –

PM: – who marches in the streets?

Evangelist: People who care. They have the freedom of assembly.

PM: You assault citizens in their homes –

Evangelist: – door-to-door campaigns are democratic –

PM: – and this violence against risk groups – members of your church, and the so-called Christian Party, are responsible. How badly do you seek power?

Evangelist: In our new age –

PM: You want power, but refuse to stand for election. Are you above it all? Or are you afraid to be tested and defeated by the democratic process.

Evangelist: I need only the love of God –

PM: (*to press*) Just get out of our lives!

Evangelist: – and the prospect of immorality. I have no mortal desire.

SCENE TWENTY-TWO

(*Delphic Hospital. Private*)

Wife: Don't go through with the test.

PM: What! When I've asked every man, woman and child to follow my lead!

(Doctor *enters*.)

Doctor: It might be best if I spoke to you separately.

PM: My wife knows everything. We'll take the test together.

Doctor: Do you love each other?

PM: Yes.

Doctor: Have you ever been unfaithful to your wife in your years of marriage?

PM: Yes. Once. Seven years ago.

Doctor: More recently?

PM: I told you – once.

Doctor: Do you suspect your wife of infidelity?

PM: No.

Wife: I have not been unfaithful.

Doctor: Then I see no reason for either of you to take the test.

PM: I believe I came into contact.

Doctor: Are you certain?

PM: No.

Doctor: Without concrete evidence, you have nothing to fear.

PM: Perhaps, but I am afraid –

Doctor: Who is this person you are afraid of?

PM: Her name is Susan Redstone.

Doctor: Does she have the disease?

Wife: He suspects Susan was the lover of a friend who recently died of the disease –

PM: – and despite our best efforts, we can't seem to find her.

Doctor: What about the police?

PM: Any investigation by my office would arouse too much suspicion – and a leak would be disastrous.

Doctor: I may be able to trace her whereabouts through Health Authority records. It could take time, but it is possible.

PM: Only if it's done with the strictest confidentiality.

Doctor: No one need know whom I'm investigating, or why.

PM: Go ahead. But be careful.

Doctor: Of course. Then we are agreed we wait.

PM: No. We still want the tests.

Doctor: It's premature.

PM: This woman has disappeared. Her lover –

Wife: – her possible lover –

PM: – has died.

Doctor: This has nothing to do with the accusations in the paper?

PM: Give me the test.

Doctor: Wait. I repeat my question. Do you love your wife?

PM: I love my wife as she loves me.

Doctor: And your children?

Wife: Your future child?

PM: You know I do.

Doctor: Taking the test could destroy your family –

PM: – I am aware of the consequences –

Doctor: – your life with them.

Wife: Are you?

PM: Please proceed.

Doctor: The test won't free you of suspicion or distress. A negative test is inconclusive. A positive test only makes the fear more tangible – every swelling, every ache a sign of disease.

PM: I am already haunted by these thoughts.

Doctor: The world points its finger and you surrender to the blame?

PM: No! Yes. My mind is a labyrinth – lead me out. I want exact answers –

Wife: Forget the accusations. Forget the past. I feel you slipping away from me. Your need for certainty –

PM: The secrets of my past lie within my grasp – answers waiting to be uncovered.

Wife: No more questions! Forget the test.

PM: I must know everything. Take my blood!

Wife: For your peace of mind – for my peace of mind.

PM: To hell with peace of mind! I want to know!

Doctor: Even if I test you, you will not know. If you test positive, the disease may never manifest. If you test negative, it may be lying dormant ...

(*Pause.*)

Wife: You already act infected. I won't take the test.

PM: The arrogance of the privileged. What's asked of the people isn't necessary for her.

Wife: This dark obsession has become the sum of your life. Your devotion to truth is a fatal as the disease. You think your past betrays you, but you betray me – again.

(*She exits. Long silence.* Prime Minister *takes blood test.*)

PM: Terror appears in many disguises – but I will unmask and face it. I will wait for the results patiently – serene and trusting – finding relief in truth.

As a child I believed I could be great – rise above common concerns and petty fears – will myself to action and triumph. I will not hesitate now, in my pursuit of truth. I will know who I have become.

SCENE TWENTY-THREE

(*Outside country motel. In background, wedding party.*)

Patrick: Does she expect me not to be jealous, not to care? I hate myself when I'm jealous, because it only tells me how much I love her. But how can I love her when I am jealous? He danced with her in the middle of dinner. The whole room stuffing their faces – me included – and before me, like a dream – no, a nightmare – they dance the first dance – him and my bride. People stare. First at them, then at me – with my mouth full of food. He just laughs it off, of course, because his father owns half of the town. Does he think I'm the village idiot? Now that he's eaten, drunk, and danced, I suppose he'll want to jump into bed with us.

Newhouse: Patrick!

Patrick: Oh Christ – what's he doing here?!

Newhouse: I have to be honest with you about Amy –

Patrick: – you slept with her – right?!

Newhouse: Not exactly, but we both know what she's thinking – she's already betrayed you in her mind.

Patrick: Her mind. I guess.

(*Pause.*)

Newhouse: We agree marriage is a sacred act, and she should be married to the one she truly loves. You may love her, but unfortunately for you, she desires me as I desire her. Ask yourself: does she love you? She doesn't love me and I don't love her, but you, Patrick, love her too much to deny her needs. The same need that made you want to marry her makes her want me.

Patrick: Have you finished?

Newhouse: I believe so.

Patrick: I wish you the best in your mutual … need – or whatever. For my part I thank you. I'd rather live alone than spend a lifetime cheated on and dissatisfied – dead. She's yours – I think –

(Patrick *leaves*.)

Chambers: A monster, that's what you've become, and what am I, by remaining silent I'm a monster's accomplice.

Newhouse: People actually believe marriage will somehow protect them. Why else would it become so popular? Do they think that marriage isn't a lifetime of indiscretion, cheating, and secrets – unions built on fear?

Chambers: The pursuit of happiness. In time, they could have been a happily married couple.

Newhouse: Happy?

Chambers: I believe that to be true.

Newhouse: I know many "good" people who are not "happy," and many "happy" people who are not "good."

Chambers: So you think.

Newhouse: Now that I've saved her from the jaws of hell, I suppose you think I should ask her to marry me.

Chambers: That would be the most honourable route –

Newhouse: – and the most deceitful. But I am honest in my affections.

(Amy *in bed alone*.)

Amy: Amy, what have you done? Patrick spent his wedding day in tears. But what does he expect me to do – I don't love him.

What am I going to do? Just take off your clothes Amy, put on your negligé, and pretend he's the one you want. If I make lots of noise he'll think I love him – maybe I should whimper.

Newhouse: Chambers, prepare the car for a journey.

Chambers: Your father ordered you to stay here – when do you want it?

Newhouse: Sunrise.

Chambers: Where are we going?

Newhouse: The Capital.

Chambers: But the police are after us by now –

Newhouse: – for what offence –

Chambers: – murder –

Newhouse: – self-defence –

Chambers: – not if Marcus has anything to say –

Newhouse: Nothing is going to happen. No scandal – or dear old Dad and the boys won't get elected.

Chambers: You have a low opinion of democracy. Every day the papers publish stories about corruption, cover-up, influence, and all sorts of sexual decadence – Do you know a good lawyer?

Newhouse: What for?

Chambers: For my trial.

Newhouse: Lawyers are for executing wills.

Chambers: All right, forget the law, if you don't believe in it, you don't, what about heaven?

Newhouse: Ouch.

Chambers: The afterlife?

(Newhouse *laughs*.)

Chambers: OK – this world, what about the Fundamentalists –

Newhouse: – the plague can have them –

Chambers: – if your father's party doesn't get elected Crane will bring in quarantine –

Newhouse: – there's absolutely no way Crane can get in!

Chambers: What do you believe in?

Newhouse: I believe that two times two is four.

Chambers: Oh, that's a fine article of faith, the multiplication table. Me, I still believe in the laws of man and nature. For example, why does the plague exist – the greatest threat to society at the end of the twentieth century –

Newhouse: I admit it makes a good campaign platform, and perhaps they can win the election –

Chambers: I'm talking about death!

Newhouse: If I have it, I have it – and I don't want to know.

Chambers: And the girl, who is undoubtedly a virgin, where is your responsibility to her?

Newhouse: She can choose not to love me.

Chambers: She would if she knew you were –

Newhouse: – a lover, a idler, a good-for-nothing –

Chambers: Oh you consider yourself so fashionable, but you're out of step. Self-sacrifice is the order of the day and you'd be surprised what you can live without.

Newhouse: You zealots – the converted who with religious fervour refuse tap water, preservatives, smoking. You broadcast your self-denial thinking that mere act of giving up confers moral virtue.

Chambers: If you no longer yield to baser animal appetites you can't help feeling better.

Newhouse: Are we morally inferior because we drink, eat red meat, enjoy additives, and avoid the gym?

Chambers: Well ... it's more than just a cholesterol-free lifestyle. People care now. They rightly congratulate themselves when they give up environmentally hostile oven cleaners, non-biodegradable detergent, coloured toilet paper, or furniture hewn from the wood of endangered rain forests –

Newhouse: – of course their next target is sex –

Chambers: – a lot of us have already given it up and amazingly we find we haven't missed it very much – it's vastly overrated, and to be quite frank, it can be very draining.

Newhouse: And when your resolve crumbles, passing inclination quickly becomes obsession.

Chambers: We only have to look at your headlong rush toward disease to know that I am leading the better life. You'll be lucky to live to forty, but you will cost our Health Authority thousands of dollars – dollars better spent on the real, blameless, innocent, honest, medically ill – rather than preserving the debauched.

Newhouse: You will live gloriously into infinite and natural old age – and one day receive a telegram from the PM.

Chambers: Preaching is all I can do since you refuse to listen to me.

Newhouse: Chambers, these inadequacies of mine – acquired and retained without denial – are in complete harmony with my nature.

Chambers: Survival is also natural, and abstinence is survival.

Newhouse: But such torture. Denial forces you to be something quite different that what you are. Oh, I would gain the respect of my father, his colleagues, and society at large, but I would become a stranger to myself – and that's quite a cost. No, I cannot be a hypocrite. Besides there are enough in the world already. Take Daddy dear, for example, he persuades the electorate that he is a man of conviction, but he really swings with the polls. Challenge his beliefs – and he alters them. And the Fundamentalists, who advocate this abstinence and all that self-mortification crap, walk around in a constant state of pain – burning with desire, obsessed with lust, their imagination duelling with pornography. Sordid secret lives are created by hypocrisy.

Chambers: You can't know how short even the longest life is, until you face death and you're avoiding it.

Newhouse: You bore me with your fears.

Chambers: If this is courage you can have it.

(Newhouse *joins* Amy *in the bedroom.*)

Amy: Patrick?

Newhouse: I'm not Patrick.

Amy: What are you doing here? – tonight of all nights –

Newhouse: Isn't this the best time?

Amy: For what?! I'll have to scream if you come any closer.

Newhouse: Have to, or want to?

Amy: If Patrick finds out –

Newhouse: Hear me out, and then I'll go – if that's your desire.

Amy: My husband is coming –

Newhouse: There is no husband.

Amy: Since when?

Newhouse: Now ... and forever.

Amy: And who arranged this?

Newhouse: Our eyes.

Amy: By what authority?

Newhouse: Our passion.

Amy: Patrick and I were legally married in church this morning.

Newhouse: Annulled. He has abandoned you already.

Amy: He has?

Newhouse: He accepts that I am dying for you –

Amy: He does? You are?

Newhouse: You know I am.

Amy: You're lying.

Newhouse: Do you believe is losing control? I want you and I won't let you throw your life away on love. Now tell me to go – or do I stay –

Amy: I don't know. I still married Patrick – it's a legal marriage.

Newhouse: Only if it's consummated.

Amy: With Patrick ... it was simple.

Newhouse: May I kiss you?

Amy: You promise me all that you said is true?

Newhouse: It's true.

Amy: Do you believe in God?

Newhouse: I believe in you.

Amy: Well ... if you're going to be my friend ... you'll have to get to know me better.

Newhouse: I'm trembling.

SCENE TWENTY-FOUR

(*Ministry of External Affairs.*)

Isabel: That's word for word the story that Ambassador Peters recited –

MEA: – we don't know who he is –

Isabel: – I'm certain that you're hiding this man's identity from me –

MEA: – you must trust us –

Isabel: I know that he had something to do with your Embassy –

MEA: You're letting your imagination run wild – your feelings of guilt, remorse about Robert are overwhelming you. The whole affair is over – let it pass.

Isabel: I want to see Robert. He can help me.

MEA: If you love Robert Baker – leave him alone.

Isabel: I must speak to Robert and this man you're concealing, or I'll go to the papers –

MEA: – that'll do more damage –

Isabel: – this is a matter of life and death –

MEA: – the slightest suggestion of sexual misbehaviour jeopardizes Robert's future.

Isabel: Robert is not at fault.

MEA: We're all protecting Robert – even the President. But the electorate is particularly sensitive. They vote for character, image, health. Do you want to take these advantages away from Robert?

Isabel: Can I talk with him?

MEA: Robert Baker refuses to see you – you'll have to accept his wishes in this matter.

Isabel: I see. And the other man?

MEA: I can't say. Security.

Isabel: But he's in danger.

MEA: National Security.

Isabel: Thank you.

MEA: Are you here for long?

Isabel: I'm not going to the papers, if that's what you mean.

MEA: No. Is there anything I can do?

Isabel: You're a real bastard.

MEA: I wish I could have been more help.

Isabel: It's enough that you were so obvious.

MEA: I am so pleased to meet you.

(Isabel *exits into the corridor.* Anna, *upset, with* Secretary, *in the corridor.*)

Anna: You're really saying he won't see me. I am Commander Gordon's wife –

Secretary: If you tell me the nature of the –

Anna: It's confidential.

Secretary: I'll make an appointment at the earliest –

Anna: It's urgent. It's about his son. It's personal. Now do you understand?

Secretary: I'm afraid you will have to wait until the Minister returns from campaigning –

Anna: – where is he? –

Secretary: – he calls regularly for messages –

Anna: Tell the Minister that unless he sees me, I'll do some thing that he'll regret. Have I made myself clear?

Secretary: The Minister doesn't respond well to blackmail, Mrs Gordon. You're hysterical, understandably, but if you don't leave now, I shall have to call the police.

Anna: His son is killing people. Tell the Minister that.

Secretary: And how would you know that, Mrs Gordon?

(Anna *exits, upset.* Isabel *walks past her, but turns back.*)

Isabel: Excuse me –

Anna: What do you want?

Isabel: The Minister is here.

Anna: Why are you telling me this –

Isabel: I came here to find a lover.

Anna: The Minister's son?

Isabel: Is that who he is?

(*pause*)

Anna: You don't know?

Isabel: – it was like a game – we weren't thinking –

Anna: – he was thinking – he's a carrier –

Isabel: – I know that –

Anna: – the game was his disguise. He knows he's a carrier, and I think he's known for a long time.

Isabel: – you're wrong – he couldn't be like that –

Anna: – everybody is protecting him – even me – I've been protecting him by keeping silent.

Isabel: How can you be so sure he knows?

Anna: He told me – he threatened me with the Health Authority – he didn't tell you his name because he didn't want to be traced – to be held responsible –

Isabel: Shut up!

(*pause*)

Isabel: I'm a carrier – have you been tested?

Anna: The man is a murderer –

Isabel: – and they?

Anna: They want us to fade away.

SCENE TWENTY-FIVE

(*Talk show.*)

Com #2:
Seven days before election
"To know is to vote!"
Shout religious rallies.
Evangelists demand candidates
Publicize test results.

PM: My opponents contend that because I decriminalized consensual sexuality, I've created a "murderer's licence." Their campaign to discredit me, and members of my party, has been ruthless – we are one step away from Kristallnacht.

Crane: I am pleased to announce my test results are negative. The people need to know what kind of leader seeks their trust.

PM: When you vote – think! Think of the children they want to quarantine. Think of the threat to your own children, your neighbour's children – segregated healthy from sick. Imagine your child branded – and then decide who is evil, and who is good. There is no simple equation for morality.

Com #1:
Rumours taint your campaign
Your reputation.
Deny them.
Release your results and remove
All doubt.

PM: Endless rumours, but without truth. I have nothing to hide.

Com #2:
A diseased woman who is
Dying
Comes forward and claims
She was your lover.

PM: Oh, another mysterious woman from my past?
Another fraud.

Com #1:
Official medical files confirm –

PM: Those medical files are confidential –

Com #1:
– or seem to confirm.
Your name
Appears in a list of her partners.
Confront her allegations.

PM: Once this circus stunt has been performed, can we discuss more vital
issues?

(*A woman's face appears.*)

Com #2:
Do you know her?

PM: Is this the woman?

Com #1:
She has been bedridden
For some time.
You may not
Recognize her –

PM: No, I don't recognize her. (*pause*) Have we ever met?
(*pause*) Did you hear me?

Susan: Yes.

PM: Have we ever met?

Susan: No. (*pause*) Not that I remember.

PM: In your files you claim that I was your lover. Now you deny it. It's unlikely you would forget a lover. (*pause*) You must tell the truth. Do you know me?

Susan: Yes, we met – long ago –

PM: Her story changes. And was I your lover?

Susan: No more questions – leave me alone –

PM: Was I your lover? They must know your answer.

Susan: Shut up! – you will destroy yourself –

PM: You can't protect me by lying. Even unanswered questions hurt me. What is your name?

Susan: – get out of here – turn off the camera –

PM: Talk! Make her talk!

Susan: Do you want everyone to know –

PM: Know what?!

Susan: – I pity you –

PM: Was I your lover? Who are you?! What's your name?!

Susan: Susan –

PM: Ask the camera to move closer. I want to be absolutely certain – Susan Redstone?! Is this the truth?

Susan: Leave me alone to die.

PM: When did you get the disease? When! –

Susan: I don't know.

PM: – from who – Lawrence – was it him? –

Susan: Please – no more questions –

PM: – I deserve to know! –

Susan: I think from Lawrence.

PM: – and were you lovers – before we were together? –

Susan: – I don't want to talk –

PM: – you must tell me! (*pause*) I am afraid, but you must say – were you lovers with Lawrence before –

Susan: Yes. He and I were lovers when you and I were lovers. On again, off again – before us, and after us ...

PM: Are you sure you got it from him?

Susan: When he tested positive, I took the test again and again – always negative. But I stopped – making love – I was too afraid. There was no one after him –

PM: So – except for him – I was the last lover you had?

Susan: Yes.

PM: Why didn't you tell me?

Susan: You were going to be Prime Minister – you seemed special – immune from such fate. *(pause)* You don't know yet if –

PM: – nothing certain –

Susan: I regret this – what can I say? I'm sorry.

Com #2:
In this time of election
Share with us
The people
Your medical tests.
Confirm or deny.

PM: I don't know my test results yet. I cannot provide the – confirmation you all desire – but – *(Exits followed by cameras.)*

Com #1:
This proud man
Pride of nation
Trips, falls
Steps into the abyss.

Com #2:
He was a good leader
We would say.
He was a great statesman
History would have told.
But now
His story rewritten
Once in pain, again in pity,
Finally in our judgement.

SCENE TWENTY-SIX

(Night. The Palace Motel. Room.)

Newhouse: What took so long?

Chambers: I had to cross town to find her – ladies like her are a little rare these days.

Newhouse: Nonsense, just more discreet. Well, where is she?

Chambers: I asked her not to come in with me and not to get too close. She'll be here in a moment.

Newhouse: So you're afraid of her for absolutely no reason.

Chambers: I'm cautious about my health.

Newhouse: You're ridiculous – provincial –

Chambers: They've cordoned off Wellington for Commander Gordon's funeral. I saw your father – he looked very drained.

Newhouse: He's worried he won't be elected after the PM's spectacular exposé.

Chambers: I'm certain he's worried about you, but if the Fundamentalists get elected he won't be the only one with problems.

Newhouse: Yes, yes. It's a wonder they haven't unearthed me yet – but I have father dear to thank for that.

Chambers: Then why are we here in Ottawa where you're known? Baker must know what you did –

Newhouse: – look – the funeral's on TV –

Chambers: – from Isabel, and the Congressman will demand extradition –

Newhouse: – no sign of Anna in the procession –

Chambers: – Marcus' father will get him out on bail –

Newhouse: – even in death she abandons him –

Chambers: – it doesn't take an analytical mind to figure out that you set him up –

Newhouse: – you don't think she's with Marcus, do you –

Chambers: – she's probably hunting you – you killed her husband. There's also Amy, the jilted bridegroom, the outraged father –

Newhouse: – Dad's on TV – he does look tired. But the Commander is doing well – peace and tranquillity – I actually envy him – if he were here he'd probably thank me.

Chambers: – probably won't look for us here –

(*Prostitute enters.*)

Prostitute: Some Palace.

Newhouse: Is it hot in here? Open the window.

Chambers: Certainly.

Prostitute: That'll be three hundred in advance.

Newhouse: Steep.

Chambers: She's the only one who would come.

Newhouse: Give her the money.

Chambers: Three hundred?

Prostitute: That's right. He looks worn out.

Chambers: He's overworked – tired.

Prostitute: Okay, these are the rules. No kissing or touching my lips, breasts, anus or vagina. (*pulling out a condom*) You wear this and pull out as you come.

Newhouse: Chambers, you've brought me a zealot, not a harlot.

Prostitute: Sorry – but safety first.

Newhouse: We'll see.

Chambers: (*handing her the money*) My employer is a free spirit. He doesn't believe in safety or caution or abstinence or basic fear. He only believes in two times two is four.

Prostitute: If he's going to watch it'll cost more.

Newhouse: Chambers – you can leave now.

Prostitute: Is he feeling okay?

Chambers: He's fine.

(Chambers *exits*.)

Prostitute: There are also some questions I have to ask.

Newhouse: I've already paid you.

Prostitute: I don't take any risks. Do what I say, or take your money back.

Newhouse: Your humble servant.

Prostitute: Any operations, blood transfusions in the last ten years?

Newhouse: Is this sex or surgery?

Prostitute: Roll up your sleeves. I have to check for needle marks. Any sores on your body, mouth?

Newhouse: No. But don't take my word for it – examine me yourself?

Prostitute: When you get undressed. (*Puts on latex gloves.*)

Newhouse: Aren't you supposed to pretend you want me?

Prostitute: Never seen these before? Get used to them – this is not exactly a relationship based on mutual trust. It's business. If you're worried about me – and I can't blame you – I could just play with myself – it's become very popular.

Newhouse: Don't you find me desirable? Touch me. I'll touch you. Skin on skin.

Prostitute: Here's your money – minus expenses. (*She begins to get dressed.*) Thing is – you guys always reveal yourselves.

Newhouse: That's your own paranoia.

Prostitute: Maybe – I've had careless friends who got it.

Newhouse: Where's the thrill?

Prostitute: Money.

(Newhouse *quickly offers her money again.*)

Newhouse: Take off the gloves – no plastics.

Prostitute: Sorry – wrong girl.

Newhouse: You're imagining things. Do I look sick?

Prostitute: You look good.

Newhouse: And I trust you. I know you don't have it

Prostitute: – I've got to go.

Newhouse: Come on – get in bed with me!

Prostitute: You're too charming – too good-looking to be desperate.

Newhouse: Take off your clothes!

Prostitute: I'm not going to die for your orgasm.

Newhouse: Here is another hundred. Five hundred.

Prostitute: No.

Newhouse: Six hundred.

Prostitute: Another statistic – fuck and die. All the Don Juans are dead.

Newhouse: Chambers! Chambers!

(Chambers *enters.*)

Chambers: What! What!

Newhouse: Get her out of here!

Chambers: Sorry. His women usually spend the whole night.

(Prostitute *exits*.)

Chambers: That was fast.

Newhouse: I didn't feel like having her.

Chambers: Are you all right?

Newhouse: I'm fine. I'm fine.

SCENE TWENTY-SEVEN

(*24 Sussex Drive. Interview with* Prime Minister's Wife)

Com:
The wife of the Prime Minister
Offers to speak with us
In this terrible hour.
Despite her condition
The upheaval in her family
She requests to make a statement.

(*Pause.*)

What are you staring at
Are you too upset to speak?

Wife: I want to beg a favour – I have no right to ask, but I must ask. He is broken – what man, what woman, wouldn't be. But if you support him, he can still serve you. I ask you not to judge him.

Com:
It is troublesome
This increasing trend.
Public figures
Judged not on politics
But on lives lived
Free of blemish.

Wife: Yes, he had an affair – surrendered to desire. But desire has many faces. Desire pushes us – as a people, as a nation – to greatness. As Prime Minister he articulated our desire – as a nation – for seven years. Think about his selfless public service. Not once did he breach his faith with you – the public.

Com:
The public
Fears that our leaders
Ignore the values
That made this country great.

Wife: What he did, he did not as Prime Minister, but as my husband. Yes — he is my husband. I bore our children. I still love him. It is for his wife, for me alone, to forgive him. As I do. I do.

(Prime Minister *enters.*)

PM: No! No more words! No more protestations! You obscure right from wrong. She does not speak for me — my feelings or my thoughts. Let there be no more words between us and them.

Wife: Why punish yourself more than you are already punished? Let me take some blame. If it is wrong, then we share in it. Banish your self-loathing — no sentence will be harsh enough — even if the world were to collapse. Forgive yourself, as I forgive you. If not — we should die now.

PM: That is our fate — we are diseased. We live, but are already dead.

Wife: All right, I will long for death — like you. Perhaps you want those who judge to stone us — or should my death come only by your hand. You say you murdered me once, then why this waiting — Strangle me, mutilate me! Rip apart this place of desire — fear — and hate. It's where crime was committed — where everything began. (*She exits.*)

PM: Have you had your fill? The feast is over.

(*Gunshot.* PM *runs off.*)

SCENE TWENTY-EIGHT

(*Palace Motel.* Newhouse *in feverish sleep.*)

Newhouse: What's that knocking?

(*Pause.*)

Chambers: I don't hear any knocking —

Newhouse: Stop the knocking — answer the door!

Chambers: Kill me if you like, but nobody is knocking.

Newhouse: I heard knocking. Open the fucking door!

(Chambers *opens door.* Commander Gordon *enters laughing — seen/heard only by* Newhouse *as an hallucination — in dark glasses, smoking and drinking.*)

Chambers: I told you, no one is there. What are you staring at?

Newhouse: Who are you?

Commander: It's me – am I welcome?

Newhouse: Of course. Chambers – It's him.

Chambers: That's enough, now get back into bed.

Newhouse: Hurry. He's our guest – get some food –

Chambers: You're seeing things – (*waving hands*) – thin air.

Newhouse: He's dead.

Chambers: The dead don't eat, so I'll just get dinner for two.

Newhouse: No, idiot – if I were dead I'd be famished. Food!

Chambers: Wait there, I'll be right back, and stay in bed!

Newhouse: I'm quite safe, Chambers. He's not alive – he's dead.

Chambers: Who is it anyway?

Newhouse: Commander Gordon of course.

Chambers: Right. Okay, wait here and don't move!

(Chambers *pretends to leave, but observes* Newhouse.)

Newhouse: What do you want from me, Commander? Hurry up – speak!

Commander: Some palace. (*pause*) I've simply come to thank you. Nothing affects me now – good or bad. The dead are alone. We are content – no despair. We smile on the concerns of the living. I'm tranquil – at peace. (*pause.*) Give me your hand – if you're not afraid of me.

Newhouse: Afraid? It will be my pleasure. I'd shake your hand – even if you were the devil himself!

(Commander *and* Newhouse *extend hands.* Chambers *rushes between them.*)

Chambers: Wake up – don't touch him, don't touch him – wake up!

Newhouse: He's leaving –

Commander: Don't worry. I'll come see you tomorrow.

Newhouse: – you missed him, Chambers.

Chambers: You saw the dead in your dreams.

Newhouse: Yes. I must have a fever – I'm hallucinating –

Chambers: You see – the fever removes your perversity and makes you susceptible to the basic good in each of us – even you. The hallucination is the last gasp of your repressed instinct for good, your remorse for all the horrible things you've done, your desire to repent. Your psyche is opening up to the universal desire for a better world – a world of responsibility, and the improvement of the soul. You saw the dead before you died and it has changed you. I have been waiting for this day, there is hope for you. tomorrow we celebrate!

Newhouse: You're right – I do have a conscience, and a little guilt. (*pause*) I'm humiliated. How that ever happened I don't know, but tomorrow I will rectify it.

Chambers: You won't be able to. Your natural goodness is oozing out despite you. Go to sleep. You'll wake up a better man.

SCENE TWENTY-NINE

(*Ministry of External Affairs.*)

MEA: (*on the phone*) Anna, I couldn't call – we were scrambling to pick a new leader. (*pause*) Anna, why would he hurt you if he loved you?

(Baker *enters.*)

MEA: How would I know he's infected? Don't – don't – don't take this to the police. Anna, your testimony would never hold up in court – (*pause*) It doesn't matter if it's true or not, Anna, once it's in the papers. Anna –

(Baker *disconnects phone.*)

MEA: Jesus – now what the fuck do you want –

Baker: We have to talk. Isabel's test confirm your son infected her –

MEA: – they only confirm she's a carrier –

Baker: – he should be charged with murder –

MEA: – premeditation is pure conjecture –

Baker: – then manslaughter, I don't care.

MEA: I don't know where he is – he's disappeared.

Baker: You're just protecting him – I want his ass.

MEA: Well, you're forgetting to protect you own. I don't want to feed the vultures – and you don't either. You're not the only one who can smell the rotting flesh, but they aren't fussy eaters and you're quite a juicy morsel, Robert Baker.

Baker: Don't threaten me –

MEA: – if word got out Isabel –

Baker: – keep Isabel out of this –

MEA: – Isabel will be deported. Back home she'd be tagged, and quarantined – I'm trying to keep all of us out of this.

(*Pause.*)

MEA: Okay, we'll do it your way – for the moment –

MEA: – when I find him he'll get what he deserves –

(Baker *leaves*. Chambers *enters*.)

Chambers: What do you think, Minister?

MEA: He won't wait long. I should have told my son the moment I knew – years ago.

Chambers: You did warn him.

MEA: And it didn't stop him, did it? I told you I wanted reports every day – you're certain he's dying?

Chambers: He's very sick, Minister, and getting worse.

MEA: Make sure he doesn't see a doctor. Give him these pain killers, and play him out. It shouldn't be long –

Chambers: Minister, are you sure this –

MEA: He'll die anyway – why prolong it – and I can't afford to have him alive. Get rid of anything the scavengers could piece together. Make sure he dies nameless.

Chambers: I have all his identification.

MEA: Destroy it.

(*Pause.*)

Chambers: Justice would be served if he just died.

MEA: Death is certainly quieter.

(Baker *meets* Angus *and* Amy *in the hallway*.)

Angus: Excuse me, I'm looking for Mr Newhouse – father or son, don't make no difference – although my daughter would prefer to see the son.

Baker: Robert Baker. Does she have a complaint?

Angus: Angus McIntyre. And my daughter Amy. I'd like to speak with the Minister.

Baker: He's occupied.

Angus: I don't give a damn. I still want to see him.

Baker: I'm a close personal friend of the Minister. Now what's the problem?

Amy: It's none of his business!

Angus: But it's damn well my business – she's no longer innocent –

Amy: – Dad! –

Angus: – and someone had better find that son of a Minister and get him to marry my daughter –

Baker: I believe I can help you.

Angus: I want to see the Minister.

Baker: Of course I'll inform the Minister immediately, but come to my office first. I'll need to now all the details –

Angus: Well – I'd prefer to fix this without too much trouble between families.

Baker: Weddings should be celebrations.

Angus: This wedding might bring in a few votes.

Baker: Just leave everything to me.

(*All exit together.*)

SCENE THIRTY

(*Later. Government Square. Candlelight vigil.*)

Doctor: Tonight the scalpel touches bones.

Com:
There is more?

Doctor: More and more. The child did not survive. She did not survive. He –

Com:
The First Lady
The Child
Are dead.

Doctor: You were not there. You did not see. I saw her faceless, I felt his body fall, his mind reel – as he tasted her blood with kisses. I heard his quiet agony swell to numbing howl.

Blinded by tears, I left him with his grief. He must have been staring at himself – he smashed the mirror with his face – and with broken shards of glass he began to stab – into his genitals – mutilating himself. He yelled out beyond the room, to you hyenas – "see me, know me, judge me – I am no more."

Life torn before its time – shoved toward a certain fate by pursuit of a terrible knowledge.

Com:
The Prime Minister ... ?

Doctor: Hospitalized, sedated. He wanted to stand before you and hurl accusations at himself, shout his story in your ears. His final words of consciousness, if you call it that, were that he resigns his leadership and seeks exile from society. And then quiet. There is nothing left to do. He must heal – alone. No one need make him suffer more.

Com:
Suicide, then mutilation.
Shock heaped on horror.
What men will do.
How much pain ... ?
Where are the limits to madness,
The borders of misery?

SCENE THIRTY-ONE

(*Airport.*)

Baker: (*holding a newspaper*) The manhunt for Newhouse has started. Look at the headlines –

Isabel: – I don't feel right about this –

Baker: – he destroyed your life –

Isabel: – but that girl Amy McIntyre – her picture's all over the papers –

Baker: Isabel, start acquiring a conscience, and you'll be quarantined too –

Isabel: – we're just using her –

Baker: – it's important Newhouse gets what he deserves –

Isabel: – important to you, Robert – I can't live like you –

Baker: Isabel, you're just depressed. Look, there are drugs that check the disease – and we can hope for a cure. Don't give in to this emotional turmoil –

Isabel: I'd like to see how you'd handle it, Robert –

Baker: I didn't betray you –

Isabel: Right.

(*Pause.*)

Isabel: But then he knew something you'll never know, Robert.

Baker: When you get back – don't call. Just disappear for a little while. You don't know my name – who I am – nothing. Understood?

Isabel: No association with known carriers, I understand. (*pause*) I always wanted you, Robert. I used to dream about you – your weight against me.

Baker: Newhouse may defy the Authority, but you have to be prepared to defend yourself if he identifies you.

Isabel: Did you dream about me? We have a little time – now.

Baker: He's unpredictable, but your secret is safe with me.

Isabel: I trust you.

Baker: You don't have much choice.

Isabel: If we cross that line – once – then we can stop dreaming. Think of us together – over and over –

Baker: Isabel, stop, please. (*pause*) I have a future.

SCENE THIRTY-TWO

(*Ministry of External Affairs. MEA fields paparazzi questions about his son – cries.*)

MEA: My son is presently suffering a debilitating, but not contagious, disease. When fully recovered, he will appear to answer, and refute, charges currently levelled against him.

SCENE THIRTY-THREE

(Newhouse *stumbles down street, and enters a cathedral.* Anna *prays at the Commander's tomb.*)

Anna: Who's there – is someone there?

Newhouse: (*flicks on lighter*) Are you surprised to see me, Anna? I came to pay my respects – I'll leave you –

Anna: No. I'm glad to see you. I'm not angry. I've changed – I've purged myself of all criminal desire. What remains is selfless – spiritual, holy.

Newhouse: That's quite a change.

Anna: God has touched me, opened my eyes – changed me. We were excessive – made fatal mistakes. I hope I live long enough to earn, through austere penance, His pardon. Turn back from passion – your ravenous desire.

Newhouse: That's rather a tall order.

Anna: Don't you feel regret – guilt?

Newhouse: No. No regrets, Anna, I'm quite content. My memories are all pleasant.

Anna: You're in denial. Accept that you are terminal – change your ways and prepare for the afterlife.

Newhouse: I'll give it some thought – in another twenty or thirty years –

Anna: Two years – three months – one week. If you continue with your crimes against life, you will exhaust His mercy.

Newhouse: Anna, you're a hypocrite. But hypocrisy is fashionable, and like all fashion, it passes for good. It must be rewarding to play the pious woman –

Anna: I won't be insulted. You're exhausted and sick. Look into yourself for whatever feeling might change you –

Newhouse: – like fear.

Anna: I loved you –

Newhouse: Stay with me.

Anna: I can't – I'm dying.

Newhouse: So am I – don't leave. We're free. Come to me.

Anna: Don't – what you're thinking is – completely beyond me.

Newhouse: Anna –

(Newhouse *falls.*)

Newhouse: I'm so hot. I feel like I'm burning up.

Anna: Lie down. Stay here. I'll call an ambulance.

(Anna *lays* Newhouse *on the tomb, and exits.* Newhouse *sees the* Commander *smoking/drinking.*)

Newhouse: Hello, Commander.

SCENE THIRTY-FOUR

(*Hospital entrance.* Doctor *with* PM.)

Com:
Why this self-inflicted
Horror?
How could you maim
Yourself?

PM: I deserve this – and more – the people know. I wish my wife never knew me. My unborn child was saved from me. The family I love, I destroyed. What remains – my poor offspring – must suffer.

Com:
Others suffer
And yet manage to
Live full lives.

PM: Reason leads to chaos. Let the plague come!

Com:
Grief and depression
Drive you
But can these passions –

PM: Endless questions. The only certainty – I killed my wife and my child –

Com:
We ask to better understand.
But I understand
Nothing.

PM: Then understand. I met a woman – felt innocent affection, joyous desire. And yet however casual or unimportant – these stolen kisses were fatal. I cannot even remember that night of love – my mind refuses – no recall of body scents, no memory of pleasure. When did insignificance become terror – the making of love an instrument of torture – I can say no more. Time to rot.

Com:
You are not alone.
People still care –
Compassionate and tolerant.
We turn to you
To lead the
Opposition.

PM: Seek nothing from me –

Com:
Only days in power
The Conservative majority
Proposes harsh measures –

Identity cards, tattoos, quarantine –
That affects your freedom –
Our freedom.
Regain your senses.
Fight to protect
Our rights –

PM: Tell the people this. I was infected and poisoned my own bed. Annihilate the freedoms that fester into disease. No more hiding, no more secrets. Drag the carriers into the open – cage them. Do what must be done – isolate the diseased! Test every citizen!

Crane: Sir, I would like a word with you. Respect what little dignity you have left, and end this public show. Members of the press, please. Is this necessary? Protect him from the public glare – shelter him. He is all but naked.

PM: Yes. Put me away – in some dark quarantine – exile – spare me your charity.

Crane: Quarantine is only required for those who knowingly spread the disease.

PM: But I am a murderer – twice! Follow the map of my disease. I am the rat, the fly.

Crane: The proposed laws of segregation are being debated. You yourself once raised crucial questions about so radical a change.

PM: Every day you delay, more die.

Crane: Your life demonstrates that no one is immune. We trust that each individual will now exercise greater caution until we have a cure.

PM: Don't use me as an example. You can't trust the people. Reject tolerance! You're Prime Minister – act with responsibility. Do your duty – lead!

Crane: I sympathize –

(Crane *joins* Evangelist *on Parliament steps.*)

PM: Don't! (*pause*) I should see my children. They will suffer too – punished by their father's crime – who will trust them – what lovers touch them –

Crane: You cannot see your children.

PM: But they must know the truth from me! I will not temper my self-abuse with apology – or seek their compassion.

Crane: Once the grief settles – the mind stabilizes – yes.

PM: They are my children!

Crane: They are now wards of the state, and will be protected until you have exorcised this pain.

PM: You rob me of my children –

Crane: – you have no rights –

PM: – my fatherhood –

Crane: – you no longer –

PM: I demand my natural rights!

Crane: The law stands above all men to protect us from nature's cruelty. Nature is the enemy today. Go home, alone, and make peace with yourself.

(*Press scrum around* Doctor *and* PM *slowly moves to* Evangelist, Crane, *and* MEA.)

Doctor:
His tragic life
Not yet ended.
The great leader
Admired, envied.
Man of great fortune pulled down
Not by disease
But by the storm of hysteria
He sought to quell.

Evangelist and **Doctor:**
There is wisdom in his story.
Shield yourself.
Watch and hesitate.
Pursue freedom
And happiness only
With extreme caution
Then boast a full life
Lived to a natural end.
Desire is dead
Passion turns to stone.
Life lived
Moment to moment
Gone forever.

SCENE THIRTY-FIVE

(Newhouse *talks to himself as he watches the preceding scene on TV.* Commander Gordon, *as an angel, watches.* Crane *introduces* MEA *to* Evangelist. Chambers *gets* MEA's *attention and they confer privately.*)

Newhouse: It's interesting that every human vice is attacked except this fashionable hypocrisy that stifles criticism and revels in the immunity of God. They cross themselves, in their religious disguise, and absolve all their earthly "crimes."

Hypocrisy would make my list of social crimes complete. If I did join them, I could hide my desires. Then I'd no longer need to defend myself from persecutors, but instead I could denounce them – publicly – defame their character, and condemn them to this famous hell of theirs. It is not in my nature to be dishonest, but the time has clearly come to give it more careful consideration.

THE END

Polygraph

Marie Brassard and Robert Lepage
Translation by Gyllian Raby

After completing studies at the Conservatoire d'Art Dramatique in Quebec, Marie Brassard began working with Robert Lepage as an author and actor in the creative process that resulted in *The Dragon's Trilogy*, and later co-wrote and performed in *Polygraph*. In 1990 she won the Jean Doat award in Montreal for her performance in both plays. She has also won the Barcelona Critics' Award as Best Foreign Actress for *Polygraph*. In addition to her collaborations with Robert Lepage, she works as an author and actress for other theatre companies, writes scripts for short films, and conceives and directs music videos.

Internationally renowned as a director who composes his own imagistic performance texts, Robert Lepage is the creator of numerous productions in both English and French, many of which have been showcased at international festivals. He studied at the Conservatoire d'Art Dramatique in Quebec and at the Institut Alain Knapp in Paris. Since 1981 he has been a principal member of Théâtre Repère in Quebec City, for whom he created the acclaimed *The Dragon's Trilogy*, which won the Grand Prize of the Festival of the Americas in 1987. Other celebrated works include the solo performance *Vinci, Tectonic Plates, Polygraph*, and the bilingual Shakespeare on the Saskatchewan *Romeo and Juliet*, which he  co-directed. He is the recipient of many awards, and was inducted as a Chevalier de l'Ordre des Arts et Lettres by the government of France in 1991. He is currently Artistic Director of French- language theatre for the National Arts Centre in Ottawa.

Gyllian Raby is Artistic Director of Northern Light Theatre in Edmonton. She is a writer and director well known in western Canada for her theatrically innovative productions, especially her theatre/ballet interpretation of Ray Bradbury's *Something Wicked This Way Comes*. She became involved with Thé- âtre Repère during the creation of *Polygraph* and was privileged to collaborate on the first version in Quebec City in 1988. Shortly afterwards, an offer to tour *Polygraph* in Europe caused her to write a complete translation. Since that time, the play has metamorphosed substantially.

Polygraph was first produced in French as *Le Polygraphe* at the Implan-théâtre in Quebec City, on 6 May 1988, by Théâtre Repère. A second version, a co-production with Montreal's Théâtre Quat'Sous, played at the Théâtre Quat'Sous in November 1988. The English translation premièred at the Quayworks festival at Harbourfront, Toronto, on 21 February 1990.

PRODUCTION

Director and Set Designer / **Robert Lepage**
Translator / **Gyllian Raby**
Assistant to the Director / **Steve Lucas**
Soundtrack / **Pierre Brousseau, Yves Chamberland**
Music / **Pierre Brousseau**
Lighting / **Robert Lepage, Eric Fauque**
Slides / **David Lepage**
Assistant Set Designer / **Jean Hazel**
Stage Managers / **Eric Fauque, Steve Lucas**
Production Managers / **Michel Bernatchez, Richard Gagnon**

CAST (TORONTO)

Marie Brassard / Lucie Champagne
Robert Lepage / David Haussman
Pierre Phillippe Guay / François

TRANSLATOR'S NOTE

I first translated *Polygraph* as it was being created, with the odd result that an English text existed before the authors considered their French production to be complete. Through the major revisions since then, the ideas under exploration have mostly remained the same (along with the majority of the words), though characters, time-frame, and situations have altered – and in our separate reality the Berlin Wall has fallen. The living performance has been allowed to metamorphose to reflect the authors' deepening perception of and relationship with their material; if it is temporarily captured here, it is to record how far we have come this past year, and to point where we are going.

Gyllian Raby

A NOTE ON PUNCTUATION

For this text, the punctuation is based on the actor's voice training for reading aloud:

During scenes when speeches intersect, as in the first scene, " – " indicates the speech is suspended in mid-breath and "..." indicates that the breath is trailing away.

A period or colon is often employed to demonstrate what the voice is doing with the shape of the thought.

Sometimes there is neither punctuation nor capital at the start of a line, because it is an uninterrupted continuation of a sentence begun on the preceding line.

Line breaks are often used as a punctuation device.

PROLOGUE

THE FILTER

*A brick wall runs right across the playing area behind a shallow platform
forestage. In a film-style introduction music plays and slides flash the play
title and actors' credits, the projections completely covering the wall. Stage
left,* Lucie Champagne *reads an inquest report describing the results of an
autopsy. Stage right, above and behind the wall,* David Haussman *talks about
the construction of the Berlin Wall.*

Lucie: The autopsy has revealed that the stab-wounds were caused by a
sharp pointed instrument which penetrated the skin and underlying tissues
–

David: After the fall of the Third Reich, little remained of its capital, Berlin, except a pile of ruins and a demoralized people.

Lucie: The body-wounds are extremely large considering the small size of
the inflicting instrument: we would surmise that the shape, depth and
width of the wounds were enlarged during the struggle –

David: The triumphant Allies enforced a new statute –

Lucie: – by the slicing action of the knife –

David: – which split up the city into international sectors: American,
French and British ...

Lucie: – as the victim attempted to defend herself.

David: ... to define their sector, the Soviets built a wall over forty kilo-
metres in length, cutting the city in two ...

Lucie: ... The victim received cuts to the left hand, the right upper arm,
and was pierced through the rib-cage and the right lung, to the stomach.
We have determined that the fatal wound was given here –

David and Lucy: Right through the heart –   -

David: – of the city.

Lucie: – between the fifth and sixth ribs.

David: The "wall of shame," as the West Germans call it, was built to
stop the human

David and Lucy: Hemorrhage –

David: – of Berliners leaving the East for the West

Lucie: – was caused by the laceration of the septum.

David: – symbolic of the division of the communist and capitalist worlds.

Lucie: The septum functions like a wall bisecting the heart, it controls the filtration of blood –

David: for almost three decades it was possible for visitors from the West to enter the Eastern Bloc –

Lucie: – from the right ventricle to the left –

David and Lucy: – but here passage is (was) one-way only. A sophisticated system of alternating doors would open and close to allow the flow of –

David: visitors from the West –

Lucie: – de-oxygenated blood –

David and Lucy: – and to impede –

David: – inhabitants of the East –

Lucie: – oxygenated blood –

David and Lucy: from circulating the "wrong" way.

(As if a continuous loop, the text of the Prologue is repeated twice, gradually increasing in tempo and volume with the drive of the music. The second time through, the naked body of François appears stage left above and behind the wall, lit only by projections of anatomical slides: bones, muscles and organs superimposed on his flesh. The scene ends with a blackout. Continuing the film script-style presentation of each scene, a projection indicates:)

Projection
PARTHENAIS, MONTRÉAL: INTERIOR, NIGHT
(Parthenais is the colloquial name for Le centre de prévention de Montréal, a remand centre located on rue Parthenais. For the purposes of this play it is to be understood as a medico-legal forensic institute.)

(Music. Lights rise first on a skeleton which is collapsed on the ground, centre stage. David *approaches it: at a signal from his hands, it rises to its feet.* David *speaks objectively to both skeleton and audience, his English is very good, and is marked by a German accent.)*

David: The body never lies. To the pathologist, and others in a police inquiry, this is obvious to us. Even in flesh which has been horribly mutilated, the architecture of the crime is there, intact.
And the shape, the disposition of the wounds tell us a true story ... which has nothing, whatsoever, to do with your cinematic realism, or fiction.
I myself, am not a forensic physician but a criminologist.
(Holds the skeleton's head, examining it in the cliché pose of Hamlet with Yorick.) And I believe it is possible also to see the truth which lurks in the mind of a criminal: to look through the skin, the skull, into his brain ...
What you are about to witness is the story of a murder. But you will not

see any murderer, neither will you see any dead bodies. Because, sometimes, it is more appropriate to let the dead rest in peace, and to practise
the autopsy on the living.

(*The skeleton flies out. Lights cross fade.*)

Projection
HAMLET, ACT 3 SCENE 1. EXTERIOR, NIGHT

(Lucie *stands in profile above and behind the wall stage left, on a moving pedestal. She is clothed in black, and holds a skull.*)

Lucie: Être ou ne pas être.
C'est la question
Est-il plus noble pour une âme de souffrir les flèches et les coups d'un sort
atroce, ou de s'armer contre le flot qui monte et de lui faire face, et de
l'arrêter?
Mourir, dormir, rien de plus.
Terminer, par du sommeil, la souffrance du coeur et les mille blessures qui
sont le lot de la chair
C'est bien le dénouement que l'on voudrait, et de quelle ardeur ...
Mourir, dormir,
dormir ... peut-être rêver
C'est l'obstacle,
Car l'anxiété des rêves qui viendront dans ce sommeil des morts,
Quand nous aurons chassé de nous le tumulte de vivre
Est là pour nous retenir
Et c'est la pensée qui fait que le malheur a si longue vie.

(*A 3 ft by 6 ft transparent mirror drops to hang above the wall stage right,
indicating* Lucie's *dressing-room. She goes to sit in front of the mirror and
starts to remove her make-up. Lights fade.*)

Projection
FRANÇOIS: INTERIOR, NIGHT

(*The sound score indicates the hubbub of a busy restaurant.* François *enters
stage left with a "table for two" over his shoulder. This he swings down in an
easy movement. Quickly setting it with plates and cutlery, he then positions
two chairs either side. When the table is "set", he immediately unmakes it,
swings it over his shoulder, and repeats the whole sequence in a different spa-
tial placement, all the while talking rapidly to invisible customers. During the
course of the scene he covers the entire stage, so suggesting a room full of tables. He is mechanically focused on the job even during the quick-fire dialogue
exchanges with* Lucie. *An entire day's work in the restaurant is accomplished
in this short double-time scene.* David *appears twice during the scene. Sliding
in ominous slow motion over the wall to sit at the table like a watching
Thought Police agent, he is obviously a product of* François' *imagination.*)

François: Vous avez bien mangé? Je vous apporte la facture m'sieur. Par ici, s'il vous plaît. Vous avez regardé le menu du jour sur le tableau? Oui. C'est pour combien de personnes? Par ici s'il vous plaît. Prendriez-vous un digestif? Deux cafés-cognac ... tout de suite ... ça sera pas long m'sieur ... Oui, bonjour. Non, malheureusement, on a plus de rôti à l'échalotte. À la place, le chef vous suggère son poulet rôti, un poulet au citron, c'est délicieux. Alors, deux fois. Allez-vous prendre un dessert? Aujourd'hui, c'est la tarte à l'orange maison. C'est excellent, je vous le recommande ... Oui. Une personne. Par ici s'il vous plaît. For two? I'm very sorry, we don't 'ave an English menu ... I can translate for you ... Deux places? Par ici s'il vous plaît. Pardon? Vous auriez dû me le dire, je vous l'aurait changé sans problèmes. Oui, la prochaine fois, d'accord. Par ici s'il vous plaît.

(Lucie *enters and sits at* François' *table, talking in double time.*)

Lucie: Salut, François, ça va bien?

François: Oui, oui, ça va.

Lucie: Aie, François, le propriétaire est venu cogner a l'appartement chez nous hier ... Y'a essayé de rentrer chez-vous avec ses clés, pis y s'est rendu compte que t'avais changé la serrure.

François: J'ai complètement oublié de l'appeler.

Lucie: Tu devrais faire attenion à tes relations avec lui, parce-que ça commence tranquillement à déteindre sur les autres locataires. Ça fait un mois que j'aurais besoin de peinture pour la cuisine ... j'y ai laissé trois fois des messages su' son répondeur, pis y me retourne pas mes appels ...

François: Excuses moi Lucie ... Je l'appelle sans faut demain matin.

Lucie: En tous cas, je te remercie beaucoup. C'était très bon. (*She goes out.* François *continues talking to customers and repositioning the table;* Lucie *quickly returns, and sits at "another" table.*)

Lucie: Salut François, ça va bien?

François: Salut Lucie.

Lucie: Aie, ça l'air que toé pis ton chum, vous êtes venus voir mon show hier ... Vous êtes pas venus me voir après, c'est tu parce que vous avez pas aimé ça?

François: Ah non! C'était magnifique ... On a beaucoup aimé l'idée de faire jouer Hamlet par une femme. De nos jours c'est beaucoup plus percutant que ce soit une femme qui tienne ces propos-là, plutôt qu'un homme.

Lucie: Ben en fait à l'origine c'tait pas prévu. Parce que moi je faisais la régie du show mais le gars qui jouait Hamlet y'é tombé malade, pis vu qu'y avait juste moi qui savait le texte par coeur, y m'ont coupé les cheveux pis asteur, c'est moi qui le fait ... Aie, François, j'ai entendu dire ... ca d'l'air qu'a CKRL, y cherchent un annonceur pour lire le bulletin de nouvelle le soir ... t'as une belle voix, y m'semble que tu serais bon la d'dans.

François: C'est gentil d'avoir pensé à moi, mais ces temps-ci c'est pas possible, j'ai trop d'ouvrage au restaurant.

Lucie: Aie, j'ai croisé Alain dans l'escalier tantôt, y m'a même pas dit bonjour ... c'tu parce qu'y'é choqué contre moi?

François: Fais-toi en avec ça ... C'est à moi qu'y en veut.

Lucie: En tous cas, j'te'remercie beaucoup, c'était très bon.
(*She goes out.* François *continues.*)

François: A bientôt, Lucie.
(Lucie *returns almost at once, and sits at a "different" table.*)

Lucie: Aie François, sais-tu c'qui m'est arrivé hier? Y'a une de mes amies de Montréal qui m'téléphone a dit tu devrais acheter *Le Devoir,* y'a une petite annonce dedans, chu sûre que ça va t'intéresser. Comme de fait ... Y'a un réalisateur de Montréal qui vient tourner un film ici a Québec, un genre de "thriller" y'aurait besoin d'une fille à peu près dans mon âge pour jouer le personnage principal ... y cherche quelqu'un pis la semaine prochaine, y vient faire passer des auditions. J'ai jamais fait de cinéma, mais y m'semble que je serais bonne là dedans ... Trouves-tu que ça serait une bonne idée que j'aille?

François: Ben, certain ... Faut pas que tu manques ça, vas-y!

Lucie: En tout cas j'te remercie, c'tait très bon!

François: A bientôt Lucie.

(François *exits with the table settings, returns, and sits at the table. The lights and music communicate that it is now the end of the day, and he is exhausted. He counts some paltry tips, then taps out three lines of cocaine, and snorts it, as the lights fade to black.*)

Projection
THE AUDITION / SAUVÉ MÉTRO STATION: INTERIOR, DAY

(*A spotlight comes up, stage right.* Lucie *enters anxiously, left, and walks diffidently into it to begin her audition. She talks to an unseen Interviewer positioned in the audience. Her English is good, but sometimes hesitant.*)

Lucie: Hi ... My name is Lucie Champagne ... My hair is shorter than in my photograph because I'm doing a show at the moment where I play a guy, and so, they cut my hair ... First, I should tell you ... I've never worked on a movie but I've done lots of videos ... I worked mainly in comedies, but I like doing drama just as much ... I did lots of videos for the government social services ... Let's see ... What would be an example ...

Oh yes! They gave me the role of this woman whose money was stolen by her brother-in-law ... Well, to us here that might seem a pretty tame crisis but for this woman it is something very dramatic and completely devastating, because ... it's her money – and well, – it's her brother-in-law ... and so I had to play this part with as much emotion as I possibly could. Oh yes! While I was still at the theatre school I worked on a truly beautiful play by Tennessee Williams called: *Talk to me like the Rain and Let me Listen*. The title is very long, but the play is actually very short. It is the story of a couple, and I played the woman, and my character, she was ... anorexic. But not by choice – I mean, she was anorexic because she hadn't eaten for four days, because she didn't have any money, because her boyfriend took off with the welfare check. I just loved playing that role.

(*She gets nervous*)

My first experience? ... Well ...
I was sixteen ... and it was with a young guy named Alain ... and at that time I was very afraid about all –
OH! ... you mean in theatre!
Okay, I'll tell you – you're going to laugh!
It was for the priest's birthday when I was in grade one; we organized a little school celebration. So, everyone in my class was in it, the other kids lined up along the wall, and they sang the first line of the song "Where are you going little Bo Peep, where are you going Bo Peep?"
And there I was out in front wearing a little white dress, and I sang back: "I am following this beauteous star and all my sheep are saying Baa"!
Oh boy! Was it heavenly! I was a kid who like to tell lies, you know – I was not a liar, but I used to be fascinated that I could say things which weren't true, but do it so convincingly that people would believe me – so I would spend my time making up all these stories ...

(*She is brought back to the present.*)

For my audition, I brought a soliloquy from
Shakespeare's Hamlet ... No, no, not the role of Ophelia: Hamlet. That is the part I'm playing in the show, as a guy.
Oh ... you would prefer an improv, euh ... Should I improvise here? What would you like me to improvise?
– To imagine myself in a tragic situation ...?
Is that so you can see if I can cry? Because, I mean, I can't cry just like that ... that is ... put me in a film where there is a sad scene where I have to cry, and I would concentrate to the point where tears would well up, yes – but I can't cry just like that.

– To imagine myself in an absolute state of panic ...?

(*She tries to joke.*)

You don't think I'm panicking enough here?

(*She gathers her concentration.*)

Okay. I'll do it.

(*Projection of a Métro logo on the wall, with the sign for Sauvé Métro station. Lucie focuses on the front edge of the stage, an expression of absolute horror on her face; she backs up to lean against the wall with an inarticulate scream. David enters, and takes in the situation downstage without expression. Solemnly, he kneels at the edge of the platform beside the "tracks," takes out a notebook and writes. Lucie continues to shout and cry about the suicide she has witnessed, in a semi-hysterical state of shock. David assesses her, finishes writing his notes, while periodically checking back to her, then goes to her. As she is sobbing for breath he pulls her from the wall to lean against him, and smooths her shoulders, rhythmically. She gradually regains control of her breathing. David checks her pulse, gives her a pill from a bottle he has in his pocket.*)

David: Take this, it's a mild tranquillizer.

Lucie: The boy – he was killed on impact?

David: (*lying*): Yes. Can I give you a lift somewhere?

Lucie: Yes.

David: Where do you live?

Lucie: In Quebec City.
I was on my way to get the bus.

David: I'll walk you to the terminal then.

(*David puts his arm round her shoulders and they move off together stage left. Lucie breaks away to stare once more at the tracks, then makes the transition back out of the memory, resuming her starting position against the wall in the audition spotlight. The Métro sign projection and other lights fall away as David exits.*)

Lucie: Was that enough?

Blackout.

Projection
THE FLESH: INTERIOR, NIGHT

(*The soundscape indicates a crowded gay bar with loud, heavy rock music, and disco lighting from hell. François enters, drinking a beer, watching bodies on the dance floor. Soon he realizes one of the crowd is assessing him; when he's propositioned to have sex in a private room, he agrees. Expressionless, he follows the man stage right where, once the door is closed, he is seized, his leather jacket pulled off, his arm twisted, and his body forced up against a wall. Slowly, and very sensuously – dropping to a kneeling position with one eye on his partner – François removes his shirt ... his belt ... which he gives away. He turns his back, and unzips his pants. As he is beaten, with each sound of the whiplash, François physically recoils against the wall. La petite morte and collapse, finally, the exchange is finished. Satisfied, soul weary, François gathers his clothes and his shreds of self-esteem. Without speaking to his partner he goes back to the bar. Lights fade as he drinks another beer.)*

Projection
THE TEARS: INTERIOR, NIGHT

(The transparent mirror which locates Lucie's dressing-room drops to hang above the wall stage right. Lucie sits behind it removing her make-up. There is a knock at the door.)

Lucie: Entrez!

David: Good evening.

(They look at one another, and search for their English language.)

Lucie: David, my God it's you! I wasn't expecting to see you here tonight! You came all the way from Montreal just to see the show?

David: Well, in fact, I had some business this week in Quebec City and I promised I would see you act one day, so here I am.

Lucie: We weren't exactly sold out tonight ...

David: Well, that just makes it more intimate theatre.

Lucie: So, what did you think? Did you like it?

David: Hm ... I thought it was quite interesting.
(Presents her with a bunch of flowers.)
Oh, – here.

Lucie: *(trying to cover her alarm)*:
Oh my God! Carnations!!

Ill at ease, David *picks up the skull on the dressing room table.)*

David: Is this Yorick?

Lucie: You know him well?

David: Of course. He's the only character in *Hamlet* who is not killed at the end of the play!

Lucie: That's nice, how you use his name. Everyone here just calls him "the skull."

David: I thought it quite clever to have a woman play the part of Hamlet. I found it brought ... a whole new dimension to the character.

Lucie: Well ... in fact – (*she lies*) We did it because we felt it has so much more impact, to see a woman grapple with those ideas in this day and age.

David: It must be very difficult for an actor to voice "To be or not to be, that is the question," – and to examine those things so fundamental to life: love, honour. Death ...

Lucie: Death ...
It's on my mind a lot. More than ever, after seeing that guy throw himself under the train in Montreal ...
Anyway ... I want to thank you for driving me all the way back to Quebec City, you really didn't have to do that!

David: Let's just say I was not acting purely out of duty; it also gave me the opportunity to get to know you a little better, and to make a new friend. Well ... (*He checks the time.*) Once again, well played, and –

Lucie: You're not going to leave – can't I tempt you out for a drink?

David: I'm afraid my bus leaves for Montreal at eleven.

Lucie: You know, buses leave for Montreal up till one o'clock.

David: Yes, but what if it should snow? If there was a snowstorm I'd be stuck in Quebec City!

Lucie: Oh, it won't snow tonight. These clouds will go away!

David: Well ... all right then.

Lucie: Do you mind waiting one second while I get changed? I'll be right back ... (*she goes out stage left and calls from offstage.*)
So, you were in Quebec City all week long?

David: Yes, I was attending a seminar on new investigative techniques. I had to do some research in the files of the City Court, also.
(*He replaces the skull on the dressing table.*)
He is quite a specimen!

Lucie: Who's that?

David: The skull.

Lucie: I'll pass it on to the props guy, he'll be thrilled to hear that from a connoisseur!
(*She re-enters the dressing room; David is looking at a small tube.*)

David: What's this?

Lucie: A special product they use in films to help actors cry.

David: Why?

Lucie: Well ... imagine doing the same sad scene twelve times. It's got to be hard to cry every time, you know? So, they put it into the actor's eyes and it makes the tears flow all by themselves.

David: Wait a minute. Are you trying to tell me that when an actress like – let me think – Jane Fonda, when she cries ... it's all a fake?

Lucie: Sometimes, yes.

David: What a deception! I really believed that, for an actor at least, tears were the ultimate proof of true emotion!

Lucie: Ah, people love these misconceptions about acting! Do you want to try it?

David: Surely you don't want to make my cry?

Lucie: Yes! You'll see, it won't hurt ... it will be funny!

David: Why not? How do I do this?

Lucie: First, I'll ask you to take off your glasses.
(*She leans forward to take his glasses; during the following, she places a few drops in his eyes.*) And now, since we are making a movie, I'll ask you to think of something sad, so the scene will be truthful ...

David: Something sad ...
Something recent?

Lucie: Whatever you want ...
... and now, I say "Quiet on the set; Sound, Camera, Action!"

(*As David remembers, there is a musical theme reminiscent of his past, and Lucie is frozen with the present moment. Holding his glasses she recedes up and away, flying from the dressing room until she disappears; and David, in another time, brings out a letter from his pocket.*
The Brandenburg gate is projected on the cyclorama behind the wall. While David reads his letter in German, English subtitles are projected upon the wall.)

"Ich weiss, dass man niemanden zue Liebe zwingen kann ... Aber ich möchte dass Sie wissen, dass ich das Gefühl habe Sie seien ein Stück von mir.
An dem Morgen, an dem Sie Ost Berlin verliessen zitterte ich am ganzen Körper. Als ich fragte wann Sie kommen, sagten sie 'Ich bin bald wieder zurück'.
Ich habe es nicht gezeigt, doch ich wusste sofort dass es eine Lüge war.
Was nicht vom Herzen kommt, geht nicht zum Herzen ... Das habe ich in

Ihren Augen gelesen. Könnte ich die Stadt verlassen würde ich mit Ihnen sein.
Sie fehlen mir,

Anna"

The Subtitles:

"I know that it is impossible to force someone into loving ...
But I want you to know that I feel you are a part of me.
The morning you left East Berlin, I was quite shaken.
When I asked, 'When will you return?' you replied,
'Soon.'
I did not let on, but at that instant I knew you were lying.
What does not come from the heart is not taken to heart ...
I can see it in your eyes.
If I could leave this city, I would be with you.
I miss you deeply.

Anna"

(David *is crying. He folds the letter and replaces it in his pocket, as* Lucie *glides back into her place in the scene and the present time frame is resumed.*)

David: This stuff really burns ... it's like getting soap in your eyes.

Lucie: It won't hurt for long ... You know, you have to suffer if you want it to look like you are suffering ... David – you should never give carnations to an actor because they bring bad luck.

David: You are superstitious?

Lucie: Well, I have just finished seven years of bad luck from breaking a mirror!

David: Then perhaps we should put some distance between ourselves and this one. Shall we go?

(Lucie *takes his arm to exit.*)

Blackout

Projection
APARTMENT #7: INTERIOR, NIGHT

(*Stage left, a washbasin full of water set in the wall with a mirror above it indicates the bathroom in* François' *apartment.* François *enters, drunk, limping and sore. He drops his leather jacket on the floor and peels off his T-shirt, craning to see the weals on his back reflected in the small mirror. There is a knock at the door. He quickly puts his shirt back on, as* Lucie *enters.*)

Lucie: François?

François: Oui ... entre.

Lucie: Excuses ... c'est parce que je viens d'arriver chez nous j'peux pas rentrer, j'ai pas mes clés.

François: Ah ...
(*He looks for* Lucie's *key inside his jacket pocket, and gives it to her.*)
Ça te tentes-tu de rester prendre un café?

Lucie: J'aimerais ça mais, j't'avec quelqu'un.

François: Ah! ... y'a quelqu'un qui t'attends ...

Lucie: Chut! J't'e conterai ça demain ...

(*She goes out.* François *again takes off his shirt and soaks it in water, then lays it across his back with a sigh of relief. The sound of laughter filters in from next door.* François *smiles and shakes his finger at* Lucie, *hesitates, then puts a glass up to the wall to listen to what's going on the other side. Sound amplification enables* Lucie *and* David *to be clearly heard from offstage.*)

David: You have a very wonderful collection of dolls here. Very beautiful, some of them ... Oh well, I guess ... I blew it! The last bus ...

(*They laugh.*)

Lucie: Oh well! Would you like to have a drink?

David: Is this a bottle of vodka I see before me?

Lucie: Yes ... you want a glass of it?

David: Yes please, with a lot of ice ...

(François *removes the glass. He's lonely. Lights fade on him standing next to the washbasin.*)

Projection
THE SNOW: EXTERIOR, NIGHT

(*A musical score plays for the snow scene. Above the wall, a light sky glows, and snow falls gently, constantly, for the duration of the scene.*)

Projection
APARTMENT #8: INTERIOR, DAY

(*Stage right, a washbasin full of water set in the wall with a mirror above it indicates the bathroom in* Lucie's *apartment.* Lucie *stands before it, washing her face.* David *enters, still hurriedly dressing.*)

David: Lucie, listen ... ! I really have to go! I promised my secretary I'd be in Montreal at ten o'clock ... it's now ten-thirty and I haven't even left Quebec City ... you can imagine how impossibly behind I am –

Lucie: (*Can't keep her hands off him*):
That's too bad, I wanted to look after you. I thought I'd make us some breakfast. I just put some coffee on ...

David: That's very nice of you but I really must go. Well! I ... want to thank you for a truly wonderful evening Lucie; I want to say that I –

(*François' voice is heard through the wall, with a pounding on the neighbouring door.*)

François: Alain! Ouvre la porte!

David: I want you to know that, last night, I –

François: Ouvre la porte!

David: What's going on?

Lucie: It's just next door. No big deal.

François: Ouvre-la ou je la défonce!

David: I see. Well, Lucie, I want to thank you for the truly wonderful evening we had and indeed, to ... to say a proper goodbye, rather than to ... disappear like thief in the night –

(*They look at each other.*)

Lucie: David. If I'm ... ever in Montreal, can I ... call you sometime?

David: I suppose so.
In fact, next week I have more business in Quebec City. Perhaps we could arrange a rendez-vous? I'll be at the morgue.

Lucie: At the morgue – I'd prefer a restaurant!

David: (*serious*):
That's what I meant. Well! all right then –

(*As they move to kiss each other goodbye:*)

François: Ouvre-moi la porte! Ouvre la porte ou je la défonce! Tu m'e-coeurera pas longtemps tabernac!

David: He's going to kill him! You should call the police.

Lucie: No, no, really. It's not a big deal. He's probably with his boyfriend, and it's just that they sometimes have ... disagreements about things.

David: You call this a disagreement; it sounds like World War Three!
(*David and Lucie lock eyes.*)

François: Lâche moi mon tabernac! J'veux pu te voir la face – !

David: Well, I really must be going ...

(*But* David *doesn't move. A long pause while he accepts he doesn't want to leave, he's looking at* Lucie. *She very gently unties her kimono, which slides to the ground, and walks naked into his arms. The lights fade as they start to embrace.*)

Projection
TRACKING IN REVERSE: INTERIOR, DAY

(*Thriller music begins in the black-out.* Lucie *stands naked, crossing slowly to stage left as she dries herself with a bath-towel. A panasonic peewee dolly tracks backwards, as she walks towards it: the camera zooming manically in and out of her face and body with the tension and drive of the music. A telephone is positioned on the dolly. Two-thirds of the way across the stage,* Lucie *thinks she hears a noise behind her, and looks over her shoulder, then leans back against the wall. High suspense. The telephone rings, catching her by surprise. She answers it:*)

Lucie: Hello ... ? Hello ... ? Hello!!

(*There is no response. She is alarmed, stands and covers herself with the towel. Anxiously, she continues to follow the dolly across the stage until she exits stage left. A second later there is an amplified, blood-curdling scream.*)

Blackout

Projection
THE WOUND: INTERIOR, NIGHT

(François *enters with a restaurant table and two chairs which he places downstage centre.* David *enters behind him.*)

François: Bonsoir monsieur. Ce sera pour combien de personnes?

David: I'm sorry ... ah ..

(*He indicates he cannot speak French.*)

François: Excuse me. Would you like a table for 'ow many?

David: For two, please.

François: Does this one suit you?

David: Yes, that's fine ... excuse me, would you take my coat please?

François: Sure.

(François *leaves with the coat.* David *sits at the table, waiting.* Lucie *runs in.*)

Lucie: Oh, David! I'm sorry I'm late ...

David: That's all right.

Lucie: I hope you haven't been waiting too long?

David: I just walked in this minute. It's nice to see you.

Lucie: We were supposed to finish at three o'clock, but it took longer than I thought. I had an argument with the director, about a scene – He wants to shoot it from above, you know, as if a murderer is lurking over this victim from the skylight, creepy ... but anyway, we fought it out. And I won.

David: Well ...

François: Bonjour Lucie.

Lucie: Ah, Bonjour François; tiens, je te présente un ami, David Haussmann, François Tremblay. He's my next-door neighbour.

David: Oh! So *you* are the one in apartment number 8?

François: Yes.

David: I heard – so much about you!

Lucie: (*quickly*):
David is the one who drove me back to Quebec City after I saw the guy throw himself in front of the Métro in Montreal.

François: Weird way to meet someone.

David: Yes ... Métro stations in Montreal these days seem to be used more for suicide than for commuting ...

Lucie: Why's that?

François: C'est la façon la plus cheap de se suicider ...

David: What?

François: ... Do you want to order something to drink before your meal?

David: Mmm, let's avoid liquor. Lucie, would you like some wine with the meal?

Lucie: Yeah. Sure.

François: I'll leave you to look at the wine list.

David: What kind of wine do you prefer?

Lucie: Oh, red or white.

David: That's what I meant.

Lucie: I like both of them.

David: How about red?

Lucie: Red? Perfect!

David: What kind of red do you like: Bourgogne, Bordeaux, Beaujolais ... ?

Lucie: I like all of them!

David: Beaujolais?

Lucie: Beaujolais, perfect!

David: What kind of Beaujolais do you prefer?

Lucie: Euh ... it's up to you.

David: How about a bottle of Brouilly? Do you like Brouilly?

Lucie: I love it!

David: What kind of food do they serve here?

Lucie: It's kind of mixed genre. A little of this, a little of that: French, Hindu, vegetarian ...

François: Have you decided on the wine?

Lucie: Yes, we'll have a bottle of – (*She looks for it on the wine list*) – Brouilly.

François: Brouilly, okay.

(François *goes again.*)

David: So! How does it feel to be a movie star?

Lucie: My God, give me a chance – it's my first day of filming! I think I felt a bit – well, silly ... !
(*She struggles for the words.*)
I found the director quite ... aggressive with his camera ... And ... oh, – I had a "difficult" scene to do and I ... I felt more observed by the crew, and the director himself, than by the voyeur in the scenario. I was being watched. Me, not the character. Do you know what I mean?

David: Watched ...
(François *comes back with the bottle, shows it to* Lucie *who simply reads the label, and nods.*)

Lucie: Brouilly.

David: What were you shooting exactly? Indoor scenes, outdoor scenes?

Lucie: We're shooting all the interiors, because the film is set in spring – so we have to wait for the end of winter.

David: What will you do if it rains all the time?

Lucie: We want it to rain, because all the scenes happen in the rain.

David: What if it never rains?

Lucie: Well, they make it rain!

David: Of course. Like they do with tears. For them, making it is not the problem, just a question of water quantity.

Lucie: Yes, for making it it's the size of the equipment that counts! (*Lucie laughs, and* François, *who holds the opened bottle, joins in as he pours her a little into her glass, to "taste."*

Lucie *is surprised not to get more.*)

Lucie: Merci!

François: Bien ... Goûtes-y.

David: Taste it.

Lucie: Oh ... yes, sure.
(*She taste it and nods.*)
Mmm. It's very good.
(*As* François *pours the rest.*)
It's even a little bouchonné!

François: Oh ... I'll get you another bottle

Lucie: No, no. It's very good. It is bouchonné ... ?
Bouchonné!

François: Yes ... but if it's bouchonné –

David: – Doesn't that mean it tastes like cork?

Lucie: Oh? Okay. Then, in that case, it can't possibly be bouchonné because it tastes just great!

David: Perhaps I should double-check ... ? It is a very expensive bottle!
(*He does so, with connoisseur's style.*)
It is an excellent wine!

Lucie: Like I said.

François: Are you ready to order?

David: Go for it Lucie.

Lucie: No, no go for it David: you are the guest.

David: But what do you mean, I am the guest. I thought I was the one inviting you out for dinner?

Lucie: No, no: I mean you are the foreigner! (*Pause. David looks at the menu.*)

David: Is this soup?

François: Yes ... Potage Crécy.

David: I'll have that please, and the filet de boeuf Brisanne. I'd like that done rare, but please, in the French understanding of the word rare – not the Canadian!

Lucie: And I'll have the same as him, but with the Canadian rare!
(François *leaves with the order.*)

David: Well, here's to your film.
(*They raise a toast. He takes a package from under the table.*) I'm not very good at this, but – here! This is for you.

Lucie: What is it?

David: What do you think it is? It's a present.

Lucie: Nnn, ye-s, but it's not my birthday.

David: It's a present time, just the same.

Lucie: No. – I mean, ...
There is no need for you to be buying me presents David.

David: Oh. Well ... I'm sorry then ...

Lucie: No ... I'm sorry ...
I'm the one acting weird here. Let me open it! Oh! A Russian doll!

David: Yes, the real thing.

Lucie: Don't these come in all different sizes, and people collect them?

David: In fact, you won't have to collect them. They are all there, packed on inside another.

Lucie: What do you mean?

David: Open it up.

Lucie: (*Opens the doll and finds another inside.*)
Oh ... it's beautiful ...

David: It's called a Matrushka.

Lucie: A Matrushka.

(Lucy *opens up each doll to discover the smaller one hiding inside, and places them in a line across the table, so as to make a wall between herself and* David.)

David: It comes from Russia but you find them in Eastern Europe also. It's a traditional doll, representing the generations. So this big one you see

here is the mother of this one, and the grandmother of this one also, because she is the mother of this one, and this one is the mother of that one, and that one, and that one ... and ... to infinity, I guess. But it can stand for many other things, I believe. Like Truth.
One truth which is hiding within another truth, and another one and another one ...

Lucie: I'm very moved. Thank you.

David: I'm glad you like it.

(*The lights and sound ambience change to reveal that suddenly the whole evening has passed. They are stirring their coffee; the desultory rhythm of the spoons evokes their languor and the lateness of the hour.* David *is mid-conversation:*)

David: ... And at one point in the film he turns to her and says: "Beware death ... she comes and goes through mirrors. Gaze at yourself all your life in the looking glass, and you will see death at work."

Lucie: That's beautiful.

David: That's Cocteau.

(François *comes in, looking at his watch.*)

François: I'm sorry, but I am going to have to close now.

David: What time is it?

François: A quarter past three!

Lucie: My God! We didn't notice the time!

David: I'm very sorry. We were completely engrossed in our conversation while digesting this excellent meal.

Lucie: Oui. Merci beaucoup, c'était trés bon.

David: Can you tell me where I could find my coat please?

François: It's in the cloakroom, I'll get it for you.

David: Lucie, you forget your Matrushka.

Lucie: Oh – my Matrushka.
(*She shows the doll to* François.)
Regarde François ce que David m'a donné ... C't'une poupé Russe, une Matrushka. Y l'a acheté à l'est.

François: C'est beau. (*To* David)
You're from Europe?

David: Yes, from Eastern Europe. But I've been a Canadian citizen for many years now.

François: What do you do here?

David: I am a criminologist. I work at a centre for scientific investigation in Montréal.

François: Parthenais?

David: (*Stopping, and giving* François *a look.*)
Yes, the Parthenais.

Lucie: Tu connais ça?

François: Oui, j'ai déjà eu affair là.

Lucie: Comment ça?

François: Pas en prison ...
(David *is trying to follow what they are saying.*)
I went there for questioning.

David: For what?

François: Because six years ago one of my best friends was murdered. Here in Quebec City. I was the last to see her alive, so I was a suspect. In fact, it was me who found her dead, in her apartment. She was tied up, raped, and stabbed a lot of times ...

David: Did they find the killer?

François: No, they never tracked him down.

David: What was your friend's name?

François: Marie-Claude Légaré.

(Lucie *recognizes the story. She turns to face the wall: her back is covered with blood.*)

David: Yes ... I think I remember. Don't worry, they'll track him down. Nobody is able to go through life with a murder on their conscience.

(Lucie *falls to the ground between the two men, whose conversation continues in the "real time" of the restaurant, despite the emotional events also being acted out, of* Lucie's *realization, and of their individual memories of the Marie-Claude Légaré case.* David *continues talking to* François *as though he never moves, but* François *drops into another reality for a moment, falling to his knees beside* Lucie, *to relive the discovery of his friend's corpse, as* David *chats on.*)

David: Well, thank you once again, and my compliments to the chef; the food was indeed excellent. And the service, impeccable. Have you been a waiter for long?

(François *resumes his position in the "present time" of the conversation.*

While he answers the question, David *in his turn kneels beside the "corpse," reliving the autopsy which he performed on Marie-Claude Légaré by ripping* Lucie*'s blood-drenched shirt from top to bottom with a scalpel.*)

François: Long enough ... three years now. Before this I was at school – University – studying Political Science and I was working part time in a Yugoslavian restaurant then.

(David *stands and resumes his former position in the real time of the conversation.*)

David: Do you intend to do this for long? I mean, waiting tables ...
(*He manages to side-step the condescension of his original question.*)
... I know how transient things are in the restaurant business.

François: (*Shrugging*):
I don't know. If I could find something else, I'd move on for sure.

(Lucie *uncoils from the floor and stands spread flat against the wall in the same "corpse" position that she had on the ground. Simultaneously, the two men each put one foot on the wall as they talk, and hold their bodies horizontal, parallel with the floor, as they shake hands over her vertical body; so creating the classic cinematic "top shot" of a corpse.*)

David: Well, it's better than no work at all. Where I come from people are starting to say things are not much brighter this side of the Wall; at least over there everybody has the right to work. Ask your Yugoslavian friends, they'll tell you the same thing.
It was certainly a pleasure to meet you François ...

(Lucie *turns around and re-enters the "present time" scene to indicate that in "reality" she has been standing listening to them all the time.*)

Lucie, if we want to exercise our own "right to work" tomorrow perhaps we should be moving along.

Lucie: (*In a strained voice*):
Salut, François.

François: À bientôt.

(Lucie *holds her finger, which is bleeding.*)

David: What's the matter, Lucie? You're bleeding?

Lucie: It's nothing ... I must have cut myself with a knife.

David: We'll take care of that.

(*He ushers* Lucie *out of the restaurant, leaving* François *alone. Lights fade to black.*)

Projection
THE RAMPARTS: EXTERIOR, NIGHT

(*A projection of the Quebec City skyline covers the cyclorama.* Lucie *and* David *enter above and behind the wall, stage left. They lean on the wall as if looking at the famous view projected behind them.* Lucie *is withdrawn and quiet.*)

David: What an exquisite city.

Lucie: I come walking here very often, but in summer generally, not winter.

David: I greatly prefer the winter. I don't know why really, but I find I like the cold ... anything cold. It's because I was born in December, perhaps. You know, when people talk about the cold it is nearly always in pejorative terms. For me, the cold evokes a kind of objective calm, wisdom ... and most of all a great gentleness. Like these snowflakes slowly falling ... Leaning against the ramparts like that you remind me of someone I once knew ...

Lucie: Who was she?

David: Someone whom I loved deeply, and to whom I ... did a great wrong. A German woman.

Lucie: (*Noting his sadness*)
I'm too nosey, aren't I?

David: It was a long time ago.
What's wrong, Lucie? Since we've left the restaurant you seem ... preoccupied somehow.

Lucie: Yes. I am ... I had a shock just now, because that story François told us is the same story that the film I'm playing in is based on. I didn't know François was involved with it; I didn't know ... And now I feel uneasy about being a part of it, playing her part ... I feel she is a *part* of him, and I am ... I guess I'm wondering if there's still time for them to find someone else.

David: That is in such bad taste. To base a film on an unresolved murder case –

Lucie: Why? Her death is something that happened: it belongs to history now – but history itself doesn't belong to anyone.

David: Yes, but in real life they haven't even identified the murderer – (*to prove his point*)
How could they end the case? How do they end the film?

Lucie: After the girl's killed, everything's set up to look as if it was ... (*She* *says this with difficulty, thinking of* François.) one of her close friends who did it ... then at the end we discover –

David: – At the end we discover it was the police who did it.

Lucie: How did you know?

David: It's a classic. When you don't know how to end a who-done-it, you always blame it on the cops. They are there, they know how it's done!

(*He explains.*)

At first, when I was a student in criminology, I too thought that those ...

(*He searches for the word.*)

Vemehmungsoffiziers – the people developing techniques for interrogation and investigation – that they were all violent brutes, that they were a product of their line of work. But, you know what?

(*His voice changes, for he is talking about an aspect of himself.*)

They are much more dangerous than that. The men leading the field of criminal research are very, very intelligent people – and that is a fact you'll never see in a thriller. It is too frightening, perhaps. Poor François. What he must have been through ... What do you want to do? Should we start back now?

Lucie: David, I'm sorry ... but I think I'd rather go home alone tonight. This has hit me hard, and I need to think it over ... but alone.

David: All right. I understand.

(*But he doesn't really. He tries to kiss her, as if in goodbye, but she pushes him away after a moment.*)

If I have to visit Quebec City again, I can call you?

Lucie: Sure ... You have my phone number.

(David *lets her go reluctantly. He stays on the ramparts stage right, staring at the view.*)

Projection
THE TELEPHONE: EXTERIOR, NIGHT

(François *enters, takes a quarter from his pocket and exits to a pay-phone in the stage left wing. A light behind him projects his shadow, his every movement, grotesquely across the entire wall. Sounds of dialing. Someone answers the phone, the voice sounds from offstage.*)

Lucie: Allô ... ? Allô ... Allô!

(François *hangs up violently. Then, he calms down and dials again.*)

Lucie: Allô ... Allô! François, c'est toi hein?

(*The phone clicks as* François *hangs up again. He steps out of the phone booth on to the stage again. He kicks the wall, again and again. Lights catch* David *who still stands alone on the ramparts, and who shares* François's *mood.* David *hangs his body over the ramparts: he is an inverse mirror image of* François. *From above and below, both men lean against the wall, pressing their faces, their bodies, against the bricks.*)

Blackout

Projection
THE LINE UP: INTERIOR, NIGHT

(*The Line Up is a re-cap scene of important visual moments from the story so far. These run in a choreographically structured, repetitive series of movement fragments. The music accompanying the scene is very important.*
First, four pin-spots lights shine on the wall from above, to reveal that the bricks are bleeding, copiously.
François *enters, to recap briefly his restaurant work,*
Lucie *re-enacts her moment of shock in the subway,* David *enters for his meeting with* Lucie,
François *kneels at the wall for the lashing scene,*
Lucie *and* David *indicate their affair;*
Lucie *falls as the corpse at the end of The Wound scene.*
François *and* David *repeat the "top shot" moment, shaking hands over her corpse.*
The speed of the movement increases, and the mood becomes increasingly desperate as the characters fling themselves around in an externalization of their introspective mental processes at this point. Excerpts from Lucie's *movie are projected on the wall at various moments, while* David *tears down parts of the wall, throwing loose bricks over the stage. The scene builds to a point of frenzy, and lights finally black out on the three characters in a line-up, alone, bewildered, dis-connected from one another.*)

Projection
THE SPRING: EXTERIOR, DAY

(François *enters with a bucket of water, with which he sluices the wall. He starts to scrub at the brickwork.* David *enters, with a travel bag and sunglasses.*)

David: Hello François.
(François *looks at him belligerently.*)
Have you seen Lucie?

François: Not for a month at least. She must be busy shooting her movie.

David: I came to say goodbye, but if she's off on location –

François: You're going away?

David: I'm going back to East Berlin. The government is sending me to organize a series of conferences on Investigative Techniques. Now that the wall has disappeared, there's a sudden necessity there for up-to-date psycho-technology. But, in fact, my motives for going are ... more personal than professional.

François: And what are the government's motives, to share technology? Or sell free enterprise? ... The art of understanding the criminal mind goes everywhere that capitalism goes.

David: Share knowledge.
(François *snorts*.)
If you see Lucie, tell her I'm here.
(*Finally, he has to ask.*)

What the hell are you doing, François?

François: I'm washing the wall.

David: Yes, I can see that, but why?

François: The landlord told me to strip my graffiti off the garden wall before I move out, or else he'll prosecute me.

David: Prosecute, for graffiti! What did it say?

François: L'histoire s'écrit avec le sang.
(David *looks blank*.)
History is written with blood.

David: And what is that supposed to mean?

François: It means that we write history through war, fascism ... and murder.

David: Are you talking about political assassinations?

François: No, I mean murder ... The smallest little killing ... of some totally unimportant person ... in a way that's still a political act, don't you think?

David: Is that what they teach you in Political Science?

François: Why are you asking me so many questions? This feels like an interrogation scene in a bad detective movie.

(*Staring scornfully at* David, François *takes his bucket and brush and exits, leaving* David *alone, and thoughtful*.)

Blackout

Projection
TRACKING FORWARD: EXTERIOR, NIGHT

(*Very creepy horror music plays as* Lucie *appears stage left, in her film costume. As she crosses the stage, wary and afraid,* François *appears behind her, so close he is on her heels. Centre stage, she stops suddenly.*)

Lucie: Everywhere I go, you are there. Leave me alone. Go away ...

(*She drops abruptly out of character, and the music cuts out.*)

That's no good. I'm sorry. I just can't seem to feel it. It's not coming.

(*She composes herself to try again and return to the stage left exit. The music starts as she enters. Now,* David *follows her.*)

Lucie: Everywhere I go, you are there. Leave me alone. Go away.

(*She stops again, as does the music.*)

I'm sorry. Let's take it again. Just give me a second.

(*She thinks.*)

Lucie: Okay.

(*She returns to enter again, with the music. This time, the camera is at her back, breathing down her neck. Her lines come as though she has been driven to the edge.*)

Lucie: Everywhere I go, you are there. Leave me alone ... Go away!

(*She steps out of character.*)

Now that one worked, eh? That's a keeper? Yah!

Blackout

Projection
APARTMENT #8: INTERIOR, DAY

(François *is packing boxes in the washroom of his apartment. The washbasin is set in the wall, as before.* Lucie *enters, with books.*)

Lucie: Salut François, j't'ai rapporté les livres que tu m'avait prêté ... "L'orgasme au masculin," j'ai trouvé ça ben interessant.

François: Tu peux les garder encore si t'en a pas fini.

Lucie: Non, non ... j'sais c'que j'voulais savoir ...
(*She looks through his cosmetics in the washbasin.*)
Ouan ... T'en as des affairs pour un gars – !
(*She pokes around in the boxes he is packing, as he puts the books in.*)
Tu marques pas ce que tu mets dans tes boîtes?

François: (*With a shrug*):
C'est pas nécessaire. Pour ce que j'ai ...

Lucie: Marque où c'est que ça va toujours, sinon tu vas être mêlé quand tu vas arriver.
She points to a box.)
Ça c'est à quoi? Des cosmétiques? J'vas écrire pharmacie dessus.
(*She writes on the box.*)
Pis, celle-la?

François: Là dedans ... des couverturs, serviettes, des débarbouillettes, des livres, des vieux journaux ...

Lucie: J'pourrais écrire "divers" – !

(*She looks inside the box, and finds a long leather strap with a strange fastening at the end. She pulls it out, curiously.*)

Lucie: Ça ça sert quoi?

(François *stops, looks at her, then decides to answer. He puts the strap around his neck and demonstrates.*)

François: Quand je me masturbe, j'me sers de ça. J'tire pis j'lâche, j'tire pis j'lâche. Pis juste avant de venir, j'tire de plus en plus fort ... Mais un moment donné, y faut qu'tu lâches – si tu veux pas venir pour la dernière fuis

Lucie: Ça sert tu juste à ça?
(François *takes the strap from around his neck and goes to the washbasin.*)

François: Viens ici.
(Lucie *hestitates.*)
Viens ici.

(*She goes where he indicates, and crouches by the washbasin. He ties the belt around* Lucie's *hands, passes it through the u-bend on the wash-basin, and wraps it round her neck before tying it off.*)

François: Là m'a serrer un peu ...

(*He puts a blindfold over her eyes, rendering her completely helpless.*)

Comme ça, t'as vraiment l'impression d'être vulnérable ...

Lucie: Pis après?

(*Above and behind the wall,* David *appears with a file. He is in his office, reading* François' *testimonies from the Légaré inquiry.* François *continues talking to* Lucie.)

François: Des fois, quand on se ramasse une gang de gars –

David: (*Reading*): Sometimes, when we get together, a bunch of friends and myself –

François: Y'en a un qui se fait attacher comme ça –

David: – One of us gets tied up just like this –

François: Pis, au hasard y'en a un qui est choisi pour aller le rejoindre –

David: Then, at random, one of us is chosen to go in and join him –

François: Celui qui est attaché, y peut rien faire.

David: The one who's tied up can do nothing.

François: Y peut rien voir –

David: Can see nothing –

François: Pis l'autre y fait ce qui veut avec ...

David: While the other one does whatever he wants ... Interrogation number eleven, fifteenth of August, nineteen eighty-two, Quebec City.

(*The light slowly fades on* David. François *stands in the trance of memory, the only sound being his hand opening and closing a metal clip he has taken from the box.* Lucie *becomes anxious in the silence.*)

Lucie: François? François – ? François ...?
(François *comes back to earth, and moves to her to release her.*)

François: Tu veux-tu que je te détache?
(*As he is untying her, she notices scars on his wrist. She takes his hands, to look more closely. Then she looks in his face.*)

Lucie: C'est tu toi qui l'a tuée?

François: Je pense pas, non ...

Lucie: Pourquoi tu dis *"j'pense"* pas?

François: Parce que des fois, je l'sais plus ..

Lucie: Moi j'le sais ...
que tu serais pas capable de faire mal à une mouche. (*She touches his face. He can't meet her eyes, they are both very moved. Slowly,* François *opens up to her, and starts very tenderly and passionately to kiss her. Lights fade to black.*)

Projection
THE RAIN: EXTERIOR, DAY

(*Rain falls steadily from the ceiling of the theatre.* David *walks alone on the ramparts, and above and behind the wall, with his umbrella. Lights fade as he completes his cross of the stage.*)

Projection
APARTMENT #7: INTERIOR, NIGHT

(Lucie *stands in the washroom of her apartment, lost in thought.* David *enters, hesitantly.*)

David: Lucie ... ! Where were you, I've been looking for you all afternoon.

Lucie: I was at François'. I ... helped him pack his things.

David: (*Comes right in*): That's right ... he's moving to Montreal, he told me this morning. Did he tell you why?

Lucie: No.

David: It's raining outside, so you will be able to shoot tonight.

Lucie: I should be there now, but I decided not to go.

David: (*Surprised*): Why?

Lucie: Because ... we are supposed to shoot the death sequence, and I feel ... I think that I don't have the right to do that.

David: Well. (*He doesn't understand.*) That's ... very courageous of you. Too bad, found some very interesting research material for you. Here ... (*He gives her the file he's brought.*) Read this.

Lucie: (*Takes it and reads*): "The autopsy has revealed that the stab wounds were caused by a sharp, pointed instrument which penetrated the skin and underlying tissues ..." What is this?

David: The coroner's report for Marie-Claude Légaré, straight out of the Quebec City police department. There you have investigative notes, interviews, interrogation records from witnesses, a list of suspects. And in the last chapter, there is written proof that François Tremblay is not guilty. (*Lucie stares at him, revolted.*)
Well? Don't you care? Doesn't that make you happy?

Lucie: I already knew that.

David: Yes, but now you have the written proof.

Lucie: No, I mean, I myself had the proof.

David: I'm not sure I understand what you mean.

Lucie: I made love with François.

(*A change in lighting and an eerie soundscape indicates that time is frozen momentarily. The source of light appears to be set in* Lucie's *back, she is silhouetted against the wall, surrounded by a bright aura which grows more intense as she steps downstage. Behind her,* David *steps out of his stunned, blank reaction, to smash his fists violently against the wall. Bricks go flying from the top, and crash down.* Lucie *slowly steps back to her original position in the scene, her light dims, and we crossfade back into "real time," where* David *still stares at* Lucie, *expressionless:*)

Lucie: Did you hear me? I, I made love with François ... (*She is both compassionate for and irritated by* David's *non-reaction.*)
Say, do something.
(David *pretends to have something in his eye; he washes it out at the basin.*)
Can't you allow yourself your own emotions?

David: What do you want me to do? You want me to be jealous of a homosexual?

Lucie: (*Turns away in disgust*): David, please!

David: (*Very tight*):
I'm sorry.

(*A difficult pause, in which* Lucie *thaws.*)

Lucie: At what time is your plane tomorrow?

David: Eleven.

Lucie: If you want, tomorrow we can get up early, and I'll come to the bus terminal with you.

(David *is having difficulty containing his emotion. He shakes his head and backs towards the door, then stops.*)

Lucie: David, if you want to cry, cry. If you want to hold me, hold me.

(*A moment where* David *understands, and accepts. Then he starts to cry, and comes slowly back to her, as the lights fade. Projection of Métro logo on the wall, and the sign:*)

Projection
BERRI-UQAM: INTERIOR, NIGHT

(François *arrives at the métro, as if to wait for a train. We hear the sound of the train approaching.* François *takes off his leather jacket, and drops it to the floor behind him, then with great deliberation, as the sound of the train becomes deafening, he throws himself off the front of the stage, under the train. The blackout is simultaneous with his jump.*)

Projection
THE POLYGRAPH: INTERIOR, DAY

(David *is in East Berlin, speaking at his conference. He stands beside a large complicated Polygraph machine.*)

David: Now, for our British collaborators, I would like to say first what a pleasure and honour it is for me to speak at this conference here in East Berlin. My name is David Haussmann. I am from Canada where I work with the Quebec Provincial Police. My official title is, in fact, that of Criminologist at the Parthenais Institute in Montreal, which one might call the nerve centre of the Quebec police forces because we're responsible for research and development in all areas pertaining to criminology.

Today, I've been asked to talk to you about this apparatus, which is commonly known as a "lie detector." This term is particularly exact consisting as it does of "poly," which is to say, "many," and "graph," which of course means "writings." Accordingly, the apparatus describes the state of a suspect by the monitoring of four physical functions; these are then transmitted into graphic form wherein any unusual activity is at once betrayed. Extensive research has enabled us to state categorically that if a witness, connected to the polygraph machine by means of electrodes, is unreliable, or actually *misrepresents* the truth, minute changes to his physical state can be perceived by monitoring the changes to these four physical states.

Firstly, the lie registers on the *cardiograph* with an accelerated heartbeat; at the *temple*, we monitor for an increase or, in the case of some subjects, a decrease of arterial pressure. *Respiration* has a direct effect on the vocal quality of the person responding to questions; this contributes yet another reading of the physical response. Lastly, we measure the subject's *perspiration*, a symptom which is often barely perceptible to the human eye; however, the polygraph can detect the most minute psycho-physical response occurring during interrogation procedures.

The wall which separates truth from fabrication is sometimes paper-thin; the consequences which could follow our mistaking one for the other are such that we cannot tolerate any approximation. For this first reason, only questions demanding an unequivocal answer must be asked of a witness, whose reply will be restricted to a simple "yes" or "no."

Some investigators have found that the mystique which has grown up around the Polygraph makes it more useful as a tactical device than an actual lie detector. For example, the law in Canada protects individuals from having to submit to the Polygraph test against their will; however, should a witness agree to participate, some detectives conclude that this person therefore has nothing to hide. Additionally, there are ways that the Polygraph can be used to apply psychological pressure. As an example, I will draw upon a test I conducted personally at the Parthenais Institute in 1982. The questioning went like this:

(*The large mirror is dropped to hang at such an angle that* François *can be seen wired up to polygraph as he sits on the up-stage side of the wall. His voice, when he speaks, is amplified.*)

David: François, can you hear me properly?

François: Yes.

David: But you can't actually see me, can you?

François: No.

David: François, are we in Canada?

François: Yes.

David: Is it summertime?

François: Yes.

David: Was it you who killed Marie-Claude Légaré?

François: No.

David: Is it nineteen eight-two?

François: Yes.

David: Are we in the month of August?

François: No.

David: Are we in the month of July?

François: Yes.

David: Are you responsible for the death of Marie-Claude Légaré?

François: No.

David: Now, the result of this polygraph test gave evidence that this witness was actually telling the truth. But the person conducting the test told him afterwards that they "did not believe he was actually lying, but that he was not telling the whole truth" – in order to use the spontaneous emotional reaction of the witness as the ultimate proof of his innocence.

(François *leaps to his feet, tearing off the electrodes, beside himself with rage and panic. He is screaming and crying that he has told the truth, again and again and again, he has told the truth, and that the truth will never be enough for them but it's all that he has ... he breaks down and stumbles out of view.*)

David: Should this latter subterfuge be brought into play, great care and compassion must be exercised. By inducing such stress one could easily trigger a damaging psychological reaction, even – possibly – a mental disorder, in the mind of a totally innocent subject. For example, I happened to come across the subject from this demonstration years after the inquiry was closed, to discover that he had started to doubt his own innocence.

However, I'm sure you will agree that this eventuality is the exception and not the rule; it certainly does not suffice to cast the shadow of doubt

upon the immense possibilities offered by North-American technology for the prevention and detection of crime.
Danke, und Aufwiedersehen.

(*Lights black out on* David.)

Projection
THE AUTOPSY: INTERIOR, NIGHT

(*The large mirror above the wall has flipped over so as to hang like a platform over a hospital gurney.*
François' naked corpse lies on the gurney. Lucie *enters, to identify the body. She looks up at her reflection next to his in the mirror, and recites the Cocteau which* David *taught her:*)

Lucie: "Beware death. She comes and goes through mirrors."

(*A soundscape of noises from the Métro begins, and develops into a musical score.* David *enters, as if to perform an autopsy on* François, *and the scene immediately becomes choreographic, expressing the relationships between* David, François *and* Lucie *which have begun and now are ending. The wheeled gurney acts as a mechanical train which cuts through each relationship before it can develop; it separates, and traps, each of them.*

The closing sequence begins with a light change; as François *lies on the gurney, a skeleton is seen through the mirror above him, in the place of his reflection.* Lucie *crouches over him, as though she has just finishes making love with him. She draws a flame out of his heart, which she holds aloft, as she stands and steps backwards off the gurney, seemingly into darkness. Balanced on the pedestal of the camera dolly, she flies backwards offstage, still holding the flame high, towards* François' *corpse, as the lights and music slowly fade.*)

THE END